IRELAND'S FIRST SETTLERS

Dedicated to

The Royal Irish Academy
The National Museum of Ireland
The National Museums of Northern Ireland

"Without them the Irish Mesolithic would be very different"

Ireland's First Settlers

Time and the Mesolithic

Peter Woodman

Oxbow Books

Oxford & Philadelphia

Published in the United Kingdom in 2015 by
OXBOW BOOKS
10 Hythe Bridge Street, Oxford OX1 2EW

and in the United States by
OXBOW BOOKS
908 Darby Road, Havertown, PA 19083

Paperback Edition: ISBN 978-1-78297-778-0
Digital Edition: ISBN 978-1-78297-779-7

A CIP record for this book is available from the British Library

Library of Congress Cataloging-in-Publication Data

Woodman, Peter C., author.
  Ireland's first settlers : time and the Mesolithic / Peter Woodman.
      pages cm
  Includes bibliographical references and index.
  ISBN 978-1-78297-778-0 (hardback) -- ISBN 978-1-78297-779-7 (eISBN) 1. Prehistoric peoples--
Ireland. 2. Mesolithic period--Ireland. 3. Excavations (Archaeology)--Ireland. 4. Ireland--Antiquities. I.
Title.
  GN806.5.W66 2015
  569.909417--dc23
                              2015022494

Printed in Malta by Gutenberg Press

For a complete list of Oxbow titles, please contact:

UNITED KINGDOM
Oxbow Books
Telephone (01865) 241249, Fax (01865) 794449
Email: oxbow@oxbowbooks.com
www.oxbowbooks.com

UNITED STATES OF AMERICA
Oxbow Books
Telephone (800) 791-9354, Fax (610) 853-9146
Email: queries@casemateacademic.com
www.casemateacademic.com/oxbow

Oxbow Books is part of the Casemate Group

Front cover: *Main picture: Hawkesworth's 1773 illustration of a Haush encampment; top right:
trihedral picks from (left) Lough Kinale, Derragh td, Co. Longford, (right) Clonava, Co. Westmeath.*
Back cover: *Portions of refitted cores from cache (?) recovered on the shores of Lough Beg, Co. Derry.*

CONTENTS

Part II
Laying the Foundations

Part III
Often an Island Too Far

PART IV
LIFEWAYS

PART V
WHERE TO NOW

ACKNOWLEDGEMENTS

Many of the images, photographs, plans and diagrams belonged to and were the work of colleagues, each of whom is thanked for their speedy permission to allow their use. The National Museum of Ireland and my former employers at the Ulster Museum (now NMNI) both provided access to illustrations and when needed to the collections. Similarly, in a positive sense, the study of the Irish Mesolithic would not be the same without the numerous excavations that have taken place, in particular, over the last two decades, This volume is enhanced by the freedom of access that many excavators gave to me as well as the support offered by the Archaeologists in both The Department of the Environment, Northern Ireland and the National Monuments Service in the Department of Arts, Heritage and the Gaeltacht. Similarly members of staff of the NRA could also not have been more helpful. Help was also forthcoming from a number of commercial companies, in particular NAC, indeed, access was denied by none. Some of the illustrations were provided from far away, in particular those supplied by Ernesto Piana, Conicet, Ushuaia, Argentina; Knut Helskog in Tromsø, Norway, Doug Price of the University of Wisconsin, Madison as well as Erik Brinch Petersen in Copenhagen, Denmark.

No book can get as far as publication without the help and guidance of a team of unsung heroes. My thanks to Kerri Cleary who read my initial draft and cleared out numerous typos and gaffs and undertook a mammoth task in getting some sort of order and system into the bibliography. Frances Healy provided an important objective overview and advice where on occasions I got lost in the detail, over-emphasised the negatives or when, in my anxiety to make a point, I got caught up in repetitions or lost the sense what I was really trying to say!

Perhaps the most daunting thought was the task of creating, scanning and borrowing what turned into 32 pages of colour and 200 other illustrations as well as colour pictures. This would not have happened without, over a period of 3 years, the constant patience and advice of Hugh Kavanagh of Landmark Survey. Others provided crucial help, most notably Kieran Westley of the Centre for Maritime Archaeology UUC who helped resolve the task of documenting coast changes while Elaine Lynch helped turn diverse drawing into images of similar style.

Funding for this project has come from two sources. These are the Dean of Arts Research Fund (UCC) and the generous support of the National University of Ireland.

Finally, without the trust, patience and encouragement of Oxbow and, in particular, Julie, I am not sure I would have got there.

Part I

IN THE BEGINNING

Chapter 1

Why?

When I first started to write this book a few years ago it was with the very simple intention of providing an easy, and hopefully accessible, introduction to many of the issues associated with the Irish Mesolithic. In part it was a frustrated reaction to decades-old interpretations of the Mesolithic period in Ireland and was intended to reach the archaeological profession in general. That profession, which existed some years ago at the height of the "Tiger Economy", is, however, no longer there! As I continued to write and think about why I still wanted to proceed with the project, I realised that, although I was in part writing it for myself, there were in fact multiple reasons to write the book. The archaeological profession, or perhaps the broader archaeological community, has always changed. Old misinterpretations will always be replaced by new ones. It has also provided an opportunity to reflect on the many ways in which "the doing of archaeology" has changed in my lifetime.

Almost exactly 50 years ago, just before I started to study Archaeology at "Queen's" and after an enthusiastic visit to the then Belfast Municipal Museum, I had rushed down to the Kinnegar in Holywood in search of "prehistory". The Kinnegar is a large ridge of sand on the shores of Belfast Lough, which runs in a south-westerly direction from the town. I would like to say that this resulted in initial discoveries of flint tools and that, ever since, I have been on a straight track attempting to elucidate the problems of Ireland's first settlers. In reality and ironically, even before my visit I had made that classic "First Year" mistake of thinking I was looking for Megaliths rather than "Mesoliths". This was compounded by the fact that everything I found consisted of natural fragments of flint nodules, so it was not until my first practical class with Arthur Apsimon that I discovered what I really should be looking for.

Shortly afterwards I was introduced to Hallam Movius's *The Irish Stone Age*. This book, with its combination of a detailed environmental history of Ireland, along with the battered and rolled bits of flint that made up the "Irish Larnian" left me wondering, is that all there was to the Irish Mesolithic and where were the traces of the settlement sites on which they lived? I had an early desire to be an Egyptologist, which was followed by a plan to work on the Palaeolithic, especially in North Africa, but the initial experiences on the Kinnegar had left me with both an abiding interest in the Irish Mesolithic and an awareness of how easy it was for amateurs to not quite understand what they had found. Having worked for 17 years in the Ulster Museum I was also very conscious that this meant both informing people of the importance of what they had found and, at the same time, trying to gently explain to someone that the bit of stone that "fitted so neatly into your hand" was more likely to be a fortuitous natural accident. I have always maintained that working as a curator in a museum is one of the best archaeological educations available. It also reinforced a belief that the interested amateur is just as important as the professional archaeologist. Similarly, I have never regretted the move to University College Cork at the other end of the island.

What has changed

In some ways, it would be simple to write an account of how many of our views on the Mesolithic period in Ireland have changed. It was apparent, however, that what was needed was more than either a retrospect or archaeological Canon or Lexicon to provide guidance.

In many ways, even though there were often local solutions, many of the problems that European Archaeology has faced throughout the last 50 years are similar. Not least of these has been the loss of the archaeological record. As economies grew, particularly from the 1960s onwards and with the changes in agricultural practices, especially within what was to become the EU, there was a growing concern over what was being lost. There has also been the consequent growth of the archaeological profession, which includes a shift from archaeological field activity being the domain of public bodies to being carried out by private companies with public authorities becoming the monitors of all aspects of activity.

In Ireland, in 1961, the year I started as a student in Queen's University Belfast, there were fewer than 25 people professionally employed as working archaeologists in Ireland. It is remarkable that in Ireland in the early 1960s there were, for a population of only 4,000,000, four university departments teaching archaeology at an undergraduate level. In Great Britain, with a population of over 50 million, there were also only four university departments teaching undergraduate courses in archaeology, with an additional two, Oxford University and the Institute of Archaeology at University College London, offering graduate training and research.

Some ten years later, as numbers began to rise, one of the debates in the early days of the then recently founded Irish Association of Professional Archaeologists (IAPA) was whether to allow those in less "tenured" positions, i.e. those employed on short-term contracts, some of whom were working in a virtual full-time capacity, to become members of the association. The assumption was that the association would provide a forum for academic debate and, indeed, it was understood that all the members should publish articles that demonstrated grounding in the broader implications of the topic, site, monument or artefact, on which they were working at the time. It was only in the mid-1980s that the first commercial companies began to appear in Ireland. Even then, archaeologists in the employment of public bodies were still in the majority. Subsequently, two interlinked economic and sociological factors were to change this ratio. These were the growing numbers of students of archaeology graduating at BA and MA level, as well as significant economic changes. Throughout this period graduate's foci changed, moving away from research topics based on catalogues of artefacts, to a concentration on field survey. This was in part due to the impact of investment by the EC/EEC/EU which, in turn, put pressure on monuments and therefore required survey and stocktaking of what survived. A few years later, by the late 1990s, the explosion of property, industrial and road developments, required a shift to impact surveys and salvage excavation. The archaeological profession was inexorably changing. The number of people working as archaeologists in Ireland had risen to over 1700 by 2007, a number which included graduates from many other countries.

Perhaps I look on some of these changes through "rose-tinted glasses" that had been coloured from an earlier time. As a student in Queen's University Belfast in the early 1960s, the Archaeology Department, and what was known as the Archaeological Survey, were all based in one house in University Square. Here, in spite of various tensions, there was a major overlap in interests, but even more so most of those working in University Square were expected to be "multi-taskers". This was particularly true of Pat Collins, Dudley Waterman and Peter Addyman or Arthur Apsimon and the same could be said for others, such as Brian O'Kelly in Cork or the staff of the two museums, the National Museum of Ireland in Dublin and the Ulster Museum in Belfast. These were people who knew the artefactual material and could excavate as well as survey and who were fairly well acquainted with the archaeological literature.

The emergence of specialists in everything from lithics or post-medieval pottery to bones and plants had strength but also a danger of losing an overview approach. In the emergence of the unfortunately termed principle "Polluter Pays", the supernovae of salvage excavations, first in urban contexts and then more generally in roads, housing developments and elsewhere, created a deluge of information that was in danger of drowning us. The shift can, perhaps, at best be illustrated not only by the number of excavations undertaken but more by the purpose of those excavations. In 1970, when the first *Excavations Bulletin* was collated on the floor of my flat, there were fewer than 50 excavations taking place per annum, while in 2006, at the height of the "building boom", there were well over 2000. The most significant change, however, was that in 1970 the majority of excavations that took place were research driven, while 35 years later, fewer than ten sites were being explored primarily as research excavations. There was a shift in expectation, from an understanding that sooner or later there would be a published report issued, to a world where the highest priority was where the next project would be. Indeed, the work of many of the field archaeologists operating during this time is to be complimented, but a perusal of many of the reports also left one with the feeling that emphasis was placed on a product that needed to show "value for money". Yes, many amazing discoveries have been made and in particular the National Roads Authority must be given credit for its scheme monographs and many useful regional and thematic compilations that are still in the process of being published. The impact of sites such as Raystown with its eight water mills in Co. Meath or the revelations of the long sought for Early Bronze Age settlement sites is immense but these and other "OMG" sites are only part of the story. What about sites recovered during other forms of large infrastructural projects, such as gas and water pipelines, major industrial developments and large-scale housing developments? Despite INSTAR (Irish National Strategic Archaeological Research programme funded by the Heritage Council of Ireland) having made inroads into turning the fine-grained detail into coherent and accessible stories, the recent downturn may have left us with a legacy in our stores that could become reminiscent of the backlog created by collectors gathering material from agriculture, industrial and infrastructural developments that took place at various times in the 19th century.

Naturally, over the years, new methodologies have emerged, as have new ways of looking at the evidence. Explanations have altered from the "Invasionist" perspectives of the post-war era to the search for more local rationalisations. The environmental-led views, along with the assumption of humans as little more than "walking stomachs" whose lives could be mathematically and rationally modelled, were found to be wanting, and so were replaced by schools of thought that belonged more to the post-modernist intellectual era. Hopefully, these approaches will merge as a collage rather than a series of mutually exclusive alternatives.

Many of the issues have been outlined by Zvelebil (2009), who evaluated the strengths and weakness of various schools of thought, ranging from the sometimes failed promises of certain "scientifically rigorous tested conclusions" of Processual and

New Archaeology to the "paradigmatic prejudices … And the Nihilism" of some post-modernist practitioners.

There are, at the local level, certain worries. In the context of what has just been discussed, more and more often, undergraduate and post-graduate papers refer to the impossibility of an entirely objective understanding of what we are exploring. This has to be a valid critique of earlier, perhaps naive expectations, but at the same time there appears to be a distancing by many from an engagement with the monuments, artefacts and excavations that form the core of our discipline.

Have the universities, which have the privilege of standing back from the day-to-day commercial world of excavation and to some extent post-excavation, been able to provide the lead in bridging the gap between Practice and Theory, or rather, between the important tasks of salvage that produces data and explaining its broader significance?

There is always the idea that getting a large grant means a major insight into new areas of research. As Feynman (1999, 214–15), in *Cargo Cults Science; Some remarks on Science, Pseudo-science and learning on how not to fool yourself* notes, throughout many disciplines, it seemed more important to get a big result that would draw in a further grant than search for a more satisfactory explanation of the problem being investigated. Incidentally, in spite of the date of publication, this is not an observation made during the last two decades! It was instead made in 1974 at "Caltech as a Commencement Address". The emphasis on requiring staff to produce articles for international "Peer Reviewed Journals" is also laudable and important to show the quality of work being undertaken here in Ireland. There appears, sometimes amongst those that evaluate our research, even here in Ireland, a lack of appreciation in the fact that there can be a difference in the meaning of the phrase "International Work", being elsewhere in the world, which is one way of looking at it, but equally, if not more importantly, the standards and the consequences of work carried out in Ireland can also be of "International Significance". The number crunching and documenting of large assemblages, or the production of a coherent report on a complex site, can also take years before they make a major contribution of new knowledge and even new insights, but they often do not fit within the timetable required for the next Quality Review or Research Assessment Exercise.

In spite of these issues, it is imperative for Irish archaeology that we can demonstrate to our peers and colleagues the quality of the Irish archaeological record and our research. This necessitates that our work is published in "International Peer Reviewed Journals".

Does the broader archaeological community read these journals? There is a need to publish or communicate our work in forms that will also be more accessible on a local level. There is, therefore, a need for a book like *Ireland's First Settlers*.

This part of the introduction is written not so much as a critique but rather derives from a series of concerns. Virtually all of the Royal Irish Academy funded research excavations of the last 75 years or more have been published. Some of them have taken a long time to appear, indeed, in some cases a very very long time! It is apparent that, for any excavation, the longer time goes on the greater the risk of non-publication. This can be due to many factors, ranging from personal circumstances such as a change of jobs and illness to accidents to the assemblages and field notes. In our case, given the collapse of the "Celtic Tiger" we do not always need massive reports, but rather we require good, relative brief descriptions of what has been found, as well as its significance. That product should be well within the ability of people who have acquired a broad range of experiences, i.e. multi-taskers.

In summary, are we in danger of being like the Ancient Mariner rather than Aladdin?

This part of the introduction is written to give a personal view on where we are today. As someone who has tended to take the glass half empty approach it may seem negative, but it is advantageous to realise that if one's tipple is in danger of running out it is better to know and get to the bar before it closes!

There have been, even within the Mesolithic, some amazing discoveries within the last 10–20 years. Many of these sites will be described later in the book. These should not obscure the accumulation of numerous modest sites and stray finds that at last begin to flesh out the distribution of known Mesolithic activity throughout the island. The danger is that, with the demise of the "Celtic Tiger", I hope we have not missed the call that time was up and the bar is now closed.

The purpose

From the inception of this book as an idea to its completion, the purpose has not really changed. It is hoped that it will provide a useful and simple understanding of the "nuts and bolts", or rather flints, stones and bones, of the Irish Mesolithic. Indeed, it will hopefully provide a bit more, including the historical context in which Irish Mesolithic studies have developed, as well as relevant comparative evidence from other regions. It will also attempt to look forward and provide an opportunity to reassess some of those comfortable self-evident truths that we have got used to. The initial reason for writing this book also still remains. While others will point to my own misinterpretations and mistakes, there are still, especially in excavation reports, numerous misunderstandings and a lack of awareness as to how much things have changed. These include a lack of familiarity with lithic technologies, for example, not understanding some of the definitions of certain artefacts, e.g. that a microlith was more than a small blade or that if one is to use the term "Bann Flake" it is necessary to realise that relatively few leaf-shaped flakes could be considered as Bann or Butt Trimmed Flakes, i.e. type fossils of the Later Mesolithic in Ireland. Of course these are not confined to the Mesolithic, thus on occasions there are assumptions that any pointed flint flake is an arrowhead. Similarly, there is still a belief that any good flint had to be brought from Antrim or that, unless there was clear uncontrovertible evidence to the contrary, all polished stone axes must be presumed to be Neolithic. Fortunately things are changing in other areas, such as a lack of understanding of the impact of calibration. Thus for many, the Mesolithic was thought to end around the calibrated date of 4000 cal BC/6000 cal BP, but still began with an uncalibrated date of 7000 BC. In effect, this resulted in shortening the Mesolithic by nearly 1000 years. (See below for an explanation of the manner in which radiocarbon dates have been used in the book)

Hopefully this volume will not result in the creation of a rigid typological and archaeological Canon, and this is one reason why some of the basic descriptions of raw materials, tools and sites are embedded in the context of a broader series of issues. At one level this approach provides an opportunity to evaluate a range of evidence and interpretations. Feynman (1999, 210–14) refers to the fact that one must, in a metaphorical sense, pay attention to the point(s) that lie off the line. It is so easy to become enamoured by the favoured theories of the day. Thus, any anomalous contra-indicators that point to alternatives which might suggest the need for further research, or bring about a realisation that matters are more complex than the researcher wants, are just ignored.

There is also a particular importance in placing Irish evidence in a broader European context. There has always been a potential tension in researching the Irish Mesolithic. For some decades one agenda was, for the author as well as others, to try to "normalise" the Irish Mesolithic. This could be, for example, by identifying a range of equipment that was similar to that used elsewhere in adjacent parts of Europe. There was, at times, almost desperation to find artefacts that were common elsewhere; indeed the ultimate touchstone was to find the equivalent of that discovered at Star Carr! Microliths, axes and barbed points had to be found before one could claim that Ireland either had a Mesolithic or had something more than the vestiges left behind by unfortunate residues of Epi-Palaeolithic societies fleeing the onset of postglacial environmental change. It took a long time to realise that, in so many ways, the Mesolithic of Ireland was very different and that when one bedded the archaeology into Ireland's distinct geography and ecology, these differences made sense. The distinctiveness of the Irish Mesolithic can best be appreciated by comparing the Irish evidence to the various processes, dynamics, etc., that may have been different in other parts of Europe. Similarly, there are aspects of excavation in elucidating traces of settlement, butchering or exchange where we can learn from other regions.

It is also important to appreciate that the study of the Irish Mesolithic has been blessed by being so strongly associated with the natural sciences. In an era in which post-modernism has dominated so much thinking, attempts at objective observation can often be dismissed. Yet, at the other extreme, there is a rich and often tetchy debate with a range of researchers in other sciences who often fail to grasp the balance required of archaeologists as they walk a tightrope. This is between the wealth of information available from archaeological sites, including the chronological structures within which we operate, and the very partial, almost quirky nature, of the surviving evidence. We have a special opportunity to engage in constructive discussions and seek parity of esteem for our viewpoints. We also can speak with authority in these areas, in fact one might even dare suggest that many of the most crucial and useful insights that come from laboratories often come from those that are part of the archaeological milieu. Pollock (2005) has shown how "uncertain" the pursuit of science can be, even in an interpretation of the contemporary world, never mind when, to paraphrase the title of Lowenthal's (1985) work, we are exploring "the Foreign Country of the Past". Of course as much as those of any other discipline, whether laboratory based or field science, our observations have their own validity but at the same time many of us have had the humbling experience of realising that our interpretations of these observations have been totally wrong!

The format

In an attempt to address a series of broader issues, as well as trying to not break up the narrative with too many details included in the wrong places, this work has been divided into five major sections:

1. Placing the Irish Mesolithic in to its historical context, as well as providing an introduction to relevant aspects of Ireland's natural history. In other words, what were the issues, social and environmental contexts within which the study of the Irish Mesolithic developed?
2. What constitutes the archaeological record to date and provides the basis for our discussions on the Irish Mesolithic?
3. A proposed and hopefully critical re-evaluation of the Irish Mesolithic, which will examine issues from a) the initial settlement of Ireland, b) the manner in which lithic technologies changed within the 4000 years of this period of our past.
4. A reconsideration of the evidence for the way of life followed during the Irish Mesolithic.
5. Thoughts for: a) how best to progress research on the Irish Mesolithic, with some emphasis as to best practices in the field, and b) suggested areas of research where Ireland may not always be able to make a contribution but at the same time where we should always keep that richer tapestry in mind.

Health warnings

It will be noted in several places that information from certain excavations and research projects is presented in a generalised manner and lacks some specific details. This approach has been taken out of respect for fellow researchers who are involved in excavation report writing or research projects. In an ideal world one should wait until they are all finished but by then other projects will be at an interim stage! Ultimately, archaeology is always a work in progress, whether it is lab based or in the field and especially in anything we write.

For some, many of the figures and facts may be familiar. At one level there is a convenience in using ones own drawing from excavation reports and other sources some of which are now approaching their 40th birthday. If nothing else, it reduces the administrative problems of sorting permission and copyright. However, another reason is that much of the information used has been scattered across various journal papers, excavation reports, buried in conference publications and, to some extent books.

Finally, there may be those who look at the way certain sites are quoted with a great frequency and then conclude that the Author never left really "The North". However while in the northern half of the island, where research has been ongoing for 150 years, in 1978 when *The Mesolithic in Ireland* was published there was in effect nothing about the Mesolithic south of a line between Dalkey Island and Galway City! The positive side is to look at how much the picture has changed in the last 40 years.

For others, Irish geography may be a mystery therefore this chapter also includes two maps to help the stranger navigate their way through Ireland's unique approach to its geography (Figs 1.1 and 1.2).

Fig. 1.1. Counties and Provinces of Ireland.

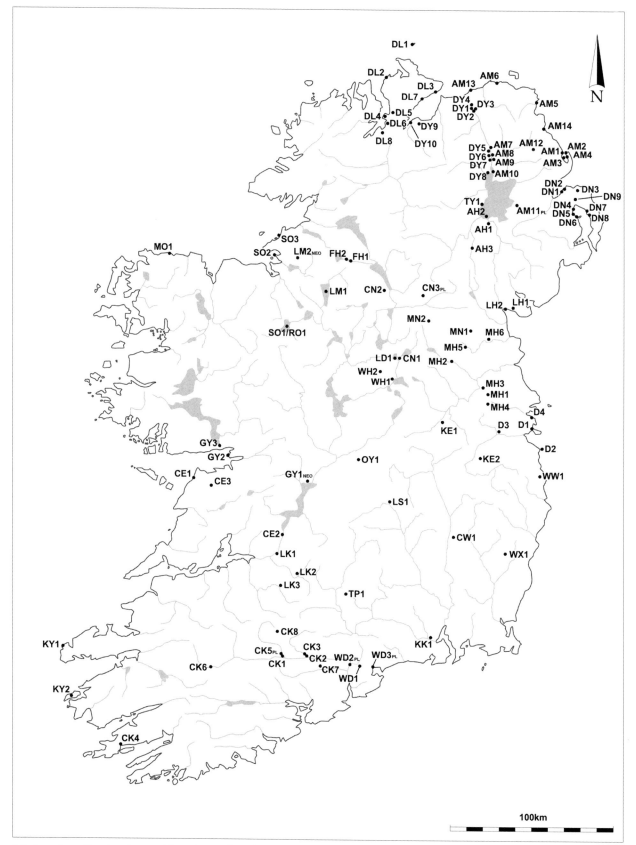

Fig. 1.2. Location of major sites and locations referred to in the text (all are Mesolithic sites except for those with a Pleistocene element marked PL and Mesolithic/Neolithic transitional and Neolithic sites marked NEO) See facing page.

For those who accompanied me

While *Ireland's First Settlers* is mostly about the present state of affairs in Ireland's earliest prehistory and where we go from here, it is also a reflection on one individual's 50 years interest in the past. Therefore, not surprisingly, while many people have helped prepare this particular review of Ireland's earliest prehistory, it is also personal reflection on a long journey where other people have accompanied me along the way.

I would like to thank my wife and family for tolerating another long episode of obsession, tantrums and absentmindedness.

The names of even some of the others are numerous and hopefully many will recognise their role in the story.

There were several "Trinitys" who like the stars in Orion's Belt were there to help and guide:

Arthur who made sure that I was grounded in the realities of what we knew

ULSTER
Antrim (AM) 1) Larne, 2) Ballylumford, 3) Glynn, 4) Ballydown, 5) Cushendun/ Castlecarra, 6) Portbraddan/Ballintoy, 7) Gortgole,
  8) Aughnahoy, 9) Newferry 3 and 4, 10) Toome bypass, 11) Agnadaragh PL 12) Linford 13) Portrush 14) Bay Farm, 15) Drumakeely.
Armagh (AH) 1) Derrinraw, 2) Coney Island, 3) Navan Fort.
Donegal (DL) 1) Inishtrahull, 2) Dunaff, 3) Eleven Ballyboes 4) Baylet & Inch Island, 5) Tievebane, 6) Ballymoney 7) Red Castle.
Down (DN) 1) Glendhu, 2) Holywood, 3) Ballyholme, 4) Rough Island/Castle Espie, 5) Ringneill, 6) Reagh Island, 7) Kilnatierney,
  8) Goldsmiths and Temple Midden, 9) Ballymaglaff and Mount Alexander.
Cavan (CN) 1) Kilgolagh and Lough Kinale, 2) Maghery PL, 3) Kilcorby.
Derry (DY) 1) Castleroe, 2) The Cutts 3) Loughan Island 4) Mount Sandel, 5) Portglenone/Glenone, 6) Culbane, 7) Newferry 1 and 2,
  8) Toome – Creagh td.
Fermanagh (FH) 1) Lough MacNean.
Monaghan (MN) 1) Ballyhoe lough, 2) Annagh ma Kerrig.
Tyrone (TY) 1) Brookend.

LEINSTER
Carlow (CW) 1) Carlow/ Tinryland.
Dublin (D) 1) Sutton, 2) Dalkey Island, 3) Cooldrinagh/ Leixlip area 4) Skerries.
Kildare (KE) 1) Kilrane Hill, 2) Morristownbiller.
Kilkenny (KK) 1) Newrath.
Laois (LX) Clonadaragh.
Longford (LD) 1) Derragh Island.
Louth (LH) 1) Rockmarshall, 2) Dowdallshall.
Meath (MH) 1) Leashemstown 2) Crossakeel area, 3) Blundelstown, 4) Clowanstown 5) Moynagh, 6) Newgrange.
Offaly (OY) 1) Lough Boora.
Westmeath (WH) 1) Lough Derravarragh/Clonava 2) Corralana.
Wexford (WX) 1) Killybegs.
Wicklow (WW) Baltyboys Upper.

MUNSTER
Clare (CE) 1) Fanore, 2) Killaloe 3) Poulnabrone NEO.
Cork (C) 1) Kilcummer, 2) Ballyderown, 3) Gortore, 4) Minane, 5) Foley Cave PL, 6) Lough Allua 7) Ballyoran, 8) Castlepook (Pl).
Kerry (KY) 1) Ferriter's Cove 2) Clynacartan.
Limerick (LK) 1) Hermitage, 2) Killuragh Cave, 3) Rathjordan.
Tipperary (TIP) 1) Cashel
Waterford (WD) 1) Ballinnamintra, Brothers/Oongalour PL 2) Kilgreany PL/Neo 3) Shandon PL.

CONNAUGHT
Galway 1) Stoney Island NEO, 2) Tawin Island NEO, 3) River Corrib/Galway area.
Leitrim (LM) 1) Lough Allen, 2) Sramore Cave.
Mayo (MO) 1) Belderrig.
Sligo (SO) 1) Lough Gara (also extending into Roscommon), 2) Rosses Point 3) Connor's Island.

Martin who always answered "you tell me"
Laurence who often said "well why not"

There is also the trinity of those who travelled in friendship:
Mike, Jim and Caroline

Amongst the students who made a difference:
Liz, Farina and Marion

The collectors who introduced me to their landscape:
Eddie Reagan in Strangford; Willie Stuart in the Glens as well as Brian McNaught and Tommy Gallagher in Inishowen

And finally:
Doug for being there in Warsaw railway station 1973
Sinead for being there at Tralee railway station in 1985
Nyree for being there when her help was needed
Nicky without whom Baylet would never have happened.
Brian O'Kelly for cajoling me into thinking about a move to Cork

In summary

Perhaps after 50 years I have become convinced that, especially when dealing with an episode of time when monuments are rare and even remote prospection often does not help, then it is the attitude not of a few researchers but rather that of the archaeological community as a whole that really matters. It has to be the belief in the "possible" that counts. In other words, a belief in the possibility that there is a richer archaeological record of "Ireland's First Settlers" and that it is a period that has much more to contribute to our understanding of human settlement in Ireland than simply finding the oldest site or seeing it as a period whose sole purpose is to be the springboard for the Neolithic.

The Irish Mesolithic is not so much the first 4000 years but rather it represents roughly 40% of the known human settlement of this Island. What can it contribute?

I hope that, in perusing this book, for every time the reader says "I knew that" there will also be a "that's interesting".

Chapter 2

Understanding Ireland's environment and ecology

Authors, such as Mitchell and Ryan (1997) or more recently Hall (2011), have provided detailed surveys of how the Irish landscape developed. The former covers from Ireland's earliest geological record to virtually the present, while the latter begins as the ice retreats after the Last Glacial Maximum and continues to the present, and indeed also looks to the future. The purpose of this short introduction is therefore twofold. First, to provide a précis of the aspects of the Irish landscape and environment that relate to the study of the Mesolithic, and second, to examine the aspects of past change, such as episodes of glaciations and their consequences, that effect both the possibility of discovering a Palaeolithic presence in Ireland and the creation of the landscape that existed in the first half of the Holocene, i.e. the landscape that existed from when people first arrived in Ireland until about 6000 years cal BP.

Ireland today

Ireland, which is the 20th largest island on the planet, has an area of 84,000+ square km and lies in the mid-50°s degrees north. It is placed in the Atlantic, on the most westerly fringe of Europe, with a climate that is ameliorated by the Atlantic Gulf stream. Not surprisingly it can be thought of as "a low flat windy mountain top with a cool pluvial environment", which is perhaps best illustrated by Kelly's (2008) overview of the Avifauna. Obviously there are mountainous areas in Ireland but almost all of Ireland lies below 500 m ASL, but a significant portion lies above 200 m ASL. Traditionally, in the teaching of geography Ireland was referred to as being saucer-shaped with the mountains usually, though not always, being placed close to the coast (Pl. 1, a). Evans (1981) refers to the fact that: "No other country in Europe has such a fragmented peripheral arrangement of mountain land".

The final form of this landscape was, in the main, created by the last ice sheets that reached their maximum extent between 27,000 and 25,000 years ago. The result was a large central plain in which the debris of the last glacial retreats had been dumped. In other words, large parts of Ireland were covered with moraines, eskers, drumlins; expanses of glacial out-wash deposits, as well as of glacio-marine deposits in certain areas.

Within this landscape the extent of Ireland's waterways is often ignored. The fact that the Shannon is the largest and longest river in the British Isles is well known. Over 50% of Ireland is within the catchment basins of six major rivers, i.e. the Shannon, Bann and Nore/Barrow/Suir systems and the Corrib, Blackwater and Mourne/Finn complex. The first three have mean discharges of more than 100 m^3 per second. The fact that Lough Neagh is the largest body of freshwater in the British Isles is also well known, but while Ireland's lakes cannot be compared with southern Finland or the great lakes of central Sweden there are few other loughs/lakes in Britain and adjacent parts of Europe that rival some of the slightly smaller Irish loughs, such as Loughs Conn, Mask, Corrib and Erne (Pl. 1, b). The Irish waterways are an often under-appreciated part of our landscape. Of course initially, as will be discussed below, Ireland would also have been littered with smaller lakes that have since been submerged under raised bogs. These bogs could have begun to develop even before the end of the Mesolithic when fen-peat began to accumulate and reduce the size of the lakes.

The other aspect of Ireland's ecology, which many appreciate less, is its climate and in particular, the rain! As Mitchell and Ryan (1997, 100–2) have pointed out, the total rainfall, even at 1400 mm per annum in the west and 700 mm in the east, is not excessive. Much of Ireland has, however, between 150 and 200 days each year on which it rains, along with high humidity and more extensive cloud cover. In other words, there was a poor rate of evapotranspiration (Pl. 1, c). Mitchell and Ryan (*ibid.*, 103–4) also noted that a consequence of the cloud cover is a reduced level of sunshine and heat that results in difficult growth conditions for many plants. Not surprisingly therefore, these climatic factors contribute to a gradation between permanent grasslands in the west with longer periods of grass growth, to areas of arable farming tending to lie in the east and south. Thus in 1970, before agricultural policies of the then EEC began to have an impact, tillage of more than 15% of available farmland in any particular area could only be found in the east of Ireland, as well as certain select areas of South Munster and North Donegal (Haughton 1979, map 63). Doyle and Ó Críodáin (2003) have noted that Ireland has the third highest percentage of land covered by "bog lands", i.e. 16.2%, with only Finland and Estonia having a higher percentage. As will be discussed below, while these different types of "bog land" evolved in different ways, and some may post-date the Mesolithic, their very existence certainly provided obstacles to the discovery of scatters of Mesolithic artefacts (Pl. I, d).

Climate, as well as human activities, has helped the development of the upland blanket peats that, in the last few thousand years, have replaced the original forest scrub that had covered significant areas of higher ground during much of the earlier part of the Holocene. In many areas the early vegetation would have been a scrub cover of pine and hazel that could have existed in harsher climatic conditions. These would have been present, especially in the west, on what Hall (2011, 64) described as wet, starved soils where the rain had washed the nutrients from the soil. In effect, any deterioration in these less developed soils in upland areas, where soil temperature would be lower and rainfall higher, would create conditions leading to the development of blanket peat. The trees would be replaced by a ground cover in which sphagnum peat spread across the ground, along with rushes and plants such as heathers, which began to grow across extensive areas of the uplands. It is of course important to realise that blanket peat covered uplands, which are such an iconic part of the Irish landscape, usually only came into existence not only after the Mesolithic but, in many areas, after the Neolithic.

The most obvious factor that conditioned the way in which many aspects of the Irish environment developed is that Ireland is an island, and may have been one for the last 16,000 years. Certainly this must have had an effect on the restricted range of species in many categories of Ireland's fauna and flora, some of the implications of which, particularly for mammals and freshwater fish, will be discussed below. In general terms, Ireland is impoverished, thus Mitchell and Ryan (1997, 111) noted that, including extinct species, 14 terrestrial mammals may be thought to be native to Ireland, while 32 could be thought to be native to Britain. While those absent from Ireland include large species such as Elk (*Alces alces*) and other, albeit extinct, species, and Aurochs (*Bos primigenius*), perhaps the almost complete absence of small mammals, such as voles (*Arvicola* terrestris and *Microtus* sp.), the common shrew (*Sorex araneus*) or the mole (*Talpa europaea*), is more striking.

The overall patterns of some other general categories, such as insects and birds, are also very different even from mainland Britain. Webb (1983) noted that for many groups of insects and other invertebrates, Ireland contains only 65% of those found in Britain. Webb also observed that, besides having a lesser variety of plants than in Britain, both islands were much poorer than a slightly more southern region, such as France:

	France	Great Britain	Ireland
Plants	3500	1172	815

It might have been expected that the bird population, which would find Ireland easier to access than land animals, might be much more diverse. Kelly (2008, 99–101) makes numerous observations about the difference between Britain and Ireland, including the fact that only 65% of the species of breeding pairs found in Britain are found in Ireland. Perhaps more tellingly, given Ireland's size relative to that of Britain, this is 5–15% lower than might have been expected. In numerous instances particular groups are even less successful, and in some cases, such as the Blue Tit, the clutch size is much smaller than elsewhere. Even though there are some good examples of the long distant migrant species of birds being present in large numbers, only 46% of the migrants that regularly nest in Britain are found in Ireland. Kelly (*ibid.*, 104) speculates on whether the "cool pluvial and virtually a/seasonal climate" associated with windy conditions and poorly drained soils are contributors to the lack of diversity of avian species in Ireland.

This observation may be relevant to Ireland's ecosystem in general. Are there other species that have failed to establish a presence because of climatic and related factors? Simon Harrison (pers. comm.) has suggested that, in the case of the common freshwater fish, most species would normally expect seasonal variations and take actions accordingly, such as existing in the mud at the bottom of the lake during the winter. They could not, as in the case of the rudd, which is an introduced species that has been relatively successful, adapt their behaviour in waters where there is not a significant seasonal variation between winter and summer. Is this part of the reason for our low numbers of reptilian species? In particular, are frog's recent arrivals, long-term residents, or failed colonists on several occasions?

There are many areas where there still seem to be no simple answers. If we look from the perspective of today's environment, even allowing for the massive human impact on the environment during the last 300 years in particular, how can we be sure that some of the absences of insects and birds may not be a product of major factors such as the loss, in recent centuries, of extensive woodland? Reilly (2008) suggests that in the case of certain woodland beetle species, they may have originally been present but loss of habitat from mid-Holocene times due to climate change and human activities, including the woodland clearances of the last few centuries, may have caused their demise. In other words, some parts of Ireland's present biosphere have been created over the millennia by human activities as well as directly by nature itself.

There is, of course, also the opposite question. How do certain species get to Ireland? Are they recent introductions or have they existed in Ireland since the onset of the Holocene or earlier? Reynolds (2008) has suggested that over the millennia numerous freshwater invertebrates were probably introduced by people. Similarly, how does one explain the presence of freshwater molluscs, even quite early in the Holocene, as demonstrated at Clondalkin (Preece *et al.* 1986)?

The development of Ireland's ecology and geography

Irrespective of the unanswered questions and the difficulties of interpreting past environments from present day Ireland, there is no doubt that many of the fundamental characteristics of Ireland's environment were, to a great extent, in existence even 10,000 years ago. Ultimately, in trying to understand the environment in which Mesolithic peoples lived in Ireland, one has to return to the evidence from, in the broadest sense of the term, palaeo-ecology.

One must also allude to the ongoing debate as to what, in an Irish context, is meant by the word "Native". As will be discussed below, there is no reason to believe that there was a single event after the "Ice Age" when, in a very short period of time, a complete suite of plants and animals, including humans, arrived, or that anything arriving significantly later than 10,000 years ago cannot be considered as "Native". Does one then use the arrival of farming and a range of domesticates as the cut-off point? In other words, if they cannot survive in the wild must they be excluded? Similarly, does the Norman introduction of rabbits (*Oryctolagus cuniculus*) and hedgehogs (*Erinacaea europaeus*) mean that they cannot be considered as native? Indeed the problem may be more with the way we use the term "Native" rather than issues of population dynamics! (See Hall (2011 37–9) for further discussion on this issue).

As noted earlier, this short review of evidence from Ireland is geared at understanding how Ireland's landscape and changing environment would have effected both the island's initial colonists, as well as whether it helped or hindered the search for traces of the Irish Mesolithic. In part, its purpose is to provide some insights into the following questions:

- How much did the last "Ice Age" mask or destroy any possible trace of a Palaeolithic presence in Ireland?
- How much did the consequent landscape and environment help or hinder initial settlement?
- What changes in the environment impacted on Mesolithic peoples living in Ireland?

The Late Pleistocene background

One of the greatest challenges in dealing with the environmental issues is that one can drown in a tidal wave of terms, names for different periods of time or events as well as variations in how the age of an object, bone or even a period is described. The purpose of this chapter, therefore, is neither to provide a full account of the Irish Pleistocene, especially the upper Pleistocene, nor to adjudicate between various interpretations, but rather to assess the types of challenges animals and humans would have faced when they first arrived. It will also consider how that environment changed.

Dating methods: health warnings and explanations

For many of us, understanding dating methods that lie outside our comfort zone are one of our biggest challenges. There has been, during my career for example, a sea change in how we name and sequence the numerous phases known as Glacials and Interglacials, that make up the geological period we call the Pleistocene. We have shifted from the pan-European Gunz through to Würm four glacial episodes or local variants (Wymer 1968, 80). The shift was initially begun with the drilling of cores from the Ocean floor which produced indications many more glacial events seem to have taken place (Shackelton 1987). The fact that these results were derived from distant ocean floors and could not be tied into an absolute chronological framework meant that there was some reluctance to accept the implications that for much of the Pleistocene there were very large numbers of very dynamic changes. Ultimately, the additional evidence obtained from coring the Greenland ice caps usually referred to as GRIP and NGRIP, where it has been possible to correlate fluctuations between Oxygen 16 and 18, referred to below as $O^{16/18}$ which indicated temperature change and provide estimates of age by counting annual layers of ice formation (Dansgaard *et al.* 1993). These provided further indications that Planet Earth had seen numerous events of extreme cold especially within the last million years.

As a result, Glacial as well as the warmer Interglacial stages are now described as MIS or Marine Isotope Stages. In general warmer, often interglacial or lesser interstadials, are designated MIS 1, 3, 5 etc. while the Glacial events are designated MIS 2 Last Glacial, 4 the Fermanagh Stadial, 6 etc.

The bread and butter of staple dating method for many of us is radiocarbon dating. The use of radiocarbon dating has also changed. The most important change was the realisation that there have been, through time, changes in the amount of carbon[14] in the atmosphere which is due to fluctuations in solar radiation. Thus the inferred age based on the level of radioactive carbon in a specimen has to be corrected/calibrated so as to provide a rough estimate of the actual age of a specimen in calendrical years. The uncalibrated dates, or determinations, are expressed expressed in years Before (a notional) Present – 1950 – simply as BP, while the calibrated dates are usually written as cal BP or, using the BC/AD Gregorian calendar, cal BC/AD.

There are instances where, either, periods studied are beyond the limits of radiocarbon dating i.e. in general beyond 50,000 years ago, or where a precise date is not being used; then dates are often expressed in a more rounded form e.g. 35,000 or 200,000 become 35 ka or 200 ka. The same system can be used in more recent times e.g. 10 ka or 8.2 ka and in these cases these are calendrical years.

There also had to be a choice on how radiocarbon dates from after the Last Glacial Maximum are to be expressed.

I have opted to express the age of samples dated in the form of cal BP. There are two main reasons. First in researching a period such as the Mesolithic, one is constantly using information that is derived from the natural sciences. In the natural sciences, dates are normally expressed in cal BP. Similarly, in researching the origins of the Mesolithic i.e. in the Late Upper Palaeolithic, one is also dealing with researchers who expressed their dates in cal BP format. The only argument for using cal BC is that cal BC is the conventional manner in which radiocarbon dates are expressed by those researching the Neolithic period and if we are to progress our understanding of the transition from hunter-gatherer to famer it is convenient to use the cal BC format. This, however unintentionally, suggests that the Mesolithic period it is of lesser significance than the issue of how it ends!

Ireland's Pleistocene background

There is no doubt that Ireland may have been extensively glaciated on numerous occasions, therefore the amount of evidence surviving from earlier interglacials is very slight and often difficult to date.

There are now also strong indications that the presumed ice limit of the last Glaciation, sometimes referred to as the Ballylanders Moraine (see Woodman *et al.* 1997and Fig. 2.1) may have been a standstill as ice retreated after the Last Glacial Maximum. Therefore deposits to the south of this limit, instead of being of last interglacial, are much later. Ó Cofaigh *et al.* (2010) suggest that deposits in the south-west of Ireland, at locations such as Courtmacsherry, CountyCork, date much later than had hitherto been suggested. They have argued that deposits previously found in the southernmost parts of Ireland, which were thought to belong to the "Munsterian" or the last interglacial, were probably created during MIS (Marine Isotope Stages) 4 or even 3 (Fig. 2.2). As the relevance will be apparent below, it should be noted that there are occasional survivals of much older deposits but they are exceptionally rare. Thus Ó Drisceoill and Jennings (2006) uncovered early deposits in two caves at Ballynamuck townland, which occur in the Vicinity of Shandon Cave (Fig. 1.2). In these caves they recovered deposits that appear to date to MIS 7/6, approximately 220–155 ka and MIS 5 e, or roughly 150 ka. While they only contained microfauna, they provided a clear indication that deposits could survive in an area that was to be subsequently glaciated.

In Ireland, therefore, it would appear that deposits from even the last interglacial, MIS 5e, are rare although not quite non-existent (Coxon and McGarron 2009, 373–6). From a potential archaeological perspective, our focus begins after MIS 5 i.e. MIS 4 (Fig. 2:2) and concentrates on the cold, but not Glacial, stages that follow the short-lived glacial Fermanagh Stadial. Coxon and McGarron (*ibid.*, 386–90) suggest this took place around or before 50 ka.

Within the following period of up to 25,000 years, i.e. 59–28 ka (MIS 3), at least three phases were recognised.

All dates quoted immediately below for these three phases are uncalibrated BP. They are used in this manner, as will be apparent, for historical reasons. These include:

An initial phase documented at Aghnadarragh, County Antrim (McCabe *et al.* 1987), where a series of deposits (Unit 6) was recorded and, from the range of dates obtained, seem to belong to a phase that may have been as old as or older than 48 ka. Woody peat detritus where organic remains existed suggested that where the conditions were warm enough to allow the establishment of a *Betula-Pinus-Picea* woodland and where the mean July temperature was +15°C to +18°C and the mean January temperature was −11°C to +4°C. The underlying gravel and diamicton produced mammoth (*Mammuthus primigenius*) remains which may be older than 50,000 ka.

The Hollymount Phase ~50? –44,000 ka, was much colder with much less woodland and an insect population reflecting colder conditions. This phase has a suggested mean July temperature of +11°C to +13°C and mean January temperature of −18°C to −7°C.

The third stage, the Derryvree Phase, ~44–28,000 ka, contains a flora that suggests a virtual tundra which was an open, treeless environment, i.e. similar to parts of the Canadian Arctic. Coxon and McGarron (2009, 388) have suggested that within this period there were other possible phases or climatic fluctuations that may, in the future, be identified. This could include instances such as a warm phase at 42 ka, which has been identified as the British Upton Warren Interstadial complex.

The faunal remains associated with MIS 3 in Ireland may be of particular significance. Some remains from the cave excavations, which are discussed in their historical context in Chapter 3, were obtained as part of the Irish Quaternary fauna's project. As evident in Woodman *et al.* (1997), virtually every large mammal that was present in Britain during MIS 3 was also present in Ireland. The most notable absence, besides humans, is the Coelodonta *Antiquitatis* or Woolly Rhinoceros. The work of the Irish Quaternary Faunas Project (IQFP) suggested a shift in species throughout time. During the "Hollymount" and earlier part of the" Derryvree" phase, which in the context of Ireland was from about 50,000 BP (uncalibrated) down to approximately 35,000 BP (uncalibrated). These dates, and those used immediately below, were for a period when the fauna consisted of mammoth (*Mammuthus primigenius*), reindeer (*Rangifer tarandus*), brown bear (*Ursus arctos*), Giant Deer (*Megaloceros giganteus*), Hyaena (*Crocuta crocuta*) and hare (*Lepus timidus*). In the latter part of the "Derryvree" phase, however, evidence from Shandon, Ballynamintra and Foley Caves included animals such as the horse (*Equus ferus*) and red deer (*Cervus elaphus*), which required more temperate conditions, though horse has only been recorded at Shandon. There was also, approaching 20,000 BP (uncalibrated), other fauna apparently present at Castlepook, which included mammoth, hyaena, lemmings (*Dycrostonyx torquatus*) and others. This was assumed to be around the time of the Late Glacial Maximum (LGM) or Glenavy Stadial. There was

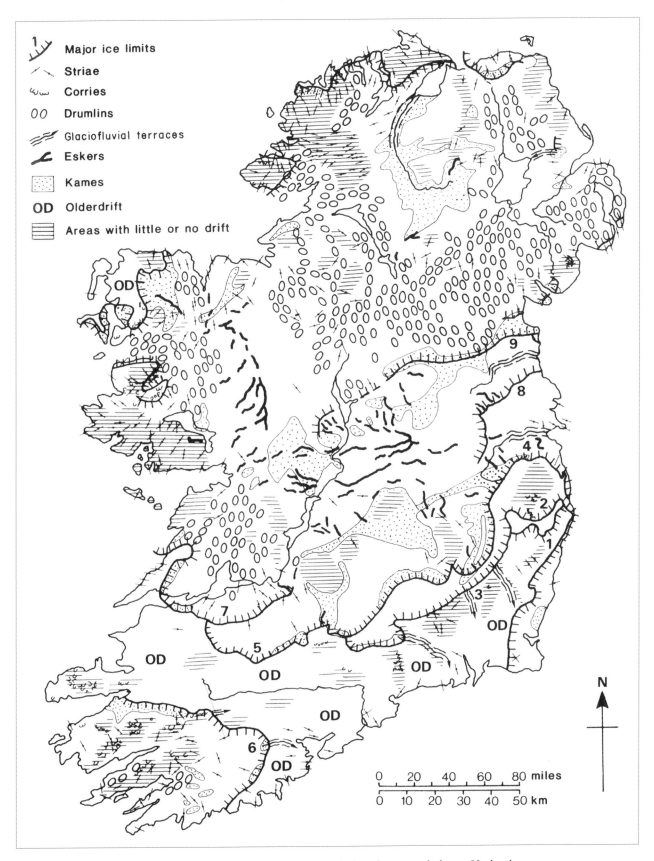

Fig. 2.1. Map showing the conventional glacial geomorphology of Ireland.

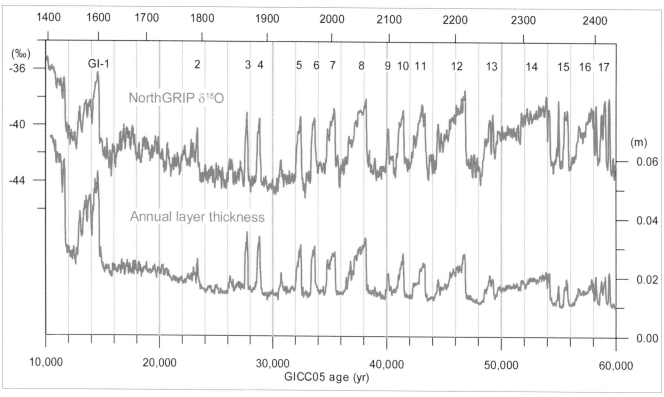

Fig. 2.2. A 60,000 year Greenland stratigraphic Ice Core Chronology (after Svensson et al. 2008). The North GRIP δ18O and the annual layar thickness profiles according to GICC05: the Greenland Interstadials (GI) are indicated.

then, as will be discussed below, a significant gap until after 16/15,000 cal BP, when no mammalian fauna is recorded from Ireland.

In the intervening two decades, since the completion of the IQFP, many "things" changed. As discussed earlier, until recently the conventional wisdom was that portions of the southern third of Ireland remained unglaciated and that the Ballylanders end Moraine marked the limit of the main "Midlandian" Glaciation. This implied that if there had been any Mid-/Upper Palaeolithic incursion into Ireland then there was a chance that some evidence might survive in South Munster (see Chapter 5). The presence of a relatively diverse fauna of MIS 3 date, present in four caves and referred to above, suggested that the area was also both suitable for human habitation and that evidence would not have been totally obliterated (Woodman *et al.* 1997). In recent times, however, the balance of evidence has swung in favour of ice not only covering virtually the whole of Ireland but that, for a time, the ice sheets could have extended well out onto the continental shelf. Indeed it is suggested that it may have extended to the edge of the continental shelf (Fig. 2.3; see Cheverill and Thomas (2010) for a review of the general issues associated with the extent and timing of the LGM). The current evidence is mainly based on observed features on the floor of the Celtic

Sea, which were, at one stage, assumed to be submerged sand ridges but, where it has been possible to examine their make-up, a glacial explanation is becoming more likely. It is possible that this tongue of ice at its maximum extent, which expanded out from the British and Irish Ice Sheet (BIIS; Fig. 2.3), may have existed for 1000 years or less and would have then contracted back towards the present Irish shoreline in a relatively short period of time (Clark *et al.* 2010). Evidence that ice flowed out onto the western continental shelf off parts of Mayo, and that gouges caused by iceberg keels can be seen well off shore towards the Porcupine Bank, would support the idea that at one stage the continental shelf off the south coast was also covered in ice.

It is beyond the scope of this volume to analyse the details of this event, most notably the spatial and chronological relationships between the Cork/Kerry Glacier, the Midlandian land based ice sheets and the BIIS. One point of interest is that, although occasional bones of mammoth have been found elsewhere, the four caves with significant quantities of MIS 3 fauna lie in one small area where perhaps the erosive effects of Glaciation were significantly less or where the area remained ice free (see Fig. 2.1).

Other changes, however, need to be taken into consideration. At the prompting of the late Roger Jacobi there was growing concern about the late phase of faunal remains from Castlepook, especially the late date from a hyaena scapula (OxA 4234), which Tony Sutcliffe (pers. comm.) has now shown to be 10,000 years older!!

So what else has changed? Several major developments have impacted on obtaining and using radiocarbon dates from the Pleistocene:

1) The use of ultrafiltration as a preparation of samples for radiocarbon dating. It had become apparent that some samples of Late Pleistocene date had retained a small degree of contamination, which in the case of samples that dated to MIS 3 could, on some occasions, have resulted in an inaccurate date (see Debenham *et al.* 2012, 302–3 for a discussion on the issue of pre-treatment of Late Pleistocene bone samples).

2) It is now possible to extend the calibration of radiocarbon dates back to 50 ka, though as yet this is by no means perfect.

3) With the availability of information from NGRIP it is now possible to at least try to correlate radiocarbon dates with the Greenland Interstadials.

A fresh look at the evidence

First we should look to see if the surviving record of Pleistocene Mammals only begins round 50,000 years ago. Doughty (2007) reviewed the occurrence of two finds of Pleistocene age, which were recovered from separate locations in the Belfast Lough area. One jaw fragment from a Palaeoloxodon was always regarded with suspicion as it came from a river close to Croft House in Holywood, Co. Down, the home of the Patterson family, a well-known family of naturalist (see Praeger 1949). The river at that point cuts quite deeply through Midlandian deposits. The discovery of such an interesting artefact or fossil in this manner emphasises that it is more likely to have been made by somebody with at least a passing interest in archaeology or natural history.

Doughty has also noted the occurrence of a second tooth, in this case of *Hippopotamus amphibious*, which was recorded as having been discovered in the Carrickfergus area in 1837. He has rightly questioned whether these finds are not chance survivals from MIS 5, about 130,000 years ago. Indeed one must wonder whether some of the other finds of mammoth or other Pleistocene faunal remains from under glacial till could not be older than MIS 3.

Perhaps the most remarkable find must be the remains of an "elephant" which was recovered from near Belturbet, County Cavan and was, as noted in Chapter 3, identified by Molyneux (1714; Woodman and Cook 2013). Adrian Lister (pers. comm.) has suggested that these teeth may also have been those of a Palaeoloxodon!

In returning to Aghnadarragh one must note that the radiocarbon dates used to establish the age of the mammoth remains are both *termini ante quo* and dates at the extreme limit

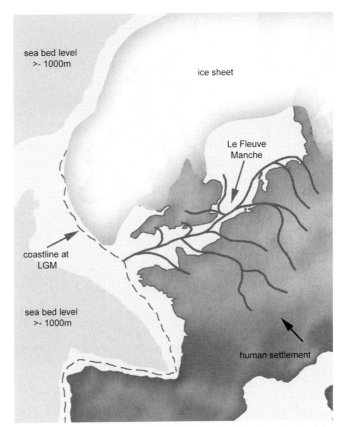

Fig. 2.3. Schematic map of British Isles showing the extent of the LGM and La Fleuve Manche (after Bourillet et al. 2003; Coxon and McGarron 2008).

of radiocarbon dating. The late Phil Doughty, in conversation, told me that Electron Spin Resonance (ESR) dates had been obtained from the mammoth teeth – a fact confirmed by Adrian Lister who informed me that the results could suggest a date from about 80,000 years ago! McCabe *et al.* (1987) also failed to mention that the skull of another animal had been found at the same time. This has been recorded in the collections of The National Museums of Northern Ireland (NMNI) as a musk ox skull *Ovibos moschatus*. Mitchell and Ryan (1997 70–2) refer, one presumes, to the same skull as *Bison priscus*. In the British Mammal Zones (MAZ) (see Currant and Jacobi 1997; 2001) musk ox occurs either much earlier, perhaps in MIS 6 which would date to more than 130 ka, or else in MAZ 2/MIS 2 which is around the time of the LGM, i.e the Dimlington stage which is significantly later than the Aghnadarragh deposits. If, however, it is a bison, then bison, which was present in Britain in the earlier part of MIS3/MAZ Pinhole assemblage, could have been present in Ireland perhaps before 50 ka. Therefore, allowing for improvements in ESR dating and the probability that the Aghnadarragh mammoth pre-dates 50 ka, is there something between the possibly potential MIS 5 fauna and the radiocarbon dated cave faunas of a slightly later date?

An ongoing programme of re-dating samples from the Irish caves is in progress and several trends are apparent. There is obviously a problem, though not a systematic one with samples from Castlepook as, in some instances, dates have shifted by between 6 and 10 ka. This is not apparent in the samples from the other caves that have so far been re-dated. This suggests that there is a particular contamination problem endemic to Castlepook Cave.

Allowing for the fact that the group of samples which have been radiocarbon dated is painfully small, certain patterns are obvious. Two factors impact on the chronological structure. These are a) there was primarily, within the Castlepook fauna, an inconsistent problem with contamination and b) it is now possible to calibrate dates back close to the limit of 50,000 years ago. Thus, possible fauna groups are becoming evident (Fig. 2.4). These include:

1. between 50 ka and approximately 35 ka pioneering fauna with hyaena, "Giant deer", hare, reindeer and bear;
2. from roughly 35 ka to 28 ka a warmer fauna, including horse, red deer, fox, lemming, etc., and
3. a still remaining cold fauna, perhaps centred on 24 ka within(?) the LGM which contains wolf, reindeer and mammoth.

Perhaps group 1 may even link back to the Aghnadarragh fauna?

As more samples are dated it is hoped that there will be greater clarity and it may become apparent which species, if any, were present throughout a period of nearly 30,000 years. Is the warmer fauna (2) to be associated with Greenland Interstadials 7–4, with earlier fauna being associated with Interstadials 12–11? How can we interpret the fact that there is some evidence that mammoth was present perhaps before 50 ka and, as can be seen in Figure 2.4, appears between 30 and 35 ka and then again at 24 ka? In examining the climatic fluctuations indicated by NGRIP (Fig. 2.2), did mammoth and other species, such as bear or even reindeer, arrive, flourish for some time, get wiped out and then may or may not re-colonise Ireland? NGRIP also emphasises that the older pollen-based Hollymount and Derryvree Interstadials, which are based on radiocarbon dates obtained many decades ago, may only represent small temporal snap-shots within a very long time period.

The third fauna, i.e. the later fauna from Castlepook, still presents the same enigma that caused this re-examination of the original Irish Quaternary fauna's project! While there may have been different advances from the BIIS and Midlandian Ice Sheets, by perhaps 22 ka at the latest, the process of large scale de-Glaciation was underway. Is the small enigmatic group of dates from mammoth, reindeer and wolf (*Canis lupus*) from Castlepook that centre on 20–22 ka evidence of a short-term re-colonisation? This may have been at a time when the ice

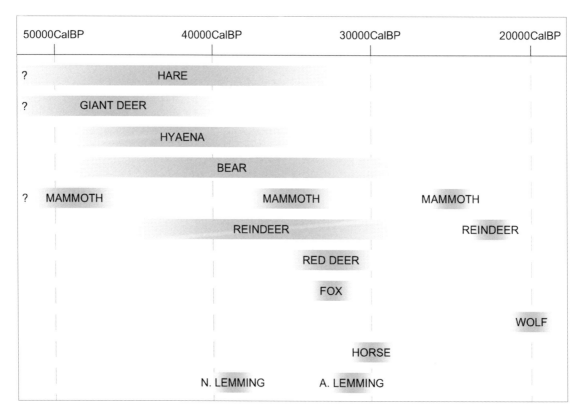

Fig. 2.4. Suggested and interim schematic revision of the chronology of mammalian presence in Ireland before the LGM (prepared by Hugh Kavanagh).

sheets had become discontinuous or even at the time of the LGM, when there were areas of Ireland where no ice sheets existed. Besides periods of ice retreat, there were occasional events, of up to a millennium in duration, of rejuvenation of the ice sheets. Many of the characteristic features of the landscape formed by the "Last Ice Age", such as drumlins, were created at this time.

Much of the discussion of Ireland's ecology and environment in a more general sense starts with Ireland's Late Glacial Period and continues into the Holocene. Many of the issues discussed below as well as other matters relating to the origins of Ireland fauna and flora can be found in a more detailed discussion in Woodman (2014). Similarly these and other relevant issues are often considered in other papers in *Mind The Gap* II (Sleeman *et al.* 2014).

Could anything survive the LGM or was there a "Faunal Atlantis" somewhere?

Areas adjacent to Ireland were also subjected to other consequences of the glaciations in Ireland and elsewhere. In particular, there has been a temptation to create refugia off the south coast of Ireland during MIS 2, but beyond the ice sheets south of the Cornubian Peninsula, a major river *La Manche Fleuve* had been in existence for some time. This was a massive river and estuary that drained, not only the British and French rivers that face onto the Channel, but other rivers, such as the Rhine, Meuse and Thames (Antoine *et al.* 2003; Lagarde *et al.* 2003). The full extent of the river can be seen in Figure 2.3 when many of the rivers of north-west Europe drained out through the Channel. While the outflow might have been restricted, due to the existence of the ice sheets during MIS 2, this would have presented a major barrier or even disincentive to the existence of an area where a range of species could have taken refuge. At the time of the LGM, when the ice sheets were extended to their furthest and when the shoreline lay a considerable distance out from the present French coast, the extremely cold waters of the Atlantic polar front (Fig. 2.5) also extended to their furthest. The Polar front's southern boundary would have reached the coast of Portugal, thus at times these waters would have been populated by icebergs that migrated this far south.

Perhaps the one lesson which is emerging from the fragmentary evidence of mammalian fauna available from the latest stages of the Pleistocene in Ireland is that it is not a simple story and was not likely to be a single event. It seems likely that from 100,000 years ago to certainly sometime before the LGM Ireland may have been populated on an intermittent basis by a range of mammals. There was therefore no single event and equally, given time, Ireland was accessible to animals and plants – and why not humans – on numerous occasions.

It was not until after 16/15 ka that the North Atlantic polar front retreated back towards Newfoundland. At this point, as can be seen from the GRIP ice core record, the now

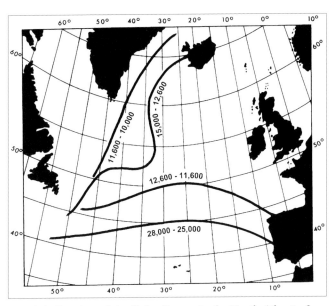

Fig. 2.5. Position of the Polar Fronts in the North Atlantic from the Late Glacial till the early Holocene.

warmer waters that began to exist in the North Atlantic would have contributed to a climate that changed with a rapid rise in temperature. In fact, the transition to warmer interstadial climatic conditions may have happened within ten years. This period, the Late Glacial, lasted approximately 3500 years, until 11,600 cal BP, which marks the onset of the Holocene (Postglacial). It could be described as a rollercoaster of rapid climatic change (Fig. 2.6).

Late Glacial background

It began with the Late Glacial Interstadial (Woodgrange Interstadial in Ireland) at whose beginning the Irish landscape was changing from one where the effects of deglaciation were everywhere and periglacial activities left their mark. For the first 1000 years, as the soils had begun to develop, vegetation was initially dominated by *Rumen* (docks) and *Juniper* (juniper) scrub. It would appear that during this first millennium of the interstadial, temperatures were at their highest. As the interstadial progressed, however, although there was a small drop in average temperature, the soils had developed sufficiently so that much of Ireland was covered by rich grassland. In places, in the east and south-west, thin woodland of *Salix* (willow) and *Betula* (birch) was also able to exist. This seemed to suggest that the climate became *warmer* as the interstadial progressed. The evidence from beetles at sites in the British Isles, however, shows that, within the earlier 1000 years of the interstadial, the range of beetle remains present included species that are today found only further south in Europe (Coope *et al.* 1998). These same beetle species are not present in the second half of the Woodgrange Interstadial, which seemed to contradict the indicators based on

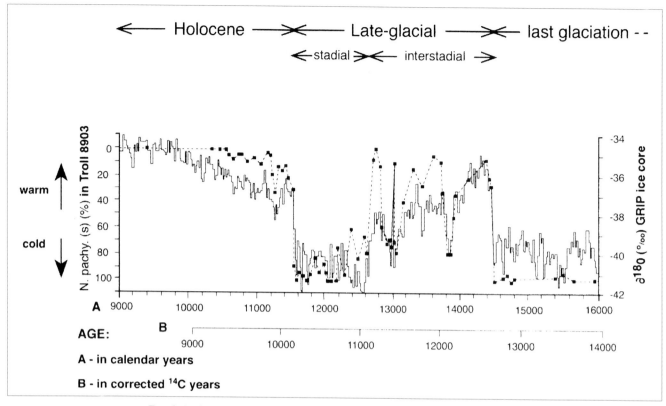

Fig. 2.6. a) Late Glacial climate changes (after Coxon and McGarron 2009).

vegetation changes. The evidence of O[16/18] from the Greenland Ice Cores changes supports the belief that the first half of the Interstadial was warmer than the latter half (Fig. 2.6 a, b). Recently, research on a sequence of Chironomid (non-biting midge fly) remains from Lough Nadourcan, CountyDonegal, which date from the first half of the Lateglacial Interstadial, also suggests that summer temperatures were at their highest (Watson *et al.* 2010). Therefore the period in which the herds of Giant deer flourished in Ireland was the second, cooler part of the interstadial.

This relatively warm phase, i.e. the Lateglacial Interstadial, came to an end just as suddenly at about 12,600 years cal BP. This final cold period, which lasted 1000 years, may have been caused by waters from the ice dammed Lake Agassiz that was being fed by the Laurentide Ice Sheet in North America, burst out through the St Lawrence River. The impact of the colder water pouring from the Laurentide ice sheets caused a massive drop in temperature in the North Atlantic. This cold stage, the Younger Dryas, in Ireland the Nahanagan, may have had mean annual temperatures that were as low as –5 to –2°C. It is also suggested that Ireland was often the coldest location in Western Europe (Isarin *et al.* 1998) and that at one point, the coldest point in the Younger Dryas, the maximum mean coldest month may have had temperatures as low –30°C. Obviously the dramatic temperature drop brought to an end the rich grasslands and left its mark in the creation of ice wedges,

polygon patterned ground pingos, etc., which are phenomenon of periglacial environments. The grasslands were replaced by tundra and alpine plants, while much of the soil that had been developing was washed away. Within a decade, around 11,600 cal BP, the Atlantic Polar Front again retreated back towards Newfoundland, allowing the onset of what we optimistically describe as "The Postglacial".

In terms of assessing the potential for human settlement, as well as the question of animal colonisation of Ireland, the Late Glacial can be seen as a relatively short period of time characterised by a roller coaster of climatic change. However, in some ways it should be seen not so much as a separate entity between Ireland's last Glaciation and the Postglacial, but rather as the real beginnings of the Postglacial period.

For Ireland it could be argued that the Postglacial really begins, not only with the rise in temperature by 15,000 years ago, but by the fact that it is highly probable that by that date Ireland was an island (Pl. II). Edwards and Brooks (2008, 24) have suggested that, during a short period of time around 15,000 years ago, three times the amount of water trapped in the Greenland ice cap was dumped into the world's ocean, significantly raising sea levels. In effect, Ireland became an island by the beginning of the Late Glacial Interstadial. Round Ireland, with the exception of the south-west, the sea often lay somewhere around 30 m below present day levels. In the north-east, where the land had been isostatically depressed to

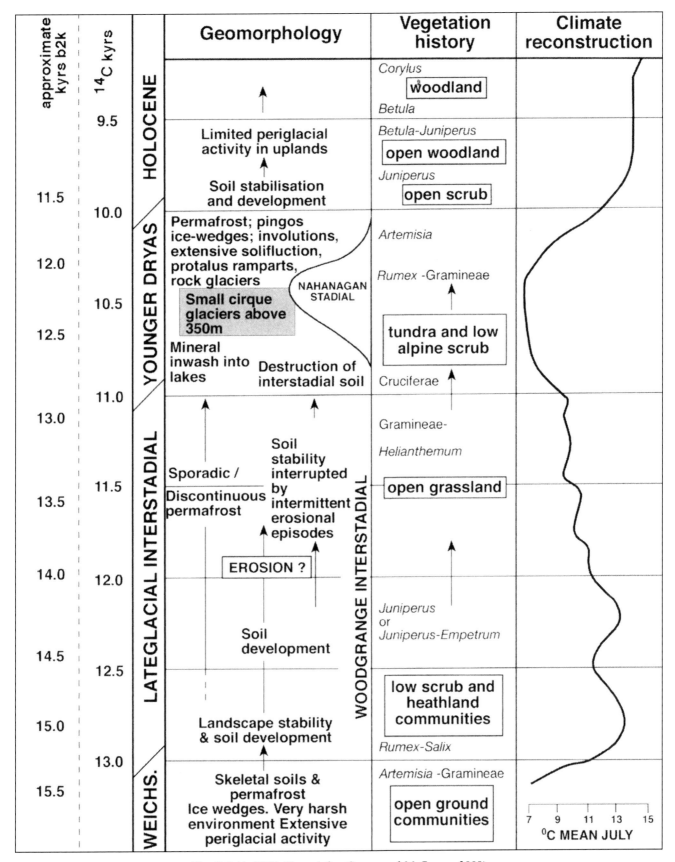

Fig. 2.6. b) GRIP Chart (after Coxon and McGarron 2009).

a much greater depth, the sea level was, relatively speaking, some metres above present day levels.

Given the short time period, climatic fluctuations, etc, it is not surprising that Ireland's Late Glacial fauna is extremely impoverished. Its arrival into Ireland also seems to be delayed. It would appear that reindeer at least had migrated back into southern Britain perhaps before 17 ka (Pettitt and White 2012, 430).

As can be seen in Woodman *et al.* (1997, figs 6 and 7) most of the large mammals found at the same date in Britain are not present in Ireland. Indeed the earliest date from Late Glacial, that of a reindeer from Castlepook, can, on redating, be placed before the LGM. The most notable difference between Britain and Ireland is the absence of horse from Ireland. Similarly, Price (2003, 92) has documented an extensive range of smaller mammals in Britain, in particular a range of voles and mice that again do not seem to have reached Ireland. It is difficult to argue for any significant mammalian presence in Ireland before 14,000 years ago i.e., during the first 1000 years of the Irish Woodgrange or Late Glacial Interstadial. One of the dominant species recorded is the Giant deer, whose presence is very obvious from finds in waterlogged deposits that date to 14,000–13,000 cal BP, i.e. the latter part of the Woodgrange Interstadial. However, besides the Giant deer, wolves, bears and hares were also present and it is also possible that stoats would have been present in Ireland before the Holocene. The presence of Red deer in Ireland at this date is extremely problematic and it probable (Ruth Carden, pers. comm.) that the Keshcorran example is, in fact, reindeer.

On the basis of stratigraphic successions observed by Mitchell (1941), as well as radiocarbon dates from the Irish Quaternary Faunas Project (Woodman *et al.* 1997), it would seem at least as if reindeer flourished during the much colder second phase of the Woodgrange Interstadial. The demise of the Woodgrange grasslands at the end of the Interstadial, may have led to the extinction of the Giant deer. However it is also possible that the reindeer and the lemming would not have survived throughout all of the Younger Dryas, never mind the onset of the full Postglacial or Holocene conditions. It should also be remembered that species such as reindeer need a very specific diet, primarily reindeer moss; therefore just because it is cold it does not mean that reindeer would be present.

The conundrum of the earliest Holocene

From the perspective of the Mesolithic, perhaps the most interesting species are those that may have survived into the Holocene. These include brown bear, stoat, Irish hare and possibly wolf. The issues associated with the presence of bear and wolf will be returned to later in this chapter. These species have attracted less attention than the earlier faunas or those associated with a human presence from the Mesolithic onwards and so fewer dates are available from the four species listed above.

Can a case be made for their presence beginning in the Woodgrange Interstadial and for their survival into the Holocene? In general, some of these species, for example brown bear, although traditionally thought of as carnivores, can be considered omnivores, which would suggest that they could adapt to changing environments and may have been able to survive the rigours of the Nahanagan stadial. It is for these reasons that it could be argued that the template for Postglacial Ireland as an island with its own distinctive ecology was established in the Woodgrange Interstadial and that what existed at the beginning of the Holocene was in fact a relict Late Glacial fauna.

Climatic changes within the Holocene

The main factor in climatic change seems to have been the shift in the limit of the Atlantic Polar front back towards Newfoundland, so there is an expectation that Ireland's climate would have been heavily influenced by the return of the Gulf Stream. However, the warmer "Atlantic" climate probably did not fully establish itself until several thousand years into the Holocene. The evidence from the Greenland Ice Cores (Fig. 2.6) suggest that, after the very sudden increase at the Younger Dryas/Holocene boundary, it took roughly 1000 years for the temperature to reach levels that were to exist for much of the Holocene. Mitchell (2009, 398) has also noted that the climate in the first millennia of the Holocene was probably drier and more continental than today. This would have resulted in warmer summers and colder winters. It would also appear that the warm "Atlantic" climate, with increased rainfall and lesser seasonal differences, did not establish itself fully until after 8000 years ago.

Of course, quite significant climate oscillations have occurred throughout the Holocene. Perhaps those of most significance for the study of the Irish Mesolithic are early "Pre-boreal" Oscillation, sometimes called the Friesland Oscillation (Reynier 2005), that took place during the first 1000 years of the Holocene and the better known 8.2 ka event. The latter event was again caused by cold fresh waters from the Laurentide Ice Cap, probably dammed in Hudson Bay, being suddenly dumped into the North Atlantic. This is thought to have caused a significant reduction in temperature for a period of 69 years. While the latter is clearly marked in the ice cores, its impact on Ireland may, surprisingly, have been muted. McDermott *et al.* (2005, 1816) were not able to detect this event in the speleotherm $\delta^{18}O$ record from Crag Cave, Co. Kerry. Until recently there was no clear evidence in the pollen diagrams – though it is possible that this may be due to poor resolution due to sampling at too great an interval (Mitchell 2009, 397–8). Recently Ghilardi and O'Connell (2012) have made a case that the significance of the 8.2 ka event could, however, be of crucial importance in coastal areas where it may have had a greater impact than simply reducing the growth of vegetation. Research off the coast of Portugal (Bicho *et al.* 2010), for example, has emphasised the significance of this type of event in disrupting the strength of the summer up-welling and levels of marine productivity within coastal Atlantic waters. Furthermore, they have suggested that there would have been a 0.5 m general rise in sea level, which would have been associated with gravity waves and extensive flooding of coastal areas. This may perhaps, have been associated with disruption of the ecology of some river estuaries. Did this 8.2 ka event, therefore, seriously disrupt the ecology of coastal areas of Ireland?

Change in sea level and its consequences

From the perspective of someone researching the Mesolithic, perhaps one of the most obvious changes in Ireland during the Holocene was that of relative sea levels. The varying impact of the change to Ireland's coastline for the period, from the onset of the Holocene at 11,700 cal BP to the end of the Mesolithic at 6000 cal BP, is usually assessed through a combination of dating relevant deposits that mark marine incursions and mathematical modelling. Not surprisingly, this is a very complex process and there is some variation in the suggested dating of relative sea level change in different areas.

Both Ireland and some parts of Great Britain are affected, from the north to the south, in different ways. Most notable is that northern areas, having been buried below ice sheets before the full effects of Isotactic recovery took place, can have had high relative sea levels. This had taken place before the Holocene and it was then followed with a comparatively limited low stand of relative sea levels in the Early Holocene. Of course, aside from the general north–south gradation in apparent sea level change, even within the north-east of Ireland, there were significant differences. Along the north coast of County Antrim Late Glacial strandlines survive at more than 10 m above present day levels, while along the adjacent east coast of Co. Down, the strandlines were much lower.

Aside from isostatic recovery, sea levels in the form of the amount of water in the world's oceans was also increased due to the massive amounts of melt water that were pouring out from the still contracting ice sheets that existed in places such as North America and Scandinavia.

In other words, the Holocene was a period when, in certain regions where isostatic recovery was still not complete and the land had not recovered to its present day approximate levels, the increasing volume of water in the world's oceans led to a period when the sea again encroached across land that today lies above sea level. In Ireland the impact varied from region to region. Along the north coast, early in the Holocene, sea levels were initially at a relative low stand, which may have been up to 30 m below present day levels, while in the mid-Holocene (8000–6000 cal BP) strandlines were created which could be up to 8 m above present day levels. It should also be pointed out that local conditions, such as the openness of the coast, the direction it faces, as well as other factors, will

cause some variation in the extent and height of local beaches. In contrast, at the same time in more southern areas, where isostatic factors did not play such a major role due to the increase in the volume of water in the world's oceans, coastal areas were gradually inundated from a much lower level off shore. This has stabilised in southern Ireland only in the last few thousand years, while along the south coast of England, where the land is still sinking albeit very, very slowly, the process is ongoing.

In summary, based on Edwards and Brooks (2008) one might suggest the following changes through time (Fig. 2.7). In the north-east sea levels at a) 11,600 cal BP were close to present day levels, while at b) 10,000 cal BP, at which date people may have been arriving, sea levels were roughly 20 m below present day sea level, and at c) the end of the Mesolithic, 6000 cal BP, sea levels may have been 5–8 m above present day levels. In contrast, in the south-west, sea levels may have been respectively at a) –60 m, b) –40 m, and c) –10 m.

The islands of Ireland, and what was to become Great Britain, differ from regions such as northern Spain where sea level change was caused simply by the rise in sea level due to the growing volume of water in the oceans. At the other extreme, in parts of southern Norway where, in spite of increasing absolute sea level, the isostatic rebound since the beginning of the Holocene has left strandlines in Oslo Fjord up to 200 m above sea level. The major difference between Great Britain and Ireland is the extent to which these changes have reduced the landmass. In the case of Ireland, one can say that the change in relative sea level since the beginning of the Holocene has reduced the size of Ireland by less than 5%. In the case of Britain, the inundation of Doggerland (Coles 1998) or the North Sea Plain, an event that took place over several thousand years throughout the first half of the Holocene, has seen the loss of a land area that is the equivalent of the size of modern England. Ireland, as noted earlier, seems to have been an island from an early date, perhaps since 15,000 years ago, while the breaching of the land connection in the English Channel, which changed Britain from being a major peninsular portion of Continental Europe into an island, happened well after the beginning of the Holocene.

By European standards the changes to the island of Ireland were relatively marginal. Perhaps the major change that took place during the Mesolithic period in Ireland would have been that in the north, from Lough Swilly in Co. Donegal to Strangford in Co. Down or Dundalk Bay, where many major estuaries and adjacent parts of river valleys would have changed to become sea loughs. Maps documenting the sea level change in Strangford Lough (Pl. IV) provides a good example of how a river valley changed to a sea lough over a few thousand years

This reconstruction and those for Lough Foyle (see Pl. XXVII), prepared by Kieran Westley, should be considered as only approximate because it does not take into account more recent sedimentation and erosion (notably the formation of Magilligan Point); because of uncertainties in the accuracy of

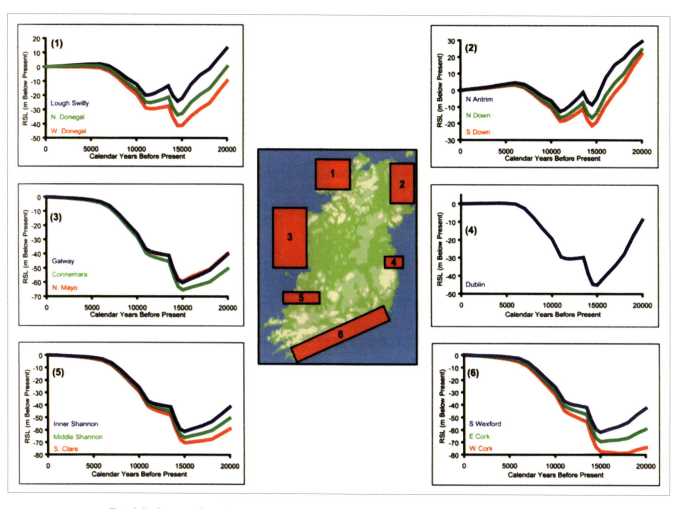

Fig. 2.7. Curves of sea level changes from round the coast (after Edwards and Brooks 2008).

the underlying sea level data and the past routes of rivers across the exposed low stand plain. Elsewhere, for at least much of the Mesolithic period, many of the major bays that exist today would have still been low-lying coastal plains and would not have been flooded by the sea until 4000–5000 years ago.

In certain areas, especially in the North, the rise in sea level, particularly after 8000 years ago when relative sea levels were above present day levels, would have meant that the fall along the lower courses of rivers as they flowed towards the sea would have been lessened. As a result the rate of silting within the valley floodplains would have increased. In particular, the fall along the course of the Lower Bann between Lough Neagh and the sea would have been only about 50% of that which exists today.

Besides sea level change and its consequences, one of the major changes to Ireland's landscape was extensive growth of raised bogs that have today completely engulfed many small lake basins. These created areas of extensive bog such the Bog of Allen which covered nearly 1000 sq. km. This process was already well established during the Mesolithic. Many of the larger loughs have also been reduced in size since the initial

settlement of Ireland. Mitchell and Ryan (1997, 104, illus. 72) also suggest that, originally, before the drainage patterns had become well established and perhaps on a seasonal basis, extensive, much larger lakes existed. In the middle reaches of the Shannon the loughs may have, as suggested by Mitchell and Ryan (1997, 104; Fig. 2.8) coalesced to form a great Lough Ree-Derg. It may be that the spectacular "Mushroom stones" (Pl. III) that are found on the lough shores at some distance above present sea levels may indicate that at one time the waters were at least seasonally much higher. In some areas, these pillars of Limestone protruded above the higher waters of the Lough. The result was that the portion which lay below water level was slowly being dissolved thus creating a narrower stalk. In other loughs, such as Lough Neagh, the evidence suggests a complexity of events. Initially, "Boreal" peat deposits, which may have formed between 9000 and 8000 cal BP and contained material that had washed up from sites further out in the lough, lined a shoreline that was lower than the present day, post-1940s drainage, lough. This creates the impression of a smaller lough but, on the other hand, the shore may have lain several kilometres much further south, beyond an area that is now covered with extensive peat deposits.

It is also apparent that throughout the latter half of the Mesolithic period these early shorelines were inundated by higher water levels. Perhaps the high point of the waters in the lough was of a seasonal nature. In the Lough Neagh/Lower Bann catchment flooding led to the creation of the Diatomaceous Clays that occur along its northern shores and further north within the floodplain of the lower Bann. These "Bann" clays, which were made up of the silica shells of diatoms, seem to have been created during the winters seasonal flooding of the river valley that left behind a layer of the distinctive white clay that often exceeded one metre in thickness. Thus, earlier in the Holocene and even today at certain seasons of the year, Lough Neagh and rivers would have been at a much higher level. It is also probable that at other seasons the Lough would have been much smaller. A further factor, as noted earlier, is that today many loughs have been reduced in size due to the existence of an extensive series of shoreline peat deposits. Thus, besides Lough Neagh, which would have extended some kilometres further south, other loughs, such as Kinale and Sheelin, may have formed one larger lake (Fig. 2.8).

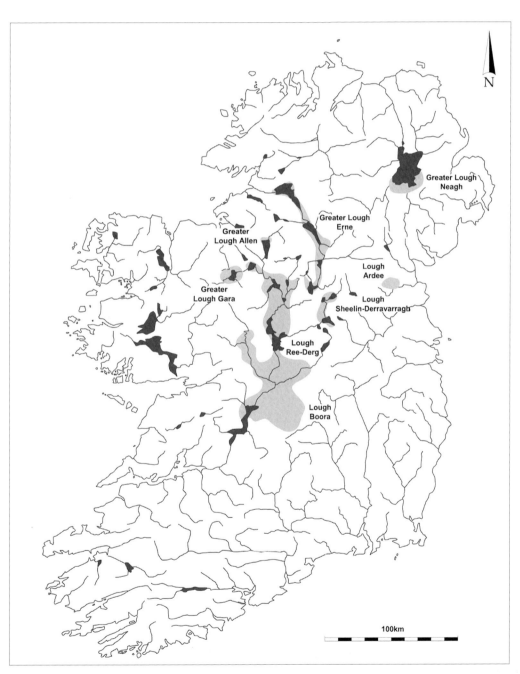

Fig. 2.8. Extent of Lough Ree/Derg in the early Holocene (after Mitchell and Ryan 1997).

Fauna and flora

The question of how and when various plants and animals got to Ireland has been one of the major debates within the study of the Irish Holocene. Perhaps this issue, and in particular the issue of the existence of a "Land or Ice-bridge", has occupied too much of the debate. As Mitchell (2009, 399) has observed, the Irish Gortian record (which is of Middle Pleistocene date) shows that a greater range of trees lived in Ireland at that time than exist today, while the MIS 3 Irish mammalian fauna (Woodman *et al.* 1997) was proportionately much richer than that which existed in the Holocene, or even today. Ireland was and is a difficult place to get to, so that the length of time available for migrations to take place may have been as important as the routes and the means by which plants and animals got here.

The mammalian fauna

The probability that some species of fauna may have survived through the Younger Dryas (Nahanagan) cold stage and continued to exist in Ireland during the Holocene has already been alluded to. As has often been noted, Ireland is characterised more by what is *not* rather than what *is* present. These absences include, as noted earlier, the large ruminants as well as smaller mammals such as moles and voles. Assuming that the four referred to earlier, i.e. brown bear, wolf, stoat and Irish hare, as possibly surviving from the Late Glacial were present; the other species that exist in Ireland today are usually added. The case of the brown bear will be returned to below. These include wild boar (*Sus scrofa ferus*), badgers (*Meles meles*), pine martens (*Mustela erminea*), foxes (*Vulpes vulpes*), otters (*Luttra luttra*), squirrels (*Sciurus vulgaris*), pigmy shrew (*Sorex minutes*), and wood mouse (*Apodemus sylvaticus*). How did they manage to get to Ireland? The major problem is that because it was usually assumed that there was a simple explanation, i.e., a movement into Ireland across a land bridge at the beginning of the Holocene, many of these species have received little attention. After all, everyone believed that they were part of a package that got to Ireland across a land bridge.

Again, as with the Late Glacial Interstadial fauna, because we tend to become fixated on how or when the species we have today got to Ireland, we are, as noted earlier, inclined to overlook what is absent. The lack of the large ruminants, such as wild cattle/aurochs (*Bos primigenius*), elk (*Alces alces*) and roe deer (*Dama dama*) which existed in Early Holocene Britain is well known but again the very significant difference between the few smaller mammals present in Ireland and the range of voles, mice and moles in Britain which occurred in Late Glacial deposits (Price 2003, 92) is an equally significant contrast.

If we are to get any sense of the ecology and the range of mammalian species present in Ireland during the Mesolithic, if not from the beginning of the Holocene, then it is necessary to step back and have a critical examination of the evidence.

For the purpose of this study, mammalian remains have been divided into three categories. Domesticates are excluded as can be both the hedgehog (*Erinaceus europaeus*) and rabbit (*Oryctolagus cuniculus*) which were brought to Ireland by the Anglo-Normans.

a) *Species which can be shown, or are thought, to be present in the Mesolithic.* These include wild boar, hare and brown bear which occur on numerous sites. Wild cat (*Felis silvestris*), which was recovered from Lough Boora (van Wijngaarden Bakker 1989), has occurred on later prehistoric sites such as in the Middle Bronze Age assemblage from Chancellorsland Tipperary (McCarthy 2008). One can be certain of the presence of otter (based on finds at Derragh Island, Co. Longford (Fredengren, pers. comm.) and at Moynagh Lough, Co. Meath (McCormick 2004). The lynx (*Lynx lynx*) from Kilgreany Cave Co. Waterford (Carden, pers. comm.) is dated to very early in the Holocene (Woodman *et al.* 1997). Stoat has, in the case of Kilgreany Cave, Co. Waterford, also been dated to very early in the Holocene, perhaps as early as 11,000 cal BP and may have survived through from the Late Glacial Interstadial (Littletonian) when it was also present (*ibid.*). The issue of Late Glacial survival and presence in the earliest portion of the Holocene will be returned to below The occurrence of field mouse at this date is based on its discovery at Newlands Cross, Co. Dublin (Preece *et al.* 1986), at depth in marl deposits of Mesolithic age. Field mouse was also recovered from Middle Bronze Age deposits at Chancellorsland (McCarthy 2008).

b) *Species that might have been expected to have been present during the Irish Mesolithic.* The apparent absence of the red deer (*Cervus elaphus*) until the Neolithic has been discussed on occasions (Woodman *et al.* 1997) while there is also, as yet, no clear evidence that the pine marten (*Martes martes*) was present in Ireland before the Bronze Age. Similarly, fox is one of the species identified by van Wijngaarden Bakker (1986) in the Newgrange faunal assemblage. Here it is assumed that they date to the Late Neolithic, though the Iron Age dates for the horse bones from Newgrange (Bendry *et al.* 2013) suggest that, in this case, caution should be exercised when assuming that the presence of any species can be considered to be Neolithic simply from its occurrence at Newgrange. In the case of the wolf (*Canis lupus*), there is a remarkable lack of clear evidence for its presence in Ireland during the Mesolithic period. This interesting apparent absence will also be discussed below.

c) *Species of uncertain origin, some of which might be recent introductions.* These include badger, squirrel and pigmy shrew (McDevitt *et al.* 2011).

Two very significant problems are apparent. Firstly, there is a remarkable absence of wolf bones. This is not confined to Mesolithic sites as the bones of this species are also absent from later prehistoric sites. On the one hand, as shown by Hickey

(2011), wolf is present in very large numbers in historic periods and as it was present in Ireland during the Younger Dryas, i.e., before 12,600 cal BP (Woodman *et al.* 1997) it might have been expected that it would have survived that cold period and been a successful carnivore throughout the Holocene. Of course, there is in the case of the wolf a consistent worry in that there is reticence in attempting to identify wolf as distinct from dog. At many Mesolithic sites, e.g., Dalkey Island, Co. Dublin and the Rockmarshall middens, Co. Louth (Hatting 1968a; 1968b) was not convinced that any of the canid bones were those of wolf while, in the case of the Mesolithic sites of Lough Boora, Co. Offaly and Mount Sandel, Co. Derry, van Wijngaarden Bakker (1989) provided equally cautious identifications. This issue is discussed in a broader chronological context in Woodman (2014) where numerous others could find no definitive evidence for the presence of wolf in what were thought to be Holocene deposits. In summary, in prehistoric Ireland and in particular during the Mesolithic a better case can be made for the presence of wolf than for red deer which does appear to be totally absent. Notwithstanding, the evidence for wolf is slender and must be regarded as inconclusive.

However the apparent absence of the wolf from Ireland's earliest prehistory is not peculiar to that species. How do we explain the apparent absence of fox, badger, pine marten and perhaps squirrel from Mesolithic sites? The discussion on the origins of these species, in particular, is by no means new (Sleeman 2008; Mallory 2013, 42–6). Is it simply the nature of the sites that the types of species listed above would be butchered, skinned and the carcasses discarded away from the settlement sites where much archaeological investigation takes place? However, none of the above species was present on the lake shore sites of Derragh Island (Fredengren 2009) or Moynagh Lough (McCormick 2004) where they might have been dumped and, of course, there has been a reluctance to invest in a dating programme based on bones of these species which have been recovered from caves. The one exception is the pine marten where Woodman *et al.* (1997) show a consistent presence in the caves from the Bronze Age. The species listed above are present elsewhere. Yalden (1999 103–4) noted that these species were amongst other wild mammals present on English Neolithic sites such as Windmill Hill, Mount Pleasant and Durrington Walls. There are also, from the Mesolithic period elsewhere in Europe, some extraordinary sites such as Ringkloster in Jutland where pine marten and otter carcasses form a significant portion of the fauna (Andersen 1974). Often in other mainland European Mesolithic sites there are small but consistent presences of the species listed above: usually 1–2% of the total.

Yalden (1999, 78) has also noted that five species, which includes those listed above as well as wild cat and lynx, were slightly late arrivals in Denmark. Could, therefore, all the species under discussion be considered as Woodland Temperate. As there seems to be little evidence for a Holocene or even Late Glacial "land bridge" to Ireland, could it be that the sea barriers and the nature of the Irish landscape at the very beginning of the Holocene inhibited their arrival in Ireland?

This discussion might seem a rather esoteric topic for a book primarily concerned with an analysis of the Irish Mesolithic. However, although their presence in archaeological contexts in many parts of Europe seems slight, it is important to remember that they form part of a broader complex series of ecological niches and even when they may not have been key elements in the food supply of humans they may have been an important link in the food chain and biodiversity of early Holocene Europe. One can assume that if they were absent in Ireland then there would have been knock-on consequences.

What survived the Younger Dryas?

A worrying methodological Catch 22 and the case of the brown bear

It is apparent from the preceding discussion that if we are to understand how Ireland's ecology and biodiversity developed throughout Irish prehistory in particular, then clarity and access to reliable data from earliest stages of the Holocene in Ireland is essential. However archaeologists rely on colleagues working in the natural sciences to create the "Palaecological Envelope" in its broadest sense and within this envelope we place humanity. Unfortunately, as is implicit earlier, certain specialities such as those studying animal and other remains rely equally heavily on material recovered from excavations. If, therefore, there is no substantial or as yet convincing archaeological presence of humans in Ireland for more than the first 1500 years of the Holocene, then there is a chicken and egg situation. Which came first, people or certain animals? In other words was there a sufficient range of species present on the arrival of humans and/or did they have to bring some creatures with them?

While the author and others have suggested that we should consider the possibility that the wild boar might have been brought by people to Ireland at a very early date, Warren *et al.* (2013) have extended this suggestion to include bears. The suggestion that they could have an Iberian origin and therefore have been imported is based on the DNA of samples of bone from the cave Poul Na Mbéar which date to the Neolithic and the Bronze Age (Edwards *et al.* 2011, table S1). Until recently, due to an inability to obtain DNA from certain samples, there appeared at times to be a major chronological gap between bears that date to the Late Glacial and those which belong to the middle of the Holocene. Therefore the idea of a deliberate introduction of bear during the Middle Holocene seems quite plausible. However if one looks as the surviving faunal evidence a very different picture begins to emerge

Looking at the archaeological record, bears, at first sight, only appear to occur on sites which date to the later part of the Irish Mesolithic. However their absence from the fauna of Mt Sandel and Lough Boora (van Wijngaarden Bakker 1989) is likely to be because of butchering practices, i.e., large mammals were usually butchered at the kill location and leave little osteological trace at settlement sites. Helskog (2012) has made the point that, in general, bear bones are poorly represented in the faunal remains from most excavations.

Information from the Irish Quaternary faunas project (Woodman *et al.* 1997) and other sources such the find from Glencurran Cave (Dowd 2010; pers. comm.) suggests otherwise. There is a series of dates available that appear to indicate a continuous presence of bear from the Late Glacial Interstadial through the Younger Dryas and into the Holocene. There is a small gap still in the earliest part of the Holocene but as several dates are slightly earlier than Mt Sandel, and even accepting the fact that Mt Sandel is only the earliest *known* site in Ireland, it seems likely that bears (which are known to survive in extremely tough environments) are part of a mammalian population that has survived through the younger Dryas and into the Holocene. Their presence through from the Late Glacial Interstadial to the mid-Holocene is illustrated in Figure 2:7, however the actual dates are listed in Table 2.1.

There are other instances of bears from later prehistoric contexts. Those associated with the Mesolithic will be discussed below in Chapter 10 but they also were recovered from several sites at Lough Gur and at Newgrange (van Wijngaarden Bakker 1974) were they could be either Neolithic or Bronze age in date while the bear skull from Kilrathmurray in Co. Kildare, which was dug up during the creation of a new channel for the River Boyne in the early 19th century (Mulvany 1852) has been dated to 4441–4161 cal BP (UBA 21047). Overall their presence in much later contexts suggest that they must have been a significant presence in Early Holocene Ireland.

This is of course only one aspect of the "Missing Millennium" at the beginning of the Holocene. What other species could have survived? Obviously the wolf remains an enigma. The hare of which a bone from Keshcorran (Plunkett Cave) which

has been dated to 12,190±130 BP (OxA 5736) i.e. during last Interstadial also survived quite well during the earlier MIS 3 (see above) and occurs again at Mt Sandel and Lough Boora (Van Wijngaarden Bakker 1989) is likely to have survived the Younger Dryas. Similarly Stoat occurs in the Late Glacial at Killavullen cave at the end of the Younger Dryas, and on the cusp between the end of the Younger Dryas and the Holocene at Kilgreany and in the earlier Holocene at Keshcorran (Coffey Cave): Killavullen Cave   (OxA 5743, 12796–12246 cal BP; Woodman *et al.* 1997, 141); Kilgreany Cave (OxA 5732, 11,822–11,221 cal BP; *ibid.*); Coffey Cave (OxA 5738, 8858–8177 cal BP (*ibid.*, 140).

Even with the possible survival of wolves and the presence of lynx and wild cat, Ireland would have had a very different range of mammalian species and an ecology which was very different from that of mainland Europe. Perhaps this is best seen by contrasting Star Carr where the full range of large mammals discussed earlier occurred and where Badger, fox, pine marten and wolf were also recovered.

Fish remains

The known fish remains in Ireland represent a similar conundrum. Many species of freshwater fish found elsewhere are not present in Ireland, even today. Others such as roach or pike are known to be modern introductions. Some local relict species may have survived from the Woodgrange Stadial and throughout the Nahanagan cold phase. These include *Coregonus Autumnalis* (pollan) in Lough Neagh and a form of arctic charr that can be found in Loughs Melvin and Conn, as well as several other lakes, and until recently would have existed in many other Irish lakes (Viney 2003, 275). There is a suggestion that in the colder waters that would have existed at times during the Late Glacial, these species would have been able to tolerate less saline waters and may have adapted to

Table 2.1 Radiocarbon dates of Lateglacial and Early Holocene bear bones.

Site	Lab ref.	Determination BP	Calibrated date cal BP
Plunkett Cave[1]	OxA-3706	11,920±85	14,004–13,556
Plunkett Cave[2]	UB 6698	11,460±57	13,438–13,171
Red Cellar Cave[1]	OxA-3704	10,650±100	12,747–12,,247
Edenvale Cave[2]	UB 6700	10, 4950± 53	12,585–12,131
Newhall Cave[2]	UB 6702	9946 ± 53	11,615–11,239
Glencurran Cave[3]	UB 13246	8999±31	10,238–9972
Donore Bog[1]	(OxA-3713)	8930± 100	10,246–9699
Derrykeel Bog[1]	OxA-3714	8880 ± 90	10,223–9687
Annagh Cave[4]	(GRA 1719)	7670± 60	8582–8383

1= Woodman 1997; 2 = Edwards 2011, table S1; 3 = Dowd 2010; 4 = Ó Floin 2012

freshwater conditions by the onset of the Holocene. A similar scenario may explain the existence of alis and Twaite shad (*Alosa alosa* and *Alosa fallax*) in the south-west in Lough Leane (*ibid.*, 285). In Lough Melvin there are also several varieties of trout: *Sonaghen, Gillaroo* and *Ferox*, as well as brown trout, all of which could be classified as *Salmo trutta*. Viney (*ibid.*, 275) has suggested that brown trout, rather than salmon, would probably be more successful colonisers of Ireland's lakes and rivers as they do not necessarily have to return to the sea. The archaeological record, especially from Mt Sandel and Lough Boora (van Wijngaarden-Bakker 1989), shows that salmon, trout and eels were present by roughly 10,000 years ago, but it is silent about any earlier presence. Could these species, like pollan, have established themselves during the Woodgrange Stadial and survived into the Holocene, or did they only find their way into Irish waters after the commencement of the Holocene? This becomes a crucial issue for the initial human colonisation of Ireland which will be discussed in Chapter 7. When, as archaeologists, we are addressing the issues of the native fish species we are inclined to forget about two others i.e. the lampreys in particular *Lampetra fluviatilis* and the three-spinned stickleback (*Gasterosteus aculeatus*) both of which are less obvious but may have played an important role in the Mesolithic (see below Chapter 10).

Flora

While the studies of animal migration to Ireland have been a much neglected discipline the same cannot be said for many aspects of the vegetational history of Ireland. Since the work of Knud Jessen (1949) and the Committee for Quaternary Research during the 1930s, more than 400 bogs and lake have been sampled, pollen diagrams constructed and, in more recent decades, radiocarbon dates obtained (www.pol.ie).

Hall in *The Making of the Irish Landscape, since the Ice Age* (Hall 2011, especially chapters 3 and 4) provides a review of how Ireland's flora arrived, spread and flourished (or not) as well as the advantages or inhibiting factors that would have existed in certain areas.

Like many other parts of Europe there has been a recognised succession of trees throughout the first half of the Holocene. As can be seen from pollen diagrams, there is a conventional general succession starting with juniper and willow and being replaced at first by birch, which could survive on more thin, nutrient poor soils. The more shade tolerant hazel then followed before 10,000 years cal BP. In turn, pine replaced the extensive birch forests within a few hundred years. Somewhat later, elm and then oak began to appear in Ireland and by roughly 8000 cal BP these species had replaced pine, to become, along with hazel, the dominant species. This is, of course, an over simplistic view. Mitchell (2009, fig. 16.3, shown here as Fig. 2.9), has shown that all these species seem to have appeared first in the south and then, over up to 1000 years, began to establish themselves throughout the island. However, as Mitchell points

out, there could be, in certain areas, competition between species, especially oak and elm, while other species, notably pine, migrated faster up the west coast than elsewhere. Pine, of course, remained dominant in many areas in the "windy and wet west". Finally, by about 7000 cal BP, alder, which had been present for some time, was beginning to be present in many of the damper environments throughout Ireland. Archaeologists are probably inclined to regard the arboreal flora and other plants as a sort of ecological background whose impacts are matters such as forest density and shading, but it should be remembered that the absence of certain trees and shrubs would mean the absence of some types of fruits, huts, seeds, etc., which may have been the staple diet of certain animals.

At any one point in time, there is considerable variation in forest composition across Ireland. At a local level, varying geology, soil conditions and exposure to wind could inhibit or encourage the spread of trees and create areas where only the more hardy pioneering species would flourish. While pollen diagrams are often used as convenient indicators of vegetation and even of climatic change, it must be emphasised that they are often overwhelmingly dominated by evidence of trees whose pollen is produced in large quantities and dispersed over large areas. Many other plants, whose pollen is rarely recovered from the bogs and lake sediments, would have existed in the understory. Trees are, therefore, only part, albeit an important part, of the ecosystem. They provide shade and protection from the wind, and at the very beginning of the Holocene the spread of trees, such as birch, would have contributed to soil development that eventually created conditions that would allow other species to establish a foothold in Ireland.

There are still many unanswered questions about the manner in which Ireland's Holocene ecology emerged and developed at a later date. It is evident from what has been presented above that archaeologist and archaeozoologists cannot, on their own, answer many of the questions we wish to examine. Other approaches are needed and, while some issues will be discussed throughout this volume, the issues and the needs for collaboration between archaeologists and geneticists is still apparent.

In conclusion

One may assume that, at the point in time when initial colonists decided to come and remain in Ireland, establishing a permanent presence would have been a challenge. The main differences that they faced would have been the absence of a range of resources that they would have been used to having, most notably amongst the mammals and fish. The other major difference may have been the much more extensive river and lake network.

The environmental changes that took place throughout the 4000 years of the Mesolithic are obvious, but it is not entirely clear if they would have impacted on the inhabitants lives to such an extent that major changes in life-ways would have

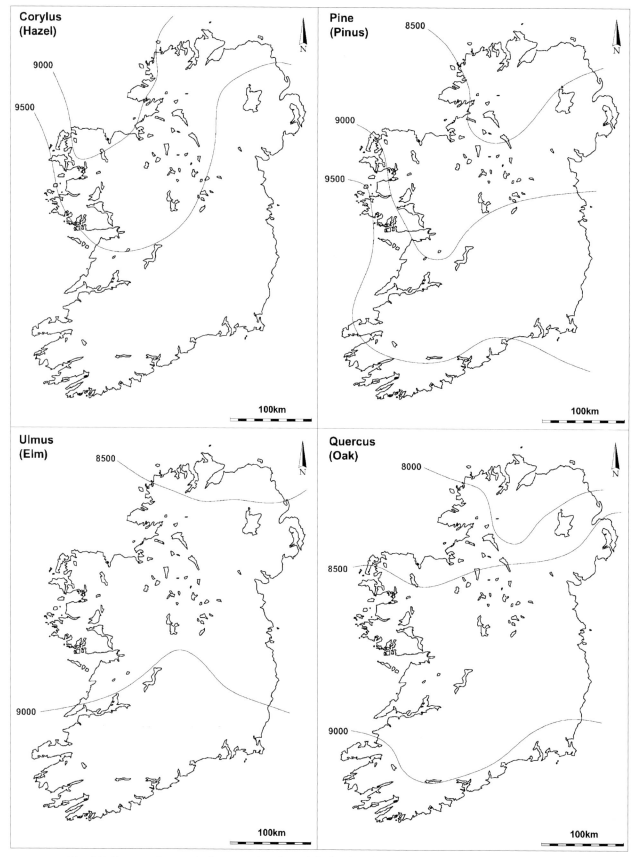

Fig. 2.9. Suggested spread of tree species through Ireland in the early Holocene (after Mitchell 2009).

been needed. The reduction in the size of Ireland, due to rising sea levels, would have been marginal, though the creation of extensive sea loughs as well as changes to the estuaries may have proved beneficial. The silting up of lakes and river floodplains was only beginning, and while some small lakes may have vanished, even today there are certain areas of extensive "lakelands" in Ireland. The shift to an Atlantic climate with higher rainfall and denser woodlands may have had an effect, but one would have to ask, what was affected?

Zealand presents an interesting contrast to Ireland. It was created as an island during the Mesolithic and initially had an extensive presence of large mammals, such as aurochs and elk. Due to a combination of the reduced size of territory and human activity, both species became extinct. Ireland was different. It was isolated from at least 16,000 cal BP, i.e., well before the commencement of the Holocene and before its fauna and flora became established. On the other hand, as noted at the beginning of this chapter, Ireland was and is one of the largest islands on the planet!

Raw materials within the Irish Mesolithic

Any examination of a geological map of Ireland shows that there is a diverse range of rocks available and it is very obvious that a number of them are suitable sources of raw materials for the manufacture of stone tools (Fig. 2.10). Yet, one of the most pervasive and enduring aspect of the Irish Mesolithic is the assumption that flint was the preferred raw material, which would be used rather than other forms of rock. There is, however, growing evidence that numerous other materials were being used and have to be seen as more than flint substitutes.

Flint

Flint has to be considered, at one level, as a variant of chert. It is not found in deposits of one particular Geologic era. In the case of north-western Europe it is assumed to be associated with Cretaceous Chalk or, in the case of Ireland, the Cretaceous Limestone (UWLF or Ulster White Limestone Formation) found in the north-east of the country.

There is still remarkable assumption that any large flint artefact would have been made from "Antrim" flint. In a sense, the over-emphasis on the size of the blades and flakes in so-called "Larnian" assemblages fed this belief in the key role of Antrim flint.

Flint, of course, occurs in bedrock now usually referred to as UWLF, which was formed during the Cretaceous Era when, in some areas, deposits of over 100 m of white limestone were laid down, but it is rare to find the complete sequence at any one location. The Antrim sources are the most obvious and longest sequences, as is apparent along the coastal cliffs of much of east and north Antrim. The reason why so much of the Antrim white limestone is only found in cliff deposits is

because it are masked by the overlying early Tertiary basalts. However, in north-east Antrim, inland along the eastern edge of the Antrim Plateau or round Knocklayd Mountain, there are other outcrops of limestone with flint. In some areas, such as Ballycastle/Torr Head, the outcrops are mostly exposed on the horizontal rather than in cliff faces. There are also significant outcrops in parts of Co. Derry, for example at Slieve Gallion overlooking Lough Neagh or the deposits on the western side of the Sperrins, such as near Dungiven. Small deposits also occur round areas adjacent to the southern shores of lough Neagh in Counties Down, Armagh, near Lurgan, and Tyrone.

The UWLF deposits are particularly hard so that there is limited evidence of quarrying to extract flint. In the case of the Ballygally site on the East Antrim coast (Collins 1978), tilted beds of flint were followed down to a depth of less than 2 m. The only other possible site where mining, or more accurately flint extraction from the rock face, is known is the 1920's extraction site on Black Mountain near Belfast (Bell and Bennett 1923). While much of the flint used, even in this north-eastern region, is in secondary sources, which will be discussed below, there must have been some extensive, though perhaps *ad hoc*, extraction of flint from the bedrock. There are numerous instances, especially within some of the caches of Neolithic artefacts (see Woodman *et al.* 2006, chapter 5), of items which retain an area of extremely fresh cortex. These pieces almost certainly have to come from a source where the original nodule was extracted directly from the bedrock. It should be noted, of course, that there is, so far, little evidence of mined flint with fresh cortex being used during the Mesolithic.

It should also be realised that not all the geological members that make up the UWLF contain good quality flint. In some cases, the deposits contain nodules which are fractured and flawed. In particular some of the flint from deposits of the early Mastrichtian stage, which occurs along parts of the north coast from Portrush to Ballycastle, is poor and not particularly reliable.

Therefore, much of the flint obtained in the northern part of Ireland comes from other secondary sources. There are two obvious sources. One would be nodules which have eroded out of the cliffs and can be recovered from the scree slopes. Along the coast, the other major source of flint is that which has been washed up into beach deposits. There is no doubt, however, that the sorting of nodules of varying quality and reliability by the action of the sea has certain advantages; it would appear that where the beach is littered with flint cobbles, there is a process of natural selection in which only the better nodules survive.

What is less clear is how much useful flint can be recovered from glacial deposits. However, as has been evident from the material recovered from many sites in the area, such as Mt Sandel, much of this type of flint is often extremely poor, very fragmentary and unreliable. One possible source of flint in an area which has to be explored is locations of clay with

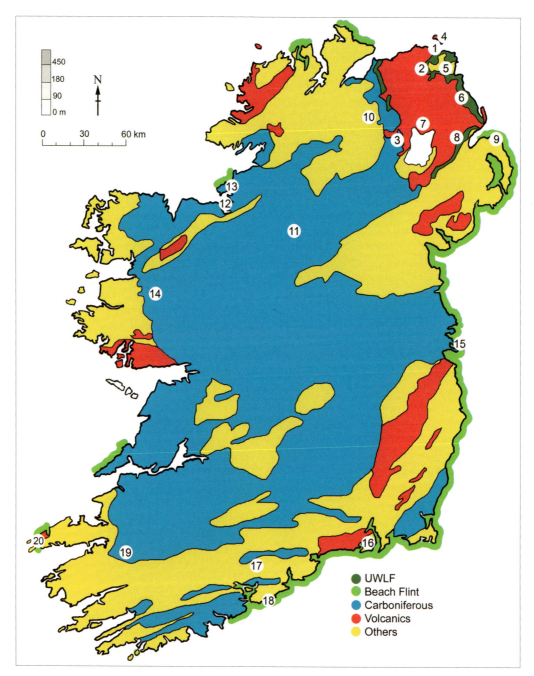

Fig. 2.10. a) Simplified geological map of Ireland with major locations of raw materials referred to in text: 1) Ballycastle/Torr Head area, 2) Knocklayd Mountain, 3) Slieve Gallion, 4) Brockley, Rathlin Island, 5) Tievebulliagh Mountain, 6) Ballygalley, 7) Tardree Mountain, 8) Black Mountain, 9) Coalpit Bay, 10) Dungiven, 11) Lough Macnean, 12) Knocknarea Mountain, 13) Dartry Mountains, 14) Tourmakeady, 15 Lambay Island, 16) Monvoy, 17) Garryduff, 18) Ballycroneen, 19 Ballydeenlea, 20) Ferriter's Cove.

flints. In this case weathering and denudation took place on the surfaces of the Limestone to create the clay with flint phenomenon and it would seem that this led on some occasions to the flint becoming highly coloured. Numerous examples of the clay with flint deposits can be identified in Antrim and Derry. This source might have been easier to exploit than the harder UWLF deposits.

Throughout the rest of Ireland extensive erosion over 60 million years of the Tertiary and nearly 1,000,000 years of glacial activity has removed a series of extensive pre-quaternary geological deposits. It has removed virtually all Tertiary, as well as many Cretaceous, deposits and even some of those from the Jurassic Era. Thus the chances of finding flint even in other sources is often very unlikely.

It would appear, however, that there were three potential sources of flint that might have occurred in the rest of the country. The first of these would have been as glacial erratics. The best known of these are the erratics that would have been carried in ice sheets down the Irish Sea. Flint nodules have been found in abundance on beaches from Belfast and Strangford Loughs in the north to beaches along the coast of Wexford in the south-east (Delaney 2000). As can be seen from the substantial size of blades at sites such as Sutton, and the large size of some of the cores (see Chapter 5), there was little problem finding a more than adequate supply of flint. Unlike other areas, notably parts of the south coast, it does not seem likely that the flint was washed in from primary offshore deposits under the Irish Sea. Similarly, flint may have been transported westwards along the coast of north Donegal. It can be found in large quantities as beach rolled nodules on Inistrahull and on beaches along the northern edges of the Inishowen Peninsula, though as Kimball (2000) has shown, while some erratic flint can be found in parts of Lough Swilly, no significant traces of flint can be found more than 25 km inland. Flint nodules are also found on the western entrance to Lough Swilly at Fanad Head, and others have been found further west by the late Tommy Gallagher (pers. comm.).

Some beaches along the south coast, especially in the east Cork coastal area, have produced large quantities of flint. Large nodules are recorded as being dredged up by trawlers based in the Kinsale area. These can be up to 200 mm across. Based in field work in the area it would appear that significant quantities of, sometimes fractured, flint nodules can be found in the sea cliff faces of the Ballycroneen till while good quality flint can be picked up from the adjacent beaches. In these cases it would seem that the offshore Cretaceous deposits that contain flint are the source. These can belong to bedrock dating to different phases of the Cretaceous from those found in the north-east. As the offshore areas off the south coast had been transgressed during the LGM flint could, as at Ballycroneen on the east Cork coast, be carried in with the till and, having been exposed by erosion caused by advancing and retreating ice sheets, more material could have been carried on shore as the sea level rose.

There are some potential differences between northern and southern flint. The northern material, as already noted, mostly dates to the upper part of the Cretaceous, primarily from the Upper Santonian to the Maastrichtian (Simms 2009, 325–31). However, along the south coast the chalk sequence begins much earlier and deposits those lying some tens of kilometres offshore begins with the older Cenomanian Chalk deposits while some of the much later deposits may have been at least partially eroded (Naylor and Shannon 2009 440–6). Field work in east Cork has resulted in the recovery of large quantities material from lithic scatters and beach collection. While flint is not a particularly homogeneous material and, in the north, ranges from black through grey to blue in colour, the material from the south includes some remarkably different material, such as

mottled blue and beige flint, rather coarser beige material and occasionally flint with a very fresh soft cortex that differs from the white cortex of east Antrim flint. While it was possible, using ESR, to distinguish between flint from east Antrim and that from east Derry such as the Slieve Gallion area (Griffiths and Woodman 1987) a similar attempt to establish differences in southern flint was not so successful (Woodman and Griffiths 1988), probably due to the complexity of the sources; it might be that simpler approaches using microfossils could identify different sources and provide useful indicators of movement of people through much of Irish prehistory.

While flint nodules have been found along the south-west and west coast they are not found in very large quantities, however, flint has been recovered on beaches from Ferriter's Cove in west Kerry (Woodman *et al.* 1999) through Co. Clare (Brett 2000) to several large nodules found on the beaches in Co. Sligo (Martin Timoney, pers. comm.). This material would also seem to have come in from offshore deposits and may again have different local characteristics.

These different sources of coastal flint may again be of immense help in tracking how this material was moved across much of Ireland, whether inland from east Antrim, northwards from the south coast to the major river valleys of Munster, or inland from the west coast to the lakes of the Shannon system. As yet the work on sourcing different types of flint from coastal and inland sites has hardly begun. But this issue, as a potential important line of research, will hopefully be of use in addressing some of the regional issues discussed below in Chapters 9 and 12.

For much of the rest of Ireland, the fact that the last glacial events in the Early and Late Midlandian did not conveniently cross surviving UWLF deposits and then move south across the Irish Midlands means that there was little chance of large quantities of erratic flint being scattered across the centre of the country.

The only other source of flint could be relict pieces that have survived the Tertiary and Quaternary denudation and erosion. The one surviving portion of Cretaceous deposits with flint in the southern part of Ireland is the Ballydeenlea deposit near Killarney in Co. Kerry. However, the quality of flint is rather poor. O'Kelly (1952) identified small, highly ground pieces of flint on a ridge adjacent to Garryduff in east Cork. These are pieces that rarely exceed 30 mm in length and would seldom be suitable as raw material for blade cores. These appear to be residual pieces of flint that survived in areas where the bedrock Cretaceous deposits have been removed. These remaniée pieces seem to have been mostly used for the creation of bipolar cores and related forms that tend to occur in later prehistoric times.

In summary, flint is available throughout much of Ireland but outside the north-east it would mostly seem to be confined to coastal areas. Even within the north-east, flint is freely available only in certain very specific locations. However, if flint is available round much of the coast and at certain inland locations, it should be remembered that flint sources are always available within 150 km of any part of Ireland. There are many areas, such as the Blackwater Valley in Co. Cork, where, as will be discussed below in Chapter 9, field work recovered a number of scatters of flint artefacts which were probable made on flint imported from the coast, which lies 40 km to the south. However not a single piece of locally occurring flint of erratic or other origin was recovered.

Chert, or is it?

While, as seen above, it is simple to work with a definition of flint that suits the circumstances of Ireland, chert presents a different set of problems. It is usually associated with a series of Limestone deposits which, in Ireland, belong to the Lower Carboniferous era – the Visean and Tournasian. Carboniferous deposits cover up to 50% of the surface of Ireland but not all of these are Limestone, in fact shales, mudstones, sandstones, etc., also form a very significant portion of the series. It also does not follow that chert occurs in all the limestones, thus it is virtually absent from the Carboniferous deposits in the north of Ireland. Many areas contain chert nodules that are small or very flawed and so would have been of limited use as a raw material.

There is also some occurrence of radiolarian chert in Silurian deposits, noticeably the 30 cm thick beds within the Glenkiln shales at Coalpit Bay on the east coast of Co. Down near Donaghadee (Anderson 2004). Certainly fine, large barbed-and-tanged arrowheads of chert have been found in east Down. In Co. Mayo there are, within the Tourmakeady and other formations of Ordovician date, quite extensive deposits which contain chert. These seem to contain relatively limited occurrences of chert but they illustrate that the tendency to assume that cherts automatically derive from Carboniferous deposits is an over-simplification (see Fig. 2.10).

There is also, in an archaeological context, no clarity as to what is meant by the term "chert". While the *ad hoc* definition of flint seems to work, the boundaries for chert seem less clear. Indeed, although not applicable in the case of Ireland, at times jasper and chalcedony have been considered as chert.

In the case of Ireland, chert is frequently, but not always, black, so there is a temptation to assume that anything black is chert. However, there are numerous examples of very dark black flint which can be mistaken for chert. Chert is usually assumed to have a lower percentage of silica but the major problem with Ireland is that there would seem to be a very diverse series of black rocks which could be considered as chert or more frequently as "cherty". There are, for example, certain distinct bands of very glossy chert to be found in the Dartry Mountain formation in Co. Sligo. This material has been used extensively in the Knocknarea area of Sligo. Nodular glossy black chert has also been used extensively in parts of Counties Clare and Limerick. There seems, therefore, to be no clear boundary between what archaeologists call chert and limestone. In many areas the description is likely to be "cherty limestones" or "dark chert argillaceous limestones". In fact the infamous Rosses Point assemblage discussed below in Chapter 3, irrespective of its age (Woodman 1998b), is based on worked limestone.

The potential differences in what might look to the unwary as a simple black cherty rock has been demonstrated by Little (2009), where at Clonava the artefacts from the archaeological site and the adjacent outcrop are different. As Little has observed casual slippage in terminology between limestone and chert can have "significant repercussions for the way in which we interpret scales of mobility, trade and settlement" (*ibid.*, 137). This became apparent during the excavations at Newferry (Woodman 1977a) where a series of non-flint black stone flakes was found. As can be seen from that site, even allowing for the fact that some of the flakes came from mudstone axes (see below for discussion on axes), there were few flakes of chert present on the site (Nawaz 1977). Of the black flakes found by Adams and others around 1900 at Toome, and which had been presumed to be chert, 50% have been identified as being of other raw materials, most notably mudstones.

Most of those which were regarded as chert from both Newferry and from the shores of Lough Neagh at Toome have been described as "Festooned chert". This has the appearance of a very distinct banded type of rock, and the term was first suggested to the author by Frank Mitchell, I think, on the basis of a verbal description of pieces from Newferry that contained very distinct evidence of multiple layers. However, it is seems that the Derravarragh "Festooned chert" from the north-east Midlands, as described by Nevill (1958, 296–7), is probably something very different.

Recent research in Lough MacNean has further demonstrated the danger of using the term chert for all coarse-grained black rocks that occur in the Irish Midlands. A series of artefacts from a type of black rock were collected from the shores of Lough MacNean on Cushrush Island. These were assumed, at the time, to be chert (Woodman 1978a, 306). However, the possibility of Mesolithic occupation on the Island of Inishee, which also lies in upper Lough MacNean, was examined by Gabriel Burns, with the geology/petrology of a series of artefacts recovered assessed by Kelly (2010). These were struck mostly from the same type of blackish stone as that found earlier at Cushrush Island. Kelly concluded that they (53%) were derived from a black siltstone that occurs in local outcrops rather than the Dartry limestones. An assemblage was also obtained through excavations carried out by Martin (2011, 112). Again, over 70% of an assemblage of approximately 150 items could be classified as being a local siltstone. The lesson from Lough MacNean is that, while sources such as chert from outcrops and Dartry limestones may exist, much of the material may have come from more local sources (Fig. 2:10; see below and Chapter 9).

In summary, while much English and Scottish chert seems to be a fine-grained and often glossy, in Ireland the term chert has been used to accommodate a range of very different rock types. Therefore, one has to consider the possibility that many artefacts that have been assumed to be chert may have been made from a range of other materials and come from a range of bedrocks in different areas. This would seem to be the case in north central England where petrological analysis is showing that different chert sources have been used (Randy Donoghue, pers. comm. and see below Chapter 9).

As Little (2009) has observed, attempts to use chert sourcing as a way of determining extent of movement and exchange systems in the Irish Mesolithic is, at the moment, fraught with danger.

Other types of raw materials

Siltstone, silicified limestone, mudstone and shales

As will be apparent from the previous discussion, there is an issue of separating cherts from other types of silicified and similar dark rocks; in particular a range of dark siltstones occur through the Ordovician and Silurian as well as the Carboniferous. Many of them, however, would be unsuitable as raw materials for the manufacture of stone tools.

It should, of course, be remembered that the older deposits are more likely to be altered. Therefore the siltstones of Silurian age of the Ballyferriter Formation have been altered and slightly metamorphosed through being exposed to two episodes of folding. Again, it would appear the mudstones within the Moffat Shales in the Longford Down Palaeozoic Peneplain, which were used for the manufacture of axes, have been metamorphosed (Woodman and Johnston 1991–2). It is, as noted earlier, obvious that there has been a limited but consistent exploitation of silicified limestones and a range of mudstones within the Bann Valley. From the 1860s onwards these mysterious black flakes and shales were being recovered from the shores of Lough Neagh near Toome. Knowles (1912) was also aware of the banded shales which were used for axes and the black flakes. In particular he commented on the very light weight of what he called "calcareous shales", which may have been examples of "decarbonated mudstones". These may well come from either the Altagoan or Desertmartin Formations which lie to the west of the Bann Valley and Lough Neagh. They seem to have been used for both the manufacture of axes and Later Mesolithic blanks, such as that illustrated by Knowles (*ibid.*, fig. 118). Indeed numerous other tool types that used these materials, for example the apparently anomalous artefacts illustrated by Woodman (2005a, fig. 9.2), could remain unrecognised.

One raw material in this group which has received relatively little attention in Ireland is slate. The realisation that there is a series of ground points (Moynagh Points) frequently produced from slate blanks indicates that, as in Scandinavia, slate was a potentially very useful raw material. As yet no serious attempt has been made to identify these sources. It should be noted, however, that similar small examples of points that are unpolished were made from other more shale-like rocks (Farina Sternke in prep. and pers. comm.).

Other volcanics and metamorphics

There is, as already noted, clear evidence of the use of metamorphosed rocks, such as baked mudstone, during the Mesolithic. This material has been used to manufacture axes and would appear to derive from sources within the Longford Down Palaeozoic Peneplain, though it seems more likely that the Mount Sandel axes could derive from much closer carboniferous deposits on the North coast in the Ballycastle area. At Ferriter's cove (Mandal 1999a, 193–4; 1999b, 201–2) and at Lough Kinale, axes made from shales and mudstones had been used, though in the former case they were derived from Carboniferous sources, while the latter may have been, again, from the Longford Down Palaeozoic Peneplain. Less attention has been paid to the green schist axes that have been found primarily in Co. Antrim, thus raising the possibility that sources in the Torr Head area in the most north-eastern part of Antrim were used. At Dalkey Island, although some of the axes may not be Mesolithic age, again mudstone/shale axes, of unknown origin, and schist axes dominate.

Therefore, while it is at the moment impossible to pinpoint the source of many of the axes, there appears to be a distinct preference for certain raw materials.

Obviously there are several major sources of volcanic or metamorphosed rocks that have been used primarily for axe manufacture. So far there is little evidence that these were used in the Mesolithic. They include porcelanite from Tievebulliagh and Brockley, as well perhaps as the mid- Tyrone igneous complex. The discovery of the Neolithic porphyry quarry site on Lambay (Cooney 2005) shows that numerous other quarries may yet remain to be discovered, although it is equally possible, as can be seen from earlier discussions, that secondary sources such as pebbles or cobbles of the right size could have been used.

Rhyolite first came to attention as a result of the excavations at Ferriter's Cove (Woodman *et al.* 1999). There is only limited evidence of its use in the manufacture of ground stone axes and so far little evidence that it was quarried in Co. Kerry. However, cobbles recovered from the beaches were used for blade and core tool production. Rhyolite artefacts and quarries have also been discovered in Co. Waterford, at Monvoy (Green and Zvelibil 1990). The major problem with Rhyolite is that there are numerous outcrops of Rhyolite from various episodes of volcanic activity and not all of these may have either been exploited or suitable for exploitation therefore can we be sure that the Monvoy quarry was used before the Neolithic. This very local distribution of Rhyolite artefacts recovered in east Waterford, in the vicinity of the Monvoy quarry site, is also evident. Here again large quantities of flint artefacts were recovered during the Ballylough Archaeological Survey (Green and Zvelibil 1990), yet in a survey area that was adjacent to the Monvoy Quarry virtually no Rhyolite artefacts were recovered. Further north, a few were recovered during National Road Authority excavations along the N25, where it formed a bypass round Waterford City. It would appear, therefore, that while there is a chance that exploitation of the Monvoy Quarry may have begun in the Mesolithic, many of the products may be Neolithic in date (Woodman 2011, 199–206).

Just because Rhyolite outcrops exist can we be sure that they were used? One of the best known examples of this problem is the Tardree Rhyolite Complex in Co. Antrim, which also contains some obsidian outcrops. In the case of the mid-Antrim area, thousands of stone tools have been collected within a few kilometres of the outcrops, but no Rhyolite or obsidian flakes recovered.

Occasional flakes of Rhyolite also turned up on the shores of Lough Gara (Driscoll 2006, 224). Perhaps in the north-west, the Rhyolite that occurs in the Tourmakeady Formation adjacent to the shores of Lough Mask in Co. Mayo could be the source of the artefacts from Lough Gara.

"Volcanics" are not just used for the manufacture of axes. Some coarse volcanic tuffs were recovered from Ferriter's Cove (Woodman *et al.* 1999), while other more fine grained tuffs constituted 50% of the assemblage from the Neolithic house site at Cloghers, Co. Kerry (Kiely 2003, 186–7).

Quartz has long been recognised as a material that was used in prehistory in Ireland. While it may not always have been recognised, it is of interest that, during Ó Ríordáin's excavations at Knockadoon, Lough Gur (Ó Ríordáin 1954; Grogan and Eogan 1987) quartz was the second most common raw material after flint. It has usually been assumed, however, that it was not suitable for blade production and in particular for the large blanks that were produced in the Later Mesolithic. The discovery by Padraig Caulfield of a Later Mesolithic site at Belderrig, Co. Mayo and its current excavation (Warren 2009) shows that, in certain circumstances, high quality quartz can be used for blade production. A preliminary survey of Irish lithic assemblages of all periods by Driscoll and Warren (2007) has recorded 150 townlands in which quartz artefacts have been recovered. While the authors have alluded to difficulties in quantifying the quartz found on various sites it is apparent that, even allowing for a relative lack of awareness and therefore identification, the majority of assemblages have fewer than ten quartz artefacts (*ibid.*, fig. 2). In general one can sense that, with a few notable exceptions such as Belderrig, quartz artefacts are quite rare on Mesolithic sites. However, although exceptionally large quantities of small splinters and waste flakes occur on a number of sites, it is of interest that in certain circumstances, such as Belderrig, relatively good quality blades could be produced. Therefore one should not assume that quartz is necessarily nothing more than a poor quality alternative to flint.

In contrast, rock crystal which has been used in the Neolithic, for example at Windy Ridge (Woodman *et al.* 1991–2), would usually not be suitable for use in the Mesolithic.

Other stone materials

In comparison to certain other regions, quartzite appears to have been used to a very limited extent in Ireland. In fact its major use seems to have been as hammer stones and it is possible that quartzite pebbles deriving from the Devonian deposits at Cushendun would have been much sought after as they were carried by glacial activity or sea current down along the Antrim coast, thus ending up in beach deposits. As was discussed with relation to flint, many of these cobbles when still *in situ* were flawed and fractured and once again the sea acted as a selection agent.

Organic material

Given that the Mesolithic population lived in a wooded environment and that a significant portion of their stone equipment may have been used to create wooden tools, weapons, utensils and structures, there seems little point stressing the obvious importance of organic materials. However, the wooden artefacts from sites such as Derragh Lough (Fredengren 2009) or the discovery of fish traps at Clowanstown (Mossop 2009a) and the Liffey Estuary (McQuade and O'Donnell 2009) helps to emphasise its significance.

Until recently few bone or antler artefacts of definite Mesolithic age were recovered from Ireland. As will have been apparent from earlier discussions on the nature of Ireland's early Holocene faunas there is no convincing presence of aurochs, roe deer or elk. The evidence that red deer were present in Ireland in any significant numbers is quite equivocal. There is an absence of known red deer antler artefacts that date to the Mesolithic. Some Late glacial Giant deer antler fragment could have been converted into artefacts at a later date. These may date to activity in the Mesolithic or be even later, as in the case of an axe of Bronze Age date (Liversage 1957).

Review of raw materials

In summary, it would seem as if the conventional wisdom of raw material availability has relied on a very simple model in which flint from the north-east of Ireland was seen as the primary raw material. The role of flint from other sources, as well as the greater reliability of beach flint, has been under-estimated. There would also appear to be a lack of clarity as to whether many of the black rocks used on sites in the interior of Ireland are cherts or other related silicified raw materials. With one or two notable exceptions there is no clear sense as to where these materials were sourced. Similarly, there is almost a dual polarity, "flint/chert" perspective. There is growing evidence that a range of other raw material was used during the Mesolithic especially, as will be discussed below, the Later Mesolithic.

As will have been apparent from papers such as Little (2009), one positive aspect of this review is that it highlights the potential for extensive areas of research which could expand the work being undertaken at the moment.

So what makes Ireland different?

It is an island but in spite of its relatively large size there seems to have been a very delicate balance between closeness and availability. On the one hand there is another large landmass close by. But there was also a relatively short period, when Ireland was ice free or not subject to exceptionally inhospitable environment conditions, when there was a relatively limited but important stretch of water between Ireland and the rest of Europe. Of course, many adjacent regions in Europe had remained ice free so that fauna and flora migrated back north and west without too much difficulty.

It would appear that Ireland's position on the Atlantic fringe may also have created a climatic environment that was not always conducive to the long term survival, and adaptation for those species that did make it was not always easy. Looking at what would have been present by 10,000 years ago, Ireland seems to have had a pioneering mammalian fauna as well as fish that seem to be, in part, something that arrived in the Late Glacial and then could have adapted during a cold phase to living in fresh water.

There is an interesting irony that most trees and large shrubs found their way to Ireland without too much delay but one has to wonder about some of the plants that might have proved important sources of food.

In contrast as already mentioned and will discussed below in Chapter 9 there was a diverse range of sources of raw material for the manufacture of stone tools. Not only were there the northern flint sources as well as erratic and beach flint but there were certain areas where good quality cherty rock and metamorphosed silt stone were available as well as one suspects other sources such as Rhyolite. In fact as archaeologists we seem to have more difficulty finding the sources than did the Mesolithic peoples who are the subject of our studies.

In summary Ireland was and is an interesting place to come to, but it is also a place where, fairly rapidly, you have to make changes.

Chapter 3

It's about time

It is always useful to provide an historical introduction to a review of any discipline. It is partly nostalgic but it has the double value of providing an understanding as to how the corpus of evidence has been created and the reasons why certain theories are in vogue. It is not intended to be another "potted" history of archaeology, or even a supplement to Waddell's (2005) *Foundation Myths: the beginnings of Irish Archaeology*, instead it is an attempt to see how ideas about "human antiquity" have developed, and in particular, how this search played out in Ireland. Perhaps it can also help one to be objective about one's own research. One can examine the struggle of previous generations in their attempts to grapple with the unknown. When their evidence appears to be in conflict with the accepted wisdom of the day, one can only be humble and appreciate their contributions. It also makes one realise that others in the future will also wonder how we could be so wrong.

This struggle for objectivity even impinges on how we interpret the surviving fragments of evidence that we have been fortunate to recover. It is possible to show that the patterns we see and which we create have been mitigated by both the debates and fixations of those working in earlier generations. The Keiller Knowles project (Woodman *et al.* 2006, chapter 1) highlighted the manner in which Victorian society organised itself in terms of transport and agricultural practices and their consequent impact on what material culture was recovered.

The manner in which ideas about ancient prehistoric settlers evolved in Ireland has not only to be seen as part of a European debate but must also be seen in the context of the shared, contested and often confusing interactions between Ireland and Britain.

Hopefully it also reminds us to ask whether, even today, if the Irish Mesolithic appears different, can we disentangle the environmental perspective, i.e. Ireland as an island, from the perspectives created by our own intellectual history and politics.

Early debates on human origins and "deep time"

The year 1859 is often seen as a pivotal date but the progress towards the acceptance that human presence on this planet had a significant antiquity was by no means a simple series of steps forward in the context of new insights. John Evans (1823–1908), a numismatist, and Joseph Prestwich (1812–1896), a geologist, visited Boucher de Perthes, a high ranking customs officer, in Amiens in April 1859. The professions of both were in the world of business, with Evans working in the family business of paper making, while Prestwich was also involved in a family business, the wine trade. Boucher de Perthes had been proposing the contemporaniety of extinct animals and stone tools since the 1840s but, due to poor illustrations and outlandish ideas – for example, claims for antediluvian works of art – and a lack of knowledge of geology, his proposals were greeted with scepticism by many geologists. During their visit, however, Evans and Prestwich were shown an artefact found in a geological context along with the bones of extinct animals which, in the words of Gamble and Kruszynski (2009), was "the stone that broke the time barrier". This evidence for a human presence at an early date was soon backed up by the discovery of the drawing of a mammoth on a mammoth tusk from La Madeleine in the south-west of France, which proved contemporaniety and finally wiped out the objections of those who argued that the Somme material could have been swept together from different sources. This may seem to have been an inevitable consequence of the Industrial Revolution ethos of "man makes himself", yet the issues of human origins and how society had developed had, in fact, been a source of discussion for over two millennia.

As far back as the 8th century BC, Hesiod had proposed a system of ages that progressed from a simple Golden Age of peace and simplicity to later ages of manufacturing and warfare, but this was not necessarily seen as a pathway to progress. Instead, it could be regarded as a decline from a Golden Age rather than an advance towards civilisation. This was to be a perspective that would haunt the debate on human origins for the whole of the Renaissance; the contrast between the fall of humanity from a Golden Age and the concept that humanity and society had developed steadily through time from a primitive state.

In Renaissance England, for example, this debate centred on the contradiction between Biblical interpretations and the search for other explanations for the origins of humanity (Fergusson 1993, chapters 1–3). In particular, Fergusson noted that even from the 14th century there was a desire for rational explanations of a dim, distant past that was, in effect, totally unknown. Thus, classical authors, with their description of the outlandish behaviour of gods, were no more satisfactory than the medieval reliance on Biblical versions of world history.

The idea of advancement by "engrafting new things on old" seemed less than satisfactory, even to Francis Bacon (1561–1626; *ibid.*, 34). Bacon seemed to flirt with the idea that "man had been led out of a brutish existence in the primeval caves and forests by individuals of surpassing intelligence who had inexplicably appeared amongst them". Thus, while there was a growing encouragement for rational demands for evidence rather than faith in respected texts, it did not mean that all scientists were converted.

Ultimately, as Fergusson noted (*ibid.*, chapter 4), these types of arguments were rendered irrelevant by the "Big Three", the compass, fire arms and the printing press, which changed the world view of Elizabethan observers.

The "Age of Explorations" created new vistas which confronted conventional scholarship with a startling array of new evidence. The impact of the Native Americans cannot be understated. Schnapp (1996, 228–30) notes the influence of travellers such as Walter Raleigh (1564–1618) on the Calvinist Isaac de Lapeyrère (1596–1676), who was to contest the theory that Native Americans were of Scandinavian origin. He therefore brought into focus the assertion that there were primitive peoples who were not part of the decline from a Europo-centric Golden Age (Livingstone 2008, 27–31). Lapeyrère, in 1655, was also among the first to use the term "Pre-Adamite" or people who existed at an earlier date than the Biblical Adam (*ibid.*, 32). Trigger (1989, 53) also noted that Lapeyrère's descriptions of the use of "Thunderstones" by "Pre-Adamite" people who existed before the first Hebrews, were probably references to stone and flint axes. This was to become a debate between "proto-evolutionists" and "degenerationists", with the latter being those who simply saw the population of the Americas as corrupt remnants of peoples who had forgotten their origins.

In England, Sir William Dugdale (1605–1686) in *The Antiquities of Warwickshire*, had postulated that what we would now recognise as Neolithic polished flint axes but had often been thought to be thunderstones falling from the sky, were made by native "Britons" as they had been made from flint that was imported to Warwickshire (Dugdale 1656; Cook 2003, 182).

As the "Age of Exploration" continued, various other peoples were "discovered". Their diversity raised further questions as to whether the origins of all peoples could be explained in terms of the Bible and a world that was created roughly 6000 years ago.

It might have been expected, therefore, that by the 18th century there would have been a more coherent search for the evidence of early and primitive forms of societies and people. In France this can be seen in the writing of authors such as

Abbé Saint Pierre (1658–1743) in the early 18th century (Bury 1932, chapter 6) and then with the works of the Encyclopaedists such as Voltaire, Diderot or Turgot, who espoused the ideals that there could be a rational progress towards a better society through science and law. In contrast some, such as Rousseau (1712–1778) who, to the consternation of the others, felt that this form of progress would not necessarily be beneficial to humanity and preferred to see society as being in decline from a "Golden Age".

In a sense, the idea of progress might have been expected to be mirrored in Britain in the Age of Enlightenment. In the Royal Society in London, Sir Joseph Banks, to the chagrin of the mathematicians, was responsible for championing natural history, as well as matters of antiquarian interest, as valid subjects of research and scholarship (Gascoigne 1994, 107–12; 119–34). It would appear, however, that Antiquaries were, in the context of natural history, not always applying "logical inductive reasoning" to the evidence from monuments and artefacts. While the work of Aubrey (1626–1697) and, in particular, Stukeley (1687–1765) had shown that Stonehenge pre-dated the Roman occupation of Britain, interests in these monuments then went in a different direction, namely more towards "end of the century" romanticism

At this time there had also emerged the growing phenomenon of the collector and his cabinet of curiosities. The mid-17th century collection of the Dane, Ole Worm (1588–1655), must have confronted those who had confined themselves to literary scholarship with a world view that was entirely different from that of "Old Europe". These types of Museums were cabinets containing materials brought back from different parts of the world, as well as fossils and other curiosities dug up from the earth. MacGregor (1994) noted that even the collections of Sir Hans Sloane (1660–1753), who had been born in Killyleagh, Co. Down, which are generally regarded as those that formed the basis of what was to become the British Museum and the Natural History Museum, really made up a *Wunderkammer* rather than a *Kunstkammer*. His collection, in his own words, included "334 volumes of dried plants, 5,439 insects, Humana viz stones of kidneys and bladders … and the like 756, 1125 things relating to the customs of ancient times or antiquities urns, instruments etc." (MacGregor 1994, 28–9). This diversity was typical of collections made by individuals, private and commercial museums, as well as those of many learned societies. Ireland, of course, did not differ from the rest of Europe. The early 19th century museums, such as those of the Belfast Natural History and Philosophical Society or the Royal Cork Institution, were closer to being cabinets of curiosities. In contrast, the growing collections of the Royal Irish Academy in Dublin were much closer to the type of archaeological collections that characterise museums today.

As the 18th century progressed, the concept of Antiquarianism and the collection of oddities were to come under attack. This was, of course, from a generation that was exposed to the grand tour and experienced the ruins that represented the grandeur of the Roman and Greek civilisations. Indeed, excavations at Herculaneum at this time were seen as organised mining to help extract the products or *objets de vertu* of that "Golden Age". Parslow (1995) in particular documents the role of Karl Weber, who was in charge of excavations at Herculaneum between 1750 and 1764. At a European level, the recovery of "objects of beauty" was heavily influenced by Johann Joachim Winckelmann (1717–1768) of whom Jenkins (1992, 19–26) felt that "His approach to Antiquity was charged with a melancholy of longing for a lost golden age. The beauty of this world serves only to remind us of that which we have lost".

It could be suggested that in England the drive was to restore, in that island, the lost glory of Greece. A pivotal figure was Horace Walpole (1717–1797) of Strawberry Hill. His concentration on the connoisseurship of *objets de vertu*, such as Etruscan vases, meant that he saw little value in "a cartload of bricks and rubbish and roman ruins" (Daniel 1962, 8), in fact he saw the Society of Antiquaries as the "midwives of superannuated miscarriages" (*ibid.*, 9). Walpole, in a letter to Sir Horace Mann, spoke scathingly of the fact that he had been appointed as a trustee to the collections of Sir Hans Sloane: "the guardianship of embryos and cockle shells" (MacGregor 1994, 48). The views of Walpole would also have been matched by others. In terms of art, society was also heavily influenced by an essay of Edmund Burke (1729–1797), published 1857, *A Philosophical Enquiry into the Origin of our Ideas of the Sublime and Beautiful*. Contemplating the "sublime" and "Terror", in the form of landscape paintings, rather than recording the details of monuments, became more prevalent.

There were, of course, those who had a broad range of interests. Earlier in the 19th century, Sir William Hamilton (1731–1803), who is more known as a collector of vases, was also passionately interested in volcanoes. For many, it may have been that they were more interested in the monetary value of the objects than in their use in helping interpret the past. When shiploads of vases and sculptures were being transported back to Britain, the problems of seeking to understand a distant time of savagery must have seemed of little significance. Waddell (2005, 49) has noted that, even in Ireland, the desire to import antiquities stretched back to the beginning of the 18th century so that Bishop Berkeley, while commiserating with Sir John Perceval of Cork who had lost two shiploads of classical antiquities, commented that "his neighbours would hardly relish feeding their eyes on rusty medals, etc.".

In summary, if the idea that human beings had developed from "primitive beginnings" at some distant point in time was to receive general acceptance then two major issues had to be addressed:

a) The concept of "Deep Time", or in other words, that Planet Earth had been in existence for a very long time.
b) A recognition of what we have come to call the "Three Age System", especially in the context of a time before written records existed. This includes the place of humanity in the natural order of things.

Concepts of "deep time"

During the latter part of the 18th century, geology had seen significant progress in the debate on the origins of various types of rocks. As Gould (1988, chapter 3) has noted, Hutton (1726–1797) in his field of research, as well as John Playfair (1748–1819) in his more popular interpretations, showed how far the study of the earth had proceeded. Hutton, who is regarded as the "Father" of modern geology, in particular with his ideas of the earth as a machine, inferred that the planet had existed for a significant length of time. This was based on the hypothesis that, rather than explain the origins of rocks in the manner that Catastrophists espoused, i.e., often through specific events such as volcanic activity or floods, it was probable that rocks were created through a long process of erosion of areas of high ground, with the deposits of sediments in the sea or elsewhere to form rocks. In turn, other regions of the Earth's crust were raised up so as to allow the cycle of erosion and deposition to continue. Based on his own observations of these processes, he felt that these events took place over exceptionally long periods of time.

At the beginning of the 19th century others, such as the canal engineer William Smith (1769–1839) (Winchester 2001) and geologists such as Charles Lyell (1797–1875) (Prothero 1990, 9–23), were helping document the stratigraphy and geological sequences of Britain. Between 1820 and 1840, due to the work of Murchison and Sedgewick, the process of recognition, naming and sequencing of periods that are still in use today took place (*ibid.*, 14–17). Lyell (1830–3) in his *Principles of Geology* expanded the ideas of Hutton and others and showed how rocks of different types and different periods had developed. Within geology there was, by this stage, acceptances that the Earth's history went back for an exceptionally long time, yet, humanity's origins were not seen as part of the quest of geology.

In Biology, many had taken exception to Linnaeus's (1707–1778) system of classification. In part this was due to the explicit use of sexual terms, but there were also major objections to the human species being classified as a mammal, implying that they were no different than cows or horses. After all, Genesis stated that "Man" had been given dominion over the beasts of the fields.

Geologists were prepared to provide reconstructions of landscapes of different eras and populate them with plants and animals. One of the more ambitious works was that of the German Professor of Botany, Franz Unger (1800–1870), whose scenes, from what is now known as the Carboniferous and later periods, appear remarkably up-to-date. They also included an illustration of the birth place of humanity, although as Unger himself said, the exact location of that paradise still remained unknown (Fig. 3.1a).

A classic example of this reluctance had consequences for Louis Figuier (1819–1894). In 1863 he published a much delayed *The World before the Deluge*. He had produced a masterly series of reconstructions throughout geological time but again it included Adam and Eve in the Garden of Eden.

The publication of his book suffered from the nightmare of a publication delay, and it only appeared after the *Annus mirabilis* of 1859, the year of the appearance of *The Origin of Species* as well as the visit to Boucher de Perthes in Amiens (see above). The second edition in 1867 replaced the Garden of Eden not only with bear skin clad individuals, but with caves, hyena and mammoths (Fig. 3.1a and b).

These were not individual statements of reluctance to include the human species within the development of creatures whose origins stretched back through an earth history that extended for an almost inconceivable length of time. The French palaeontologist Georges Cuvier (1769–1832), who provided reconstructions of various extinct species such as the Giant Sloth or the Mastodon (Fig. 3.2; Rudwick 1995, 31–7),

Fig. 3.1. Two reconstructions of the Garden of Eden (from Figuier 1863 and 1867, after Rudwick 1995).

Fig. 3.2. Reconstruction of the Deluge (after Rudwick 1995).

and Dean William Buckland (1784–1856), the first Professor of Geology at Oxford and a consummate field geologist whose stratigraphic observations helped lay the foundation of English geology, both believed that the existence of different species of fossils in different geological strata was a result of a series of catastrophic floods which may have required either large-scale movements of animals of a new range of species to repopulate devastated areas or perhaps even Divine intervention. Buckland had also observed the phenomenon of deposits of mixed origin and age (Fig. 3.3), therefore, even after discovering the "Red lady of Paviland" in the Goats Hole in south Wales, apparently in association with extinct animal bones and stone implements, he still felt that the deposits had been disturbed and that the skeleton was contemporaneous with the Roman invasion (Buckland 1823, 87–92). Cook (2003, 181) felt that Buckland, as a Clergyman, was required to be cautious and that, in a later work in 1837, he was prepared to recognise the importance of the fact that the human remains had been stratified. In reality, of course, other excavations were producing indicators that human antiquity stretched well back in time, such as that at Paviland, was quite frequent. Father McEnery (1796–1841) excavated at Kent's Cavern between 1824 and 1829, and this was only one of several investigations of caves in South-West England in which McEnery was involved (Walker 2009, 26). The world, however, was not yet ready for the concept that humanity had existed well before the suggested Biblical origins of 4000 BC. (For fuller accounts of the role of these mid-Victorian pioneers of cave explorations see Hosfield *et al.* 2009).

The Three Age System

In one other way, concepts of time were altering. Thomsen's (1788–1865) "Three Age System", consisting of a sequence of Stone, Bronze and Iron Ages, as published in 1836 in the guidebook *Ledetraad til Nordisk Oldkyndighed*, and in 1848 in its English translation, must have implied that humanity was likely to have been around for a significant length of time. As Daniel (1962, 39) noted, this idea was not universally received.

In England, as Briggs (2007) has documented, in the early 19th century the Society of Antiquaries languished in the doldrums and, in particular, had little interest in prehistory. This was in spite of the activities of "Barrow Diggers" such as Cunnington and Colt Hoare and others. There were collectors of what were regarded as prehistoric artefacts of stone and bronze but even when they were put on display as part of a major exhibition they did not bring about the expected reaction. In fact in the minds of the more general public, the prehistory of Ancient Britons was not treated in a favourable light. Volume 1 of *Old England: a Pictorial Museum* (Knight 1845) provides numerous descriptions of monuments such as Stonehenge or Avebury which, in effect, were often a step back from the observations of Stukeley. The chapter on Ancient Britons ends with the following observations: "We look back upon these earliest records of a past state of society with wonder, not unmixed with awe, with shuddering but not with hatred" (*ibid.*, 23).

In particular indications of the possibility that humanity's existence could be extended back into geological time were not

Fig. 3.3. a) Cartoon of Buckland entering the Hyaena den, b) Illustration of excavation at Paviland Cave (Buckland 1823).

only treated with caution but were, in fact, totally dismissed. Perhaps one of the strongest indications that the issues around the possible existence of "Pre-adamite Man" were not those that occupied the attentions of a significant number of antiquaries can be seen in the cautious approach to earlier discoveries. While it is not surprising that the Conyers discovery of elephant remains with a handaxe at Grays Inn in 1673 was originally dismissed as being associated with Claudius and the Roman invasion of Britain, though, as Cook (2012) has noted, Sir Hans Sloane was not to be convinced by this explanation (see below). Again John Frere's (1800, 204–5) observations that the handaxes found with extinct animals at Hoxne in 1797 belonged to "a very remote period indeed", even beyond that of the present world, could not be supported. They did not fit in with the conventional wisdom of the time; therefore they too were forgotten in a similar manner to the Grays Inn axe.

The Amiens visitation referred to earlier preceded Darwin's *Origin of Species*, which was not published until November 1859. Prestwich had presented their observations to the Royal Society of London on 26 May, while Evans spoke to the Society of Antiquaries on 2 June. While Prestwich's presentation drew an audience of, to quote Evans, "Geological Nobs", or an audience containing many distinguished geologists, the attendance a week later at the Antiquaries was average (*ibid.*, 471–2). Gamble and Kruzynski (2009) have also noted that, while waiting for the commencement of the June lecture at the Society of Antiquaries, Evans noticed a case containing some handaxes. Enquiries revealed that they were Frere's long ignored handaxes from Hoxne. Briggs also notes (2007, 246–51) that, in the decades following 1859, neither Evans nor Sir John Lubbock, the author of *Prehistoric Times* received the recognition that might have been expected. Briggs (*ibid.*, 249) makes the interesting observation that, because of the religious groups, not only did *Prehistoric Times* receive a lukewarm reception but it may have impeded Lubbock's early Parliamentary career.

In the latter part of the 19th century in particular, the "Antiquity of Man" was only part of the debate. O'Connor (2007, chapters 1–2), for example, has documented the discussion over the origin of the series of "Diluvial/Drift" deposits. From the 1830s Louis Agassiz (1807–1873) had been making the case that these deposits were often created by land ice (Agassiz 1840). After the acceptance of the importance of glacial activity, much of the remainder of the century was a continuous series of discussions as to the origin of the different types of deposits and to their age Were some of those deposits older than others, or especially in the case of the river deposits in the south of England, were some of them of post-glacial date (O'Connor 2007, 65–8)?

In summary, virtually until the 1880s there was no real consensus as to the chronological framework that could be used for the British Palaeolithic. It is also the case that by the last decades of the 19th century, Ireland was beginning to develop its own archaeological debate.

Ireland's place in the debate on the "Antiquity of Man"

Ireland's contribution to these great debates seems at first sight to have been relatively limited. Interests in the Irish landscape and its natural history often had, even from the 17th century, a different focus from that found in Britain. In fact three other questions, in addition to those posed earlier, which were particular to Irish interests, became entangled in the discussion. These were:

1) Who were the first people to settle Ireland? (In many ways this was the least contentious question).
2) Who built the many distinctive monuments, such as the megalithic tombs, round towers, etc.?
3) How did the indigenous wild animals found in Ireland get here?

As noted earlier, in this chapter it is not intended to provide a detailed account of nearly two millennia of research into Ireland's past, especially when so much of it has been covered by Waddell (2005). In the case of Ireland, it would also seem that archaeology and the natural sciences were much more closely associated than in certain other parts of Europe. However, it will also be seen below that, in Ireland, religion and politics were never far from the surface of many historical debates.

Of course this does not mean that all religious figures were a negative influence in these debates. Two of the most significant figures reflect the different ways in which the past can be viewed. The first known discussion on how wild animals got to Ireland was posed by the 7th century Irish Monk, Augustin. His ideas survived when his work on miracles mistakenly became an appendix to the writings of Saint Augustine of Hippo (354–430). Unlike many of those in classical and medieval times, who relied on the texts for their interpretation of the past, Augustin seems to have relied on observations of nature and from these he drew his own conclusions (Moriarity 1997, 71–3). In writing about miracles, he felt that some apparently miraculous events recorded in the Bible were simply products of nature. Thus, he felt that, after "Creation", the landscape continued to change and that islands in particular were formed by being cut off from the continental mainland. Species such as deer, "forest pigs", badgers and others therefore became isolated on the island of Ireland and there was no reason to believe that they had been brought in by human agency.

Obviously, any survey of Ireland's contribution must also include James Ussher (1581–1658), Archbishop of Armagh and Primate of all Ireland, as well as, on occasions, Vice Chancellor of Trinity College Dublin. His suggestion that the world was created on the morning of 23 October, 4004 BC, has often been ridiculed and almost demonised by many of those writing centuries later. Yet, as Chesney (1997, 367) has noted, Ussher was not an isolated figure. He maintained contacts with persons such as the influential German intellectual, Samuel Hartlib, who lived for some time in Cromwellian England, as well as others who had adopted Francis Bacon's philosophy of observing and collecting information as well as using this knowledge for man's progress to fulfilment. These included individuals who were to form the Royal Society of London in 1660.

Gould (1993a, 187) has pointed out that Ussher's suggested date for the creation of the Earth, though not necessarily the precision to that particular year of that millennium and the specific day, 23 October, was almost the conventional wisdom of his time. The Jewish calendar suggested a date of 3761 BC, with another version extending back to about 5500 BC, while the Venerable Bede suggested 3952 BC. It also fitted in easily with the concept of six days of creation, each one of which represented 1000 years, *pace* 2 Peter 3:8 *"One day is with the lord as a thousand years"* (*ibid.*, 189). The four years was simply a correction based on the realisation that, as Herod had died in 4 BC, the conventional 4000 BC did not work. Of course, based on biblical scholarship, the creation of the Earth was usually thought to have taken place in the autumn, in September. Gould (*ibid.*) also suggested that Archbishop Ussher had been given "a hard row to hoe" and was constantly aware of papist plots, one of which was the Gregorian calendar of Pope Gregory XIII. Thus, a correction of 30 days was needed to keep it in line with the Julian calendar.

There were in Ireland, even in the 17th century, large-scale natural histories and surveys such as those carried out by Gerard Boate (1604–1650) a member of a Dutch family who had moved to London and then purchased land in Ireland. Boate's *Natural Histories of Ireland*, written in the 1640s, was not published until 1725 (Boate 1725). Waddell (2005, 44) described it as:

> not an entirely apolitical exercise. There was also the mapping of Ireland by Sir William Petty (1623–1687), perhaps better known as the Down Survey of Ireland (Mendyk 1989, 185–192). In many ways these were excellent, but they were more like stock-taking by new owners that were taking over a set of strange and, at times, very different properties…!

Surveys of Ireland's natural history had also been carried out by what could be described as "Native Scholars". These included for example, Roderick O'Flaherty's (1684) *H-Iar Connaught* and Philip O'Sullivan Beare's unpublished manuscript *Natural History of Ireland* translated from Latin and edited by Denis O'Sullivan (2009). Both of these works, which were compiled in the 17th century, provided detailed descriptions of birds, fish and animals present in Ireland and were often intended to correct observations made in the work of Giraldus Cambrensis's (Gerald of Wales) (1188–1223) account of Ireland in *Topographia Hiberniae*. While there has been much discussion as to whether wild peacocks and other species really were present in Ireland, his text still provides one of the few insights into the wild life of Ireland 800 years ago. For many centuries, however, his opinions created a shadow over Ireland's natural history. O'Sullivan Beare described the contribution of Gerald of Wales as:

"Deliberately more biting and bitter everywhere he writes about the Irish nation".

Giraldus Cambrensis was, therefore, to have a long lasting influence on the continuing discussion about both history and natural history, and especially the significance and origins of many types of archaeological monuments in Ireland. He wished to ascribe the origins of ringforts and other monuments to the Danes, with *Danesfort* still occurring as a place name in Ireland. As Waddell (2005, 19) noted, this tied evidence of some degree of "civilisation back to other previous invaders of Ireland". In essence, there was and will always be a constant tension between the new owners/colonisers and the "Natives", especially when the former is placed in a situation where there is a lack of understanding of how this different landscape and its peoples worked.

It might have been expected that the 17th century in Ireland, starting with the end of the Nine Years War, including the Cromwellian War, and ending shortly after the Williamite War, would not have been a century of intellectual debate and scientific exploration of the history and natural history of Ireland, never mind more cosmic issues. Yet, in the mid-1680s, a group of like-minded individuals met and formed the Dublin Philosophical Society. The membership of this society originally consisted of 14 individuals. Sir William Petty (1623–1687) became its president and William Molyneux (1656–1698) was its first secretary. The membership included Thomas Molyneux (1661–1733) (Pl. V), William's brother, Narcissus Marsh (1638–1713), founder of Marshes Library, and Robert Boyle (1627–1691), a son of the Earl of Cork, one of the most respected chemists of the 17th century and a close associate of Robert Hooke of the Royal Society. The Dublin Society flourished for roughly 25 years. Cabot (1997, 472–6) sees them and their contacts outside Ireland almost as an extension of the "Invisible College" in the tradition of Samuel Hartlib, who had died nearly 25 years earlier. Much of the documentation associated with the society that survives is lodged in the library of Trinity College Dublin with printed versions of their correspondence being included by Thomas Molyneux in his publication of *Boate's Natural History of Ireland* (1725). Their own correspondence and meetings brought them into contact with the philosopher John Locke, in exile in Leiden (see below), as well as Edmond Halley. At this time, Halley (1656–1742) was enquiring into the age of the Earth and felt that, assuming sea water only obtained salt gradually over time and if one could establish the rate of input of salt into the oceans, then one should be able to use this to estimate the age of the Earth (Gould 1993b).

As was usual for this time, and for some time afterwards, the study of antiquities was also part of the remit of this type of society, therefore it is not surprising to find records of contact with the Welsh antiquary, Edward Lhuyd, who published the first account of Newgrange (Lhwyd 1710–12). He concluded that the occurrence of a Roman coin on top of the mound was a clear indication that Newgrange pre-dated the presumed

Danish age that was frequently given to many of the enigmatic mounds to be found throughout the countryside. The society made various attempts at surveys and its records include many county surveys that are, at times, uncannily reminiscent of those produced roughly 150 years later as memoirs by the Ordnance Survey

Other activities and interests included botany, indeed Sir Arnold Rawdon, who was an accomplished botanist, imported plants from Jamaica and, in the 1690s, established at Moira, Co. Down, one of the most outstanding gardens in Europe, including a hothouse for 1000 plants (Reeves Smyth 1997, 557–8).

Within the Dublin Society, Thomas Molyneux (Pl. Va) is the perfect example of someone who was grappling with issues that could not easily be understood within the received wisdom of the day. He was a polymath whose interests ranged through various branches of natural history to Ireland's own early history and, like many gentlemen of his time, included knowledge of the classical authors. In 1725, shortly before his death, he became a founder member of the Royal Dublin Society, where more practical purposes were inclined to be substituted for the spirit of the natural philosophers.

To archaeologists he is best known for his comments on Newgrange (Molyneux 1725; Herity 1974, 12; O'Kelly 1982, 27) where he asserted that the Roman coin found there was a later intrusion and that the monument was built by the Danes.

This, however, was not based on the opinions of Giraldus Cambrensis but rather was due to his acquaintance with a relative of Olaus Worm in Leiden where he learnt that similar, though smaller, monuments existed in Denmark. For geologists he is reputed to be the first to suggest that the Giant's Causeway was not a human artefact but rather a product of nature (Wyse Jackson 1997, 92), while in zoology his name is associated with the first full description of Giant deer (Molyneux 1697) which he named *Cervus Platyceros Altissimus*. It was the issues raised by the discovery of Giant deer along with a paper he published in 1701 which was a critique of the idea that giants had lived in Ireland and elsewhere and then, finally, the discovery of large teeth near Belturbet which he identified as those of an elephant (Fig. 3.4) (Nevile 1714; Molyneux 1714; see also Woodman and Cook 2013 for a fuller description of the discovery of the elephant teeth) These discoveries caused Molyneux to think about their implications and obviously raised the issue as to how elephants could get to Ireland. He dismissed the notion that they were brought in by Greeks or Romans to "an island where Greeks and Romans had never set foot" (*ibid.*, 377). It was this observation that led Sloane a few years later to doubt the explanation that the Grays Inn elephant was brought to Britain by Claudius.

As Molyneux was writing these communications he also wondered, in the context of the biblical chronologies, how

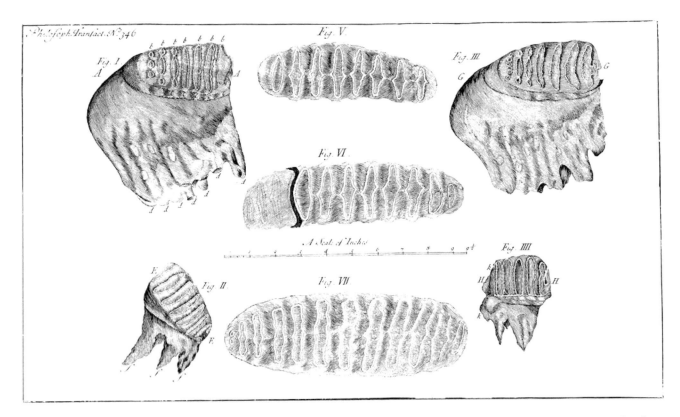

Fig. 3.4. Elephant's teeth from Cavan published by Molyneux in 1714 (three teeth in the centre are comparative examples from a modern elephant).

plants that were found only in Iberia or North America could turn up in Ireland, indeed he wondered if the Irish Giant deer were related to the American moose and he also noted the discoveries of mammoth elsewhere in Europe and Russia. Like Augustin over 1000 years earlier he wondered if even since the "Deluge" could there have been dry land that connected islands to continents.

In terms of a human presence in Ireland Molyneux was not impressed by the view that the people of Ireland had an exotic and distant origin. In the spirit of the Royal Society he was looking for substantial evidence and even though exotic artefacts and pottery were turning up, Molyneux (1725) showed his impatience with the manner in which national history was perused, especially in Ireland. Therefore, apparently reacting against a trend he noted that most nations "Had been apt to fall into the vanity of deriving themselves from a more antient [sic] origin than truth or credible will vouch for"; he re-iterated his belief that Ireland was first occupied at quite a late date by Celtic Peoples.

The divisions over the origins of the Irish were to consume many scholars for over the next 100 and more years but there were other debates. In terms of geology, the debate was between those perceived to be in favour of Neptunism (rocks were formed under the sea) and those who supported Vulcancity (a volcanic origin). This may not appear to relate to the place of humanity and deep time but as the issue was whether the rocks formed fast or, as suggested by Hutton, over a very long period of time. Belief in an ancient humanity could only exist if the world itself had existed over a much longer period of time. In Ireland, one intellectual battle centred on the north coast at the Giant's Causeway and nearby Portrush. Besides the origins of the Giant's Causeway, rocks protruding onto the beach at Portrush provided an interesting conundrum. These rocks looked as if they were formed by volcanic activity, yet they contained fossils, such as ammonites, that should be found in sedimentary rocks. Ultimately, in the early 1800s, it was determined that they were indeed embedded in what had been a sedimentary rock, however this had been heated and altered (metamorphosed) so that it had a similar appearance to basalt (Wyse Jackson 1997, 92–4).

Throughout the 18th century, many antiquaries were continuing to record, collect and illustrate artefacts and monuments (see Waddell 2005, chap. 4). The issue of the age and the origin of many of these monuments continued to be a source of acrimonious debate, which perhaps reached its peak in the debates between Charles Vallency, (1725–1812), who was to propose a Phoenician origin for the peoples of Ireland, and Edward Ledwich, who preferred to look for the origins of these monuments amongst the Danes.

O'Halloran (2004) has shown that, in the context of the *Act of Union*, much of the debate related to supporting the idea of an Ireland with a venerable pedigree for its past made a powerful case for Catholic emancipation. The level of vitriol in these discussions can be clearly seen in Ledwich's second edition of the *Antiquities of Ireland*, published in 1803, i.e. just after the 1798 rebellion and the subsequent *Act of Union* in 1800. In the introduction he stated that:

> When Hibernians compare their present state with their former condition; their just and equal law with those that were uncertain; the happy security of peace with the miseries of barbarous manners, their hearts must overflow with gratitude to the author of such blessings: nor will they deny their obligations to the fostering care of Britain. The happy instrument of conferring them. (*ibid.*, 2)

While on issues such as colonisation he stated: "Let others enjoy the gibberish of oriental etymologies and the company of Milesians, Phoenicians and Magicians in that Gloomy Cave" (*ibid.*, 31).

Although these statements pre-date the debate on concepts such as the Stone Age and human antiquity they helped create an intellectual environment where there was little inclination to search for evidence of "Pre-Adamite man".

McGuinness has suggested, in terms of prehistory, that the period immediately preceding the early 1830s had been a state of stagnancy (2010, 29). Indeed the debates around what Leersen (1996, 91) has described as "Irish Phoenicianism and English Teutomania", in other words the vociferous nature of the debates in the early 19th century, such as that between Sir William Betham (1779–1853) and George Petrie (1790–1866) over the origins and purpose of the Irish round towers, bedevilled much of the historic debate throughout this period.

There were two notable exceptions. First, Thomas Pownall (1722–1805), was heavily influenced by the lifestyle that he saw amongst the Native Americans during his time as Governor in the American colonies. He preferred to see "Celtic Wood-men" being influenced first by Phoenicians, who introduced agriculture as well as other aspects of what was presumed to be civilisation. While he had no sense of the chronology, he had been influenced by the fact that there were Native Americans living without recourse to agriculture. In his mind, once again, it was possible to envisage within the British Isles a period before the spread of agriculture.

Secondly, in the earliest decades of the 19th century, one of the few that suggested something different was the collector and landscape painter, John Bell (1793–1861) of Dungannon, Co. Tyrone. Bell, who was a son of a wealthy landowner in Falkirk, seemed to have moved to Ireland in the early 1800s. He "excavated" some of the megalithic tombs in South Armagh (Fig. 3.5) and had come to the conclusion that they were used as places of burial, furthermore, to the astonishment and disbelief of his contemporaries, he felt that Newgrange was a place of burial that, in spite of its cruciform plan, pre-dated Christianity (Bell 1815; 1816). Furthermore, he also proposed a Three Age System of Stone, Bronze and Iron Ages.

In Ireland, even within the earth sciences, few looked for evidence of "deep time" within geology or archaeology. Frequently, however, and especially under the influence of Sir

Fig. 3.5. Reconstruction of Annaghcloughmullam Tomb (Bell 1816).

Robert Kane, the primary concern was to produce geological surveys that would be of economic use. Herries Davies (1995, 214–20) has demonstrated that there was, along with all the usual clashes of personality, extensive survey work carried out in Ireland, but there seems to have been very little clear acceptance of the nature of Irish Quaternary deposits and a slow reluctance to accept Louis Agassiz' explanation that these deposits were the remnants of events that took place in an Ice Age. Thus, in spite of the presence of George Du Noyer (1817–1869) (Pl. Vb) and George Kinahan (1829–1908), both of whom were involved in archaeology in different ways, the issue of "human antiquity" was not a matter of great concern. Kinahan and Du Noyer, a few years before Du Noyer's death, were, however, to make a contribution to this debate (see below).

The Three Age System and the search for an Irish Stone Age

From early in the 19th century, along with bronze artefacts and items of later periods, large quantities of stone tools were being collected. There was even then an almost fatalistic assumption that these were to be primarily found in the "north" of the island. This profusion was best illustrated by the quantities of stone tools that were put on exhibition during the British Association for the Advancement of Science meeting held in Belfast in 1852. The catalogue produced by Sir William

Wilde (1857) again illustrates the quantities of stone tools that were already in the collections of the Royal Irish Academy (for the role of collectors see Woodman *et al.* 2006, 8–22; Woodman 1993a).

If the question of the Three Age System had been ignored in Ireland, a visit by Jens Jacob Asmussen Worsaae in 1846, which was shortly before the publication of his seminal treatise referred to earlier, obviously ensured that antiquaries and others were aware of it. The visit was primarily to explore the similarities of so called "Viking" material in Scandinavia and the British Isles, but his impromptu lecture to the Royal Irish Academy on the 30 November 1846 allowed him to talk about the Three Age System and observe the similarities in Stone Age artefacts from across much of Europe. His talks to the Academy were published in 1848. It would appear that he found the collections of the Museum of the Royal Irish Academy "a finer and better arranged collection than [was] to be seen in London or Edinburgh" (Briggs 2007, 241).

Wilde (1815–1876; see Fig. 3.8a), who had initially prevaricated about the Three Age System, took an interest in the question of who were the first Irish and, in preparing the catalogue of the collections of the Royal Irish Academy, made use of the Three Age System (Wilde 1857, 5). He stated that: "All primitive nations throughout the world, so far as we know … must in the absence of knowledge of harder materials have employed weapons and tools of flint and stone".

In the 1857 catalogue, Wilde also envisaged progress from hunters through nomads to farmers and, as noted elsewhere (Woodman *et al.* 2006, 34), these views of Stone Age hunter-fishers being the first settlers in Ireland were further expanded at the British Association meeting in 1874. As was common for much of the next 50 years, there was a sense of there being one "Post Ice Age Stone Age".

There were also debates on the validity of the Three Age System within Ireland. One of the most notable criticisms was by Monsignor James O'Laverty (1828–1906) (Pl. V), where the author felt that the stratigraphic sequencing of metal and stone tools from the mid-19th century dredging of the River Bann did not accord with ideas of the Three Age System (O'Laverty 1857). He also felt that the system was not in accordance with the Bible evidence.

As full importance of Amiens became clear, it is interesting to note the contrasting reactions of Wilde and O'Laverty. In May of 1859 Wilde presented a paper: *Upon the Unmanufactured Animal Remains Belonging to the Academy*, which was, in general, a listing of the bones of bears, pigs, marten, etc, but also a return to the very large collection of the remains of "Gigantic Irish Deer or Fossil Elk" (Wilde 1860, 195). He noted that most naturalists felt that they were not contemporary with man but that, in fact, the opinion tended the other way. He also commented that it seemed as if they were either "Pre-Adamite" or anterior to man's occupation of Ireland. He observed:

> But if the discoveries lately said to be made in the gravels at Abbeville should prove to be true, this theory respecting our Irish fossil deer is untenable; moreover these fossils show that man is much older or several fossils much younger. (*ibid.*, 195)

Wilde's paper was almost certainly prepared before the two London lectures of Prestwich and Evans had taken place, and he was, at the very least, aware of the significance of their visit to Abbeville a few days earlier, at the end of April.

In contrast, Monsignor O'Laverty (Pl. Vc) held firm that his observations of the stratigraphy and sequence of artefacts found at Portglenone left him in no doubt that the Three Age System was not valid. In his introduction to *A History of the Diocese of Down and Connor* he dismissed, very forthrightly, arguments in favour of a prehistoric presence in Ireland, stating that "Rejecting as unworthy of any credit the stories regarding an Antediluvian colonisation" (O'Laverty 1878, xi). He preferred to retain the belief that Ireland was first settled by Parthalon "in the year of the world 2520" (*ibid.*). In Volume III, when describing the history and antiquities of the parish of Portglenone (O'Laverty 1884, 368–72), he went so far as to republish an edited version of his 1857 paper. As O'Laverty built up a collection of prehistoric antiquities, which were auctioned after his death in 1906, one must wonder whether he eventually changed his mind, or whether the politico/religious furore that was to consume Belfast from the mid-1870s left him, like so many others, in an entrenched position.

While Irish Archaeology has always had its own dynamic, whether in the study of its origin myths or aspects of the "Golden Age" of Early Christian Ireland, with the development of the postal services and more reliable communication by land and sea, many Irish researchers also involved themselves in the London intellectual milieu, which, as noted earlier, provided them with a convenient method of exporting Irish antiquities. Some, such as Thomas Crofton Croker of Cork, who seems to have exported a very large number of antiquities, moved to London on a permanent basis. Rowley-Conwy (1996) brought to our attention to a fellow Corkman of Crofton Corker's: Hodder Westropp, who is credited with being the first to use the term Mesolithic. While this is normally associated with his 1872 publication *Prehistoric Phases*, he had used a similar though not identical term six years earlier in 1866 when he suggested the term "Mezolithic".

The presence of many Irish figures, such as Lord Talbot de Malahide, as members of London societies was a conduit which allowed new ideas to be discussed in Ireland but, at the same time, as will be seen below, there was a degree of continuity of some traditional prejudices. Conversely, staff at the Queen's Colleges of Belfast, Cork and Galway not only worked on Irish issues, for example, William King (Fig. 3.6c), the first professor of mineralogy and geology at Queen's College Galway, was the person who first proposed the term *Homo Neanderthalensis* at the 1863 meeting of the British Association.

Within the decade following the 1859 "Amiens Visit" the issue of the "Antiquity of Man" was raised on a number of occasions in Ireland. George Morant, in collecting from the shores of Ballyhoe Lough on the Monaghan/Meath borders, wondered whether what was an obviously Mesolithic core borer, could be a *Coup de Poing*, like those from Amiens (Morant 1867; Woodman 1998a). John Evans, during a business trip to the north of Ireland that took place shortly after his visit to Amiens, visited the southern shores of Lough Neagh and was acquainted with the discovery of stone tools from that area. On a subsequent visit to the northern end of the Lough (Pl. Vd) he was able to recover larger quantities of stone tools; indeed over the following years he amassed a large collection that became part of the collections of the Ashmolean Museum (Evans 1867). His paper contains a meticulous description of a range of implements, many of which can be identified as Mesolithic. He prophetically wrote that he had, in 1867, discovered similar flakes on the shores of Lough Kinale in the Irish Midlands and that he had no doubt that "A search, properly conducted, would prove nearly or quite as remunerative, in some other of the Irish lakes" (*ibid.*, 404).

Not surprisingly, while early cave excavations were undertaken with a particular interest in the "extinct fauna", there was always hope that evidence for a Palaeolithic would turn up. This was a particular interest of Andrew Leith Adams (Fig. 3.6a), who, in the short period before his untimely death, explored several caves in Munster. Leith Adams was Professor of Natural History at Queens College Cork from

Fig. 3.6. a) A. Leith Adams, Professor of Natural Philosophy, Queen's College Cork (Portrait from Department of Geology, BEES, UCC), b) Robert Harkness, Professor of Geology, Queen's College Cork (Portrait from the Heritage Office, UCC), c) William King, Professor of Geology, Queen's College Galway (Coutesy of NUI, G), d) Sir Bertram Windle, President and Professor of Archaeology, Queen's College Cork and UCC (Portrait from the Heritage Office, UCC).

1878 to 1881, a friend of the English "cave explorer" Boyd Dawkins and received support from the British Association for the Advancement of Science (BAAS) for work at Shandon Cave, Co. Waterford, which had first been opened in the 1850s (Adams 1876). At Ballynamintra Cave (Fig. 3.7a), Co. Waterford (Adams *et al.* 1881) he thought he had found traces of early human activity as some splintered *Megaloceros* (deer) long bones looked as if they were worked. Some pieces of stone found in Ballynamintra were also thought to be worked (Woodman *et al.* 1997) though, in retrospect, they have turned out to be natural.

Even though we now know that many of the shell midden sites are much later in date, they attracted significant attention. William Harte (1866), the county surveyor for Donegal, explored shell middens on Lough Swilly, while the geologist, George Kinahan, along with colleague Hugh Leonard, worked at shell middens in West Galway. It was claimed, in one instance, that a midden 200 ft long, 70 ft wide and 8 ft (61 × 21.3 × 2.4 m) thick near Creggauns, which lay on the shores of Galway Bay, had produced, at a point below high water mark, several crude stone tools (Leonard 1868). Robert Harkness (Fig. 3.6b), the second Professor of Geology at

Fig. 3.7. a) Ballinamintra Cave, b) James Ussher during excavations at Castlepook Cave (original photograph in Grove White 1915–18).

Queen's College Cork, besides carrying out excavations in the Lough Gur area of Co. Limerick (Harkness 1869), also took an interest in shell middens and, in particular, reported his observations on a shell midden that occurred on the intertidal shore at Ballycotton, Co. Cork (Harkness 1871, 151–2). It is apparent that many natural scientists and antiquaries were well aware of the Danish Scientific Commission on shell middens that had been established 1848, as well as the belief that they were of Stone Age date.

At Larne, Co. Antrim, William Gray (1830–1917) (Pl. VIa), an engineer attached to the Office of Public Works, claimed to have found stone tools as far back as 1865 (Movius 1953a, 7), while material from Kilroot, Island Magee, Holywood and Strangford were found in the following three years (Movius 1953b, 7–23; Woodman *et al.* 2006, 32–6). It is of interest that the geologist, amateur archaeologist and draughtsman/artist, George Du Noyer, may have been the first to recognise the existence of the water-rolled flint flakes at Larne, perhaps as early as 1863 (Du Noyer 1868). However, according to Gray (1867), it was with difficulty that he and members of the Belfast Naturalists Field Club (BNFC; see below) persuaded Du Noyer that these were artificial. However, there seems to be a better case that it was George Du Noyer who first recognised that the material from the raised beaches was different from material found on higher ground away from the beaches. The first group Du Noyer (1869, 169–72) attributed to an early period when people lived on a shore, now buried beneath the sea, they had a simple technology and most of the artefacts were "the rejecta of that manufacture during countless ages". He also identified that similar flakes could be found amongst material on the shores of Lough Neagh at Toomebridge and along the Lagan River at Moira. Du Noyer noted that his second and later group of much fresher material included more finished implements which were, along with rude pottery, amber, etc., to be found in "sepulchral tumuli and megalithic chambers" that were to be attributed to the Neolithic. In effect, he was identifying what we would now recognise as the Later Mesolithic, as distinct from artefacts that belonged to the Neolithic and Bronze Age. Twenty years later this same suggestion of two separate series of implements was made more clearly by W. J. Knowles (1832–1927) of Ballymena (Knowles 1885, 436–44; Pl. VIb). Knowles, of course was the most energetic collector of the late 19th and early 20th centuries and the most prolific writer on the subject of "Human Antiquity in Ireland". He was also an amateur geologist with a deep interest in place names and dialects (Woodman *et al.* 2006, chap. 1) In this case the water-rolled flint flakes in the raised beaches were considered as the "Older Series", while the "Younger Series" could be distinguished by the different "Neolithic" forms that were much fresher and stratified in the overlying sand hills.

Not everyone was prepared to rush into identifying an Irish Palaeolithic, or even a Stone Age of some antiquity. In some cases, such as Gray (1879), there was a great degree of scepticism as to whether the water-rolled flint flakes found in the raised beaches genuinely belonged at a great depth in the gravels and could therefore be presumed to have a great antiquity.

Evans had another perspective, which is one that has bedevilled Irish archaeology. As noted earlier, Evans had actually first collected material from the southern shores of Lough Neagh in May 1859, but his paper on this material was only published in 1867 Evans is, however, remarkably coy in his concluding summary. Quoting Moryson's descriptions of the Irish (and Ireland) at the end of the 16th century, whom he saw or believed lived in extremely impoverished conditions with no bread and only eating the flesh of dead animals, Evans reluctantly finishes with:

> Until, however, we have a greater number of facts at our command in connection with the discovery of stone implements, arms and utensils in Ireland, I think it is the safest plan while placing on record these the character of these discoveries in Lough Neagh, to abstain from expressing any opinion as to the degree of Antiquity which is to be attributed to the implements which I have described. (*ibid.*, 408)

Although not stated as strongly, Wilde (1857), in the Royal Irish Academy catalogue, also put forward a similar *caveat*, while Leonard (1868), having noted the crude artefacts from the Galway midden, felt that they were similar to those which he maintained were still in use in the Arran Isles.

In other words, there was an implicit assumption in the minds of many that things in Ireland could be significantly later than elsewhere. This is a view of Irish prehistory that continued to be present up until the 1960s.

Although artefacts that might potentially be of Stone Age date were turning up across a large part of Ireland, the core of the debate on the "Antiquity of Man" in Ireland gradually centred on Larne. As a result, the Antrim coast was, for a period of 100 years, to become the focus of much of the research on the Irish Mesolithic.

Politics and religion

The debate on the "Antiquity of Man" and the creation of the world was not confined to academia and the halls of learned societies. These debates took place within a world where politics and religion played a major role in the life of the community. This debate was not necessarily reflecting just two different views i.e. complete acceptance of the words of Genesis or that humans had existed and developed over an almost unimaginable period of time.

It should be remembered that 1859 was not only the *Annus mirabilis* for Darwinism but it was the year of the beginning of a major evangelical revival in Belfast. In the years that followed, which Livingstone (1997, 390–4) described as the "Lull before the storm", i.e., the events of 1874, there were numerous debates about matters such as the appropriateness of certain types of behaviour at religious gatherings, such as swoons, convulsions, etc. Darwinism was seen by some as the touchstone which marked the advance of more atheist and strident assertions by some, such as T. H. Huxley (see below). However, many theologians and clergy men, in particular, John Joseph Murphy, the secretary to the Church of Ireland Diocesan Synod, while uncomfortable with Darwinism sought to find ways of accommodating scripture and science. Murphy, who

was also a member of both the Belfast Naturalists Field Club and the Belfast Natural History and Philosophical Society addressed issues around topics such as scripture and the idea of a longer history for the earth, as well as finding no problem with the law of natural selection

J. S. Moore (1867), writing in the *Proceedings of the Royal Geological Society of Ireland*, stated that he was prepared to explore ways of accommodating scripture and the succession of geological periods. Moore argued, in particular, that there are in existence a diverse range of races of different colours, forms and languages which are well adapted to their climate and environment. Therefore, these races could only have evolved over a considerable period of time. "Are we not at liberty to infer that there were other races of man on the face of the earth" i.e prior to Adam and Eve (*ibid.,* 20)? These races were often referred to as "Pre-Adamite". Moore noted that on the 6th day beasts were created before man (male and female), in this case Adam and Eve. These creatures would have been created within a "Mosaical" day that lasted 516,000 years, which contained evidence of an ice age that was preceded by a time when mammoth and other animals lived. Moore was also aware of the discoveries at Abbeville and so not surprisingly he observed that "It is all but certain that over the plains and through the forests of the old world man hunted the Irish Deer and speared the mammoth" (*ibid.,* 21). At the same time he had no difficulty in accepting the creation of Adam, which took place with great solemnity at the close of one of the zodiacal cycles that "brought an ancient era to a close", thus uniting their several courses at the vernal equinox of 4004 BC (*ibid.,* 24). Moore finished with the observation that:

> The Almighty has given us in the Holy Scriptures all the information necessary for our salvation; but he has not forbidden us to search into, and investigate, and admire his wondrous works. (*ibid.*, 29)

So in spite of the religious revival, there would appear to have been a broad and diverse range of opinions on these matters.

However, when the British Association for the Advancement of Science (BAAS) met in Belfast in 1874, the presidential address was given by John Tyndall (1820–1893) (Fig. 3.8c) and it was attended by a number of like-minded scientists, such as Thomas Henry Huxley (1825–1895). This address proposed a dominant role for Science over religion; "All religious theories schemes and systems which embrace cosmogony … must … submit to the control of Science". This produced an immediate backlash from several leading Presbyterian ministers, such as the Rev. Professor John Watts, and alienated a number of those who sought to bring science and religion together. This group included John Joseph Murphy, whom it seems was already wavering, though the Rev. Canon McIlwaine who was an enthusiastic collector of prehistoric artefacts, besides castigating Tyndall for debating a religious question in a scientific arena, still held out that

"Christianity was … ever the elder sister of true science" (Livingstone 1997, 394).

These events created what Livingstone (*ibid.*, 405) described as "a long shadow over the intellectual life of Belfast". This included a winter series of lectures, primarily intended to counter the views of Tyndall, Huxley and others, in Rosemary Street Presbyterian Church. Livingstone (*ibid.*, 401) also suggests that this provided an opportunity for the Presbyterian hierarchy, in the context of how it related to other denominations, to define its theological boundaries. This intention became even clearer when the Catholic hierarchy became involved and supported the view that religion and science should be compartmentalised. It

would, therefore appear that the search for a Stone Age and the "Antiquity of Man" in Ireland took place in a society where there were many different views and not all of those views would have been well received.

Tyndall, forever the "controversialist", involved himself in other matters which were to impact on the search for an Irish Stone Age. In this case he was not the "prime mover". Foster (1997, 408–9), refers to Tyndalls's involvement in the manner in which science and natural history were taught in the Catholic University of Ireland. Tyndall noted that students complained that the "Faculty did not contain the name of a single Professor of the Physical or Natural Sciences". It would appear that

Fig. 3.8. a) Sir William Wilde, President of the Royal Irish Academy (by permission of the Royal Irish Academy), b) Robert Lloyd Praeger, Belfast Naturalists Field Club (by permission of the Royal Irish Academy, c) Professor John Tyndall, President British Association for the Advancement of Science, d) Cardinal John Henry Newman.

in spite of Newman's (Fig. 3.8d) ideals and his extensive discussions in his "Discourses and Lectures on the role of Science in a Catholic University" in *The Idea of a University* (Newman 1873, republished 1976), the fact that most science by been taught by Protestants seems to have created certain reluctance towards the teaching of science in the Catholic University. There was a fear that the teaching of science might infect the piety of Catholic students! Is it not surprising, as Foster observed (1997, 428–9), that Gerard Manley Hopkins, a poet of nature who had converted to Catholicism and was the author of *Binsey Poplars,* felt at times conflicted and out of place when appointed to the staff of the Catholic University.

It would also seem that, on a more secular political level, the reluctance to teach science would have sat comfortably with a prevailing attitude of many cultural nationalists. Thomas Davis (1814–1845) of the Young Irelanders was keenly interested in the monuments of Ireland and had been extremely concerned about potential destruction taking place at Newgrange (Waddell 2005, 123–6). In his *Cultural Institutions* essay, Davis (1846) proposed that the Royal Irish Academy divorce itself from science and that science would revert to Trinity College. Natural history would be entirely separate from the Royal Irish Academy and the Royal Dublin Society and would be accommodated in a separate Institution with its own Museum (Foster 1997, 425–6). The Natural History Museum was built in the 1850s, with the foundation stone being laid in 1856 and the formal opening took place on the occasion of the meeting of the British Association in Dublin in 1857. Although it was not the official name, it is of interest that the *London Illustrated News* in May 1856 referred to the intended building as a National Museum. For nationalists, however, the study of Ireland's past was to continue within language, literature and related areas. It is, therefore, not surprising that as Foster (*ibid.*, 426) observes, notwithstanding the appointment of some catholic scientists: "science appears to have been culturally ceded to the Anglo Irish and Ulster Scots".

The divisions within the so called "Ulster Scots" have already been noted, but one must wonder about the role of the Anglo Irish and their relationship to the rest of Irish Society. Tyndall was, of course, born in Carlow and would today be considered Irish. He was a member of the Orange Order and was completely opposed to Home Rule. His attitude to his Irish origins was probably quite similar to that of the Duke of Wellington. Many of Tyndall's confidants, such as Huxley, also opposed Home Rule. In contrast, W. E. Gladstone, who was open to Home Rule, was not in favour of Darwin's ideas.

One of the consequences of *Annus mirabilis* was the idea that if evolution of animals or humans had taken place then it was possible that certain races of humans could, in an evolutionary scheme, be regarded as more primitive and inferior. This was a commonly accepted view of many natural scientists, especially those associated with the Ethnological Society and later the Anthropological Society of London. It would also have been the view of others, such as Louis Agassiz. Certainly Huxley

was not complimentary about the Irish and, as Foster (1997, 435) notes: "in 1860 Charles Kingsley mixes comments about human chimpanzees with a kind of paternalistic attitude towards the Irish, whom he seaw in the vicinity of Markree Castle in Co. Sligo".

The creation of the Dublin Museum of Art and Industry might have, in itself, been expected to encourage an interest in Ireland's past. However, as many have observed, the initial purpose of this institution, established under the rubric of South Kensington, was primarily to display the glories and deeds of the British Empire, as well as promoting an interest in industry (Crooke 2000, 121–8); Many were not happy with the Royal Irish Academy and the Royal Dublin Society passing over their collections to the new Museum. The magnificent collection of antiquities that had been on display in the Royal Irish Academy in Dawson Street (Fig. 3.9) was, when moved to the new Museum and located beside Leinster House, relegated to a room on the upper floor, while under the direction of South Kensington the Rotunda and Central Court were given over to displaying the "Glories of the British Empire".

The appointment of George Coffey (1857–1916) as Superintendent of Antiquities in 1890 resulted in the presence of a figure of nationalist persuasion with a strong interest in the archaeology of Ireland, while the director from 1907, George N. Plunkett, also added a figure of known nationalist sympathies and, as Crooke (*ibid.*, 137–8) noted, the shift to a more Irish focus began. There is a certain irony that, with the establishment of the Irish Free State in 1922, antiquities and natural history were to suffer different fates. Following from the 1927 Lithberg Report (see Crooke 2000, 141–7), the purpose of the now National Museum was deemed to be "to accumulate preserve, study and display such objects as may serve to increase the knowledge of Irish Civilisation, of the natural history of Ireland …". As Crooke (*ibid.*, 144) noted, the new emphasis on Irish antiquities resulted in both the removal of certain artefacts which had glorified the Empire, and the shift of Irish antiquities from the upper floor to their present location on the ground floor. In contrast, natural history was to suffer from pragmatic expediency. After a degree of independence was obtained to some extent this was to the detriment of portions of the natural history collections and certainly in the case of geology, specimens of worldwide significance were often stored in what was internationally accepted as inferior even entirely inappropriate locations.

The appointment of George Coffey to the now National Museum of Art and Science, as well as the interest of several staff at the Royal College of Science, focused attention on matters where natural history and archaeology overlapped. Coffey's appointment also coincided with the spread of the Field Clubs, especially those based in Dublin, Cork and Limerick. The next two decades did see a period when, under the enthusiastic leadership of William Knowles (Woodman *et al.* 2006, 25–31; Pl. VII), coastal sites were searched for and explored throughout the island. Of course we now realise that they were exploring a coastal landscape that often only

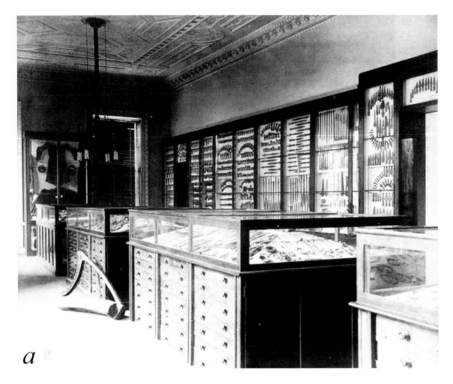

Fig. 3.9. a) Royal Irish Academy museum display (by permission of the Royal Irish Academy), b) The newly founded Dublin Arts and Industry Museum (by permission of the National Museum of Ireland).

contained material dated to what we now call the Neolithic but, along with material from many periods, it did produce significant evidence of how some Stone Age peoples lived and used the sea.

Besides the surveys carried out under Knowles' enthusiastic direction, the Limerick Field Club investigated sand dunes at Ballybunnion, Co. Kerry, and found artefacts that we might now recognise as later Mesolithic (Windle 1904). Furthermore, Sir Bertram Windle (Fig. 3.6d), Professor of Archaeology and President of University College Cork, along with his student, Joanna Brunicardi (Née Holland), carried out their own extensive investigations of the "shore dwellers" of Ireland (Windle 1910; 1911; Brunicardi 1914).

In summary, one could suggest that, post-1859, the search for the earliest traces of human settlement in Ireland did not take place in an atmosphere that was always conducive to research and an open spirit of enquiry. Within the North, the debate and the search took place, as noted earlier, under the long shadow of the BAAS 1874 Belfast meeting. There is no doubt that many of those who participated in this search and discussions were devout Christians and many were ministers or priests of various denominations, but they must have been aware that their opinions and activities were frowned upon by others. Elsewhere, it would seem that this search was not a high priority. On the one hand, energy and interests were focused elsewhere and issues around the teaching of science may have helped create an attitude of mind that did not encourage delving into areas where prehistoric archaeology and natural history

met. Similarly, significant elements of the so-called Anglo Irish, while trained in the sciences, may have also felt that searching for traces of the original Irish was not a worthwhile pursuit.

It was also apparent that, by the end of the 19th century, there was little trace of a Palaeolithic in Ireland and that, in spite of some issues that were common to both islands, the search for the earliest peoples of Ireland was set on a very different course from that taken by British prehistory.

The Older Series of flint implements and Eoliths

It may be that the events of 1874 impacted on the issue of the age of Irish Stone Age material, yet surprisingly, in the absence of any chronological framework, some people, such as the Rev. Leonard Hassé (1850–1908), wished to place the Irish water-rolled material in the Palaeolithic (Hassé 1885). Indeed Hassé was of the opinion that human origins, instead of being sought in the tropics, might be found in northern Europe! At the other extreme, the Rev. George Buick (1843–1904) saw some of the Younger Series of implements, which were found in the sand dunes in north-east Ireland at locations such as Dundrum and Portrush, dating as late as the Iron Age (Buick 1887; 1891). Knowles and many others, however, continued to believe that many of them belonged to a part of the Neolithic that pre-dated farming.

The debate on the age of the Larne Gravels continued until 1890 with, in particular, Gray's continued scepticism as to whether artefacts could be found at a significant depth. A key

Fig. 3.10. The second examination of the Larne Gravels at the Curran Point/Railway Cutting, Larne, Co. Antrim by the Belfast Naturalists Field Club (by permission of the National Museums of Northern Ireland).

development was the extension of the railway line from Larne Town to the new Larne Harbour (Fig. 3.10). This necessitated cutting through a series of sand and gravel deposits at the upper end of Curran Point and allowed access to sections which could be examined for the occurrence of artefacts. The second committee of the Belfast Naturalists Field Club, which included Robert Lloyd Praeger (1865–1953) (Fig. 3.8b) returned to the "Railway Cutting" at Larne and showed conclusively that flint flakes could be found at more than 20 ft (6 m) below the surface (Praeger 1890, 198–210), thus confirming their antiquity. Praeger's (1892) survey of the raised beaches published 2 years later was the final confirmation that the raised beaches were of Holocene Age. In a later paper, Coffey and Praeger (1904) strongly suggested that the material in the raised beaches belonged to an early phase of the Neolithic.

At this stage it is worth noting how much of research into Ireland's earliest inhabitants was being carried out by a combination of amateurs and professionals who were grounded in the natural sciences. There is no doubt that early research was to a great extent based in the Belfast and Ballymena Field Clubs and their successors. Praeger (1949), in his biographical accounts of Irish naturalists, lists the luminaries of these societies as stretching from Templeton through William Thompson to the Patterson Family and Samuel Alexander Stewart, and many others, all of whom made major contributions to the natural history of Ireland. In Ballymena, Knowles was as much an amateur geologist as a prehistorian, while Cannon Grainger's first interest had been in geology. Praeger, who was originally trained as an engineer, in his introduction to *The Way That I Went* (Praeger 1937, 9–10) reminisced about the difference between the Dublin Field Club and that in Belfast. This was a contrast between the "sturdy amateurism of Belfast" and the Dublin Society that relied heavily on the Royal College of Science, who provided members such as Professors Haddon (zoology) and Sollas (geology).

Still looking for an Irish Palaeolithic

Even after the second excavation at the Larne Railway Cutting, Knowles retained the belief that at least some of the material was of an extreme age and, as a result, he was a participant, even if it was at a remove, in one of the most acrimonious debates of British and Irish prehistory, namely the "Eolith Debate" where, first in Kent, it was claimed that tools which were more ancient had been found in gravels that pre-dated those which contained handaxes. Later in the early 20th century similar claims were made for artefacts recovered in early deposits in East Anglia (see O'Connor 2007, chapter 5 for a fuller account of the Eolith debate).

As a result Knowles, to the end of his life, believed that a series of heavily rolled nodules in his Older Series of flint implements were exceptionally ancient. In particular he believed that some crude items that were very similar to Eoliths

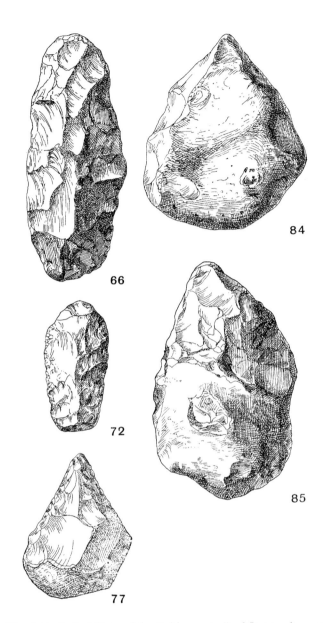

Fig. 3.11. Rolled flints of the "older series" of flint implements illustrated by Knowles (1914): 66) core axe from Island Magee, 72) small core axe from Holywood Co. Down, 77) core borer from Island Magee, 84 and 85) crude water rolled "hand tools" from Kilroot Co. Antrim.

and which he had recovered from the beach gravels belonged to the Palaeolithic (Knowles 1914; Fig. 3.11).

The possibility of an Irish Palaeolithic was to remain on the agenda through to the late 1920s. First there was a claim by Burchell for an Irish Mousterian at Rosses Point (see Woodman 1998a for a discussion of this topic). Here, in essence, amongst large numbers of naturally fractured pieces were recovered a few large humanly struck artefacts but there was no independent contextual evidence to suggest that they dated to the Palaeolithic. Burchell, along with Reid Moir, also went on to claim that a series of flint nodules from various locations in Co. Antrim could be regarded as Eoliths and other primitive tool types which suggested that evidence of a Lower Palaeolithic survived in Ireland (Burchell and Reid Moir 1932). Movius (1942, 105–8) provides a useful critique of the material presented by Burchell and Reid Moir and suggested that these artefacts are either natural or else found in a Holocene context. At the same time Edgar Kingsley Tratman was to claim that two burials he found at Kilgreany Cave were of late Upper Palaeolithic age (see Dowd 2002 for a recent review of the history of the exploration of this cave). Movius (1935) was also able to show that the Kilgreany (A and B) burials were not contemporaneous with the "Ice Age" faunas, as Tratman had presumed. This was also eventually confirmed by Radiocarbon dating. For a summary of the archaeology and stratigraphy of Kilgreany see Dowd (2002).

In passing one can only observe that the 1920/30s search for an Irish Palaeolithic, probably created an attitude that lasted for decades, where anyone considering searching for an Irish Palaeolithic, or thinking that they had found it, would think more than twice about becoming publicly embroiled in such an issue. In other words it killed the question stone dead! The issue of an Irish Palaeolithic, which will be returned to in Chapter 6, therefore became dormant but there was still the question of the age and significance of all the other stone implements that did not look quite like the implements from the "sandhills Sites".

An older Neolithic, proto-Neolithic or…?

The abundance of lithic artefacts from the River Bann and Lough Neagh, summarised by Knowles in 1912, and much of which we now know to be Mesolithic in date, sat uneasily in the Irish archaeological record. It should, of course, be recognised that his material, while better documented than most others, only represented a fraction of the stone tools to be taken from this region during the previous 50 years. As noted earlier, extensive collections of antiquities had been created and sold on through much of the 19th century (Woodman *et al*. 2006, 8–12). However, in the north-east of Ireland in the decades from about 1880–1910, there was a period of extensive collection, much of which, though not all of it, was based on the membership of the Ballymena Field Club (*ibid*., 13–22). They collected extensively from the mid-Antrim area and also from across parts of adjacent counties. It was only in this period, and perhaps only towards the end of it, that there was a consistent effort to record the provenance of the artefacts. Of course, others, notably Adams who was based in Antrim Town, also kept a record of the location of his discoveries, as did Gray and Patterson (1835–1918), who lived in the Belfast area. Unfortunately Buick and Grainger (1830–1891), perhaps mainly because of their untimely deaths, left very little information.

One major disadvantage of these collections (see Woodman *et al*. 2006, chapters 1 and 2) is that much of this material, especially that from the Bann Valley, was purchased from intermediary individuals, such as peddlers, and aside from a few "super Locations", much of the material was recorded only to the nearest townland. In the case of the treasure house of Lough Neagh and the Bann Valley it is possible that in excess of 50,000 items may have ended up in collections outside Ireland and can be found in museums right around the world. A significant portion of this material, such as the implement types illustrated in Knowles's 1912 paper, would now be recognised as Mesolithic in age (Figs 3.12 and 3.13). These included Mesolithic core and flake axes, microliths, numerous small blades and small single-platformed cores. From what we would now recognise as Later Mesolithic they had collected a range of Butt Trimmed and other Later Mesolithic forms, as well as a series of picks and core-borers. He was also aware of some instances where quite similar objects were found in southern Britain. Thus he included examples of the "Thames picks" (Fig. 3.13, 90) which, of course, are now thought to be Neolithic in date. It would appear that several thousand polished/ground stone axes were also collected. These implements were found during peat and diatomite cutting, dredging, collected at times when water levels were low or dug out of Quaternary deposits. It was apparent to Knowles that, although forms that were instantly recognisable as being similar to those from Neolithic and Bronze Age assemblages in the later sand dunes of Portstewart and Dundrum were present, there was also a very significant residue that must be considered as different and probably older. He stated enigmatically near the beginning of his paper that a number of the implements suggested to him that they might have been the products of the descendants of the manufacturers of the "older series of flint implements" found on coastal sites and that they were brought to the Bann Valley "by peoples entering the river system from the Bann Estuary" (Knowles 1912, 196). There was no doubt in his mind that they pre-dated what was conventionally recognised as Neolithic assemblages.

It is unfortunate that the one person who had developed a particular interest in these assemblages in their context did not follow up on his work. This was R. D. Darbishire, who was attracted to the Bann Valley because of his interest in the "diatomaceous clays". In 1909 Wilfred Jackson published a paper on the artefacts that Darbishire had recovered from the "diatomaceous earths". This material still resides in the collections of the University Museum in Manchester. Initially, he was interested in the deposits themselves but he became fascinated by the fact that there were artefacts associated with them. While he recorded the stratigraphic sequence of these deposits, in particular in the area of Culbane, my visit to the museum in the early 1970s revealed that most of the records seem to have been inadvertently destroyed. If he had retained an interest in these deposits, and documents survived, it is possible that the chronological position and

Peter Woodman

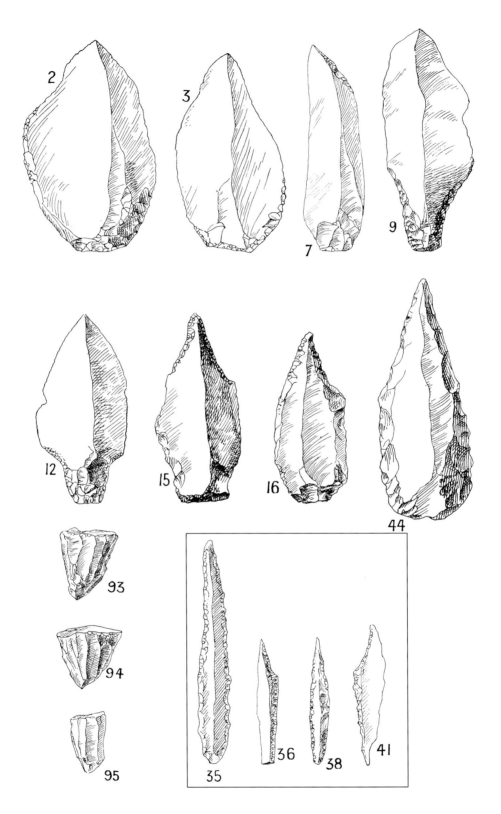

Fig. 3.12. Selection of Mesolithic implements illustrated by Knowles (1912) 2, 3, 7, 9, 12, 16, 17, and 44) series of Later Mesolithic forms; 35) micro-awl, 36, 38, 41) Microliths, 93–5) small prismatic cores. Locations: 2, 7) Coleraine, Co. Derry, 36) Gortgole, Co. Antrim, 3, 16, 36) Culbane, Co. Derry, 41) Glenone, Co. Derry, others) locations not specified.

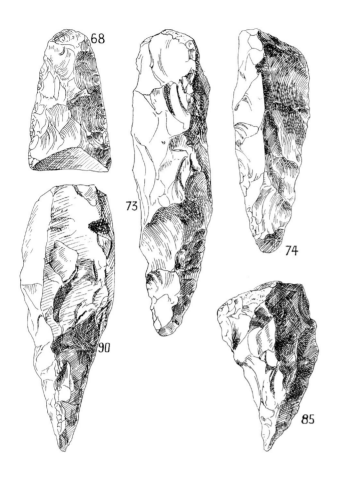

Fig. 3.13. Further selection of Mesolithic implements from the Lower Bann Valley illustrated by Knowles (1912): 68) Flake axe ("Kitchen Midden Axe"), 73–4) core axe/pick, 85) core borer. Locations: 68, 73, 85) Culbane, Co. Derry, 74) Lower Bann opposite Ballymoney; 90) is a pick from the Thames Valley.

full significance of this material might have been realised at a much earlier date.

A general consensus had emerged that the material from Larne and other locations belonged to some form of an as yet undefined Neolithic and was Holocene in date (Coffey and Praeger 1904). Discussions in Ireland were to mirror those taking place elsewhere in Europe; was there a need to have a defining term that described the archaeological assemblages of post-glacial hunter-gatherers? Rowley-Conwy (1996) has showed that the term "Mesolithic" first proposed by Westropp was not greeted with much enthusiasm. Smith (1960) has documented in detail the chequered history of the term. Numerous different schemas were proposed and, as Smith noted, one of the definitions that would be closest to what was to be used from the mid-20th century was proposed by the Argentinian anthropologist, Florentino Ameghino, who was in fact born in Sardinia but his family immigrated to Argentina when he was a child.

Many excavators in Denmark preferred to simply incorporate what we now know as the Mesolithic assemblages within a phase of the Neolithic. Similarly, Knowles (Woodman *et al.* 2006) had, aside from the "Older Series" no difficulty in accommodating the first settlement of Ireland after the "Ice Age" within a Neolithic.

Smith suggests that ultimately it was Macalister (1921; Fig. 3.14) who first used the term Mesolithic in the context of a series of lithic assemblages that seemed to belong to the early part of the Holocene and pre-date the spread of farming. In an Irish context, even without using the term Mesolithic, Macalister in 1928 showed a detailed knowledge of assemblages from across Europe. These are what we would now consider to be Mesolithic. He described a range of assemblages that would be recognised today, even if in some cases the names are no longer used. They included the Azilian, Maglemosian, Obanian as well the Asturian and the Campignian. One interesting observation by Macalister was that the so-called Pygmy flints found in Ireland were nothing to do with the "Azilian", but rather were something of a similar type at a later date.

However, Macalister used the term rather reluctantly. He offered an explanation for having "The Mesolithic Period" as the title to chapter x in his *Text-Book of European Prehistory* Vol. 1. He felt that it had "at least the advantage of brevity over 'Epi Palaeolithic' and 'Proto Neolithic' preferred by some authorities", that it was "the most convenient term that can be found" (Macalister 1921, 517) and that, in essence to summarise his opinions, it was preferable to stick with something that had received some use rather than try to impose something new. It is of interest that in an equivalent chapter on the Mesolithic of Ireland in the *Archaeology of Ireland* (Macalister 1928) as well as in his *Ancient Ireland* (1935) he seems to have abandoned the term Mesolithic.

In the case of Ireland, it was Claude Blake Whelan (1933a) who really established the term Mesolithic. In Britain, M. C. Burkitt had, in 1925, also shown resistance to the term, preferring to call the relevant chapter "Transition to the Neolithic". By 1932, however, he and Gordon Childe, in their overview of the Stone Age published in *Antiquity*, were prepared to live with the use of the term Mesolithic. The fact that it was seen as a term of convenience by Grahame Clark is shown by the fact that, in 1936, he also saw the Mesolithic as a "point in time" rather than an evolutionary stage (Milner and Woodman 2005, 4).

Spikens (2008, 4) has outlined the way in which the basic template for the Mesolithic period was created and resulted in minimal expectations for the period. As she noted, even Grahame Clark was prepared to accept the notion of a Mesolithic characterised by a "low level of Culture", while Mortimer Wheeler, who worked primarily in Iron Age or on Romano-British archaeology, used the adjective "squalid" to describe the British Mesolithic.

Fig. 3.14. a) R. A. S. Macalister, Professor of Archaeology, UCD (by permission of the Royal Irish Academy), b) A. E. P. Collins (by permission of the Ulster Journal of Archaeology, c) Dr Adolf Mahr, Director of the National Museum of Ireland (by permission of the National Museum of Ireland), d) A view of the excavations at the Warren, Cushendun, Co. Antrim (after Movius 1940a).

The story of the Irish Mesolithic

In many ways, Lawlor's (1928) review in *Ulster: its Archaeology and Antiquities* reflects many of the issues that dominated the study of "Early man and the Stone Age in Ireland". Lawlor found it difficult to know where to place both the Larne artefacts and those from the River Bann. On the one hand they were not Palaeolithic, yet there was no sign that they belonged to what people identified to be typical on Neolithic sites, namely pottery (*ibid.*, 13). Of course, at that time there was still a belief that the megalithic monuments belonged to the Bronze Age. Perhaps Lawlor's other, more enduring contribution was to state quite clearly that "man first arrived in Ireland, let us say perhaps 10,000 years ago, he arrived in primitive boats

to procure flint" (*ibid.*, 12). It is also implicit that they were confined to the extreme north-east and like many at that time he envisaged dense forests containing dangerous animals "against which the settlers had not sufficient means to defend themselves" (*ibid.*). This view carried with it the presumption that the initial settlers had come from adjacent parts of Scotland

It was only in the 1930s that there was a clear consensus that the initial settlement of Ireland could be categorised as belonging to the Mesolithic. In the case of Ireland, the chronological framework and the sites that were to form the back bone of the Irish Mesolithic for the next 40 years were identified by various workers, such as J. P. T. Burchell (1931), who described assemblages from mid-Holocene deposits at

Island Magee and, more importantly, Cushendun. Claude Blake Whelan (1930a; 1938) identified an assemblage from below what was perceived as Late Boreal peat deposits found on the shores of Lough Neagh at Toome and along with Burchell was among the first to realise the significance of Cushendun.

As was common at that time, in the case of Cushendun and Island Magee, Burchell was inclined to see a Magdalenian influence in the assemblages while, at Toome, Whelan felt that he could detect Aurignacian elements in the assemblage. He also went on to comment on the assemblage from the Lower Gravels at Cushendun and suggested that besides Magdalenian elements there was evidence of Mousterian and Aurignacian influences.

In Ireland, even at earlier dates in the late 1920s, the search for origins and influences on the material culture of the Irish Mesolithic was to a great extent based on finding comparisons from across Europe. One of the first of these papers was that by Walther Bremer (1928), where he noted the similarity between the triangular-sectioned Asturian picks from the north coast of the Iberian Peninsula and a series of pick-like flint implements from Larne Lough in particular. This was an idea that also temporarily attracted the attention of others such as Whelan (1930a; 1931) However, most authors, such as Macalister (1928), identified the Campignian as a possible source of a range of core and flake axes found in Ireland. This was a culture/technology from northern France that sat uneasily between the Mesolithic and Neolithic. Other analogies included the similarity between some of the Larne axes and the Nostvet Culture of southern Norway.

One slightly anomalous claim was that some assemblages that had been picked up in fields on the Castlereagh Hills in Co. Down could be associated with the Tardenoisian (Whelan 1933a, 201–2). In reality many were small naturally shattered pieces of flint that had a fortuitous resemblance to microliths.

These comments might, in the light of present day knowledge, seem outlandish, but it should be remembered that similar claims for everything from Mousterian to Gravettian were being made for the Komsa culture in Arctic Norway (Bøe and Nummedal 1936; Woodman 1999). In fact the possible parallels in research history were one of the things which attracted me to working in Arctic Norway.

The real decade of development was the 1930s. Amongst the many who contributed in this decade of change, Claude Blake Whelan (1895–1954) was in many ways the key figure, indeed "the unsung hero". He was, throughout the 1930s, trying to create a framework for the Irish Stone Age. Born in Co. Wicklow he trained as a lawyer and after serving in the First World War, he became a member of the Northern Ireland Civil Service. Although much of his career was spent as a professional civil servant, many of his own activities were as an amateur, but he did take a professional responsibility for the archaeological implication of the 1930s Bann Drainage and amassed in particular a crucial collection of bone and stone implements from near the Cutts at Coleraine (see below

Chapter 9). He was also a founding member of the International Congress of Prehistoric and Protohistoric Sciences, which held its first meeting in London in 1932.

It was the excavations under the direction of Hallam Movius of Harvard that established a firm chronological framework. These were excavations of a series of coastal sites, Cushendun, Glenarm, Curran Point and Rough Island, as well as at Newferry on the River Bann. This major series of excavations could be impressive exercises in their own right, as at Cushendun (Fig. 3.14d), carried out in 1934 and 1936, led to the publication of both a series of excavation reports and of *The Irish Stone Age* in 1942. The project had the advantage of being supported by a parallel initiative established by the Royal Irish Academy. This was the Committee for Quaternary Research, which was chaired by Lloyd Praeger. The committee had invited Professor Knud Jessen to carry out research on Irish bogs and as a result, not only was there a general pollen sequence established for Ireland (Jessen 1949), but detailed analysis was carried out at Cushendun and Newferry, as well as at Whelan's site on the shores of Lough Neagh. In passing it should be noted that, while Jessen assisted Whelan and Movius in providing a series of palynological reports which were published in the 1930s or early 1940s, in the interim and for his final definitive paper (*ibid.*) he revised the nomenclature he used for the various Pollen Zones. This can be a source of confusion as Movius in *The Irish Stone Age* used the earlier schema; however, the 1949 schema became the standard for the following 20 years.

The Curran Point assemblage, due to the quantity of material recovered from a series of raised beach deposits, impressed Movius (1953a) and as a result the name "Larnian" was used to describe the Irish Mesolithic (Movius 1940a, 75). The key site, however, was undoubtedly the Warren at Cushendun. At this site Movius uncovered the following series of deposits (Fig. 3.15b):

1) Topsoil containing a Neolithic assemblage, which also included some elements that might be seen as similar to the Bann Culture.
2) A series of raised beach gravels containing similar material to that found at Curran Point, i.e. of Late Larnian age.
3) Upper Lagoon silts. Jessen (1949, 135–9) suggested that the pollen recovered from this layer was typical of a date that was earlier than PZ VII a (Atlantic).
4) Lower Gravels, not necessarily of marine origin, containing a slightly lighter more laminar industry. This had already been identified by Burchell (1931, 282–7).
5) Lower lagoon silts containing a relatively fresh, large blade industry associated with pollen of PZ VI c (Boreal age).
6) A Boreal peat deposit

Palynological research was first carried out by Gunnar Erdtman (1934) and then by Jessen (1949) provided several other key chronological markers. These included the observation that the Toome material was associated with a Boreal peat deposit, which was felt to be slightly older than the deposits from Cushendun.

Fig. 3.15. a) Amateur flint hunters at Newferry, Co. Derry (Photograph R. J. Welch, 8-9-29, Collections of the Ulster Museum, by permission of the National Museums of Northern Ireland), b) The Harvard excavations at the Warren, Cushendun, Co. Antrim showing the stratigraphic sequence identified during the excavation (after Movius 1940a).

Crucially, there was a sense that the lithic artefacts from the "Bann Culture" lay at the Atlantic/Sub Boreal transition and so could be contemporaneous with the Neolithic. Jessen (1949, 122–3; pl. xi, diagram 8) even suggested that the "Bann Culture Artefacts" were associated with diatomite that were laid down during the sub-Boreal and in some cases date as late as the Bronze Age. The Bann Culture was seen by Piggott (1954, 316–7) as part of the "secondary Neolithic". The presumption of a Neolithic date was also in part based on the presumed contemporaneity of the Bann Flakes with so-called decorated Neolithic (Sandhills) pottery. This pottery was thought to be found at stratigraphically the same level as the lithics from the Movius excavation. The pottery, however, was found over 100 m away from the excavation, near the river in a less certain context (see Woodman 1974a).

One commentator seems to have been somewhat hesitant. Adolf Mahr, in his Presidential address to the Prehistoric Society 1937, was not prepared to entirely accept the growing consensus that the Bann Culture was late. He recognised that much of it could date to as late as the Bronze Age and felt that in general the large blade tradition was a product of the availability of quantities of good quality flint in the North-East of Ireland. He also noted that:

> there is something uncannily Maglemosian about many of the characteristics of this culture, and the presence of polished stone implements is, on the other hand, no evidence against a pre-Neolithic … The art of stone polishing is now recognized as antedating the so called stage quite considerably. (*ibid.*, 307)

In retrospect, while Neolithic and Bronze Age elements were also recovered from the diatomite, the result was that the vast majority of material from the Irish Mesolithic was misplaced and pigeon-holed as "secondary Neolithic" for a period of 35 years. This was, perhaps, the most significant *Cul de sac* to be created within Irish prehistoric research.

In summary, Movius in *The Irish Stone Age*, laid out the following, in the context of the Irish Mesolithic, being subsumed into one culture called the "Larnian":

1) The archaeological material from the mid-Holocene could be divided into an Early Larnian and a Late Larnian.
2) Based on palynology, and mainly on the assemblages from the lower lagoon silts at Cushendun and Whelan's Toome site, it would appear that the human settlement of Ireland began sometime before 6000 *uncalibrated* BC.
3) The Early Larnian looks like a derivative final Palaeolithic industry.
4) The Later Larnian, based primarily on the excavations at Curran Point, Larne, is mainly characterised by being a heavy, large bladed industry.
5) The so called "Bann Culture", such as that found in the excavations at Newferry (Movius 1936), should be described as later Neolithic.

6) Implicitly, the Harvard excavations seemed to reinforce the idea put forward by earlier authors, such as Lawlor (1928), that people came first to Ireland from adjacent parts of Scotland and that it was the availability of large quantities of flint along the Antrim coast that attracted them. Settlement was confined to the north-east to facilitate access to sources of flint.

The result of *The Irish Stone Age* was to produce, in many ways, a minimalist set of perspectives for the Irish Mesolithic. Perhaps the most important perspectives could be summarised as follows:

a) The Irish Mesolithic was seen to be of marginal significance as it was confined to a small region, was based on being in areas where flint was accessible and incapable of penetrating the "dark forests" which were inhabited by ferocious animals. We now realise that the distribution in Ireland of artefacts recovered in the second half of the 19th century (see Fig. 3.16) and which we now know to be Mesolithic artefacts, was much wider than the presumed distribution in 1950.
b) The assemblages were crude and primitive. They were thought to derive from Late Palaeolithic survivals and so had very little similarity to what was becoming the conventional microlith-dominated Mesolithic of many adjacent parts of Europe. Microliths had, however, been recovered by Knowles and a small selection of microliths from the River Bann were also published (Batty 1938). Perhaps, most importantly, virtually the whole "Bann Culture" was removed from the Irish Mesolithic with the core axes and particularly flake axes being seen as part of the Campignian.
c) For the next 25 years the Irish Mesolithic remained in a limbo. Papers by Mitchell (1949a; 1949b) and Hodges (1953) demonstrate the problem. There was a constant need to see how Irish material of putative epi-Palaeolithic origins could relate to the Azilian, the Tardenoisian or even the "Forest Culture" and this was confused, at times, by a desire to link Irish and Scottish material. The poor chronological framework for the Mesolithic of western Europe did not help. It is salutary to remember that there was no real understanding of how the Maglemose and Ertebølle related to each other. There is a certain irony that, in spite of the misplacement of the Bann Culture Jessen's work combined with the Harvard mission's activities created a potentially better chronological framework for Ireland than was available in much of the rest of western Europe. Perhaps the most insightful comments from the period were made by Hodges (*ibid.*, 29):

> "Thus it would appear that in the entire peripheral areas one can detect borrowings from the "Forest Culture" people. There can be no doubt that such influence was never great in the Hiberno-Scottish area … How much of the Larnian material is due to this borrowing, and how much to native ingenuity, is hard to tell; and until many more good Irish sites have been excavated such assessment is bound to remain very largely a matter of conjecture".

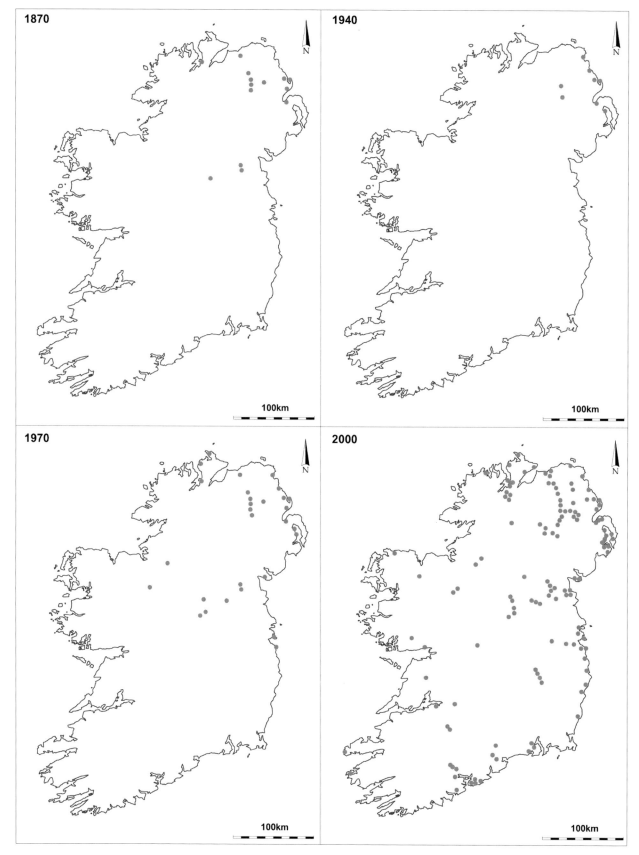

Fig. 3.16. Distribution of the numbers of known locations of Mesolithic material 1870s–1980s (prepared by Hugh Kavanagh).

Was there a Mesolithic in Ireland?

The result of these perspectives, especially the very limited north-eastern distribution and the absence of anything that resembled the English or Continental European Mesolithic, was a serious suggestion that the so-called "Larnian" was little more than a local industrial facies of the Neolithic. This was proposed by De Valera in his revision of Ó Ríordáin's (1979, 1) *Antiquities of the Irish Countryside*. Therefore, there was a serious suggestion that there was no reason to believe in a human presence in Ireland prior to the Neolithic. By the beginnings of the 1970s Mitchell (1971; Plate VIc) was defending the presence of a Mesolithic in Ireland on the basis of two locations. These were 1) Whelan's Toome site, where the assemblage was stratified below peat that Jessen had placed in his Pollen Zone VIa/b, as well as his own excavations in the area in the early 1950s and 2) the lower Lagoon silts from Cushendun, which were placed in Zone VIb/c.

In the interim, since the publication of the *The Irish Stone Age*, Mitchell (1947; 1956b; 1972a) at Rockmarshall, Co. Louth and Sutton, Co. Dublin, as well as Liversage (1968) at Dalkey Island, had been excavating a series of coastal shell middens that produced implements which seemed to be like those associated with the "Larnian". The presence of polished stone axes in several of these sites led to a presumption that they were likely to be of Neolithic date, as did a belief that many of these sites post-dated the Littorina Transgression, which was assumed to date to the end of the Mesolithic period. This in turn led to the suggestion that these sites must, at best, be transitional and might date to the Early Neolithic. Various other sites fed into this perception that much of the Mesolithic material was of a late date. Although radiocarbon dates had been obtained from sites such as Dalkey Island D38 (charcoal: 5300±170 BP; 6411–5664 cal BP; Liversage 1968) the early dates for Neolithic settlement at Ballynagilly lay between 5700 and 5200 BP suggested a Neolithic presence perhaps by or before 5500 BP or well before 6000 cal BP (Apsimon 1976) Thus much of what we knew as Late Larnian really was contemporary with the Early Neolithic.

One site that seemed to fit into this category was Ringneill Quay, Co. Down, where there was a suggestion that the bones of domesticated cattle and sheep were found under beach deposits and associated with a date of 6498–5946 cal BP (Q770, charcoal; 5470±120 BP). Unfortunately, the association of these dates and the faunal remains is not entirely clear (see Woodman 1978a, 17–18) and the crucial faunal remains were subsequently lost in a sewage pipe burst and flood of a basement store room belonging to the Geography Department at Queen's University Belfast.

Similarly, chert assemblages had begun to turn up in the midlands. Major areas were initially found at Loughs Gara by Cross (Fredengren 2002), at Kinale by Maghee (Raftery 1972) and by Frank Mitchell at Lough Derravarragh (Mitchell 1972b), as well as other occasional Bann Flakes of flint and chert from the midlands, had been considered to belong to a final or "Ultimate" phase of the so called Larnian.

By the late 1960s there was little agreement as to the extent of the Mesolithic in Ireland. Besides the possibility that it did not exist, two sets of material appeared anomalous. The first of these were the "Bann Flakes" and other related forms that were not turning up in any numbers on Neolithic sites, yet at the same time they existed in very large quantities in museum collections and, even before the Movius excavations, amateurs had been drawn to Newferry (Fig. 3.15a).

It was becoming necessary to look for another explanation of the place of this material within the Irish Stone Age. An excavation during the 1960s in diatomite deposits on the Antrim side of the river at Newferry Site 4 had produced a roughly similar assemblage to that found by Movius at Newferry during the 1930s, i.e., large blades, Bann Flakes/Butt Trimmed forms and polished stone axes (Smith and Collins 1971). In this case, a similar range of material was found towards the upper part of the sequence (Level V), with Smith and Collins (*ibid.*, 21) able to obtain a date D36 charcoal 5280±170 BP from this level. In contrast, much of the material excavated by Movius (1936) at Newferry Site 1 came from the base of the diatomite. At Smith and Collins' site which was later designated Newferry 4, while substantial quantities of artefacts were found in Level V, the excavators also noted that a number of flakes were recovered at lower levels in the excavations, including some flakes in a Boreal peat deposit (Smith and Collins 1971). This suggested that possibly the so-called "Bann Culture", as defined by Movius, might have an antiquity that extended back into the Mesolithic. At a time when there were serious doubts as to the existence of a Mesolithic the chance to discover an *in situ* assemblage from the "Boreal" period was deemed to be a priority. At the time it was thought that if we excavated down through the Newferry deposits there would be greater evidence of classic diagnostic Mesolithic implements, such as Core axes and fewer of the implements that were associated with so-called "Bann Culture". In particular, it was assumed that polished or ground stone axes, a presumed sign of a Neolithic presence, would be absent. As so often, the story was to be somewhat different.

A New Mesolithic chronology

Additional excavations at Newferry Site 3, adjacent to Smith and Collins' Site 4, were carried out in 1970 and 1971 (Woodman 1977a). On the basis of an extraordinary series of diatomite and peat deposits interleaved with sand banks there was confirmation of a series of activities that had taken place over a long period of time (Pl. VII).

1) A range of large blades, Bann Flakes (later to be called Butt Trimmed Forms), as well as a series of related tool types and polished stone axes were found throughout the diatomite deposits as well as in underlying sand banks and peat deposits.
2) Therefore, while there were some changes in the form of implements, the direct percussion blade production, Butt

Trimmed Forms and, most importantly, ground stone axes were found throughout the complete series of phases of occupation that began by perhaps 8500 cal BP and supported by a series of radiocarbon dates and the palynological sequence, activities in this locality continued for more than 2000 years.

3) Neolithic elements, both pottery and lithics, including a hollow scraper and leaf/lozenge arrowhead, were only found in eroded and disturbed deposits at the top of the sequence.

These Newferry Site 3 excavations therefore placed the "Bann Culture" and, along with other associated artefacts, a range of "Bann" and Tanged flakes, often now referred to as Butt Trimmed Forms, firmly and primarily within the Mesolithic.

There remained, however, one obvious conundrum. Another suite of artefacts, including microliths as well as core and flake axes, were, to my surprise, not associated with the "Bann Complex". Knowles had occasionally found microliths and, as noted earlier, Batty (1938) had published a small selection from the Bann Drainage. One small area in particular remained noteworthy by being different. After Seaton F. Milligan's initial discovery of a series of axes in the vicinity of Mount Sandel (Gray 1888) that area, on the Bann Estuary south of Coleraine, was to remain an area of interest. Between the various collections, nearly 100 core and flake axes exist. These elements, along with the microliths and small prismatic cores which had also occasionally turned up elsewhere, were instantly recognisable as the types of implements that would be found in a European Mesolithic assemblage.

In 1959 A. McI May came upon an area of landslip on the outer side of Mount Sandel Fort, where it over looked the River Bann. On examination, this area was shown to contain all the elements that had been found earlier by the collectors. Excavations in April of that year revealed that a ditch cut round the fort had truncated a series of brown–black occupation soils and gravels. These layers were backed up against a slope that dropped precipitously down towards the flood plain of the Bann Estuary. Some Neolithic potsherds appeared to be associated with this material. Flake axes were conveniently thought to belong to the final stages of the Mesolithic, e.g., in the Ertebølle in Denmark or the "Campignian" in France. The maximum age of the English narrow blade/geometric industry was yet to be established, but the conventional wisdom was that it occurred in the later part of the English Mesolithic. In 1968 further trenches (A and C) were opened by A. E. P. Collins. These revealed a similar sequence, with again prehistoric pottery found in association with microliths and other artefacts of presumed Mesolithic age. Therefore, as discussed elsewhere (Woodman 1974a) there was also the possibility that two very different types of Mesolithic assemblages were present in Ireland at the end of the Mesolithic. In other words, was there a very late phase of the Irish Mesolithic in which the microlithic industry existed side-by-side with the late phases of the Bann type industry? Sometime in 1971, during the Newferry excavations, radiocarbon dates were obtained from three samples from what

came to be known as Mount Sandel Lower. Given the mixed nature of the site and, in particular, the presence of later material along with "Mesolithic artefacts", the fine particulate nature of the charcoal and the large standard deviation of two of the dates: (UB 591, charcoal 8370±525 BP, 10,782–8175 cal BP and UB 592, charcoal, 7720±695 BP, 10,522–7313 cal BP) the dates were treated with some caution. Another date, (UB 532, 8370±200 BP, 9893–8773 cal BP) was based on charcoal that came from the base of Cutting C. This date, although it seemed somewhat more reliable, was also treated with caution. While Early Christian or medieval pottery had already been found, in this case a shale bracelet fragment of Early Christian or later date was recovered mixed in with Mesolithic material, which emphasised that extensive disturbance may have taken place at a late date.

The excavation at Mount Sandel Lower was finished in 1973 and it was at this time that the Mount Sandel Upper excavations began. The latter site lies in fields behind and to the east of Mount Sandel Fort and was the area where it is suspected the collectors had found large numbers of implements, At Mount Sandel Upper the same range of Mesolithic artefacts was associated with hearths and other pits (Pl. VIII) It had been expected that the assemblages from Mount Sandel would be roughly contemporaneous with the Newferry assemblages and that they would be the product of different range of activities or perhaps although even then it was a questionable idea different groups of people. The key was the absence of a firm Mesolithic chronology in Britain and a widely held belief that were flake axes existed in particular in Scandinavia they were associated with the latest phases of the Mesolithic. The words consternation and amazement come to mind to describe our reaction when dates from this excavation revealed that in fact the flake axe, core axe and microlith assemblages were in existence before 8500 cal BP, in fact some of the dates obtained at the time suggested a possible age just before 9000 BP. Issues associated with the site and its re-dating will be discussed in more detail later, but in essence the Mount Sandel sites established clearly for the first time that two distinct chronological phases could be identified in the Irish Mesolithic:

1) An *Early Mesolithic* phase existing primarily between 10,000 (?) and some after 9000 years cal BP In this phase, besides the small core and flake axes, a number of sites produced microliths, including both internationally recognisable forms such as scalene triangles and local forms such as needle points.

2) A *Later Mesolithic* phase in which composite tools had been replaced by large blanks that were produced by a hard hammer percussion technology. This phase was in existence by 8500 cal BP A slight modification suggested by Woodman (2012) will be discussed below in detail in Chapter 8.

Ground stone axes existed in both phases and their occurrence in Ireland was in no way associated with the spread of farming.

As a result the term "Larnian" had become irrelevant and should be replaced by these terms.

By the mid-1970s Michael Ryan's (1980) excavations at Lough Boora, Co. Offaly had produced a somewhat similar assemblage based mainly on the use of chert (Pl. IX). At this site microliths and polished stone axes were found buried below peat on the edge of an earlier lake basin. Radiocarbon dates showed that by 9500 cal BP there was a human presence in the Irish Midlands. As a result it was possible by the end of the 1970s to pose some new questions which required immediate and further investigations:

1) Would we discover a Mesolithic presence throughout the whole of Ireland? *This issue was quickly and fully addressed by the discovery of microliths at Kilcummer, Co. Cork* (Woodman 1989) *and by the excavations at Ferriter's Cove, Co. Kerry* (Woodman et al. 1999). (Pl. X)
2) Is there any evidence of an earlier presence in Ireland, either during the earliest phases of the Holocene or even is there reason to believe that there was a Palaeolithic presence in Ireland? *Research has increased our understanding of the issues surrounding the potential of a Palaeolithic presence in Ireland, but, as yet, no substantive remains have been discovered. This also holds true for attempts to find a Mesolithic presence that pre-dates Mount Sandel.*
3) Could there be any progress in understanding the nature of the transition from the Earlier to the Late Mesolithic? *In this case, recent excavations have shown that, instead of there being a rapid shift from an Early to Late Mesolithic technology, change would appear to have taken place over at least one millennium* (see below Chapter 8).

Conclusion

For many, this chapter may seem irrelevant to today's research on the Irish Mesolithic, but hopefully it will be seen as more than an attempted teleological account of how our ideas changed and developed. It is hoped that some lessons can be identified and that questions arose that deserve careful examination.

Our research or philosophy, like most experimental subjects, is always constrained by the conventional wisdom of the day. Two relevant examples are given below.

• There has been a long held belief, while perhaps prejudice is too strong a term, that regions on the edge of Europe are only occupied late and usually by groups that have failed to adapt to environment changes elsewhere.
• Certain aspects of the archaeological record become "self evident truths". In this case it was the presumption that the polished or ground stone axe was a type fossil of the Neolithic period and that its presence on any Stone Age site was a clear and unequivocal indicator that farming was taking place.

It is also evident that, without a reliable chronological framework suitable for the needs of the time, it is difficult to advance the discourse. In this instance Thomas Molyneux provides an interesting case study of an astute observer whose ideas could only be developed within the almost universally accepted Creationist 6000 year long chronology for "The World".

As shown earlier in this chapter, the prevailing values and priorities of society must have played a role. It may be an over-simplification to suggest that the almost complete absence of a Mesolithic presence over much of the southern half of Ireland was because of the rarity of flint along with both a late rise in sea level combining with no raised beaches of the right date that contained artefacts. The reality was that few people looked. The suspicion of the role of science throughout much of Irish society must have had an effect. The emphasis on other aspects of Ireland's past as well as the probable lack of interest by many seems to have created an environment in which there were few opportunities for making discoveries which would help us to understand how or when Ireland was first colonised. These attitudes seem to have been the mindset of many throughout the second half of the 19th century and it could be argued that it coloured the thinking of many well into the 20th century.

These attitudes have not been confined to one part of the political spectrum in Ireland. The often proposed assumption that the initial colonisation of Ireland took place from Scotland into the north-east of Ireland has been used to suggest that the original population of Ireland can be found in the Stone Age. While it has become apparent that the initial human footfall may not necessarily have happened in the north-east there is good reason to be believe, that, during later prehistory, as there is no evidence of substantial movements of new peoples into Ireland after the Stone Age, many such as myself (Woodman 1988) have argued that the Stone Age population must have left a significant contribution to Ireland's modern gene pool. Authors such as Adamson (1991) or Hall (1994) have argued that the descendants of the "Stone Age Peoples", the Pretani, pre-dated the late arrival of the Celts who pushed up through Ireland from the south eventually driving out the indigenous population. The validity of this suggestion is the subject for another debate but as a result of this perspective the returned "Ulster Scots" could be seen as the descendants of Ireland's earliest settlers. In Ireland the distant past is never far away!

Perhaps the lessons of the chapter can be summarised as follows. We should be humbled to see how often conventional wisdom constrained the exploration of alternative ideas and approaches. Each generation works within the accepted wisdom of the day, whether that of society in general or the particular discipline.

Making changes to the "accepted view" was and is often not easy and there can be many barriers. For example O'Connor (2007), in her study of the research history of the British Palaeolithic, has identified a series of significant factors, such as the role of the super sites or the role of major figures who dominate the discipline.

At least for the author, it provided a salutary lesson best summarised as, to again quote Feynman's (1999, 211) directive, "that one should not ignore the point that is off the line", namely not to be so convinced of one's opinions that one ignores evidence that points in another direction. The real heroes are those who can see the flaws or contradictions in the accepted views of their world and, while working across the grain, seek to find ways of resolving the contradictions.

To conclude the most dangerous argument, or the one that should be critically examined, is the one that begins with "*it is reasonable to presume that...*"

Part II

Laying the Foundations

Anyone who has been involved in the academic planning of new course or particularly new degree programmes will have run across the conundrum of "front loading". This is simply the issue of what do you introduce first. Do you introduce theory, methodology, etc., first at the risk that there is no appreciation of the relevance of these approaches to the particular subject which is being introduced? Alternatively do you bury them in factual details and leave the methodology and some forms of critical analysis to later? Although I have admitted that the reasons for writing this book have changed, there are elements within the work that relate to a number of the on-going debates within the study of the Irish Mesolithic and there are hopefully some issues which are raised that provide alternative explanations or suggestions for further research. However one of its major purposes is still to introduce the first 40% of Irelands known history to a broader audience within the archaeological profession and to an important interested amateur community. For that reason, much of Part II is devoted to describing the types of evidence that exist within the Irish Mesolithic as well as discussing how certain biases may have developed. It is more a set of factual references rather than being a contribution to some of the Meta issues which will be considered later.

Chapter 4

Where did it all come from?

In any country or region, the corpus of archaeological material that is available for study from any period or culture is, as suggested in Chapter 3, a product its time, with its own interests, priorities and other socio-economic factors. In the case of the study of the Irish Mesolithic these perspectives have to be combined with changes to the landscape, both those that were the product of the natural alterations that took place over time and, in certain instances, changes in the manner in which the landscape has been used. Therefore, it is not surprising that the material available for Mesolithic research in Ireland was gathered through a very different process, in comparison with the manner in which it was created in different parts of Britain or other areas such as Denmark or Norway.

Creating the database

As noted (Woodman 2009, xxxvi), the Irish Mesolithic could be characterised by the following; *collectors and townlands, bogs and beaches, islands, flint*. In other words, the manner in which museum collections were built up differed from many other regions of Europe. The availability of the townland as a local unit within the landscape, with all its variations (Fig. 4.1), adds a particular dimension to Irish Stone Age studies.

First find your site

There is a curious quirk to the nature of locational information from Ireland. Up until the 1980s artefacts and excavations included, as part of their location, both the county and the name of the townland within which the finds were made or the excavation took place. Since then, this information has been supplemented by the additional use of the Irish Grid. In recent years, in Northern Ireland, for the convenience of the postal service there has been a shift from townlands to rural addresses based on road names and house numbers. This was combined with the earlier 1970s' abolition of County Councils i.e., where the traditional county was an administrative unit. Therefore, in Northern Ireland there has been a greater shift to a reliance on the use of the Irish Grid references, while the county and townland name are often not included.

However, most individual and surface collected finds are still recorded to townland with, in a few cases, location to a more precise position such as farm or bog, while others are recorded to parish or even, unfortunately, just County.

How is the material found?

Unusually, in Ireland the role of excavations and of "field walkers" was, as will be shown below, quite limited.

In many countries, excavations would be the main source of information about the Mesolithic period. In Ireland, a Mesolithic database, which it is hoped will be online in the immediate future, has documented nearly 1000 "sets of information" that may belong to the Mesolithic. This term "sets of information" has been used because of the fact that it is often unclear whether or not assemblages built up by different collectors came from the same findspot or, conversely, whether two slightly different locational references actually refer to the same findspot. One has to admit that much of the material in museum collections is poorly documented.

The role of collectors and the associated problems has been discussed in detail in Woodman *et al.* (2006, chap. 1). This illustrated the significant role played by collectors in the formation, as well as the preservation, of the archaeological record. Primarily these collections are now held in the National Museums of Ireland and Northern Ireland. Collections of archaeological artefacts had been well-established in Ireland even in the late 18th century and while even in the early part of the 19th century there were a number of professional middle-men travelling throughout the country, with the intention of selling on their purchases from farm labourers to those interested in having collections of artefacts, very little emphasis was placed on scientific recording of the places of discovery. Thus, even in the 1850s when substantial collections of Stone Age artefacts were in existence, as witnessed in the Belfast Exhibition of 1852 or Wilde's (1857) catalogue of the collections of the Royal Irish Academy, few records were kept of the locations of discoveries. Similarly, an extensive collection of stone tools belonging to the Royal Dublin Society frequently lacked detailed information as to where they

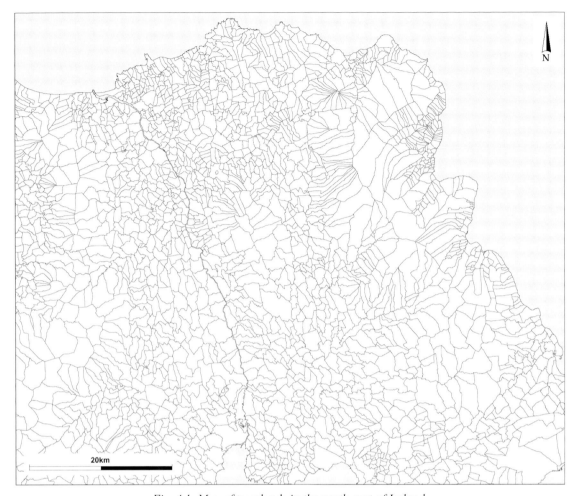

Fig. 4.1. Map of townlands in the north-east of Ireland.

were found. This was further compounded by the fact that, throughout much of the 19th century, collectors outside the north-east of Ireland did not place such a great emphasis on stone tools – a fact that was, late in the 19th century, lamented by the dealer and collector, Robert Day (1891).

Yet, even in the north-east, in spite of all the scientific attention to detail, that practice was common amongst many active field workers in the field clubs until virtually the beginning of the 20th century; recording provenance was not regarded as a priority. Besides Gray and Patterson, a number of others kept very limited records, for example, Grainger, Buick and Raphael of the Ballymena area. Where records existed, they were usually in the form of information written on the artefact or on a label stuck to its surface. William Knowles, who published prolifically, usually kept records in this form. He also only seems to have begun this practice more regularly as late as the beginning of the 20th century. Thus detailed records were often only kept during the last 100 years. Having purchased many of the artefacts from the "ragmen" it was common for much of the material to be recorded only to townland, a unit that was at times useful, but could also vary

from tens of hectares through to thousands, meaning it was often of limited value (Fig. 4.1).

Although there were notable exceptions, such as Buick's collection of large quantities of Neolithic and Bronze Age artefacts at Rose Cottage, Glenhugh td (Woodman *et al.* 2006, 262), few of that generation actively field walked but instead visited classic honey pot sites, such as the sand dunes or raised beaches. Even the prolific locations in the River Bann, such as Portglenone, Culbane and the shores of Lough Neagh near Toome, were usually visited to purchase material from workmen rather than involving the collectors in the active pursuit of collecting for themselves. There were, of course, notable exceptions, such as a visit by Knowles and others to Lough Neagh during the extremely dry summer of 1911 (Knowles 1912; Fig. 4.2).

Obviously, as the 20th century progressed so recording improved, notably in the Adams collection, though it must be admitted that, as noted previously, the shift to the discovery of a possible Palaeolithic led many researchers, such as Whelan, to concentrate on artefacts which looked early. There were few who collected in their own locality. Perhaps the most notable

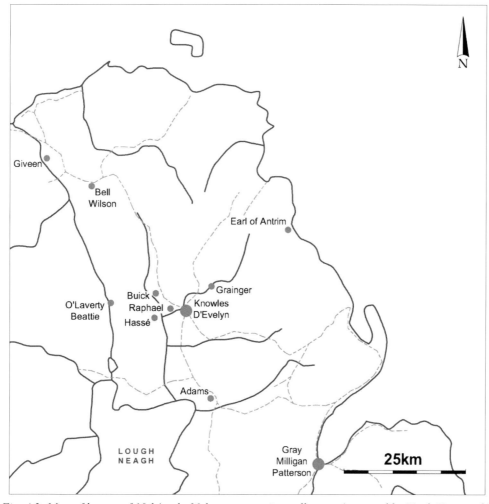

Fig. 4.2. Map of homes of 19th/early 20th century major collectors (prepared by Hugh Kavanagh).

example from the inter-war years was Kirk of Newtownards, who built up several collections from numerous sites round the shores of Strangford Lough. In some instances the place names he used were idiosyncratic, thus Kirk used the name "Goldsmiths", the surname of a local Clergyman, and fields were identified according to their proximity to his house. Another example of somebody who made a contribution during the inter-war and immediate post-war years was Gracey from Kilrea. Unfortunately, with some exceptions, much of the locational information associated with this collection was lost. Two individuals, Claude Blake Whelan and A. McI May, both of whom worked in the public service, also amassed collections. Even at this late date, however, some collectors did not keep detailed records of where material was discovered, the most notable, perhaps, was Dr Stuart of Portglenone.

Amateurs, such as Stuart of Carnlough, Carr of North Down, Reagan of Strangford, the Ards Hodgers (1973; 1994) and McCrainor of Co. Louth and McNaught, Gallagher and Harkin of the Inishowen/Derry area must also be recognised. These few individuals were the backbone of the search for Stone

Age sites. They were and are rare individuals in comparison to other countries. As was noted by Woodman (1978a, 2–5), field walking and related types of exploration either took place at known "hot spots" or relatively close to the homes of the followers of these pursuits.

Even within the last 50 years the number of professional or amateur field walkers has always remained quite limited. On a professional level, four major projects can be identified. These are 1) Cooney (1990) with the Mount Oriel Project, 2) Green and Zvelebil (1990) with the Ballylough survey, as well as 3) the Barrow project (Zvelebil *et al.* 1996) and 4) Kimball (2000) in Lough Swilly. To these projects could be added the more limited work of Woodman (1989) in the Blackwater area and the east Cork coast (Fig. 4.3).

It will be apparent, however, that aside from material found on lake shores there were relatively few Mesolithic sites found through surface collections. Two other factors help create the absence of an extensive network of field walkers in Ireland. Firstly, the limited number of locations producing Mesolithic material in Ireland is best seen by comparing the fact that, at

Peter Woodman

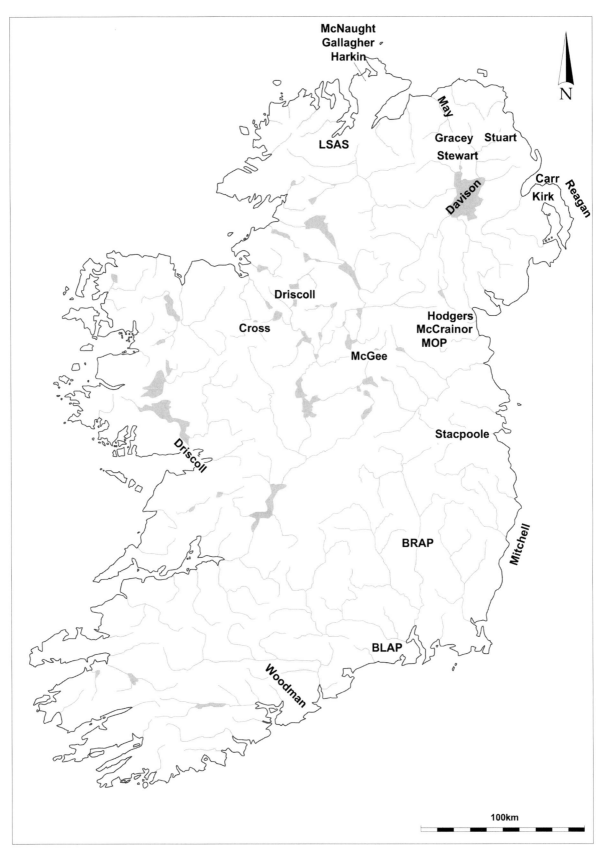

Fig. 4.3. Locations of organised 20th century surface collections Ballylough archaeological project: BRAP = Barrow River archaeological project; MOP Mount Oriel = project; LSAS =Lough Swilly Archaeological survey (prepared by Hugh Kavanagh).

most, 900 locations of all types are known in Ireland, which has a land mass of over 80,000 sq. km. In contrast, McCartan (2003) has recorded nearly 350 find spots from the Isle of Man, which has a landmass of less than 600 sq. km. In other words, *pro rata*, Mesolithic find spots are 15 times more common in the Isle of Man than in Ireland! Again, Prescott (2011) has recorded 800 locations in an area about 1500 sq. km of the central Pennines alone. In Contrast, there are few places elsewhere in north-west Europe that have produced 10,000s of artefacts. In Ireland, at places such as Culbane, Toome and Portglenone, it is highly probable that these numbers of artefacts, have, by one means or another been recovered. Comparisons are always invidious!

As in Scotland, in Ireland there also are extensive areas where there are limited populations and therefore areas where it is less likely that there will be a milieu which will develop or foster this type of archaeological field work. Again, as in other parts of the "Highland Zone" of the British Isles, arable farming is confined to areas in the east of Ireland, while in much of the west the land is either under permanent grassland or bog. It is also highly probable, therefore, that the nature of the Irish Mesolithic may have contributed to the difficulty of site discovery and contributed to the surprisingly low number of Mesolithic sites or assemblages known from Ireland.

Of course, in assessing a region one can ask how is it possible to balance the quantity of artefactual evidence and relative richness when, in one region, sites may be defined by a small number of microliths which only represent one or two composite tools with, on the other hand, a region such as north-east Ireland where, at some spots, up to 10,000 artefacts have been found and each of which may have been hand held tools in their own right.

The role of excavations

Obviously there are sites where significant Mesolithic assemblages were recovered inadvertently, but if one only considers excavations, irrespective of whether they were research or primarily rescue excavations, that have an initial or a primary purpose in excavating a site of Mesolithic date, then, in Ireland, over the last 125 years, fewer than 30 excavations have been carried out. As will be discussed below, while numerous developer-led excavations have taken place in the last 15 years, excavations primarily centred on the Mesolithic during this period of time represent only eight in total. Of course, in Ireland this is in part due to licensing controls on excavations, which distinguish it from areas like England, where there are very limited controls on excavations. Therefore, unlike the Pennines or the greensand of southern England, where numerous amateur excavations have taken place, a very limited series of excavations has been carried out in Ireland. Numerous other sites have produced some traces of Mesolithic occupation or artefacts. In total, in spite of the remarkable increase in development-led excavation, there

are relatively few sites that have produced any Mesolithic material. Indeed, just over 200 excavations have produced any traces of Mesolithic material (Fig. 4.4), but the low incidence of sites primarily designed to explore an aspect of the Irish Mesolithic is, in part, a statement of the low priority given to a period that lasted for 40% of the known human history of Ireland.

As can be seen from Figure 4.4, excavations have been associated with little more than 20% of the discoveries of Mesolithic material from Ireland. While this might look like an impressive number, as will be shown below most of the material comes from a very limited number of excavations. If one separates off those excavations that had a specific intention to explore aspects of the Mesolithic, along with those where discoveries led to particular attention being paid to elucidating aspects of the site that were associated with the Mesolithic, then, as will be seen below, the numbers fall off quite radically. What is of particular interest, however, is that in spite of the exponential rise in the number of excavations that have taken place during the last 25 years, especially the decade between 1998 and 2007, the numbers of sites making a significant contribution to the Irish Mesolithic remained relatively constant.

The Mesolithic database, if it had been created 25 years ago, would have shown that the vast majority of finds of Mesolithic date were chance finds that often passed through several hands before ending up in collections. There were, and had been up to the early 1980s, a limited number of crucial research excavations for most periods. For a long time these were dominated by excavations on National/Historic monuments that were usually prehistoric sites, a small but significant number of excavations of Mesolithic sites also took place. With the increased economic activity there was a realisation that, along

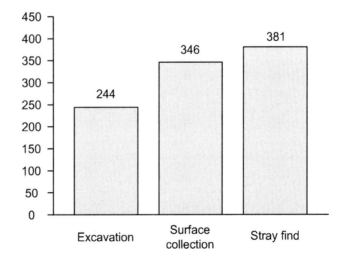

Fig. 4.4. Histogram of the manner of discovery of Mesolithic artefacts: excavation, surface collection, stray finds (prepared by Hugh Kavanagh).

with clearance of services and other planning requirements, archaeological excavations were, when appropriate, a necessary prerequisite to development. Ed Bourke (pers. comm.), of the National Monuments Service, has prepared figures for the period 1985–2009 based on licences issued. In all 25,000 licenses were issued in this period. These demonstrate the rapid rise in excavations that took during this period. These numbers would have been driven by urban renewal schemes of the late 1980s, expansion in housing and industrial development, as well as the better known NRA (National Roads Authority) road developments.

Inevitably, trying to estimate the actual total number of sites investigated in Ireland in recent decades and the nature of these investigations is more complex. Furthermore, the introduction of licensing through Ministerial Directions on road construction by the NRA, where a single license was issued for a stretch of road that could include a number of separate sites

Licenses were also issued for a number of purposes; as in many cases, especially from the 1980s onwards, they were granted to carry out excavations before one knew whether there was anything of significance present. Many of these, whether watching machines or small test excavations (monitoring) where nothing was found, have been listed as having produced "nothing of archaeological significance". They did, however, explore small or large portions of the landscape and the absence of an archaeological presence of any period or artefact type is still a significant statement..

In contrast, estimating the numbers of excavations prior to 1985 presents different challenges. In short, up until 1970 establishing the numbers of excavations is based on the number of licenses issued, i.e. one per excavation site irrespective of the number of years taken for the excavation reports. This was supplemented by an examination of journals in which excavations were reported. Of course, not all excavations were published. The figures, therefore, are a rough estimate. *Excavations.ie* on the other hand provides information on almost all excavations carried out each year.

For this reason information has been placed in three roughly 25 year periods. There are five excavations that pre-date the 75 years examined below. These were mostly at the Curran Point. It should be noted that the numbers of excavations in each period are approximate, especially as types of information available earlier than the establishment of the *Excavations Bulletin* (subsequently developed into *Excavations.ie*) is very partial. It might, therefore, have been expected that there would have been a very significant increase in the number of excavations where significant attention was paid to the Mesolithic component evident at the site.

The whole changing nature of excavations, from research with its own priorities, to the emphasis on recovery of evidence in danger of destruction, along with various other topics, are well worth more careful examination, however in this case the analyses are confined to how Mesolithic material was recovered:

1) The total number of excavations carried out and/or reported.
2) The total number of excavations which have produced Mesolithic artefacts or other indicators.
3) The number of excavations where either the primary purpose was to contribute to Mesolithic research or where after discovery the excavator invested a significant effort in recovering traces of a Mesolithic presence.

Based on Table 4.1 certain trends for the Mesolithic are obvious. Until the most recent period, from 1985 onwards, excavations with an interest in the Mesolithic were almost entirely carried out as research excavations, as were most excavations undertaken in Ireland overall.

When examining the sites which could be regarded as making a significant contribution in the early period, before 1960, the Harvard Mission excavations, in this case under the direction of Hallam Movius, as well as those carried out by Frank Mitchell, dominate. In the middle period, most of the significant sites were also research excavations or became excavations with the intention to elucidate aspects of the Irish Mesolithic. However, since 1985, only one of the excavations in the significant category could be regarded as being begun as a research excavation. It might have been expected that, with the massive increase in excavation during the 1985–2012 period, there would have been a considerable increase in sites which would have made a significant contribution. Across the three periods the number of excavations that have made major contributions to the study of the Irish Mesolithic has been almost constant. However, the extraordinary change in the ratio of sites producing Mesolithic artefacts against the total number of excavations speaks for itself, i.e. a shift from roughly 1:10 to over 1:80.

James Eogan, in a presentation on the nature of excavations in Ireland as documented in *Excavations.ie* (Lecture April 2013 to IAI Institute *of Archaeologists of Ireland*), highlighted a number of points that are worth considering in the context of the contribution of excavation to the study of the Mesolithic. It is worth noting one rather curious point.

More than 40% of the excavations carried out took place in an urban environment. Surprisingly, virtually none produced any trace of Mesolithic artefacts whether *in situ* contexts or in secondary later deposits. Yet many Irish towns and cities, especially those of medieval origins, were located at spots where Mesolithic communities were likely to have lived i.e., at key points on rivers or on river estuaries. Of course, in some

Table 4.1. Presence of Mesolithic material from excavations between 1932 and 2009.

Excavations	1932–1959	1960–1984	1985–2009
Total No.	250?	750?	15,000?
Mesolithic presence	27	28	176
Significant presence	10	10	15

cases, landscaping may have taken place and destroyed much of the archaeological record or the excavators did not have to go deep enough. At the moment the number of urban sites producing Mesolithic artefacts is fewer than ten!

Which sites create the framework for the Irish Mesolithic

If we consider the sites from the last 80 years where extensive excavations have taken place as well as the sites that have in their own way made a significant contribution then, admittedly on a personal basis, 25 excavation sites can be identified.

These are:

1. *Ballydown*, Co. Antrim, 1990s. Later Mesolithic and Neolithic settlement site overlooking Larne Lough (Moore 1999).
2. *Bay Farm*, Co. Antrim, 1970s–1980s. Later Mesolithic settlement and chipping floors (Woodman and Johnston 1996).
3. *Baylet*, Co. Donegal, 2000s. Later Mesolithic shell midden, on-going post-excavation. (Milner and Woodman 2007).
4. *Belderrig*, Co. Mayo, 2000s. Later Mesolithic coastal settlement, on-going post-excavation. Preliminary publication by Warren (2009).
5. *Cushendun*, Co. Antrim, 1930s. Stratified series of marine and other deposits containing a range of artefacts from throughout much of the Irish Mesolithic (Movius 1940a).
6. *Dalkey Island*, Co. Dublin, 1950s. Shell middens, primarily of Later Mesolithic date (Liversage 1968).
7. *Derragh Island*, Co. Longford, 2000s. Later Mesolithic–Neolithic lakeside platform, on-going post-excavation. Preliminary report by Frendengren (2009).
8. *Drumakeely*, Co. Antrim 2010s Later Mesolithic settlement on the Banks of the Cloghwater River (Dunlop in prep.)
9. *Clowanstown 3*, Co. Meath, 2000s. Later Mesolithic fish baskets and other related features as well as a platform (Mossop 2009b).
10. *Fanore*, Co. Clare, 2010s. Later Mesolithic and transitional Mesolithic/Neolithic shell middens place on the western edge of the Burren. Excavations still on-going (Lynch: *Excavations.ie*).
11. *Ferriter's Cove*, Co. Kerry, 1980–1990s. Mesolithic coastal settlement (Woodman *et al.* 1999).
12. *Hermitage*, Co. Limerick. 1990s Two cremation burials of Mesolithic date (Collins and Coyne 2003; 2006; Collins 2009).
13. *Kilcummer*, Co. Cork, 1980s. Scatter of Early Mesolithic artefacts overlooking the junction of the Blackwater and Awbeg Rivers, on-going post-excavation. Preliminary report by Anderson (1993).
14. *Killuragh Cave*, Co. Limerick, 1990s. Small cave containing, amongst other material, Early and Later Mesolithic human remains and artefacts on-going post excavation. (Woodman 1997).

15. *Lough Boora*, Co. Offaly, 1970s. Early Mesolithic lakeside settlement, on-going post-excavation. Preliminary report by Ryan (1980).
16. *Moynagh Lough*, Co. Meath, 1990s. Later Mesolithic lakeside platforms stratified below crannog, on-going post-excavation. Preliminary reports by Bradley (1991;1999).
17. *Mount Sandel*, Co. Derry, 1970s. Early Mesolithic settlement site adjacent to the Lower Bann (Woodman 1985a).
18. *Newferry 1*, Co. Derry, 1930s. Excavations of Later Mesolithic artefacts from diatomite (Movius 1936)
19. *Newferry Sites 3 and 4*, Co. Antrim, 1970s. Stratified riverside site having been reoccupied for 2000+ years (Smith and Collins 1971; Woodman 1977a).
20. *Larne, a) The Curran*, Co. Antrim, 1930s. Excavation of chipping floors and rolled flint artefacts from raised beach deposits (Movius 1952); *b) Port of Larne*, Co. Antrim, 2000s. Chipping floor and traces of settlement site at the entrance to Larne Lough dating to the middle of the Mesolithic, on-going post-excavation (McConway in prep.).
21. *Rockmarshall*, Co. Louth, 1940s. Excavations of Later Mesolithic Shell middens (Mitchell 1947; 1949a).
22. *Spencer Docks*, Co. Dublin, 2000s. Evidence of fishing facilities (McQuade and O'Donnell 2009).
23. *Sutton*, Co. Dublin, 1950s, 1960s. Excavations on a later Mesolithic shell midden (Mitchell 1956b; 1972a).
24. *Toome (Creagh)*, Co. Derry, 1940s. Excavation of a Mesolithic shoreline site with radiocarbon date (Mitchell 1955).
25. *Toomebridge Bypass*, Co. Antrim, 2002. Multiple traces of Mesolithic occupation on a drumlin close to the Lower Bann and Lough Neagh (Dunlop and Woodman 2015).

Several patterns can be seen. The bias towards Co. Antrim is not as strong as might have been expected but as in so many ways the Province of Connacht is poorly represented. Though some of the sites are extremely important, the contribution from excavations associated with infra- structural developments (site names above in bold italics), is not as great as might have been expected. Their contribution seems to have been more in documenting a presence across the landscape.

Environmental issues and the creation of the Mesolithic

As will have been apparent from the previous chapter, much of the research on early prehistory was based primarily on a particular set of contexts, notably those associated with the Holocene raised beaches and deposits in the Bann Valley, i.e., in secondary contexts. Therefore, until the 1950s much of the emphasis was on the age of the material, so that the occurrence of artefacts in a secondary context did not represent a problem. Similarly, as will be apparent later, much of the settlement in Ireland during the Mesolithic was closely associated with rivers and lake sides, as well as sea shore activities (Fig. 4.5).

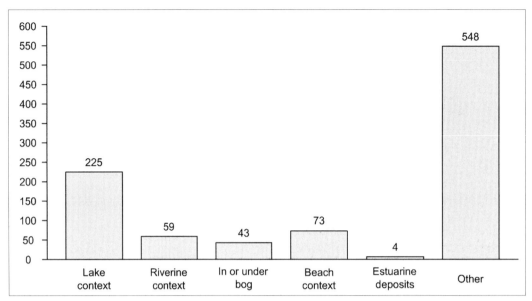

Fig. 4.5. Histogram of geological and other contexts of Mesolithic finds contexts (prepared by Hugh Kavanagh).

This had the extra effect of burying much of the evidence of a Mesolithic presence below a series of quaternary deposits and thereby creating a series of problems.

The Bann Valley had the advantage of commercial hand cutting of diatomite combined with the acquisition of fuel for brick kilns in the form of peat cutting in adjacent bogs. Most other river valleys that contained extensive, undisturbed layers of silt and other forms of Quaternary deposits were not exploited in the same manner. So much had been recovered from the River Bann and its vicinity over the previous 100 years, the drainage and dredging activities of the 1930s were monitored by Whelan on behalf of the Department of Finance, as well as interested amateurs, such as the May family of Coleraine.

There are few instances of significant quantities of material being recovered from dredging elsewhere. In the case of some river valleys, such as the Boyne and the Shannon, one must ask whether the limited recovery of artefacts from those rivers was based more on the expectations of discovery rather than on a genuine absence Bourke (2001) clearly demonstrated that large number of objects of other periods were being recovered from the Shannon There is also the small selection of artefacts from the dredgings of the Tyrone/Armagh Blackwater (Bourke, C. 2001; *Excavations.ie*), while the dredging of the river between Loughs Sheelin and Kinale, especially at Kilgolagh, produced a range of Later Mesolithic artefacts (Woodman 1978a; Little 2010).

The infilling of lakes and the extensive development of bog of considerable depth, especially raised bogs, has had another effect. In the latter case it is very apparent that, in spite of the extensive commercial exploitation and removal of peat bogs mostly by *Bord Na Móna*, there are few instances where bogs have been lowered to the point where traces of shoreline Mesolithic settlement can be found. It is worth noting that the

Early Mesolithic site of Lough Boora was only exposed because of the drainage of a lake within the peat bog, which brought to light a shoreline that lay some distance below the surrounding peat. In the case of Corlanna, Co. Westmeath, the actual site of Later Mesolithic settlement (Warren *et al.* 2009) has not yet been exposed but rather the material has been spewed out on a higher surface through a process of deep drainage.

The extensive nature of many of the midland bogs may also help, in part, to explain the relative lack of early prehistoric sites that were or are being recovered along the new road systems. In theory, it might have been expected that significant quantities of material would be found round the shores of many Irish lakes. Some material has been recovered from these locations and certainly the fact that much of it is of a poor quality chert-like material that does not always survive well does not help in identification. It should be noted, however, that perhaps the three largest concentrations from lakes shores were each recovered as a result of drainage schemes that created very short windows of opportunity. At Ballyhoe Lough (Morant 1867; Woodman 1998a) material was recovered after a drainage scheme in the 1860s left large areas of lake shore exposed. A similar process at Lough Gara in the 1940s (Cross 1953; Fredengren 2002) and Derragh Lough in the 1960s (Fredengren 2009) produced very large numbers of artefacts. A visit to many of these locations today will reveal that extensive shoreline reeds and marshes now cover the areas where the artefacts were recovered (Pl. XI). Interestingly, Driscoll (2006; 2009) has documented a clear example where substantial quantities of material were recovered from the shores of Lough Allen. Here only six find spots were recorded as producing Mesolithic artefacts. In this case, during one summer period of low water, he recovered material from numerous find spots, which varied from individual finds to small groups of artefacts (Fig. 4.6). In

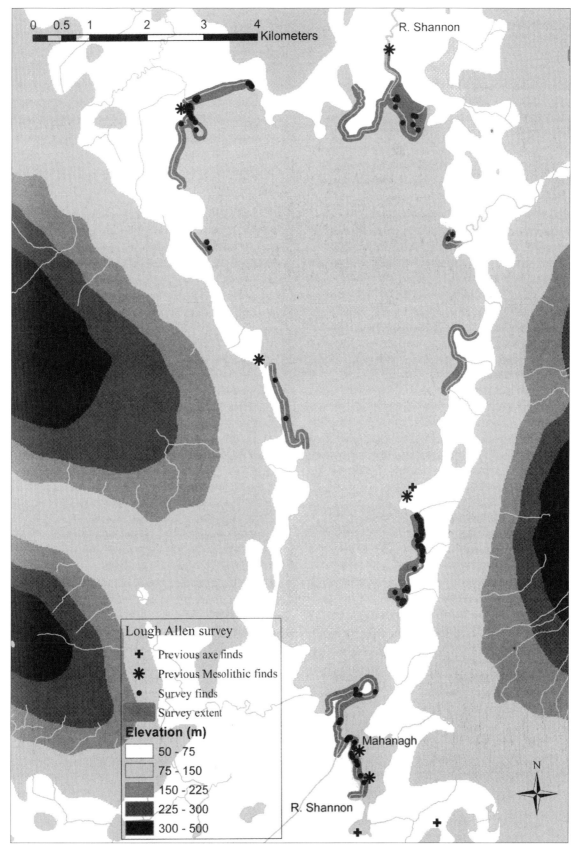

Fig. 4.6. Find locations from the shores of Lough Allen (from Driscoll 2009).

many cases it is difficult to assess how many sites originally existed. Obviously townlands are too large a unit. No matter which way one calculates sites, Driscoll's map of Lough Allen shows that each area surveyed produced numerous locations where Mesolithic artefacts were recovered and that therefore anywhere between 20 and 40 separate sites may have been identified. Therefore, if one took lake shore environs as a separate sub-category these constitute nearly 250 find spots.

As Evans noted in his 1867 paper, there is still the possibility that other lakes that are subject to seasonal change and which temporarily expose extensive areas of shoreline may well produce many more Mesolithic assemblages. Thus, in comparison to lakeshore finds, locations where artefacts were actually collected from the surface of ploughed fields are very much in the minority. This clearly emphasises the distinctive nature of the Irish Mesolithic.

There are also other environmental factors that have reduced the chance of finding Mesolithic sites. Perhaps the most obvious is the relative scarcity of sites along the Leinster and South Munster coastline. There are a number of well-known sites in the vicinity of Dublin Bay and at one or two other find spots. Elsewhere they are surprisingly sparse. While sea levels stabilising at a late date may have contributed, it is probable that coastal erosion may have removed numerous sites that had originally been close to the shore. This is particularly evident along the east coast of Ireland from Co. Down to Wexford. This is further complicated by the fact that around the coast of Ireland many protected bays, where erosion has not taken place, are filled or cut off by extensive barrier sand dunes that can, in turn, cause extensive marsh deposits to develop behind them. This again reduces the chances of discovering the locations of coastal sites of Mesolithic date. Therefore, a site such as Ferriter's Cove (Woodman *et al.* 1999) is remarkable both for its survival and its discovery, again in this case by a geologist Peter Vernon who had in interest in archaeology.

Distribution patterns

The overall picture of the Irish Mesolithic has also changed. In fact, one of the biggest problems is how to present the information. Even while making allowances for the possibility of the same find spot being represented several times, usually due to a lack of precise information or where it is uncertain whether material from different collections comes from one or several different locations, there is still a striking general distribution of Mesolithic finds throughout the island and there is no single county which has not produced at least one find spot. Representing this distribution is more problematic. Dots representing find spots (Pl. XIIa) are useful but there is often a failure to understand that they are not distribution patterns like those for megalithic tombs or leaf-shaped swords, where there is now a very limited chance of making a series of new discoveries. One person could, in one year, add a significant number of new locations to Mesolithic distribution maps.

Counties also vary so much in size, i.e. from Louth at 820 sq. km to Cork at 7420 sq. km. Therefore numbers of find spots per county are not an accurate representation (Pl. XIIb). This can be moderated by dividing the number of find spots from each county by the number of 1000 sq. km units in each (Pl. XIIc). However, the best reflection of both where sites have been found and the activity of collectors, etc., is perhaps on the basis of a 25 × 25 km grid square (Pl. XIId).

While certain patterns are obvious, such as the concentration of sites in coastal/riverine/lacustrine areas, which will be discussed below, another pattern which emerges is that most sites lie at less than 100 m ASL, while sites above 300 m ASL are extremely rare (Fig. 4.7). Two other patterns can also be seen. There is a strong east–west divide which, in part, relates to population density and to the extent of arable farming. There may have been an expectation that the linear building programme of the NRA (Fig. 4.8) might have been more apparent in the distributions of Mesolithic sites (Fig. 4.9), as it is in the sudden appearance of linear patterns of sites belonging to other phases of Ireland's prehistory, for example the presence of assemblages associated with Beaker pottery.

Three remarkable facts emerge in any over view of the Irish Mesolithic:

1) A very high percentage of the material comes from secondary contexts, whether that is raised beach material, dredgings or shoreline discoveries.
2) Where locational information is known a very significant percentage of the material comes from very unspecific locations, i.e., townlands.
3) Extremely large quantities of artefacts come from a limited number of these locations.

The excavation record

Habitation sites

Three stake-holes do not make a hut and many huts do not leave stake-holes

As will be seen below, a very rich, diverse range of settlement sites have been found in Ireland. At the same time, it has to be admitted that Mount Sandel, with its circular structures that were over 5 m across, central hearths, large pits, quantities of artefacts and, while the material is burnt, a significant concentration of plant and animal remains, is still the most significant Mesolithic settlement site in Ireland. Unfortunately, Mount Sandel has, like Star Carr in England, become the "little house on the prairie" that is held up as "typical" of the period. However, even after some recent re-interpretation based on revising the chronology of the site (Bayliss and Woodman 2008), Mount Sandel is still of exceptional importance.

At Mount Sandel (Pl. XIII), although the most interesting area is the central area where most traces of huts, hearths and pits were found, scatters of chipping floors, other pits and post-

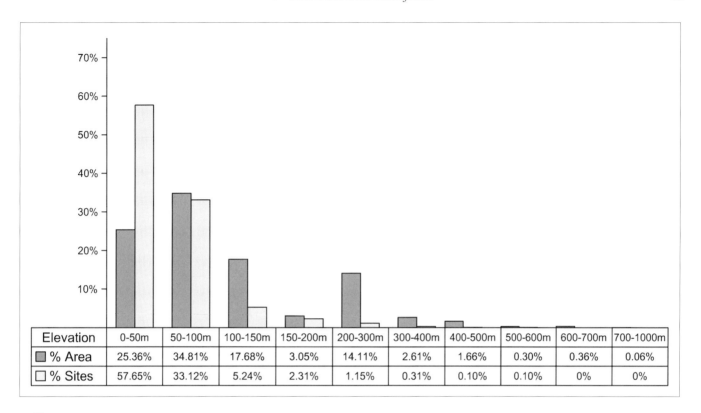

Elevation	0-50m	50-100m	100-150m	150-200m	200-300m	300-400m	400-500m	500-600m	600-700m	700-1000m
■ % Area	25.36%	34.81%	17.68%	3.05%	14.11%	2.61%	1.66%	0.30%	0.36%	0.06%
□ % Sites	57.65%	33.12%	5.24%	2.31%	1.15%	0.31%	0.10%	0.10%	0%	0%

a

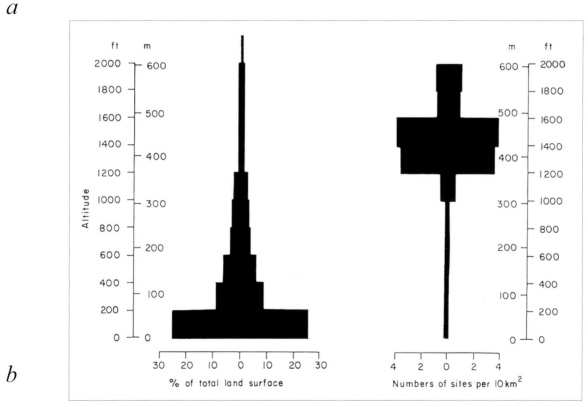

b

Fig. 4.7. a) Histogram of altitude of sites and percentage of land at various altitudes in Ireland, b) pennine comparison (after Jacobi et al. 1976) (prepared by Hugh Kavanagh).

Fig. 4.8 Road schemes with archaeological mitigation (by permission of the National Roads Authority, Ireland).

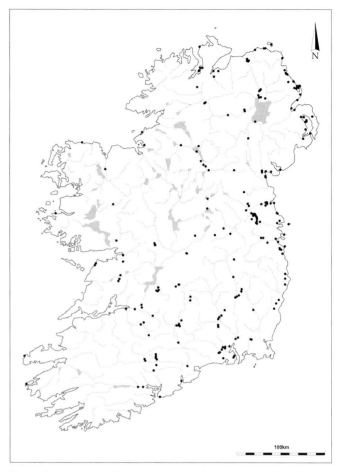

Fig. 4.9. Locations of excavations producing traces of Mesolithic activity (prepared by Hugh Kavanagh).

holes were found within an area 25 × 25 m across (Fig. 4.10). The most intact of the huts was centred on the main hearths, F56/2–7, were in what seems to have been a shallow, perhaps artificially enlarged depression (Fig. 4.11). There also still seems to be no evidence that there was ever more than one large hut present at any one time at this location. Other hearths that may have been at the centre of huts, such as F83 and F91, are in positions to the north of the main huts. A partially surviving arc of post-holes was probably associated with these hearths (Fig. 4.12). Similarly, F31/1, which cut across the main arc of stakes, as well as F32, may have also been central hearths. Mount Sandel has produced a very large number of what should be more properly referred to as a range of stake-holes of different sizes. Many of those associated with the huts are relatively narrow and can be up to 200 mm or more in depth. They are often cut into the subsoil at a slight angle which, as will be discussed below in Chapter 11, is relatively unusual, as are the runs of tiny stake-holes that lie between the larger ones.

Excavations extended 10–15 m in each direction from the main hut area, but these uncovered no other clear evidence of huts. However, as will be discussed later, they did reveal traces of other activities, for example, shaded areas (Fig. 4.10) which could be described as chipping floors.

It now seems most likely that the use of the main hut area lasted between 60 and 120 years (Fig. 4.13; Bayliss and Woodman 2009). At the time of the excavation it was assumed that a scatter of large deep pits, as well as a series of smaller ones (Fig. 4.14), was contemporaneous with the huts. In the case of the smaller pits there was a sense that many of them post-dated the main phase of hut building and occupation (Fig. 4.15).

It later became clear that, on stratigraphic grounds and re-dating (Bayliss and Woodman 2009), the small pits in general post-dated the huts, perhaps by 100 years. It had also seemed probable that each hut would have had a large (storage?) pit, such as F74 or F56/1 (Fig. 4.16), and been associated with a number of the smaller examples, such as F31/2–4, F46 or F100/3–5. The chronological position of the larger pits is less clear, but only some of them may have been the same age as the huts and they also definitely ran later in date. In fact are some of the latest dated features on the site. As with so many traces of Mesolithic settlement, these pits are a particularly

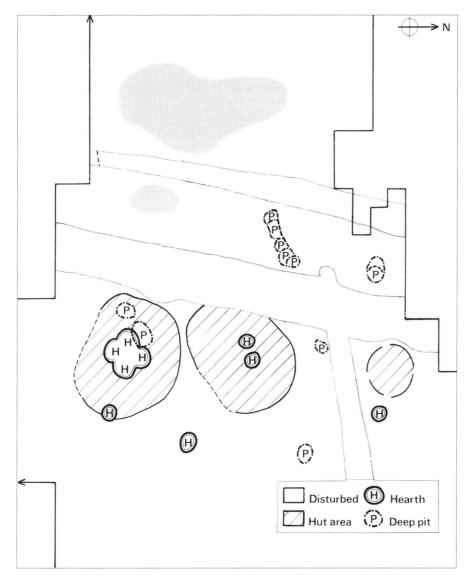

Fig. 4.10. Schematic plan of Mount Sandel excavations (Woodman 1985a).

different phenomenon. In one instance, F.74 had been refilled with the local gravel. The large pit complex to the north-west of the huts was, to say the least, even more impressive. As part of the re-dating programme (*ibid.*) samples were taken from the very extensive F209/211 pit (Fig. 4.17) complex which had seemed at the time to be so large that there was an intuitive feeling that they were later. However, these were shown to have been more likely to be Early Mesolithic in date. This raises the question as to whether, in Ireland, large pits, such as those excavated at Bay Farm, Co. Antrim (Woodman and Johnston 1996), could also be, as at Crathes in Scotland or other locations, Mesolithic in age. The recent discovery of a very substantial pit at little Dartmouth Farm in Devon that was almost 3 m across and 2 m deep shows that Mesolithic hunter-gatherers could dig large holes (Tingle 2013).

Perhaps, one of the lesser known aspects of the Mount Sandel excavation was the identifications of several hollows created by tree falls or throws. One in particular, F 29, clearly cut across the Mesolithic occupation layer. It also contained significant quantities of Mesolithic artefacts that had been washed back in. From its irregular shape and the manner in which it refilled it could be seen, however, that it was not a dwelling hollow (Woodman 1985a, 18–9, fig. 11 B). It provides a clear warning that one should not be too enthusiastic or hasty about identifying dwelling hollows.

Unfortunately, as mentioned already in Chapter 3, the material recovered by Collins (1983) from the other side of Mount Sandel Fort, i.e., up to 50 m away, was in a disturbed secondary context. It may have represented another living area but it is uncertain as to its extent or purpose. Not only was the

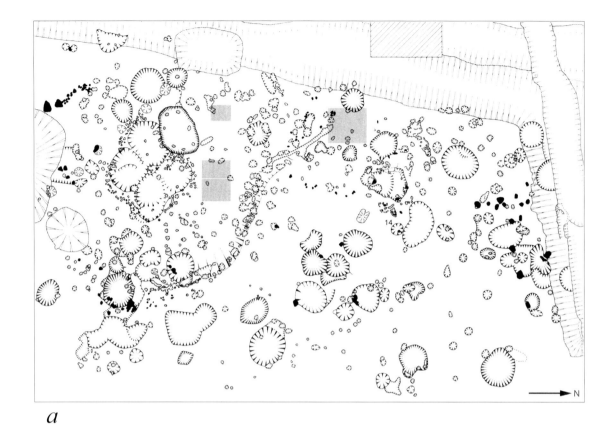

a

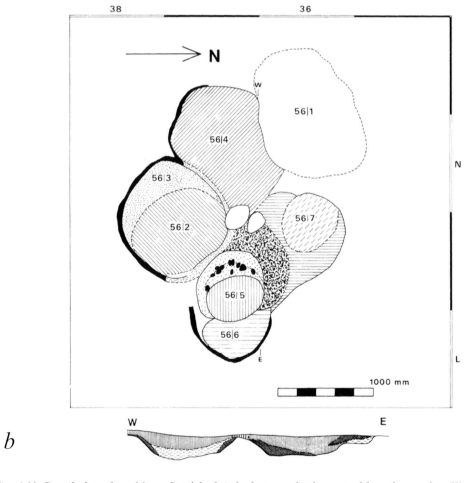

b

Fig. 4.11. Detail plans from Mount Sandel of a) the hut area b) the central hearth complex (Woodman 1985a).

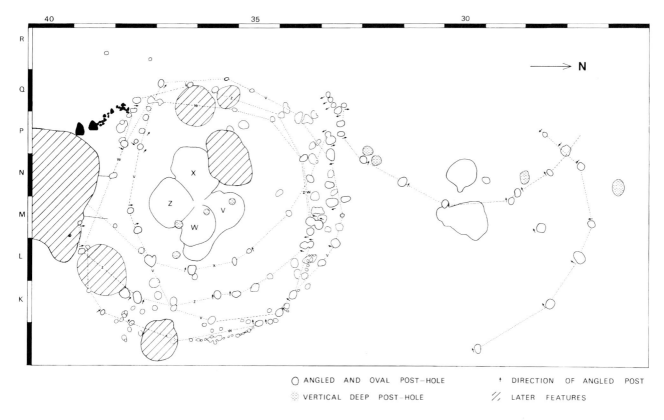

Fig. 4.12. Plan of post-holes and potential outlines of various huts in the central area at Mount Sandel (Woodman 1985a).

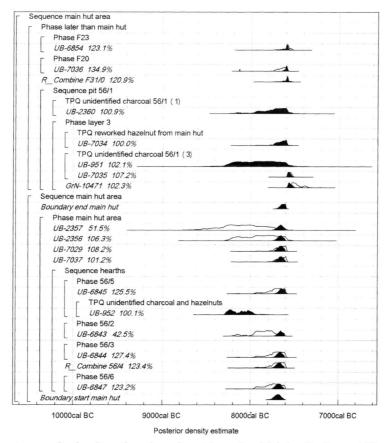

Fig. 4.13. Bayesian graph of radiocarbon dates from Mount Sandel (after Bayliss and Woodman 2009).

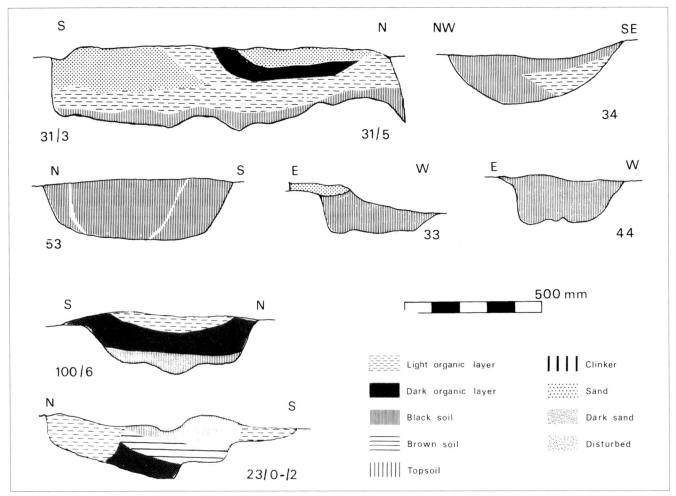

Fig. 4.14. Sections through a selection of smaller pits from Mount Sandel (Woodman 1985).

material in an extremely fresh condition but, unlike the hut site at Mount Sandel Upper where the microliths were often broken and burnt, those from Mount Sandel Lower were generally in a remarkably fresh, intact condition. It raises the question as to whether, even if they were not of the exact same age, there were other huts of a similar type built in the immediate vicinity. Similarly, the small area rescued at Castleroe (Woodman 1985a), which lies on the other side of the Bann, produced the remains of several small pits. It may be that, for a number of centuries, the area at the upper end of the Bann Estuary had a special significance.

Within the British Isles there are, at the moment, fewer than ten convincing structures that combine robust walls and/or are sunk below the surface and that approach 5 m in diameter. This re-emphasises the question as to what type of evidence should we expect when looking for dwellings? Most other, presumed, settlement sites are much more partial and in many instances one cannot even be sure whether actual dwellings were erected on them.

One of the most convincing evidence of a substantial structure or dwelling of Mesolithic age in Ireland is, unfortunately, only known from written accounts. In the 1890s R. M. Young and colleagues excavated on the edge of a quarry and exposed what appear to have been traces of Later Mesolithic settlement (Pl. XIV). This was located on a ridge placed back from the seashore and which, even in the Later Mesolithic, would have overlooked the outer estuary of the Bush River. This area is often referred to as the "Bushfoot" (Young 1892; Woodman 1978a, 273–7). Many of the artefacts that came from this area were of Later Mesolithic character, such as large blades, Butt Trimmed Forms, a greenstone chisel that may have been made of schist and a "sandstone polisher". At the same time, there is no reference or record in the collections of pottery or diagnostically later artefacts. In the Ulster Museum, notably in the Adams collection, there is a group of Mesolithic material that seems to have been collected from the Bushfoot area in October 1892 and June 1901. Besides finding artefacts, explorations at this find spot also uncovered a hearth and at one particular location

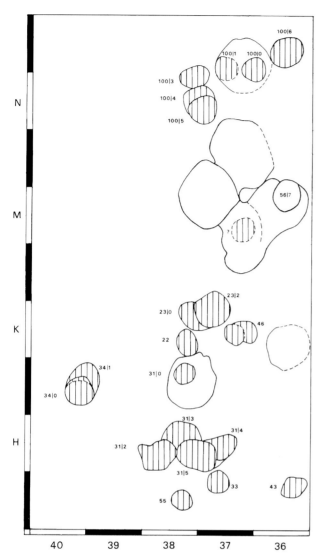

Fig. 4.15. Plan of the stratigraphic position of small pits located in the main hut area at Mount Sandel (Woodman 1985a).

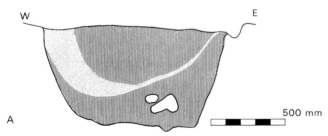

Fig. 4.16. Section through Pit 56/1 at Mount Sandel (Woodman 1985a).

exposed a floor in a deliberately made hollow that was defined by a bank of stones. Young was convinced that this was the location of a hut which was several metres across. This site had only been preserved because of the overlying sand dunes.

Similar preservation is also evident both in the case of Lough Boora (Ryan 1980) and Ferriter's Cove (Woodman *et al.* 1999). At Lough Boora, which was placed on the edge of a lake and where several hundred square metres was excavated, the site was protected by a thick layer of peat which was being removed as part of peat extraction. Besides scatters of artefacts and burnt bones and some traces of hearths, little evidence of artificially created structures was found. It is quite possible that very light wind breaks and shelters were erected, but no trace of them has survived.

At Ferriter's Cove, the original old ground surface and soil horizons were preserved under several metres of sand. An extensive area was opened, yet only three post-holes were found, while no dug hearths or large pits were noted, though occasional small groups of what might have been holes created by small stakes were also noted (Fig. 4.18). Some of these might have been left behind as a result of the erection of a light wind break, for example in the M–P/16 area, and it could be argued that a line of stakes ran across the southern area (F–M/22–24; Fig. 4.19). Others look as if they were associated with a series of activities around small open air fires, while some, such as the hearth at Feature 5, were patently outside. This could be viewed in the manner noted by Binford (1983, figs 89 and 91) at the Mask site, a Nunamiut Eskimo hunting stand, in which certain large or messy types of debris had been tossed outwards by those close to the fire. In this case a prevailing south-westerly wind had also blown quantities of charcoal from the fire itself. Many other enigmatic features were recovered from the site, including small shell heaps or mounds and occasion little piles of burnt hazel nutshells. There was also a series of small platforms up to 1 metre across. These were made of stones packed together and set into the underlying gravel surface. Nothing was found on top of them. There was no trace of burning on them; therefore they were not the bases of fire places. One must conclude that, if this site had lain under a few centimetres of topsoil, then virtually every one of the features listed above would have been obliterated.

Even where ploughing has taken place, however, traces of settlement sites may occasionally be recovered. The Toome By-pass sites (Dunlop and Woodman 2015) are one of the few excavations which have revealed extensive, though still partial, traces of settlement. An excavation in advance of a road scheme ran along a large drumlin which overlooked an extensive area of boggy land that ran off towards the edge of the present day Lough Neagh (Pl. XV). The area exposed was 350 × 50 m (Fig. 4.20). Obviously this area had been cultivated in the past and, aside from the northern edge, the limits of the area where excavations were required did not permit examination of the more low lying waterlogged organic deposits below the boggy surface. Therefore, not surprisingly, on the drumlin itself a number of the archaeological features had been partially truncated. However, the fortunate collection of material from the topsoil showed that many of the artefacts were in extremely fresh condition and had not been moved over considerable distances.

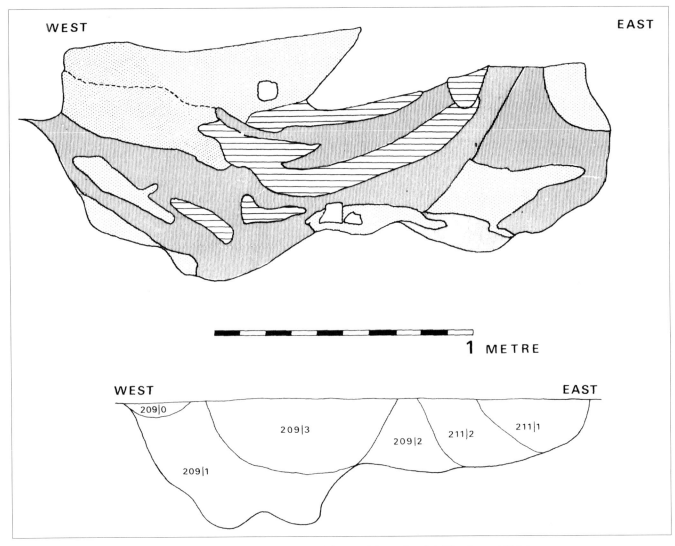

Fig. 4.17. Sections through Pits 209/211 at Mount Sandel (Woodman 1985a).

Earlier Mesolithic material is sparse. This may be because, at 9000 cal BP and earlier, the lough level would have been significantly lower and, as at the Mitchell (1955) site on the other side of the Bann settlement, it would have been concentrated closer to the then lough shore. In contrast, during the Later Mesolithic, especially at or after 7000 cal BP, when the lough level was much higher, the drumlin itself would have become a prime location for settlement. In this case, there is a significant scatter of Later Mesolithic artefacts and possible related pits and post-holes. While in the southern area there were very small scatters of Later Mesolithic material associated with Features 2 and 4, one of which produced a Later Mesolithic radiocarbon date, the main concentration lay in the northern area of the site. In particular, one area, 60 × 40 m (Fig. 4.21) across this part of the site, that sloped up from the surrounding bogs to the high point of the drumlin, contained the most artefacts.

Four features or complexes were noted in this area. Upslope, on a flatter terrace there was a major concentration of artefacts in an area 20 × 20 m. It was dominated by Features 3, 5 and 7.

The area was dominated by F5 (Fig. 4.22), a large, almost rectangular structure, 6 × 4 m defined by a trench up to 350 mm in depth and with a clay floor inside. This feature produced a series of radiocarbon dates (Table 4.2).

As can be seen from Table 4.2 the dates from Feature 5 range in age from 11,243–10,921 cal BP (Beta 228742, 9720±50 BP) to 4086–3857 cal BP (Beta 206328, 3640±40 BP). Two samples, one of Later Mesolithic date and one that is slightly later, came from the basal sediments in the trenches, Context 694. The area around the structure, the topsoil and the excavated *in situ* contexts also contained the largest concentration of Later Mesolithic material found during excavations on this drumlin prior to the building of the Toome Bypass.

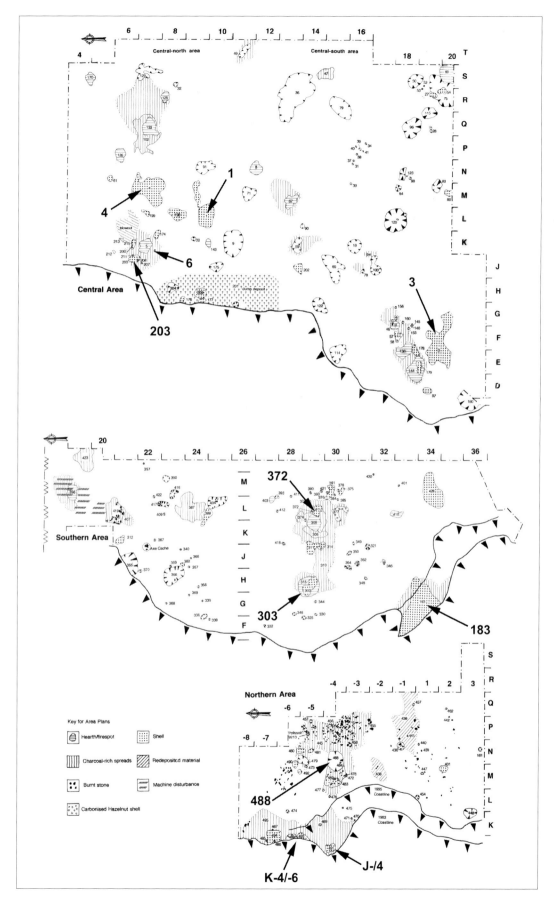

Fig. 4.18. Simplified plan of features from excavations at Ferriter's Cove, Co. Kerry (Woodman et al. 1999). Emphasis placed on features with large numbers of shells.

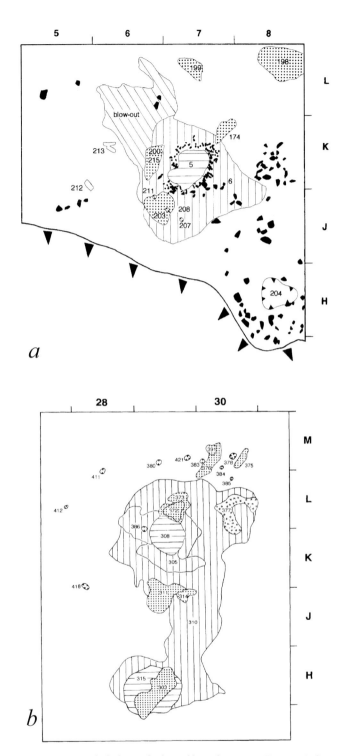

a

b

Fig. 4.19. Detailed plans of selected hearth areas at Ferriter's Cove
a) Feature 5 b) centred on hearths F308 & F315 (Woodman 1985a).

Fig. 4.20. (right) Overall plan of excavations at Toome Bypass,
Co. Antrim, showing the location of various feature complexes
(Dunlop and Woodman 2015).

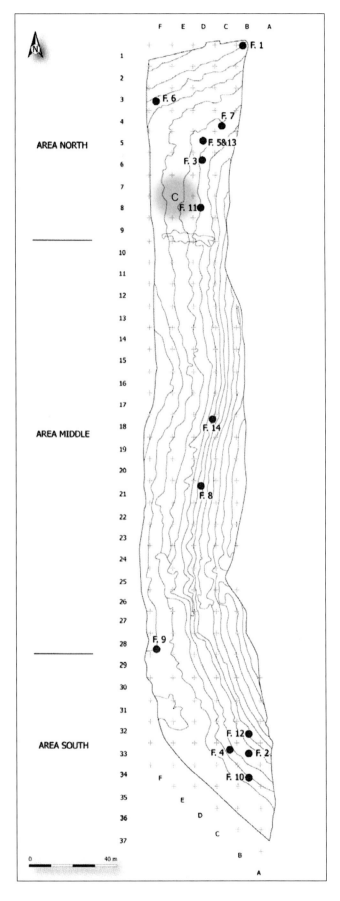

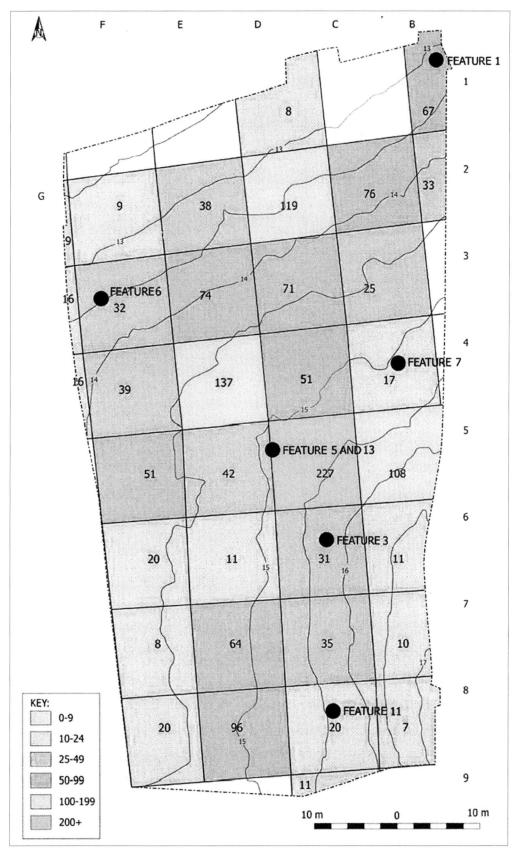

Fig. 4.21. General plan of northern area of Toome Bypass excavations (Dunlop and Woodman 2015).

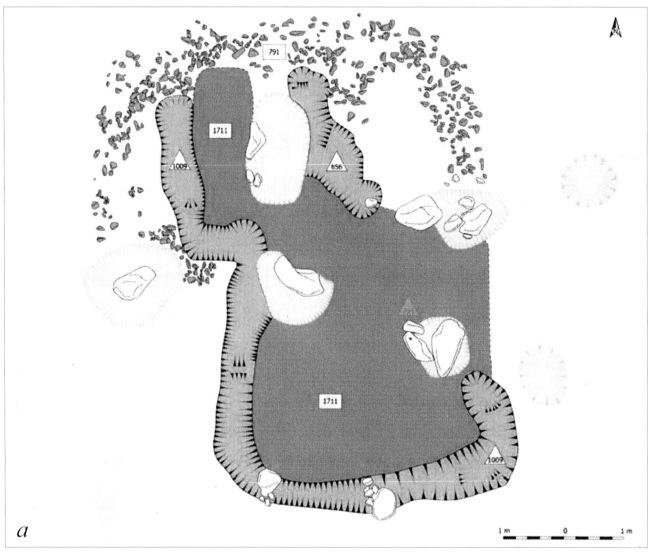

a

b

Fig. 4.22. a) Plan of Features 5, b) Feature 5 area at the end of excavation at Toome Bypass (Dunlop and Woodman 2015).

Table 4.2. Radiocarbon dates from the Toome Bypass excavations.

Context	Material	Lab. ref.	Determination BP	Date cal BP
Feature 5				
694	Charcoal	Beta 228741	5000±40	5893–5625
694	Hazel nut	Beta 206327	6110±40	7158–6871
855	Charcoal	Beta 219472	3880±40	4420–4159
1010	Charcoal	Beta 228742	9720±50	11,243–10,830
1010	Grain charred	Beta 206328	3640±40	4085–3857
Feature 6				
949	Charcoal	Beta 219462	5880±40	6795–6560
1030	Charcoal	Beta 219464	5670±90	6657–6300
Feature 7				
663	Charcoal	Beta 219466	5770±70	6728–6412

How does one interpret this structure? Is it possible that it is of Later Mesolithic date? First one should note that the locality of Feature 5 contained the largest concentration of artefacts from the excavation both from the topsoil and *in situ* contexts. This ranged in date from mostly, if not overwhelmingly, Later Mesolithic through to the Early Bronze Age. The obviously very early date that just post-dates the Younger Dryas could be seen to be anomalous. Both that and the Early Bronze Age date (Beta 219472) came from context 1010, overlying C694 which lay at the base of the main Trench (context 1009). The other Bronze Age date came from the upper level of a narrow, shallower trench (context 856). It might be tempting, on the basis of Beta 228741, to see the structure as belonging to the transition from Mesolithic to the Neolithic but is the fact that it was obtained from wood charcoal, i.e., a date based on old wood, sufficient to place it in the Early Neolithic?

Unfortunately, virtually all the artefacts were recovered from contexts that were late in the sequence, notably contexts 1010 and 855, but one remarkable aspect of the assemblage was that so much of the Later Mesolithic material was in a relatively fresh condition. Given its location on an island close to the edge of Lough Neagh and the almost complete absence of lithic artefacts of Neolithic date as well as of pottery, the balance of probability still favours that this structure dates to the Later Mesolithic.

Other concentrations of Mesolithic activity were also present at the site. The most noticeable is that of Features 7 A and B (Fig. 4.24), a series of small pits and post-holes that cover an area 20 × 20 m. It could be suggested that in the northern area (7A) a series of larger pits almost delineates a rectangular area while the more prolific smaller pits of differing size could be suggested to form a pattern that is "open to interpretation". Relatively few artefacts were recovered from this area.

In contrast, slightly further up slope in a less protected location, there was a further, smaller concentration of Later Mesolithic material (Concentration C; Fig. 4.20). Here no relevant archaeological features survived and the of focus of settlement was only recovered from the topsoil material.

Finally, down slope there were traces of another enigmatic group of trenches, pits and post- holes (Feature 6; Fig. 4.23) which contained two parallel trenches or slots (C207 and C1029) as well as 20 pits and stake-holes. Some of the latter were quite narrow and could exceed 200 mm in depth. Between the two slots, which were 5 m or more in length and relatively shallow, was a circular shallow pit (C 325) which contained quantities of charcoal. Again, while some material was recovered from the topsoil, few *in situ* artefacts were recovered. These included a tanged Butt Trimmed Form as well as two possible Blade points/Bar forms. The manner in which some locations could be re-used can be seen in the small but residual scatter of often weathered blades that would seem to be typical of the Earlier Mesolithic.

It was noticeable that the thin scatter of "Early" Mesolithic material from these excavations, which would date to a time when the Lough level was lower, tend to be found on the lower fringes of the drumlin closer to the present day marshy land which surrounds it.

There is one further site of a different character which may also earlier in date than the Later Mesolithic and which also lies on the edge of the lowlying marshes. This is Site 1, a stone jetty or platform whose significance in terms of its associated lithic assemblage will be discussed below in Chapter 8.

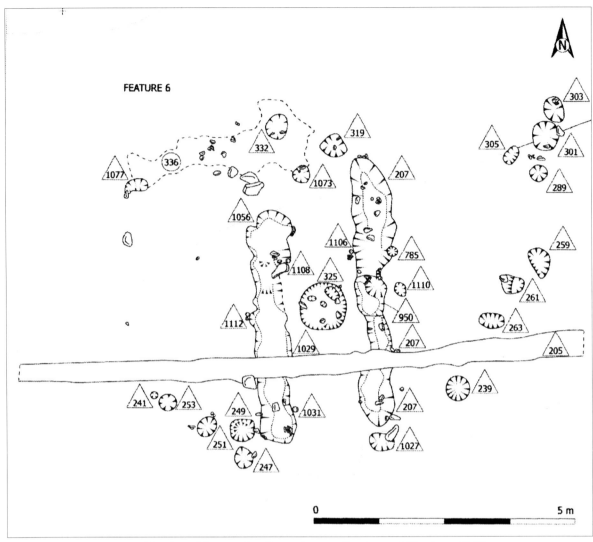

FEATURE 6

Fig. 4.23. Plan of Feature 6 at Toome Bypass (Dunlop and Woodman 2015).

The lessons that can be learnt from the Toome site include the fact that:

1. Topsoil material can make an important contribution and, in some instances, may be the only indication that settlement had taken place at a particular location.
2. Later Mesolithic material, as in areas such as around Toome, may be highly curated and so will not necessarily be discarded in quantities at any settlement location.
3. The interpretation of post-holes and stake-holes from this site raises many problems. Individual small features that might have retained posts vary in size and depth and one must wonder whether they may have been put in place for varying purposes. There is always the temptation to try to invent dwellings but perhaps we should consider whether, besides some that were associated with huts, we are recording evidence of other types of structures that were used for storage, drying meat or fish or other purposes.

Stake-holes and post-holes have been found on several other Mesolithic sites. In most cases, however, they do not form a coherent pattern or, more usually, there are not enough found to form a judgement. This can simply be because there was an insufficient area opened, as at Sutton (Mitchell 1956a), Bay Farm (Woodman and Johnston 1996) and Baylet (Milner and Woodman 2007). In other cases, such as at Mitchell's (1955) site at Toome, there may have been little else than an open fire present.

Perhaps, as noted earlier, one of the most remarkable aspects of the archaeological work carried out in the late 1990s and much of the 2000s is the relatively lack of traces for Mesolithic sites that have been recovered. Some of the reasons for this paucity will be discussed below. While the recovery of Mesolithic artefacts has been relatively rare, the number of sites producing pits, post-holes or hearths of Mesolithic date are exceptionally uncommon. The evidence when it occurs, in most instances, is scant. It may include irregular Mesolithic

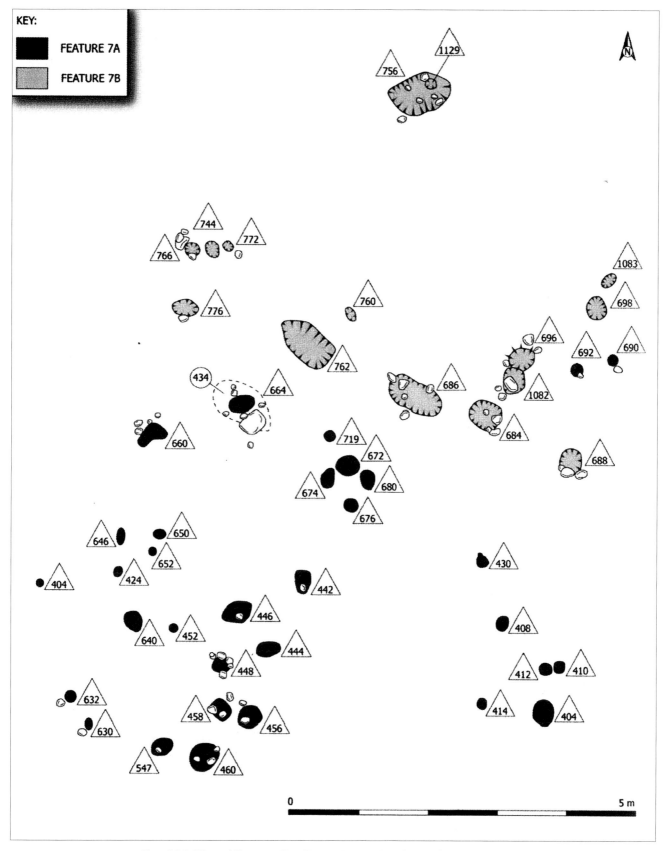

Fig. 4.24. Plan of Features 7 at Toome Bypass (Dunlop and Woodman 2015).

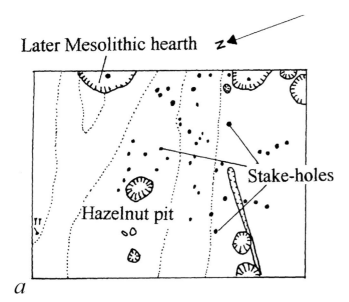

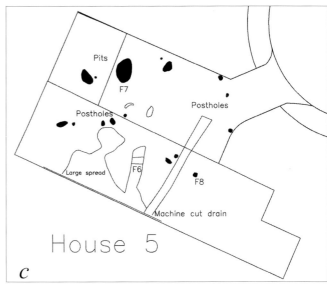

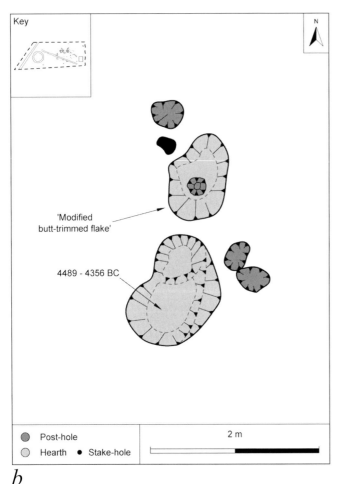

Fig. 4.25. Site plans of areas of Mesolithic activity at a) Linford, Co. Antrim (Moore 1999), b) hearth area at Cakestown Glebe, Co. Meath (by permission of IAC and NRA; prepared by Hugh Kavanagh), c) Possible Mesolithic features at Kilcorby, Co. Cavan (by permission of Farrimondmacmanus Ltd).

pits, such as that which has produced a Mesolithic radiocarbon date of at Curraghprevin (O'Neill 2013; Beta 201071, charcoal, 7320±60 BP, 8200–7990 cal BP). Three associated post-holes of possible similar age were also found. Pits were also found at Cakestown Glebe, Co. Meath (Fig. 4.25b). In total, however, out of approximately 2000 licenses issued for NRA excavations (Rónán Swan pers. comm.), while a number of artefacts have been recovered, few sites have uncovered any structural traces that could be presumed to be associated with huts. Other sites of importance found during the NRA excavations have been found, such as Clowanstown, which will be discussed later.

One potential hut at Kilcorby, Co. Cavan (*Excavations.ie* 2005) (Fig. 4.25c) which might have been Later Mesolithic in date, was found in the footprint of a new house during the building of an estate. Several other pits which might possibly be of Mesolithic date were also recovered elsewhere on the estate that was placed close to the Woodford River. But only one artefact that might be associated with the Later Mesolithic, a Butt Trimmed Form, was reported to have been recovered.

The problem of identifying what might be Mesolithic in age can best be seen in Co. Antrim at Ballydown, where traces of both Mesolithic and Neolithic phases of activities were uncovered. Here Moore felt that a series of post-holes in this intensively occupied site were Mesolithic. A scatter of small stake-holes was also found at altitude at Linford (Fig. 4.25a). Perhaps one of the most remarkable sites was found during the expansion of a container park at the Port of Larne (Pl. XVI c–d; McConway in prep.). Here, traces of Mesolithic activity were uncovered as several metres of Mid-Holocene storm beach shingle were being removed. The remnants of chipping floors, scatters of artefacts and pits were recovered in association with one particular layer (C5012). This surface seems to have been reused for a period of over

1000 years, most notably from between 9000 and 8000 cal BP. It contained, besides one very distinct chipping floor (CF1) and discarded by-products from tool production and a few retouched tools, a plethora of irregular pits and hollows, some of which contained fish bones. Is this a settlement or an industrial site? Excavations revealed that an area over 30 m across had survived and appeared to lie across the eroded surface of a ridge of glacial deposits that had been buried by rising sea levels. While, as will be shown in Chapters 8 and 9, the site has made a very important contribution to our understanding of the chronology of the Irish Mesolithic as well as the exploitation of the sea at that time, it is difficult to see how any traces of dwellings might have been identified. One might be tempted to draw parallels with structures such as those investigated by Von Rust (1972) at Poggenwisch or Borneck in the Hamburg area of Germany. At those sites large stones were collected to create the base of structures, while at the Port of Larne, boulders would have to be removed. However, as will be seen below, there is evidence that artificial platforms were created during the Mesolithic.

In returning to the question of trying to identify dwellings, the lesser known more westerly area at Mount Sandel provides good examples of activity areas where dwellings were not present. This includes small runs of post-holes, pits and chipping floors. As will be discussed in Chapter 11, one of the major challenges for the future is to find ways to interrogate settlement sites, but this will require awareness of the issues during the excavations rather than relying on post-excavation analysis. The ethnographic evidence suggests that, not surprisingly, human activity in and near their dwellings is and was much more complex than we would wish.

Of course, there are always going to be sites that can only be noted in a short interval of time when some development, building or even bog cutting is taking place. Examples include what may have been a hut that was discovered while the ground was being prepared for the construction of a garage in Derrinraw td, Co. Armagh (Declan Hurl, unpublished report submitted to Historic Monuments NIEA). Besides a small scatter of what could be Later Mesolithic blades and a large stone implement, the family recalls observing a circular structure, perhaps up to 3 m across which was delineated by a series of small stakes. In the sides of the trenches the stakes could be seen extending for up to 300 mm down through a sand layer. This site was located on a slope overlooking the floodplain of the Upper Bann. It lay at a narrow point and that was close to its exit into Lough Neagh. A somewhat similar example may have been observed during peat cutting near Finnea Village in Co. Westmeath (Maghee letters on file in NMI). Here again stakes and traces of what may have been fireplaces were noted. What is important about both these sites was that they were found in the former case by the land owners while in the latter it was a local amateur.

Other structures on habitation sites

As was noted earlier, at the Toome Bypass site many of the post-holes could be interpreted as parts of other types of facilities rather than dwelling

Examples that illustrate these points are three linear alignments of posts that may date to the Mesolithic. Excavations at Eglinton, Co. Derry (Northern Archaeological Consultancy, unpublished report prepared 2010), overlooking the Foyle estuary and adjacent to the Muff River, produced a site that reflects some of the problems just referred to (Fig. 4.26a). Traces of prehistoric settlement producing evidence for Neolithic and Bronze Age activity were found during an extensive excavation. One area (Area 7), however, produced two clusters of small stake-holes which were often less than 100 mm in depth and diameter. They are most likely to represent windbreaks rather than small huts. One radiocarbon date was obtained from each complex (Beta 230119, charcoal, 5690±40 BP, 6629–6400 cal BP and Beta 230121, charcoal, 5360±40 BP, 6278–6004 cal BP). What appeared to be a linear row of stake-holes representing perhaps a 9 m long fence, abutted onto the area where the stake-holes were found. None of these stake-holes, or the area in general, has produced any artefacts. The existence of a fence of Mesolithic age may seem improbable, though the lengths of "fences" that we would regard as fish weirs, for example that at Spenser Dock in Dublin Docklands, suggests otherwise. Indeed, a similar, though shorter, alignment was uncovered from below the chipping floors at Bay Farm (Woodman and Johnson 1996; Fig. 4.27). A further possible instance of a fence are the alignments of post-holes recovered at Glendhu (Fig. 4.26b), overlooking the shores of Belfast Lough (Woodman 1985b). Here a 10 m stretch of post-holes was recovered, some of which were paired. Some of these appeared to pre-date a phase of very late Mesolithic settlement that was associated with a small oyster and cockle shell midden. A date obtained from the shell midden (Beta 148672, shell, 5670±70 BP) when calibrated, and making allowance of 400 years for the marine effect, was 6278–5882 cal BP These post-holes were rather more substantial than those at Bay Farm.

There is one recent suggestion that may require that we look more carefully at our settlement sites. Hawkes (2014) has recently pointed out that there are a number of sites where an argument could be made for heated and roasted stones being of Mesolithic date. Profusions of burnt stones occur on many Mesolithic sites. Ferriter's Cove (Woodman *et al.* 1999) is a good example of a site where scatters of burnt stones can be found. Occasional Mesolithic artefacts have turned up in burnt mounds or, as at Liscahane, Co. Cork, have an associated Mesolithic date (i.e. OxA 2204, charcoal, 6870±90 BP, 7851–7584 cal BP).

As was raised by Woodman and Anderson (1990, 384–6), the probability that curated technologies, where often relatively limited numbers of diagnostic artefacts were discarded where

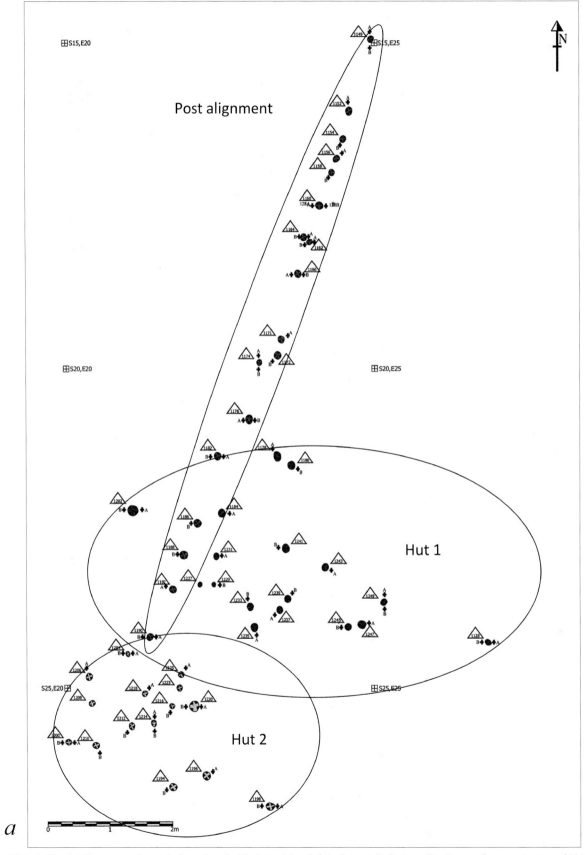

Fig. 4.26. a) Alignment of post-holes of probable later Mesolithic date at Eglinton, Co. Derry (by permission of NAC).

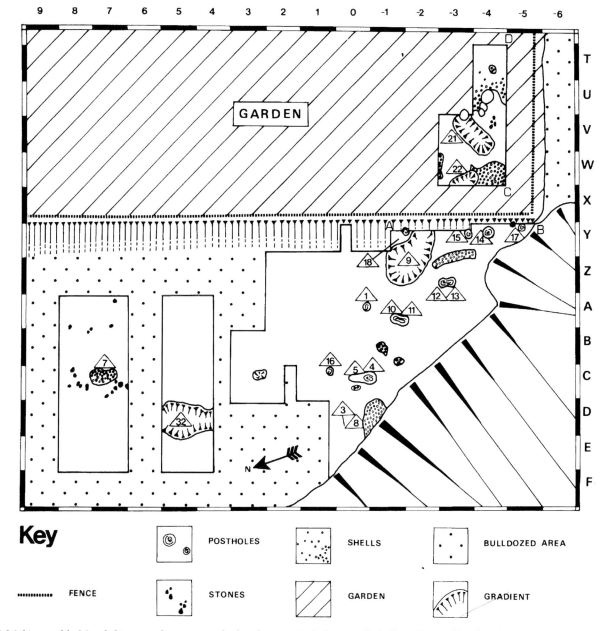

Fig. 4.26. b) possible Mesolithic post alignment and other features including small shell midden at Glendhu, Co. Down (Woodman 1985b).

they had been used, creates a challenge as often no diagnostic artefacts will be recovered. This happened at locations like Mitchelstowndown where a brushwood platform produced a date of 7563–7431 cal BP (GRN 14902, wood, 6585±30 BP), but where no artefacts were recovered. (Woodman and Anderson 1990).

Caves

In many parts of Europe, where easily identifiable sites can be hard to find, there is an assumption that traces of hunter-gatherer settlement, or other activities, will be found in caves

or shell middens. The excavation of caves has been the default means of exploring parts of prehistory. Obviously this approach has produced a wealth of information from the Mesolithic in countries where caves are numerous, such as France and parts of Belgium.

In parts of both Britain and Ireland there are numerous caves but, in contrast with Britain, relatively little contribution to our knowledge of the Mesolithic has been made through the investigation of Irish caves. There are several reasons for this. Until recently, much research on Irish caves was focused more on the recovery of Pleistocene animal remains. These were often recovered deep in cave systems, rather than in the

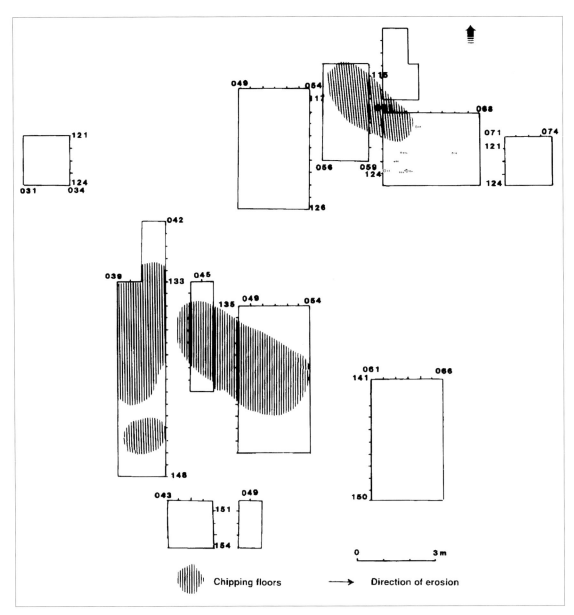

Fig. 4.27. a) Plan of excavations at Bay Farm, Co. Antrim showing the position of chipping floors (Woodman and Johnson 1996).

entrance areas where human settlement is more likely to have taken place. A number of the caves explored are in relatively low-lying areas and not in suitable locations, or else are narrow fissures which would not be used for settlement. Thus while some caves, such as Portbraddan (Pl. XVII a–b), look like the popular image of caves, others are more like Killuragh (Pl. XVII c–d). The absence of Mesolithic material of any form from the Keshcorran and Knockmore Caves, which are placed slightly higher, is striking. Similarly, suitable caves in the southern part of Ireland, for example, Kilgreany (Dowd 2002) and Ballinamintra (Woodman *et al.* 1997) have a surprising lack of evidence of use during the Mesolithic period.

There are, therefore, few certain signs of Mesolithic settlement within caves (see Dowd 2015; Woodman forthcoming

d). In fact there are approximately 10 caves that have produced artefacts that could be Mesolithic in date. In some cases, such as Brothers Cave in Waterford, a potential Early Mesolithic flake axe is so rolled and degraded it is likely to have washed into the cave. Similarly, two of the tanged Butt Trimmed Forms from the Ballintoy caves (Potter's Cave and Boat Cave), are stratified above layers containing material from the last two millennia and are likely to have been deposited within the Caves at a more recent date. In total, only five caves have produced artefacts that could be of Mesolithic date and which did not find their way into the cave at a later time. These sites contain a limited number of blades that might be Early or Later Mesolithic. In the case of the Earlier Mesolithic, the two blades from Carrigagour in Cork and the blade core from Brothers

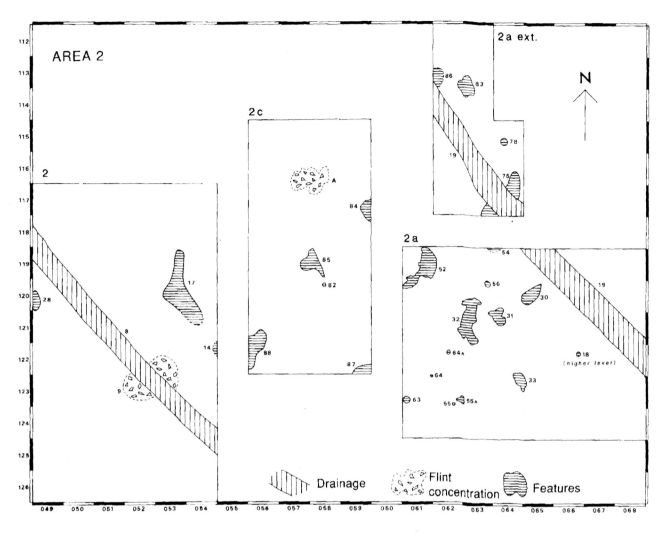

Fig. 4.27. b) Plan of excavations at Bay Farm, Co. Antrim showing the position of post-holes (Woodman and Johnson 1996).

Cave in Waterford could belong to that period. One blade from the Neolithic burial cave at Annagh, Co. Limerick might also be Early Mesolithic in date. In this instance the presence of a bear bone dated to the Mesolithic can be interpreted as either evidence of a Mesolithic presence or the placing of a bear bone in the cave at the same time as the Neolithic burials (see below, Chapter 10). A case could also be made for a Later Mesolithic date for the two large blades fragments from Foley Cave in Cork (Gwynn *et al.* 1942) and possibly the two chert blades from Knockninny in Fermanagh (Woodman forthcoming d).

There are other caves that could have been used during the Mesolithic. The most obvious of these must be Portbraddan Cave on the north coast of Co. Antrim (May 1943). In this instance, an extensive layer of beach shingle, presumably from the highest strandlines of the "Littorina Transgression", lay within the cave that lies at a slightly higher level than most of the north Antrim caves. Besides pig bones, which have not survived or are no longer available, small caches of limpet

shells and occasional crude blades were recovered from within the beach shingle. These might be of Mesolithic age.

In spite of the large number of bones that patently have a Holocene date, Irish caves contain little clear evidence of the discard or butchering of faunal remains that could be considered a product of Mesolithic settlement. Obviously the presence of animal remains in caves which date to the earlier part of the Holocene present a conundrum (Woodman *et al.* 1997). The bear bones may be remnants of animals that died in the caves during hibernation, but, as will be discussed below, there is little evidence for this. Equally, it is more difficult to assess the significance of the metapodial of the wild pig from Kilgreany Cave, which has been dated to 9530–9034 cal BP (OxA 4240, bone, 8340±110 BP), This site has produced no material culture that could, unequivocally, be dated to the Mesolithic. It is, therefore, uncertain whether it was part of the remnants of a creature left behind after human use of the cave or represents something that was dragged in by a bear or wolf.

Even at Killuragh Cave, which has produced both Mesolithic microliths and human remains of Mesolithic date, is still a conundrum (see Woodman http://heritagecouncil.ie/ unpublished_excavations/section3.html). This cave appears to be a group of small conjoined fissures that contained, in a disturbed context, a range of both human bones and artefacts of Early Mesolithic to Middle Bronze Age date, along with a faunal assemblage that seems to be mainly of Bronze Age date. There are very limited numbers of human bones from at least four individuals of Mesolithic date. These are three early dates and two that date to the latest part of the Mesolithic. They range from 9084–8650 cal BP (GrA 2434, bone, 8030±60 BP) to 6396–6124 cal BP (OxA 6749, bone, 5455±50 BP). Does this material derive from settlement or ritual activity associated with the cave *per se*, or from the platform that lay outside its entrance?

Shell middens

The other major source of material which is often associated with the Mesolithic period is shell middens. There are probably close to 500 shell middens known in Ireland. There is, unfortunately, a tendency to associate shell middens with the Mesolithic and the alliteration of "Mesolithic middens" is fatally attractive. A shell midden site is defined as one where the accumulation of shells forms the major attribute of the site. This does not, of course, imply that the sites have to be Mesolithic in date. In reality, most of the very large middens found in Ireland are much later. The midden at Culeenamore in Sligo which, in places, approaches 3 m in thickness, (Burenhult 1984, 326–46) began in the Neolithic and continued through to the Iron Age, while those in Cork Harbour usually begin in the Iron Age and continue through into the medieval period (Milner and Woodman 2007). Unfortunately, some of the particularly large middens, such as those recorded by Harte (1866) in Lough Swilly, were already removed by the 1860s but, based on evidence from other sites, such as those referred to above, it seems likely that the very large middens are of a more recent date. In many instances shell middens also lie within rather than under sand dune systems, which we now recognise developed later in the Holocene, while the frequent presence of domesticate species clearly indicates that they post-date the Mesolithic (Knowles 1901; Brunicardi 1914).

The image of "Mesolithic middens", based on Danish examples, is that they are massive, however, while they can stretch for considerable distances, such as the Børnsholm midden (Andersen and Johnson 1990) can be quite thin. Irish middens of an early date are rarely very long and few exceed 1 m in thickness. Often, as in the case of Ertebølle itself (Andersen and Johansen 1986), they can be thrown up against a bank and so it is unusual for them to stand high in the landscape. The Cnoc Sligeach midden in Oronsay is a contrast as it seems to have been a mound, and even within the Obanian group of middens it is an exception (Wickham-Jones 2007, 87) as many

are much thinner. Several of the classic Obanian middens, such as those around Oban, were found in caves, as are the Asturian middens in northern Spain. In reality, the Muge middens of Portugal (Rolão and Roksandic 2007), which are amongst the largest and deepest shell middens to be found along the Atlantic seaboard, are the exception rather than the rule.

The most obvious Irish Mesolithic examples are the three shell middens from Rockmarshall (Mitchell 1947; 1949a), the two, one each from sites II and V, at Dalkey (Liversage 1968) and that at Sutton (Mitchell 1956a; 1972a). One of the Rockmarshall middens, site III, was about 25 m in length, 10 m in width and up to 70 cm thick (Fig. 4.28a). The Sutton midden was much larger, though still of the same approximate thickness. Its length was roughly 100 m and originally it may have been approaching 40 m in width. Its seaward edge was eroded at the time of the maximum Holocene transgression (Fig. 4.28b). The two Dalkey middens were much smaller. They were only partially excavated but would seem to have been 5–10 m across and originally been 50 cm thick.

In Lough Swilly, especially in the immediate vicinity of Inch Island, a number of large middens had existed. It is of interest that the *Ordnance Survey Memoirs* (Day and McWilliams 1997, 147) refer to the fact that the best Irish oysters come from dredging in the Farland Channel, i.e., from Ballymoney td up past Inch Island. The remains of a midden, which lies in the townland of Ballymoney, is apparent from the beach running along the cliff face as well as in test pits in the field. This showed that the midden ranged for a distance approaching 150 m (Pl. XVIIIa) though, from what can be seen along the cliff edge. It contained different types of shells at different points. Radiocarbon dates, although based on shells, suggest, after making an allowance of 400 years for the marine effect,

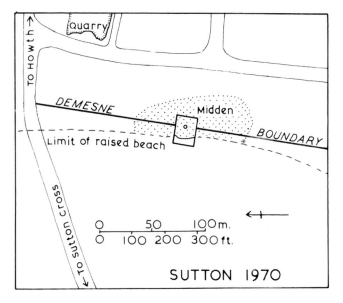

Fig. 4.28. a) Plan of shell midden at Sutton, Co. Dublin (after Mitchell 1972a).

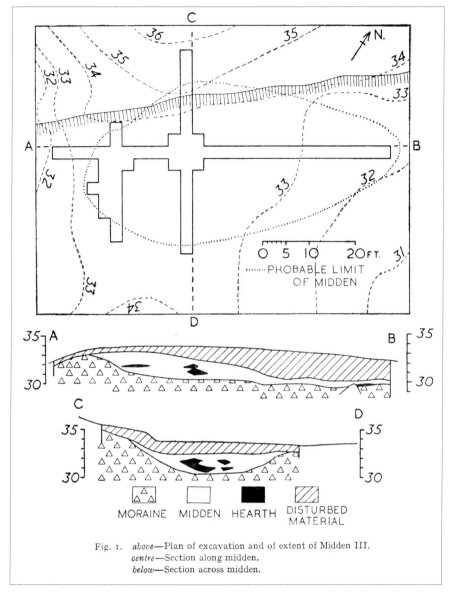

Fig. 1. *above*—Plan of excavation and of extent of Midden III.
centre—Section along midden.
below—Section across midden.

Fig. 4.28. b) Plan and section of shell midden at Rockmarshall, Co. Louth (after Mitchell 1949a).

that the midden began in the latest part of the Mesolithic (Beta 161646, shell, 5760±80 BP, 6746–6358 cal BP) and continued to form well into the Neolithic (Beta 151925, shell, 5100±70 BP, 5991–5662 cal BP).

Excavations at Baylet (Pl. XVIIIb) on Inch Island, on the surviving portion of a very large midden, revealed a long and complex history (Milner and Woodman 2007). This can be seen in how the landscape changed over a period of several thousand years (Figs 4.29–4.30). Unfortunately, in this case, based on Harte's (1867) observations, it was a midden that was originally "more than 3ft [0.9 m] thick and up to 100 yards [91.4 m] long". Even in his time it had been largely removed. Settlement at this site began with Late Mesolithic activity, which was identified underneath the midden whose

Mesolithic component was little more than 300 mm thick. A date based on a pig (*Sus scrofa ferus*) phalange showed that the midden had begun to accumulate on top of a ridge which would have overlooked the shore relatively early in the Later Mesolithic (GrA 21490, bone, 6450±50 BP, 7436–7271 cal BP). The midden then continued to develop through the final part of the Mesolithic and may originally have had a Neolithic component on top, which was removed in the mid-19th century (Fig. 4.31). A second example, Baylet II, was discovered some metres behind the main midden. This had become buried in hill wash. Baylet II seems to have developed in the middle of the Neolithic Period.

Some Irish middens were either thrown up against low banks, for instance, Rockmarshall III. In the case of the Baylet

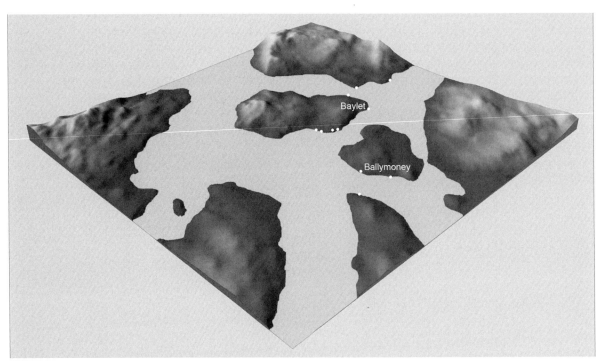

Fig. 4.29. Map of Lough Swilly area in Co. Donegal during the final stages of the Irish Mesolithic (prepared by Hugh Kavanagh and J. Fenwick).

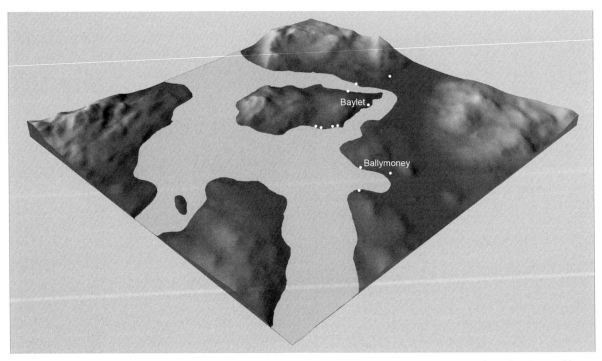

Fig. 4.30. Map of Lough Swilly showing present day sea level (prepared by Hugh Kavanagh and J. Fenwick).

midden (Fig. 4.31) the history was more complex, a midden had been created by being thrown up against a bank but the rising sea level eroded away the lower portion of the midden,. If nothing else, this shows how shell middens are usually not the creation of simple, single events but often have a much more complex history.

The other area where numerous midden sites exist is in Strangford Lough (McErlean 2003a). These middens are mostly undated. Mallory (pers. comm.) in his excavations at Rough Island suggested that the midden there is Neolithic in date. Milner and Woodman (2007) have shown that, on examination, many of the most impressive middens are later in date than the

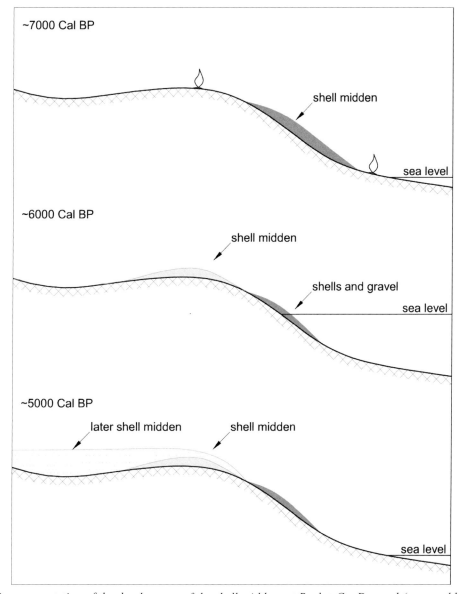

Fig. 4.31. Schematic representation of the development of the shell middens at Baylet, Co. Donegal (prepared by Hugh Kavanagh).

Mesolithic, indeed some are not even prehistoric. In Strangford, in spite of these caveats, some middens are known to date to the Later Mesolithic. One excavation, at Kilnatierney, Co. Down (Murray 2011), has produced pig bones of Mesolithic date (UB6835, bone, 5386±36 BP, 6286–6021 cal BP and on burnt bone UB6836, 5546±36 BP, 6403–6291 cal BP). At other sites such as the Temple midden (Woodman 1978a, 302) a Later Mesolithic assemblage appeared to be associated with the shell midden.

It is questionable as to whether the small mounds of shells found at Ferriter's Cove (Woodman *et al.* 1999) could be used to describe the site as a midden site. The largest mound was less than 3 m across. Similarly, the small mound of shells at Glendhu (Woodman 1985b) is insufficient to represent it as a midden site (see Fig. 4.26).

It is probable that along the west coast other shell middens will be discovered that date to the latest stages of the Mesolithic and earliest Neolithic, as in the case of the Lynchs' work at Fanore in Co. Clare (Woodman and Milner 2013).

Therefore, while the remains of perhaps up to 500 middens are known in Ireland perhaps fewer than ten can be shown to date to, or contain a component that dates to, the Mesolithic period. In part this is caused by the fact that most shell middens are placed close to the then shoreline and as the sea transgressed much of the coast at a late date, especially round the southern half of Ireland, pre-existing Mesolithic shell middens would have been eroded away or buried.

In summary, the Lough Swilly and Strangford Lough areas seem to be the only two regions where there is potential for a large number of shell middens of Mesolithic date to survive.

The information from the sites is limited in a number of ways. Often only a small proportion of the site was excavated and usually there was no sieving policy. The implications of the latter will be discussed in Chapter 10.

Other sites

THE BANN VALLEY DIATOMITE

With the very large quantities of Mesolithic artefacts that have been recovered from the shores of the Bann, particularly between Newferry and Portglenone, some traces of settlement would be expected. As this material has come from the flood plain of the river, the traces might be expected to be ephemeral, especially within the diatomite deposits which were created during winter floods. In many areas where the diatomite flats have been exploited, virtually no traces of settlement or artefacts have been recovered. In the case of Newferry Site 3 (Woodman 1977a) one large hearth, more than 600 mm across, was found. In this case the layer of charcoal was on top of a very well defined patch of sand which, in turn, preserved a small patch of soil that lay on the diatomite. Although no traces of a structure were associated with this hearth, the fact that a soil horizon existed suggests that it lay at a location that was more than a transitory muddy flat edging the River Bann.

It is of interest, therefore, that Movius (1936) also found a number of traces of hearths within the diatomite on the other side of the Bann at Newferry Site 1. He also discovered areas where the diatomite had been turned to a bluish colour, which led him to suggest that they were fire spots, i.e. places where fires had been lit but whose traces had vanished. He also found other slightly less ephemeral traces. These were located at the base of the diatomite and on the surface of layers of peat and would have been created at a point in time when the winter water levels of the Bann started to reach levels that caused the creation of the diatomite flats. He uncovered two enigmatic structures/features (Fig. 4.32); these were two deliberately created shallow, relatively well defined oval hollows. Pit A was 4.90 × 3.25 m while Pit B was 4.50 × 2.20 m. Both were cut into the underlying peat and seem to have cut through an ash spread that lay at the base of the diatomite. They were also cut at a time when diatomite had just begun to form. Both were filled with black ash that could be up to 400 mm thick. It seems likely that the hollows were used on several occasions. Four hearths could also be identified in Pit A. Both pits contained Later Mesolithic artefacts, usually blades, bar forms and Butt Trimmed Forms. They also contained quantities of burnt flint as well as numerous small, often badly decomposed, cobbles that were up to 150 mm in diameter. These were not pot boilers and while some of the quartzites could have come from the Dungiven area 30 km away, many of the cobbles would have to be brought to the site from the general area, even if that was only 100–200 m away. Although they were not worked in any way it is always possible that they could have been used as net sinkers.

In the case of Newferry Site 3 these peat deposits on the shore margins had been consolidated (Fig. 4.33). In comparison with Derragh (see below) the evidence from Zone 7 at Newferry Site 3 is less impressive, but there is no doubt that a significant number of stones were brought in and laid on the peat surface, presumably to help consolidate its surface. It is probable that these stones would have been brought from the edge of the flood plain which lay several hundred metres away. Thus, the creation of this layer, or floor, on top of the peat was not a simple casual act. Again hearths were created and in this case, unlike higher levels where flint artefacts were brought in as finished blanks, flint nodules were brought to the site and various implements were manufactured. This suggests that the visits may not have been totally transitory. It is just possible that, at the Newferry sites, there was a change from the basal layers, where some investment has taken place, to a different type of use of the area, as witnessed in the type of evidence found in the overlying diatomite. One can be certain that, if it was possible to excavate equivalent surviving deposits further north at Culbane and around Portglenone, similar types of evidence would be found.

A slightly different type of site was also found at the Toome By-Pass excavation. Here Feature 1 consisted of a layer of larger stones which was laid down to form either a pier or a platform jutting out into the water that may have formed part of a more extensive Lough Neagh. These waters would have, at least in part, surrounded the drumlin on which such extensive Mesolithic settlement had taken place.

Obviously, many of the Mesolithic sites cannot be placed in very specific categories. Is Ferriter's Cove either a transitory settlement or should one emphasis the industrial debris left behind? Again, many of those along the shores of Strangford Lough could be seen as settlement sites, middens or even industrial sites. There are of course many "special" Mesolithic sites which in some instances are more obvious than settlement sites. The recent excavations at the Port of Larne Container Park (McConway in prep.) also provided such an enigma.

INDUSTRIAL SITES

There is such a profusion of flint debris from a number of sites along the Co. Antrim coast that, even allowing for the fact that much of this material has been incorporated into beach deposits, there are still a number of sites that could be considered as industrial sites. Perhaps the most obvious example is at Bay Farm (Woodman and Johnson 1996; Pl. XVIa) where a series of small overlapping chipping floors was found. The site mostly contained by-products, such as cores, primary flakes and hammer stones, with only a few retouched tools (Fig. 4.34).Within an area of roughly 500 sq. m., that was only partially excavated, in excess of 25,000 artefacts were recovered, yet it only produced roughly 50 retouched tools. Similarly, the slight traces of fires, which seemed to

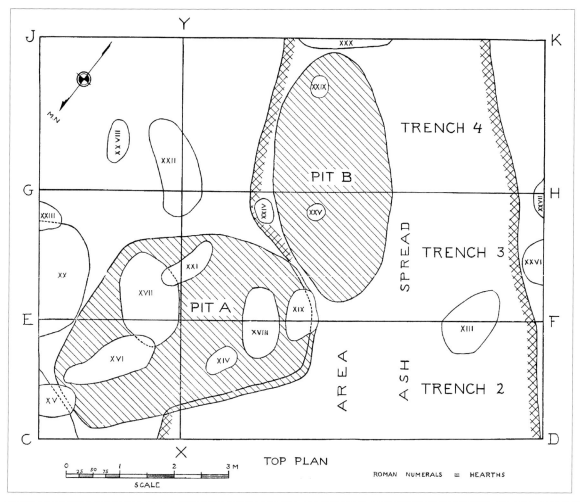

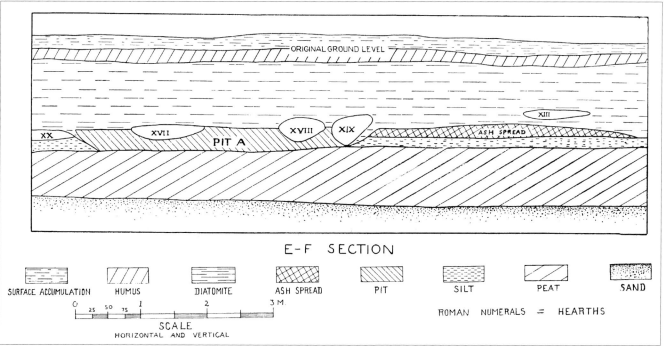

Fig. 4.32. Plan and sections of the Harvard excavation at Newferry (Site 1), Co. Derry (after Movius 1936).

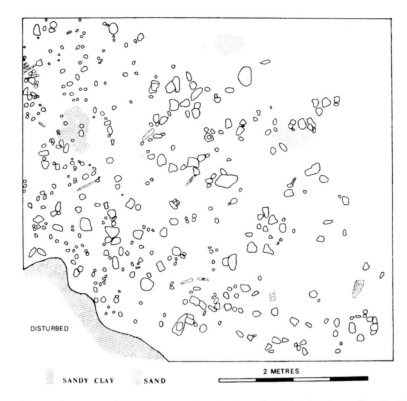

Fig. 4.33. Plan of area of stones embedded in peat, Zone 7, Trench J-K/6, Newferry (Site 3) (Woodman 1977a).

be more like dumps of hearth material, and the stake-holes, found especially in Trench 2a (*ibid.*, fig. 7), appear to be part of a long run of stakes rather than part of a house. It might be thought that areas like Bay Farm are the centre of a major nexus of industrial activity, but analysis of the assemblages (Johnson 1988; Woodman and Johnson 1996) suggests that, rather than being "industrial" zones they seem to consist of a series of small events in which each nodule worked may have only produced between five and ten useful flakes.

There are other chippings floors that dated to the Mesolithic and the most obvious concentration is those from Curran Point at Larne. Again, where they survive these are small chipping floors, usually less than 5 m across, which suggest short-term visits to the coast as part of visits for other purposes. Several have been recovered from within the storm shingle of the raised beach (Woodman 1978a, 63) and, more recently, during excavations as at the Port of Larne (Woodman, lithics report in McConway in prep.).

There are chipping floors and quarrying of other raw materials that might, at least in part, date to the Mesolithic. Some sites, such as Clonava, Co. Westmeath (Mitchell 1972b), are quite rich but as Little (2009) has pointed out it seems probable that much of the material has been quarried from the nearby Knocklyon Hill and then, after a degree of preliminary knapping, was brought to Clonava Island. In this instance the Clonava site retains a high proportion of useable tertiary blades and flakes, therefore it cannot be considered

as primarily an industrial site. It is probable that at Derragh Island, Co. Longford, Site A falls into the same category. In the case of the Monvoy quarry in Co. Waterford, which Kador (2009, 37–40) has claimed was used from the Mesolithic, the degree to which this exists as an extensively used source in the Mesolithic is not yet clear.

FIXED FACILITIES

The most significant examples of "fixed facilities" are those at Spenser Docks in Dublin Dockland, where a partially preserved complex of wattle fencing and basket fish traps was recovered from the edge of the Liffey estuary (McQuade and O'Donnell 2009). Their discovery was in a location where nothing of archaeological significance was expected to be recovered. They were found during the removal, by mechanical means, of extensive deposits of more recent date. This illustrates how little chance there is of recovering such sites. The remnants of this system were recovered from an area 60 m in length (Fig. 4.35). These were dated to around, or just after, 8000 cal BP. The four dates ranged from 8042–7861 to 7934–7714 cal BP (NZA 22112, wood ,7144±46 BP; NZA 22114, 6989±45 BP) . One point of interest that emerged from this site is that it is possible the choice of hazel round wood was based on the availability of deliberately coppiced hazel shrubs; however it has been suggested (Warren *et al.* 2013) that the choice of wood might have been more opportunistic.

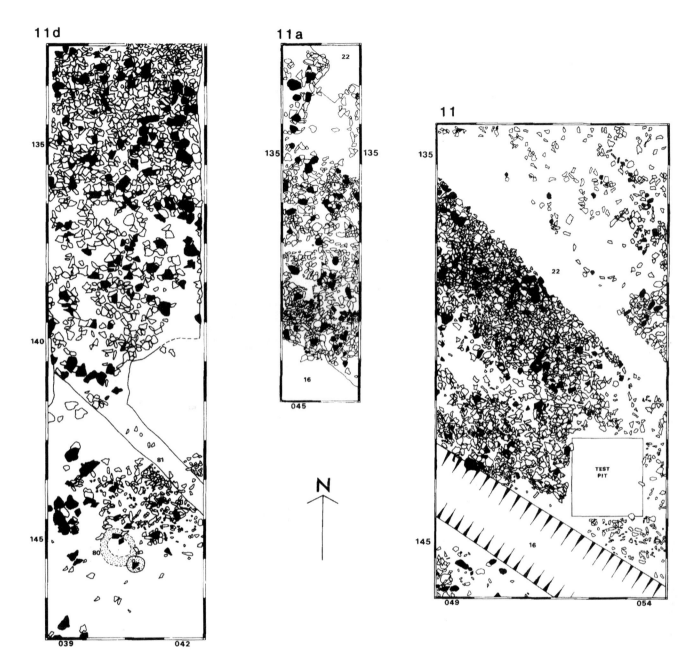

Fig. 4.34. Chipping floors at Bay Farm, Co. Antrim (Woodman and Johnson 1996). Aside from infilled (black) stones, all other material recorded is flint.

These are also amongst the oldest known fish traps in Western Europe. The Danish Mesolithic examples that Fischer (2007, table 5.2) has documented from 11 locations tend, with the exception of Kalø Vig, to date to after 8000 cal BP. This may be because, by 8000 cal BP, the relative sea levels were beginning to approach present day levels and the rate of sea level rise was decreasing. Therefore, the chance of inter-tidal structures being uncovered, when they were preserved only a few metres below present day levels, would be significantly increased. Similarly, these structures would be found within estuarine deposits that dated to the later half of the Mesolithic.

Another site of a somewhat similar character was found during excavations at an inland site at Clowanstown, Co. Meath (Mossop 2009a). This site lay in a boggy area which was investigated as part of the archaeology associated with the M3 motorway. Here four basket fish traps, as well as a series of substantial posts, were recovered along with a natural platform of sphagnum (moss) that had been consolidated with a layer of

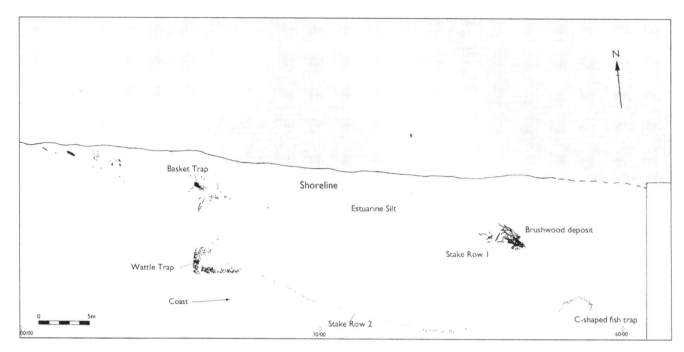

Fig. 4.35. Plan of fish traps found during excavations at Spenser Dock, Dublin Docklands (after McQuade and O'Donnell 2009).

burnt timbers (Fig. 4.36). The fish traps and posts appear to be radiocarbon dated from 7246–6961 to 6931–6677cal BP (Beta 231957, wood, 6190±50 BP; Beta 231948, wood, 5970±50 BP). They were found during road building in a boggy area that had developed on the location of a small lake that would have existed during the Mesolithic and appear to date to the Later Mesolithic. If we compare the size of the Clowanstown examples such as Basket 3 (Fig. 4.36b) with a reconstruction drawing of an Ertebølle fish trap (Fig. 4.36c) being made in Vedbaek in Zealand (Knudsen 1980), it seems likely that the Clowanstown fish traps may have been used in a different manner to those in the Liffey Estuary.

As noted earlier, the remains of many midland lakes that would have existed at an earlier date now lie buried under extensive peat deposits or clogged by shoreline fens that are often too deep or extensive for any chance discovery. It is therefore probable that many other examples of these types of sites were uncovered and went unrecognised. As noted (Woodman 2003) it is possible that a fish weir uncovered during quarrying adjacent to the shores of Lough Beg and recorded by David Liversage, was of Mesolithic date. A perhaps more fanciful suggestion is that some wood found in waterlogged deposits at the base of the Newferry sequence in Zone 9 (Woodman 1977a) could have been the washed out remains of a fish weir.

There are of course many fish traps recorded from round the coast of Ireland. Tidal foreshore traps were used to catch fish behind them in the tidal zone as the waters retreated from high tide. Many other fish traps have been documented, notably by

Went (1964). He recorded the existence of around 50 working or extant head weirs in the earlier part of the 20th century. In an overview of the traditions of salmon fishing, he also recorded that most of the head weirs were concentrated in the estuaries of the major rivers in the southern half of the Island (Went 1963, fig. 8). Of course, as noted earlier in Part I, as sea level stabilisation happened at a later date around the south coast the chances of recovering any fixed fish traps of Mesolithic age is even less. Within the last 20 years there have been extensive inter-tidal surveys in the Shannon/Fergus estuaries (O'Sullivan 2001) and Strangford Lough (McErlean and O'Sullivan 2002). The latter, very detailed survey, has documented numerous examples of both wooden and stone foreshore fish weirs. It would appear that the stone weirs tend to be later than the wooden ones. The stone weirs can be substantial structures, extending for more than 200 m in length. The foreshore tidal fish weirs in Strangford Lough have generally turned out to date to within the last 2000 years. Went (1964) also identified and listed numerous examples of fish traps associated with salmon fishing along a number of the major rivers, though noticeably not along the River Bann where most of the modern weirs are associated with catching eels. While the discussion on recent fish weirs may seem irrelevant, they do show, by their simplicity, that they could have existed at any point in prehistory.

PLATFORMS

As mentioned above, there is evidence of consolidation of a surface in the Irish Mesolithic: at Newferry Site 3 where

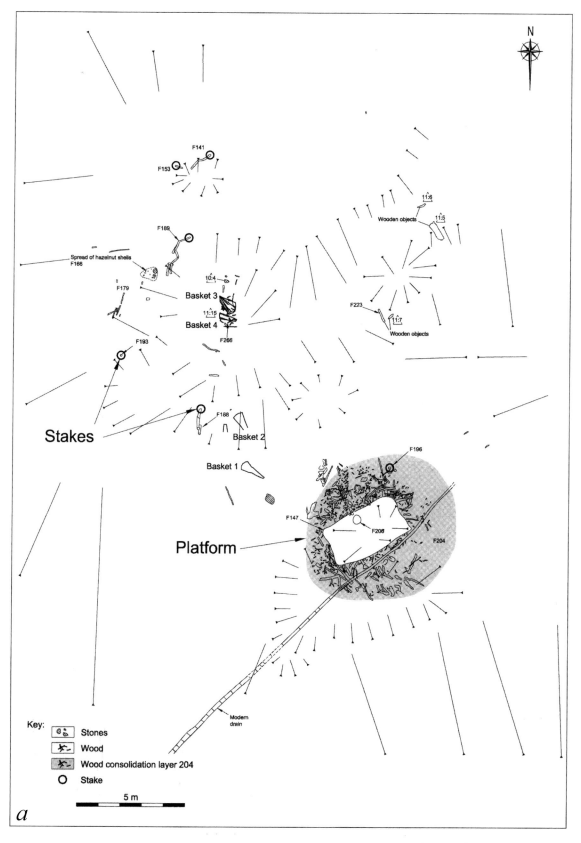

Fig. 4.36. a) Plan of the excavated area at Clowanstown, Co. Meath (after Knudsen 1980).

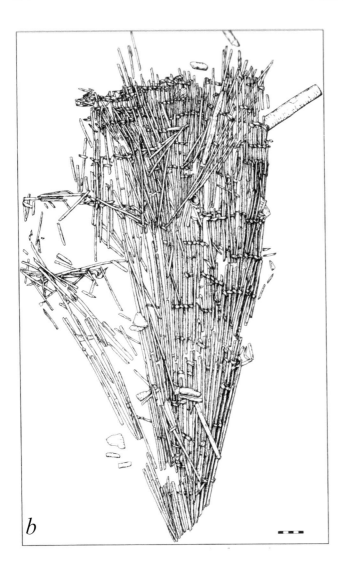

Fig. 4.36. b) detailed plan of a fish trap recovered during the excavation (after Mossop 2009), c) reconstruction of making a basket fish trap on the shores of Vedbaek Fjord (after Knudsen 1980).

the surface of the peat was consolidated through placing a large number of stones in Zone 7 (Woodman 1977a) while, at Belderrig (Warren 2009), a continuous layer of stones was laid down on top of a rich horizon containing Mesolithic occupation.

One possible, more substantial, timber structure, of human origin, was documented in the mid-1990s. This was found in the bank of the Dargle River, near Bray in Co. Wicklow during operations to widen the river course. Here, beneath several metres of deposits and resting on compacted glacio-fluvial gravels, 17 oak timbers arranged in two groups were recovered. A radiocarbon date was obtained from one timber (UB 4038, wood, 5642±46 BP, 6530–6335 cal BP). This may have been at a time when the relative sea level in the area was at its maximum height. Although there was always a slight doubt that this was an artificial creation, the fact that the evidence in the long standing debate at Star Carr has shifted in favour of human intervention in creating a platform at that site and growing evidence of worked timbers Conneller *et al.* (2012) suggest that the Bray example should receive serious consideration.

The platform found by Mitchell (1989) at Clynacartan on Valentia Island is rather more enigmatic. It has produced two dates. This was a stone platform where Mitchell noted several large slabs had to be pulled into place and the piece of oak found in the platform was dated to 10,372–9550 cal BP (I 14391, wood, 8910±150 BP), which has been sealed by peat which has been dated to 7660–7262 cal BP (I 14082, peat, 6560±120 BP. At the moment it is unclear why, on top of phragmites peat, a platform would be created at this particular location.

These types of sites of Mesolithic date are rarely found elsewhere. In some instances, such as in Lough Gara, Later Mesolithic artefacts have been found on deliberately created shoreline platforms and this suggests that they may be of Mesolithic date (Fredengren 2002, 131–7). Two other sites can be certainly associated with the Mesolithic First, the Discovery Programme excavations of a platform at Derragh Island (Fredengren 2009; Pl. XIXb) has shown that, at one particular spot, a deliberately created mound was built up over a period of several hundred years. An area about 20 m across on the edge of the modern lough was consistently heightened by throwing down layers of brushwood and other organic material and which was capped by a rather enigmatic stone platform that contained material of different periods. Due to the richness of the site, it was only possible to excavate across a portion of the mound but even the limited excavation revealed numerous stakes which could delimit either the partial edges of huts or wind breaks. While the upper stone platform produced very large quantities of artefacts and lithic debris of both Neolithic and Mesolithic date, the lower levels mostly produced a limited number of large blades and flakes reminiscent of those recovered at Newferry. The excavator (Fredengren 2009) reports that the phase of development of this site which seems to have begun on a small peaty island sometime before 7000 cal BP and finishes with a stony platform of as yet uncertain origin which contained at its edge cattle bones that date to the Mesolithic–Neolithic transition. Given its location in an area that would have been susceptible to seasonal flooding, it is likely that this location would have been used annually on a persistent basis at certain seasons. This would make the investment in maintaining one particular spot very worthwhile. One can assume that a number of the other platforms identified by Fredengren (2002) in Lough Gara also fall into this category.

Another potential site includes three platforms based on knolls that may have been artificially enhanced. These were found under the early medieval crannóg at Moynagh Lough (Bradley 1991; 1999; Pl. XIXa). This site lies within the dried out remnants of a lake that originally would have been more than 2 km long and 500 m wide. Platform 1, that was fully excavated, was 8.3 × 5.5 m. The excavation identified three occupation layers which were separated by peat layers and was edged with brushwood. It is possible that timbers also layer under the deposits that made up the knoll though it was not clear whether these were the collapsed trunks of trees that grew on the lake edge. Unlike the quite small stakes that were recorded at Derragh Island a scatter of quite substantial post-holes and a few stake-holes occurred. A total of 56, along with two small pits, were recorded. Scatters of Mesolithic material and faunal remains were found running off into lake shore deposits especially south-west of Platform 1 (Fig. 4.37). This phase of activity based on a charcoal sample dates to the very end of the Mesolithic (GRN 11443, 5270±80 BP, 6275–5907 cal BP). This date came from Platform 2. The possibility that Platforms 1 and 2 were contemporaneous could be suggested by the timbers recovered in the gap between them. While there is less evidence as to how much the knolls were deliberately heightened, it would appear that they may have had their shape altered. In other words, it looks like a location that was deliberately altered with the intention of return.

Evidence of other platforms would include the example from Clowanstown which dates to several hundred years after the fish baskets (Beta 246999, charcoal, 5310±40 BP, 6208–5960 cal BP).

In summary the evidence for Ireland in terms of houses is not impressive but, on the other hand, the range of evidence for a diversity of activities is quite significant. In particular between the fish weirs, the platforms and certain other sites, such as Newferry, there is evidence of continuous or repeated use of specific locations.

SUBMERGED LANDSCAPES

Perhaps one of the most surprising relative absences is the comparative lack of sites or material from submerged landscapes. Indeed sites where material is still close to being *in situ* on the inter-tidal shore are also scarce. Obviously, as discussed earlier in the chapter, there are numerous lakeside locations where quantities of Mesolithic material has been recovered and at the same time material has been dredged

in large quantities from the Lower Bann. The presence of submerged landscapes belonging to the Irish Mesolithic is rare, however, while artefacts from the sea bed are almost non-existent. There are a certain number of submerged forests of Early Holocene date but these are relatively restricted. Examples are known from The Ballyholme area at the exit of Belfast Lough, while others have been noted in the middle region of Strangford Lough (McErlean *et al.* 2002; Fig. 4.1). The Strangford situation is interesting as it is a very shallow sea lough with, at its northern end, an extensive intertidal zone, though in many areas earlier Holocene deposits are covered by extensive recent silt deposits. In the Greyabbey area on the eastern shores, however, it is possible to walk across Early Holocene deposits. In Belfast Lough, as noted by Praeger (1892, 228–37), in many accessible areas it would appear that Early Holocene ground surfaces and shorelines may be buried under several metres of marine deposits, as could be seen for example in the excavations of the Alexandra Dock. In fact it looks as if in many places the flat bed of the lough that may have existed in the very earliest parts of the Holocene and may have often been limited by quite steep sides. Therefore, in many areas marine deposits may have built up quite quickly and attractive locations for shoreline settlement may have been rare. The one exception would seem to be the Sydenham Station site found by Patterson (1892; Woodman 1978a).

It is very clear that around most of the coast the traces of prehistoric remains on inter-tidal shores really only begins in the Neolithic (Westley and Woodman forthcoming). This is particularly evident in the Discovery Programme's inter-tidal survey of the Shannon Estuary where there is only the slightest indication of a Mesolithic presence with an axe of possible Later Mesolithic date at Meelick Rock (O'Sullivan 2001, 61–3) and a plank radiocarbon dated to the Later Mesolithic at Carrigdirty (*ibid.*, 71–2). The inter-tidal finds, apparently associated with peat deposits from Bigstone Bay on the eastern shore Strangford Lough (Woodman 1978a, 23, 299) are one of the few indications that there is much more to be found in key inter-tidal locations.

Elsewhere, a number of sites that have been recovered, such as from the Severn Estuary, where sea level changes were taking place at a similar rate to many parts of Ireland. At the moment, the assemblages of artefacts and ecofacts, as well as the footprints, found at Gold Cliff (Bell 2007, 218–47) are the most notable. Almost certainly there are similar types of locations waiting to be discovered in Ireland.

The one abiding image of underwater archaeology in the Mesolithic must be the photograph on the front of *Man and the Sea* (Fischer 1995). However, the Danish situation is different to Ireland. Unlike Denmark there is only a narrow shallow sea bed off the coast of Ireland and today's fishing practices are likely to recover few significant finds – indeed this is true of finds of any period. The ongoing project run by *The Centre for Maritime Archaeology* (University of Ulster, Coleraine) at Eleven Ballyboes is the only instance where, on the basis of

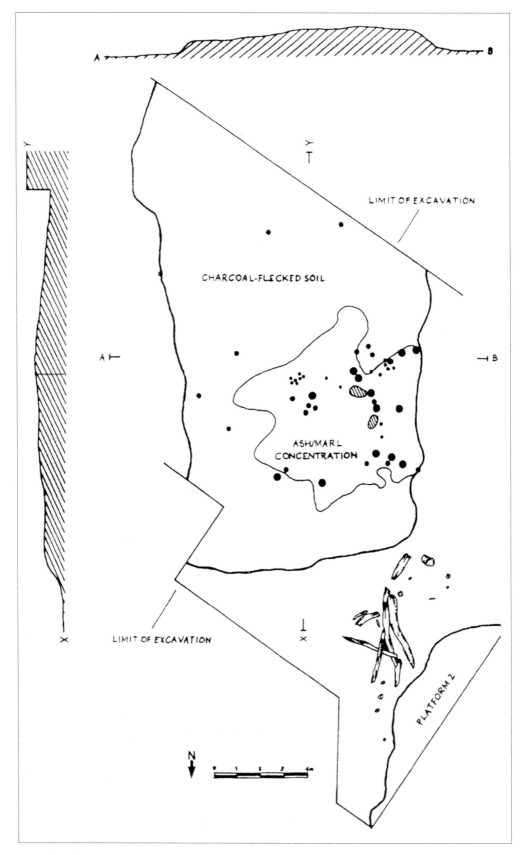

Fig. 4.37. Plan of features recovered from top of platforms at Moynagh Lough, Co. Meath (after Bradley 1999).

the profusion of "Early Mesolithic" artefacts washed up, there is an attempt to find traces of *in situ* deposits of Mesolithic date (Westley 2013; Pl. XX). Here the presence of so much material in such a small area, along with the fact that some material is relatively fresh, has led to underwater surveys of the sea bed in the hope of identifying intact deposits and evidence of settlement from the Early Mesolithic. Some *in situ* off-shore peat deposits that date to earlier than 9000 cal BP have, however, been identified (Westley 2013).

Conclusion

In summary, there are numerous settlement or other types of sites that do, or could, belong to the Irish Mesolithic. Many are very partial and most do not contain large quantities of organic remains while the number with structural features is relatively small. However, it is also apparent that there is a diverse range of sites of different types to be found in Ireland and, as will be seen in Chapter 9, in the context of their local and regional landscapes it is possible to see that they bring new perspectives to the study of the Irish Mesolithic.

Chapter 5

Chronology, flint facts and other artefacts

While the study of artefacts has been the backbone of Mesolithic research and in spite of using other dating methods, we still rely implicitly on radiocarbon dating. Therefore one has to consider how our use of radiocarbon dates helps create the chronological framework within which we work.

Radiocarbon dating

After the radiocarbon dates for Newferry (Woodman 1977a) and Mount Sandel (Woodman 1985a) became available, the Irish Mesolithic was conventionally and conveniently divided into two phases. There is an "*Early*" Mesolithic phase which began sometimes around or after 8000 cal BC or about 10,000 cal BP and ended at an as yet unknown date. This may have been before or after 7000 cal BC (9000 cal BP). The Later Mesolithic would appear to have developed by 6500 cal BC (8500 cal BP) and is difficult to trace beyond 4000 cal BC (6000 cal BP). As will be shown below, particularly in Chapter 8, there is growing evidence that we need to change the way we look at the chronology of the Irish Mesolithic and see it as a continuum of a human presence during which time a number of changes took place.

Some of these issues associated with establishing an up-to-date chronology for the Irish Mesolithic were outlined in a recent review (Woodman 2009). However, in attempting to establish the defining characteristics of each period it is still useful to consider some of the problems associated with establishing a chronological sequence.

One major change is that, in the last two decades, many new dates have been obtained and many of these were obtained from short-lived material, generally from precise contexts. AMS dating has provided dates with very significantly smaller standard deviations.

The problem of matching the AMS dates with ones obtained in earlier decades has been partially rectified through a return to older excavations where samples of organic material of short-lived duration, notably bone and burnt hazel nutshells, have helped provide what is hoped to be the basis of a more secure chronology based on more precise dates from reliable samples. The most notable example are the recently published project results based on the provision of 30 new dates from Mount Sandel (Bayliss and Woodman 2009), which has helped clarify some chronological anomalies associated with that site.

It has also exposed the weakness of the working assumption that, even in the case of some smaller sites, a single date, especially based on wood charcoal, is sufficient. In reality it does not begin to approach an acceptable standard of thorough investigation of the possibility of a site being a product of a complex series of re-occupations through time. The dates obtained from both the Dalkey Island and Sutton middens as part of the Irish Quaternary Faunas project (Woodman *et al*. 1997) have also shown that the long-held presumption that the shell middens along the Leinster Coast dated to the latest phases of the Mesolithic was erroneous. This assumption had been based on a combination of wood charcoal dates as well as a belief that, if these sites were significantly older, they could not have survived the Littorina transgression. The presence of domesticates was also seen to suggest that these sites belonged to a transition phase between the Mesolithic and Neolithic. The recent series of relevant AMS dates obtained by the Irish Quaternary Faunas Project from the early Holocene therefore suggests that the Dalkey middens, in spite of their limited size, were created and added to over a period of 3000 years. Although it is not as clear, the dates from Sutton also seem to suggest that the midden built up, perhaps intermittently, over several thousand years (Woodman *et al*. 1997). Perhaps the important lesson is that a radiocarbon date is only as good as our capacity to place it in its archaeological context.

At the moment one can estimate that there are 300–325 dates which could be used with some reliability though, in some cases, one is limited in how they can be used because full information is not always available

Figure 5.1 (a and b) shows how much the use of radiocarbon has increased over the decades. It shows for each decade how many sites had provided radiocarbon dates and how many dates were obtained. Radiocarbon dates are attributed to each decade on the basis of when they were likely to have been obtained rather than the date of the excavation. Thus, as already mentioned above, older excavations could be returned to and new dates obtained.

While the numbers of dates seem impressive, our pattern of research has also created a skewed picture. First, approximately 50% of all dates come from just eight sites, one of which (Mount Sandel) alone has produced 15% of the total!

As can be seen Figure 5.1, while there has been an increase in the use of radiocarbon dates over time, the 2000s represent the most notable increase. Prior to the 2000s virtually every date was obtained from research excavations or other forms of research. Dates from infrastructural projects only become a major factor during that decade. However, surprisingly, since 2000 the majority of sites excavated which have produced dates are a product of developer-led archaeology but at least 100 radiocarbon dates obtained in the same period come from research.

Given the potential biases, due to research concentration on a very few sites, if one simply counts the number of dates available within each millennium then the impact of those few

sites (most notably Mount Sandel) will skew the evidence. Also, in some instances, there is only partial information available for dates from some sites. Therefore, Figure 5.1b is based on much cruder figures i.e. the number of sites which have produced dates in each millennium. Naturally, some sites (notably Newferry) have produced dates within a number of different millennia.

Not surprisingly, there are many more sites dated to the last millennium of the Mesolithic. This is a topic that will be explored in more detail in Chapter 8. Leaving to one side the sites or artefacts that are strays, e.g. bone points, and sites such as platforms and fishing facilities etc. (i.e. sites without a lithic component) then the increase in the last millennium becomes even more striking.

The conventional typology

To those working outside Ireland, the typologies used for the Irish Mesolithic may sometimes seem similar to that used in Britain but, on occasions, bafflingly different. The reason why the British typology has not been followed is simply, as will be seen below, because many of the elements that characterise the British Mesolithic are not present in Ireland and, at times, there are various elements that are peculiar to the island of Ireland. One of the major problems that bedevil the Irish Mesolithic is the tendency to use aspects of the lithic technology or reduction strategies as attributes which indicate a particular age for an assemblage. Thus a common assumption has been 1) that small blades can be confidently associated with the *"Early"* Mesolithic, while 2) the Later Mesolithic is characterised by large blades produced using a hard hammer stone, thereby creating blades or blade-like flakes which retain large striking platforms that often have prominent bulbs of percussion. If these represent the Irish Mesolithic then the question must be how do we identify the technological attributes of a Neolithic assemblage?

"Early" Mesolithic

The Irish *"Early"* Mesolithic is usually thought to begin sometime after 10,000 cal BP and may have ended by 9000 cal BP (see below for discussions on problems associated with chronology). It is usual to begin with an examination of the primary technologies but in this case as the period is most clearly defined by the range of retouched tools (distinct type fossils); these implements will be considered first. The *"Early"* Mesolithic is still characterised by the range of artefacts from the excavations at Mount Sandel. In the future other excavations may lead to a need to revise the typology of certain aspects of the Irish Mesolithic.

1. Microliths

Unfortunately, within a portion of the Irish profession there is a mistaken assumption that all small blades, less than 25 mm in length, are microliths. In many areas of Ireland, especially

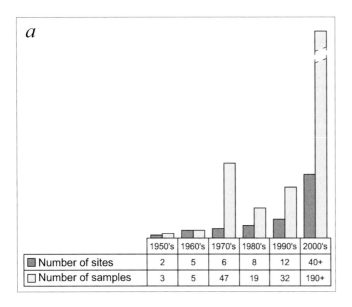

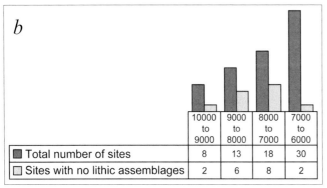

Fig. 5.1. Histograms of a) excavations with radiocarbon dates by decade and number of radiocarbon dates obtained in each decade, b) number of radiocarbon dates within each millennium (cal BP) (prepared by Hugh Kavanagh).

	1950's	1960's	1970's	1980's	1990's	2000's
■ Number of sites	2	5	6	8	12	40+
□ Number of samples	3	5	47	19	32	190+

	10000 to 9000	9000 to 8000	8000 to 7000	7000 to 6000
■ Total number of sites	8	13	18	30
□ Sites with no lithic assemblages	2	6	8	2

in parts of Munster and Leinster where flint is often present as remaniée pebbles, the use of a bipolar technology tends to produce small bladelets. These are usually Neolithic or, more likely, Bronze Age in date. Only small blades or portions that have been retouched, preferably into a distinct shape, can be considered as microliths. The commonly used schema for British microliths, devised by Clark (1933), is much more complex than that used in Ireland and served particular needs in the English Mesolithic. The Clark typology is divided into eight major groups, A–H, though only groups A–D are relevant to Ireland (Fig. 5.2).

A. Obliquely trimmed
B. (1) Continuously backed on one edge (B 2–3) retouched
    on two edges
C. (1–2) Curved back with or without blunting across the base
D. (1) Isocèles Triangles
D. (2) Crescents
D. (3) Scalene triangles
D. (4) Range of rhomboids

It is notable that Clark did not regard this typological sequence as an absolute system that must be applied to all assemblages; in the case of Star Carr, for example, he used a more limited set of criteria. These were obliquely blunted, triangles and trapezes (Clark 1954, 102). This raises an issue that will be returned to on numerous occasions. As the need for any typology is that it provides a useful set of categories that allow the description of a particular group of material, then, as in the case of Ireland, it is necessary to use more locally relevant sets of criteria.

In the case of Mount Sandel and other sites, the following types of microliths can be identified (Fig. 5.3):

- *Obliquely retouched points* (Clark type A), this includes broad examples retouched across the full width of a portion of the blade or those retouched at a more acute angle down a portion of one edge of the blade or blade fragment. Figure 5.3, 5–7 came from one of the smaller pits at Mount Sandel, which tended to be later in the sequence.
- *Rods* (Clark type B1) retouched along one edge, such as Figure 5.3, 19.

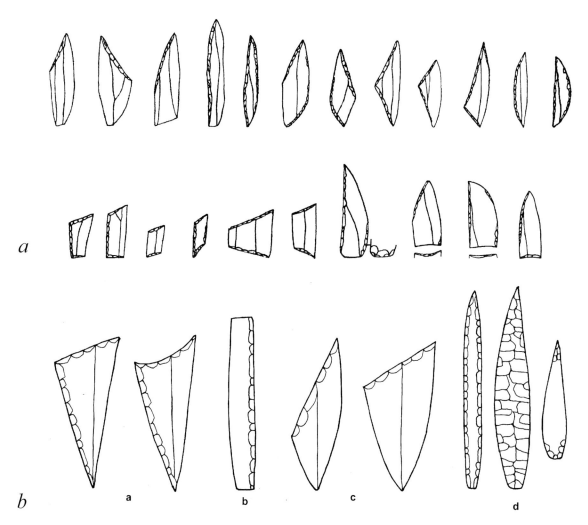

Fig. 5.2. Schematic diagram of microlithic types a) British, b) Irish.

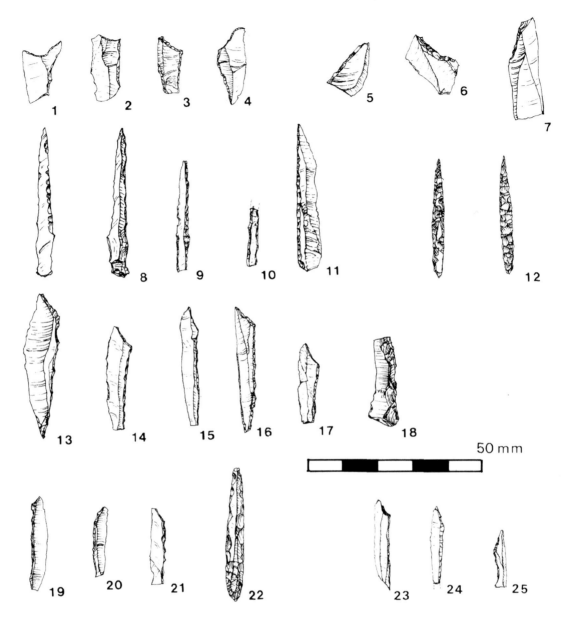

Fig. 5.3. A selection of microliths from various contexts at Mount Sandel Upper, Co. Derry: 1–4) F31/3, 5–7) F100/5, 8–11) F22, 12–22) F56/1, 23–25) F/31/0 (after Woodman1985a) (drawn by D. Warner).

- *Needle points* Some simple types (type a), such as Figure 5.3 9 and 10 bear some resemblance to Clark's type B2. The Irish examples often include areas of surface retouch. In the case of type b, (Fig. 53, 12) this is limited and usually occurs on examples with a quadrilateral section, while in the case of type c) they almost resemble small narrow leaf-shaped arrowheads (Fig. 5.3, 22).
- *Scalene Triangles* (Clark type D3), In this case all examples vary: from those with a concave short edge, such as Figure 5.3, 1–4 that could be placed in one sub-category, to the other more elongated forms which might be regarded as something slightly different. These differences could be regarded as representing forms from slightly different dates but, in the case of Mount Sandel, it also seemed likely that these differences could be nothing more complex than the work of different tool manufacturers (Woodman 1985a, 47–8).

One could argue that the difference between the Irish typology and that of England must be, in part, due to the author being a "Lumper" while the other, at the early stage of establishing a detailed typological framework for English microliths being a "splitter" was preferable. Since the Mount Sandel report was written, other ways of classifying microliths in Great Britain have been suggested e.g. Finlay (2000a).

As will be discussed below in more detail, one of the most remarkable aspects of the Irish forms is the narrow range of types, where the earliest forms, i.e. trapezes, Isosceles triangles and some of those that can occur in the later phases of the English Later Mesolithic, for example rhomboids and crescents, are absent. What is perhaps of greater significance is, as noted earlier, the scarcity of excavated sites that have produced microliths.

WHAT WERE THEY USED FOR?

These items were parts of composite tools but this does not necessarily mean that they were used for projectile heads especially focused on hunting large animals. The alternatives have been discussed extensively by Finlay (2000b). One must ask, in the case of Ireland, what large animals would they have been hunting?

As was discussed by Woodman (1985a, 46–9) there may be some reason to believe that, on occasions, they were used as parts of projectiles. The Mount Sandel (upper) examples are not the most attractive as many are broken. While by far the largest numbers look as if they are discards that have been removed and dumped, apparently under the eaves of the hut, the other major source was the groupings of a limited number of in several pits and hearths. Two patterns would seem to be present. Within each of a number of pits, small numbers of very similar triangular microliths were recovered (see Fig. 5.3) but the shape of these microliths in each pit is different from those in the other pits. It could be suggested that, in each case, 4–6(?) microliths were used within one projectile head.

While it is not clear cut, there seems to have been a higher incidence of triangles in pits with pig bones (Woodman 1985a, tables 5 and 6) but that where rods occurred more frequently, they were often found in pits containing fish bones which could suggest a different purpose. In fact as can be seen from table 6 in that paper, one could also argue for microliths being used in plant processing. Unfortunately, with so many microliths being burnt, Dumont (1985) was able to recover relatively limited micro wear traces which would have elucidated their purpose. Similar problems were encountered by David (1998) when micro wear analysis was carried out on a group of triangles and a group of rods found embedded in peat at Seamer Carr, Yorkshire.

Therefore, microliths may have, at any one time, been used in different ways i.e. hunting, plant food gathering and on-site processing.

2. Micro-awls

As described in the Mount Sandel report (Woodman 1985a) these are steeply trimmed small blades which are usually retouched to a robust point. These blades are often about 50 mm in length. Given their size many more micro-awls than microliths have been recovered as stray finds (Fig. 5.6, 5–12).

3. Scrapers and burins

These are rarely discussed within the context of the Irish Mesolithic but they can occur. Many of the burins are simple angle burins (Fig. 5.4, 3–4). They also occur in the secondary context in the lower gravels at Cushendun and were found during Whelan's excavation at the Creagh near Toome. These will be returned to in Chapter 8.

Scrapers include small flake scrapers whose functional edge is of a more irregular form than would occur in the Neolithic, as well as some examples of small blade scrapers at several sites such as Lough Boora or again in the Lower Gravels at Cushendun. There are also occasional end of blade convex end scrapers, for example from Mount Sandel, whose retouch is confined to the distal end and which look different to many of those found on Neolithic sites (Fig. 5.4, 1–2). These, as with the examples from Ballyderown, Co. Cork (Pl. XXIIc), may be early in date. The question is whether, if one has found a small number of end-of-blade scrapers like those from Balleyderown and if there are a small number of small blades, this constitutes an "Early" Mesolithic assemblage?

4. Axes and other core tools

Within the "*Early*" Mesolithic there are a range of different axe types:

CORE AXES (FIG. 5.4)

In spite of their name, these are not necessarily made directly from nodules of flint. The use of the term "core" is based on the fact that their cutting edge is created by the removal of one or two flakes at right-angles to the longitudinal profile of the axe. Thus the axe is finished by the removal of two flakes in a core-like fashion, where the convergence of these flake scars created the cutting edge. They can also be resharpened in the same manner. The result is the creation of very distinctive sharpening flakes (see in particular Collins 1983, fig. 18). It is, however, first necessary to clarify the names for these types of axes. In Britain they have traditionally been called "Tranchet axes/adzes", however, the term "Tranchet" is used in French to describe either small transverse arrowheads (Petit Tranchet) or large flake axes, typical in the infamous Campignian, which were referred to as Grand Tranchet! The term "core axe" was never applied to the few examples known in France. The Irish use of the term is in line with the term used in Denmark (*Kaerneøkser*). Irish examples tend to be confined to the north and north-east and they are characterised by being relatively small, usually less than 100 mm in length, and usually bilaterally symmetric. Many examples (as noted by Woodman 1978a) have also been reduced in width so that the cutting edge is frequently less than 20 mm wide. This was also noted by Collins (1983). Many of these small core axes of Mesolithic date have actually been made on flakes. This is a practice that was common even as far back as the

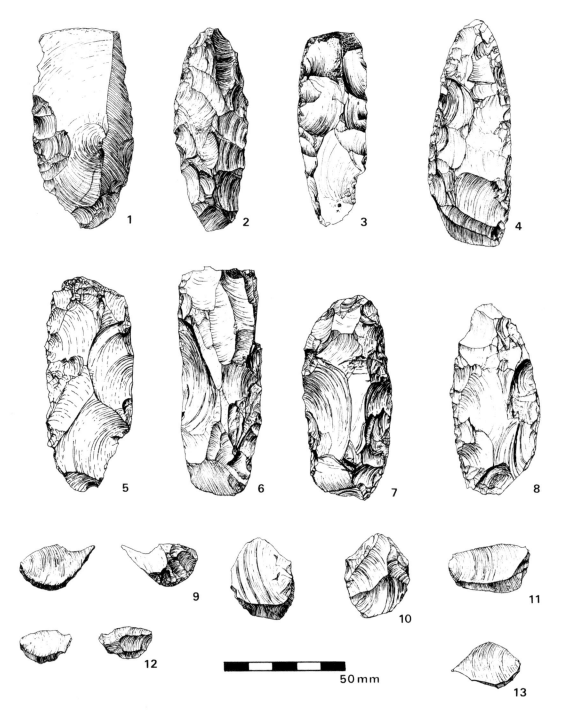

Fig. 5.4. Early Mesolithic core axes from Mount Sandel Lower: 1–8) core axes, 9–13) axe sharpening flakes (after Collins 1983).

Lower Palaeolithic, where hand-axes were often made on large flake blanks.

FLAKE AXES (FIG. 5.5)

The term flake axe in Ireland is in line with its use in many parts of mainland Europe. While core axes can be made on large flakes and are characterised by the formation of a cutting edge created through flake removals, flake axes are almost invariably made on flakes and are produced through a careful reduction strategy that leaves a portion of an original flake edge to form the functional edge (see Woodman 1978a, fig. 16). This portion of the edge often retains a high angle between the ventral and dorsal face. The intended edge is

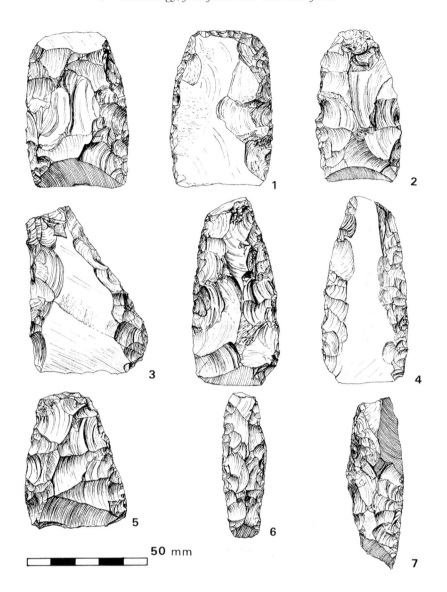

Fig. 5.5. Early Mesolithic flake axes from Mount Sandel Lower (after Collins 1983).

asymmetric with the lower ventral surface forming a straight adze-like edge, the axe is then shaped round this portion of the original flake edge. The rest of the body of the axe is retouched, often on both faces though rarely overall on the ventral face. They are, unlike the core axes, often splayed, with this functional edge forming the widest part of the implement.

OTHER CORE TOOLS

It is apparent from the Mount Sandel excavations that a series of small pick-like implements also occurred in the Mesolithic. These can be small, double-pointed implements that have also been found at several other locations, along the Bann Valley in particular. In this case there is less certainty as to whether these smaller implements always belong to the Mesolithic.

GROUND STONE AXES

On the basis of the discovery of axes at both Mount Sandel and Lough Boora we can be certain that ground stone axes were in use in the "*Early*" Mesolithic. One Mount Sandel axe is a small well-made axe ground overall, while the Lough Boora axes are little more than large cobbles where an edge has been ground onto the cobble and few other alterations have been made. Interestingly one of the largest axes from a Mesolithic context in Ireland is that from Pit A at Hermitage, which also contained a cremated burial (Collins and Coyne 2006), while a similar large axe was recovered from Ferriter's Cove (Woodman *et al.* 1999, 63; fig. 4.4), where it was buried below the Later Mesolithic occupation layer. One can only say that the latter example pre-dates the main occupation at Ferriter's Cove but it is impossible to say that it was "*Early*" Mesolithic in date.

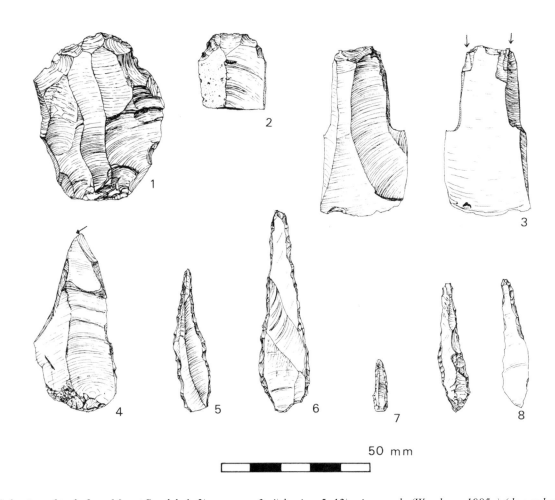

Fig. 5.6. Selection of tools from Mount Sandel: 1–2) scrapers, 3–4) burins, 5–12) micro-awls (Woodman 1985a) (drawn by D. Warner).

One possible early example is a triangular adze-shaped ground stone axe from excavations at Gortore, Co. Cork (Sternke forthcoming) on a site that overlooked the Awbeg River (Pl. XXI). It was found in proximity to a series of possible "*Early*" Mesolithic blades. Unfortunately there seems to have been a very poor association between this potentially "early" artefact and a series of radiocarbon dates which could suggest a presence quite late in Early Mesolithic. Irrespective of its exact age this is a doubly interesting artefact as it looks like an attempt to make something that resembled and would have the same purpose as a flake axe.

5. Other forms

The artefacts described above are the most distinctive forms that would characterise the Irish "*Early*" Mesolithic. Other forms, however, may also be associated with this period and these include small retouched blades. One type which might superficially seem similar to something which occurs in the Later Mesolithic is the bevelled ended pebble from Mount Sandel (Woodman 1985a, 52, fig. 33.4). However this is much smaller and has a more carefully ground edge than is usual in Later Mesolithic examples.

Technology

The "*Early*" Mesolithic, based primarily on the Mount Sandel assemblage (Woodman 1985a), seems to be characterised by a series of small blades that are usually less than 15 mm in width and where in excess of 75% of the blades are 60 mm or less in length. This would seem to be valid irrespective of the type of raw material or its accessibility. It has been noted (Woodman 1978a, 29–31, figs 8a, 9a) that the platforms on these blades were usually quite small and Costa *et al.* (2001; 2005) have shown that this is a product, not of a punch percussion technique as previously suggested (Woodman 1978a), but rather through the use of a soft hammer stone and careful platform edge preparation. Punch percussion, characterised by diffuse bulbs of percussion and lips on the inner edge of the platform, is rare in Ireland. There seem, however, to be some Neolithic assemblages, i.e. associated with Neolithic pottery, where equally small blades have been created, but these often retain proportionally larger platforms which lack platform edge preparation and are rather less regular in outline, for example at Townleyhall (Eogan 1963). This presents a problem that will be returned to in Chapter 8. It should also be noted that tiny blades produced by bipolar core technology are not typical of the "*Early*" Mesolithic. There is also little evidence that bipolar cores were used in any part of Ireland before the Neolithic period.

Again the distinction between cores of the "*Early*" Mesolithic (Fig. 5.7), in particular with reference to those found on many Neolithic or Bronze Age sites, is a mixture of qualitative and quantitative attributes. In essence, the "*Early*" Mesolithic examples tend to be better quality blade cores though there is some variation between assemblages. There is also a higher tendency to find single platformed cores along with a small but significant number of dual platformed examples. In the latter case the platforms are opposed to each other. The cores can vary in size from those found at Mount Sandel where the raw material was transported from the coast (Fig. 5.7) to larger but similar examples from Glynn (Woodman 1977b). In general, the Neolithic assemblages often seem to include a greater number of multiple platformed cores though as will be seen below this can result in confusion between some Neolithic and Mesolithic assemblages.

One aspect of the production of cores during at least part of the "*Early*" Mesolithic is that, on occasions, where they have to be transported from locations where flint is available, it would seem that, instead of bringing nodules of flint, the core pre-forms could be very large flakes. Examples were recovered at Mount Sandel (Woodman 1985a, 32; fig. 10.3). One particularly interesting example was recovered by Vincent Macalister in field walking at Culbane. In this case, three large flakes were refitted and one of these had already been used as a small core from which a number of small blades had been removed (Pl XXII, see also Fig. 5.7, 5).

It has already been noted that, within the last two decades during which excavation has increased exponentially, there are certain challenges in identifying the period (or even periods) into which most assemblages can be placed. There are many regions in the southern part of Ireland where, as will be seen below, access to good raw materials was limited and where assemblages of substantial size of any period are, with a few notable exceptions such as Gortore, Kilcummer or Cloghers, extremely rare. This is compounded by the fact that much of the material was found in the topsoil, where artefactual recovery rates are likely to be lower.

This presents a problem that impact on assemblages of potential "*Early*" Mesolithic date. These are quite small groups of material where a significant number can only be accepted as "*Early*" Mesolithic with some degree of reservation. Therefore, in returning to the criteria outlined earlier, degree of reliability can be gauged in falling probability as follows:

1) On the presence of a contexted assemblage containing diagnostic artefacts.

2) The presence of a series of diagnostic artefacts in a poor or secondary context. In this case not all the pieces can be presumed to be Mesolithic in date.

3) A preferably contexted assemblage of smaller blades associated with a significant number of single and dual platformed blade cores. The blades are produced with soft hammer percussion, elongated, and in general less than 60 mm in length. Degree of reliability is to a great extent dependant on assemblage size and integrity.

Small assemblages of blades, even where evidence of soft hammer percussion exists but with no other diagnostic elements associated and often in a poor context, should be accepted with reservations. In fact, an assemblage which contains a limited number of smaller single platformed cores which are conical and cylindrical as well as dual platformed blade cores is more likely to date to early in the Mesolithic than an assemblage with nothing more than a few small blades.

Later Mesolithic

The Later Mesolithic is known to have existed by 8500 cal BP if not, as will be shown in Chapter 8, probably earlier. It conventionally seems to have ended around 6000 cal BP. Unfortunately, other than the assemblages from the lower part of the sequence at Newferry (Woodman 1977a) there is a limited range of sites from the first half of the Later Mesolithic. This period is therefore frequently identified

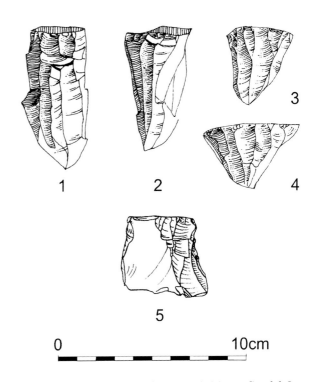

Fig. 5.7. Selection of cores from: 1–4) Mount Sandel Lower, 6) Mount Sandel upper.

with assemblages that belong to its last 1000 years. Unlike the "*Early*" Mesolithic, where there is no clear chronological sequence through time, the excavations at Newferry provide an insight into how certain aspects of the Later Mesolithic changed over a period of roughly 2000 years. Therefore, while there are certain attributes that occur consistently throughout this period, it can also be seen as a period of gradual change. Some implications of these changes will be discussed below in Part III. There is one issue that will be a constant question. This is whether the implications of the 2000 year long sequence of artefacts recovered from Newferry Site 3 forms a reliable scaffold on which to build the typology of the Later Mesolithic. In the absence of anything else, however, one must rely on Newferry Site 3. Figure 5.8 provides a simplified section though the sites with approximate ages of each zone. In this case, rather than providing a range of examples of each specific implement type in turn, the range of implements from selected zones is illustrated (Zones 7 (main) = Fig. 5.9; Zone 6 = Fig. 5.10; Zones 3 and 2 = Fig. 5.11). A simplified sequence is provided in Figure 5.12.

The more prolific Later Mesolithic forms immediately present a different set of problems to those found in the "*Early*" Mesolithic. Many of the distinctive implements are peculiar to Ireland. In essence, Later Mesolithic forms are a range of artefacts made on larger blades or flakes. Many of these implements have been associated with the term "Bann Flake", which has a number of drawbacks but it is a term that has also shown remarkable resistance to change.

The case of the Bann Flake: creeping towards an accidental definition

For many the term "Bann Flake" has become synonymous with the Later Mesolithic, however, there was never an actual decision that this term would be used for a very specific, clearly defined implement. Antiquaries such as Knowles,

as can be seen in his 1912 review of the implements from the River Bann, never used the term. Instead he headed this section "Large Flakes slightly dressed at the base" (Fig. 3.12). In his description he noted that they were slightly dressed at the base on both sides (*ibid.*, pls xii and xiii). He also noted the presence of examples with tangs and obliquely blunted distal ends and suggested that they had served as both knives and spearheads. Neither Movius (1936), in his report on the Newferry excavations, nor Whelan (1938), in his review of the Irish Stone Age, used the specific term "Bann Flake". Movius (1936, 24) speculated, on the basis of the small groups of blades or flakes, that one use for these implements might have been as tips of fishing spears, but he did not see this as their only purpose.

It would appear that the first explicit use of the term "Bann Flake" was by Raftery (1944) when he published *The Bann Flake outside the Bann Valley*. Within the paper, however, the word Bann was followed by Flake, flake and point. In this paper and *Prehistoric Ireland*, published in 1951, where again he used the term "Bann Flake", the emphasis was on thinning the butt so that they could be used as spearheads (Raftery 1951, 71). Mitchell continued the use of the term as a leaf-shaped flake until he witnessed, in 1971, a flint knapping demonstration by Mark Newcomer, who was striking from the core a leaf-shaped flake that resembled a "Bann Flake" (Mitchell 1971, 278–80). In fact, around this date, it had become clear that the use of hard hammer percussion would, irrespective of the period, produce a certain number of leaf-shaped flakes. As part of this process, the removal of flakes from the dorsal face at the butt prior to the removal of the flake is part of the normal process of hard hammer percussion. Even as late as the 1970s it was quite usual, when cataloguing lithic assemblages, to apply the term "Bann Flake" to any large leaf-shaped flake which had been thinned on the dorsal face. I previously suggested that 1) these implements should be characterised by limited retouch along the lateral edges near the butt (Woodman 1974a; 1978a,

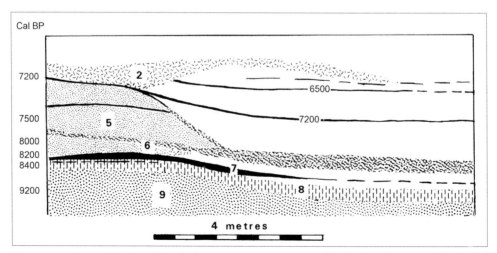

Fig. 5.8. Schematic section of Newferry Site 3 showing approximate age of each Zone (prepared by Hugh Kavanagh).

82–97) and 2) as the term "Bann Flake" has no clear definition it should be replaced. The admittedly more cumbersome term *Butt Trimmed Form* was suggested.

Butt Trimmed Forms

In general the important characteristic of the "Butt Trimmed Forms" is that they are retouched near the butt *after* the flake has been struck off from the core. Often, though not invariably, the retouch is peripheral and quite steep, is used to shape or round off the butt of a flake and usually extends for 20–40 mm along each edge. The flakes tend to be pointed or leaf-shaped and to be 50–100 mm in length. As will be apparent from Figures 5.9–11, they change in shape through time. Within this general description the shape of the Butt Trimmed Forms changes from narrow, steeply retouched forms (Zone 7; Fig. 5.9, 1, 2, 4) through, in Zone 6, to the occurrence of broad examples that are more tanged (Fig. 5.10, 2) as well as, in general, a series of less diagnostic forms, while the exceptionally broad examples occur very late in the sequence (Fig. 5.11, 1, 8). In the case of the final form there may be an argument, as previously suggested (Woodman *et al.* 2006, 120–3), for retaining the term "Bann Flake" for these very large, broad examples of Butt Trimmed Forms, where the width is more than three-fifths the length and the retouch near the butt tends to be very light and does not significantly alter the shape of the flake.

Obviously other occasional flakes have some signs of peripheral retouch at the proximal end but these can be thicker and not necessarily tapering to a point. Those from the putative "Bann Blade Cache" (Costa 2006, 238–41), which are 160 mm in length, are Neolithic in date and good examples of pieces that are different from Later Mesolithic forms. There are also other forms that can be seen as part of the same group. These include the following types which are also illustrated in Figures 5.9–11.

Distally retouched

These may also have some traces of retouch at the butt end but the main characteristic is the presence of an area of oblique retouch at the distal end of the blanks, which are usually rather laminar in outline. These occur from the bottom of the Newferry sequence (e.g. Fig. 5.9, 5–6; Fig. 5.10, 4; Fig. 5.11, 3). In the latter part of the Later Mesolithic they become less bladelike.

Backed flakes

These are usually squat, quite thick flakes which often have quite heavy retouch running along one edge. They tend to be less common than the Butt Trimmed and distally retouched forms (Fig 5.9, 7 and Fig. 5.10, 3).

Bar forms

These are heavily retouch blanks that have been trimmed into a thick bar and quite heavily retouched on both faces. They are not usually retouched to a point. In general they are 50–100 mm in length. This particular form only occurs in the upper part of the Newferry sequence (e.g. Fig. 5.11, 5). These implements seem to occur on inland locations and to be virtually absent from the coast.

Blade points

In this case, large blade or blade-like flakes have been retouched, usually on the distal half of the blank. This steep peripheral retouch is used to create a point at the distal end (Fig. 5.10, 7).

Other miscellaneous blade/flake tools

STRANGULATED PIECES?

There is other perhaps almost unique retouched tools made on blades but one that should be singled out is an example of a broken blade which appears to have been used intensively on either lateral edge. Occasional examples were recovered from Newferry, notably in Zones 5 and 6. It might be regarded as a chance, almost on-off item, except that three blade fragments from Castlecarr on the Antrim Coast (see below Chapter 9) were also retouched on their lateral edges, though in their case not quite as invasively.

NOTCHED PIECES

As can be seen from, for example, the selected material from Zone 6 (Fig. 5.9, 13), large, heavily notched flakes occurred at Newferry. They have also been found on coastal sites (see below) such as Ferriter's Cove and Bay Farm.

It would, however, be a mistake to assume that the Newferry/Bann valley sequence is something local. As can be seen from even the distally trimmed forms, like the Butt Trimmed Forms, they can be found elsewhere in Ireland (Fig. 5.13), such as the distally trimmed chert form from Lough Kinale and a related similar example from Ferriter's Cove.

IMPLICATIONS OF THE BUTT TRIMMED AND RELATED FORMS

This range of implements is so distinctive that on sight they provoke an immediate demand to know what they were used for. While this matter will be discussed below one must admit that, sadly, we are still in the foothills of a momentous task in trying to establish with some confidence why they were made and how they were used. Initially, Knowles (1912, 200) put forward the suggestion that they were rather similar to the quartzite knives used by Native Australians, where the handle

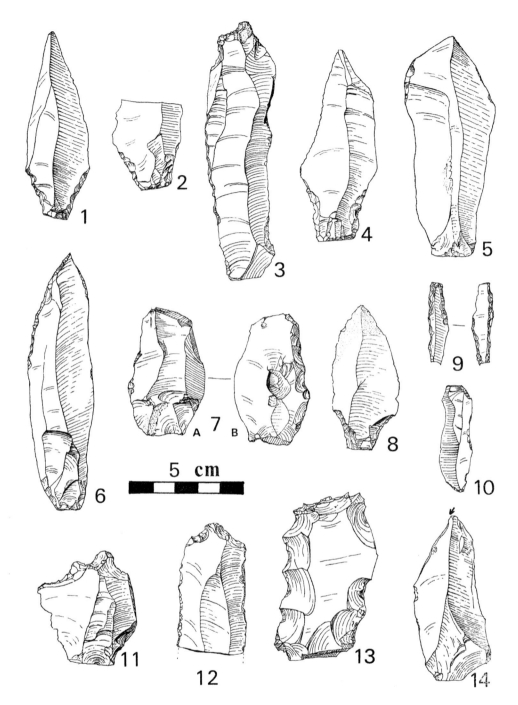

Fig. 5.9. Selection of implements from Zone 7, Newferry Site 3: 1, 2, 4, 8) series of Butt Trimmed Forms, 5–6) distally trimmed forms, 7) backed flake, 9) micro-awl?, 10) retouched bladelet, 11) notched scraper, 12) nosed end of blade scraper with some lateral edge damage or use, 13) large notched flake, 14) flake with possible burinal flake scar (Woodman 1977a) (drawn by D. Warner).

was created by encapsulating the butt in a ball of gum (Fig. 5.14a). He also noted the discovery of an Irish example from the River Bann. This is a large flint flake with a moss handle which would tend to support this view (Fig 5.14b). It was found in the middle of the 19th century and is included in the Wilde (1857) catalogue of stone tools that were, at that time, in the Museum of the Royal Irish Academy. In fact, Gabriel Mortillet (1867, 153) noted its display at the Paris exhibition: "un éclat grossier de silex, emmanché dans un bourrelet de mousse". This particular flake raises an issue associated with how handles were made or hafted. Knowles also claimed to have found a wooden handle or rather a globular piece of wood

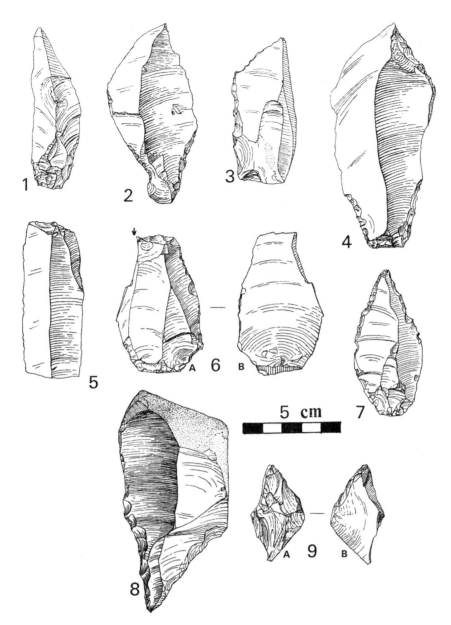

Fig. 5.10. Selection of implements from Zone 6, Newferry Site 3: 1–2) Butt Trimmed Forms, 3) backed flake, 4) distally trimmed flake, 5) end of blade scraper, 6) probable burinal tool, 7) blade point, 8) large flake trimmed to point at proximal end, 9) sharpening flake from tip or butt of flint core tool (Woodman 1977a) (drawn by D. Warner).

with a hole in it (Fig. 5.14a). His experiments seem to suggest that this was perfectly suited as a handle for a tanged Butt Trimmed Form. However, Doug Bamforth (pers. comm.), at an early stage of micro-wear analysis of a range of Butt Trimmed Forms, has observed that there is little evidence that these pieces had wooden handles or hafts. If handles were usually made from soft vegetable material, such as moss or hide, then little trace of hafting would be apparent, even under microscopic examination. One other possible parallel can be found within the Ertebølle of Denmark where several examples have been found in graves and are also presumed to be knives.

Perhaps a reason for the change from tanged forms to examples that have little more than very slight peripheral retouch near the butt is associated with a change in type of handle? The change to the butt was documented (Woodman 1978a, 87–91) through the Newferry sequence. It was noted that in the lower Zones 8, 7lr, 7 and, particularly, in 6, numerous tanged examples occurred. They were virtually absent in Zones 5, 4 and 3. From the tanged examples in the lower part of the sequence it was apparent that, while flake and blade width altered, the width of the tang remained the same. This would give credence to Knowles's suggestion that his globular piece

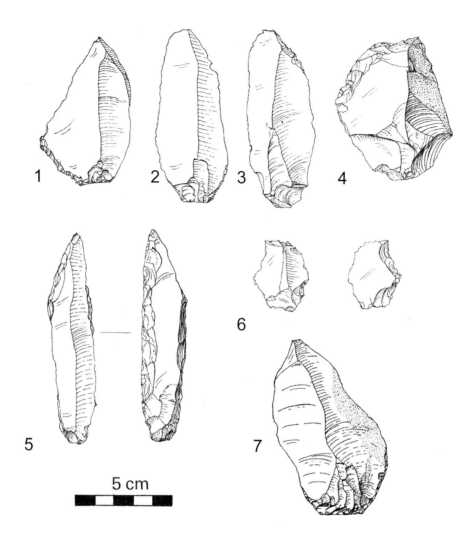

Fig. 5.11. Selection of implements from Zones 3 and 2, Newferry Site 3: (Zone 3): 1–2) Butt Trimmed Forms (no. 1 = Bann Flake?), 3) distally trimmed form, 4) larger scraper like flake, 5) Bar form, 6) small notched scraper; (Zone 2): 7) Butt Trimmed Form (Bann Flake?) (Woodman 1977a) (drawn by D. Warner).

of wood was a handle for tanged Butt Trimmed Forms. It is also probable that the light, very peripheral retouch found on so many of the simpler, more leaf-shaped, forms may have been to blunt the edges where the butt was wrapped in softer material and reduce the possibility of a sharp edge of the flake cutting through soft materials. The obvious question must be: were the tanged and more leaf-shaped Butt Trimmed Forms little more than the same implement which had different types of handles?

With a few strategically chosen illustrations one could make a case that significant changes were made throughout the Newferry sequence. Therefore, at a time when objective measurements seemed to be the best way of establishing typological criteria, simple sets of attributes were chosen. As often happens when there are no clear questions there are no clear answers, but, by simplifying the process it is still possible to see changes throughout the Newferry sequence. The simplified version is as follows:

a) Mean length of Butt Trimmed Forms and unretouched blanks.
b) Mean width of Butt Trimmed Forms and unretouched blanks.
c) Degree to which the Butt Trimmed Forms are pointed (based on two measurements, the width at i) mid-point and ii) 80% of the length and dividing the latter by the former).
d) Width of tang at 15 mm from the butt.

Material from the sequence was divided into six groups:

1) Zones 8 and 7 (lower and main)
2) Zones 7 (upper) and 6
3) Zone 5 (lower)
4) Zone 5 (upper)
5) Zone 4
6) Zone 3

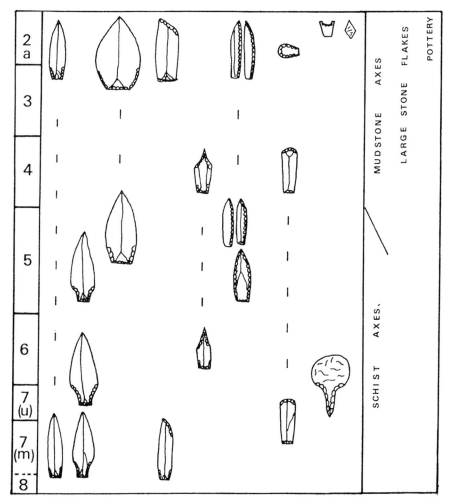

Fig. 5.12. Schematic sequence of implement types from Newferry Site 3 (Woodman 1977a).

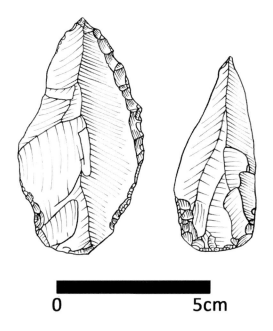

0   5cm

The graph presented in Figure 5.15 confirms more subjective assessments that Butt Trimmed Forms became, on average, shorter and broader, with the more tanged or narrow butt specimens tending to be confined to the lower part of the sequence. However, the tendency to be pointed remains the same throughout the sequence. One other observation is that, in general, the unretouched pieces tend to be slightly shorter and narrower than the Butt Trimmed Forms. The significance of this point will be returned to later.

To some extent, there is a double "cop out" by using the knife attribute as a blanket explanation. One must wonder about the very broad examples where it is suggested that the term "Bann Flake" is retained. These examples, which are much broader than the normal Butt Trimmed Forms and have a lower edge angle are, as noted earlier, confined to the final part of the Newferry sequence and one must consider

Fig. 5.13. Later Mesolithic forms from elsewhere in Ireland: Backed and Butt Trimmed Form from Ferriter's Cove.

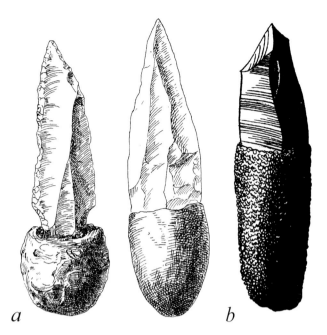

Fig. 5.14. a) Reconstruction by Knowles of tanged Butt Trimmed Form with wooden handle found in the Lower Bann Valley (after Knowles 1912), and Australian example, b) example with moss handle found in the early 19th century in the Lower Bann (Raftery 1951).

the possibility that they had a different purpose. In particular, one flint example from Kilgolagh td in North Cavan is approximately 70 mm in width. As no flint sources are found nearby this raised the question as to why such a large example was moved over a considerable distance and for what purpose was it intended?

It is of course possible that these are just atypical extremes. However, significant numbers of the "Bann Flakes" were found in the Urbal Cache (Pl. XXIII) while, in the Dalkey Cache, three examples were found along with ten blades (Fig. 5.16). This suggests that these implements were produced with a particular purpose in mind. Anderson (1994, 188–9) went further and suggested that towards the end of the Later Mesolithic reduction strategies altered so that the broad Bann Flake could be consistently produced. This issue will be returned to below when the question of the purpose of the so-called blanks is discussed in more detail.

Movius's claim that one purpose of these pieces was as the tips of fish spears became the accepted view – a view that is still accepted by some authors. To some extent the apparent discovery of fish spears in a log boat at Toomebridge by the late Dr Townsley helped underpin this view. However, examinations of Townsley's manuscripts, which are housed in the Ulster Museum, were less than convincing that this

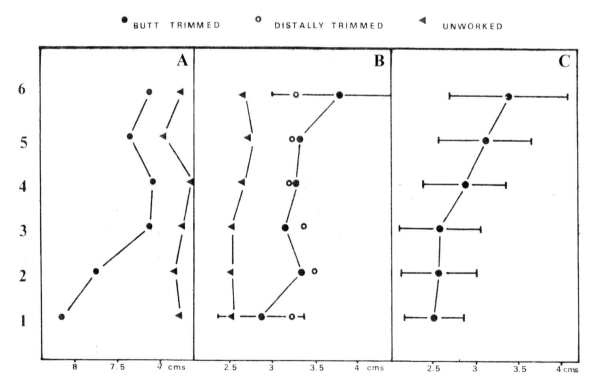

Fig. 5.15. Graph of changes in Butt Trimmed Forms, distally trimmed forms and blanks from Newferry Site 3: a) mean length, b) mean breadth, c) mean width of butt at 15 mm from butt end.

Fig. 5.16. Cache of Later Mesolithic artefacts from Dalkey Island excavations (after Liversage 1968).

patinated it was possible to see "use wear traces compatible with experimentally produced woodworking polishes ... on some retouched blades and flakes". As noted earlier, Doug Bamforth found little evidence as to how these implements were hafted but micro wear should be the best way to find evidence as to how they were used. It is unfortunate that, in spite of Van Gjin's observation, upon visual inspection of a selection of stone tools from Clowanstown, that some traces of wear might be present, there was no follow up (Warren *et al.* 2009).

In spite of all these uncertainties, there is little reason to believe that these caches provide evidence that so-called Bann Flakes were used in groups as tips on fish spears (Movius 1942, 244). Although, as Finlay (2003) has noted, there are some instances of caches where three examples, and multiples of three, seem to re-occur, it should be noted that they would often have been inappropriate as part of fish spears, for example, the squat blade and two Butt Trimmed Forms found together at Drumakeely in mid-Antrim (Figure 5.24, below) or the many oblique distally retouched examples, as in the Raphael Cache.

Although the issue will be considered in more detail in Chapter 9 one must also remember that there are a small but significant number of Butt Trimmed Forms found away from the coast and major areas of water, which again suggests that they are not just simply fish spears!

A frequently asked question is whether other leaf-shaped flakes could have been used in a similar manner. From a functional perspective, any flake of a roughly similar shape might have been similarly used. While it is also possible that they date to the Later Mesolithic, without the secondary retouch they cannot be unequivocally classified as Later Mesolithic in date.

was the case (Woodman 1978a, appendix 4). The dugout is a well-made form that would be more typical of later periods, while the fish spears, which were rather short at less than one metre in length, could alternatively be either branches or paddles. One flint flake was found in the boat. The purpose of certain forms appears relatively obvious. The smaller, often squat and crudely backed, examples appear to be cutting tools, while the often more laminar, distally-trimmed edge, made to provide a blunted area where an index finger could rest, seems also to have been a cutting tool. This still does not explain the purpose of the other Butt Trimmed Forms and related artefacts within the Later Mesolithic forms group. Attempts at micro-wear analysis have met with limited success. The Bay Farm assemblage (Anderson 1996), which consisted of material left on chipping floors, mostly contained material that was either weathered or had not been used. Anderson (*ibid.*, 235) did, however, note that while the Newferry Site 3 assemblage, like most River Bann material, was heavily

Burins, scrapers and notched pieces

BURINS

In the "*Early*" Mesolithic burins are quite rare but in later Mesolithic assemblages they are virtually non existent and where they are thought to occur they maybe more accidental. One of the few distinctive examples is shown in Figure 5.10 (No. 6).

SCRAPERS

There seem to be very few scrapers and in general they are irregular in shape. However, there is also some end of blade scrapers. Three were associated with the Lough Beg Cache and from the lower zones at Newferry. One recovered from Zone 7 at Newferry (Fig. 5.9, 12) has a slightly nosed outline to the working edge. Retouch on these examples is usually steep but less regular than the retouch found on Neolithic examples.

NOTCHED PIECES

These are amongst the least known forms from the Mesolithic. They can vary from small, almost scraper-like examples, such as one from Zone 3 at Newferry (Fig. 5.11, 6), to heavily notched portions on large blades or flakes which have been found in some number at Newferry Zone 6, or at Bay Farm and at Ferriter's Cove (Fig. 5.17). In some cases, such as Bay Farm, these can be exceptionally large ranging being more than 50 mm thick and up to 150 mm in length.

Core tools

In this case there is a presumption that many of the large core tools found, in particular in the north-east, are of Later Mesolithic date, but they are often not found in closed contexts. They have neither been found in association with "*Early*" Mesolithic artefacts nor on Neolithic sites. Instead, they have been particularly common in certain parts of the Bann Valley or in Larne Lough where a small number were found at the

Curran Point in the "Larne Gravels" themselves (Woodman 1978a, 107). Besides the core-borers many of the core tools from the later Mesolithic are quite elongated and, at the same time, robust. As I suggested (*ibid.*, 98–108) many of these implements grade from narrow, roughly parallel-sided axes through to picks. Knowles similarly commented (1914) that the name "Larne Celt" was erroneous as "they have not a broad cutting edge like Celts. On the contrary one or both ends are pointed".

CORE AXES

Unlike the small axes of the "*Early*" Mesolithic, these are often quite large, exceeding 150 mm in length, and can either have a symmetrical lozenge-shaped or rectilinear section. Because of the way they are made, on occasions with a trapezoidal section, the cutting edge can appear to angle diagonally across the end of the axe. Troels Smith (1937) noted a similar phenomenon in certain classes of the Scandinavian core axes.

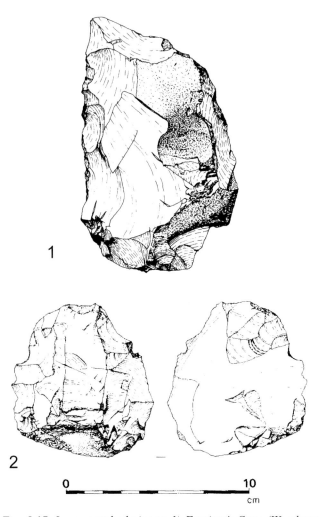

Fig. 5.17. Large notched pieces: 1) Ferriter's Cove (Woodman et al. 1999), 2) Bay Farm (Woodman and Johnston 1996).

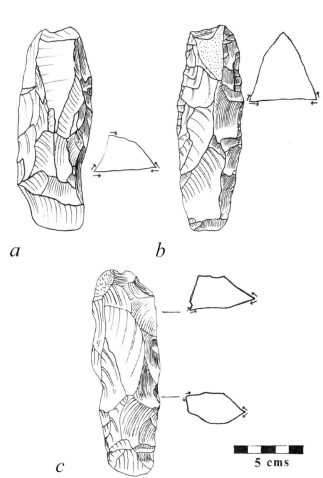

Fig. 5.18. Core axes from the Lower Bann: a) Gortgole td., b) Portglenone, c) Kilrea (after Woodman 1978a).

Core axes, as is evident from Knowles's 1914 paper and in the Keiller Knowles Collection, were found in large numbers in Larne Lough (but the better preserved examples, though they are fewer in number, come from the Lower Bann (Fig. 5.18)). In the former case, i.e. Larne Lough, Woodman (1992a, 99) recorded 98 examples. Unfortunately few good examples were recorded in the Keiller Knowles collection (Woodman *et al.* 2006) and they remained within the collection donated by Matilda Knowles after her father's death. Many, mostly from Larne Lough, were heavily rolled and so did not receive the attention that they should have. The rectilinear-sectioned core axes from the Lower Bann and Larne Lough are narrower than the Neolithic roughouts (Woodman 1978) and unlike many Neolithic roughouts they are worked, for their size, to a relatively narrow cutting edge.

Three possible examples made from other materials are known from outside the north-east These are two of chert, including a particularly fine example from Clowanstown (Warren *et al.* 2009) while a possible unfinished example made from made in Rhyolite was found at Ferriter's Cove (Farina Sternke, pers. comm.).

PICKS

As noted elsewhere (Woodman 1978a, 100–6) these come in various forms. Many are up to 150 mm or more in length and have a large, sometimes cortex covered, butt and are trimmed down to a narrow edge (Fig. 5.19). These are created by the removal of transverse flakes to form an edge which is less than 20 mm across. Others, which have a trihedral section,

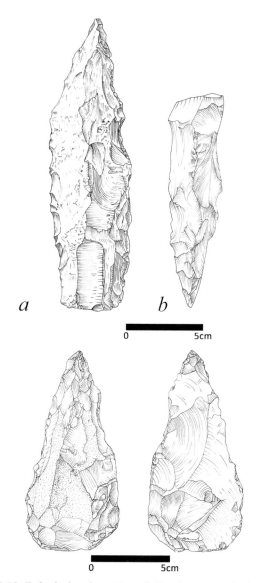

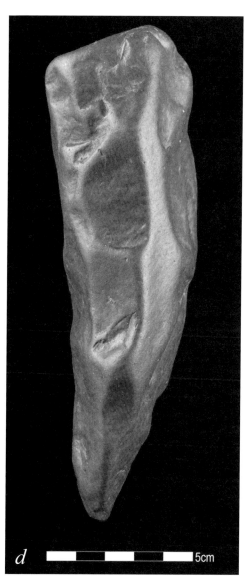

Fig. 5.19. Trihedral picks: a) Lough Kinale, Derragh td, Co. Longford, b) Clonava, Co. Westmeath, c) Newferry Site 3, d) water rolled specimen from the beach at Ferriter's Cove (drawn by Elaine Lynch, photograph by Hugh Kavanagh).

are retouched to a point. This is created by forming three edges, each of which was worked in both directions to form a triangular section that tapers to a point. One example was found at Newferry in the disturbed Zone 2 deposits (Fig. 5.19), however, a possible tip of another pick was found in Zone 6. A few examples made in other materials are known. These include chert examples from the midlands while a Rhyolite example was found at Ferriter's Cove (Fig. 5.19, d). Besides these major types, occasional double ended picks were also found. Some of the smaller examples probably belong to the "*Early*" Mesolithic.

CORE-BORERS

These are rather squatter implements that have, in proportion to their size, a large heavy butt. They are usually less than 100 mm in length. While some give the impression of being made from used large cores, on occasions they may also have been made from large flakes. Core-borers are trimmed from this large butt to a constricted, narrow but quite strong point which is often triangular in section. Examples of these have been found in Newferry (Woodman 1978a, fig. 7, 7). Again, one example made on a piece of black rhyolite was recovered from Ferriter's Cove, while a tip of what seems to have been another example was also recorded on the same site. Micro-wear analysis strongly suggests that these were used as heavy duty boring tools (Douglas Bamforth pers. comm.).

HOW DO YOU MAKE THE CORE TOOLS?

As many of the Later Mesolithic core axes and picks are quite large, in some cases with a length greater than 150 mm, it is very apparent that the initial starting block would have had to be as much as 300 mm in length and, if they are like some Palaeolithic handaxes, they may have been made on large flakes rather than by simply reducing a nodule of flint. Indeed, in some instances one can see an original ventral flake surface on the basal face of a triangular pick. This suggests that, in the case of the flint examples, they could only be made in areas where large flint nodules were available namely parts of the East Antrim coast. Nodules of erratic flint found further south along the east coast of Co. Down and Leinster, though suitable for blade production, would not have been an adequate source. In contrast, large blocks of good quality chert, as found at Moynagh Lough (Bradley 1999), could have been used, while Rhyolite blocks, such as those found in the Dingle Peninsula, would also have been ideal.

The technology of the later Mesolithic

Perhaps one of the most enduring sets of misconceptions about the Irish Mesolithic is those that surround the technology of the Later Mesolithic.

There has been, perhaps going back to Movius (1942) and *The Irish Stone Age,* an assumption that the Irish Later Mesolithic is based on the production of very large blades and blade-like flakes. Therefore, the production of large blades was

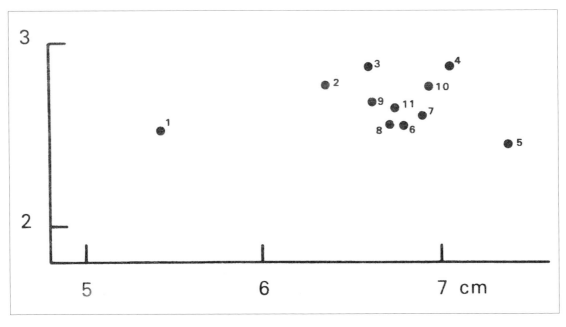

Fig. 5.20. Mean length of blades and bladelike flakes from Later Mesolithic sites: 1) Sutton, 2) Curran Point, Harvard chipping floor, 3) Lough Beg, 4) Lough Derravarragh, 5) Newferry Site 1, Newferry Site 6–11, 6) Zone 7, 7) Zone 6, 8) Zone 5 lower, 9) Zone 5 upper, 10) Zone 4, 11) Zone 3.

a reliable attribute of the Later Mesolithic, indeed it was often assumed that the bigger the blades the more likely they were to be of Later Mesolithic date. However, as was evident even in the 1970s, in flint-rich areas the purpose of blade production was to produce blades that were usually between 50 mm and 80 mm in length and in general 20–30 mm in width. Thus there is little difference between those from Curran Point, where a chipping floor was found in the beach (Woodman 1978a, fig. 24), and sites elsewhere. Indeed, due to the selection process, which resulted in blades being carried into the Bann Valley, at places like Newferry the mean blade size is slightly larger. Further south, along the east coast where erratic flint was used, the blades may be smaller, though at Sutton these tend to be only 10 mm shorter on average. In the Strangford Lough area they were shorter again but it is noticeable that, in all cases, the width tends to decrease to a much lesser extent. In contrast, from locations along the Antrim coast, such as at Mad Man's Window, there are Neolithic assemblages where much larger blades can be found (Woodman 1992a; Woodman and Johnston 1996). The significance of the issue of blade size and preparation will be discussed below in the context of changes that took place throughout the second half of the Irish Mesolithic.

The obvious problem is that, frequently, individual blades are found and it can be difficult – in some cases, impossible – to attribute them to a period. One major problem is that one cannot assume that because blades with large platforms and evidence of hard hammer percussion exist in very large number in the Later Mesolithic then any blade with those attributes will automatically belong to the that period. Large blades were found at the Neolithic house site at Ballynagilly and in the Ballynease cache (Woodman 1992a). Somewhat similar blades have been found in other Neolithic assemblages, thus, on occasions, other than relying on subjective assessment, there can be a degree of uncertainty as to whether they are Later Mesolithic or Neolithic in date. In some cases, as in the large blades from the Bann Valley (Costa 2006, fig. 6:5), platform preparation can be shown to have taken place. Intensely facetted platforms were also found on some blades and flakes in the Killybegs "hoard" (Woodman 1967) and in the blade cache from Ballyalton Court Tomb (Woodman 1992a, 89–91). Thus, platform preparation and a softer form of percussion seem to occur, *on occasions*, in the Neolithic period. In a similar vein, these forms can often be rather thinner than the typical blade and blade-like flakes of the Later Mesolithic while, certainly in the north-eastern region where flint is common, the existence of fresh cortex on blades or flakes of Later Mesolithic date seems to be remarkably rare.

In contrast, while there are certain limits to the size of blade production in the Antrim coast, i.e. the nodule size, in chert/ silicified Limestone areas, where large blocks are available, such as at the Clonava site excavated by Mitchell (1972b), blade size can be larger. At Clowanstown in particular, a location where Butt Trimmed Forms and large blades were brought to the site (Warren *et al.* 2009) has shown that the chert examples were significantly larger than those in flint. One group of large quite elongated blades with large platforms was recovered from the Neolithic levels at Clowanstown and illustrates the difficulty when it comes to ascribing large blades to a particular period. In this case, as they were also found in the Mesolithic levels, can they be Mesolithic artefacts in a secondary later context or do they demonstrate that similar large chert blades exist in the Neolithic? The problem here is that there does not seem to be any other group of similar large chert blades in any other securely contexted Neolithic assemblage!

There is obviously no simple solution to this conundrum. One can only be careful and not assume that because a blade is large and has a large striking platform it must be Later Mesolithic in date.

Another misconception, which was in part created by the author, is that the flat uniplane single platformed core or a so called "Larnian" core is a type fossil of the Later Mesolithic. There is no doubt that where flint nodules of sufficient size are available it is quite common to find a significant number of cores where the flaked surface is flat and, often, more than 50% of the circumference is still covered with cortex. It had been assumed that this was a deliberate creation, thus the term "Larnian" or "uniplane" core. As Johnson (1988; Woodman and Johnson 1996) noted, the typical large blades produced in the Later Mesolithic need to be removed from cores where the platform of the core has some curvature. When the core developed a flat working surface and the curvature on the platform vanished then the core was abandoned rather than being rejuvenated (Fig. 5.21). This was a phenomenon of the areas where flint nodules were freely available rather than a characteristic of the Later Mesolithic. It also would appear to have been used in the case of the Lough Beg cache (Pl. XXV).

It is noticeable that in the collections from Lough Kinale and Clonava, where cherty-type materials are used, these uniplane cores are quite rare and more globular cores occur in some numbers. Similarly at Ferriter's Cove the siltstone and Rhyolite multiple-platformed cores are more common, while they are rarer amongst the flint cores (Woodman *et al.* 1999, Chapter 3). It should be noted that, as yet, there has been no study as to how blades were produced from these coarser raw material and why so many globular/multiple-platformed cores exist.

Four other questions

Aside from the major categories of the tool types described above there are four more general questions which should be considered at this point.

Was there evidence of extensive flint knapping at Newferry?

The author has, in the past and later in this book, relied heavily on the suggestion that many of the artefacts, both retouched tools and blanks, found on sites in the Lower Bann Valley were

Fig. 5.21. Refitted core reconstructions from Bay Farm (after Johnson 1988).

Zone 7 at Newferry is very different from the remainder of the sequence in that knapping *was* taking place in that particular zone and it therefore presents an interesting contrast (Table 5.1)!

The pattern evident in the upper levels of Newferry Site 3 is also replicated at Newferry Sites 1 (Movius 1936) and Site 4 (Smith and Collins 1971) while cores that would be types need to produce large blades and flakes used in the Later mesolithic were also absent from Toome bypass (Dunlop and Woodman 2015) One crucial point that will be returned to in Chapter 8 is that Zone 7 is remarkably different in that extensive flint knapping did take place. The pattern for the latter part of the Later Mesolithic seems to have been very different.

Caching of flint artefacts in the Later Mesolithic

Although there are a few caches of other artefacts, notably ground stone axes and Moynagh Points (see below), a more significant number of caches of Later Mesolithic forms and blanks have been recovered. As will be seen from Table 5.2, while there might be a tendency to identify the more eye-catching caches dominated by Butt Trimmed Forms, they are quite diverse in character. They vary in size, types of artefacts and in the history of their discovery (many of these are already listed in Woodman (1978a, appendix 6) and Woodman *et al.* (2006, Chapter 5)).

In addition, the Ordnance Survey of Co. Derry noted the discovery of a "Peck of well-shaped flints and two polished stone axes" in Altduff td. These could have been a Later Mesolithic cache (Woodman 1992a, 89).

Two examples are also excluded. Since publishing the list of "hoards" in 1978 (Woodman 1978a, 342) another piece from the Aughnahoy Cache (incorrectly described as Portglenone in Finlay 2003, table 7) has turned up (Woodman *et al.* 2006, 203). It was concluded that it is highly probable that this was a cache of Neolithic date. Warren (2006) has included a group of 24 pieces from a pit at Glendhu (Woodman 1985b), however, as originally noted, there was no clear evidence to suggest that it was Later Mesolithic in date but that it was more reminiscent of *"Early"* Mesolithic or Neolithic material such as the cache found at Moynagh Lough, Co. Meath (Bradley 1991). There are numerous instances of caches of Neolithic blades and flakes.

Furthermore, perhaps the Lough Beg "Hoard" should be put to one side. It was a chance find during peat cutting and it is not certain that the whole assemblage was recovered. There is no evidence that it was a portion of a settlement site but the

produced elsewhere and brought into the valley. However, Kador (2010, 149) has wondered if the manner in which the data from Newferry (Woodman 1977a) has been tabulated has created a potentially biased impression in which retouched tools have been given an enhanced status and the role of on-site knapping has been played down. This is based on the fact that the figure for "waste" pieces was given in weight rather than numbers though, in fact, numbers of actual small waste flakes from manufacturing was quite low. This is because so many of the smaller pieces were fragments and burnt so the presentation in terms of absolute numbers seemed rather spurious. Kador's implication was that a much broader range of activities were carried out at Newferry.

At one level, one can note that out of a roughly estimated 60 kg of flint artefactual material only 6 kg constituted waste which, as noted above, included burnt and broken pieces as well as small flakes. Certainly it does not swamp the retouched tools and blanks. It is only Newferry Zones 6–3 that are considered as being typical of the movement of blades and large flakes.

Table 5.1 Mesolithic flintwork from Newferry by zone.

Zones	7	6–3
Retouched tools	54	400
Blade and flakes	334	1006
Cores	17	20

Table 5.2. Later Mesolithic and probable Later Mesolithic Caches.

Name	Discovery	Total	BTF	Distal	Other	Blades & flakes
N.Ferry (1) a	Excavation	6	–	–	–	6
N.Ferry (1) b	Excavation	5	2(?)	–	–	3?
N.Ferry (1) c	Excavation	3	–	–	–	3
N.Ferry (3) a	Excavation	4	–	1	–	3
N.Ferry (3) b	Excavation	5	–	–	–	5
Largy	Diat. cutting	7	–	–	–	7
Toome (Whelan)	Chance	10	10?	–	–	–
Toome Castle	Drainage	15(4?)	–1	–	–	10
Moneygran	Chance	3	–	–	–	3
Kells	Chance	6/8?	2?	–	–	4
Dalkey	Excavation	13	3	–	–	10
Raphael	Unknown	4	4(?)	–	–	–
Urbal	Chance	34	18	4	–	12
Lough Beg	Chance	138	1?	2	4	131

range of material, varying from small blades through to large irregular pieces, does not seem to have gone through a process of selection of useable high quality blades or other pieces that could be turned into Later Mesolithic forms, as usually occurs in Later Mesolithic caches. The Lough Beg assemblage is dominated by blades made using a hard hammer percussion and, in several instances where refitting was possible, they seem to have been removed from cores that could be described as "Larnian", i.e. removed from one platform but not from a cylindrical core (Pl. XXV). The question of refitting should also be clarified. Although roughly 100 pieces could be refitted these were spread across 17 different cores (more than three items refitted) or groups (three items refitted) along with seven pairs of refits. The largest number refitted into one core being 15 in Core 3 and only five cores had more than five pieces refitting. This phenomenon of partial refitting of only a portion of the material is not unique to the Later Mesolithic. In the case of similar Neolithic assemblages, the Killybeg "Hoard" (Woodman 1967) is a good example where refitting was not particularly successful. This was also evident in three large Neolithic hoards of flint flakes and other items from the west coast of Scotland (Saville 1999). The Later Mesolithic forms are also uncertain and the Bar Form may have been added later. The three end of blade scrapers, which are retouched in a very steep manner only at the extreme distal end, though not unknown, are not particularly common in the Later Mesolithic.

There must also be a slight reservation about the composition of the Toome Castle material. This group seems to have been found during mid-19th century dredgings at Toome (Pl. XXIV)

and was described, amongst the material recovered from the dredging that had taken place throughout Ireland, as: "Fifteen flint knives found with several others in one mass, found on the old hard gravel of the river not far from Toome Castle" (Mulvaney 1852, lxiv).

Eleven of the pieces seem to have the same distinctive grey patina that is typical of material that has not been disturbed, while the rest are more heavily patinated and some show signs of damage. The 11 pieces may be those which were *in situ* while the others may have been added. What is noticeable is that, as in many of these caches, there are no retouched forms.

Most of the caches consist of much smaller numbers and, as can be seen from Table 5:2, usually consisted of blades and blade-like flakes. In fact just Toome and Raphael caches contained only Butt Trimmed Forms – notably these are tanged examples. The group of narrow blades and Butt Trimmed Forms that may have been found at Kells (Woodman *et al.* 2006, 208–9) would also seem to pre-date the latest phases of the Later Mesolithic (Fig. 5.23). The only occurrences of the broader so-called "Bann Flake" forms which occur in the final stages of the Later Mesolithic are in the large and virtually unique Urbal Cache (*ibid.*, 214–5) and three examples in the Dalkey Cache (Liversage 1968; Woodman 1978) and perhaps Cluster 2 from Newferry Site 1 (Movius 1936; Fig 5.22).

It is hard to explain the reason for the Urbal and Lough Beg Caches. Unfortunately many of the pieces from them have extensive, heavy post-depositional damage and so it is difficult to establish if they had already been used. Perhaps they should, for the moment, be put to one side.

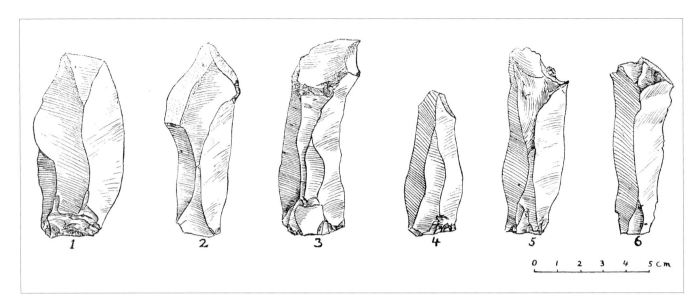

Fig. 5.22. Cache 1 of flint blades from Newferry Site 1 (Movius 1936).

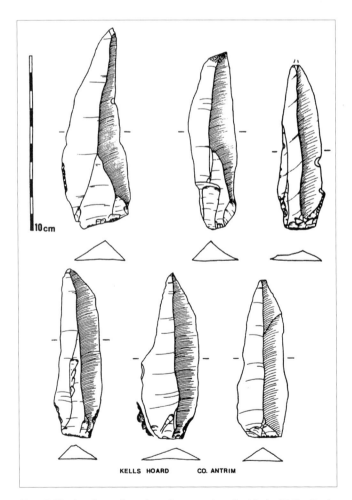

KELLS HOARD   CO. ANTRIM

Fig. 5.23. Artefacts thought to be associated with the Kells Cache (after Anderson 1994).

Strategies would be developed to facilitate movement of raw material in the form of pre-prepared tools or items that would only be finished when there was a clear idea as to what they would be used for. It is ironic that Australian knives illustrated by Knowles (1912; Pl. XIII), as comparanda to the Butt Trimmed Forms in the Bann Valley, were often acquired from quarry sites in a similar manner. A large number of these knives were carried back to the camp sites wrapped in leaf packaging or, in some cases, placed within the fuzzy hair of those who had received the implements!

Perhaps, if one is looking at personal packages of a similar type from the Irish Later Mesolithic, Whelan's Toome cache would qualify. This cache, which originally comprised ten artefacts, seems to have been left as a group that had been brought to the Toome area wrapped up as a bundle (Whelan 1930b). It could also be that the main part of the group, found in the mid-19th century (i.e. that recorded by Mulvaney from near Toome Castle and referred to earlier), were also left in a bundle. The Dalkey and Kells caches may again have been something similar.

The Caches discussed here are probably only a tiny fraction of those that were discovered. Indeed, during recent excavations of a shell midden and settlement site at Fanore 2 seven chert blades (referred to in Chapter 2) were found lying together (Michael Lynch pers. comm.). As these seem to have been lodged in a crevasse in the limestone they may be another cache, while Moore (1998, 58) observed that several other blades, as well as Butt Trimmed Forms and some debris, were found in a crevasse during excavations at Castle Carra in Co. Antrim (Hurl and Murphy 1996).

If it was simply a question of caches being created, was this part of a procurement strategy based on production in one location for use elsewhere, or as part of an embedded procurement strategy where they were cached against future use? If the latter, one might have expected a greater number of larger caches of material, but many of these have quite small numbers of artefacts.

If it were not for excavations the smaller caches at Newferry would never have been noted, therefore, one must wonder how many others were missed during the exploitation of the Bann Valley diatomite deposits.

Perhaps the most enigmatic group was from Newferry Site 1 Cache 1 (Fig. 5.22), which consisted of six blades. Movius (1936, 24) described their positioning as follows: "With one exception, these were found in a vertical position, bulbar end down, and with the upper surfaces all facing in the same direction, Nos. 1–3 in front and Nos. 4–6 behind." Something similar was noted in the Dalkey cache.

It is tempting to offer ritual as an explanation and it should be emphasised that this may also be, in part, an explanation for the other small caches. Are "Ritual" and "Caching", against a return to a frequently visited location, mutually incompatible? Although it will be discussed in more detail below, the excavations at Newferry and other evidence suggests that much of this material was cached on land surfaces rather than thrown into the water.

At the settlement site of Drumakeely in Co. Antrim (see Chapter 4) three pieces (two Butt Trimmed Forms and a large quite rectangular blade) were recovered during NAC's excavation on the banks of the Cloughwater River (Dunlop in prep.; Fig. 5.24. b). These lay close proximity in a pit (Woodman in prep.).

The Dalkey Island cache described earlier, shows that this use of caching of groups of Later Mesolithic artefacts and blades was not something particularly developed to deal with resource availability in the geographical area of the north-east. As became evident in the analysis of the equivalent Neolithic groups (Woodman *et al.* 2006, Chapter 5), it is highly probable that many other cached groups of material were uncovered, especially if the numbers of items in each find was quite small, their significance not recognised and the groups split up. One must wonder whether some of the smaller groups of artefacts recovered along various motorway schemes in Leinster (described in Chapter 9) may not also have been deposited together.

As became evident in the analysis of the equivalent Neolithic groups (Woodman *et al.* 2006, Chapter 5), it is highly probable that many other cached groups of material were uncovered, especially if the numbers of items in each find was quite small, their significance not recognised and the groups split up. In summary, these Later Mesolithic caches are diverse in size and do not contain just one artefact type. They also do not come from one particular phase within the Later Mesolithic. It is also evident that there is no consistency in their composition.

THE ROLE OF "BLANKS"

It is apparent that one of the most important aspects of Later Mesolithic reduction strategies is the creation of usable blanks that could also, where necessary, be transported over long distances (see Chapter 9). It appears that the creation of these blanks was achieved by a number of different choices and reduction strategies that were suited to local circumstances. It is also possible that these choices were made throughout much, though not all, of the Later Mesolithic (see Chapter 8).

The term "blank" is preferred to "blade" because, while many of the unretouched items are blades, a significant proportion is blade-like in character, rather than true blades. Throughout much of the Later Mesolithic, especially within the Bann Valley, there is little evidence of knapping and the production of blanks. Therefore, Newferry and the other Bann Valley assemblages provide an important insight into the purpose of these artefacts, i.e. they were brought to the area with particular intentions in mind. It also raises the question: were they more than simply the blanks for a range of tools? Another way of asking this question is whether there was an intention to deliberately produce blanks of different shapes. As has already been noted, throughout much of the Newferry sequence, the blanks were in general smaller than the Butt Trimmed Forms (see Figs 5.15 and 5.16).

This is an issue which has been explored both explicitly and implicitly. Mitchell (1956a) in his description of the Sutton assemblage categorised his "blanks" as pointed and straight sided. Johnson (1988) and Anderson (1994, 188) felt that the blanks from which the classic Bann Flakes were made were deliberately produced at a specific stage in the core reduction sequence and this led to the creation of the uniplane core.

These large blades or blanks also occur consistently within the caches described above. They range from the examples of narrow blades associated with Butt Trimmed Forms in the Kells cache through larger examples found with the Toome Castle cache to the very large forms associated with the retouched tools from the Urbal cache (Pl. XXIII). While in each instance there were pieces that could be regarded as spares which could be converted into retouched tools such as the range of Later Mesolithic forms, many were the wrong shape, too small, etc., and would have been kept for use in their own right. The Dalkey cache assemblage provides the clearest evidence that blanks for Bann Flakes were deliberately created and selected and, therefore, that many of the other pieces could be used in their own right for different purposes. As described earlier, this cache of ten blades and three Butt Trimmed Forms was found below the midden (Liversage 1968). The blades/blanks tend, like the Newferry material, to be 50–80 mm in length. This suggests that, on the basis of the blanks that were selected, there was a preference for blades and blade-like flakes that were usually 60–80 mm in length and 20–35 mm in width. The crucial point is that these are all narrower than the "Bann Flakes" in the cache (Fig. 5:24). This pattern is also repeated

Fig. 5.24. Cache of three Mesolithic artefacts from a pit at Drumakeely, Co. Antrim (by permission of NAC).

was discussed and where it was noted that throughout the sequence the unretouched pieces were consistently narrower than the Butt Trimmed Forms.

Without a detailed analysis it is difficult to quantify, but even this more casual examination of the material suggests that a significant number of these imported blanks could not be converted into many of the other classes of retouched tools with which they were associated. These would include Bar Forms which would have required production from larger thicker flakes. Similarly, many sites have a number of large, heavily notched pieces which would have to be made from much larger and thicker flakes. An equally obvious indicator that blanks were produced for purposes other than conversion into a specific tool type is also evident in Strangford. Here, especially in the Kirk Collection, there are quite a number of large Butt Trimmed Forms while, given the small size of nodules that are usually available, the blanks are relatively small, often little more than 50 mm in length. Yet they often have widths that are close to 30 mm.

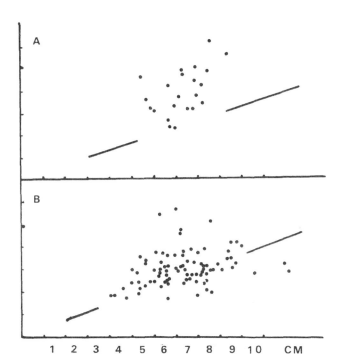

Fig. 5.25. Scatter diagrams of maximum length/breadth ratio of a) Butt Trimmed Forms, b) blanks from Newferry Site 1 (after Woodman 1978a).

in other assemblages, such as at Newferry Site 1 where there is a tendency for the Butt Trimmed Forms to be broader than the blanks, thus it seems that they may have, at least in part, been intended for other purposes (Fig. 5.25). Was this something just associated with the final stages of the Later Mesolithic? This pattern has already been alluded to (see Fig. 5.15) where the sequence in Butt Trimmed Forms from Newferry Site 3

EDGE ANGLES, BLANKS AND BUTT TRIMMED FORMS

It appears that the most important attributes searched for were width and thickness and, by inference, edge angle. Thus length, although impressive, was not essential. Anderson (1994, 161) also notes that, in Papua New Guinea, White and Thompson had recorded that stone tool users were more concerned about the edge angle than tool morphology.

Large unretouched blades and blade-like flakes are certainly not unique to the Irish Mesolithic and can occur in the Neolithic phases of the Swifterbant Sites S2 and 3 (Devriendt 2013, 127–40) where large flint blanks have been imported from some distance away and often show evidence of extensive use. They also occur in significant numbers within the Danish Late Mesolithic. Micro-wear analysis carried out by Juel Jensen (1986; 1994) showed that many of these blades had been used, possibly in a number of different ways. Many authors, such as Juel Jensen (1986, 28), have recognised, on the basis of micro-wear traces, that differing edge angles were preferred for different tasks:

Group I: acute angle around 20° for fresh hide and meat
Group II: 30–40° for wood and dry hide
Group III: 40–50° for siliceous plants and bone

Thus lower angled pieces could have been used for cutting, especially softer materials, or for other purposes such as fish gutting. In contrast, higher angles may have been used for whittling, cutting siliceous plants such as reeds, or for other tasks such as splitting branches and basketry and even scraping. In fact, the production of perfectly symmetrical blanks, while a sign of the quality of skill of the knapper, may not be as essential as one might expect. Juel Jensen (1986, 73), for example, also suggests that a series of blades with a concave edge and, in general, having edges of a higher angle than would usually be associated with knives, were probably used for "Whittling, shaving, splitting and trimming of plant stems such as reed, rushes and wooden twigs". She notes that, among a large number of blades from Ertebølle which might have had associated fish traps nearby, a number of blades showed signs of the transverse working of wood or plant and that these had concave edges (*ibid.*, 74). She also suggests that distinctive traces of evidence of cutting siliceous plants other than cereals, in particular reeds, were present at certain Mesolithic sites that were located close the water's edge (*ibid.*, 79). These are places where reeds could be collected, and possibly used in the manufacture of mats, baskets or even for thatching.

Anderson (1994, Chapter 4) has also shown there are interesting changes within the Newferry sequence. Figure 5.26 shows the edge angles of the Later Mesolithic forms and the

unretouched blades and flakes. As can be seen from Figures 5.26 (b–d), the balance between the predominant edge angles of retouched and unretouched artefacts, shifts through time. Thus, in Zone 7 the retouched forms tend to have a higher edge angle than the unretouched pieces, while in the slightly later Zone 5 there is more of a balance but, in the latest *in situ* Zone (3) the edge angles are reversed in that the retouched forms have an average lower edge angle. In other words, while the edge angles of the unretouched material remains roughly the same there is a shift amongst the retouched category to pieces with a lower angled thin edge. Does the purpose of the Butt Trimmed Forms change? Equally importantly, both the retouched forms and the blanks from all levels at Newferry 3 tend to have a lower edge angle than the Danish examples described above? Most of the items have an edge angle of 35° or less, while Danish

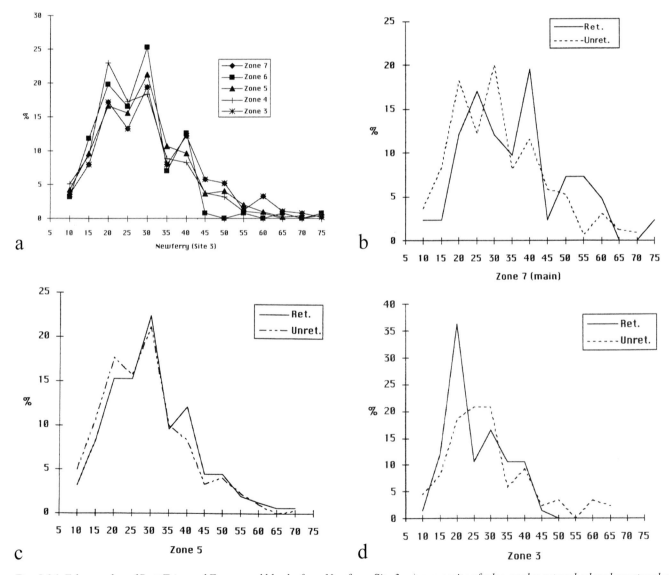

Fig. 5.26. Edge angles of Butt Trimmed Forms and blanks from Newferry Site 3: a) composite of edge angles retouched and unretouched from Zones 7–3, b–d) edge angles of retouched and unretouched from Zones 7, 5 and 3 (after Anderson 1994).

examples normally lie between 40° and 60°. This is a crucial difference. It suggests that many of the blanks found at Newferry were used for cutting and gutting rather than for gathering and processing a range of materials such as reeds or certain plant foods with stalks. Perhaps the most enigmatic pieces are the broad Bann Flakes where the width can exceed three-fifths of the length. These also have particularly low angled lateral edges and may have been deliberately produced, which could suggest that they were used for very specific purposes such as filleting fish or certain other animals. Of course Newferry may have been placed well out in the centre of the flood plain and had a particular purpose, while at other locations, such as at the fords where traps may have been placed; Later Mesolithic blanks may have had different shapes and different purposes.

One assemblage, "The Lough Beg cache" appears different. As noted earlier, one cannot even presume that it should be regarded as a cache but the pattern of angles and degree to which these pieces are pointed is just that little bit different. While, as was shown above, up to 60% of the retouched and unretouched pieces from Newferry Site 3 had edge angles of 30° or less, in the Lough Beg assemblage only 30% fell into that category. Similarly, the Lough Beg material was less pointed. While, due to the condition of the material, it was felt that micro-wear analysis was not likely to be successful it was noted that, to the naked eye, many of the pieces showed evidence of damage that was likely to have been caused by robust use. This type of damage was never noted at Newferry. This assemblage was also recovered from a location that lay at the edge of the flood plain at the south-western corner of Lough Beg. This would be a location where very different activities would have taken place.

In spite of the limitations of the Irish material, the evidence from Denmark provides a clear indication that many unretouched pieces found in the Irish Later Mesolithic, especially in contexts like the Bann Valley, should be regarded as potential tools in their own right! One must observe that we have been working with a very narrow selection of sites and, if other assemblages were looked at, it may well be observed that some of the implement types being used for very different purposes.

In an Irish context, these issues will need to be explored more extensively both in terms of morphology and micro-wear.

Other stone tools

Although some of these implements were first published in Woodman (1977a) and when the issue of a broader range of artefacts was addressed in Woodman (2005a), it is not usually recognised that a range of coarse stone tools played a very significant role in the Irish Later Mesolithic, or that the variety extends beyond the ground stone axes. There is also a problem in coming up with a term that, on the one hand, provides an overarching category and on the other provides a terms that describes each individual class. Does the term "coarse stone tools" encompass ground stone axes? In this case it has been decided to leave *Ground stone axes* and *Ground stone pointed implements* as separate categories, while other types are placed in a third category *Other coarse stone tools.*

Ground stone axes

These are particularly prolific during the Later Mesolithic. The 40+ axes that were found at Newferry must represent one of the largest concentrations of axes from any part of the Irish Stone Age, especially if one excludes the numbers from quarry sites, such as the porcelanite outcrops or the Lambay Quarry site. Thus fewer than half the number of axes that were recovered from Newferry was found at two prolific Neolithic sites, i.e. at the adjacent Lyles Hill and Donegore Hill. It is also probable that the vast majority of the 500+ axes collected by Knowles from Culbane belong to the Later Mesolithic. Elsewhere they appear to occur in the same profusion: 15 axes were collected in the 1960s from Lough Kinale (Woodman 1978a) while many of the axes from Dalkey Island (Liversage 1978) were almost certainly Mesolithic. At Ferriter's Cove the discovery of 15 axes doubled the number of axes previously known from Co. Kerry.

The axes use a diverse range of materials, including shales, mudstones, siltstones and schist, though there is no evidence for the use of any of the raw materials which were to become common in the Neolithic (Figs 5.27 and 5.28). Given the range of sources available it might seem that there was a tendency simply to use what was available locally, but many have been transported for some distance. While the full implication of the choice of resources will be discussed below, and the fact that many axes are made from baked mudstones has been long established. It is worth noting that there is some evidence that other materials were also preferred and, in some cases, moved over some distance.

The most obvious example is Chlorite Schist:

- *Dalkey Island*: Three out of four axes from the midden are made from schist while 11 out of 16 strays from Sites II and V are either shales, mudstones or schist.
- *Moynagh Lough*: Bradley (1998) noted that one of the three ground stone axes recovered from Mesolithic levels was green in colour and partially decomposed. This was a phenomenon which was also observed at Newferry (Woodman 1977a).
- *Ferriter's Cove*: Axes are either shale or mudstone made from locally derived carboniferous deposits.
- *Newferry Zones 8 and 7*: Ten axes made from schist and two from shale.
- *Newferry Zones 6 and 5*: Nine axes made from schist and two from mudstone.
- *Newferry Zones 4 and 3*: Nine axes made from mudstone and one from schist.
- *Port of Larne:* One certain axe of schist was recovered from context 5012 and two other much decomposed fragments were also noted.

Fig. 5.27. Stone axes from the lower part of the sequence at Newferry Site 3 (Woodman 1977c).

Fig. 5.28. Stone axes from the upper part of the sequence at Newferry Site 3 (Woodman 1977c).

While some axes have been ground, overall there is little evidence that they relied to any great extent on quarried sources, but rather large pebbles have generally been used and sometimes it is possible to identify the water-rolled portions of the original surface. In general, the axes tend to reflect the manner in which raw material can be used: those made from banded shales tend to look different to those from baked mudstones or from schist.

It appears that, as at Newferry, axes tend to be relatively small: less than 150 mm in length. This can also be seen the Ferriter's Cove cache (Fig 5.29). As noted (Woodman 1978a) at both Newferry and Kinale, axes fell into two class sizes with, in both cases, a significant gap in maximum length: around 70 mm at Kinale and 90 mm at Newferry. In this latter case the gap exists irrespective of the raw material used (Fig. 5.30).

Certain attributes (Woodman *et al*. 1999) seem to be associated with axes from this period. These seem to occur throughout Ireland rather than being confined to one region (Fig. 5.31):

1) There is a notable tendency to grind flat facets onto the surface rather than produce a fully rounded, smooth profile.

In some cases, as at Ferriter's Cove, this can be seen in an extreme form where the edges are formed by a series of long flat facets.

2) One long edge may retain extensive traces of battering or bruising.

3) In certain areas, especially where schist axes have been used, a distinctive pointed butt axe with a rounded cutting edge can be found. These axes can also have an asymmetrically formed cutting edge where one face is flat while the profile of the other is convex (see above Fig. 5.27).

As yet no large-scale project has tackled the questions of differences between Mesolithic and Neolithic ground/polished stone axes in an objective manner. There is also a tendency to illustrate and concentrate on axes that, in the broadest sense of the word, resemble forms that are considered "axe-like". However, from the Bann Valley in particular and perhaps elsewhere, there are many axes that appear to have been made from elongated rectangular slabs of banded stone and where virtually the only alteration is the creation of a cutting edge. Knowles (1912, pls xvii and xviii) illustrates a selection of these, while Jackson (1909, pl. iii, 4–9) seems to have collected numerous examples from the diatomite deposits at

Fig. 5.29. Cache of ground stone axes from Ferriter's Cove.

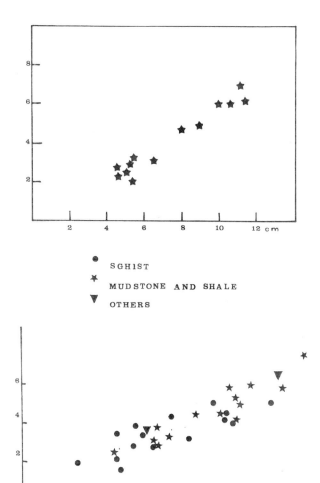

● SCHIST

✱ MUDSTONE AND SHALE

▼ OTHERS

Fig. 5.30. Size differences in axes from Newferry Site 3 and Lough Kinale assemblage.

Culbane. Examples were also recovered from the excavations at Newferry Site 3 (Woodman 1977a).

While a small cache of five axes was uncovered at Ferriter's Cove (Woodman *et al.* 1999, 63–5), few other caches of Mesolithic axes are known. One group of four axes that were found in a small area at Belderrig (Warren 2009) are thought by the excavator to be another dispersed cache. Knowles (1912, 219; pl. xix) noted one nest of six axes from the Culbane area, which are similar to those found in Mesolithic contexts at Newferry Site 3 (Woodman 1977a). These may, though it is by no means certain, be associated with a grinding stone. Flanagan (1960) has noted other examples where a single axe is associated with a grindstone.

One aspect of the large numbers of ground stone axes made from mudstone, siltstone and related materials is that, in places, they occur in very large numbers and there is a temptation to assume that they could not possibly be Mesolithic. In part this is due to Mahr's (1937) contentious creation of the "Riverford Culture". The most well-known example must be at the ford at Killaloe on the Shannon where up to 900 axes are reported to have been recovered (*ibid.*, 297–300). It is apparent from the records in the National Museum that these axes were part of an active commercial process where workers on the Shannon drainage knew they would be rewarded for handing them in. This large concentrations of axes, at or near the sea or rivers, seems to be a common factor in many parts of the west of Ireland. Driscoill (2006, 149–78; 2013) has explored the issue as to why a large percentage of the ground stone axes from Co. Galway were concentrated in the Tawin Island/Maree area which lies on the coast in Galway Bay. These axes came into the National Museum in the 1930s. During field walking, which has also produced large quantities of chert lithic debris in this area, more axes were also found. In this instance it would seem that the majority of the material post-dates the Mesolithic and provides a warning that not all mudstone and axes of similar materials need necessarily be of Mesolithic date.

Lynch (2002) has also noted that a similar concentration of axes that were recovered from the shores of Lough Inchiquinn in Co. Clare could be of Mesolithic age. Similarly, the axes found by D'Evelyn, Knowles and others at Fisherstreet could be regarded as being of the same age.

Therefore, where large numbers of axes have been recovered from the types of contexts where other Mesolithic material has been recovered, one should, perhaps, suggest that there is really no evidence that those axes are *not* Mesolithic in date!

Ground stone pointed implements

These are a significant and very diverse group of artefacts. Initially it was thought that there were simply a few well-made, very distinctive implements that were given the name "Moynagh Points" and some cruder, chipped examples that it was suggested could be called "Kerry Points" (Woodman 2005a, 131–3). It seems probable that these should be placed within a large group of artefacts. At the moment Sternke (in prep.) has identified over 70 items which can be placed in this broader category.

One should perhaps approach this category with an element of caution. Rather like the ground stone axes from rivers and diatomite cutting, where one can presume that many are of Mesolithic age, some ground pointed and related implements have been found in contexts dated to the Later Mesolithic and are found at locations where a Mesolithic date seems probable. There are some that are completely without context but on sites where material from a number of other periods are present – most notably the particularly fine specimen from the A32 near Dungannon, Co. Tyrone, which was in a pit of Bronze Age date (Pl. XXVIa). It is important that we recognise that this technology was definitely present in the Irish Later Mesolithic even if, on occasions, it reappears at a later date.

Moynagh and related types of points

Moynagh Points are a series of elongated, thin, pointed implements that are usually 150–200 mm in length (Fig. 5.32). In many instances they are less than 10 mm thick and can range in width between 20 mm and 40 mm. They have been made of fine-grained silt and slate. They were first chipped into a rough shape and then ground to their finished form (Sternke in prep.). They have often been dredged from rivers and one particularly fine example was dredged up off Beare Island, Co. Cork (O'Brien 2012, 41; Pl. XXVIc). Although Wilde (1857) listed several examples in his Museum Catalogue, the significance of these implements was first recognised by Raftery in a paper in 1942. However, while there was a feeling that they might be Mesolithic, it was only with the discovery of a cache of six examples at Moynagh Lough that a strong case could be made for a Mesolithic date (Pl. XXVIb). This cache lay within a layer that contained significant quantities of Later Mesolithic artefacts (Bradley 1999). Again, when they are found in association with other artefacts, they are usually only found with Later Mesolithic artefacts. The term "Moynagh Point" was first suggested in 2005 (Woodman 2005a, 130–2). More recently they have begun to turn up in other excavations, such Derragh Island, Co. Longford (Sternke and Woodman unpublished) and at Fanore on the coast of Co. Clare (Woodman in prep.). Both of these examples occur on sites that date to the latest/final phases of the Mesolithic though the Fanore example was quite broken and weathered and may be earlier than the date of the main phase of the site which was approximately 6000–5800 cal BP. Again, the Derragh example belongs to the roughly contemporaneous stone platform at the top of the Derragh Island sequence. In one instance, a fragment was recovered during excavations at Gortore which overlooked a key location on the Funshion River in Co. Cork (Sternke forthcoming) While there were a series of unassociated radiocarbon dates which centred more on 8000 years cal BP there was no clear evidence that the Moynagh Point belonged to that chronological phase of the Irish Mesolithic.

Fig. 5.31. Lateral edge of ground stone axe from Ferriter's Cove.

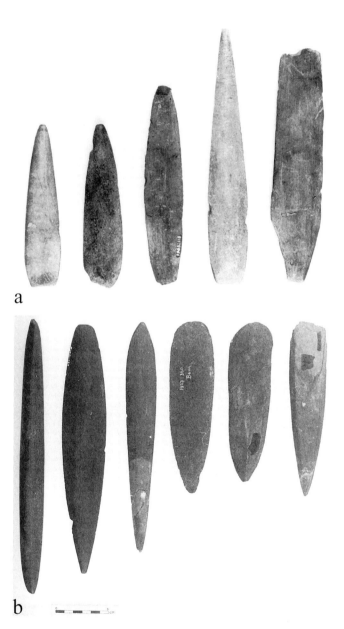

Fig. 5.32. Selection of examples of Moynagh points from collections of the National Museum of Ireland: a) Clonaddaron td, Annaholty, Lough Naglack, near Moira, near Moira, b) Corrib River Rahoonagh td., Corraghy td., Bann River, unprovenanced (provided by the National Museum of Ireland).

Moynagh Points are relatively rare in north-east Ireland and were not noted or included in many of the collections based on material from that part of Ireland, notably Lough Neagh and the River Bann (e.g. Adams, Evans and Day), while they were only given a passing mention by Knowles (1912, 218).

There is also some evidence of other forms which do not quite fit into the Moynagh Point category. This can even be seen in the examples from the Moynagh cache (Pl. XXVI) which appear to have been of varying shapes. Those illustrated from the collections of the National Museum again show a diversity of shape (Fig. 5.32). At this stage it would be a mistake to assume that they were also projectile heads as the term "*point*" suggests, Knowles, for example (*ibid.*), regarded the few he was aware of as knives.

There are others which may not date to the Mesolithic. One example, from Cloonarragh, Co. Roscommon approaches 300 mm in length and is quite thick. Is this a particularly large example of a Moynagh Point or is it a well-made example of something else? A fragment of a similar example was found during drainage work in Gardenfield td, Co. Galway (Mulvaney 1852, lxiii). This was a middle section measuring 145 × 33 × 18 mm and was probably originally about the same size as the Cloonarragh example.

Kerry Points: Is there such a thing?

At Ferriter's Cove simple pieces of siltstone were chipped into shape (Fig. 5.33). It was tempting to regard these as anomalous local products, but similar chipped points have been collected from the shores of Lough Neagh at Toome (Fig 5.34) and one possible but rather eroded example was found by Movius during his excavations at Newferry Site 1 (Woodman 2005a). As mentioned above, further fragmentary examples were found during excavations at Fanore and at Derragh Island.

It would be tempting to describe these as roughouts for Moynagh Points but they are usually thinner and shorter as well as made from a more laminated friable material. Van Gijn and Keiser (1999) report finding wear traces round the butt of one of the Ferriter's Cove examples and it appears that this example may have been used as a knife.

Other ground stone tools

There are also occasional examples of extremely large, thicker implements. The surviving portion of one large fragment dredged from the River Bann is 300 mm in length and could have exceeded 500 mm (Fig. 5.35a). It is also 20 mm thick. It is one of those anomalous items kept in the bottom drawer in museum stores and there was no sense of its actual age, however, an artefact from the recent excavations at Belderrig, Co. Mayo (Warren 2009, 149, fig. 15.6) may be a fragment of a similar tool. The crucial information about the Belderrig example is that it comes from a Mesolithic context, which

should give us the confidence to consider the strong possibility that these examples from dredged or uncertain contexts are also Mesolithic. Certain other implements may also fall into this category. One example would be that found in early 19th century drainage works associated with Lough Aclaureen in Co. Galway. This example is recorded as being "23″ long by

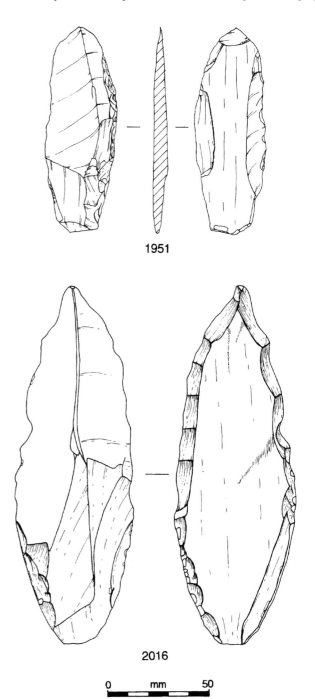

Fig. 5.33. Kerry points from Ferriter's Cove (after Woodman et al. 1999).

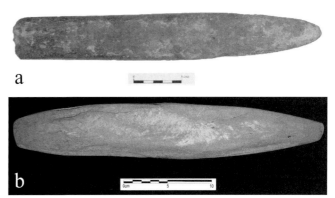

Fig. 5.35. a) Portion of a elongated ground stone implement dredged from the river Bann near Coleraine (by permission of National Museums of Northern Ireland), b) elongated ground stone implement dug from the edge of the Upper Bann floodplain, Derrinraw td. (photograph by Vincent McAllister).

Review of the ground stone tools

Obviously, we cannot presume that each and every item in the classes discussed above is Mesolithic in date, though it is a reasonable presumption that many of them do belong to the Later Mesolithic.

Using flint as the template, the first reaction to them must be to see these implements as very different items, perhaps a series of inferior tools that were substitutes for the norm. In particular, it would be very easy to see them as a substitute for flint. However, while some forms are found predominantly away from the north-east, the fact that they all also occur within a region where flint has always been available, suggests that there is more to them. One could argue that the use of other material removes some of the constraints imposed by flint, in particular the fact that, throughout much of Ireland, the size of the nodule is not particularly large.

One might go even further and observe that, in terms of the manufacture and use of lithic artefacts, Ireland lies across a significant border. Away from the European flint rich "Heartland", there is another more northerly region, almost a Clark's Techno-complex where ground stone tools exist in some numbers. This can be defined as a region that includes Lake Onega in the Russian federation, where at sites such as Oleneostrovski Mogilnik (Gurina 1956) a range of slate artefacts were recovered. After tools made from flint, slate tools at 33.4% are the most the most common (O' Shea and Zvelebil 1984, table 9). Implements such as slate daggers, some of which are quite spectacular, occur towards the end of the Older Stone Age, i.e. perhaps before 6000 cal BP, had even reached Finnmark in Arctic Norway. No one would suggest that the appearance of ground slate artefacts in Ireland is as a result of direct cultural contact but it is an interestingly similar response.

Fig. 5.34. Kerry points from Lough Neagh at Toome (by permission of National Museums of Northern Ireland).

1 7/8″ thick" (Mulvaney 1852, lxii–lxiii; Wilde 1857, 35). It is not entirely symmetrical in shape, has a more lenticular section than the examples referred to above and had been ground or smoothed overall. It is worked to a narrow point and has a flat butt which seems to have been formed by the original surface. It has had a hole drilled in it in recent times.

Although it may be pushing too many different forms into the one category, a recently discovered example from Derrinraw, on the edge of the upper Bann's estuary into Lough Neagh, could be regarded as part of the same group. Interestingly, in this case the implement has been ground to a narrow bevel at either end (Fig. 5.35b). Again, a somewhat similar artefact was recovered by MacNaught and Gallagher from a field on the western shores of Lough Foyle in the Red Castle area. This particular field had produced a very large selection of Later Mesolithic artefacts.

Overall, these implements were not hafted projectile heads and must have served a different purpose. It would seem likely that, while many are at least narrow or roughly pointed, they may have served very different purposes.

Chipped coarse stone tools

Again individually and taken in the context of particular sites, these tend to be seen as interesting anomalies, but if a more objective look is taken then it becomes clear that the following range of tool types is something which forms an important and crucial part of the Irish Later Mesolithic. They present a particular set of problems. Some, such as the elongated pebbles and other similar slabs, may have received scant attention from the collectors, indeed Knowles (1912) in his "Stone implements from the River Bann" paper makes little reference to them and many other collectors do not seem to have collected them. A further problem is that some of these implements are so simple that they may well have been used in other periods. Many of these simple forms can only be considered as Mesolithic when they are found in context. At the other extreme some are so idiosyncratic that there is a temptation to regard them with suspicion and assume that they are forgeries or at the very least be placed in the "Riverford" implements category, which in effect condemns them to be regarded as suspect.

For certain categories of coarse stone tools Clarke (2009) have provided a good overview of the British evidence, which illustrates some similarities between Britain and Ireland and in some cases shows that there can be quite significant differences. One apparent and significant difference is that certain classes of chopper tools are not found in Britain and while Skaill Knives are known from both sides of the Irish Sea they appear to exist in Scotland in later contexts, such as the Bronze Age, while they have been found in a Mesolithic context in Ireland at Ferriter's Cove.

On the other hand, what has been described at countersunk pebbles, which only exist in Ireland in later periods, occur at Mesolithic sites such as at Sand in the Hebrides in Scotland (*ibid.,* 15–16, fig. 2:1).

Perhaps the lesson from these differences is that certain implement types, especially various forms of coarse stone tools, may not be typical of a particular period but may be created either deliberately or through use, according to needs, at different times. The forms known or thought to have been used during the Irish Mesolithic are listed below:

Chopper and related tools

The most distinctive examples were found at both Newferry and Ferriter's Cove (Fig. 5.36). These were either unifacial or bifacially chipped along one edge. They were usually made on flat, coarse stone cobbles with a maximum dimension of approximately 150 mm. Some have what could be regarded as a rounded butt that would provide a comfortable hand hold. At Ferriter's Cove (Woodman *et al.* 1999, fig. 4:7) several examples were chipped along one or both lateral edges.

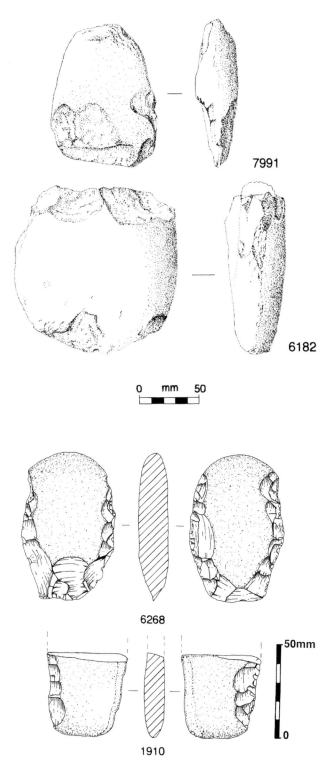

Fig. 5.36. Coarse stone "chopper" tools from Ferriter's Cove (Woodman et al. *1999) (drawn by R. Cronin).*

"Skaill" knives

This is amongst the most elusive class of artefact. These distinctive large flakes of coarse stone were first recognised on an Orcadian site at Skaill. These were first documented in Ireland at Ferriter's Cove (*ibid.*, 55). In one sense they are little more than large, 100 mm in diameter, often sub-circular flakes that are, if anything, slightly broader than long. They are usually relatively thin but retain the slightly thicker rounded outer surface of the original nodule along one edge. The Ferriter's Cove examples include only one example which shows signs of retouch. While rather opportunistic, these artefacts could be used as cutting or butchering tools. Also, while one cannot assume that individual stray finds belong to the Mesolithic period, it is of interest that May (1939) noted that numerous examples of what he called "discoidal flakes" were recovered at Loughan Island during the "Bann Dredgings" and he illustrates those from the Cutts (*ibid.*, fig. 3:1 and 3) while another was found further upstream at Camus Ford (*ibid.*, fig. 3:4). Mitchell (1972) mentioned in passing that at least one similar artefact was recovered during his excavations at Sutton.

The lesson of the Skaill knives is that we often identify, list and illustrate our diagnostic tool types and can be over cautious in identifying other simple forms. Thus with recent work at Fanore in Co. Clare, where work is still in progress (Lynch and Woodman in prep.), there is a series of large tools made from coarse stone raw materials. These can seem like simple large flakes from the surface of cobbles which have some casual damage to their edges but how many have to be found before one can call them an artefact?

Other flat disc shaped pieces have normally been found in sand dunes of a later date yet even a casual examination of some assemblages from the Later Mesolithic is beginning to uncovered similar objects.

Elongated pebble tools

These are amongst the least considered tool types in the Irish Mesolithic, yet on some sites they are amongst the most common implements to be found.

BEVEL ENDED TOOLS

The most obvious forms have in Ireland been called "Elongated Bevelled Pebbles" (Anderson 2000; Fig. 5.37) or on occasions "Bevel Ended Tools".

These are sometimes confused with limpet scoops such as those found on so-called Obanian sites in western Scotland, many of which can be made from bone. Usually these artefacts have been found on Later Mesolithic sites in Ireland though one small, very well-made example was found at Mount Sandel (Woodman 1985a, 52, fig. 33:4). Kador (2010, 150–1) has compared this example to forms found in the Irish Later Mesolithic, but at 105 mm it is much smaller than the vast majority of Irish Later Mesolithic forms, which are often in excess of 150 mm in length.

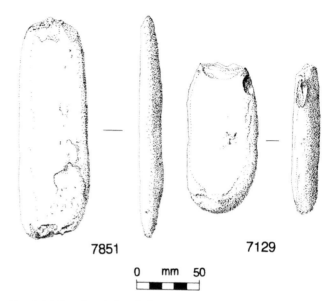

7851   7129

0   mm   50

Fig. 5.37. Bevel ended tools from Ferriter's Cove (Woodman et al. 1999) (drawn by R. Cronin).

In the few sites in Britain where coarse stone tools have been documented there is no consistent pattern in the presence of bevel ended tools. As (Clarke 2009, 15, fig 2.1) has noted, at Sand on Skye, although other forms of coarse stone tools are present, bevel ended tools were not recorded. In contrast, at Kinloch on Rhum both ground and flaked edged examples were recovered, along with elongated pebbles which had surface pecking (*ibid.*, 18, fig. 2:3). At Howick in Northumbria, 19 examples were documented, all of which seem to have ground or worn edges (Clarke and Waddington 2007, 110–12). These examples ranged in length from 95–140 mm.

The Irish examples are found only on coastal sites. Surprisingly, however, in Ireland these forms are only known in any numbers from four sites; Sutton, Dalkey Island, Rockmarshall and Ferriter's Cove. It is also very noticeable that none are known from the whole of the Strangford Lough area, which perhaps has the largest concentration of Later Mesolithic coastal sites in Ireland. Anderson (2000) examined examples of "elongated pebble tools" from the three east coast sites. The fact that they were all particularly large is evident from her results listed below. Unfortunately the sample from Rockmarshall is quite small and perhaps because these were the first excavations carried out by Mitchell (1949a) there is a chance that some, especially the apparently unaltered and unused ones, may not have been recognised. The major groups in her study therefore came from Sutton and Dalkey Island.

One question which Anderson addressed was whether or not these were just a random selection of beach pebbles. Samples of pebbles were obtained from beaches adjacent to Sutton and Dalkey Island. It is apparent that they reflect the local geology. At each location both the beach pebbles and the archaeological examples occurred in roughly the same numbers with quartzite, sandstone and shale dominating at Sutton, while schist, sandstone and limestone were the most common at Dalkey Island. However, at Dalkey the limestone may not have been entirely suitable and is not present amongst the selected examples (Anderson 2000, 20, table 3:2). A small sample of actual artefacts were examined (*ibid.*, table 3:3) and these appeared to again reflect the local geology. What was also apparent is that while these implements are usually referred to as "Elongated Pebbles", Anderson also observed that a sizeable minority could not be fitted into that category. This again would have reflected what could be found on the beaches.

It was also apparent that while elongated examples were preferred this was not to the exclusion of others. In the case of Dalkey, 56% could be classified as elongated while at Sutton the figure was higher, at 71%.

In general, Anderson (2000) noted that worked edges appeared to have been created with a combination of methods and perhaps uses. Of the 183 examined, only 30 had an edge created solely through grinding. Examples which had chipping and/or flaking first before grinding was much more common... Anderson also suggested that the grinding process only happened after the edges had been created.

At Ferriter's Cove (Woodman *et al.* 1999) only three out of 23 examples showed signs of having been ground down, again either as a deliberate process in making the implement or through use. Anderson also noted that the flaked edges varied, with some being straight and at a right-angle to the perpendicular length of the pebble, while others had edges which ran at an angle.

Obviously the most contentious issue surrounding these artefacts must be the question of what were they used for? The explanations, as Clarke (2009) has noted, vary from limpet hammers, an idea that Saville (2004, 191) has pointed out goes back to the 19th century, through use in knapping or hide working (Roberts 1987). Experiments carried out as part of the Southern Hebrides Mesolithic project favoured, on balance, the likelihood that many were used as "limpet hammers" though in at least one case an example could have been used for hide preparation (Barlow and Mithen 2000, 520–1).

Anderson (2000) observed that, in the case of the Irish examples, the grinding process which only happened late would suggest that the grinding may have taken place during use. In Ireland, the fact that bevelled forms were found on sites where limpets had been collected in some numbers must also weigh in favour of these implements being mostly used in rocky shore environs where limpets would be collected. It is of interest that while simple unaltered elongated pebbles were found on all sites, at Sutton, where oysters were the overwhelmingly dominant species in the midden, only 17 out of the 64 pebbles collected had a manufactured edge. If there were other uses then experimental work in Ireland is required if a case is to be made for alternative explanations.

SIMPLE ELONGATED PEBBLES

There are also, alongside the bevelled forms, a series of simple elongated pebbles. Clarke and Waddington (2007, table 15:1) categorised the 15 simple forms from Howick as "blanks", however, as Clarke (2009, 15, fig. 22) has shown in the case of the Kinloch assemblage, some pebbles though not always elongated have pecking on their flat surface or have facetted sides. On coastal sites, such as Sutton (Mitchell 1956) or Ferriter's Cove (Woodman *et al.* 1999), one might be tempted to see these items as casual introductions from the nearby beaches. They were, although not included by Kador (2010, 149, table 14:1), also found on inland sites such as at Newferry (Woodman 1977a; Fig. 5.38) and five examples were also recovered from the inland lake site of Moynagh Lough (Bradley 1999), as well as six examples between the original surface collection on Lough Kinale and the Discovery Programme's Derragh Island excavation (Fredengren 2009; Sternke and Woodman forthcoming). Some examples from the Newferry excavations were quite large and two were over 180 mm in length. While these implements do not look impressive their occurrence on inland sites may be significant. Certainly there is no obvious location along the portion of the lower Bann from which they could be collected and those from Newferry are made from relatively soft materials, usually schist (Woodman 1977a, appx 2). At the very least these implements could be classed as "Manuports", in other words items that have been deliberately collected at one location, but not altered, and brought to another location for use.

It is tempting to see them as serving the same function as similar elongated stone items known as "Priests", which until recently were used on the lower Bann to stun eels and even salmon. However, this may be too simple a solution, particularly as one portion of a broken example from Newferry, where both portions were recovered, has been ground down along one lateral edge. Again, examples from Ferriter's Cove show evidence of other types of use as several retain areas of damage on their flat surfaces (Woodman *et al.* 1999, fig. 4:7; Fig. 5.38) as does one example from Sutton (Mitchell 1956). This damage is more like that caused when the stones are used as "anvil stones". Yet, why use an elongated pebble as an anvil stone?

What about the Riverford Implements?

Implements associated with the term "Riverford" were regarded by many with suspicion. There is a strong belief that at least some of the large axes, in particular those collected in the 1930s by Dr John B. Stewart of Portglenone, may have been forgeries. I would also have been in that category, particularly as a local farmer informed me that they were made by grinding, using a rotary grindstone that was powered with the aid of a bicycle! However, Simpson (1993; see also Woodman 2005a, 134–5) in his review of the so-called Riverford material has shown

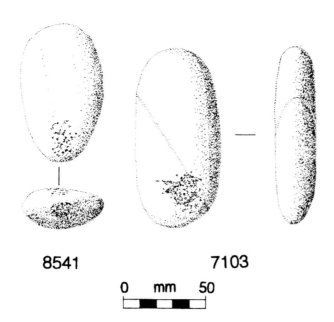

8541   7103

0   mm   50

Fig. 5.38. Elongated pebbles from (left) Ferriter's Cove (Woodman et al. 1999) and (right) Newferry Site 3 (Woodman 1977a) (drawn by R. Cronin).

quite clearly that some of these large crude implements could belong to the Stone Age and probably the Mesolithic. Most have been dredged out of rivers, and might be considered to be of unknown age but occasional examples having been found on excavations, notably at Newferry (Fig. 5.39). These range from simple, large pieces of stone, such as those found at Newferry, to the amazingly long example from Culbane in the Darbishire collection in Manchester. One particularly striking example that is 550 mm long comes from the Blackwater River near Charlemount, Co. Armagh (Wilde 1857, fig. 5). There are also a series of these large, almost club-like, implements that again have been mostly found in the River Bann and Lough Neagh. Similarly, Jackson (1909, 13) and Knowles (1912, 213) refer to examples of the same size.

Mahr (1937) suggested the term "Riverford Clubs" for this particular series of large implements. Indeed, there would seem to have been a debate as to whether they could be considered as axes. Perhaps the term "Riverford club" is, at the moment, the term that most adequately describes them. However, it is also quite difficult to distinguish large axes from clubs. Mahr (*ibid.*, pl. xxii) has illustrated that there are some quite long implements that are thicker and may

Fig. 5.39. Selection of coarse stone tools from Newferry Site 3: a) "chopper tool", b) polissoirs/grindstone, c) artefact of petrified wood, d) elongated pebbles.

have been axes. It is highly probable that there are occasional implements that differ from the elongated clubs yet are too large to be considered as axes.

The so-called "clubs" may seem to represent the boundary for exotic forms that do not fit comfortably into the European Mesolithic's typological lexicon, but there are others? There are certainly anomalous, large, thick triangular, almost wedge-shaped, pieces, examples of which were identified by both Knowles (1912, pl. xviii) from the Bann and by Mahr from the Barrow River (Fig. 5.40). As mentioned above, these have been noted as far back as the mid-19th century when O'Laverty (1857, 122), in his analysis of implements from the Bann Drainage at Portglenone, noted several of these large artefacts. Is the example that was illustrated by O'Laverty (Fig. 5.40b) a club or something else?

Rather like the elongated pebbles, there are probably forms that are not recognised. Occasionally flat slabs that may exceed 500 mm in length and extend from a narrow "handle" to a broad flat surface, have been noted, such as at Ferriter's Cove and Derragh Lough. Knowles (1912, pl. xviii) illustrates a quite regular example but many of these pieces are almost fortuitous manuports that usually show only some limited signs of alteration.

The weird and the wonderful

Part of the reason for returning to examine the classes of implements that had been dismissed as anomalous implements of a late date, was the discoveries at Ferriter's Cove. Here implements made from a range of raw materials, as well as rather striking items such as the chipped slate points (Kerry Points), raised questions as to whether other "odd" items could be Mesolithic (Woodman 2005a) These include some very distinctive items, such as one made from decarbonated chert that was dug up from the diatomite at Toome and another that was dredged from the Bann (Fig. 5.40e and f). Both are in excess of 250 mm in length. The hesitancy in accepting these objects may reflect more on the debate as to whether there really was a Mesolithic in Ireland, as well as the belief that, if it was present, our Mesolithic should be like that found in Britain. Needless to say, the belief was that it should look something like Star Carr. There is a certain irony that many of our British colleagues are still, 60 years later, looking for something like Star Carr!

Of course there was also the disdain in which Mahr's Riverford Culture was held. I have to admit that several really weird "things" found at Newferry were objects so strange that they were best ignored (Fig. 5.40c and d). Both of those illustrated have, along with their strange form, clearly been worked at one end to form a handle. These have raised the question as to whether other equally "odd" items still remain to be rehabilitated. As to their purpose, that's another question!

Grindstones/polissoirs

Grindstones can be used for a number of varying purposes and in different periods (Fig. 5.41). The discovery of several in Later Mesolithic contexts at Newferry (Sites 1 and 3), however, shows that they were used during the Mesolithic. Several examples were also found at Dalkey Island and while none was found in the middens that seem to have been primarily Mesolithic in date, several were found, along with large numbers of Later Mesolithic artefacts, in the disturbed deposits. Flanagan (1960, 59), in noting one acquired from the Bann Valley in 1959, pointed out that an example had also been found with a stone axe at the Bushfoot in Co. Antrim. Again both Knowles and Jackson referred to a number of examples, especially from the Culbane area. Jackson refers to six examples between his own and Robert Bell's collection, while Knowles claims to have had 21 in his possession. In general these are dished pieces of sandstone that are generally less than 150 mm across and usually about 50 mm thick. At Newferry Site 1 a smaller rather thicker piece, less than 100 mm across and of triangular section, shows signs of having been worked on all three surfaces (Fig. 5.41a). At the very least this suggests that the raw material for these grindstones is not immediately accessible?

The better known example is that of Knowles (1912, 219) which is ground into a slight concavity on both faces and is over 300 mm across. As noted earlier, this example was found close to "a nest of six stone axes", which led Knowles to speculate that the grindstone had been used in the production of the axes. This view was repeated by Raftery (1951, 71, fig. 72). Flanagan (1960, 55), in cataloguing the example for the collections of the Ulster Museum, pointed out that some are so small that they could not have been used for grinding down a roughout of an axe or have been used for sharpening, but could be used for plant processing or other purposes and need not necessarily be associated with axe grinding. This was a view that was supported by Woodman and Johnson (1991–2), who pointed out that many of the axes which were likely to be Later Mesolithic in date were made from a series of baked mudstones that were probably brought from sources south of Lough Neagh to an area where there were few roughouts. Interestingly, the Ulster Museum example is made from chlorite schist, as may the nest of the axes recorded by Knowles (Preston 1960). One example, however, stands out as different, namely the Jackson example from Culbane. This is slightly larger, nearly 400 mm in length, has much more linear grinding surfaces which are more typical of the type of grindstone that is known to have been used to help in the process of manufacturing axes (Woodman *et al.* 1999).

It is noticeable that while these forms are usually dish-shaped the example found at Ferriter's Cove is much more linear (Fig. 5.41b). This example is also elongated but smaller and seems to have deeper facets than the Jackson specimen. Could this example, or some of the others, have been used

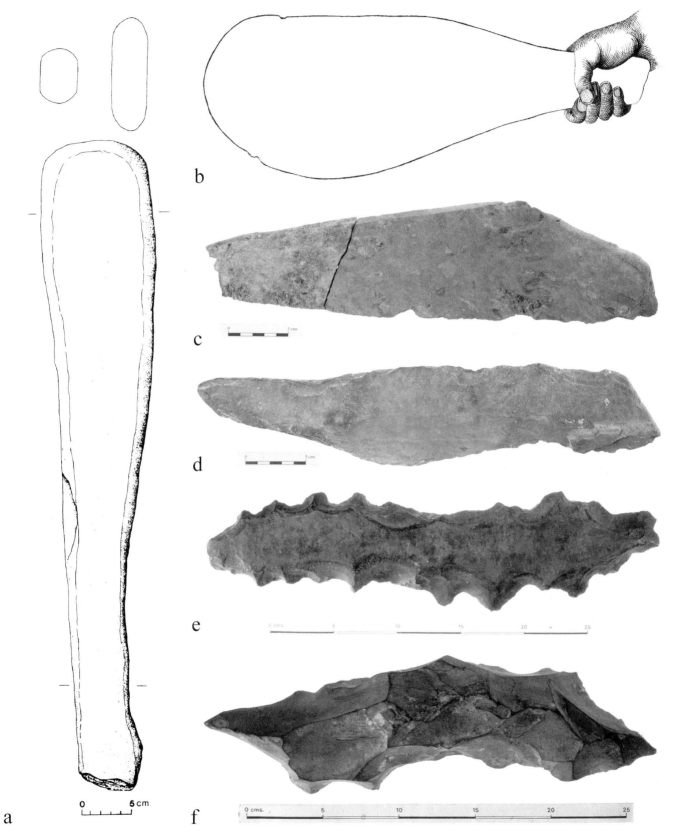

Fig. 5.40. a–b) So-called salmon clubs from the Lower Bann from Simpson (1993) and O'Laverty (1857), c–d) two club like implements from excavations at Newferry Site 3, e) dredged from the Lower Bann near Coleraine (by permission of National Museums of Northern Ireland), f) from the diatomite at Toome.

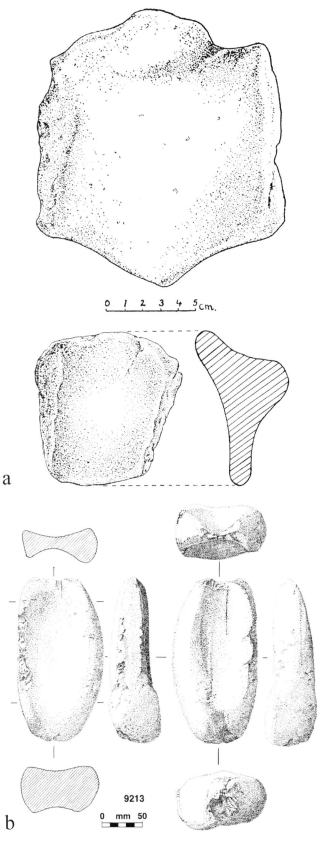

a

b

9213

0   mm   50

Fig. 5.41. Polissoirs: a) Newferry site 1 (Movius 1936), b) Ferriter's Cove (Woodman et al. *1999) (drawn by R. Cronin).*

for grinding slate or bone? The example photographed in the Museum in Kalundborg, which is roughly 1 m in length, illustrates how large these axe polishers can be (Fig. 5.42).

Although it was not found in a Mesolithic context the flat and thin slab recovered from the central area during excavations on the Toome Bypass, irrespective of its actual age, could have had a different purpose. It is highly probable that similar slabs have been uncovered on a number of other excavations but, especially in coastal area and riverine sites, were just assumed to be brought there by nature.

It is possible, therefore, that grindstones were used throughout the Irish Later Mesolithic and possibly, like some of the other implements discussed above, during the whole of the Irish Mesolithic. It should not be assumed, though, even

a

b

Fig. 5.42. a) Axe polishing stone from Kalundborg Museum, Denmark, b) from excavations at Toome Bypass (Dunlop and Woodman 2015).

if they are lumped together under the same heading, that they had only one purpose. Some may have been used for the other stone implements and as will be seen below many of the bone points also show signs of grinding.

Bone implements

There are surprisingly nearly 200 worked bone implements in Ireland which may be of Mesolithic date. From Rockmarshall (Mitchell 1947), there are two worked or altered pieces of bone, one of which is a needle-like bone sliver and the other the epiphysis of the limb bone which has been trimmed to a point. The vast majority of the bone implements are bone points that, along with a small number of irregularly worked bones,

were recovered from the 1930s Bann Drainage. Whelan (1952) only recorded that about 90 were dredged up at one specific point, at the Cutts on the lower Bann, though a series of over 125 broken and complete bone points, besides the other worked and unworked bone fragments, survive in the Collections of the National Museums Northern Ireland (NMNI). A further smaller sample, perhaps 17 items, that was also published by Whelan (*ibid.*, 12–14) was recovered about 1 km south at Loughan Island. A selection of these items from Whelan" s 1952 is illustrated (Fig. 5.43).

Whelan (*ibid.*, 5–6) records that these implements were fortuitously recovered from a specific area. At one spot, exploratory drilling had shown that a series of soft deposits existed instead of the usual reefs of basalt outcrop and

Fig. 5.43. Bone points dredged from the lower Bann (after Whelan 1952).

therefore the usual blasting was not required. The area was, instead, de-watered within a coffer dam and the deposits were removed with the use of a dipper dredger/grabline (?). Whelan (*ibid.*, fig. 3; Fig. 5.44) recorded two layers within the bed of the river. These were an overlying layer of gravel which, in places, exceeded 500 mm in thickness, with an underlying layer of soft "fluviatile silt" that was slightly thinner in places, approaching 500 mm. Fortunately, at this point the bed of the river had been inspected after the river had been de-watered and before the dredger went into action. Whelan reported that nothing of archaeological significance was noted, i.e. that on and in the upper gravels there were no archaeological artefacts but he (*ibid.*, 6) was also sure that: "There are no satisfactory indications from Site I, though such may well have existed, of the association of bone artefacts with flints and polished stone axes of the Bann culture."

In other words, the bone implements seem to have been dredged up from the underlying "fluviatile silt". At nearby Loughan Island, as no extensive silt deposits had been noted, this area had been blasted rather than simply dredged. No record of an *in situ* silt deposit was recorded, though Whelan suspected that small unidentified patches may have existed. He also noticed that numerous stone tools were recovered. While many of these were rolled, damaged or heavily patinated, a number of Butt Trimmed Forms, including tanged examples as well as blades, were in an extremely fresh condition and are likely to have been buried in undisturbed deposits for the last few thousand years. These were so fresh that it would be tempting to see at least some of them having been part of a cache of the type referred to earlier. The Loughan area also produced a, so far, unique ground stone point that in some ways simulates some of the bone points.

May (1939) also note that occasional examples had turned up during dredging elsewhere along the Lower Bann? Since then a number of other examples have been recovered, including two and a possible third from Lough Gara, one from Ballyholme on the shores of Belfast Lough and from between Loughs Sheelin and Kinale in Kilgolagh td. Most recently, one example was found on the inter-tidal shore at Glynn in Larne Lough (Sinéad McCartan pers. comm.). Perhaps most importantly three fragments recovered from Zone 5 at Newferry Site 3 (Woodman 1977a, fig. 11) showed that at least some of the bone points could be presumed to date to the Mesolithic, in this case at some point between 8000–7000 cal BP. Given the fact that the dates from Zone 5 were based on charcoal rather than bone and had probability errors of approaching 200 years, any more precise estimate of age would be spurious

An on-going research project on these objects, which includes NMNI, UCC and CNRS Nanterre, is beginning to provide an understanding of the significance of these objects (David *et al.* forthcoming). From this project it is apparent that many of these pointed bone implements were made from fractured fragments of bone which were chipped and then ground into shape.

At present a radiocarbon dating programme is confirming that, in general, most of these artefacts are of Mesolithic Age. Currently 11 dates have been obtained and of these eight were from samples collected during the dredging programme in the Coleraine area. Some of these are illustrated in Figure 5.45. Of the other three dates, two were samples collected on the shores of Lough Gara, while the third was on an example collected from a garden on the shores of Belfast Lough at Ballyholme, Co. Down (Fig. 5.46). Remarkably, all dates could be regarded as being within the Mesolithic, though one example which is not quite the same as the other points (UBA 7395, 5036±30 BP, 5895–5665 cal BP), from Rathtermon, Lough Gara, dates very late, to an interim period which lies on the cusp of the transition between Mesolithic and Neolithic (see Chapter 11). The remaining samples lay between 9000 and 7500 cal BP. One exceptional example (Fig. 5.43), recovered from Loughan Island, consists of a human ulna that has been shaped and has produced the date of 8048–7870 cal BP (PUBA 7562, 7157±43 BP), which falls within the general range of dates (Fig. 5.45). It is possible that bone implements of this type were used extensively throughout the Irish Mesolithic, though if one relied entirely on the dated examples listed in Table 5.3 one might feel that they belonged to the middle of the Irish Mesolithic. There are also possibly two other examples from Moynagh Lough (Bradley 1999) and Derragh Lough (Christina Fredengren pers. comm.) Both came from excavated sites that belong to the later part of the Irish Later Mesolithic. As yet neither of these items has been examined. Also, given the limited number of excavations and the very acidic nature of the soil in many parts of Ireland, it could be argued that Irish archaeology is surprisingly fortunate in the number of these implements that have actually been recovered (Fig. 5.44).

At this stage, as can be seen from Figures 5.43–6, a series of different types can be identified There are various attributes which can be considered. These include condition, methods of manufacture and shape. In the absence of a completed

Table 5.3. Radiocarbon dates of bone points and related froms.

Cutts	GR29189	7460±40	8289–8176	Bulbous
Cutts	UB 7561	6386±40	7430–7176	B.holme
Loughan Isl.	UB 7562	7157±43	8160–7851	Human
Ballyholme	UB 7563	6949±45	7935–7666	B.holme
Cutts	UB 19470	7363±40	8342–8026	El.flat
Cutts	UB 19471	7004±40	7959–7689	Worked bone
Cutts	UB 19472	8033±49	9125–8641	Splinter
Cutts	UB 19473	7103±45	8041–7790	Bulbous
Cutts	UB 19474	7376±48	8361–8021	Splinter
Shroove	UB 7396	7246±32	8175–7968	narrow

Bulbous = Bulbous point, B. holme = Ballyholmetyhe, Human = made on human bone, El. flat = Elongated flat section, Splinter = made on bone splinter.

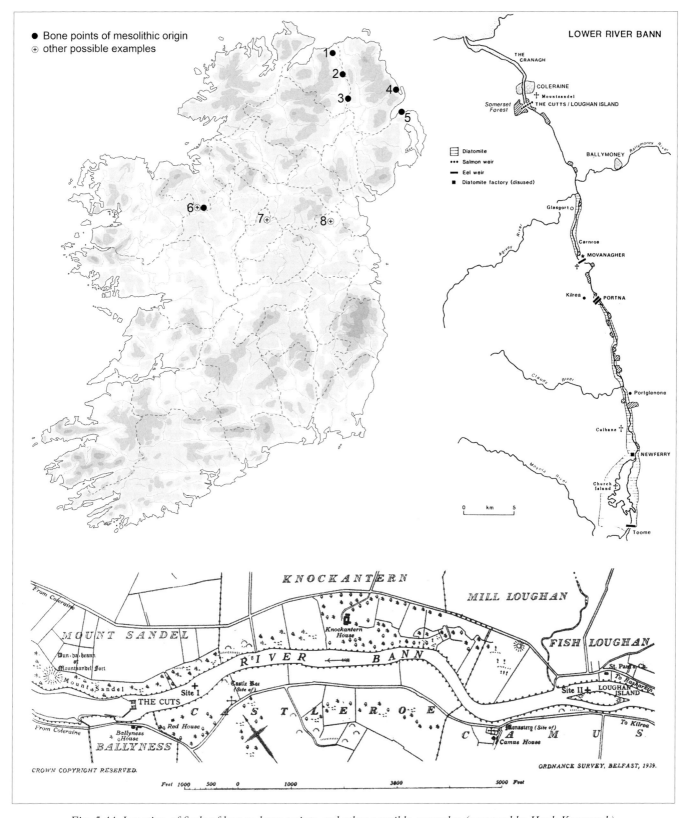

Fig. 5.44. Location of finds of known bone points and other possible examples (prepared by Hugh Kavanagh).

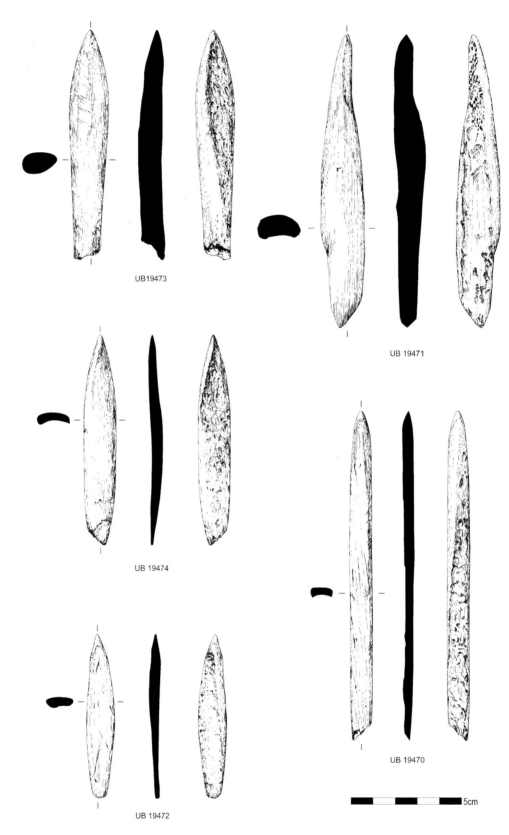

UB19473

UB 19471

UB 19474

UB 19470

UB 19472

5cm

Fig. 5.45. Selected radiocarbon dated bone points (drawn by Vincent McAllister).

definitive study, one can simply observe that they range from small examples, often approximately 100 mm in length and which have been made on small flakes of bone, through to large spatulate examples, one of which is 250 mm in length. Many of the larger forms have quite obtuse, very thick points. In between are a range of different shapes which vary from narrow examples, such as the Ballyholme example (Fig. 5.46) whose points can again vary in character. There are also some examples which are double pointed. Again, some are extensively ground over most of their surface while others concentrate on a very careful shaping of the leading edge with the remainder of the body receiving much less attention. These shapes may be a product of both methods of manufacture and purpose. At the moment the radiocarbon dating programme is not indicating that different forms occur at different times.

One observation can be made. This is that while bone points of various types can occur on many sites of later periods, many of the forms that have been noted above are not known to occur on sites of later periods.

The question will and has been asked as to which bone and species of mammal has provided the raw material. While the experimental manufacture aspect of this project has only begun, the two species for which a case can be made are the wild boar and brown bear. Certainly (Eva David pers. comm.), it seems probable that some of the larger specimens may have been made from bear metapodials. While these observations refer to the manner of obtaining a blank, whether a small flake or a more carefully produced elongated splinter, there is also the problem of the manner in which these implements were ground down to their final shape. Could some of the stone "polissoirs" that have been found on Later Mesolithic sites have been used?

The one clear observation that can be made about these points is that they differ from those found in many other parts of Europe. In general, while some of the smaller, lighter examples could have served as the tips of projectiles, it seems unlikely that they would have been used as fish spears, even aside from the absence of barbs, since elsewhere they were

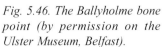

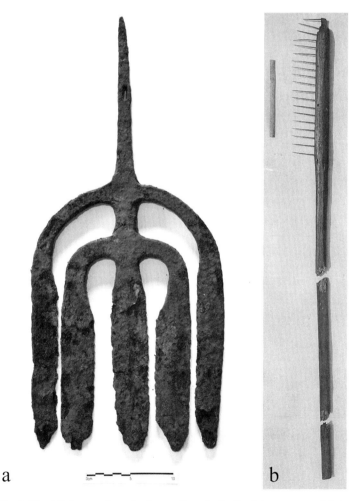

a

b

Fig. 5.46. The Ballyholme bone point (by permission on the Ulster Museum, Belfast).

Fig. 5.47. a) Eel spear from the Lower Bann in the Portglenone area (photograph by Vincent McAllister), b) eel rake (from the Collections of the Ulster Folk and Transport Museum, by permission of National Museums of Northern Ireland).

usually much longer. Instead, they may represent the types of multi-pronged forks that were used for catching eels on many rivers in Ireland and perhaps, as existed on the Bann, as the teeth in eel rakes (Fig. 5.47). The full implications of these suggestions will be explored in Chapters 10 and 11. Even at this stage of the project one other observation can also be made. This is that there is little evidence of impact fractures on the end of these points, while many have been broken laterally around the mid-point of their length.

Summarising the Later Mesolithic

Besides the fact that there is a much greater diversity of artefact types in the Irish Later Mesolithic than has generally been appreciated, there are still many issues which require further investigation. As well as the issue of purpose of use of many artefact types and the refining of the chronology, some of which will be explored below, there are other areas that present difficulties. One of these is the identification of whether a smaller assemblage without distinctive and diagnostic tool types is actually Later Mesolithic in date.

Hopefully, on the basis of this review, one of the lessons that will be apparent is that "Bann Flakes" are only a relatively small part of the story of the Later Mesolithic. Although it is only possible to produce evidence from a limited number of excavated sites, Table 5.4 shows that some of the lesser known artefact types are a consistent presence.

There are many small assemblages, however, that can be difficult to attribute to the Later Mesolithic. As with the "*Early*" Mesolithic, the decision to call an assemblage Later Mesolithic, where independent dating is not available, is surrounded by varying degrees of probability:

1) An assemblage containing diagnostic artefacts along with a range of blades and flakes in a secure context.
2) Assemblages of similar character in disturbed contexts.
3) Assemblages in the north-east in particular, where a series of blades is found along with a group of uniplane cores, are probably of Later Mesolithic age.

4) Dependant on the size of the assemblage and context, a series of blades found on their own may need to be attributed to the Later Mesolithic but with some reservation.

Is the Later Mesolithic homogeneous?

This question was recently considered by Kador (2010) and several observations made in that paper have been dealt with but the question about the Later Mesolithic in general is valid. There is a simple answer YES and NO!

The question could be asked in either a chronological or geographical context. The chronological context has already been touched on and as noted earlier, given the absence of a good selection of sites that pre-date 7000 cal BP, one ends up coming back to Newferry where the shift from flint knapping took place from in Zone 7 to a much greater reliance on importation of blanks. Even within the later Newferry phase there are changes, such as the appearance of bar forms, changes in the presence, absence of tanged Butt Trimmed Forms, and even a shift in the preferred raw material from which ground stone axes are made. This is an issue which will be considered again in Chapter 8.

Geographically, there has always been the worry that "The north-east" is "calling the shots" too much. When I moved to Cork and started to excavate at Ferriter's Cove I expected that, while an "*Early*" Mesolithic might look the same across the whole island, we would find, as can happen in other regions of Europe, a much greater diversity within the Irish Later Mesolithic. The big surprise of Ferriter's Cove was the similarity of so much of the assemblage to what has been found in the north-east. While there may be a few small differences whose significance will be considered below in Chapter 9, in general the similarities within the Later Mesolithic right across the island are quite striking. One of the most eloquent statements can be seen in the very distinctive Trihedral picks (Figs 5.19–20). These are an example in flint from Newferry, two examples in chert from the Midlands and a rather water rolled example made from Rhyolite which was recovered from the shore at Ferriter's Cove.

Conclusion

When considered in its entirety, there is no doubt that Later Mesolithic assemblages are very different from not only the "*Early*"/Earlier Irish Mesolithic but from most other European assemblages. Besides the occurrence of a series of large ground and chipped stone tools ranging from Riverford Clubs through chipped coarse stone pebbles and Moynagh Points to grindstones, this period is characterised by a series of artefacts made on large blades and other blanks. These forms, many of which are often associated with the term "Bann Flake", seem to have been general purpose tools perhaps, as noted earlier, frequently associated with heavy duty tasks such as wood working, possibly in the creating of fixed facilities. They are strongly suggestive of a major shift between the Earlier and

Table 5.4. Range of coarse stone tools from selected Later Mesolithic sites.

Site	GSA	CST	Grindstone	Bone point	EP	BET
Ferriter's Cove	C	P	P	–	C	C
Moynagh	P	–	P	P (?)	P	–
Newferry	C	P	C	P	C	–
B.down??	P	–	C	–	P	P
Dalkey Island	C	–	P	P (??)	C	C
Derragh Island	C	–	?	P	P	–

GSA= ground stone axes; CST = coarse stone tools; EP = elongated pebbles; BET = Bevel ended tools; P = present; C = common

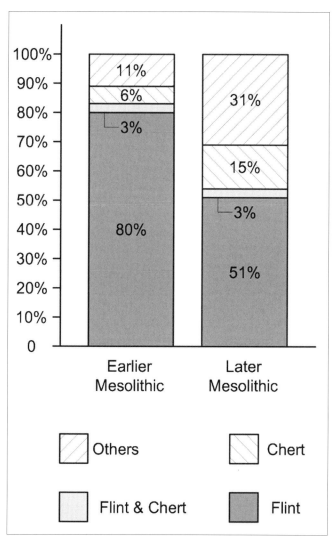

Fig. 5.48. Ratios of the presence of different raw materials: a) Earlier Mesolithic, b) Later Mesolithic (prepared by Hugh Kavanagh).

Later Mesolithic in the manner of procurement of resources, whether raw materials or sources of nutrition.

There is one final, less obvious and perhaps apparently quite mundane, change between the Earlier and Later Mesolithic. There seems to have been a shift in how, in terms of lithics, the appropriate raw materials were procured. Figure 5.48 shows that during the Later Mesolithic there was much less reliance on the use of flint than was the case at an earlier date. This suggests that after an initial period of reliance on tried and tested raw materials there was a shift to more local resources though (see Part III below). There was also, perhaps, a more structured system of bringing particular materials to a group's particular area of settlement (see Chapter 9).

These issues can only be fully pursued once other matters are considered. These include examining in more detail how and when Ireland was first settled, as well as the manner in which changes took place within the Irish Mesolithic.

Part III

OFTEN AN ISLAND TOO FAR?

Is research to be concentrated solely on establishing the evidence for the beginning of the continuous human settlement in Ireland, or should the possibility of an Irish Palaeolithic be explored? These two priorities require very different approaches.

The latter avenue of study, that is the question of identifying a human presence in Ireland before the beginning of the Holocene, is quite simple. Can traces of earlier artefacts of any part of the Palaeolithic be found in Ireland? It goes without saying that any artefacts recovered or recognised must also be shown to be incontrovertibly within geological or other contexts that help confirm their age.

In contrast, as will be shown below, questions associated with the Holocene colonisation of Ireland are qualitatively different. Unlike the search for an Irish Palaeolithic, the presence of a Mesolithic in Ireland is beyond doubt. It is always possible that an earlier Mesolithic presence will be identified and, while on a regional level there is still a lot of attention paid to the discovery of "the earliest", "the first", etc., discussions at a European level (see Larsson et al. 2003; McCartan et al. 2009) have lead to a very thoughtful exploration of what is meant by the earliest Mesolithic settlement in any region. This includes topics such as the distinction between exploratory and pioneering phases of settlement and the establishment of a permanent presence on the "Island of Ireland". There are not only simple economic issues around the question of how to survive in a different land, but there is also the question of technological responses to a new environment.

Chapter 6

Anything earlier?

Perhaps the pursuit of an Irish Palaeolithic seems like a self-indulgent search for irrelevant trivia. It is apparent from earlier descriptions of Irish Quaternary geology that there is little chance of discovering a significant missing, yet to be discovered Palaeolithic. The possibility of a post-Last Glacial Maximum (LGM), i.e. late glacial, presence falls into a separate category. It has to be borne in mind that there is a qualitative difference between investigating a potential late glacial presence and the possibility of evidence from the much older pre-Last Glacial Maximum periods. Different strands of evidence have to be found in each case.

The significant mammalian faunal presence from MIS 3, discussed earlier, will always act as an indicator of a potential human presence, at least in the period 60–25,000 years ago (60–25 ka) but even in the apparently ludicrous task of attempting to identify an Irish Lower Palaeolithic there are contributions that can be made towards a broader European debate on the nature of the presence of modern humans and their ancestors in middle and early upper Pleistocene Europe. In particular, given the fact that Ireland was often isolated as an island, any clear indication of a human presence at an early date would be a major contribution to our understanding of the use of the sea by early humans and their capacity to cross significant stretches of open water.

A summary of the questions surrounding an Irish Palaeolithic was provided over a decade ago (Woodman 1998c), however recent work in both Ireland and Britain, renders it worthwhile to set out a framework within which future research can take place.

Before the Last Glacial Maximum

For the earlier periods two problems exist:

1) The chance of discovery
2) The reliability of the artefactual evidence.

The chance of discovery

It has always been tempting to simply dismiss the possibility of an Irish Palaeolithic. However, even within this one heading there are two particular considerations, a) the possibility that an early human presence had existed on one or more occasions in Ireland, and b) perhaps more importantly, the possibility of the survival and/or recovery of evidence for such an early human presence.

It may be felt that the total destruction of any traces of an early Palaeolithic settlement renders this discussion pointless but this is too simplistic an approach simply because the "absence of evidence is not evidence of absence". It has always been simpler to work within the unspoken assumption that major gaps in the archaeological record are a product of genuine absences of human activity. This is a theme that will not be considered here but will be returned to on several occasions below. Numerous good reasons will be advanced to explain the lacuna in question. It should be remembered that in the case of Ireland, research in the last few decades has had the lesson of the "empty landscape of the southern part of the island", where no Mesolithic presence was known! The absence of a Mesolithic was not questioned, but as discussed in Chapter 3, was explained away on the basis of the absence of appropriate raw materials and loss of potential evidence below rising sea levels. The real lesson should be that if a perfectly obvious Mesolithic could be overlooked, why should there not be something earlier? However, the search for evidence of a human presence that pre-dated the last ice age would require constant vigilance rather than being simply dismissed.

The second problem is that, even if there were, in certain regions, surviving traces of early humans, there would also be a requirement that the deposits in which they were embedded would be exposed. Burial below tens of metres of quaternary deposits would, unless some other agency intervened, render them inaccessible as evidence.

Recent research in Britain has illustrated how our views of early settlement can be significantly revised. Two areas in particular have shown how regions that were either relatively neglected or dismissed can still provide new insights. The midlands of England, which have been glaciated on numerous occasions and were always regarded as the poor relation of the English Lower Palaeolithic have, in recent years, seen a revival of interest. In particular, through the careful examination of relatively few artefacts, such as those from Waverly Wood near Birmingham (Keen *et al.* 2006), it has become apparent that Lower Palaeolithic settlement did take place along the now vanished Bytham River, which was obliterated during the "Anglian Glaciation" (MIS 12; Bridgeland *et al.* 2006, 439). The recovery of a number of Andesite handaxes has raised broader issues than might have been expected (Keen *et al.* 2006, 467–9).

There appear to be no local bedrock sources of Andesite as a raw material and while it is possible that the implements could be made from glacially derived boulders it is equally possible that these artefacts were originally made either closer to the Lake District or in north Wales. In other words, this suggests a more extensive area where there was a Lower Palaeolithic presence in Britain than might have been expected (Fig. 6.1).

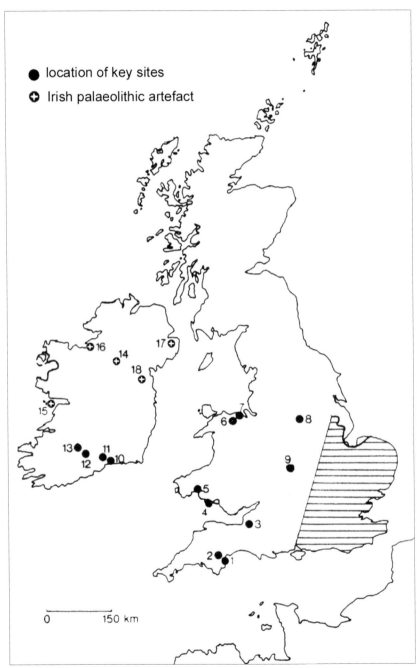

Fig. 6.1. Map of the British Isles showing the locations of some key Lower and middle Palaeolithic sites in the west: 1) Kents Cavern, 2) Torbryan Valley caves, 3) Hyaena Den, 4) Paviland Cave, 5) Coygan Cave, 6) Pontnewydd Cave, 7) Cwynn and Ffynnon, 8) Creswell Crags, 9) Waverley Wood, 10) Shandon Cave, 11) Ballynamintra Cave, 12) Foley Cave, 13) Castlepook Cave, 14) Maghery, 15) Dun Aenghus, 16) Rosses point, 17) Newtownards flint flake, 18) Drogheda flint flake.

The rediscovery of the significance of the north Wales site of Pontnewydd (Green 1984; Aldhouse-Green *et al.* 2012) is another example. Here, earlier excavations paid little attention to a range of artefacts that were made from a series of raw materials such as Rhyolite or Ignimbrite. It was only through Aldhouse-Green's re-investigation that a significant assemblage dating to MIS 7, approximately 200,000 years ago, was recognised to be associated with the cave! If the syntax of discourse is based almost entirely on the language of flint then much will be missed. The broader archaeological implications of Pontnewydd will be explored further below.

Evidence can also be dismissed as not really being that old. Thus, the return to the often contentious issue of an early "Pre Cromerian" human presence from coastal regions of East Anglia, which was one of the battle grounds for the Eolith dispute, is a good example. Yet, at Pakefield (Roebroeks 2006, 428) a small but *in situ* lithic assemblage was incorporated in deposits that could date to at least MIS 17, or approximately 700,000 years ago. This would pre-date the conventionally presumed earliest human presence recovered at sites such as Boxgrove in Sussex (*ibid.*). Perhaps the crucial difference between the East Anglian coast and elsewhere is that the *opportunity* for new discoveries along the Cromer coast is, through coastal erosion, continually being refreshed in a manner that is difficult to replicate elsewhere.

In returning to some of the issues associated with "opportunity", it is also rarely emphasised enough that southern England presents a remarkable chance to recover evidence of a Lower Palaeolithic. In particular, the combination of an area where there is an abundance of flint and a convenient series of river terraces of varying ages going back through the middle Pleistocene has provided one of the best laboratories for the discovery and study of Lower Palaeolithic artefactual assemblages. Admittedly these artefacts are usually in secondary contexts but the profusion of the material makes it impossible to ignore. How many other parts of Europe have this convenient convergence of opportunity and exceptional quantities of artefacts?

In summary, the destruction of the contexts in which Palaeolithic artefacts might occur does not necessarily exclude the possibility of occasional chance remains being uncovered or remove the possibility that human settlement did take place. The lack of expectation of the chance of discovery may be as big a barrier as those posed by geomorphological factors.

The reliability of the artefactual evidence

This includes not only the artefacts themselves but also the context within which they were recovered. As will have been apparent from earlier discussions, for much of the time in which Knowles and others pushed for a substantially greater antiquity for many of these disputed artefacts, little understanding of the chronology of Irish glacial deposits existed. Thus, besides pseudo-artefacts there will always be a series of potentially genuine artefacts, such as the occasional handaxe (see below), but these are frequently chance finds out of context whose pedigree in terms of association with deposits of Pleistocene age is unclear. These are potential signposts for an earlier presence but not a guarantee that it existed.

There is also the often unappreciated fact that artefacts of roughly similar shape can be created at entirely different points in time. Artefacts, or even the apparent technological process of their manufacture, are not a certain guarantee of a particular age. There are too many instances of unfortunate similarities being used to create either false chronological or cultural associations. The examples from Ireland include the claims by Knowles that that some of the picks and core-borers that we now recognise as belonging primarily to the Later Mesolithic were handaxes, and Burchell's attempts (Burchell and Reid Moir 1928; 1931) to classify what we would now regard as natural pieces of limestone found amongst some struck flakes at Rosses Point as either handaxes or Mousterian side-scrapers (see Woodman 1998b). In the case of Wales this is a particularly difficult issue, as Aldhouse-Green (1993) has shown there are a number of artefacts along the south Wales coastal area that could be placed in either of the above categories.

In the Upper Palaeolithic and perhaps the Mousterian there are different problems. The chances of any form of scraper, knife or projectile head, which is presumed to be a type fossil, being confined to a specific period is a presumption fraught with danger. Therefore, suggestions of an Upper Palaeolithic in Ireland should not be based on the single presence of one distinctive type fossil. Leaf points that resemble *Blattspitzen* and tanged points that look somewhat like Font Robert Points, for instance, may be little more than bifacial forms or slightly anomalous plano-convex knives of Neolithic date respectively (Woodman *et al.* 2006, 167–9). The difference between the Irish Later Mesolithic tanged Butt Trimmed Form and the Font Robert Point is sufficiently subtle to warrant caution in attributing an individual artefact to the Gravettian.

In summary, the search for traces of a Palaeolithic of pre-Last Glacial Maximum date in marginal areas is never easy. It has to be a fine balance of an open mind without giving into "messianic" convictions that it is really there.

So! What is the case for Ireland?

In the case of Ireland, there seems to be little chance that any remnants of an earlier Palaeolithic would survive. As has been shown in Chapter 2, there has been extensive destruction of older Quaternary deposits caused by the actions of Midlandian Glaciation, plus the fact that a significant number of surviving deposits are of glacio-marine origin. It seems probable (see Chapter 2), that the ice sheets of the last major glaciation not only extended over the whole of Ireland but southwards offshore for a considerable distance. The surviving deposits may be the result of a complex series of events but, in total, they result in a landscape where any *in situ* traces of settlement in the period 60–25 ka (MIS 3) are unlikely to have survived.

It is of interest, therefore, that while occasional individual finds of bones of a probable Pleistocene age have been found elsewhere, all the caves containing MIS 3 fauna only exist south of the Ballylanders Moraine and come from a small area in north-east Cork and west Waterford.

So, is there any convincing evidence of an Irish Palaeolithic? Again, any examination of these problems can be divided into:

a) the problems of the Lower and Early Middle Palaeolithic, where surviving deposits are rare but where occasional distinctive artefacts might just survive;

b) The flake and blade industries of the Mousterian and Earlier Upper Palaeolithic which might just survive the effects of the LGM.

An Irish Lower Palaeolithic? Surely not!

We are faced with the sad fact that, as Coxon and McGarron (2009, 368–86) and others have shown, there are in Ireland few surviving traces of Quaternary deposits which pre-date MIS 3. Lower Palaeolithic assemblages, as well as those with a Middle Palaeolithic Levallois element, come from a much earlier date, notably between MIS 13 and 7, or roughly 500,000–200,000 years ago. Even in Britain this early human presence is only intermittent and its extent, even during more favourable "interglacial conditions", is still subject to discussion.

There is also the fact that the last warm stage, MIS 5e, where deposits do occasionally survive in Ireland, is the one period in which human settlement seems to be absent or virtually absent from Britain. One of the very few possibilities would seem to be an assemblage of artefacts from Dartford in south-east England which may date to MIS 5d–b (Wenban-Smith *et al.* 2010). In spite of all the negative factors which reduce the chances of finding evidence for an early human settlement in Ireland, there are occasional indicators that suggest that such a presence was not impossible!

Unfortunately, the two genuine handaxes that have been recovered from Ireland also fail the test suggested earlier. These are the Aran–Dún Aonghasa handaxe and the Araglin example (Woodman 1998c, 147–8). The former is claimed to have been recovered from the surface in the interior of the aforementioned hillfort, while the latter was recovered from the base of the topsoil in a garden. Both are genuine artefacts, in fact the Araglin object (Fig. 6.2b) is not only a particularly large and fine example but it does not look as if it has survived several glaciations. It also appears to be made from a type of flint that is found in the Hampshire river systems (Derek Roe pers. comm.). The Dún Aonghasa example has the appearance of coming from river gravels, which makes it, seem out of place on top of a limestone plateau in the hillfort!

Two possibly genuine artefacts have been recovered. These are the "Mell Flake" (Mitchell and Sieveking 1972) and the recently discovered "Scrabo Flake" (Stirland 2008). The former is a large, water-rolled and weathered flint flake that

was discovered in the top of glacial deposits in Co. Meath. These deposits are thought to be Glacio-Marine and would be associated with the Midlandian Glaciation, MIS 2. They are, in spite of their relatively young age, deposits which could retain material that may be much older. These objects may, however, not have been made or disposed of in Ireland. It is also unfortunate that the Mell Flake was suggested to be "Clactonian". If the Clactonian exists, there is a chance that it would not have continued in south-east England to a date much later than MIS 11. It would be preferable, therefore, to see this as a large flint flake of indeterminate age that may be Lower Palaeolithic and which was transported into, or even around, Ireland for some significant time before being deposited in eastern Ireland. Similarly, the Scrabo Flake may have been transported from somewhere else and then deposited during the Midlandian Glaciation. This piece was found during archaeological testing and while it cannot be stated with absolute certainty, it seems highly probable that it was brought to the surface by a machine that had cut into the underlying glacial gravels. Farina Sternke (pers. comm.) feels that this piece shows many of the attributes which would be associated with a Levallois reduction strategy. This could suggest manufacture during either MIS 9 or 7.

While much of this discussion may seem over-optimistic and clutching at evidential straws, it should not be forgotten that this issue relates to much larger debates. Not the least of these is the whole question of the Irish Sea as a barrier. The presence of a rich diverse mammalian fauna in Ireland during

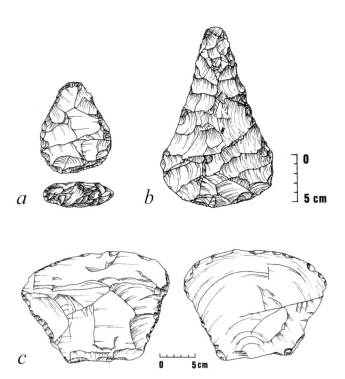

Fig. 6.2. a) Handaxe from Dun Aonghusa, b) handaxe from the Funshion River, c) flake from Rosses Point.

at least part of MIS 3 has already been described. Its presence clearly indicates that the Irish Sea may not have been a major barrier to mammalian colonisation, even at a time when the climate was not particularly accommodating. These occasional, earlier remains, such as the Hippo and Palaeoloxodon discussed in Chapter 2 suggest that entry into Ireland, irrespective of the nature of the so-called Irish Sea barrier, would have been quite possible.

This, in turn, raises questions about the capacity of predecessors of modern humans to use the sea as a staple source of food, as well as whether they had the capacity to confidently and consistently cross large stretches of water. At the moment there is an assumption that, as in the case of Jersey, humans walked across dry land at times of lower sea levels while animals swam (Callow and Cornford 1986). Erlandson and Fitzpatrick (2006) have documented that the sea was a major resource throughout a large portion of the Pleistocene. Examples of utilised marine resources can occur as far back as the Middle Stone Age of Africa, at 80–90,000 years ago. Again, 30–50,000 years ago, there is evidence for the spread of humans through parts of the Pacific Islands, such as western Melanesia and the Ryukus Island, and in some cases even importing species of animals. While this may not have extended to Bjerck's (2009) fully maritime type economy, there is evidence that the sea was exploited and served as a vector for movement from an early date. Therefore, a presence of a Lower Palaeolithic in Ireland would be an important indication that the sea played a significant role at an early date along the coasts of parts of Europe.

Realistically the answer must be that a presence in Ireland, or certainly the survival of that presence, seems unlikely. As referred to earlier, however, the excavations at Pontnweydd (Green 1984; Aldhouse-Green *et al.* 2012) show evidence for an MIS 7 occupation in an area of north Wales. Here, made in what were often thought of as quite intractable materials such as Rhyolite and ignimbrites, handaxes, as well as a Levallois flaking technology, was recovered. This shows that a Lower Palaeolithic did extend relatively close to Ireland.

The question from an archaeological perspective is – did humans cross to Ireland at any stage of the Lower or Middle Palaeolithic? The answer is that the chances of finding evidence of a lower Palaeolithic presence in Ireland are tiny but not impossible.

The case for an MIS 3 human presence in Ireland

There is a qualitatively different case to be made for a human presence during MIS 3, i.e. roughly 60–25,000 years ago, based on the fact that most of the larger mammalian fauna found in the rest of Europe during that period has been found in Ireland (Woodman *et al.* 1997; Woodman 1998c). It is possible that not all the species were present at the same time, notably the horse, which has only been found at Shandon Cave while Hyaena was only found at an earlier date.

Given the presence of these animals, the argument can be made that the lack of a known human presence at this time is somewhat anomalous (*ibid.*). This is further emphasised by a small but significant series of Palaeolithic sites in areas not too distant from Ireland. In south-western Britain, there are sites such as the rich artefact assemblage from Kent's Cavern in Devon and the Goats Hole, Paviland in south-west Wales, which contained the famous "Red Lady" burial and an array of distinctive bone, ivory and antler artefacts as well as stone tools. These sites, amongst others, have produced a range of artefacts of earlier Upper Palaeolithic attribute. These assemblages along with a series of radiocarbon dates (see Jacobi *et al.* 2006; 2009; Jacobi and Higham 2009 for a recent review of the radiocarbon evidence) suggest an intermittent presence in south-west Britain in the early part of the English Upper Palaeolithic.

Recent reviews (Pettitt 2008; Pettitt and White 2012) suggest a chronology for these archaeological periods, which existed within what was traditionally called the earlier Upper Palaeolithic (*pace* Campbell 1977). Figure 6.3 illustrates a range of typical implements. The evidence may be summarised:

1) The earliest phase, (*c.* ~42–43 ka) is characterised by a series of leaf points that are made on blades and are retouched on their ventral face. They are associated with end of blade scrapers and burins. Jacobi (1990) has noted that they are generally found south of the limits of the glaciers of the LGM. Because of their early date it is not clear whether assemblages of this date were being created by a population of Neanderthals or modern humans and a debate centres on the maxilla fragment from Kent's Cavern dated to 35,000+ BP (Stringer 2012, 39–40) though recently Pettitt and White (2012, 382) have suggested that it could date to anywhere between 46 and 41 ka.

2) An Aurignacian phase, *c.* 34+ ka? (*ibid.*, 402). It appears that there was a gap between the leaf point phase and the first phase that can be clearly associated with modern humans. So far only eight sites with relevant artefacts have been associated with this phase. These are found primarily in the west of Britain and are characterised by nosed shouldered scrapers and *burin busqué*. They appear to be typical of the Late Aurignacian.

3) A Gravettian phase 33–34 ka (*ibid.*, 411–21) which is characterised by Font Robert Points (tanged points). Again, few sites have been found, though in this case they are distributed across southern Britain. The site of the cave burial at Paviland in south Wales belongs to this phase and appears to be associated with a rich mammoth steppe fauna.

The British leaf point complex might seem to have the most potential for being also present in Ireland, especially if, as Pettitt (2008, 22) suggests, this group arrived in Britain by paddling along the west coast. However, it appears that the earliest stage of the Irish MIS 3 fauna that would be contemporaneous with the leaf point assemblages were very poor, with a limited number of species present. At the moment, only bear, reindeer, hyaena, mammoth and giant deer has been documented to before 35 ka. The greater likelihood, therefore, is that of a movement by peoples associated with either the Aurignacian or Gravettian phases, which is a period when there is evidence of a series of intermittent human presences during part of the Upper Palaeolithic of Britain and some evidence that these

activities occurred not too far from Ireland. Not only is there the question of whether there was a viable population and sufficient reasons to cause a movement from Britain to Ireland but there is also that of sustainability of a population within Ireland or even its short term attractiveness.

The most tantalising piece of evidence is the $\delta^{13}C$ result from human remains at Paviland ("Red Lady": −18.4‰) and Paviland 5 (−19.4‰; Richards 2000, 71–5). These suggest a marine element in the diet of the human population represented in this area: but is this evidence of exploitation of the inshore coastal areas rather than a confident use of the open sea?

In returning to Ireland, there are several questions relating to the chances of survival of evidence. In particular, surface scatters of material from the equivalent of the British earlier Upper Palaeolithic would be unlikely to have survived, bearing in mind also that their occurrence outside caves is extremely rare in Britain. However, while the deposits in the Irish caves show signs of disturbance, which was presumably caused at the time of the LGM, they just might contain some artefacts from before that time. Given the extent of survival of faunal remains of MIS 3 in the southern caves, could it be that the

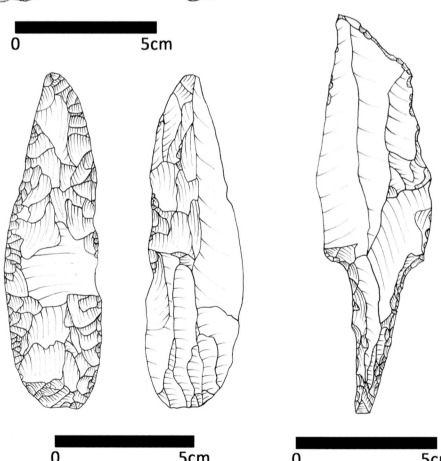

Fig. 6.3. British Early Upper Palaeolithic artefacts (after Campbell 1977 and Elaine Lynch).

ice sheets in south Munster, especially in the south central area of east Cork and west Waterford, were less destructive than elsewhere or even absent? If so is it possible that traces of a human presence might yet turn up within that limited area?

Summary

The case for early settlement for each of these two periods under discussion can be summarised as follows. The chance of the recovery of a clear and definitive presence during the lower and early Middle Palaeolithic is slight, indeed improbable, but at the same time not entirely impossible.

While the archaeological potential for a late Middle and Early Upper Palaeolithic settlement in Ireland is at best limited, the rich faunal remains from MIS 3, especially in parts of Munster and in a period of several thousand years, as well as the closeness of contemporaneous settlement in western parts of Britain, must constantly give us pause for reflection.

Perhaps, from an Irish perspective the biggest barriers to the study of this topic are mental! If there is an ingrained assumption that no human settlement took place before the Mesolithic then a self-fulfilling prophecy that there is nothing there will ensure the chance of the discovery of earlier settlement will remain minimal. Given problems of raw material and the absence of a cohort of individuals on the ground who have the capacity to recognise the evidence, the chances of recovery are slight. How many are prepared to tackle the thankless task of examining quarry spoil, usually of a later date, for the extremely unlikely occurrence of an artefact of early date? The presence of the informed amateur or the field archaeologist who is prepared to look beyond conventional wisdom may be as important as the chance survival of evidence.

Just delayed, not missing?

From the onset of the LGM, i.e. MIS 2, and leaving aside the curious short-term presence of a very cold fauna in the Castlepook area around 25 ka, there seems to have been no possibility of a human or even mammalian presence in Ireland until the Woodgrange/Allerød Interstadial. The process of colonisation after the LGM in Ireland, i.e. the late and post-glacial periods, is remarkably different from most other parts of north-western Europe. Much of Scotland may fall into the same category though the recent discoveries at Howburn Farm (see below; Ballin *et al.* 2010) are an indication that there may have been occasional early forays at least south of the midland valley of Scotland. Parts of Fennoscandinavia provide an interesting contrast as, within that region, there is only a short chronological gap between extensive areas of new land becoming available and the arrival of the first human communities (Woodman 1998b; Bjerck 2009; Rankama 2003). The nature of these first arrivals will be discussed below but at this stage it is sufficient to contrast the rapid movement that took place within certain parts of Norway, Sweden and Finland

with the several thousand year apparent delay in initial and or continuous settlement in Ireland.

It could be argued that the human colonisation of Ireland should be seen in terms of the millennia required to populate the island, not just with people but with plants and animals. The late glacial interstadial was a seesaw-like process that lasted for more than 3000 years and it has been suggested (Woodman 2008) that, rather than being seen as an *event*, it is a *process* that began during that interstadial and even continues today. After the rapid expansion of ice to its limits at the LGM, there was an almost equally rapid dissolution of the ice sheets, so that by before 16,000 cal BP Ireland was ice free and, with significant inputs of meltwater, the Irish Sea had become a significant major barrier (Edwards and Brooks 2008).

Although there are differences between the pursuits of issues that pre- and post-date the LGM, there are two remarkably fundamental similarities. These are:

a) In the context of early human colonisation, did the Irish Sea represent a significant barrier?

b) As throughout MIS 3, was the settlement of England and Wales during the Late and early post-glacial so marginal that it would have not been likely that even pioneering investigations of Ireland did not take place?

In this case, the late glacial fauna of Ireland is remarkably sparse. This paucity is further emphasised by contrasting it with the late glacial fauna of southern Britain, which was extremely rich at times.

Within Britain, after the LGM and until the earliest known human settlement of Ireland, four phases of settlement can be identified. Jacobi and Higham (2009) have suggested that, shortly after the recolonisation of the Paris Basin and parts of Belgium, the first human presence had been established in parts of southern Britain, most notably in the Cheddar Gorge area where it can be dated to a period of up to 200 years around 14,700 cal BP (Pettitt and White 2012, 431).

There are three phases that are usually associated with the later Upper Palaeolithic of Britain. The first two contain a range of distinct implements and there is an extensive series of sites known from much of England (Fig. 6.4), and to a limited extent from elsewhere, associated with these phases. These are as follows:

1) The Creswellian phase (Magdalenian; *pace* Jacobi and Higham 2009) (Fig. 6.5) where there seems to be a significant pulse of human expansion westwards to south-west Wales from the area around Mendip, of which extensive traces have been found at sites like Gough's Cave, and northwards into the Peak District and the southern Pennines. Kendrick's Cave at Great Orme on the north coast of Wales, near Llandudno, also contains material from this period. This phase of late glacial settlement has been extended further north into southern Scotland. Recently, an excavation of an open site at Howburn Farm, which lies in the northern

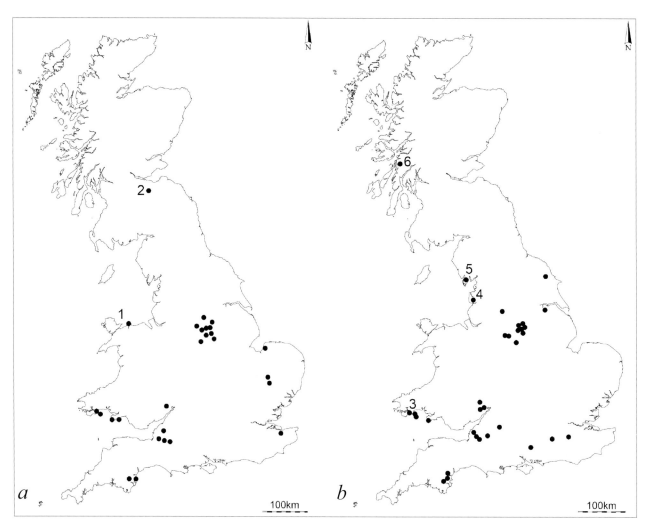

Fig. 6.4. Map of Late Glacial Interstadial archaeological sites in Britain: a) Creswellian/Magdalenian, b) Federmesser/Penknife Point.
1) Kendricks Cave, 2) Howburn Farm, 3) Priory farm, 4) Poulton Fylde, 5) Kennis Cave, 6) Kilmelfort Cave.

foothills of the southern uplands, has produced a mixed selection of artefacts (Ballin *et al.* 2010). It includes what the authors have described as an assemblage that relates to the Havelte or Late Hamburgian, which is similar to material found in parts of Denmark. These assemblages are associated with a high quality blade industry, with distinctive forms such as Creswellian and Cheddar points. These assemblages, which are particularly, though not exclusively, known from caves, seem to be associated with the hunting of animals such as horse and, to a lesser extent, reindeer and Arctic hare on steppe grasslands.

2) Penknife Point industry (Federmesser: *pace* Jacobi and Higham 2009), which belongs to the later part of the Allerød Interstadial, is found throughout southern Britain though its presence within cave sites is not so extensive. These artefactual assemblages are characterised by small penknife points and small flake scrapers. Recently, Saville and Ballin (2009) have suggested that the lithic assemblage

from Kilmelfort Cave near the west coast of Argyll, which Coles (1983) had tentatively suggested was Mesolithic in age, should be regarded as more likely to be Federmesser in date. It is probable that a more temperate fauna, including red deer, elk and wild boar, was exploited at this date in the late glacial interstadial.

3) The third phase is associated with the Younger Dryas and appears to have been characterised by assemblages associated with the long blade or *lame mâchuré*, and small tanged points that are often thought to resemble Ahrensburgian Points (Fig. 6.6). There are also occasional large, simple microlithic forms. This phase of settlement seems to have been confined to eastern England, especially the south-east (Fig. 6.7) and as a result of a recent re-dating programme they may also be limited to only the latest part of the Younger Dryas. From the limited faunal remains available, reindeer and horse, along with Arctic hare, would seem to have been the main sources of food.

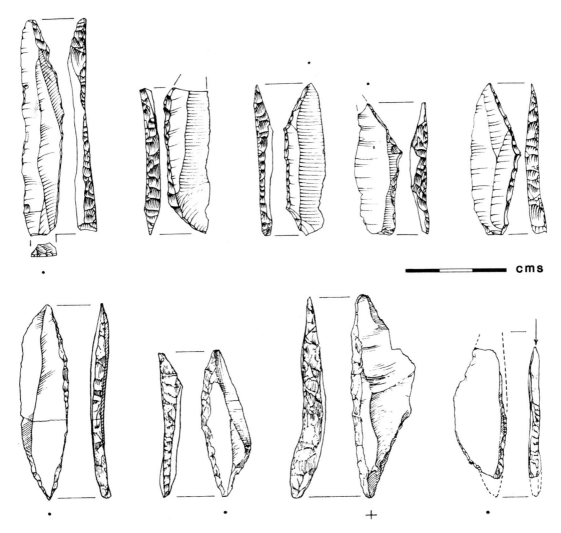

Fig. 6.5. British Later Upper Palaeolithic artefacts (after David 1991).

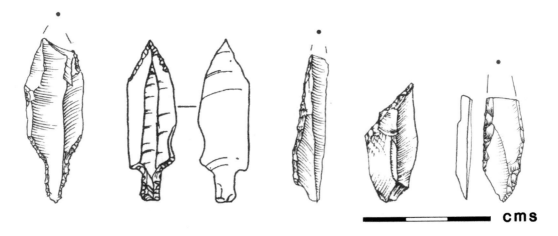

Fig. 6.6. Typical artefacts of Ahrensburgian type (after Barton 1991).

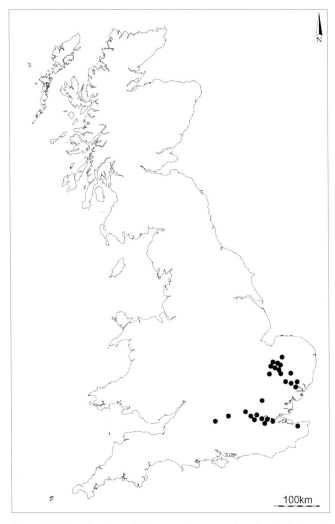

Fig. 6.7. Distribution of Younger Dryas archaeological sites in Britain.

Could they have made it into Ireland during the late glacial "False Dawn"

At the time of the establishment of the initial Creswellian/Magdalenian settlement in Britain, i.e. just after 15,000 cal BP, little is known about Ireland's fauna and flora. The only date that appeared to be convincingly before 14,000 cal BP was on the reindeer from Castlepook (F21124) dated to 15,142–14,147 cal BP (Oxa 3602, antler, 12,480±130 BP). This same bone has now been shown to to date much earlier: 24,538–24,038 cal BP (Oxa 20891, 20,220±90 BP; and to date to close to the end of the Last Glacial Maximum. It is possible that, in Ireland, bears, hares, wolves, stoats and perhaps a small red deer population existed alongside giant deer during the latter half of the late glacial interstadial. In comparison with even the early fauna found at Goughs Cave, Ireland's fauna is extremely impoverished.

In this case, the early emergence of an Irish sea (Edwards and Brooks 2006), which would have been in existence by 16,000 years ago, would have been in itself an extremely hostile environment for those not *au fait* with maritime environments. Ireland must also have seemed like a very unattractive landscape that had very little to offer. Unlike MIS 3, the late glacial interstadial was a short period of time which perhaps would not have allowed the establishment of a suitable ecology that would have attracted late glacial hunters.

It might have been possible that the less diagnostic but perhaps more prolific Federmesser/Penknife phase of settlement would potentially have represented a more likely group to move to Ireland. They would have been contemporary with the large herds of giant deer and their predators, along with other species that were to make up the initial phase of Ireland's late and post-glacial fauna.

There is an implicit assumption that all the Magdalenian/Federmesser economies were based on terrestrial hunting or, in the case of hares, trapping. Could there have been use of other resources During the earlier part of the Late glacial interstadial, i.e. when there is a very definite Hamburgian presence in Britain, there is, given the subsequent rise in relative sea level, little evidence of a presence in what would then have been coastal locations. As the Bristol Channel would have been a low lying broad valley, most of the south Wales sites and those in the Mendip Hills were placed well away from the coast. It is not surprising that a coastal dimension is rarely discussed.

In contrast, in north Wales, it is of interest that Kendrick's Cave which, while it would have faced inland, was on a high promontory (Great Orme), that would have protruded out into the plains that existed at a time of a lower sea level. The Great Orme would overlook this plain which would have extended for some tens of kilometres to the sea. It is therefore of interest that the human remains from this cave, dating to the end of the Magdalenian phase, have produced a series of δ¹³C results ranging from -17.7 up to -17.0‰ which would strongly suggest a significant marine contribution to the diet (Jacobi and Higham 2009, table 4).

There are also some indications of a presence of the slightly later Federmesser complex along the west coast of Britain. In the most westerly part of Dyfed, in south Wales, the Priory Cave has produced a Federmesser assemblage. This cave would have overlooked a narrow valley that today is the long sea inlet of Milford Haven, that would have opened out onto a narrow coastal plain. So far there is no evidence from the cave that the adjacent shoreline and sea were used during the late glacial period. Further north, along the coast in Lancashire, the Poulton le Fylde elk and associated barbed points (Barnes *et al.* 1971) can also be associated with the late Allerød. The most interesting indication of a Federmesser presence on the western coast is the recent suggestion that the assemblage from Kilmelfort in Argyll (Saville and Ballin 2009) should be associated with the Federmesser complex.

Aside from the question of which phase of the British later Upper Palaeolithic might have provided that springboard, two questions can be asked.

1) Was there a significant human presence along the west coast of adjacent parts of Britain?

Pettitt (2007) suggests that many of the sites in the Magdalenian in the north and west of Britain may have been hunting camps and special short-term campsites created by groups who, on a seasonal basis, moved up from the south. It has been shown that the flint used in Creswell Caves in the north midlands of England derived from south-west England. Were these presences little more than the "furthest throw of the dice" by land-based hunters pushing west and was Ireland little more than a distantly seen landfall filled with mystery but never really visited? Alternatively a late glacial interstadial presence in Ireland would be a clear indication that other maritime adapted late glacial hunter gatherers existed.

2) Were there, at that date, sufficient resources available to attract them to Ireland?

Could there have been a coastal dimension where other resources such as birds and fish were also used? Perhaps these resources were exploited at different times of the year and in different places. Bratlund (1996) has suggested that in Scandinavia game hunters needed a diversity of species. Therefore was there a local maritime adaptation to a coastal lowland basin which was fringed by high ground in virtually every direction?

What about the last cold snap and the date of the long blade assemblages

As noted in Chapter 2, it is assumed that, during the Younger Dryas, the giant deer herds that had been so common in Ireland would have been wiped out. It appears that, for at least part of the Younger Dryas, there would have been some groups of reindeer present in Ireland and that some of the other species referred to earlier would have survived through this cold phase. Yet, the Younger Dryas seems the least likely phase for a human presence in Ireland. The confined spatial and chronological distribution of human settlement in south and east Britain suggests an absence of any Younger Dryas human presence in Ireland, where it is thought that even harsher environmental conditions existed.

Relying on the presence of individual type fossils, such as the small Ahrensburgian tanged points, as an indicator of early human penetrations is very tempting, especially in the context of the recovery of several examples from north and west Scotland. If these were genuine then one might assume that there would be an equally strong probability that a similar movement of reindeer hunters into Ireland might have taken place. Indeed, many researchers (Wickham-Jones and Woodman 1998) suggested that such a presence may have existed in Scotland. The redating of the English material to a local and short phase late in the Younger Dryas must point to the need for extreme caution in making claims for an Ahrensburgian in Scotland and, by inference, also in Ireland. These objects appear primarily in the north of Scotland and, as they are undated, one might be more easily persuaded that they relate to a tentative movement from western Norway, where the Fosna culture contains similar small points that may ultimately be of Ahrensburgian derivation. The Fosna culture exists at a very early date in the Holocene (Bjerck 1986; 1995) and it is probable that it was well established before 11, 000 cal BP.

The known human settlement of Ireland seems to have been delayed by up to 5000 years later than the post-LGM human recolonisation in southern Britain. There is nothing that can be attributed with any certainty to this period. Occasional well made end of blade scrapers could belong to an Irish Creswellian, or some fragmentary backed pieces might be penknife forms, but the former are more likely to belong to the Irish Neolithic, while backed fragments could easily belong to the lopsided and elongated classes of petit tranchet derivatives (Woodman *et al.* 2006, 150–5). Other occasional pieces, such as the large backed blade from Newport cannot be placed in the late glacial with any confidence (Woodman 1989, 119). Similarly, there is no evidence that punch percussion technology, often characterised by blades with lipped platforms and diffuse bulbs of percussions, have turned up.

An afterthought

There is a fourth phase: i.e. roughly the first 2000 years of the Holocene, and it is towards the end of that time that the first convincing evidence of human settlement in Ireland can be documented.

Chapter 7

The first arrivals

The beginning of the Holocene is notionally designated as the point at which the archaeological period of the Mesolithic began. The Early Holocene in southern Britain, and much of the adjacent areas of north-western Europe, contains a series of lithic industries in which microliths occur in significant numbers. In Britain this phase is often referred to as the "Early" Mesolithic though often also as "non-geometric or broad blade assemblages". The Early Mesolithic appears to last until sometime around 10,000 cal BP, although a case can be made for either an earlier end to the phase or, in some regions, a continuation until well after that date (see below). This phase is not characterised by one particular suite of microliths.

The British "Early" Mesolithic

Within Britain at least three potential groups have been distinguished by Reynier (2005) and these are:

a) Star Carr assemblages where a significant number of large isosceles triangles and trapezes occur;
b) Deep Carr assemblages where there is an extremely high percentage of simple obliquely trimmed or non-geometric points;
c) The more southern Horsham group characterised by the presence of hollow based points.

Reynier suggests that the Star Carr group pre-dates the Deep Carr group and he notes that both can be found in the north and south of England. The Horsham types, characterised in particular by the presence of distinctive hollow based points (*ibid.,* 119–20), seem to be confined to the south and are chronologically later in date. A fourth group which, until recently, received little attention, is also thought to exist at the end of this phase and is primarily associated with the midlands. These are the Honey Hill assemblages, which were first identified by Saville (1981) and were distinguished by the presence of numbers of distinctive microlithic basely trimmed points. Although it is beyond the scope of this rapid survey to adjudicate on the relative merits of regionalism

and chronological variations in the British Early Mesolithic, it is worthwhile noting the division between the early/non-geometric/broad blade and the later/geometric/narrow bladed Mesolithic in England, as proposed by Mellars (1974) and Jacobi (1976). This division, which was made a time when there was no clear chronological schema for the English Mesolithic, was an important step forward. However, the manner in which it has been used in more recent times suggests that the division may have become more rigid than was intended. In illustrating the range of microliths in use throughout the "British" Mesolithic, Mellars (1974; Fig. 7.1a) drew a line between what came to be known as the Early Mesolithic and the Late Mesolithic. This may have inadvertently over-emphasised the division and suggested a sudden and quite radical shift in the use of microliths as well as other differences. It should also be remembered that in other parts of north-western Europe, notably in the Maglemosian and related assemblages, there is no evidence of a similar radical change in technology. Even the shift from the Maglemose to Kongemose that took place in parts of southern Scandinavia after 9000 cal BP was a much more gradual transition. This more gradualist approach used in Denmark was also in use in the 1970s and can be seen in Petersen's chronological chart of the Danish Mesolithic which was constructed about the same time (Fig. 7.1b).

The economy of the British Early Mesolithic is heavily influenced by the assemblage from Star Carr. In particular, a diverse range of large mammals was exploited, notably aurochs, elk, red deer, roe deer and wild boar. In the following millennia the role of aurochs and elk was to diminish if not disappear entirely, as in the case of Zealand. The fauna has been subject to a number of re-interpretations (Legge and Rowley-Conwy 1988). It appears that the hunting of large mammals, such as aurochs and elk, played a very important role. This is not peculiar to England, as indicated by other sites elsewhere in the region, for example Lundby in southern Denmark where several butchered elk carcasses have been excavated (Hansen and Pedersen 2006).

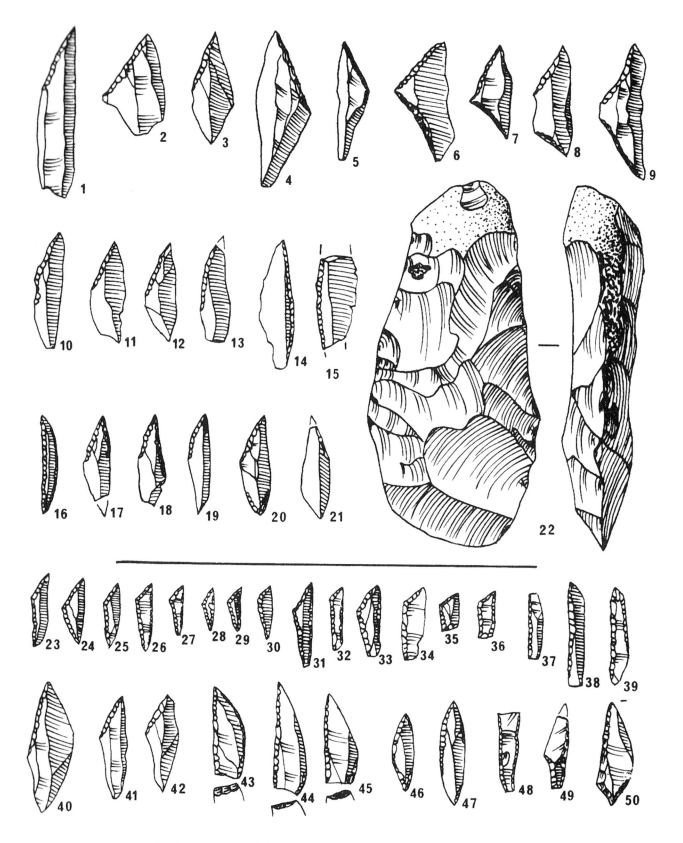

Fig. 7.1. a) the division of microliths between the Early and Later Mesolithic in Britain (Mellars 1976).

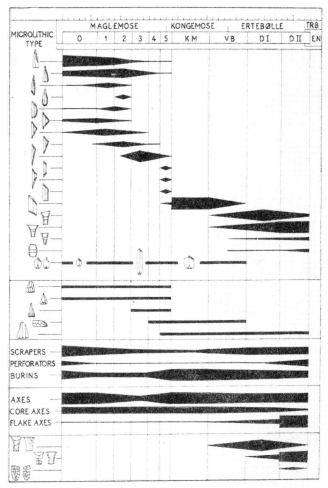

Fig. 7.1. b) chronological chart of the Danish Mesolithic (Brinch Petersen 1973).

The earliest Holocene human settlement in Ireland

At present, Ireland seems to have remained unoccupied for close to 2000 years after the commencement of the Holocene at about 11,600 years ago. This absence of a human presence in Ireland is perhaps more curious than the lack of a Palaeolithic. While there are occasional older radiocarbon dates these will be shown to be somewhat spurious as indicators of settlement in the earliest part of the Holocene, therefore the dates from Mount Sandel remain the earliest firm indicators of human presence on the island. Perhaps the earliest huts were being erected at or just after 9750 cal BP (Bayliss and Woodman 2009). There occur, however, a number of local implement types, most notably the flake axes and the surface retouched needle points found at sites such as Mount Sandel Upper (Woodman 1985a, fig. 29: 12 and 22). It can be presumed that these are indicators that a period of local adaptation took place, so sites that are slightly older, but still based on the narrow blade/geometric tradition, should be expected to be found in Ireland, though these need not necessarily be as early as 10,000 cal BP.

One question must be: was there any human presence in Ireland that belonged to the first 1500 years of the Holocene? One advantage of having so much material in the two large institutions of the National Museums of Ireland and Northern Ireland (formerly the Ulster Museum), means that a thorough search of their collections has revealed no trace of an assemblage that closely resembles those of the British Early Mesolithic, i.e. assemblages that are likely to significantly pre-date 10,000 cal BP. It is particularly unlikely that an earlier phase of the Mesolithic will be found in Ireland. The identification of very early assemblages from a single artefact type is not without problems. This has been especially evident in Scotland where a number of large trapezes and isosceles triangles, which are similar to those found at Star Carr, have turned up at Lussa Bay (Mercer 1971) and Glenabatrick (Mercer 1974). While it has been tempting to place these assemblages in an earlier phase of the Scottish Mesolithic there has been no independent corroboration that they pre-date the existing sequence. This issue will be returned to in more detail below.

The problem with attempting to find Deep Carr type assemblages, i.e. those dominated by simple non-geometric points and where the other forms do not exist, is that these are so non-specific it requires a large assemblage to be certain that it really belongs to the Deep Carr phase of the British Early Mesolithic. Occasional non-geometric points occur in Ireland, but one distinctive group that was found in a pit (F100/5) at Mount Sandel (Woodman 1985a, 43–5) appears, on stratigraphic grounds, to date late in the sequence at that site, possibly as late as 9550 cal BP. Therefore, their occasional presence in Ireland cannot be taken as a clear indication of an early date, especially one that would suggest a human presence before 10,000 cal BP.

Until very recently e.g. Reynier (2005, 27–9) there was no clear evidence of a very early presence for the Honey Hill type assemblage in Britain. However, recent excavations at Ashfordby near Milton Mowbray in the north Midlands suggest that this type of assemblage could be in existence by just before 10,000 cal BP (Cooper 2013, 11–12). Besides the basely trimmed points the assemblage is dominated by obliquely truncated and backed points though on visual inspection of those illustrated there also appear to be some elongated scalene triangles. Therefore, as will be discussed below, a case could be made for seeing some affinities between Honey Hill and the Irish "*Early*" Mesolithic microlithic assemblages.

There is, in contrast, little evidence that the Horsham assemblages date to very early in the Holocene, and they have not been found anywhere near Ireland.

It is possible that Ireland's prehistory could be extended earlier by some other form of evidence for a human presence, such as undiagnostic artefacts of some form found in a securely dated context, but at present the boundary line for the earliest human settlement is particularly fuzzy.

The background, or where did Ireland's first people come from?

A number of authors, such as Oppenheimer (2006, chap. 4), have suggested on the basis of comparisons of modern DNA taken from various sources throughout Europe, that the most likely area of origin for the first Irish Mesolithic colonists would be the so-called mountainous Basque regions of northern Spain. Oppenheimer (*ibid.*) has, however, given this a stronger coastal dimension, which comes across most strongly in his figure 4:2, where there is a curiously out of date and inaccurate assumption that the development of forests in the Early Holocene forced increased coastal exploitation. The 2009 RTÉ TV programme *Blood of the Irish* also centred on the implied relatively rapid movement of people up along the Atlantic coast. This could have been by boat, as inferred by *Blood of the Irish*, or along the narrow coastal corridor hemmed in by forests, as implied by Oppenheimer. Mattiangelli *et al.* (2008) have shown that the Irish genome is a mosaic which is typical of northern European populations rather than something deriving initially from Cantabria. This coastal scenario ignores the evidence for extensive Mesolithic settlement right across the *whole* of continental Western Europe. Kozłowski (2009), for example, has documented the diverse series of settlement sites and technologies scattered across mainland Europe for the whole of the Mesolithic. Figure 7.2 illustrates the distribution of just one of his early typological groups.

The problem here is that (as noted by Woodman *et al.* (2006, 36)) even in the late 19th century many authors, such as Knowles, were aware of the fact that the re-colonisation of north-western Europe began with human populations spreading out from regions such as Cantabria. Radiocarbon dating programmes, such as Housley *et al.* (1997), have documented this spread. Indeed much of the area adjacent to the British Isles in "continental" north-western Europe had been occupied continuously since before 15,000 cal BP. In fact even at the LGM, when human settlement is thought to have been driven to its furthest south, there is evidence in the form of the very distinctive Solutrean culture of human populations being present as far north as Lyons in the Rhone Valley and, significantly, in Charente well north of Bordeaux.

While similarity or difference in lithic artefacts is not always a reliable indicator of a relationship, or the lack of it, between two populations, it should be noted that there is very little in the way of similarity between the very distinctive Asturian industries of coastal regions of northern Spain and the microlithic complexes typical of the British Isles and adjacent

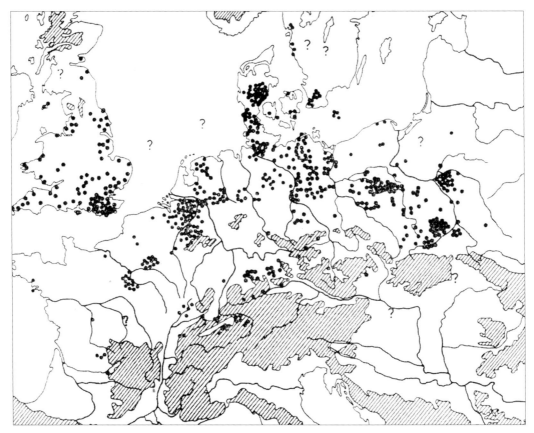

Fig. 7.2. Distribution of certain microlith types in the "Early/Middle" Mesolithic from across the north European mainland (after Kozłowski 2009).

areas. Therefore, in returning to the main body of evidence, in spite of some local variations there is a close affinity between what was described earlier as the Irish "*Early*" Mesolithic and the earliest phases of Britain's later Mesolithic. There are occasional similarities at this point in time between Irish material and assemblages along the west coast of France but, until there are some other indications of a direct connection at this early stage of the Holocene, our working hypothesis must be that the earliest phases of the Irish Mesolithic has strong associations with Britain, which was still at that stage part of mainland Europe.

Assessing the Irish evidence

It is worth returning to the questions of expectation when searching for traces of early settlement. Besides the biases inherent in dealing with a partial landscape, Rankama (2003, 38–9) has also made the point that when, in the context of colonising new lands and archaeologists are assessing the attractiveness of new landscapes, our own personal biases play a significant role. The landscapes that we are comfortable within tend to be those that are presumed to be the most attractive to early hunter-gatherers. Rankama in particular juxtaposes the strongly coastal perspective that exists within Norwegian archaeology with the viewpoints of those working in inland regions just freed from ice in Finland. In essence, both sets of archaeologists feel more confident about early exploration taking place in the environment in which they themselves feel comfortable.

As discussed earlier, surprisingly, the earliest reliable dates remain those from Mount Sandel and until recently these early dates suggested a presence at and before 10,000 cal BP. These dates were not matched by similar early dates in Britain (see Woodman 2004). Recently, dates from Howick East in north-east England and East Barnes in south-east Scotland (Waddington 2007) show that the British later Mesolithic assemblages were in existence before 9700 cal. BP, in the case of the former (Waddington *et al.* 2007), and slightly earlier at East Barnes (Gooder 2007). Perhaps Filpoke Beacon, which is also situated in north-east England, could also be added to

this group, though this is based on a date obtained many years ago and which has a large standard deviation (Q1474, charcoal, 8760±140 BP, 10,220–9490 cal BP; Jacobi 1976, 71). At the moment the older dates from Crammond in south-east Scotland, which suggest activity in the 85th and/or 84th centuries BC, are still regarded as slightly problematic (Saville 2008).

From the north coast of Wales there are several quite late dates from apparently Early Mesolithic assemblages, i.e. Trwyn Dhu and Rhuddlan, but at the moment it seems simpler to regard most of these dates as spuriously late (see below). Further south, along the south coast of Wales, there is evidence for an earlier Mesolithic presence, notably at sites such as Nab Head (David 2007) and on Caldey Island (*ibid.*; Schulting 2009), whose significance will be discussed below (Fig. 7.5). These dates, in general, combined with the re-dating of Mount Sandel to about 9700 cal BP at the earliest (Bayliss and Woodman 2009), provide a more coherent chronology across the northern part of the British Isles and at least create a framework within which the colonisation of Ireland can be discussed.

Does anything in Ireland pre-date Mount Sandel?

There are dates which could suggest a human presence at a significantly earlier date than Mount Sandel (see Table 7.1). Each of these dates is somewhat suspect and often not clearly associated with any artefacts. This phenomenon of dates that seem to suggest earlier arrivals than had previously been expected is not unusual. Anderson (2003, 177) has provided a good example in relation to the human settlement of Polynesia. In this instance, a process of "Chronometric hygiene" suggested that dates from the Society Islands, Marquesas, Hawaii and New Zealand that were between 1500 and 500 years too old needed to be discarded.

The Toome Bypass sample, which came from a large rectangular trench (Dunlop and Woodman 2015; see Chapter 8) forming the Feature 5 complex, is spectacularly early, dating to nearly 1500 years before than any of the Mount Sandel dates (Bayliss and Woodman 2009). It comes from a feature that has produced other radiocarbon dates which range from later

Table 7.1. Pre Mount Sandel Radiocarbon dates.

Site	Lab. ref.	Material	Determination BP	Calibrated date BP
Toome Bypass	BT 219463	charcoal	9720±50	11,143–10,830
Ballyoran	UB 6780	wood	8958±53	10,220–10,131
Lufferton	LU 1809	charcoal	9440±100	11,105–10,313
Clynacartan	I1 3641	wood	8910±150	10,297–9548
Lough Boora	UB 2268	charcoal	8980±350	11,161–9290
Port of Larne	UB 11668	charcoal	8806±29	10,118–9695

Mesolithic (1) to Early Neolithic (1) to Bronze Age (2). The very early date was based on charcoal, unlike the date from the Later Mesolithic which was based on a hazel nutshell fragment. Much of the lithic assemblage found in this feature suggests a date from either the Later Mesolithic or Neolithic. Nothing that could be considered diagnostic to the first millennium of the Holocene has been recovered from Feature 5 in general.

The dates from Lough Boora have been excluded as it had a very large standard deviation of 525 and 695 years. The Ballyoran sample is based on brush wood which may not be an artificial creation, an associated 'worked' giant deer bone of likely Woodgrange Interstadial age. The giant deer bone cannot be securely dated to the "*Early*" Mesolithic and as Liversage (1957) has shown, these bones can be re-used at a later date.

The Lufferton or Woodpark sample was obtained during exploratory excavations as part of the Carrowmore Project of the early 1980s. Claims that the date was associated with an artefact (Burenhult 1984) can be discounted as the so-called artefact, which may be a natural piece of chert, was recovered some considerable distance from the trench that produced the charcoal used for dating. Not only was there no artefactual association but the charcoal was in a beach deposit that was likely to have been created several thousand years later than the date obtained on the charcoal! The Clynacartan sample that produced the early date was based on oak wood from the lower part of a platform that was partially excavated by Mitchell (1989) in Emlagh Bog on Valentia Island, Co. Kerry. Again, an overlying sample produced a date that was significantly later in the Mesolithic. Both of these dates were produced from wood or wood charcoal that was not, in one way or another, clearly associated with other forms of archaeological material.

Perhaps the most improbable date (not listed in Table 7.1) is that from the NRA excavation at Ballynamona 1, Co. Cork (Hanley 2013a, 377). This date (Beta 201088, charcoal, 9690±100 BP, 11,240–10720 cal BP) was based on a piece of oak from a cork drying kiln!

The final example is one of a pair of dates from a chipping floor (CF2) excavated at the Port of Larne (McConway in prep.). Like some of the other dates its probability range at 95% extends back beyond those of Mount Sandel (Bayliss and Woodman 2009). In this case it is a wood sample associated with a context that is stratigraphically later than the main phase of occupation which lay at a lower level. This lower level produced a series of radiocarbon dates which in some cases could be up to 2000 years younger that the date listed in Table 7.1 (see below). Typologically, the CF2 assemblage belongs to the Later Mesolithic. Again this date may be best explained as a combination of an old wood factor and/or contamination from an earlier context.

In summary, none of the very early Irish dates referred to above, is convincing. It is possible that initial colonists were using *ad hoc* and unrecognisable technologies but, as discussed earlier, it would seem likely that new arrivals would continue to use the established technologies that they brought with them. In this case, the earliest documented sites with assemblages have a lithic technology that, with certain notable exceptions, is similar to those associated with sites such as Howick and East Barnes (see below). When the information on the earliest phases of the Irish Mesolithic is placed in a broader context it must be admitted that there is now, unlike the 70s–90s, much more information available about the earlier parts of the Mesolithic in the west of Britain.

It is therefore important to note that there was nothing pre-ordained about the rate of expansion of human settlement throughout the so-called marginal regions of Europe. It could be argued that movements to the north (Scandinavia) and the north-west (Scotland and Ireland) were driven and/or constrained by different factors.

Factors constraining movement to new lands

It is apparent from historical sources that, even when large scale invasions are removed from consideration, population movements are not a simple phenomenon. The initial spread of Early Holocene hunter-gatherers can be considered under a number of headings.

What factors would lead to movement to new areas?

Demography does not exist in isolation. There is little evidence of sudden, rapid rises in population throughout the Mesolithic; in fact many of the apparent increases may be more due to certain parts of the archaeological record of the Mesolithic in any region being more accessible than others. In Demark, due to sea level rise, the final stages of the Mesolithic, the Ertebølle, is more accessible than the older Kongemose culture where sites are more likely to have been inundated by the sea or buried under more recent deposits. In contrast, the very rapid isostatic rise of the land in parts of Norway and Sweden created numerous fossil shorelines during the first few thousand years of the Holocene. These, in turn, provided both attractive areas for settlement sites and are easily available to archaeologists for survey and exploration. This was followed by a period sea level rise that buried or destroyed many of the slightly later Mesolithic settlement sites in the same areas (Bjerck 1986). There can, of course, be landscape loss, such as the inundation of the North Sea and the loss of the coastal plain along the coast of Provence and neighbouring Genoa. Changes may also be a lot more subtle, such as the infilling of certain major water systems, as at Ringsjon in Scania, which must have removed a preferred area for hunting, fishing and wildfowling or left them buried and often quite inaccessible. As a result tracking changes in population levels in a relatively restricted area or ecological niche may be fraught with problems.

The historic record still suggests that social pressure, consequent on population increase, resulting in alternative available niches being filled, could result in a fissioning of a community. If the size of the social grouping increased too much, the resultant tensions could lead to the departure of a portion of the community. Is it even possible that religious difference could have caused some sections of a small community to move on to new areas? In this case it is questionable as to whether bands lived in large enough groups to experience issues such as "scalar stress" early in the Mesolithic.

In what manner did the peopling of the new landscape take place?

In general, there is little support within north-western Europe for the idea of the colonisation process being a single event. Suggestions have been made for recognising a more gradualist approach. Fuglesveldt (2003) has suggested that, in the case of south-west Norway, the shift from the flat North European plain and associated area would have been so abrupt that preliminary exploratory visits to an entirely different land of high mountains and sheer cliffs, as well perhaps of a different coastline, would have been required. These first visitors, who were exploring outside their normal territory, would have brought back information about these new regions which would have become part of the learned knowledge of the group. Housley *et al.* (1997), in considering the north-westwards expansion of the Creswellian, suggested that there would also have been significant pioneering phases in which certain resources could be followed or procured. Thus substantial movement into a new area would probably include people who would be well acquainted with the differences, advantages and pitfalls that they would face. It is also probable that any major settlement that was occupied for a significant portion of the year may have lain elsewhere within the annual territory used by these early hunter-gatherers. The earliest sites in new lands will not necessarily be base camps but, more likely, will be rather transitory in their nature, or may be specialised sites. It is always possible that the earliest sites from any area will be rather atypical and may have no associated major base camps. For fuller discussions on these issues see the relevant "New lands" sections in Larsson *et al.* (2003) and McCartan *et al.* (2009).

Were there local adaptations?

Issues such as getting to new areas will be discussed below, but little attention has been paid to the manner in which new arrivals adapt. In many parts of Europe there will be no particular change in the environment, but for some it would have meant a shift from land based to marine environments, a change in the ranges of land animals or even a requirement to change to procuring new raw materials.

Ackerlund *et al.* (2003) have discussed this issue in the context of new arrivals populating newly emerging landscapes in western Sweden where different raw materials were available. The issues in these instances were two-fold:

1) Retain the form of the artefact types from the homeland area.
2) Adapt rapidly to the constraints of new raw materials.

The question posed was based on a choice between retaining a pre-existing technology, which would have needed to be adapted to local circumstances, or using the new materials, in this case quartz, to develop a new technology more suitable to local raw materials. A number of authors, notably Pellegatti (2009) in relation to Croatia, have identified the fact that in an initial phase of colonisation the earliest Mesolithic groups seem to have preferred to rely on raw materials similar to those that they were already accustomed to using. It has also been suggested that newly arrived farmers had to learn a new landscape and that they may have brought in raw materials from some distance away (Andreasen 2009). In this case, initial phases of settlement were associated with flint that had been imported from a considerable distance and probably, in some cases, across difficult terrain. Sandmo (1986) identified a similar pattern in northern Norway where flint, which would have been a particularly rare material, occurred in greater abundance than expected in the earliest sites. At Rissole, in northern Finland, initial occupation seems to use a technology that required imported flint rather than local quartz (Takala 2009). Thus, where there is a choice, some groups may chose to retain as much of their pre-existing technology as possible and this may include the retention of preferred raw materials even when access to these materials can be quite difficult.

At the very least communities would be able to adapt their technologies. Perhaps this would be based on experience gained during an early pioneering phase of exploration. This may have happened along the Norwegian coast (Fig. 7.3). A case can be made for a very rapid expansion along the Atlantic coast of Norway and to the part of the Kola Peninsula facing northwards into the Barents Sea (Olsen 1994; Woodman 1999). This may have taken place within a few centuries. Prosch-Danielsen and Høgestøl (1995) have suggested that Galta 3, near Stavanger in south-west Norway, which has many of the attributes of the Ahrensburgian, could be dated to before 11,500 years ago (10,200–9800 BP), while there is good reason to believe that human settlement was established well into the Arctic within a few hundred years, for example perhaps by 11,000 at Slettnes which lies above 70 degrees north (Hesjedal *et al.* 1996), and there is no reason why this had not extended to the Kola Peninsula. The movement northwards in Norway, over a distance of more than 1500 km, may have happened within less than 500 years and may have, within that period, extended eastwards for another 500 km. It seems that, at least initially, there were many similarities between the earliest stages of the Fosna in south and west Norway and what may have been a primary, very early phase, which pre-dated the better known classic Komsa/Olsen Phase 1. This initial phase (Phase 0),

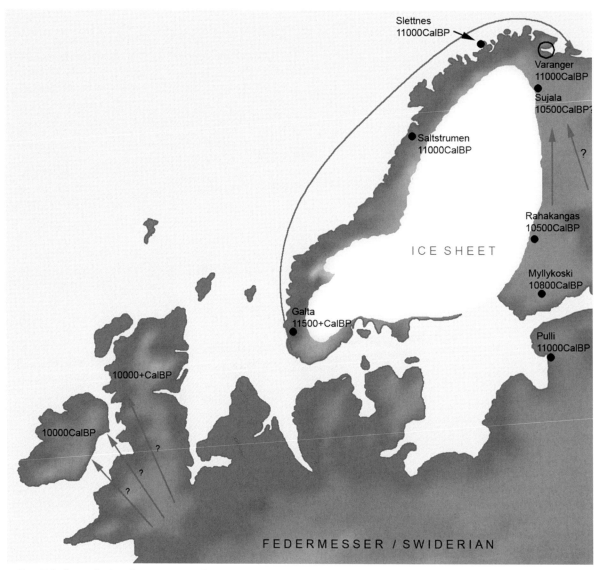

Fig. 7.3. Spread of settlement in North-West Europe: Britain, Scandinavia, Ireland (prepared by Hugh Kavanagh).

which is known from very few sites, again had many similarities with the earliest phases of the Fosna (Woodman 1999).

As Bjerck (1995) has pointed out, this expansion northwards would have only been possible when a technology had been developed that was capable of exploiting marine resources. In essence, the emergence of new land from beneath the sea or from below the ice did not necessarily result in immediate colonisation. This standstill can be seen in the manner in which large parts of the Canadian arctic islands, such as Baffin and Ellesmere Islands, were not populated until the development of the bladder float technology that allowed effective exploitation of sea mammals. Fuglesveldt (2003) has noted, if good sea-going canoes were available then large area of new coastlines could be explored very rapidly (Fig. 7.4).

Economic changes may not be as radical as those associated with lithic technologies and one also presumes that social networks would frequently have been retained. However, in areas where expansion occurred at a very rapid pace, such as along the Atlantic coast of Scandinavia, more fundamental adaptations may have taken place after a very short period of time. In contrast, in an adjacent regions of South Scandinavia i.e. from Scania to parts of southern Norway, a relatively short distance of little more than 100 km, the development of very different technologies could suggest that, besides constraints imposed by varying resources, other factors may have also contributed. Thus new social networks may have been established quite rapidly.

Did islands create any special situations?

Even within the context of the issues normally associated with the Mesolithic, the initial settlement of islands and

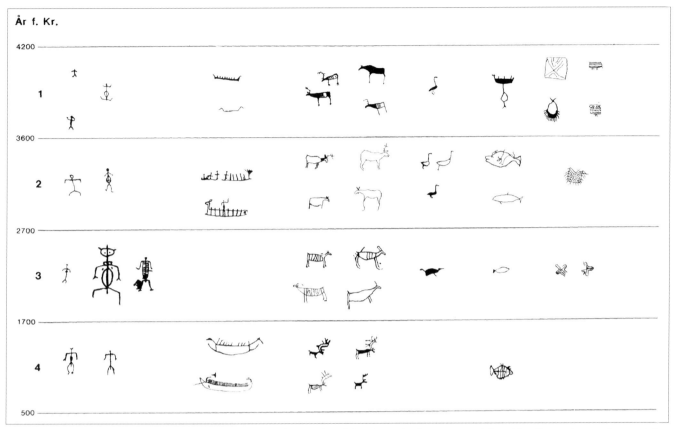

Fig. 7.4. Older Stone Age rock art from Alta showing boats, the oldest from the latter part of the older Stone Age at the top (after Helskog 1988).

those surrounding the date of their first colonisation, have always attracted a disproportionate interest. These can often be quite controversial, as can be seen in the case of many of the Mediterranean islands as documented by Patton (1996). A good example would be the difference of opinion on the date of the initial human settlement of Corsica, indeed the whole Tyrrhenian island complex. Some, such as Bonifay (1998), have claimed that there is evidence for a Middle Palaeolithic presence, perhaps 70,000 years ago, based on typological comparisons of artefacts from, in particular, La Grotte Corsica. Others, such as Patton (1996) and more recently Costa (2004), strongly suggest that human occupation began as late as the Holocene. Patton (1996) has also outlined the various theories, such as the island biogeography theory of MacArthur and Wilson but, while these seem to have certain validity in Mediterranean islands, it is questionable as to how useful these theories are in a context such as Ireland. The Mediterranean or the Pacific islands were available for colonisation for an indefinite but quite long period of time, while the time available for initial human settlement in Ireland, or perhaps Newfoundland is, as seen above, restricted to a portion of the late glacial and Holocene.

In settling new lands there will always be barriers, but the movement to islands and the establishment of new communities in these circumstances may present special problems. Given the

manner in which humanity has spread to various island groups it seems likely that the sea itself was not the greatest barrier. It is apparent that, for the Early Holocene, there is still a dearth of knowledge about the nature of marine craft. While paddles have been found on sites that date quite early in the Mesolithic, in the case of Ireland dugouts/log boats have been recovered from many locations but most of these date quite late (Fry 2002). It may seem quite simple that a boat can be made from a log, but there is a question as to both the appropriate material and its availability. Most log boats in Ireland have been made from oak, but as Gregory (1997), in his extensive study of log boats and especially their buoyancy, has shown, oak is quite dense and boats made from oak tend to settle low in the water. While they are very stable they are susceptible to shipping water in rough seas and sinking. They are most suitable for inland waters and sheltered coastal areas rather than the open sea. In the right circumstances log boats could be used but would they have been viewed as the normal and consistent means of transport? Gregory (*ibid.*, 127) has also noted that, while sails could be used, there is no evidence in any early log boats that there was an effective means of fixing or stepping a sail within the boat.

There is also the question as to whether suitable trees would have been available. How prevalent was oak round the Irish Sea before 10,000 cal BP? McGrail (2001, 174) in this context has suggested that the earliest log boats were more likely to have been made from pine such as those from Pesse in the Netherlands and Noyen sur Seine which date to earlier than 9000 cal BP. Scots pine, which would have existed at the time, would have suffered the same problems as oak, while other trees would be much slimmer. It is of interest that the Danish Later Mesolithic canoes from Margrethes Naes on Halsskov fjord are made from Lime. The sides and bases of these canoes varied between 5 mm and 20 mm in thickness (Pedersen and Fischer 1997, 157–63). The slightly later and well known Tybrind Vig boat (Andersen 1987, 274–6), which was complete at 10 m in length, was made in a similar manner, also from lime. Obviously lime trees were not really available in the earlier part of the Holocene – indeed have never been prevalent in Ireland – but they illustrate an important point, namely that they would have been like skiffs or canoes that rode high over the water and, in competent hands would have been safer. It is highly probable that boats that ventured out into the Irish Sea on a regular basis would have been more like canoes but made from what materials? As McGrail (2001, 181–3) has noted "the record on hide covered or even bark covered boats especially from the Mesolithic is insubstantial and obviously it will be difficult to find even a fragment of one". Ireland would have presented its own problems. The absence of most large mammals from Ireland would mean that boats built in Ireland would not have had easy access to the hides of large land mammals. Bark or seal skins would have been the only alternatives. One could argue that the prospective first explorers would first be able to make allowances for tides and weather and then use the small skiffs to visit Ireland. In the context of attempts at a more long term settlement, one can assume that there would be knowledge of what could be obtained and used on arrival, but it is still possible that with larger numbers of people and the need to bring certain utensils, tools, etc., with them, the boats used would have been bigger. Again, could these large boats exist?

There are some indications, most notably from Norway, that, in that region at least, Mesolithic communities had evolved new technologies (in Norway this period is usually referred to as the "Older Stone Age"). The technological change is based on the shift from Bjerck's (2009) littoral stage to a full maritime adaptation, i.e. from simple shoreline navigation, or even visitations to convenient islands, to a capacity to use the resources of the open sea as well as those of archipelagos and shorelines. This is clearly demonstrated by the extensive use of the island of Vega which lies out into the open Atlantic, just below the Arctic Circle, some 15 km from the Norwegian mainland (Bjerck 1990). An important point is not only the fact that they got to that island at all but that many of the locations for habitation sites were chosen to provide safe havens for boats. In some cases these were placed so as to provide, dependant on weather conditions, a choice of two havens. While not a direct indicator of a marine technology that regularly used the open sea, there is a widespread distribution of ground stone axes north and south for several hundred kilometres from the axe factories at Bømlo and Flora (Olsen and Alsaker 1984). Similarly, rock art in Finnmark, at locations such as Alta, illustrate that (albeit in the later part of the "Older Stone Age"), a series of large sea-going craft that were used for deep sea fishing were more than adequate for carrying large numbers of people or cargo (Helskog 1988, 32; 90–4; Fig. 7.4).

If one adopts a fatalistic perspective and recognises that Mesolithic groups got to many islands, quite a number of which were surrounded by less than tranquil seas, then one must assume that their sea-going skills and craft were more than adequate for most tasks. Perhaps the discovery of Irish "*Early*" Mesolithic material on the small island of Inishtrahull, located 10 km north of Malin Head (Woodman in prep.) in a very similar location to Vega, is a strong indication that Mesolithic communities in the Irish Sea and adjacent part of the Atlantic were regularly able to use the open sea in a confident manner.

There has been research on the feasibility of sea travel along the coast of western France and around the British Isles. This has, however, centred more on the spread of the Neolithic at or around 6000 cal. BP. There are some key differences, notably that this indicates contact between areas where there is a known human presence and where much of the emphasis has been placed on long voyages of up to 10 days or more. As will be discussed below, the patterns of voyages of exploratory, pioneering or initial settlement would have been different. Callaghan and Scarre (2009), in their simulation studies, have made several important observations. Perhaps the most important is that journeys of a particular length may be virtually impossible or unwise during certain seasons of the year when prevailing winds or currents would have driven boats back towards, if not past, their point of departure. These were, however, long voyages from Brittany northwards where certain seasons of the year were more likely to be suitable. In the Irish Sea they suggest that two routes Argyll–Antrim and Anglesey–Boyne would be worthy of attention. In good conditions 1–2 day voyages could be taken at any time of the year but there would have been seasonal preferences when the prevailing winds would have been favourable and then, later in the year, blew in a reverse direction. It should be noted that, as the authors themselves (*ibid.*, 369) are not convinced that sailing predated the 1st millennium BC, there is an assumption that paddled craft were used. This view, that more emphasis should be placed on phases of movements and shorter journeys, is also expressed by Garrow and Sturt (2011). If nothing else these studies again show the improbability and problems of the long voyages across the Bay of Biscay from Iberia to Britain and Ireland, as suggested by authors such as Oppenheimer (2006) or implied in the 2009 TV series *Blood of the Irish*.

At this point it is worth considering the manner in which Mesolithic maritime adaptations are viewed. A belief that was more common in the past was that highly maritime adaptations tended to be much more common very late in the Mesolithic, which is the period when, due to rise and stabilisation of world-wide sea levels, most evidence along shorelines is preserved.

There may be some instances where this happened, or where there was an intensification of the use of specific sources, for example the Oronsay middens in Scotland (Richards and Mellars 1998). In contrast, there would seem to be a growing tendency to presume that the exact converse is true and that highly adapted marine economies would have existed for much of the earlier Holocene. As noted earlier, Erlandson and Fitzpatrick (2006) have pointed out that there is evidence that the sea and its resources were used even before the Middle Palaeolithic, but the question is more whether these resources, even if they were the predominant ones, were key elements in their economy.

What is the evidence?

Unfortunately, for much of the European coastline, the rise in sea level throughout the Early Holocene has destroyed or put out of easy reach many of the sites that could have provided information. In parts of western Sweden, however, some information survives. These are often sites that have been buried by a rising sea level and where, fortunately, the settlements have not been eroded away and there is some preservation of organic remains. These include Huseby Klev (Hernek and Nordquist 1995) where spectacular evidence survives from an event of Early Boreal age when, apparently, a dolphin pod was driven ashore and killed. This may, of course, represent a single event that did not actually produce a consistent source of food throughout much of the year.

Further south, different information came from sites near Gothenburg such as Bua Våstergaärd at around and Balltrop which are dated to between 9000 and 7500 years ago. Some sites were buried below deposits created by an advancing sea level. These sites are often placed within an archipelago of islands and contain significant quantities of both terrestrial and marine fauna. Wigfross (1995) suggests that these are seasonally occupied locations. There may be some local specialisation but there does not seem to be a broad regional heavy reliance on marine resources throughout much of the year. There are some sites, such as Bua, that have a fauna dominated by marine resources, while Balltrop has a more mixed coastal and mainland fauna. One site in the same general area and of the same general age as those listed above, at Dammern (7600–8000 cal BP), produced the remains of a dog which has a $\delta^{13}C$ ratio of -13.2‰, which may be a proxy that indicates that the human population also lived extensively on marine resources. At Tågerup (Karsten and Knarrstrom 2003, 54–5), also on the west coast of Sweden, the $\delta^{13}C$ ratios of the human and dog remains from the Kongemose levels, about 8500–8000 cal BP, were between -17.6‰ and -21.1‰, which would suggest a significant reliance on terrestrial resources with some marine input.

The complexity and difficulties in assessing the role of the sea is perhaps best illustrated by Schulting's (2009) work in south Wales. Here two regions, Worms Head and Caldey Island, have each produced a number of human remains that date to the Mesolithic. Both locations would have been situated relatively close to the coast throughout the Mesolithic. The remains from Worms Head are earlier, predominantly *c.* 10,800–10,200 cal BP, as against those from the caves on Caldey Island at 9700–8500 cal BP. Both sites are relatively early in the Mesolithic but the $\delta^{13}C$ results from the Caldey Island remains are much more marine (–14‰), as against those from Worms Head at –19‰ to –18‰. Schulting has suggested three possibilities:

1) The absence of a suitable technology during the 11th millennium cal BP;
2) The human remains from Worms Head date to a point in time when the shoreline might have been much further from the their location;
3) There may have been a cultural difference in choices of food.

As Schulting (*ibid.*, 357) has noted, the actual explanation maybe a product of all three reasons.

In summary, while there are instances of highly specialised marine exploitation at the end of the Mesolithic, there is also extensive evidence that the sea was being used as a major source of food from early in the Mesolithic. It is therefore probable that by 10,000 years ago the Mesolithic communities of the Irish Sea would not necessarily have been shore bound.

Why the delay in getting to Ireland?

If travelling to an island is not the major obstacle then alternative explanations must be sought for the frequent, significant delays in establishing human settlement on islands. This is very apparent on certain quite large Mediterranean islands which are within sight of continental Europe. These include the Tyrrhenian islands of Corsica and Sardinia which lay only a short sea voyage from Elba. In both cases no successful long term settlement took place until the Mesolithic and in the former case, Costa (2004, 39–41) suggests that, there is an immediate adaptation to marine based economy. *Prolagus sardus* (an extinct member of the lagomorph family) being the only mammal present on the island and relatively small in size, was not sufficient to support a land based economy. Takamiya (2006) has noted that, in the case of parts of the Pacific, early farming communities were more successful colonisers than hunter-gatherers. It would, therefore, seem probable that in areas where the new lands contain meagre resources, those who arrive with their own economic package, frequently, though not exclusively farmers, are more likely to be successful in the long term.

One must therefore conclude that the successful settlement of islands depends on a crucial combination of a series of factors and that the so called "sea barrier" is only one of them. One must also consider:

1) Distance from the nearest landmass. Islands such as Madagascar or the New Zealand islands would have required a well-developed maritime technology and may have needed an established "tried and tested" economic

package which could be transferred. Distance and other elements could have seriously inhibited the range of fauna and flora that would have existed prior to human settlement.

2) In some cases the islands need to have been available for a significant length of time to allow for various attempts at explorations, as would have happened in Micronesia and Melanesia. In contrast, ice sheets would have denied access to other islands, such as those in the Canadian Arctic. In this context, islands that could be colonised while they were available with a dry land connection or "land bridge" and which had been mostly free from ice sheets for some considerable time before human colonisation cannot, in this instance, be considered as islands. Thus, for the purposes of this discussion, mainland Britain is not considered as an island as it only became separated from the European mainland at a late date. Similarly, islands such as Tasmania, which had never been extensively covered with a large ice sheet and which only became separate from mainland Australia long after a human presence was established, are not in the same category as Ireland.

3) Size of the island would also be a major factor. It may have been a limiting factor in the presence of an ecology that would not always form a viable basis for a hunter-gatherer economy. Curet (2004) has noted that, in the case of the West Indies, on certain smaller islands there may have been a rapid over-exploitation of even some littoral resources such as sea otters. It is thought that the emphasis on sea otters was not so much as a source of food but rather so that their pelts could be used for cloaks. He also noted that transfer of populations to other islands may have, on arrival in new locations, required significant changes in economic strategies.

4) Location within oceanic or marine systems such as warm and cold water currents could play a significant role as their productivity would condition the relative availability of marine or littoral resources. As noted earlier, the rapid human expansion into Arctic Scandinavia took early communities north of the Scandinavian ice sheet. It is therefore probable that climate in itself would not have precluded the development of a successful society in that apparently inhospitable region.

5) The environment in its broadest sense will, along with many of the other factors, determine island ecology and may in certain circumstances inhibit the establishment of a range of flora and fauna, which in turn might deter an early initial settlement. It is also probable that during their initial phase of occupation, new or first arrivals would face other challenges as they try to a) retain or develop a new social network; b) retain links with established ones or c) cope with the need to retain the broad range of skills (Woodman 1981). In some instances, success might require that the "colonisers" remain embedded in a larger community.

Problems in colonising Ireland

As indicated, there are a number of factors impacting on how and when colonisation takes place and in the case of islands there are additional matters to be taken into consideration. Ireland seems to have been a very particular case. It cannot be described as a small island, in fact, as noted in Chapter 2, it is one of the larger islands in the world. It cannot be described as being out of sight of adjacent settled areas. As will have been apparent from earlier discussions, it was accessible and ice free for a considerable time before it appears that a continuous human presence was begun. It is also not one of those areas where climatic conditions and the available resources would have conspired to delay settlement until a suitable set of technologies had developed.

On the basis of various constraints no two islands are exactly the same; however, even allowing for some leeway in the definition of location, such as latitude, size and difficulty in access, as well as availability, there are some similarities. Newfoundland, as well as the larger islands of the West Indies are also examples. These islands also have a restricted fauna and flora as did the larger Japanese islands of Honshu and Hokkaido.

If the present archaeological record is a relatively accurate reflection of early human activity in Ireland then there are reasonable explanations as to why a relatively late arrival took place. In the context of the late glacial period, if one starts from the working hypothesis that hunters categorised under the Magdalenian/Creswellian and Federmesser/penknife point cultures were primarily land based hunters, then it is possible to see why Ireland would not have been attractive. Even allowing for the meagre information available, the faunal range documented in Chapter 2 is so restricted that survival would have required a major shift in procurement strategies. The absence of species such as horse and the apparent lack of reindeer contemporaneous with the Creswellian, along with the absence of elk and the relative lack of red deer later in the Woodgrange Interstadial, would have required a very different economy. It is of interest that even the apparently ubiquitous giant deer seems to be confined, or perhaps at its most prolific, to a very short period of time at the very end of the interstadial. Ireland also seems to have been a very open landscape in which, even at the most optimal of times, there were few stands even of birch trees and it may have been subjected to very windy conditions. In southern Britain birch occurred in some quantities during one part of the interstadial but it did not have a significant presence in Ireland.

The possibility of other limiting factors in the marine ecosystem will be discussed below. Again, the absence of information about coastal environments of these early dates remains as one of the almost unanswerable questions.

Given the large number of assemblages that have become available during the last two decades, the apparent absence of any group of diagnostic artefacts seems to be a clear indication that there was no significant late glacial human presence in Ireland. Pettitt (2007) has suggested that much of the Creswellian/Magdalenian presence in the southern Pennines and Peak District represents short term seasonal extensions northwards from more established communities based further south in areas such as Mendip. This suggests that a substantial and semi-permanent presence in Ireland would be unlikely. This does not preclude the possibility of a limited pioneering visit but the occasional possible lithic piece, such as the backed bladelet from Newport referred to earlier, cannot be used as an indicator of rare pioneering visits excursions to Ireland.

As already mentioned in Chapter 6, because of humanity's very limited presence in space and time in Britain during the Younger Dryas, it seems extremely unlikely that there will ever be found a human presence in Ireland that related to that final phase. The absence of an equivalent to the British Early Mesolithic presents a number of challenges. Aside from an inferred slightly earlier phase pre-dating Mount Sandel (see above) there is in Ireland an actual gap of at least 1500 years from the beginning of the Holocene to the earliest confirmed settlement. Given all the constraints that could inhibit or delay settlement it is of course tempting to explain the delay by suggesting that Ireland was not only an island but lacked potential for early settlement within its ecosystem. In spite of the severe effects of the Younger Dryas it is unlikely that Ireland, at the beginning of the Holocene, could be regarded as a totally barren landscape or one that at that suffered from severe tectonic events, such as landslides, earthquakes, etc., that were induced by crustal re-adjustment due to the wasting away of such massive ice sheets. It also seems likely that, in spite of the climatic fluctuations during and after the Younger Dryas, several mammalian species survived through into the Holocene (Woodman 2008).

In Part I we saw how there has been a demise of the concept of a colonisation event by plants and animals primarily at the commencement of the Holocene. There has been a move towards seeing Ireland's re-colonisation as a process that began during the late glacial, survived in part through the Younger Dryas, and continued slowly throughout the Holocene. Therefore, it is apparent that only a small selection of mammals would have been present in the earliest part of the Holocene. Indeed it is possible that, with the exception of the wild boar, most of the fauna would have consisted of the species that may have survived the Younger Dryas.

So often the evidence for the presence or absence of certain species is dependant on what has been recovered from archaeological sites. These are hardly random records, as factors such as preferences in what was hunted or gathered or how animals were butchered, or fish gutted, will preserve a biased record of the contemporaneous fauna. Also, there is the added problem that it is very difficult to obtain information about indigenous fauna or flora that pre-dates the archaeological sites. As noted earlier, the virtual absence of any stratigraphy in most Irish caves means that, short of a massive programme of radiocarbon dating on species such as fox, badger, otter, etc.,

it is difficult to get a sense of how long certain species have been present in Ireland. Therefore the faunal record for the Holocene mostly begins with sites like Mount Sandel.

There is also the question of climate. As discussed in Chapter 2 it seems probable that, during some of the initial phases of the Holocene, the climate in Ireland may have been somewhat more continental, i.e. drier with hotter summers and colder winters, but this would not have been of a sufficient order of magnitude to cause a serious delay in settlement. Several factors need to be considered, including the pre-Boreal oscillation as a phase of climatic deterioration that occurred during the first millennium after the beginning of the Holocene. In Britain, Reynier (2005, chapter 5) has suggested that the pre-Boreal oscillation, along with poor soil development and hydrological factors, may have been one influence on the delay of the spread of human settlement in Britain during the Early Mesolithic.

It is also apparent that this period is associated with what many have described as the "Missing Millennium", which is a period when, due to variations in the creation of radiocarbon in the upper atmosphere, it can be difficult to obtain precisely calibrated calendar radiocarbon dates. There also seem to be problems in many areas where the earliest sites may be buried under an extensive series of Quaternary deposits of various types. Thus, in many parts of north-western Europe, the archaeological record for that first millennium can be extremely scanty. This is evident in discussion of the chronology of the earliest Holocene in Denmark (Hansen and Pedersen 2006, 105) and somewhat more widely in Denmark and northern Germany (Terberger 2006, 127–8).

The potential of Ireland and the Irish Sea

Can we assume that the Irish Sea was always a rich marine environment? At that date, the Irish Sea would not have been radically different to today. Sea levels, 12,000–10,000 years ago, would have been slightly lower and, aside from the extra area of land to the east of the Isle of Man, the channels to the north and south would have been slightly narrower. This may have led to stronger tidal currents. Much of the Irish Sea basin may have had a more enclosed area of water which, in turn, was less subject to marine influence (Pl. II). There is also a possibility that the influence of the Gulf Stream was not as strong at that time. If, due to the huge impact of the Younger Dryas, the slow rise in temperature after the significant initial increase and then the pre-Boreal oscillation resulted in a vegetation cover round the Irish Sea basin that was limited, other factors may have affected the nature of the basin. In particular, there may have been increased rates of freshwater run-off that may have led to much higher mineral content in the water. Freshwater layers can also act as a barrier to sunlight. Therefore, one could ask whether the marine environment would be conducive to the occurrence of rich populations of phytoplankton and other micro-organisms that were essential to the extensive fish and sea mammal populations.

In the case of the marine environment there is often an assumption that it will always have been very productive. However, in the period when ice was melting at an accelerated rate it is possible that the mineral input into the north Atlantic would have precluded the development of a rich marine bio-sphere. It is perhaps unlikely that this would have continued to a significant degree into the Holocene but, at this stage, should one assume that there was a rich littoral and marine eco-system during some few centuries after the beginning of the Holocene?

As one needs a fully developed rich food chain for coastal settlement to flourish, one has to keep in mind the possibility that just because many coastal areas have been extremely rich in the later part of the Holocene, one cannot assume that it would have been the same during the Holocene's earliest stage. As has already been noted by Bjerck (2009) there is a significant difference between the use of the shoreline and the waters immediately offshore and venturing regularly out into the open sea on a regular basis as a necessary part of their life ways. Thus, there is a significant difference between, on the one hand the use of the littoral, where shellfish collecting, fishing from the rocks, targeting populations of beached or breeding sea mammals or perhaps even the driving inshore of pods of dolphins, such as at Huseby Klev in Bohauslan (Hernek and Nordquist 1995) and, on the other hand, an economy that confidently uses the open sea on a regular basis.

One might, on the other hand, ask when substantial fish populations began to develop in the rivers and lakes. The existence of several relict late glacial species, such as *Coregonus Autumnalis* (Pollan) in Lough Neagh (Wilson 1985, 53–8; see Chapter 2), shows that at a very early date some marine species may have populated a series of Irish and British lakes. The date of the establishment of other species, such as Salmonids and eels, is another question. Mellars (1985) noted the relative absence of fish bones from the late Upper Palaeolithic sites in south-west France and contrasts this with the Azilian, which would in part date to the Irish Woodgrange (Late Glacial) Interstadial and suggest that substantial fish populations were present by the end of the late glacial. There is, of course, the continuing enigma around the absence of fish remains from Star Carr which led Wheeler (1978) to suggest that certain species may not have established themselves until much later. Unfortunately, as well as Ireland, in so many other areas there is simply no evidence available to allow us to ascertain whether there were viable resident or migratory fish stocks present in the river systems during the earliest part of the Holocene. Reynier (2005, 75), for example, found few instances of fish bones from British Early Holocene deposits. Bennett (1983) noted that, while Wheeler (1978) had suggested that many of the fresh water species of fish found in Britain were introduced by a human agency, the presence of pike at Sea Mere in Norfolk in quite early Holocene deposits suggested that, especially on the east coast of England, many species found their own way into lakes at an early date.

This may seem a slightly esoteric question but the presence or absence of certain species can, of themselves, be key indicators of the extent to which ecology has matured or degraded. Glavin (2000, 45–71), in discussing the forests of the Pacific north-west, has noted the key role that salmon play in that environment. There is a complex balance between the spawning salmon and their death, which influences the extent of the avian fauna and other species such as bears. It is suggested that this inter-dependence in itself helped the spread of the forest zones that now dominate the area.

This, as in the case of Star Carr, raises again the question of when do salmon populations begin to establish themselves in the rivers of northern and north-western Europe? The absence of salmon and perhaps eels from the rivers of the earliest part of the Holocene would have, in the context of the lack of most other freshwater species of fish, created a major lacuna in Ireland's fauna. It is difficult to identify both pre-Boreal coastal and inland faunas in many regions. This is particularly true of the marine component. The Danish evidence is mostly later and is also very representative of areas that were significantly inland, while many coastal regions in Norway have no faunal remains surviving on sites that are early in the Holocene.

It is also noticeable that, in Ireland, three relatively substantial groups of fish bones from Mesolithic coastal sites – Port of Larne, Ferriter's Cove and Baylet – have produced a range of inshore sea fish (see Chapter 9). However, there is either a limited presence of salmon or none. In general, coastal sites in north-western Europe rarely produce salmon bones in any number.

One region which gives some sense of what was available and exploited is again the Bohauslan region on the west coast of Swedish. Many marine species have been recovered from sites in this region and changes in species caught can be documented through time (Jonsson 1995), but again there are no significant occurrences of salmon bones. Here, although the sites are generally in the island archipelagos, there seems to be a lack of evidence that salmon were being caught and this could be seasonal, i.e. salmon may not have been coming in towards rivers at the time of year when the islands of the archipelagos were being occupied. A similar pattern can be seen at Kotedalen on the west coast of Norway. Here over 5500 identifiable fish bones were recovered from the earliest three phases of settlement, dating to between approximately 10,000 and 8000 cal BP. These were overwhelmingly from the *Pollachius* and *Gadidae* families with only 10 bones of Salmonidae being recovered (Hufthammer 1992).

As will be discussed more fully below, salmon fishing in the open sea requires a relatively sophisticated technology while river estuaries provide more manageable locations. There are, however, few sites from the Early Holocene that are placed on river estuaries. In part, this absence is due to rising sea levels round many part of the European coast in the Early Holocene. Thus the estuarine locations from the beginning of the Holocene will be buried below more recent deposits or have been washed away. Mount Sandel with its salmon bones, which is placed above the Bann estuary, is one of the few estuarine sites known from early in the European Mesolithic. It is of interest that, in locations where early estuarine locations might be available, such as parts of Norway, there are no known settlement sites in similar locations to Mount Sandel, i.e. on the major river systems such as the Tana River. Settlement along these rivers seems to begin in the Younger Stone Age.

In summary, the presence of significant communities on the eastern seaboard of the Irish Sea is dependent on the post-glacial biological and ecological development of the Irish Sea basin. If it was a rich environment that encouraged deep sea fishing and hunting mammals from boats, then exploration and colonisation was likely to happen quickly, but if they were more confined to butchering of stranded sea mammals, shoreline fishing and shellfish collecting, then movement would have been much slower. Obviously the other side of this scenario would be whether the resources in Ireland would have been sufficient to attract groups to make a permanent move across the sea.

Was there anyone there?

A further question must be whether, early in the Holocene, there was a significant presence in western Britain and, in particular, in coastal areas facing Ireland. Although there is an obvious British Early Mesolithic it can hardly be described as well-documented even throughout England and Wales. It relies heavily on a limited number of sites, some of which may have been used over a significant portion of time, such as Star Carr, or were reoccupied at different dates, such as Thatcham (Dark 1998; Reynier 2005, 54–7). It also has little information on dated sites from the first 1000 years of the Holocene, indeed even Star Carr's radiocarbon dates belong to a point in time well after the beginning of the Mesolithic. Is it possible the spread of human settlement from the core areas occupied during the Younger Dryas may have happened relatively slowly?

Aside from the question of differences in distribution, as noted earlier, Reynier (2005) has recorded that there is little evidence of an Early Mesolithic to the north and west and has suggested that, in general, Early Mesolithic assemblages lay outside the maximum limits of deposits laid down during the Devensian glaciation. Reynier (*ibid.*, 85–96; fig. 6, 2) suggested that the poor development of soils within the recently glaciated area may have inhibited further movement north and west.

There may also be, allowing for the typological variation within the British Early Mesolithic, too much of a tendency to see it as one entity. Thus, even within the area where Early Mesolithic assemblages occur, the concentration of dates from the earliest known part of the British Early Mesolithic, i.e. significantly before 10,500 cal BP, tends to be in the east (Fig. 7.5). At Worm's Head (Schulting 2009), aside from one apparently anomalous very early date (see above), the human remains date to approximately 10,500 cal BP. Dates from Nab Head and Caldey, as well as those from Mendip, notably

Aveline's Hole, are later in the 11th millennium cal BP (Reynier 2005, table 4.1; Schulting 2009, fig. 53.2; 2005, figs 34–8; Conneller 2009a, fig. 103, 1). Two sites in north Wales had, for many years, perhaps over-emphasised a potentially very late Early Mesolithic in at least the northern portion of Wales. These came from Rhuddlan on the north-east Coast and Trwyn Du on Anglesey. In essence the five dates obtained tended to suggest ages between 10,000 and 9500 cal BP. However, numerous authors (e.g. David and Walker 2004, 302–3) have suggested that, between problems in the process of obtaining the date and the probability of samples containing material of mixed age, only one sample from Rhuddlan Site E (BM 691, charcoal, 8739±86 BP, 10,160–9530 cal BP) is reliable.

There is one interesting indication of a human presence in north-west England which is only slightly later than the date of 10,500 cal BP. Re-examination of the older excavation at Kent's Bank Cavern in southern Cumbria has, amongst a series of radiocarbon dates of Mesolithic age, produced one date on a human bone of 10,200 cal BP (Smith, O'Regan, and Wilkinson, Lecture to Palaeolithic/Mesolithic Conference, British Museum, November 2011).

There is also one tantalising indicator from within the Irish Sea. This final piece of evidence consists of two potential worked pieces of chert dredged from the seabed off Arklow, Co. Wicklow (Campbell 2004). While one piece is not convincing, the other appears to have been worked, albeit in a very crude manner. These could be indicators of a very early human presence on the floor of the Irish Sea. Campbell has, however, noted that it is unclear how these pieces arrived at this location and that they may have been inadvertently dumped there at a much later date. Although the Irish Sea basin is very different from Doggerland there is always a strong possibility that, one day, artefacts of an early date will be dredged off the floor of the Irish Sea.

The date from the Kent's Bank Cavern and those from Wales suggest that, certainly by 10,000 years ago, there was a human presence on the western shores of England and Wales, but the question remains as to whether this is an indication of substantial settlement or a product of exploratory or pioneering visits.

There is also the question of the date of the initial Mesolithic settlement of the west coast of Scotland (see Finlay *et al.* 2002 for a full discussion on this question). In general, the early site on Rhum (Wickham-Jones 1990) which dates to approximately 9500 cal BP has often been considered to be the oldest known Mesolithic site in the west of Scotland. There is, however, as noted earlier the issue of the date of microlith assemblages that resemble those from Star Carr and, in particular, the presence of large isosceles triangles along with the occasional trapeze. The most contentious example is represented by the dates from Morton in eastern Scotland (Coles 1971) where a series of microliths that are reminiscent of those from Star Carr was recovered but where the radiocarbon dates from the same site generally lie between 8000 and 7000 cal BP, i.e. more than

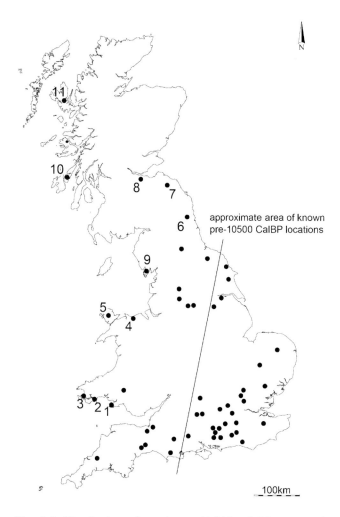

Fig. 7.5. Distribution of mostly pre-10,000 cal BP sites in the more north-westerly portions of the British Mesolithic: 1) Worms Head, 2) Caldey Island, 3) Nab Head, 4) Rhuddlan, 5) Trwyn Du, 6) Howick, 7) East Barnes, 8) Crammond, 9) Kent's Bank Cavern, 10) Lussa Bay, 11) An Corran.

Mesolithic. Other similar groups of material were recovered from Glenabatrick (Mercer 1974), also on Jura. A small sample of similar artefacts was also recovered from the base of the shell midden, An Corráin, on Skye (Saville *et al.* 2012), but unfortunately no radiocarbon dates could be obtained from these basal levels. The questions about these assemblages are 1) are they Early Mesolithic in typology; 2) if so, does this mean that they are the same age as the English Mesolithic; or 3) could they pre-date 10,500 cal BP?

In summary, there is as yet little substantial evidence that there was, before 10,500 cal BP, a significant human presence along the eastern shores of the Irish Sea. This does not mean that there was not a human presence by 10,000 cal BP or certainly well before settlement began in Ireland. The question remains as to the age and location of assemblages that are similar to those found at Mount Sandel.

In the case of Ireland at least it is possible that there may have been little pressure to push across the Irish Sea until quite a late date. As noted earlier, the very partial survival of coastlines contemporaneous with events around 10,000 cal BP in part hinders this investigation. On the positive side, and again based on earlier discussions, were there coastal communities along the west coast of Britain who would have been capable of exploring and settling within Ireland?

The question is, therefore, really about what caused an eventual movement into Ireland. One event that has been suggested is the loss of Doggerland and the North Sea basin through flooding. Numerous authors have noted a coincidence in this inundation and the apparent expansion of Mesolithic Settlement during the 10th millennium cal BP (Waddington 2007, 219–24). This may have been a factor that, along with an ongoing slow rise in population, caused small groups to seek new lands to the west and north. Waddington (*ibid.*) has suggested that this should be associated with the emergence of the more geometric forms of microliths that became increasingly common in the British later Mesolithic. While this is an interesting suggestion, there are difficulties. Not the least of these is that sites like Asfordby in Leicestershire (referred to earlier) seem to have a geometric microlithic element already before 10,000 cal BP while the main assemblage from Cass ny Hawin II, which dates to around 10,000 cal BP, already contains numerous geometric Microliths.

The abrupt or rapid transformation between the British Early and Later Mesolithic seems, in part, to be a curious phenomenon confined to Britain. It can be contrasted with other parts of Europe, from Denmark and the Netherlands to the eastern side of Germany, at sites such as Freisac (Ghelen 2010), and beyond into Poland, as well as southwards into France (see Reynier 2005, chapter 7 for comparisons of European typological sequences). In essence, the larger number of well-documented and dated mainland European sites suggest a series of changes during a long period of time within the Mesolithic. Denmark, as noted earlier provides a good example of a series of changes throughout the whole of the Mesolithic.

2000 years later than Star Carr. At Morton, does the settlement contain an assemblage that represents i) a late survival of Star Carr type microliths, ii) is there no association between the microliths and the radiocarbon dates or, iii) is this a case of a fortuitous reinvention of a range of microliths that just happen to be similar to those found at Star Carr? There are several assemblages in western Scotland that could, potentially on a typological basis, be earlier in date than the Kinloch assemblage from Rhum (Wickham-Jones 1990). No radiocarbon dates are available, but the presence of a series of large isosceles triangles and some trapezes at Lussa Bay on Jura, where it seems probable that the material came from a site that pre-dated the Holocene rise in sea level (Mercer 1971), suggests that the assemblage is not late within the Mesolithic. There is a resemblance between this material and the artefacts from Star Carr, which suggests that it could belong to the British Early

Petersen (1970, fig. 7:1b) documents the change in microliths but shows that changes in other parts of the technology, such as methods of blade production, did not necessarily coincide with those changes. Therefore, as there is no dramatic event in the change in microlith types, the fact that these changes are going on over a large part of Europe suggests that they have little to do *per se* with the loss of Doggerland.

Problems on arrival

If the development of Ireland's Holocene ecology, in which the initial human settlement was one element, can be seen as a part of a process, then a different perspective can be brought to bear on a number of issues previously raised (Woodman 1981). Many of those issues still exist and include:

1) A small population that belongs to a tiny genetically closed group may have biological problems in sustaining itself. The larger the size and the more diverse the initial population, the less is the risk of the emergence of recessive genetic traits. Where these populations become isolated at an early stage, it is usually necessary to increase the total population relatively quickly. Kelly (2003, 51) has observed that any initial group would need to consist of up to seven foragers, but the group might also contain children, some of the woman and elderly individuals, thus making up a group of roughly 25 people.
2) Small populations may not contain, within themselves, the full range of skills required. These skills could range from hunting and fishing techniques through acquiring plant foods to technological skills, of which stone tool manufacturing, was only one. In fact, sea-going populations even today would be very susceptible to sudden and significant loss of a key number of members of a small population. In Ireland the loss of the lives of several men from Inistrahull seems to have been one of the factors that led to the island being abandoned early in the 20th century.

The more gradual process of exploration and colonisation suggests that contacts existed for quite some time and, as discussed earlier, it would have been an informed, considered process that could even include several failed or abandoned attempts. This would seem to be supported by Rockman's (2003, fig. 1.3) observation that any new population arriving into an empty landscape would have to surmount several obstacles. While social problems and levels of population would, as discussed above, present barriers, the major problem would be a lack of knowledge of new lands (Fig. 7.6), including knowledge of how to fish the rivers and lakes, especially if the incoming population had either been living primarily on the coast or were more adapted to a land based economy. Rockman (2003, 19) noted that some of the major problems would have been in establishing where key plant resources could be found. Given Ireland's more impoverished flora this could have been a major difficulty for any new arrivals. Surprisingly, she noted

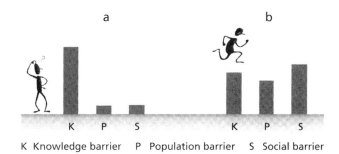

Fig. 7.6. Rockman's diagram of issues for new colonists (Rockman 2003).

that knowledge about the location of sources of lithic raw material was one of the least transferable types of information. This may not have been such a problem in Ireland. As already discussed in Chapter 2 flint, the most obvious material, was reasonably accessible throughout many, particularly coastal, areas in Ireland.

Much of the discussion on colonising islands has taken place in the context of small islands that are sometimes located a considerable distance from their starting point, for example, the West Indies (Curet 2004) and Polynesia (Anderson 2003, 182). In both instances the authors describe numerous cases where, because of the small size of the island, an apparently prolific but time-finite resource was exterminated in a relatively short period. This is less likely to happen during an initial phase of settlement in an island the size of Ireland.

Routes?

Several aspects of the "*Early*" Mesolithic in Ireland have changed radically since 1981. Then, the characteristic "*Early*" Mesolithic assemblages were confined to the northern half of Ireland and elsewhere, aside from Lough Boora, the Mesolithic was quite poorly documented (see Part I). Now, some traces of the "*Early*" Mesolithic have been found throughout most of Ireland, including west of the River Shannon. This leaves open the possibility of movement from a number of areas (Figs 7.7 and 7.8). Today's sea levels are higher, but 10,000 years ago even a drop of 20 m in relative sea level would not change the choice of routes significantly. Some of these routes are:

1) Islay to Rathlin (30 km).
2) Mull of Kintyre to Torr Head (20 km).
3) Galloway to Isle of Magee or the Ards Peninsula (35 km).
4) The Isle of Man basin, where most of the then coastline and its environs have since been submerged: Peel to Ardglass (55 km).
5) North Wales, including the Isle of Anglesey, to south Dublin (90 km).
6) The south Wales areas, including Pembrokeshire, Ramsey Head to Censure Point (80 km).

None of these routes is impossible and, as noted previously (Woodman 1981, 97), especially if one takes into consideration awareness of another large land mass and the fact that much of the Irish Sea is surrounded by significant areas of high ground. This means that new lands were visible from points of departure on coasts or near that point, rather than only when the journey was already half complete, as is the case in some parts of the West Indies.

In the intervening 30 years since (Woodman 1981) our knowledge of the Mesolithic of the western shores of Great Britain has changed and there are numerous relatively early sites known from the later Mesolithic in the western parts of Britain As a result, perhaps the routes into Ireland could be distilled into three choices.

The Scottish routes

Perhaps the discovery of a relatively early site on Rhum (Wickham-Jones 1990), even if it is not as early as Mount Sandel, suggests that the Scottish routes should not be dismissed. It should also be remembered that, on the basis

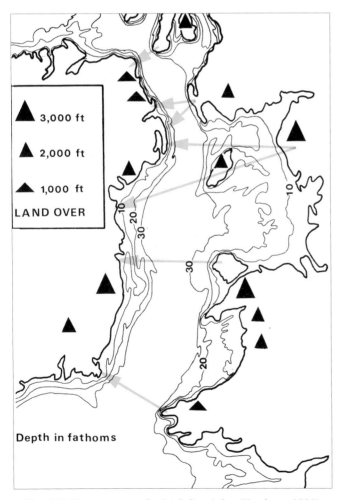

Fig. 7.7. Routes across the Irish Sea (after Woodman 1981).

of assemblages from Lussa Bay on Jura and elsewhere, a case can be made for the presence of groups using so-called British Early Mesolithic "broad blade" tool kits at a date of 10,000 cal BP or slightly earlier. The shortest route, Kintyre to Torr Head, may, in terms of rough seas and steep cliffs, be the least likely. Besides these open sea crossings to Ireland, the one alternative almost "archipelago like" route would be to the north coast of Antrim through the Islands of Jura, Islay and Rathlin. This would assume that there was an already well-established population in the Scottish Southern Hebrides.

The Isle of Man basin

The existence of English later Mesolithic sites in the Pennines that were not that much younger than Mount Sandel suggested the possibility that there could have been a movement across the Isle of Man basin onto the east coast of Ireland. Unfortunately the fact that there were no coastal sites left one with one of those awful proposals that "it made sense to see a movement across the Isle of Man basin but unfortunately the relevant sites lie below present day sea level"! It was hoped that an examination of the one high point, i.e. the Isle of Man itself, would provide a stepping stone. Examination of the Manx collections and the follow up excavation at Cass ny Hawin I house site (Woodman 1978b; 1987), while producing some important results, did not find that chronological stepping stone. However, it has now turned up at Cass ny Hawin II less than 300 m south of my excavation. Here, possibly, two new sites were recovered. These excavations have uncovered, from within a new house site, what appears to be an assemblage that, in its blade production, is both similar to the English later Mesolithic (narrow blade) and at the same times could be ancestral to the Mount Sandel type assemblage. The assemblage contains numerous scalene triangles of various sizes. some of which are quite broad. A small number of inversely trimmed points are also present. Sinead McCartan (pers. comm.) had suggested that there might be some link between the Manx material and the Honey Hill assemblages. The crucial point is that the assemblage has produced five radiocarbon dates which centre on 10,000 cal BP. There were samples from a pit in the nearby third site dated some hundreds of years later (Frazer Brown, pers. comm.).

The west coast of Wales

In the case of Wales, the archaeological evidence is slightly different in that there is one site from the later Mesolithic that is as early as Mount Sandel and none of an earlier date. As noted above, there are, in Wales, assemblages which seem to date to the latest stages of the Early Mesolithic though perhaps after 10,500 cal BP. The Prestatyn site has also produced the earliest known later Mesolithic dates on the western shores of mainland Britain (OxA 2268, charcoal, 8700±100 BP, 10,150–9490 cal BP; OxA 2269, charcoal 8730±90 BP, 10,150–9530 cal BP).

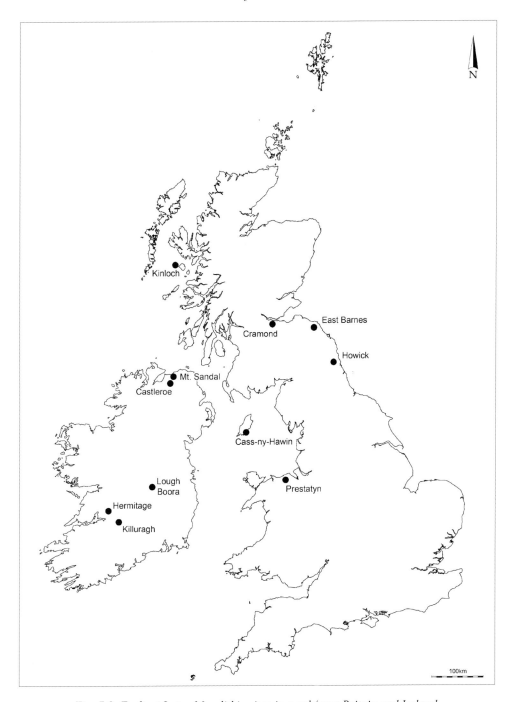

Fig. 7.8. Earliest Later Mesolithic sites in north/west Britain and Ireland.

Although it may be a very personal and subjective observation, there are interesting elements in the lithic assemblage from the preceding earlier Mesolithic of Wales. Jacobi (1980) and David and Walker (2004) have documented a small but important number of core axes and axe-sharpening flakes from sites located round the coast of Wales. Although many of these have been found in south-west Wales, notably in Pembrokeshire, they have also occurred at Trwyn Du and possibly at Rhuddlan on the north coast. A number of these Welsh axes and sharpening flakes tend to be made from Tuffs and Rhyolite rather than flint. Although the Welsh evidence cannot be put together in a neat chronological package that provides the perfect antecedent to the earliest Irish Mesolithic, the occurrence of the axes and the presence of micro-awls/*meche de forets* suggest some sort of link (Fig. 7.9). Indeed, although one must wonder whether they remain to be identified elsewhere in Wales, the presence of ground stone axes at the later Mesolithic Nab Head II site must also give us pause for thought (Fig. 7.10).

Elsewhere, further north along the east coast of Britain core axes, associated with what could be regarded as Early Mesolithic assemblages, seem to be unknown in north-west England and western Scotland.

An overwhelming case cannot be made for any of these routes but each has both advantages and disadvantages.

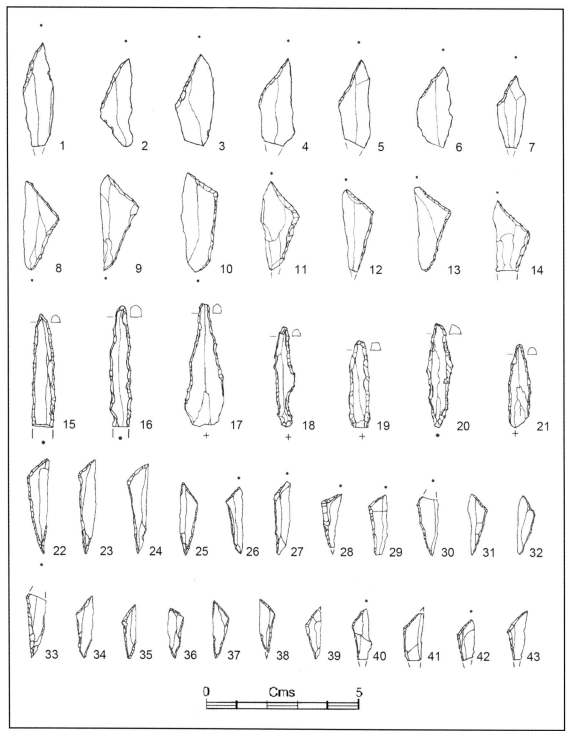

Fig. 7.9. Nab Head Site 1: 1–14) microliths and micro-awls, 15–21) Mèche de Foret, 22–43) microliths from Prestatyn (after David and Walker 2004).

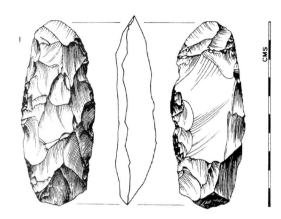

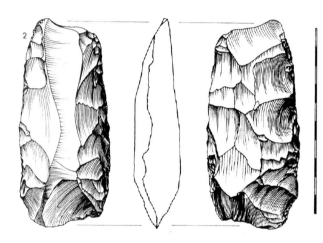

Fig. 7.10. Axes from Trwyn Du, Nab Head Site 1 (after David and Walker 2004).

a) The Northern routes had the advantage of being the shortest but are there earlier presences in adjacent parts of Scotland?
b) The Manx route has an assemblage that in part resembles the Irish Earlier Mesolithic but is a slightly longer journey.
c) The Welsh assemblages have elements which can be paralleled in Ireland but they would require the longest sea voyages.

A suggestion?

Rather than seeing the initial movement to Ireland as being from the Mesolithic equivalent of one "Invasion Sea Port", is it possible that there were groups of hunter-gatherers living within the Manx basin – which would have included a presence on the shores of north Wales as well as on the Isle of Man, which would already have been an Island? The Isle of Man would, perhaps, have been much bigger and extended closer to the coast of north-west England. Cass ny Hawin II suggests an early knowledge of seafaring and it could be argued that the presence on Man was more than seasonal. The preference for this area as a point of origin should be evident from discussions

earlier in the chapter. Some of the distinct elements of the Irish "Early" Mesolithic seem to have parallels in Wales, i.e. micro awls/*meche de forêt*, core axes and just possibly the use of ground stone axes. The range of needle points, described in Chapter 5, which appear to have developed in Ireland, could owe their origins to earlier simple forms found at the earlier site of Cass ny Hawin II. These, as noted earlier, could derive from similar forms found in Honey Hill assemblages.

In retrospect there may have been, in Ireland, an over reliance on the rigid division into an Early and Later Mesolithic that existed within the British Mesolithic. This resulted in a lack of appreciation of the series a gradual and perhaps local changes that were taking place in Britain either side of 10,000 cal BP and as a consequence we were searching for a type of point of origin that did not exist.

The main problem would be in maintaining that initial population within Ireland and, if necessary, keeping in regular contact with the "Homeland".

The challenges of surviving on the island

One of the avenues of investigation discussed previously (Woodman 1981) was that of population levels and in particular, based on admittedly modern examples, the need to build up a substantial population within the island relatively rapidly. Given the possibility of lower levels of fertility, along with higher infant mortality, it is quite probable that this would have taken much longer than, for example, the relatively modern colonisation of the Bass Strait Islands. To some extent, the Irish "*Early*" Mesolithic represents the archaeological record of the initial phase of the colonisation of Ireland. Therefore, its extent and the quantity of material must reflect the success of this phase and provide some indications of its growth. Kelly (2003) has also suggested that the chance of the survival of one small group, notionally containing 25 individuals, would not be great, but that one large group living together may also not have worked, and he therefore suggests that there would have been a need to develop to a point where there were several small collaborative bands.

Ultimately, one must return to both the type of economy and extent of population present along the western edge of Britain and the nature of the Irish Sea basin during the first millennium of the Holocene. One must also assume that, within the Doggerland and adjacent parts of northern England, the economy was primarily based on terrestrial sources; therefore the Irish Sea basin would not necessarily have been an attractive area to which people could adapt quickly.

Similarly, with a lower sea level, the narrowness of the Irish Sea during the earliest part of the Holocene may not always have been a beneficial factor. Waddell (1991–2) has noted that the tidal currents that run north–south, up and down the Irish Sea, would help movement up the channel but even today the narrow points, such as that between parts of Antrim and Scotland, are subject to extremely strong tidal currents which may have been worse more than 10,000 years ago and an effective knowledge of boats and the environment would have been essential. In this case a second set of factors should also be considered.

The second requirement, as noted earlier by Bjerck (2009), is the fact that it is the availability of the appropriate technologies, in terms of boats and equipment for hunting and fishing, that shifts an economy from a coastal to a maritime one. A good example can be seen along the Beagle Channel in Tierra del Fuego. Piana and Orquera (2002) have suggested that, while it may seem obvious that the Yamana should have relied extensively on the hunting of sea lions in Tierra del Fuego, it does not always follow that communities living in the archipelagos and using their small bark-covered canoes would have had that capacity. They noted that it was probably the development of the large, heavy hunting spear/harpoon that allowed the Yamana to hunt sea lions successfully. Bjerck (2009) has noted that archipelago environments would have been very suitable for sea-based hunting communities. Did the Irish Sea, represent a different, more open type of seascape that would have either inhibited the use of the sea or more likely encouraged a capacity to sail open water?

One can assume from the existence of paddles that boats did exist and, as noted earlier, some of the rock art in Scandinavia strongly suggests that large substantial boats existed there by the later part of the Older Stone Age of northern Norway. The problem, as already alluded to, is how to know, in the context of the north-western Atlantic fringe, at how early a date seagoing technologies existed. Ames (2002), in reviewing boats in the Pacific north-west, has shown that while large wooden canoes were used, large Umiaks or skin-covered boats that could carry several tons of items also existed in the recent past. Could boats of this type have existed in the Irish Sea? In returning to the rock art of Arctic Norway, is it possible that similar, though not quite as large, skin-covered boats existed in the Early Holocene? Moss and Erlandson (2009) have argued for an early fully developed maritime economy along the Californian coast. Perhaps this is best exemplified by the early colonisation of small Channel Islands, such as that discovered at Daisy Cave on San Miguel Island, about 50 km off the coast of California, where there is occupation from at least 12,000 cal BP Can we assume that, in and around the Irish Sea basin, that these elements would have been present at the beginning of the Holocene?

While only one possible wooden boat fragment is known from the Irish Mesolithic, that from Woodend on the shores of Lough Neagh (Fry 2002), recent discoveries of "*Early*" Mesolithic material on the tiny island of Inistrahull, which lies roughly 10 km north of Malin Head, provide some interesting indications of a well-developed capacity of open sea faring economy.

Summary

In borrowing Mitchell and Ryan's (1997, illus. 73) concept of a steeplechase; several obstacles or challenges needed to be faced in order to bring about a successful colonisation of Ireland:

a) The life ways of the established communities on the western edge of Britain.
b) In terms of the ecology of the region, the ease of the development of a maritime economy.
c) The potential for a more open sea-going technology to both successfully reach Ireland and provide a constant link to the original area of departure.
d) That the fauna and flora of Ireland had matured and developed to a point where human communities could be maintained on a long term basis.

If, however, in recognising the various factors that influence discovery of early settlement and the reasons that may initially limit movement to the west and north in the British Isles, we must recognise the fact that by 10,000 cal BP there was likely to have been a human presence in Ireland. It is also apparent that, within a relatively short period of time, settlement had spread throughout the island and a series of local adaptations were taking place.

Chapter 8

Settling in

"Pioneers always try to use the past as a template by which to cut the future." Wallace Stegner (1955, 288) *Wolf Willow*

On the basis of discussions in the previous chapter, one of the major issues which has so far received little attention is the documentation of how and when changes took place within the totality of the Irish Mesolithic. Instead, much of the focus has been on a perceived rapid change associated with the transition from the Early to the Later Mesolithic. Of course there has also been, as elsewhere, extensive discussion on the transition from the Mesolithic to the Neolithic.

These discussions may, however, have deflected research from a series of equally significant questions. The quotation from *Wolf Willow* above, although written in the context of the European settlement of an area of Canada on the borders of Saskatchewan and Alberta, points to a fundamental question for all periods. How much do the pioneers in a new region bring with them and continue to use the technologies, economies and even the social organisation of the regions from which they came? On a more local level, it is also possible to ask whether, as our chronologies improve, it is possible to see evidence of a continuous series of changes taking place throughout the Irish Mesolithic.

Given Ireland's distinctively different ecology, it should come as no surprise that Irish lithic technology should, as discussed in Chapter 7, have different lithic technologies to those used at the same time in adjacent parts of Europe,

As discussed in Chapter 7 there are many instances where, during an initial phase, non-local but long-familiar raw materials such as flint were used. Ireland seems to represent a very different case study. Indeed, the first peoples to actually settle within Ireland, as distinct from the "explorers" and "pioneers" discussed earlier, would probably have been aware of the existence of a better range of raw materials within Ireland than would have existed along the opposite shores in western Britain. While the Antrim coastal cretaceous flint is exceptional in its abundance, there would also have been significant quantities of erratic flint to be found along the eastern seaboard and even on most of the beaches along parts of Wexford to at least east Cork. Other raw materials in the interior would also not have been difficult to find.

Therefore, arrival in Ireland would not have been like the move from the flint-rich south in Sweden through to the quartz dominated regions further north. Instead there might be an expectation that the same range of tools would be used in Ireland as, for example, in Britain. However, as discussed below, new implement types seem to emerge quite early in the Irish Mesolithic.

It is now apparent that there is an "*Early*" Mesolithic presence at some level (Fig. 8.1) throughout the whole island, though the pace of the process of expansion across Ireland and

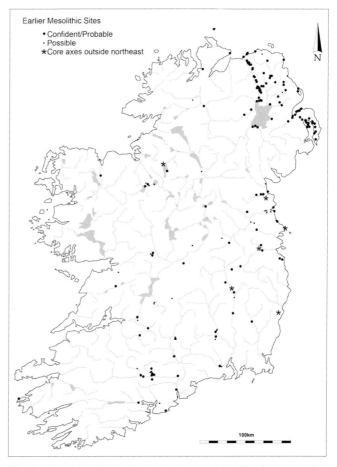

Fig. 8.1. Early Irish Mesolithic site (prepared by Hugh Kavanagh).

the resultant population size are really unknown. However, especially within the conventional framework discussed in Chapter 5, there seems to have been neither an immediate radical change nor a continued long term total reliance on the technology and economic strategies that settlers brought with them. Instead, given Ireland's size and its proximity to the European mainland (peninsular Britain), it seems that changes within Ireland may have been gradual. It could be argued that, even within the limited archaeological record available from the first two millennia of Ireland's known human settlement, it is possible to show that change started shortly after initial settlement and then continued. The "Early" Irish Mesolithic should not be seen as a homogeneous chronological period of time within which no changes took place.

What is the evidence?

The Irish "*Early*" Mesolithic is notably and unfortunately different due to the small number of assemblages with a substantial component of diagnostic artefacts. While certain types of core axes and, in particular, flake axes seem to be distinctive forms of "*Early*" Mesolithic artefacts, they are (especially in the latter category) confined to a small part of Ireland, i.e. Antrim and Down. It is obvious from their presence at Mount Sandel and Lough Boora that ground stone axes were used throughout the "*Early*" Mesolithic, but it is difficult at this stage to identify all those that could belong to this earliest stage of the Mesolithic in Ireland (see Chapter 5 for a more detailed description of the range of artefacts normally associated with the "*Early*" Mesolithic). The most reliable indicator of an "*Early*" Mesolithic presence is the microlith and perhaps the micro-awl. These at least have a variety of forms that might help not only to identify an early presence but also to indicate changes through time. Yet, as noted above, there are other problems, specifically the poor quality of the information that survives from this period.

There are now over 130 entries in the Irish Mesolithic database (see Chapter 4) which can be associated in some way with the "*Early*" Mesolithic. Not all of these can be attributed with certainty to this period. Well documented assemblages with diagnostic artefacts are actually extremely rare. There are few sites, such as Mount Sandel and Lough Boora that fulfil all the criteria listed in Chapter 5:

1) preferably coming from a secure context, usually an excavation;
2) containing diagnostic artefacts;
3) containing a significant number of diagnostic items.

The Mesolithic database can provide several insights. As noted, there is now evidence of an "*Early*" Mesolithic presence throughout Ireland, though it is both very partial in terms of excavated assemblages and other relatively closed groups and it relies heavily on material in secondary contexts, surface finds, stray finds, etc. While, as noted in Chapter 5, this is part of a general pattern for the Irish Mesolithic, it seems to be more pronounced in the earlier period.

Quite a large number of the database entries are based on single or multiple stray finds recorded only to townlands (Woodman *et al.* 2006). In certain cases these can be an individual microlith, such as the examples from Donegore or Loan Hill tds in the Knowles collection. At the other extreme, more substantial numbers of diagnostic artefacts were recovered from Culbane, Glenone, or, to a lesser extent, Gortgole, but these have the disadvantage of possibly being from a multiplicity of sites. It is also apparent, when looking at the microliths found or purchased by the collectors and comparing them with those coming from the excavated sites, that there is a distinct bias towards larger forms; in fact the majority are not even genuine microliths but are micro-awls.

Within the database there are roughly 400 locations where material has been collected from a specific find spot. Only roughly 10% have any possible association with the "*Early*" Mesolithic, and in a significant number of cases these are also from locations where the material is in a secondary context, such as on a lake shore or in coastal raised beach deposits. Perhaps the most notable site that falls into this category is the Glynn Rugby pitch in Co. Antrim, where an extraordinary number of core and flake axes were recovered from a field in which beach deposits had been bulldozed to create rugby pitches (Woodman 1977b).

A similar situation exists at the shoreline site of Eleven Ballyboes, Co. Donegal, where Brian McNaught has collected a very large quantity of material washed up from what seems to have been a settlement site that is now under water (Costa *et al.* 2001). As noted in Chapter 4, Kieran Westley has identified early peat deposits in the area (Westley 2013) and future work will hopefully determine whether any of the assemblage is associated with the peat. Perhaps the most extreme case is in the assemblages from the shores of Lough Neagh at Toome, where many thousands of artefacts from the whole of the Stone Age were collected over a long period that began as early as the 1850s.

There are a few excavations that have produced some evidence of a Mesolithic presence, i.e. roughly 220 sites, but only 43 have some evidence relating to the "*Early*" Mesolithic. In some cases, such as the Warren at Cushendun, Co. Antrim (Movius 1940a), the material is again in secondary deposits, while at the Toome Bypass site an interesting but small scatter of microliths was recovered from an excavation that extended across a strip of land which was over 300 m in length (Woodman 2015). In the latter case, all were found in the topsoil and could not be associated with a specific dated feature. In many cases these are little more than one stray object, such as one or two microliths from the ringfort at Lislear, Co. Tyrone (Ivens and Simpson 1988, 66). These can be interesting objects and of some significance, for example the occasional little core axes that were found along the east coast, such as that recovered from beside a hearth during exploratory excavations at Killybeg in Co. Wexford (Fig. 8.2). They can represent a clear indication of an "*Early*" Mesolithic presence in a particular area but they contribute little to the issue of change throughout that period. Similarly, at the later prehistoric site of Tullywiggin, Co. Tyrone, the discovery of a small assemblage of scalene triangle microliths, possibly the lithic components of one composite implement (Woodman 1978a, 256–7), was a particularly important indication of early settlement in the foothills of the Sperrins.

In effect, of the sites which have produced microliths less than ten sites are known to have more than ten microliths! These include Mount Sandel Upper and Lower, Castleroe, Lough Boora and Kilcummer. Researching the "*Early*" Mesolithic is therefore not helped by the scarcity of microliths. Is their absence due to the fact that they were only used for a short period of time or, at least in part, are there methodological explanations for the absence, or low rate of recovery, of microliths from so many sites?

There has also been, on occasions, a tendency on the part of many excavators to assume that any small bladelet is a microlith. In examination of the assemblage it often becomes apparent that these tiny bladelets, such as examples from Curraghprevin (Woodman 2013), have been produced from bi-polar cores which tend not to be in use in the Irish Mesolithic.

A number of assemblages have therefore been placed in the probable/possible categories. In general these consist of a series of small blades with reduced platforms that seem to have been produced by soft hammer percussion. They are reminiscent of the types of blades found at sites such as Mount Sandel. A good example would be the two small blades found during an excavation in the Bishop Street area within Cork City. The site lies on a bluff that overlooks the River Lee (O'Donnell 2001: Excavations.ie). Similarly, a small series of chert blades was found in excavations on the Cashel Bypass in Co. Tipperary (Woodman forthcoming). At this stage these assemblages have been placed in the "*Early*" Mesolithic on the basis of technology, though it is always possible that a similar technique was used during the Neolithic, a period when a diversity of knapping techniques were employed. Often the tendency to place them in the Mesolithic has been helped by the fact that they were found in locations where Mesolithic material might have been expected to occur.

The body of reliable "*Early*" Mesolithic material from Ireland is obviously quite limited. The narrowness of the sample of potentially useful "*Early*" Mesolithic assemblages is further emphasised by the fact that only four sites have secure associations between microliths and radiocarbon dates. These are: Mount Sandel Upper (Bayliss and Woodman 2009); Castleroe (Woodman 1985b); Lough Boora (Ryan 1980); and Hermitage (Collins and Coyne 2003; 2006; Collins 2009).

Within this group, the Castleroe material comes from a small one-day rescue excavation, while the Hermitage site produced one certain and one probable microlith from a cremation burial at Site A. In addition, one late date from Mount Sandel (F109) and those from Killuragh Cave can only be regarded as probable

associations, the significance of which will be discussed below.

While the Mount Sandel dates are marginally earlier than the others it would be unwise to assume that this indicates an earlier Mesolithic presence in Northern Ireland than elsewhere. It is unfortunate that the Kilcummer site in Co. Cork (Woodman 1989; Anderson 1993; Fig. 8.3) while producing

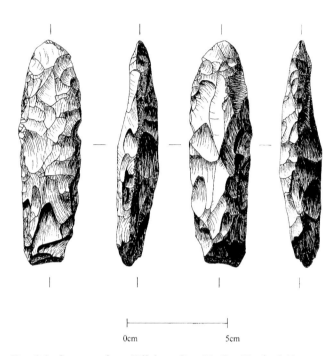

Fig. 8.2. Core axe from Killybegs Site 50, Co. Wexford (drawing supplied by Valerie J. Keely Ltd and by with permission of the NRA).

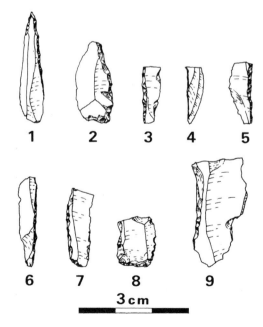

Fig. 8.3. Microliths from Kilcummer, Co. Cork.

quite a number of simple microliths, did not, on excavation, reveal any significant *in situ* deposits which would produce material suitable for dating. Kilcummer and other sites such as Hermitage still show that there was a human presence in the South West of Ireland at an early date.

Was there just one group of arrivals into Ireland?

When the Mesolithic of Ireland was perceived as being confined to the north-east, it seemed reasonable that the Mesolithic presence was based on just one small movement into the island but one must ask whether the movement of people to Ireland in the Early Holocene could have been more complex.

This is an issue that has not received any serious consideration since the mid-1980s, by which time (Woodman 1986) it was possible to see that there was an "*Early*" Mesolithic even in the south-west of Ireland. Dismissing a personal light-hearted suggestion (that students often took too seriously) that one could make a case for an origin coming from western France and an arrival on the south coast, as shown in Chapter 7, our knowledge of the earliest phases of the Mesolithic along eastern shores of Great Britain has improved immeasurably.

Without wishing to dwell on what may appear to be a dated "Invasion hypotheses", one further question raised previously (Woodman 1981) was whether the settlement of Ireland was a product of one simple movement. If there is an, as yet unknown, but slightly earlier phase of settlement in Ireland and we are simply looking at an archaeological record that dates to the first centuries of a mature and established presence, then this question verges even more than usual on speculation. There is no doubt that, with the exception of variations in raw materials in axe manufacturing, there seems to be little regional difference within Ireland's "*Early*" Mesolithic. This, and the appearance of similar local forms of microliths such as the needle points recovered from both Mount Sandel on the north coast and Lough Boora in the centre of Ireland, suggests a single point of origin.

It may be that much of the relevant portion of the western seaboard of Britain was occupied by populations that made up, through kinship networks and exchange systems, one extended group. Were there were small groups using shared information coming from one specific spot, or arriving from along an extended area of coast line, these options may just represent two extreme versions of one process?

How long is the "Early" Mesolithic?

It is clear that documenting change throughout the "*Early*" Mesolithic is difficult and there is a degree of uncertainty over the length of this phase. The challenge is whether the quite sparse archaeological record for the "*Early*" Mesolithic is a product of a relatively small population and/or a short period of time.

It is tempting to blame the limited record on the relative lack of attention that has been paid to this period in the past. Two other factors suggest that this is an explanation that might have a limited shelf life. "*Early*" Mesolithic assemblages are, unlike Later Mesolithic ones, often associated with quantities of manufacturing debris should be relatively easy to find. Yet, through extensive developer-led archaeology numerous lithic assemblages (probably several thousand) have been recovered, in general, very little of certain "*Early*" Mesolithic material has been identified.

An explanation might be that much of the new material comes from salvage excavations where it is highly probable that a high proportion of the material was in a secondary context i.e. in later features or, perhaps more importantly, the topsoil. With the limited expectation of a Mesolithic presence is it possible that one of the key elements for discovery (see Chapter 1) was not present, namely "The expectation of discovery", i.e. if nothing is expected nothing will be found. It is quite remarkable that microliths are almost unknown from developer-led excavations; none has been found in the topsoil collection. Notably, those from the Hermitage Site A were discovered during sieving of a cremation burial.

The question associated with this "settling in phase" is therefore: *is it possible to see a series of local developments?*

The earliest colonisers of Ireland will have been required to make some changes to what and how they procured their sources of food and one assumes that some changes in lithic procurement and related strategies may have also been required. The economic changes will be discussed below (Chapters 9 and 10), but it is of interest to see that, within the slightly more abundant lithic record, several small but significant changes took place quite rapidly.

Axes and core tools

Perhaps the most remarkable changes are in the occurrence of axes. Saville (2003) has made the pertinent observation that the profusion of axes in the Irish Mesolithic in general might be due to the absence of red deer within Ireland. It is probable that, elsewhere, red deer antlers and the bones of Aurochs would have been used as the raw material to make axes and related implements. However, some distinct forms of core tools do occur within the Irish "*Early*" Mesolithic.

Core tools, such as axes, are found throughout much of the Danish Mesolithic but in much of Britain they appear to be of limited occurrence within the Early Mesolithic. Similarly, they occur within one of the earliest phases of the Mesolithic of north-west France (Ducrocq 2010, 350–3). It is, therefore, somewhat surprising to find that they occur within the Irish "*Early*" Mesolithic, whose most likely antecedents belong to the British later Mesolithic – which in adjacent areas, appears to lack core axes. Indeed it could even be suggested that the British core tool tradition was already vanishing by the time Ireland was settled and a series of local tool types had to be created. What is most noticeable about the core axes from Mount Sandel (see Chapter 5, Fig. 5.4) is that, in contrast to the British and other north-western European examples, such as those from Thatcham (Fig. 8.4), the Irish examples often tend to be quite small, usually less than 100 mm in length, and are frequently retouched into a bilaterally symmetrically-sectioned form. Furthermore, the Irish examples have often been created with a very narrow cutting edge, frequently less than 20 mm across, and are usually also symmetric. They are often trimmed to a narrow pointed butt. Their small size has little to do with flint availability as much larger axes and picks were made from the same sources during the Later Mesolithic and large, highly polished flint examples were made during the Neolithic.

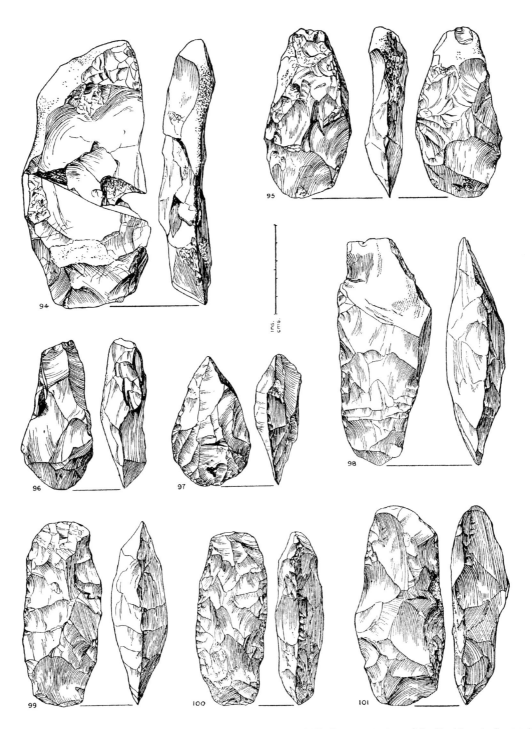

Fig. 8.4. Core axes from Thatcham, Berkshire (after Wymer 1962) (by permission of the Prehistoric Society).

The flake axes represent an even more distinct difference. As noted in Chapter 5, Irish flake axes are more than axes made on flakes. These implements cannot be paralleled in Britain. The early Danish so-called flake axes from sites such as Barmosen (Fischer 1978) or Nørregård (Sørensen and Sternke 2004) are really more irregular forms than those occurring in Ireland. Many of the Hensbakka/Fosna/Komsa flake axes from Norway and Sweden are more similar to the Irish examples, but again these forms date to a much earlier point in the Holocene and, while the Irish examples are associated with woodworking (see below), it is possible that they were also used for butchering carcasses (Woodman 1992b). Dumont (1985, 62–3) has shown that the Irish core axes were used as chopping tools while the flake axes were used as adzes, indeed one example in particular has traces of damage caused by hafting (Fig. 8.5).

It is fortunate that a number of these core and flake axes have been recovered from the main hut area at Mount Sandel, indicating that they were probably in use at an early stage in the known Irish "*Early*" Mesolithic. These forms have been found in some profusion at various locations in the Bann valley, on the shores of Lough Neagh and at Glynn in Larne Lough, as well as on the shores of the Belfast and Strangford Loughs in Co. Down.

Only five similar core axes that look to belong to the "*Early*" Mesolithic are known from outside the north-east even though an "*Early*" Mesolithic presence can be documented across most of Ireland (Fig 8.1). These include one made from chert found at Cormongon on Lough Allen (Driscoll 2006) while the others occur on the east coast from Ardee in Co. Louth,

through Leixlip and Kenure in Co. Dublin to Killybeg in Co. Wexford. One might assume that this is simply a matter of a lack of good flint in many parts of the east but here we can return to the evidence from Wales, where a number of core axes have been recovered (see Chapter 7). In Wales, where again flint would have been in limited supply, a number of the axes were made from Rhyolite or volcanic tuff. These raw materials also occur in the geology of south-east Ireland. This does not mean that sources other than flint were used but we should take note of the apparent absence of core axes made from materials that would have been available and equally suitable as flint. As discussed in Chapter 7 there often seems to be a pattern of incoming groups using the material that they were most acquainted with and, in many cases, where they would not be fully aware of the range of local sources they would have opted for a least risk solution and used flint which could be found on the local beaches.

Perhaps, as discussed in Chapter 5 and especially outside the north-east, even at an early date they began to use ground stone axes? The best documented example from Mount Sandel occurs in a pit that has been cut into the main hearth complex (Fig. 8.6). The Lough Boora examples are clearly associated with an "*Early*" Mesolithic assemblage. There are also many other stray examples of ground stone axes that may have been made during the initial phases of settlement but these lie unrecognised and are difficult to identify.

It is at this stage it is impossible to find exact parallels outside Ireland and the very interesting examples from Nab Head Site II (David and Walker 2004, 324–5) are almost unique and later in date than the earliest Irish examples (Fig. 8.7).

Other differences

There are also other less obvious differences between the range of implements found in Britain and Ireland. The micro-awls found in some numbers on Early Mesolithic sites do not occur after the earliest stages of even the British Mesolithic. Certain

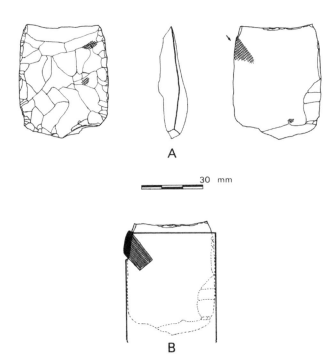

Fig. 8.5. Shaded areas mark places where lasting damage took place (Dumont 1985).

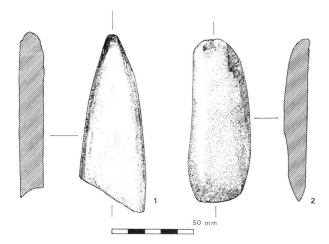

Fig. 8.6. Ground stone axes from Mount Sandel Upper.

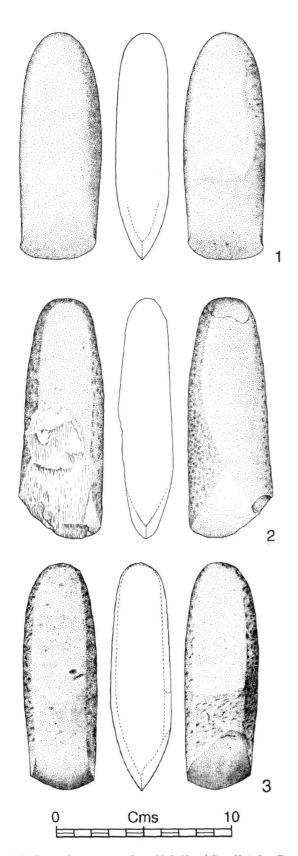

Fig. 8.7. Ground stone axes from Nab Head Site II (after David and Walker 2004).

forms of microliths, such as some of the needle points, are also distinctly local to Ireland. Although their origins may be found within the British Mesolithic but the very distinctive examples with some slightly invasive retouch seem to be confined to Ireland. Again, one must wonder if these were a local development for a set of needs that were particular to Ireland. Finally, as in some adjacent areas, such as parts of Scotland and the Isle of Man, scrapers, especially end scrapers, as well as burins, are relatively uncommon, even in the Irish "*Early*" Mesolithic (Chapter 5).

In summary, the lithic technology of the Irish "*Early*" Mesolithic seems to be made up of three elements. The first is the continuation of the use of microliths and small blades as part of composite tools in a manner similar to that which existed in Britain. This includes a similar procurement of raw materials, in the main flint or occasionally chert, whether from some distance away or close at hand. Second is the relative paucity of certain tool types, including scrapers and burins. Third is the development of a unique range of core tools and related artefacts. This category is the one which appears to illustrate how, even in a relatively short period of time, forms particular to Ireland emerged.

Identifying the demise of the microliths

Most of the classic assemblages, notably from Mount Sandel and Lough Boora, date to before 9400 cal BP, there is the issue of whether microliths continued to be used.

It is difficult, with such a limited series of sites, to establish the type of chronological sequence used in many parts of Europe (see Chapter 7). In England, where microliths continue in use throughout the whole period, there seem to be recognisable changes in the first 1000 years of the later Mesolithic, i.e. the appearance of small isosceles triangles, rhomboids and crescents may have happened around 9000 cal BP. In both Britain and Ireland the shift to the larger cutting rhombic and trapeze projectile heads, that were typical of so many adjacent parts of mainland Europe, is not present.

In Ireland, unlike Britain, the addition of the small, more geometric microliths does not occur but there is, in contrast, a small indication that the scalene triangles, needle points and rods might have disappeared at an early date. One of the stratigraphically later small pits (F100/5) from Mount Sandel (Woodman 1985a, 46–7) contained, in one layer, six simple non-geometric points. The one complete microlith from the cremation deposit at Hermitage Site A is a very simple piece. Here (Collins and Coyne 2006, 21) the cremation burial (Pit A) is dated to 9480–9270 cal BP (Beta 214236, cremated bone, 8350±40 BP.

Again, though the association is very poor, the microliths from the cave at Killuragh are also quite simple (Fig. 8.8).

At Killuragh Cave there was no direct unequivocal association between the microliths and radiocarbon dated human bones that have produced dates belonging to the

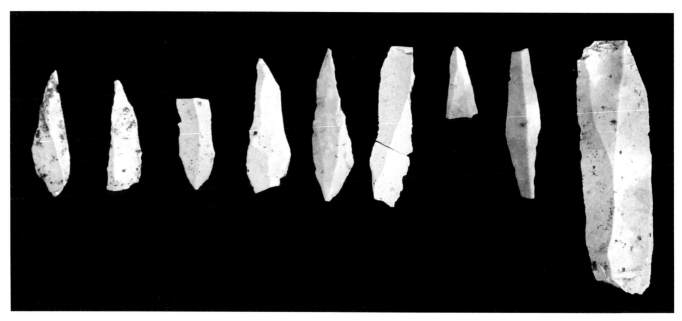

Fig. 8.8. Selection of microliths and blade from Killuragh Cave, Co. Limerick (Courtesy of the National Museum of Ireland).

earlier part of the Mesolithic (Woodman 1997; Woodman and Dowd in prep.; see also http://www.heritagecouncil_excavations/3.2html). There are also other, later dates on human remains from the site, including dates from the Later Mesolithic, Neolithic and the earlier half of the Bronze Age. Bronze Age pottery and Neolithic artefacts were also recovered along with faunal remains, primarily from the later part of the Bronze Age as well as the historic periods. In the case of the earlier dates, the same individual may have been dated twice (GrA 2434, bone, 8030±60 BP, 9035–8650 cal BP and GrA 27215, bone, 7955±45 BP, 8989–8648 cal BP, while another individual produced a slightly later date of 8978–8555 cal BP (GrA 2433, bone, 7880±60 BP). Can we associate the microliths or blades found on the site with the earliest dates quoted above?

Although the evidence is quite scanty it could be argued that even before 9000 cal BP microliths seem to have been very simple and it appears from the Port of Larne excavation (see below) that they may have, by that date, been beginning to disappear from the lithic repertoire of the Irish *"Early"* Mesolithic.

It is of interest that at Hermitage the excavation produced no other microliths apart from those from the cremation burial, even though much of the blade material from the area around the cremation in Pit A could be placed within what would be expected in an *"Early"* Mesolithic assemblage. Interestingly, a second cremation burial, in this case from an adjacent area in Pit B, dated to 9250–8700 cal BP (Beta 214237, 8070±40 BP), produced no microliths and none was found in the vicinity. Again one must return to the issue raised earlier, that the absence of microliths from so many presumed *"Early"* Mesolithic sites is remarkable. Is this a methodological creation

from the manner in which many of the sites were explored, or is there a genuine case to be made for a very early disappearance of microliths, i.e. an abandonment of certain tool types?

While it is difficult to track the exact point in time when the use of microliths vanished, there is a definite impression, based on both their scanty occurrence on certain key sites and their relative scarcity in general, that composite tools using microliths were quite scarce, perhaps even before 9000 cal BP!

In summary, while the initial phase of settlement has a superficial resemblance to a common "techno-complex" found in adjacent parts of Europe, even the initial phase identified at Mount Sandel contains a number of local attributes, namely the local forms of microliths as well as a range of axes. In other words, solutions based on the large scale importation of a pre-existing economy and technology do not seem to work. Instead, the imported technology was adapted to local needs and seems to have then mutated into something very different. Thus, not only did the microliths disappear but, in the north-east where they are most prevalent, it also appears that the small symmetric core axes as well as flake axes did not survive. At this stage it is impossible to gauge any change that may have taken place within the ground stone axes.

The issue of "the gap"

The author's oft-quoted statement that the change from the Early to Later Mesolithic technologies within Ireland was one of the most "Radical changes within the European Mesolithic" may have been based on an assumption that there was a sudden and major shift at one point in time. Instead it now appears that the *"Early"* Mesolithic was a period during which a series of changes had already begun to happen. Again, it cannot be sufficiently emphasised that there are very few instances where there is a radical shift in the technology used during the European Mesolithic. There is usually a significant degree of continuity.

Perhaps in Ireland a radical shift in lithic technologies in a very short period of time may be magnified by a poor or unrefined chronological framework. The major problems in documenting the changes that took place within the Irish Mesolithic are associated with the archaeological record of the 9th millennium BP. As noted in previous chapters, this is probably one of the most poorly documented periods of Irish archaeology. The problem stems not so much from the absence of dates but rather from the absence of dates that are associated with a series of substantial and/or distinctive assemblages that can be used to track the change between the earlier and later parts of the Irish Mesolithic.

It is also important to remember that the recognition of this gap took place at a time when knowledge of the Irish Mesolithic was mostly confined to north-east Ireland. At the time, a number of simple assumptions were made. These included a belief that there would be a radical shift from an *"Early"* Mesolithic technology to a later form and that this would take place over a very short period of time. The problems of this period or "The Gap" have been discussed on numerous occasions, notably by Woodman (1981), Costa *et al.* (2005) and most recently Woodman (2010).

Over the decades various suggestions as to the reasons for the change and the context in which it would happen have been put forward and include:

1) A disappearance or dying out of the initial population (Mitchell 1986, 82–3), though Woodman (1981) showed that it was possible to document at least a human presence throughout the so-called "Gap".
2) A major climatic or natural event such as the short term and very distinct climatic downturn known as the 8.2 ka Event (see Chapter 2) Warren (2003) suggested that while the 8.2 ka Event may not have been the prime mover it may have had some effect on the creation of a new technology.
3) A change in the economy and/or methods of procurement (e.g. Mallory and Hartwell 1997, 4–5).
4) Changes in technology, such as the shift from a constrained technology based on composite tools to a more flexible one based on a range of procurement strategies for raw materials and the use of large blanks (Costa *et al.* 2005).
5) The argument was also put forward that certain sociological factors must be taken into consideration (Woodman 1981). Britain has, throughout the Later Mesolithic, roughly the same sort of technology in use from the Isle of Wight to the Orkneys or Hebrides. Yet there must have been significant differences in the economy of these various diverse regional landscapes. Therefore, it may be the combination of a significant, though not impassable, sea barrier with the build-up of a permanent population that

spread throughout the whole island and reached sufficient numbers. The Mesolithic population of Ireland could then function as a more self-contained entity outside the social networks of what became the island of Britain.

Of course these explanations are not mutually exclusive and some are all could be regarded as contributor factors which brought about change. However, what hopefully will be apparent below, is that it was unlikely that there was a sudden a rapid event that brought about change.

Gaps, transitions, adaptations or a Middle Mesolithic?

While it is, as yet, impossible to document all the changes that took place and put them in a chronological framework, it is now possible to see a number of very significant changes that did take place.

The concept of a radical shift initially became less tenable with the result of two pieces of research. The realisation that red deer did not play a significant role in the Irish Mesolithic (Woodman *et al.* 1997) brought into question the belief that the blade production of the *"Early"* Mesolithic was based on indirect punch percussion. It had been assumed that the blades had been produced by antler punches. Independently it was noted that the blades in *"Early"* Mesolithic assemblages, notably that from Eleven Ballyboes, Co. Donegal (Costa *et al.* 2001), had been produced using a soft hammer stone. Early stages of core preparation were probably carried out using hard hammer, followed by platform edge preparation and then blade production percussion using a soft hammer stone. Therefore, the change in knapping strategies between the "Early" and Later Mesolithic was not as great as had been thought.

It was also apparent even in the early 1980s (Woodman 1981) that there was no gap in human settlement, as some dates fell into categories that clearly demonstrate a human presence. In general, however, they still seemed to add little to our understanding of the changes in lithic technology that took place at this time.

1) The hearth loosely associated with flint flakes and blades excavated by Mitchell (1955) at the Creagh td, Toome, which produced a date of 8767–8208 cal BP (Y95, charcoal, 7680 ±110 BP). These artefacts have generally been perceived as being relatively undiagnostic (though see below).
2) A "stone setting" noted in the top of a sand bank at the base of the Newferry Site 3 excavation (Zone 9) and associated with a date of 9467–8662 cal BP (UB 888, organic mud, 8175±145 BP; Woodman 1977a).

Overall, the evidence for this period has been very unsatisfactory but it can be asked if this is because of expectations that a change would be clearly associated with a change in the series of diagnostic tool types. There are other periods when research has been be-deviled by expectations of something diagnostic and therefore obvious. One perfect example was the manner in which recognition of the presence of a Hiberno-Norse settlement in Cork took place. This was only established from dendrochronological dating rather than primarily from artefacts. This growing recognition is demonstrated in the account of excavations that took place in Cork City through the 1980s and '90s (Cleary and Hurley 2003). Similarly, the question of identifying 14th century AD settlement and activity in medieval Ireland was made more difficult by a failure to recognise that distinctive ceramics were not used at the time

However if microliths were to cease to be used at an early date there were two anomalous dates.

At Mount Sandel the main focus of discussion has been on when the site was first occupied and the date of the huts but, reuse of the site continued until perhaps close to 9500 cal BP. Features from these later phases included pits that contained numerous microliths (Woodman 1985a; Bayliss and Woodman 2009). There was one anomalous date from a pit (F109) to the north of the main site. Here, charcoal returned a date of 9014–8436 cal BP (UB 2359, charcoal, 7885±120 BP), along with a number of small blades and microliths. With the loss of the overlying occupation layers in that particular part of the site, it was never possible to ascertain whether the microliths were from the main phase of occupation or if the charcoal came from later use. In a more extreme parallel, a palisade that was also recovered at Mount Sandel, the mixture of activities from

two very different phases was evident. This was a later feature associated with an Iron Age radiocarbon date but which also contained numerous microliths. The palisade had evidently cut through the much older Mesolithic occupation layer. Lithic artefacts constantly hang around and turn up in patently later assemblages and contexts.

Again, in returning to Killuragh Cave there is no clear evidence that the microliths were associated with the human remains dated to around 9000 cal BP.

A case can be made, therefore, that, in Ireland, the use of microliths began to wane relatively quickly and that this possibly took place as early as 9000 cal BP.

It appears that changes also took place throughout the period from 9000 to 8000 cal BP. This case is based on the examination of the evidence from a key series of excavations, which illustrate the fact that stratigraphy and technological change can still contribute to discussion as much as classified sequences of chronological type fossils. Most of this evidence has already been considered in some detail in Woodman (2012).

The Port of Larne

The excavations in the early 2000s at the Port of Larne Container Park entailed the removal of extensive areas of the famous Larne Raised Beach (see Chapter 3). During excavations of the beach shingle (primarily in 2000), it became apparent that the raised beach material covered a ridge of glacial deposits. Initially this ridge may have formed a high point on a peninsula protruding into a marshy valley floor that pre-dated the formation of Larne Lough. As sea levels rose, this area became an island (suggested name Praeger's Island) in the entrance to Larne Lough. As sea levels rose further the island became covered with several metres of beach shingle (Fig. 8.9).

In one location, below the raised beach shingle, a complex series of layers, most notably Context 5012, extended across the ridge to cover an area c. 30 × 25 m (Fig. 8.10). Within this layer, or associated with it, was a series of stone tools and a number of pits and hollows, dotted between numerous boulders. A very small residual and often weathered scatter of blades was recovered, typical of those associated with the earliest Mesolithic such as at Mount Sandel but most of the assemblage differed from that found at Mount Sandel. The main phase of use of this island (associated with C5012) seems to post-date Mount Sandel. As this surface existed for a considerable period of time it is hardly surprising that numerous traces of activities of different dates had accumulated.

These show that activity on the island, mainly within C5012, took place between 9200 and sometime after 8000 cal BP when Praeger's island ceased to exist. The number of distinct retouched tools recovered from C5012 was relatively small and these were often scattered across the area excavated, the lithics consisting primarily of cores, cortical flakes and other knapping by-products, as well as a series of blades. These varied in character from large, sometimes cylindrical cores to

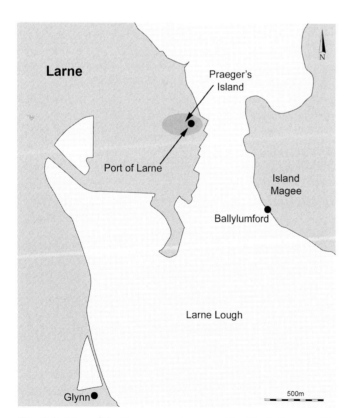

Fig. 8.9. Map of the Larne area (prepared by Hugh Kavanagh).

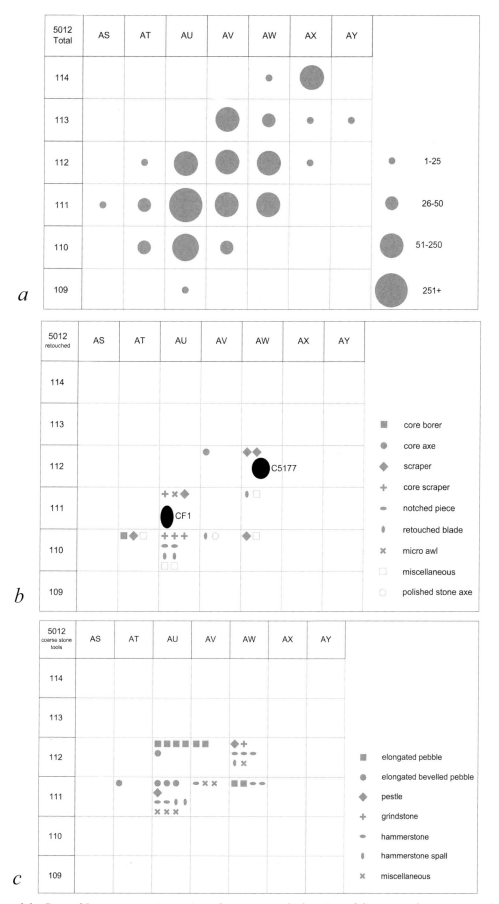

Fig. 8.10. Plans of the Port of Larne excavations: a) total per square, b) location of diverse implement types, c) location of coarse stone tools (prepared by Hugh Kavanagh). Each square is 15 × 15 metres.

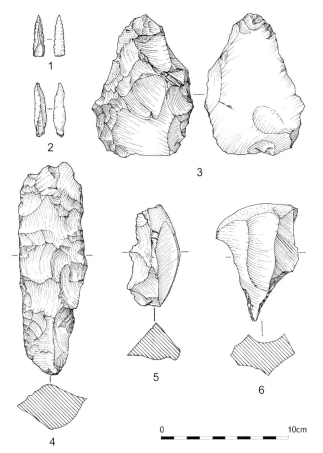

smaller, more irregular examples and with smaller irregular blades and bladelets occurring as well as much larger examples. The scatter of retouched tools included a number of artefacts, in particular a core borer and large core axe that would also be typical of the Later Mesolithic (Fig. 8.11). One complete example of a schist ground stone axe was also found, as were several other possible fragments. Similar axes were found in the lower half of the Newferry sequence. Interestingly no Butt Trimmed Forms were recovered.

Two major concentrations were noted within this spread of material. These were: to the west, chipping floor CF1 and associated pit 5129, and *c.* 10 m to the east, a series of pits and artefacts.

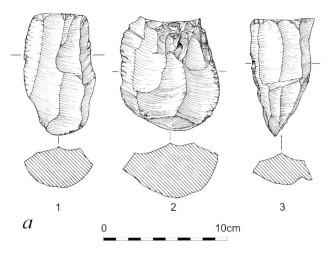

Fig. 8.11. Selection of Later Mesolithic artefacts from Context 5012, Port of Larne (drawn by R. Cronin).

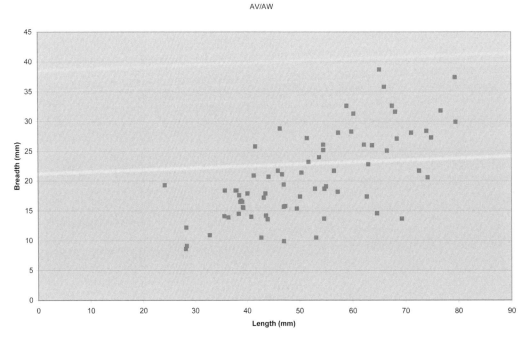

Fig. 8.12. a) (above right) Cores and b) length/breadth scatter diagram of blades from Context 5012 (east), Port of Larne (drawn by R. Cronin).

Unlike the somewhat diffuse activities in the eastern area, the key portion of the western concentration, CF1 was mostly confined to an area of 6 m². It was dominated by the production of small blades. Unlike the cores from sites such as Mount Sandel, which consist primarily of very regular single platform and some dual platformed cores, much larger numbers of more irregular cores were present in CF1, many of which were dual platform (Fig. 8.13a and b). Again, the blades differed from those at Mount Sandel in that there was a profusion of blades less than 30 mm in length (Fig. 8.14a and b) that lacked platform edge preparation and seemed rather more irregular in outline (Figs 8.15 and 8.16). The small scatter of retouched tools in the vicinity did not include any type fossils that would provide a clear indication of age. In particular there were no microliths. Besides one retouched blade and a small micro-awl, there were a number of small convex end scrapers and notched pieces, and a small series of what were originally taken to be large heavy "carinated" scrapers. After micro-wear examination (van Gjin forthcoming), it seems more likely that they are the remnants of a distinct type of core (see below).

Had it not been for the stratigraphic location under several metres of raised beach shingle, the material from CF1 might have been considered as just another *ad hoc* variant of Neolithic knapping techniques. Indeed the presence of many multiple platform cores which are common on several Neolithic sites would have led the author to ascribe a Neolithic date to an assemblage where no type fossils had been recovered. Fortunately it was possible to obtain five dates on burnt hazel nutshells from within CF1 and from within a nearby pit, C5129. These range in date from 9255–9021 cal BP (UBA-12298; 8173±31 BP) and 9011–8776 cal BP (UBA-12300, 8019±30 BP).

It might have been expected, given the availability of flint in the vicinity on beaches and in the nearby cliffs, that assemblages in the Larne area might always contain larger blades than elsewhere. It is therefore interesting that, as shown in Figures 8.14–8.16, if blade lengths from CF1 and a sample from Mount Sandel are compared the trend is for a higher percentage of small blades, i.e. less than 30 mm in length within the CF1 assemblage. In contrast to the availability of flint in and around Larne Lough the flint used at Mount Sandel may have been brought from coastal locations up to 10 km away.

Unfortunately, the other local "*Early*" Mesolithic assemblage, Glynn, was in a secondary context having been washed up into raised beach deposits so that the assemblage had been geologically sorted and the finer elements were missing (Woodman 1977b). Platform edge preparation is not effected by marine sorting, and it is also possible to see that at both Glynn and Mount Sandel the blades had small reduced platforms which would usually be associated with platform edge preparation (Fig. 8.16).

The dates from the Port of Larne, from CF1 and C5129, indicate that before or, at the latest, by 9000 years ago,

techniques of blade production had begun to change and that large numbers of very small blades may have been produced to serve the same needs as microliths.

Sites in different types of locations where flint is not so easily available also show the same pattern. There are, therefore, clear indications that the technology associated with the Port of Larne CF1 was used elsewhere, although the complete absence of microliths cannot be verified. Much of the evidence is located at the northern end of Lough Neagh in the area around Toome where three sites make an important contribution (Fig. 8.18).

Toome Bypass (Feature 1)

The Toome By pass excavations have already been mentioned in Chapter 4. Material from the most northerly Feature (F1: Fig. 8.19) seemed to be similar to that from CFI at Port of Larne. Feature 1 was centred on a small stone platform which may have extended into open water. It appeared to be stratified below two organic layers (Fig. 8.19b). The upper layer (1657) produced a date of 6789–6567 cal BP (Beta 219463, charcoal, 5870±40 BP), and the lower layer (1598) a date of 7926–7681 cal BP (Beta 219465, charcoal, 6950±50 BP). Stratified in and below these layers was a simple undiagnostic industry that was initially suspected of being Neolithic in date. Because of the overlying dates it was re-examined and seen to closely resemble that from CF1 at the Port of Larne (Woodman 2015).

The slightly higher adjacent area that overlooked the stone platform produced a much larger selection of artefacts, though these were recovered from topsoil contexts. Some quite weathered remnants of what might be an "*Early*" Mesolithic blade assemblage were found but, in contrast to the types of cores that were usually found on so-called "*Early*" Mesolithic sites, there was a very large concentration (24), of small cores of polyhedral type (generally <50 mm across). Though heavily patinated, they are much fresher than the occasional, more distinctive, classic "*Early*" Mesolithic material.

The Lesson on this assemblage is that it was initially assumed to be Neolithic in date, as multiple platform cores occur in the Neolithic as do small irregular blades. They occur, for example, under the passage tomb at Townleyhall, where they were associated with globular, decorated Middle Neolithic Bowls and diagnostic flint tools such as transverse arrowheads and hollow scrapers (Eogan 1963).

The Creagh td (Mitchells)

In light of the context of discoveries at the Port of Larne and as the Mitchell assemblage from Creagh seemed, as noted earlier, to date to within the "Gap" in the Irish Mesolithic. In total, 68 pieces came from Mitchell's *in situ* levels, while another 66 were found in other levels. The assemblage had similarities to the Port of Larne CF1 assemblage; the small blades, of which 14 were recovered, were again quite irregular

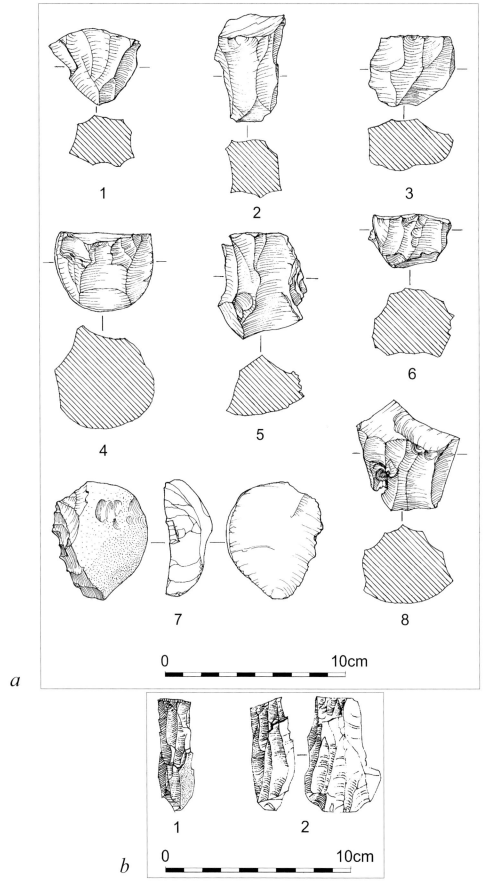

Fig. 8.13. Cores from a) Chipping Floor 1 (CF1), Context 5012 at Port of Larne (drawn by R. Cronin), b) Mount Sandel Lower (after Collins 1983).

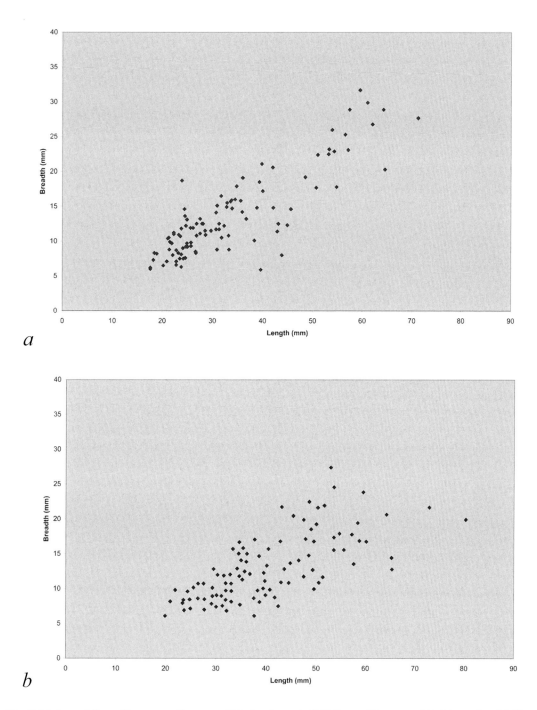

Fig. 8.14. Length/breadth scatter diagram of blades from a) CFI, Port of Larne and b) Mount Sandel Upper.

and usually without platform preparation (Fig. 8.21). Although some flakes removed from the face of cores showed signs of parallel removals of blades, the cores, of which six were found, were either reduced to multiple platformed or irregular cores and fragments. Only one retouched piece was noted, which may have been a burin.

In order to check the validity of the original date obtained by Mitchell, as the sample used was on wood charcoal and the date was obtained in the pioneering early days of radiocarbon dating i.e. the early 1950s, three hazel nutshells from *in situ* contexts were selected for dating. The dates obtained were: D/4 mid-sand: 9000–8659 cal BP (UBA-15653, hazel nut shell; 7980±37 BP), D/6 sandy mud: 8756–8646 cal BP (UBA-15654, hazel nutshell, 7844±36 BP), and J/6: 8748–8543 cal BP (UBA-15655, hazel nutshell, 7837±36 BP). These dates seem to suggest that the simple lithic technology from Mitchell's site, which appears

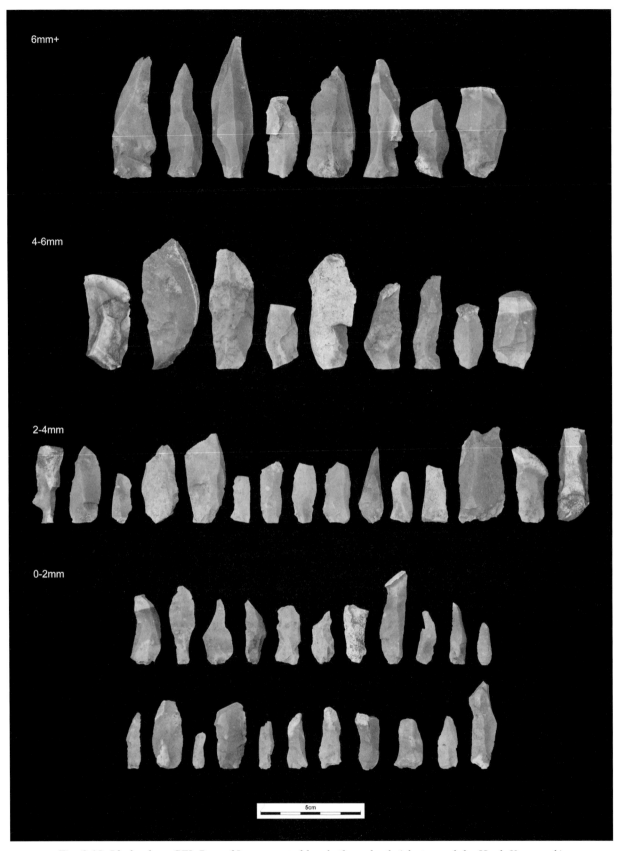

6mm+

4-6mm

2-4mm

0-2mm

5cm

Fig. 8.15. Blades from CFI, Port of Larne, sorted by platform depth (photograph by Hugh Kavanagh).

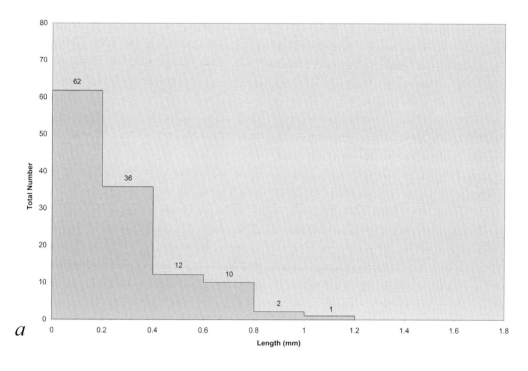

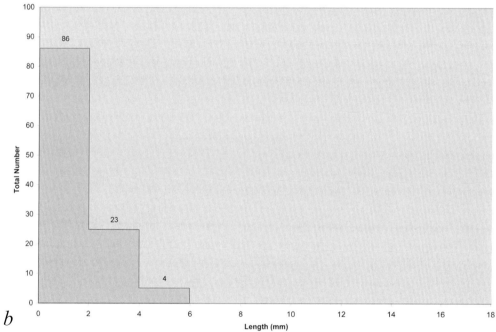

Fig. 8.16. Platform depths of a selection of blades from a) CFI, Port of Larne, b) Mount Sandel Upper.

somewhat similar to that from Port of Larne CFI, continued in existence after 9000 cal BP. Conversely there was no evidence of Microliths or the type of blade technology used at Mount Sandel.

Other sites and assemblages

There are other assemblages who appear to have the same range of artefacts but these are not necessarily as well contexted.

Whelan (1938) had in 1930 excavated in roughly the same area as Mitchell was to explore i.e. on the shores of Lough Neagh in Creagh td. (The Creagh Whelan's) Jessen (1949, 120) suggested that the peat deposits had formed during the Boreal (PZ VIb/c) and undoubtedly at a time when the lough levels were lower. Today it is difficult to attribute an actual date to this layer but Jessen felt that it was older than the Lower Lagoon Silts at Cushendun but there appears to have been

Fig. 8.17. A selection of blades from Context 5177, Port of Larne (photograph by Hugh Kavanagh).

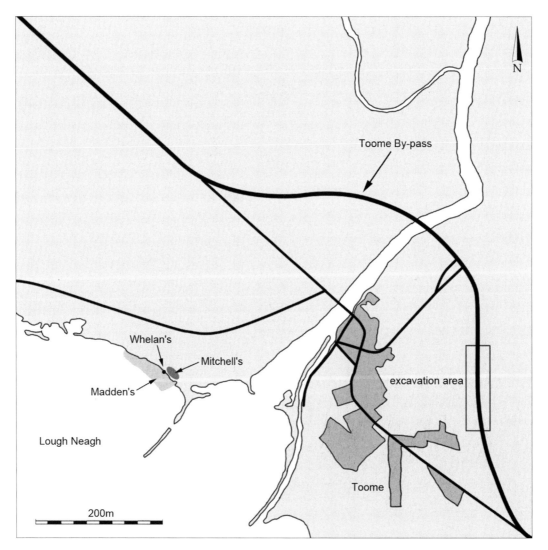

Fig. 8.18. Map of the Toome area showing locations of sites (by permission of NAC).

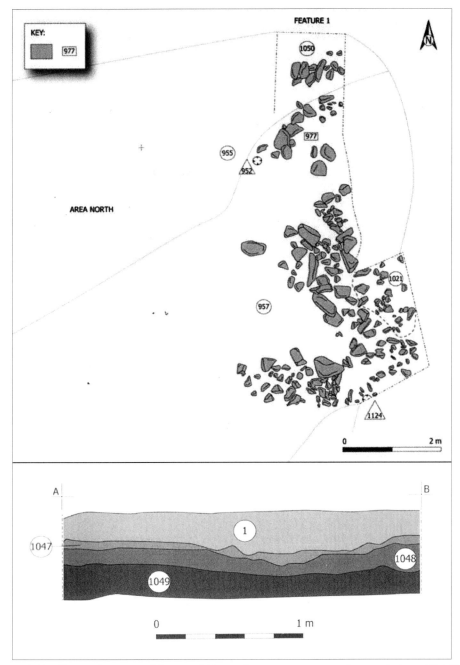

Fig. 8.19. Plan and section of Feature 1,Toome Bypass excavations (by permission of NAC).

both later and earlier elements present Indeed the presumed contemporaneous red deer bone (Whelan 1938, fig. 6) has produced a date from the early medieval period (UBA-20318, bone, 1269±44 BP, 662–873 cal AD). Some pieces, such as the core axe and some of the cores, would have seemed at home at Mount Sandel, thus the deposits and the assemblage may not have been as much a product of one event, as thought by Whelan and Jessen, However, the majority of items looked similar to both the Port of Larne and Mitchell's material, consisting of

small burins and notched scrapers as well as mostly irregular cores and the infamous domed or "carinated" cores/scrapers of presumed "Aurignacian" origin, all of which bear a striking resemblance to the other assemblages under discussion (Table 8.1; Fig. 8.22, 1–7).

In the 1972 excavations at The Creagh Madden's revealed that, in roughly the same area, artefacts were often not *in situ* but had been embedded in the sandy gravels on the floor of the lough, dredged up from the floor and were being spewed out

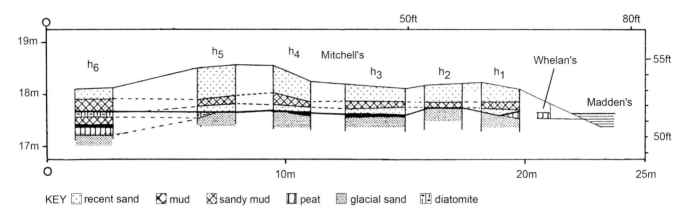

Fig. 8.20. Schematic section through the area of exploration and excavation in Creagh td., Co. Derry.

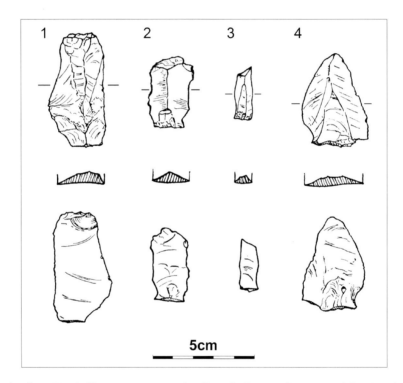

Fig. 8.21. Selection of blades from Mitchell's excavations at the Creagh, Toome, Co. Derry (after Mitchell 1955) (by permission of Ulster Archaeological Society).

from a grader. We then paddled in the lough and once again recovered (to our surprise) a mixed assemblage different from what we had expected. It included a range of small irregular scrapers, burins and, in one area in particular, cores that included single and dual platformed types as well as multiple platformed examples (Fig. 8.23), all of which were, in some way, similar to those found by Mitchell.

In summary, at present, the range of radiocarbon dates of varying quality, precision and association makes it difficult to provide a detailed and reliable chronological framework for the events occurring around 9000 cal BP. A case could, however, be made for the use of microliths ceasing before that date and that, while simpler composite tools continued in use without microliths, the needs in blade production changed from that associated with Mount Sandel to that found in CF1 at the Port of Larne. In fact the large number of small bladelets recovered from CF1, and the presence of the scraper-like cores from which they may have been struck, could be evidence of the use of small unretouched bladelets rather than microliths.

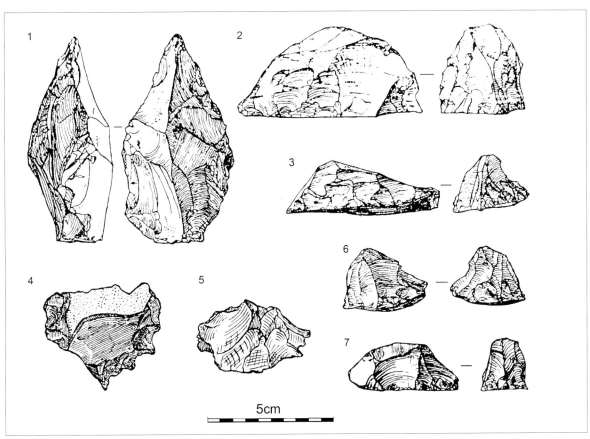

Fig. 8.22 Artefacts from Whelan's excavations in Creagh td., Toome, Co. Derry (Whelan 1938).

Fig. 8.23. Peter Woodman and Mike Baillie exploring the shoreline at Toome (Autumn 1972).

The beginnings of the Later Mesolithic

In searching for the origins of the Later Mesolithic, there has also been an expectation that one is looking for the origins of the classic "Larnian" technique, which may, as noted in Chapter 4, be little more than a regional development (Woodman and Johnston 1996). Furthermore, the strategy of having chipping floors where blanks are produced and then transferring to settlements or other forms of procurement sites may be neither a *sine qua non* of the totality of the Later Mesolithic nor of the whole of the Island. These very distinctive reduction strategies existed in the north-east of Ireland during much, though probably not all, of the Later Mesolithic (Griffiths and Woodman 1987) but such strategies are currently less evident in the chert-rich Irish midlands or at Ferriter's Cove in the south-west (Woodman *et al.* 1999). Numerous blanks, either large blades or Butt Trimmed Forms, made from flint and other materials have, however, been found as individual items or in small numbers throughout many parts of Ireland, but there is no widespread clear evidence that the knapping strategy resulted in the creation of many uniplane "Larnian" cores. The "Larnian" technique is not of itself, therefore, a product of the change to the Later Mesolithic.

Cushendun and the Port of Larne again

At the Warren, Cushendun, the Lower Lagoon silts produced a key assemblage. These observations are based on the material lodged in NMNI in Belfast though other rather rolled items are still housed in the Peabody Museum in Harvard. The NMNI assemblage consists of 40 struck items though there are several other more questionable pieces. Of these 19 are relatively fresh while 21 are rolled and patinated white. The fresh material was probably washed in from the edge of an adjacent shoreline settlement which lay to the south. Its presence would also be suggested by the occurrence of charcoal within the silt. The presence of several fresh cortical flakes seems to indicate flint knapping which, in itself, is interesting as the nearest sources of flint lay several kilometres further south. While no diagnostic retouched tools were found, nine fresh and rolled narrow blades were recovered (Fig. 8.24). These were all narrow and elongated with a length/breadth ratio of six being 3/1 or greater. Only one had any evidence of platform edge preparation. The Lower Lagoon Silts also produced two radiocarbon dates (I5134, charcoal 7670±140 BP, 8972–8185 cal BP and UB689, wood, 7395±65 BP, 8361–8047 cal BP). The crucial aspect of the material from the Lower lagoon silts is that like the Port of Larne assemblage it provides evidence that a macrolithic technology was in use sometime before 8000 cal BP.

The recent excavations at the Port of Larne, also referred to earlier, have shown quite clearly that the hard hammer large blade technology was in existence closer to 9000 cal BP. More importantly, however, the dates stratified at a lower level from the pit complex centred on Contexts 5177 and 5127 ,which also had produced significant quantities of fish bones, produced small quantities of a large blade assemblage (Fig. 8.17) and a series of four dates based on burnt hazel nut shells between 9000 and 8600 cal BP (C5177; e.g. UBA12304, burnt hazel nutshell, 7891±30 BP, 8951–8595 cal BP and UBA 12303, burnt hazel nutshell, 7866±30 BP, 8768–8588 cal BP). Two more dates, again from burnt hazel nut fragments were obtained from C5127/8 (UBA 12307, burnt hazel nutshell, 7812±31 BP, 8646–8480 cal BP and UBA 12308, burnt hazel nutshell, 7788±35 BP, 8635–8460 cal BP). These dates suggest that the large blade technology was in existence sometime before 8500 cal BP.

It appears that Praeger's Island continued in use until sometime after 8000 cal BP. Although they are slightly inverted in date, there are two radiocarbon dates available. This is based on evidence from another chipping floor, i.e. C5110-CF2, which lies at the base of the overlying beach deposits, about 10 m from CF1, and is, in the main, stratified above the layer C5012. There is a radiocarbon on a pig bone of 7963–7844 cal BP (UBA 14826, 7072±30 BP), from the base of the shingle and another date on pig bone which came from the underlying C5012 at the same spot produced a date of 7673–7591 cal BP (UBA-14827, bone, 6788±25 BP).

In fact a slightly less concentrated scatter of material appeared to be associated with the eastern area was also dominated by large blades and cores that would have been expected from the Later Mesolithic. However, instead of the flat, so-called "Larnian Uniplane" cores that are found in the latter part of the Later Mesolithic, this area produced a significant number of large, more elongated and cylindrical cores, which suggested an earlier date (Fig. 8.12), while a series of large blades was also found in the same area (Fig. 8.12b). These can be paralleled material from across Larne Lough at Ballylumford on Island Magee (Burchell 1931); Ballylumford had produced cores and blades from a series of so-called "Early Atlantic" deposits. These were of similar character to the quite elongated blades and cores that were recovered from the eastern portion of C5012.

Therefore based on the evidence from these two sites one can suggest that reliance on large blades produced by hard hammer percussion were already in existence in the middle of the 9th millennium cal BP. Although these dates were by no means as precise as would have been wished (Woodman 2010) they did at least suggest that large blade production existed before the 8.2 ka event which, as Warren (2003) felt could, constitute a possible contributor to the origins and development of the Irish Later Mesolithic.

Other possible evidence

There is a danger when a possible chronological lacuna has been identified, such as that perceived to exist between roughly 8000 and 9000 years ago, that there will a rush to fill the hole with all sorts of assemblages, In this case there are other groups of material for which a case can be made for their

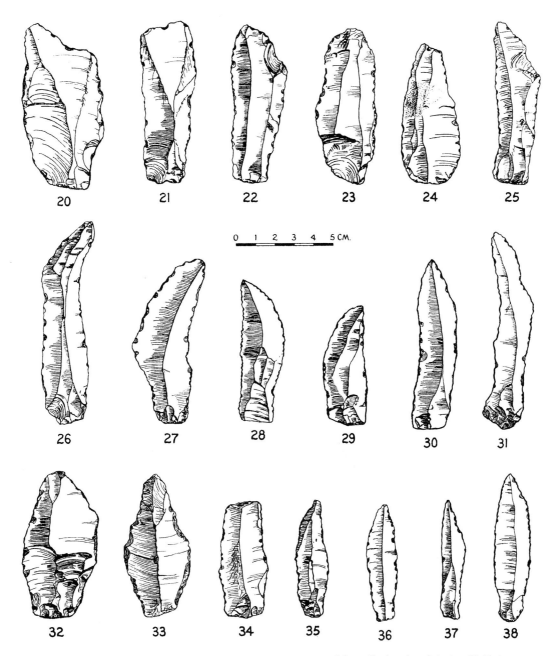

Fig. 8.24. Selection of blades from the Lower Lagoon Silt at Cushendun (Movius 1940a).

inclusion in this transitional phase. In the 1960s an amateur, Eddie Reagan of Greyabbey, collected a series of flint artefacts from the lower limits of an intertidal beach at Big Stone Bay in Strangford Lough (Woodman 1978a, 299), while 70 years earlier Patterson (1892; Woodman 1978a, 290) recovered an assemblage from the intertidal shore at Sydenham Station on Belfast Lough. In the latter case there was also a small bone assemblage, including deer, ox and horse. Radiocarbon dating has shown these to date to Early Historic times (Woodman *et al.* 1997). Both assemblages are relatively fresh and based on

blade production that has more in common the Later Mesolithic. The fact that they both come from below present day sea level suggests that they are in contexts that pre-dated the sea level rise. This strongly suggests a date within the transitional phase. There are also concentrations of narrow, more elongated blades, such as those found in Concentration C at Toome Bypass (North) (Fig. 4.20), as well as the elongated blades in a number of the caches, such as the Kells Hoard. Though limited in numbers they look similar to those from the lower Lagoon silts at Cushendun.

If one is to summarise the changes that were taking place in the period just before 9000 cal BP and which had been completed perhaps by, at the latest, 8500 cal BP, it would appear to be based mostly on a technological shift rather than in the initial appearance of a series of distinctive type fossils or retouched tools. In this case composite tools, in which microliths and possibly small bladelets (as in the case of Port of Larne CF1), were abandoned and replaced by the production of large, perhaps quite elongated blanks that constituted hand-held tools. The scatter of more cylindrical large blade cores and the series of large but narrow elongated blades found in small numbers across C5012 may also belong to this phase.

It is even possible that some of the contexts where the smaller blades are found alongside larger examples may not be a case of the mixing of material from slightly different ages but rather represents the transitional nature of the technologies of the early 9th millennium BP.

Suggested renaming of phases within the Irish Mesolithic

A case can be made for a long transitional phase between the two conventionally accepted phases of the Irish Mesolithic that have been used for over 30 years, namely the *"Early"* Mesolithic and the Later Mesolithic. There is obviously a need to reconsider the terms used to describe the chronological phases of the Irish Mesolithic.

The possibility that there could be regional variations in how the lithic technologies developed has already been mentioned and we should also not expect to be able to draw hard lines between chronological phases. Figure 8.25 shows the main spread of dates primarily from the major sites in each of the first three stages discussed above. The existence of potential overlap can be seen. A small micro-awl (see Fig. 5.9, 9) and an obliquely retouched bladelet (Fig. 5.9, 10) were found in Zone 7 at Newferry while a similar micro-awl and retouched bladelet (Fig. 8.11, 1 and 2) were recovered from the general scatter of artefacts at the Port of Larne excavations in context 5012, At neither site was there any evidence of a significant presence of the earliest phase of the Irish Mesolithic. Therefore it is important to remember that we are looking for gradual changes through time.

Are we justified in labelling a new phase as "Middle Mesolithic" or "Transitional Mesolithic"? This would define a phase that began perhaps before 9000 cal BP and in which microliths and possibly several other classic "Early" Mesolithic implements had ceased to be used and was followed, certainly well before 8500 cal BP and perhaps as early as 8800 cal BP, by a phase when the use of smaller blades had been abandoned and larger blades were being produced using hard hammer percussion. The classic implement types, such as those found at Newferry, i.e. the range of butt and distally trimmed forms, did not yet occur.

Or, by way of contrast could the two existing phases be extended and changes within *each part of the Irish Mesolithic be recognised*? In this case the distinction between the Early and Later Mesolithic would be based on the abandonment of the large scale production of small blades and the reliance solely on hard hammer percussion as the initial defining point of the beginning of the Later Mesolithic.

On balance it would seem best to adopt a more conservative approach in which there are just two contiguously chronological phases to the Irish Mesolithic. These could, with one minor alteration, retain the existing terms. Thus the two main phases of the Irish Mesolithic would become:

Earlier Irish Mesolithic: 9800(?)–8800/8600(?) cal BP
Later Irish Mesolithic: 8800/8600(?)–6000 cal BP

The advantage of this simple system is that it takes into consideration the current paucity of sites that at the moment produce any quantities of material from this point in time, between say 9500 and 8000 cal BP. It is possible, of course that the transition from Earlier to Later Mesolithic may vary in date and character across Ireland.

In returning to the suggestions for change outlined earlier in this chapter

Some, such as social factors and population growth, must have played a role, while procurement of raw material may have also contributed. Even the short term climatic deterioration of the 8.2 ka Event, discussed in detail in Chapter 2, which only happened at the end, if not after, this period of change, can be seen as another factor that may have had consequences. There has been a suggestion (Bicho *et al.* 2010) that as the 8.2 ka Event is associated with changes in water temperature and temporary surges associated with sea level rise? Thus, productivity in the North Atlantic may have changed. Perhaps the migration patterns of fish, such as salmon or eels, were disrupted at this point in time but it is difficult to envisage an effect that would cause a major economic shift. In fact, the date of the Dublin North Wall fish traps, which just post-date this event, and the concentration of material at locations where fish traps would be placed, as in the River Bann, suggest a greater reliance on fixed facilities associated with fishing. *Was there a significant shift in the resources procured?* The surviving evidence is sparse and the range of animal species that could be procured is very narrow, there also seems to be little evidence that there was a major shift in food sources from the Earlier to the Later Mesolithic.

The major problem is, as is evident to prior discussions in this chapter, the absence of a distinctive range of implements making it difficult to track change in the 9th millennium BP. The few lesser diagnostic assemblages described above can only be used when they are clearly associated with secure and reliable sources for independent dating, such as in a sealed archaeological context or, as in the case of the Lower Lagoon Silts at Cushendun, in a stratified context.

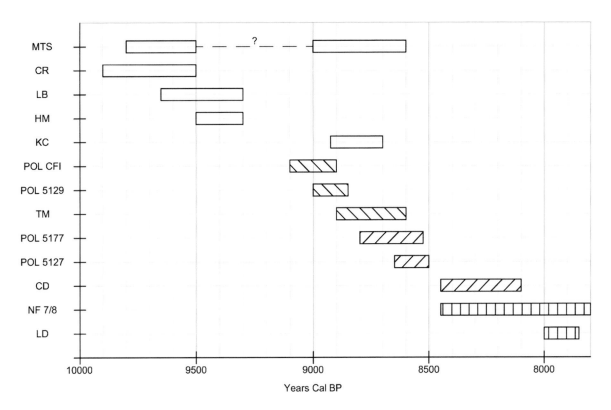

Fig. 8.25. Schematic sequence of radiocarbon dated ages of major Mesolithic sites for the first 2000 years (Mount Sandel Facies): MTS, Mount Sandel; CR = Castleroe; LB = Lough Boora; HM = Hermitage; KC = Killuragh Cave(?); (Creagh Facies) POL = Port of Larne CFI, C.5129; TM = Toome, Mitchell's (Cushendun Facies); POL = Port of Larne C.5177, C.5127, CD (Lower Lagoon Silts); (Newferry Facies) NF = Newferry Zone 3, 7 and 8; LD = Linford.

This relates to a more general shift that may have taken place within the Irish Mesolithic. It appears that there is little evidence of settlement away from valley bottoms during the Later Mesolithic, or perhaps we should say, little *recognisable* evidence of settlement (Woodman and Anderson 1990). The implications of this point will be examined in more detail in Chapter 9, however, at the moment it should be noted that if this shift took place early, i.e. between 9000 and 8000 cal BP, then by 8000 cal BP these assemblages will often be buried deep in valley floors or under other forms of Quaternary deposits. Sites in Ireland of the earlier parts of the Later Mesolithic will be difficult to find. However, the reward would be that they may well be securely stratified and therefore easier to date.

These issues imply that there is a series of barriers to the proper investigation of the issue of the 9th millennium BP and there are some genuine difficulties in researching this topic but, aside from good luck and chance finds, it is probable that progress will only be made through keeping these difficulties in mind.

Gone native

The consequence of accepting that there was a series of ongoing changes within the first 2000 years of the Irish Mesolithic is that it requires a reconsideration of many aspects of the Later Mesolithic. Perhaps the most important is that the Later Mesolithic is seen too much as a static phenomenon. This could, however, be a product of an implicit assumption that there will be various forms of pauperisation or stagnation on an island which, through time, appears to have become even more isolated.

It could be argued that, having undergone a series of adaptations within the 9th millennium BP, technology and lifestyle had developed which were more suited to Irish conditions and therefore became very stable and not likely to change.

There are two particular areas that can be explored:

1) The development of the technology normally seen as typical of the Irish Later Mesolithic.
2) The appearance of and changes to the suite of retouched tools usually regarded as typical of some part of the Irish Mesolithic.

Investigating these issues, as will have been apparent from earlier discussions, can be quite difficult. The problem is to assess whether observed differences are due to changes through time rather than regional strategies and preferences.

One major difficulty is, as was noted in Chapter 5, that the final stages of the Later Mesolithic provide much more evidence than the rest of the Later Mesolithic and indeed the whole of the Irish Mesolithic. There is a natural tendency to look at the latest sites and assume that they are typical for the whole of the Later Mesolithic.

In addition Newferry has a very distinct type of assemblage where, with the exception of Zone 7 where some blade production took place, most of the tools are made from imported blanks. However in spite of the limited ranges of evidence for lithic reduction, the Newferry sequence is the chronological backbone of the Irish Later Mesolithic (see Chapter 5).

The Newferry sequence

The radiocarbon chronology for Newferry 3 was established on the basis of radiocarbon dates that were obtained more than 40 years ago. The fact that they were obtained from bulk samples and were based on wood charcoal has on occasions lead to reservations about their reliability, although usually nothing specific is mentioned. It is, however, worth looking at the reliability of the Newferry dates.

First, individually, these dates must be treated with caution and the fact that they also often had a large standard deviation limits their value (e.g. dates associated with the bone points from Zone V which were discussed in Chapter 5). If they are examined as a sequence, on the other hand, then it can be seen that there is a consistent shift through time from the bottom of Zone 9 to Zone 3. The chronological sequence is independently supported at each end. At the base the pollen in the Zone 8 a peat layer is typical of the latest stages of what would have been called the Boreal Zone VI (Smith and Collins 1971, 254) which suggests that the peat deposit could date to around, or just before, 8500 years ago. Towards the top of the sequence, in Zone 2, was an eroded river channel that contained Neolithic pottery and artefacts. Therefore, one can presume that Zones 8–3 accumulated throughout a period extending for at least 2500 years,

The question is how much reliance can be placed on the dates of the individual zones? If one accepts the relatively poor precision of many of the dates and the fact that there could be an old wood factor, then they give us a rough estimate for each zone but, aside from three samples, the stratigraphic progression of the dates forms a sequenced coherent pattern. The radiocarbon dated samples can be seen in Figure 8.26 where they are placed in their stratigraphic sequence.

It should be noted that the three dates to be treated with caution are UB 636 from Zone 7, which is not only at variance with other dates from Zone 7 but, more importantly, is much

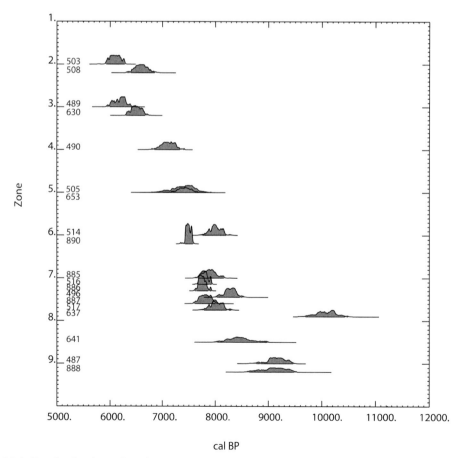

Fig. 8.26. Graph of radiocarbon dates, in their stratigraphic sequence, obtained from Newferry Site 3.

older than the dates from both the underlying peat Zone 8 and even the dates from a small pond in the basal sands (Zone 9) that was sealed by the peat. The other samples excluded are UB 503 and UB 508 which come from the top of the sequence. This problem was discussed by Woodman (1980). These samples were obtained from small trenches excavated in the first season before it was realised that the bulk samples were taken in an area of erosion, belonged to Zone 2 and were very likely to contain charcoal from earlier sources.

Given the large standard deviations, it is not surprising that there is an overlap between contiguous stratigraphic zones. The age of an assemblage in one Zone or Layer should not be based solely on an individual radiocarbon but one can suggest that there are three main phases: Zones 8 and 7, Zones 5 and 6 and Zones 3 and 4. It is also possible to document the general sequence of artefacts and their changes throughout that sequence.

Were there changes in technology throughout the Later Mesolithic?

There are, as already mentioned and discussed in Chapter 5, certain, perhaps erroneously, perceived images of the Later Mesolithic. One of the most obvious is the belief that Irish Later Mesolithic technologies produce particularly large blades. However, as was apparent even in the 1970s (Woodman 1978a, figs 24 and 33; Fig. 8.27) the majority of blades and flakes from a range of sites tended to be 60–90 mm in length. It could be argued that the simplicity of the technology masks the fact that there was a specific purpose to producing blades and blade-like flakes of a certain size.

As noted in Chapter 5 the range of retouched tools from Zones 7 and 8 at the base of the Newferry sequence differs in some ways from assemblages later in the sequence. Anderson (1994) has also shown that the blade forms and reduction did

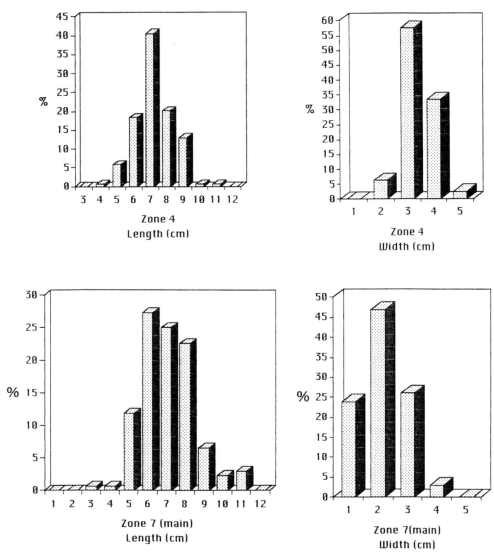

Fig. 8.27. Blade sizes from selected zones at Newferry Site 3 (Anderson 1994).

change through the sequence. There is a difference between the main part of the Newferry sequence Zones 3–6 (Anderson's Unit 1–2) and the blades from Zones 7 and 8 (Unit 3). Platform preparation is a lot less common in Anderson's Unit 3 i.e. Zones 7 and 8 at the base of the sequence, roughly 30%. In Unit 1 Zones 3 and 4, platform preparation reaches 75% or more (Fig. 8.28). This, not surprisingly is paralleled in that there is a reduction in platform depth in the upper parts of the Newferry sequence.

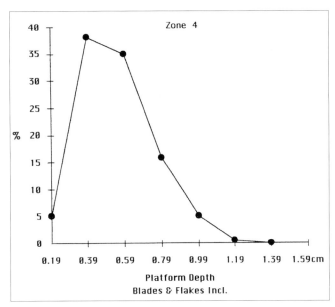

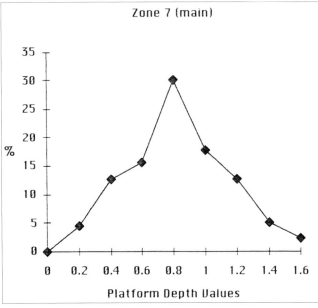

Fig. 8.28. Platform preparation and depth from Newferry Zones 4 and 7 (after Anderson 1994).

In spite of the presence of individual artefacts, such as the particularly elongated distally retouched piece which is more than 100 mm in length, the graphs at first sight do not seem to show that blades in Unit 3 were significantly longer than in other later assemblages at Newferry. Anderson has, however, noted that in Zone 7 there is a presence of a substantial number of long but importantly quite narrow blades. These elongated blades were not as evident in the upper part of the sequence in Units 1 and 2.

This presence of more elongated blade is paralleled other assemblages. Thus similar blades occur from Port of Larne context 5177 and from the Lower Lagoon Silts. These latter two assemblages, also, as in Newferry Zone 7 lack extensive use of platform edge preparation present in the upper part of the Newferry Sequence. Therefore, the presumed shift away from the more elongated forms of blades really only began to happen sometime after 8000 cal BP.

It should of course be remembered that while the chronology of change has absorbed much attention, the reasons for the change in blade form has been almost totally ignored!

The technological changes throughout the Later Mesolithic is also reflected in both the presence of knapping activity solely at the base of the Newferry sequence and in the types of cores that were present. The validity of this assumption and Kador's (2010 149) suggestion that the figures do not support this assertion has already been discussed in Chapter 5 but the nature of the material is worth further consideration.

As noted by Anderson (1994), there are also clear indications that, in the earliest part of the Later Mesolithic, notably in her Unit 3 assemblages from Newferry (essentially Zone 7), there is a diversity of core types, including six single platform cores, some of which are worked round the whole circumference, as well as eight dual platformed examples and two others (Fig. 8.29). At Newferry, in assemblages that post-date Zone 7 cores are virtually non-existent. They are quite rare at the other Newferry excavations as well as from the Toome Bypass (Woodman 2015). It seems that, while initially more local materials were being used, perhaps again at or just after 8000 cal BP i.e. in the upper levels, blanks and perhaps some already retouched tools were imported.

This parallels the evidence from Port of Larne and Ballylumford which was referred to earlier. The changes in core type and the nature of the blades are part of the same series of technological changes that took place throughout the Later Mesolithic in the north-east but as most sites outside that region belong to the final stages of the Later Mesolithic, there is as yet no clear evidence that there are similar changes taking place elsewhere. In other words is the Newferry Site 3 sequence local or typical of the whole of the Irish Mesolithic? This is a crucial issue which will be returned to in Chapter 9.

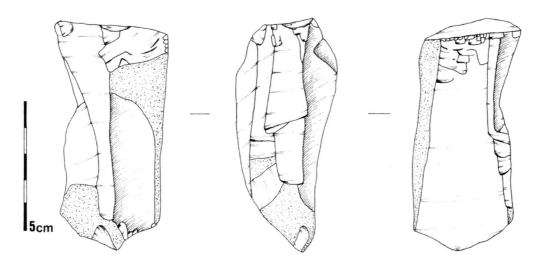

Fig. 8.29. Cores from Newferry Zone 7 (after Anderson 1994).

Changes in retouched tools

The major problem in assessing changes in retouched tools is, as we have seen, that the suggested series of changes through time is based almost entirely on the sequence at Newferry Site 3. Numerous examples of tanged Butt Trimmed Forms have been found in dredgings and diatomite cutting as well as on the shores of Lough Neagh and in both the Toome and Raphael hoards. However, at present, the occurrence can only be documented at Newferry Site 3 at the bottom of the sequence and by an apparent association of similar radiocarbon dates with two other examples from Linford (Moore 1998). Perhaps the strongest case for change in the types of Butt Trimmed Forms is the absence of the tanged forms from numerous sites that date to the last 1000 years of the Later Mesolithic.

There are many unanswered questions about the changes in implement types found at Newferry. Do the bar forms in particular, which only occur in the upper part of the Newferry sequence, really only appear in the final part of the Later Mesolithic? Is their absence from Newferry Site 1 a functional or chronological phenomenon? Similarly, are the classic broad Bann Flakes only associated with the last few centuries of this period and are they a new implement type added to the repertoire of Butt Trimmed Forms or a replacement for earlier forms?

There are some implements where it is as yet impossible to establish whether or not they are typical of the whole of the Later Mesolithic. Ongoing research indicates that pointed bone implements were not only being used throughout the Later Mesolithic but may have been in existence by 9000 cal BP.

The ground (Moynagh) and chipped (Kerry) points, with one possible example from Newferry, so far belong to the latest phases of the Mesolithic but there is no reason to believe that they could not belong earlier in the Later Mesolithic. The drop off in the use of schist as the raw material for axes and the appearance of baked mudstone axes in the upper part of the Newferry sequence seems to reflect different exploitation strategies that were particular to that part of Ireland. This change may not have happened in the rest of the island; indeed other strategies may have been devised elsewhere.

In conclusion, there is some evidence that numerous, quite significant changes took place during the Later Mesolithic but it is also evident that the changes may have been gradual.

An overall assessment

It is possible then that the use of composite tools with microliths continued throughout the first 1000 years of human settlement but that, throughout that period, their usage became less common. Perhaps another, simpler, alternative technology and tool types had emerged even before the common usage of larger hand-held tools that were made from blanks and struck using a hard hammer technology.

At this point it is worth considering the different technological journey that Ireland took during the centuries on either side of 9000 years ago. Differences between Ireland and Britain are not confined to the abandonment of microliths in Ireland and their continued use in Britain. Even allowing for an early disappearance, they are remarkably rare in Ireland which suggests that moves to different procurement strategies were happening from quite early in the Irish Mesolithic. Fischer (1989) showed that, in south Scandinavia, projectile heads were present throughout the Mesolithic and, indeed, back into the Late Upper Palaeolithic. The forms changed very significantly through the Maglemose, Kongemose and Ertebølle. There were changes in the environment, especially as Zealand became an island, but the role of hunting and use of bows remained throughout the Mesolithic.

Obviously, unlike Britain or many adjacent regions in Europe, in Ireland it seems likely that it was the development of a very different way of life which entailed the development of implements that were particular to the needs of people living in an insular environment.

Not only were composite tools replaced by large hand-held implements, that were used as unretouched blanks or retouched into particular forms but there is an impression that there was a greater use of a series of core tools, i.e. picks and borers as well as axes and adzes of both flint and ground stone. It is also of interest that polissoirs and other forms of grindstones seem to occur more frequently in the Later Mesolithic. To these can be added elongated and bevelled pebbles, only one of which has been found in an early context (i.e. at Mount Sandel). There is a series of clubs and simple, slightly altered slabs of stone. At present ground Moynagh points and chipped Kerry points also seem to belong to the Later Mesolithic.

This range of artefacts that can be associated with the Later Mesolithic could best be described as "heavy duty equipment" whose purpose was probably entirely different from that associated with the Earlier Mesolithic in Ireland. From a different perspective, the relatively common occurrence of caches of Later Mesolithic artefacts, especially in the north-east, along with, in the same areas, the common practice of producing blanks that were then transported to areas of settlement, suggests that the landscape may have been used in contrastingly different ways during the Later Mesolithic (see Chapter 9).

One other perhaps less obvious change seems to have taken place. Burins are quite rare in the Irish Mesolithic, though we may not be recognising some, but where they occur they usually seem to belong to the Earlier/*"Early"* Mesolithic. Not only do they occur at Mount Sandel (see Fig. 5.6) but they were also present in Whelan's assemblage at Toome. They were also found at in the Lower Gravels at Cushendun (Movius 1940a; Woodman 1978a, fig. 85).

Again, while some small notched scraper-like pieces exist in the Later Mesolithic they seem to be more common in the earlier Creagh Phase and at sites like Lough Boora (Woodman 1978a, 324, fig. 99). There also seems to be a limited presence of end of blade scrapers during the Earlier/*"Early"* Mesolithic while they are only known from the Lough Beg cache in the Later Mesolithic.

These are not the really eye-catching changes that have been referred to earlier but the shift is probably of equal significance. Their relative absence from the Later Mesolithic leaves one asking "what were they actually used for?" In the case of the "burins" one has to ask, were these tools used for bone working or were they discards whose primary function

was to allow the production of small bladelets? Again, with the scrapers, was it the lateral edge rather than the retouched distal edge that was important? Their virtual absence from the Later Mesolithic is something of significance.

In summary, the story of the Irish Mesolithic, is one of a rapid adaptation to local conditions followed by several millennia of continuous change, which did not contain any radical shifts, but where we can assume that there may have been, by its end, a very different set of life ways than those practiced by the first settlers.

A proposed chronology

As described earlier, there is no simple chronological sequence such as can be observed in the Danish Mesolithic. Instead the two major stages of the Irish Earlier and Later Mesolithic are retained, but it is also recognised that changes take place within each stage. As a further refinement of that referred to previously, the proposed sequence for the Irish Mesolithic is:

Irish Earlier Mesolithic 9800–88/8600(?) cal BP

Mount Sandel Facies: This is characterised by the range of implements found in the Mount Sandel excavations and includes a range of core and flake axes, microliths of varying forms, as well as platform edge preparation and soft hammer stone production.

Creagh Facies: This is based on the assemblages from Port of Larne context 5012 (CF1) and in the Toome area, most notably those found by Whelan and Mitchell in Creagh td. Assemblages are characterised either by a paucity in numbers or types of microliths or by their absence. Blade production seems to be by a more *ad hoc* process that lacks core platform edge preparation. This usually results in smaller, more irregular blades. One also has to be cautious and not assume that there was a simple synchronous shift from Mount Sandel to Creagh facies. It is possible that blade technology changes and the abandonment of microliths proceeded at a different rate. Some might feel that the discoveries at the Port of Larne would warrant the use of the term "Larne Facies" but as we have only managed to divest ourselves of the images created by the term "Larnian" it seems safer to use Creagh!

Irish Later Mesolithic 88/8600–6000(?) cal BP

Cushendun Facies: This is based on the material recovered from the Lower Lagoon Silts at the Warren, Cushendun and the eastern assemblage in Context 5012, Port of Larne. It is typified by the use of hard hammer percussion leading to the creation of relatively elongated, though often irregular-shaped, blades. It also lacks core platform edge preparation and appears to lack the diagnostic range of forms that are often regarded as typical of the Later Mesolithic.

Newferry Facies: This is based on the assemblage from Newferry Site 3 and is characterised by the range of Later Mesolithic forms recovered from that site. These include, most notably, the Butt Trimmed Forms that occur on so many Later Mesolithic sites. Blade production and platform edge preparation became more regular during this phase. It may also be associated with a greater use of ground stone tools.

It will be evident that these facies cannot be assumed to be water-tight chronological phases; there are likely to be fuzzy boundaries and overlaps and changes may happen at different rates in different regions. In other words, it is as yet unclear if there is a simple sequential series of changes or phases of *ad hoc* experimentation.

It is therefore evident that the chronological schema proposed for Ireland differs from both the British schema, with its two major blocks of time, and the more fluid Danish one. All three have their own strengths and are a product of the way Mesolithic communities developed as well as the nature of the archaeological and environmental contexts in which they were constructed.

Part IV

LIFEWAYS

One particular problem in assessing "life ways" in the Irish Mesolithic is that there is every reason to dismiss the concept of a single Irish Mesolithic economy that was homogeneous through time or throughout the island. The Mesolithic period is the longest single period in the human history of the island, incorporating approximately the same time span as the Neolithic and Bronze Age together. It also is a period in which much more radical environmental changes took place. The often unspoken challenge is the fact that, as the 20th largest island on the planet, it is a land area where assumptions of similarity throughout the island in technology or economy should also be subject to question.

It is obvious from the review of environmental evidence in Part I that any hunter-gatherer settlement in Ireland may have necessitated the development of a series of different procurement strategies. In Part II this was reflected in the manner in which a new series of technologies developed. It also seems probable that these were a series of gradual changes that took place throughout the Irish Mesolithic rather than the original Early/Later Mesolithic as was first envisaged in the 1970s. Thus one can start with the observation that any analysis of the possible lifeways developed in Ireland will be different from other parts of Europe and that the questions will always centre on 1) how different and 2) why? These potential differences have been apparent from the 1970s, both in the distribution of Mesolithic artefacts and in the range of faunal remains recovered.

There are also other issues which should receive attention, as they should in other parts of Europe. The most obvious is the relative lack of information about the structure of settlements sites and dwellings of this period (see Chapter 4). There are also areas that are rarely considered. In the Irish context, especially, there is the problem of the paucity of human remains making it difficult to address questions of health, life expectancy, etc., while issues of belief or cosmology may seem beyond consideration. Many of these will be addressed in the next two chapters.

In spite of the sparse archaeological record, the resources available do allow some insights into the life ways of Mesolithic Ireland. These include what can be gleaned from a) the distribution patterns of Mesolithic artefacts and the significance of the objects themselves (Chapter 9) and b) the role of the flora and fauna in providing sustenance for the population (Chapter 10).

Chapter 9

Patterns in the landscape

As noted, not too many large scale excavations of Mesolithic sites have taken place in Ireland and of these a relatively small proportion of sites contain significant quantities of organic materials. Therefore, we often have to rely to some extent on what can be learnt from the scatters of Mesolithic artefacts that have been recovered from across the landscape.

Sites and artefacts: patterns at an "island" level

As will have been apparent from the discussion on the history of research, the limited range of fauna and distribution of Mesolithic artefacts were partially masked by a double assumption. These were that Mesolithic settlement was primarily confined to areas where flint was obtainable, i.e. the north-east, where the initial settlement was also presumed to occur; and, secondly, a common assumption that impenetrable forests inhabited by unspecified dangerous animals inhibited movement away from coastal areas and major waterways. A clear indication of the predominantly low-lying occurrence of Mesolithic artefacts was discussed in Chapter 4 could be seen in the plotting of some Mesolithic artefacts from the north-east of Ireland as far back as 1970s (e.g. Woodman 1978a; maps included in Fig. 9.1). These maps showed very clearly that, unlike Neolithic finds, the distribution of Mesolithic material in Ireland was confined to the lowlands.

Even in the 1970s the evidence from England where, in many regions amateur field archaeologists had collected extensively, provided a contrast. These were in areas such as the north-east, the Pennines (see Fig. 4.7b), the Peak District of the north Midlands, portions of the Home Counties, south of London, and even in the south-west. In all these regions Mesolithic sites were found in both lowland locations and in the local uplands. The difference with the Irish distribution encouraged another perspective on the Mesolithic material in Ireland, namely the realisation that land mammals would have played a lesser role here and that there may have been a greater reliance on coastal resources of all types, i.e. molluscs, fish and sea mammals, as well as the resources to be found at or in rivers and lakes.

Given that the patterns observed in the 1970s were initially based on a small area in north-east Ireland it could be argued that the results are biased and perhaps based on what might have appeared to be a very local phenomenon. Today the Irish Mesolithic database, which has gathered material together from throughout Ireland, still shows the same trend with most of the material being found in lowland contexts.

One observation that has been made on a number of occasions is that the low-lying riverine/lacustrine and coastal distribution may be inherently biased by collectors always returning to particular "hot spots" and that they may have ignored other landscapes. This is a point that has often been raised in conversation but rarely in print though it has recently been made again (Kador 2010, 154). Kador's crucial point was that collectors were biased in the preferences for the types of locations searched. The weakness in the "we have not looked" argument can be seen in two ways (Woodman *et al*. 2006, chapter 7, 245–304). First, in the north-east, while there were "hot spots" (i.e. the Larne or Portstewart sand hills), much of the material acquired from the mid-Antrim/east Derry area came via the "Ragmen" who travelled across the whole region and purchased artefacts from agricultural labourers. Thus, if the material found by peat and diatomite cutters is included, material was recovered from across the whole landscape not just from low-lying "hot spots". The absence of the distinctive Later Mesolithic forms away from the Lower Bann, in areas on the edge of the Antrim Plateau which lie to the east of Ballymena was, even in the late 19th century, a matter of constant comment.

This difference can be best illustrated in Figure 9.2 (compiled from Woodman *et al*. 2006, table 7:26). This is a comparison between artefacts in the Knowles collection, from the Bann Valley floor (–25 m OSL) and an area on the edge of the Antrim Plateau centred on Clough and Glenleslie, which has a mean altitude of 200 m OSL. Figures for Mesolithic artefacts axes, microliths and Later Mesolithic forms are compared to leaf/lozenge shaped arrowheads, javelin heads, hollow scrapers and invasively retouched/plano-convex forms. This shows that, while roughly 33% of Neolithic material can be found in the floor of the Bann Valley, the converse is not true, as the Mesolithic forms are less than 5% of the total number of artefacts found on the upland edges. Collectors

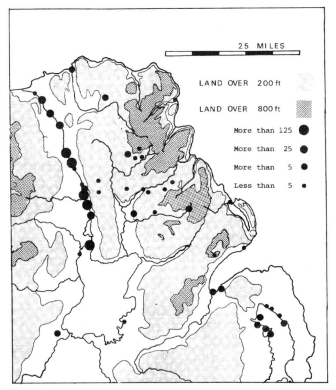

Fig. 52 Distribution of butt trimmed forms in the North East of
          Ireland.

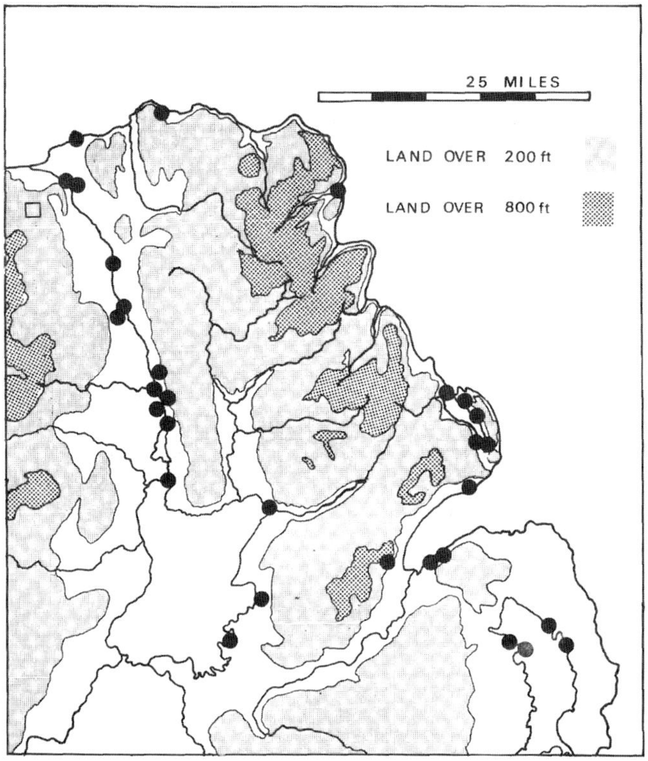

Fig. 53 Distribution of core borers in the North East of Ireland.

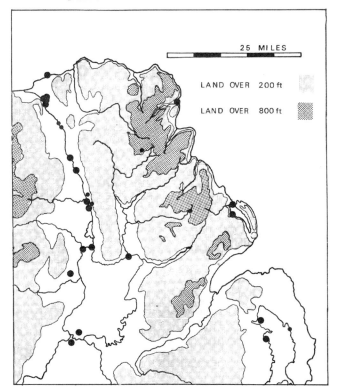

Fig. 54 Distribution of early Mesolithic material in the N.E. of
          Ireland.

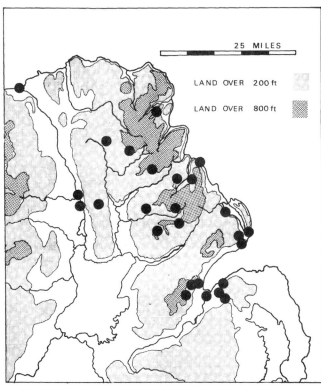

Fig. 55 Distribution of known Neolithic and later surface collections.

Fig. 9.1. Distribution of Mesolithic artefacts in north-east Ireland (after Woodman 1978a).

were obtaining Neolithic lithic artefacts in large quantities in the uplands. Thus it is obvious that other locations, away from the preferred "hot spots" such as the Antrim Uplands (i.e. away from valley floors and coast) were being scoured for stone tools. In comparison to the very large quantities of Mesolithic artefacts from the lowlands, relatively few pieces of Mesolithic date were recovered from the edges of the Antrim Plateau. As shown in Figure 4.7, though the evidence from elsewhere is often quite scanty, throughout Ireland Mesolithic artefacts and their locations of discovery is overwhelmingly confined to lower altitudes.

There is also, in this oft-repeated observation, an implicit though probably unintended assumption that upland presences will only be detected by professionals or very interested amateurs. I suspect that the reality is different. There are areas, like the top of the Antrim Plateau or a large part of north Mayo, where lithic scatters of any period will be difficult to detect because the original ground surface lies under blanket peats that often exceed 1 m in thickness. However, there are many areas such as the Mournes or the Wicklow mountains where extensive areas of peat deflation have taken place. It seems unlikely that an extensive upland Mesolithic would have been entirely missed on a national level, not just by archaeologists but all the numerous walkers, amateur botanists, geologists and even tourists.

There is, of course, evidence of a Mesolithic presence away from low-lying locations but the totality of artefacts is quite low. This does not mean that Mesolithic communities avoided these other areas; rather they were not subject to the same repeated/persistent visits as seen at places like Toome and Culbane. One very clear example of this is the discovery of at least 10 tanged Butt Trimmed Forms (Fig. 9.3) during excavation of a multi-period site at Linford 4 *AN 11*, which lies at 250 m ASL. Further examples will be alluded to later in this chapter. The main lesson that can be drawn from these distributions is that areas away from major areas of water, including the highlands, were used to some extent during the Later Mesolithic. However, even given the highly curated nature of the way in which communities used a range of Later Mesolithic artefacts, i.e. retained them for further use or carefully cached them against return visits, the use of many parts of the landscape seems to have been relatively slight although more than as areas of transit. This is an issue which will be returned to below especially in discussing the local distributions of artefacts in the Later Mesolithic.

Settlement patterns throughout the Mesolithic in Ireland

This discussion can be divided into two topics: a) where are the sites located and, from the way in which they are positioned, is it possible to establish the existence of specific limited groups of sites within a small area? b) are there, on a regional basis

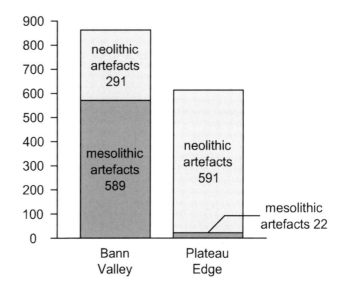

Fig. 9.2. Histogram of upland and lowland distribution of Mesolithic and Neolithic artefacts (prepared by Hugh Kavanagh).

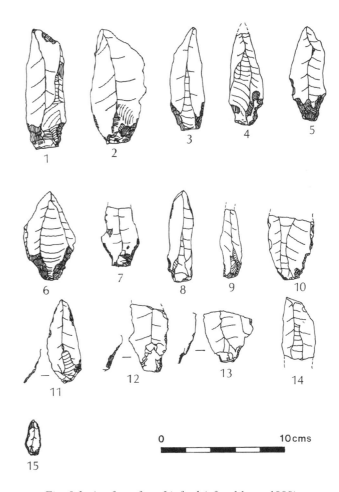

Fig. 9.3. Artefacts from Linford (after Moore 1999).

and especially on the basis in which various raw materials were obtained and used, any hints as to the extent of territories that might have existed?

From Chapter 4 and in particular Plate XVI, it is apparent that there are areas of Ireland where very few Mesolithic sites or even stray artefacts have ever been uncovered. In certain parts of Europe a case could be made for equating areas without finds with a presumption that these were empty landscapes where there was a very limited presence during the Mesolithic. However, in Ireland as perhaps in parts of Scotland, these empty landscapes are as likely to be a product of areas of low, sometimes very low, modern population density with portions which are virtually uninhabited. Similarly many of these gaps in a Mesolithic presence are in extensive areas of virtually permanent grassland as well as expanses of both raised bog and blanket peat. Thus the recognition of a Mesolithic presence requires both the opportunity to find something and people who have an awareness of the significance of a chance find that comes their way.

As discussed in Chapter 4, so much of the Irish material is made up of chance finds. The problem is further complicated by the fact that there are relatively few sites from the Earlier Mesolithic and that (Chapter 8), the classic microlithic phase where diagnostic artefacts occur is only known with certainty from remarkably few sites. At the moment one also has to admit that this is primarily a contrast between the more conventional "Early" Mount Sandel Facies, i.e., earlier than 9000 years ago and only the latter part of the Newferry Facies, i.e., certainly sometime after 8500 years ago. Therefore, in spite of the suggested reconfiguring of the Mesolithic outlined in Chapter 8, large chunks of the Irish Mesolithic are still poorly documented.

Ireland is a relatively large and diverse landscape with, as far as the Mesolithic is concerned, a very varied regional research history. In the previous chapters it was suggested that, throughout a period of nearly 4000 years, there had been constant change. Is it not possible, therefore, that, in different parts of island, the landscape might have been used in different ways? There is little point yet in trying to draw upon smaller pieces of evidence which have been taken from across the whole of the island. Instead several specific regions have been selected. These are areas where there is sufficient evidence available to make some type of assessment as to how that landscape was used. The areas selected are:

1) The extreme north of the island from Inishowen to the Antrim coast and as far south as Belfast Lough and Lough Neagh
2) The northern end of Strangford Lough
3) North Leinster as far south as the Dublin area and inland to the upper reaches of the Shannon River tributaries

References will also be made other areas which may, in some instances, become relevant these are a) the Barrow/Burren rivers area, b) the Limerick/north Cork area c) the Loughs Gara and Allen area.

What do we know about the settlement patterns of the Earlier Mesolithic?

It will be apparent that the distribution of Earlier Mesolithic sites and, in particular, what we know of the choice of location, is different from the Later Mesolithic (see Chapter 8, Fig. 8.1 for the location of sites referred to below). In the case of the Lower Bann River system, most of the sites that significantly pre-date 9000 years ago, such as the Mount Sandel sites and Castleroe *DY1-4*, are placed on ridges overlooking the river. Again, what must have been a major site of similar age to Mount Sandel (Knowles 1889; Woodman 1978a, 279) at Springhill Portrush *AM13* even today lies on slightly higher ground overlooking the sea.

Elsewhere along the Lower Bann Valley, sites with the same range of artefacts are also found in similar locations. In spite of the fact that microliths were never high on the list of "Collectibles" a number of locations have produced a selection. These are often the larger forms, such as needlepoints or micro-awls (Chapter 5). Knowles and others found a number of microliths and cores, as well as flake and core axes in the Culbane area. McAllister (2008) has clearly shown, in his examination of a strip 20 m wide running back from the River Bann for 100 m, that the material from his most inland area (Zone 1) contained a range of material of Earlier Mesolithic date. This included microliths and a range of cores similar to those from Mount Sandel. In contrast, the riverside area (Zone 2) contained numbers of Later Mesolithic artefacts as well as Neolithic and Bronze Age diagnostic artefacts This pattern, can also be seen on areas of higher ground in the area of Portglenone Ford *DY5*, thanks to the work of MacErlean and others.

Similarly, a thin scatter of typical early material, i.e. microliths as well as two axes but few blades and cores, was recovered from an area of several hundred sq. m. during the Toome Bypass *AM10* excavations (see Chapter 4). This drumlin is set back from the shores of Lough Neagh but, during the earliest phases of the Irish Mesolithic, would have been placed well back from the shore.

The obvious question about the concentration of early material at locations that overlook the floodplain must be: if water levels in lakes and rivers were much lower, is it possible that numerous early sites lie buried at a greater depth in the valley floor, or were they washed away as the waters in lakes and rivers rose? The fact that dredging along the Bann regularly produced diagnostically early artefacts such as flake axes, cylindrical cores, and the occasional microlith (Batty 1938) is a clear indication there had been a presence along the edge of the early, contemporaneous river and lake shores. Similarly, the early artefacts washed-up on the shores of Lough Neagh, suggest that sites were occupied at a time when the level of the lake was much lower.

Elsewhere there is no evidence of Earlier Mesolithic material being dredged up from river floors and few traces of potentially early artefacts being recovered from lakes shores. One of the few exceptions is a small group of artefacts from the shores of Lough Allen (*LM1*) notably at Cormongon td (Driscoll 2006, 184). However the same pattern of earlier Mesolithic sites on ridges adjacent to rivers can still be noted. In north Leinster there are several sites in similar locations. The most significant must be in the Leixlip area (Cooldrinagh *D3*) where a small Early Mesolithic core axe was recovered at one location overlooking a key series of rapids on the River Liffey while, on the other side of the river, a series of blades likely to be of Earlier Mesolithic date was also recovered.

In the Limerick/north Cork area, Kilcummer *CK1* in Co. Cork (Woodman 1989; Anderson 1993) is situated on a limestone cliff overlooking the junction of the Awbeg with the River Blackwater. In Limerick the Hermitage *LK1* site is similarly located adjacent to a series of rapids on the River Shannon (Collins and Coyne 2003; 2006). Although it is a site that might be more ritualistic in character, the Killurragh Cave *LK2* assemblage is also on a limestone reef overlooking the Mulchair River (Woodman 1997). Ó Ríordáin (1948), during his excavations of a series of ring barrows at Rathjordan *LK3*, Co. Limerick, which lie close to the floodplain of the Camogue River, also uncovered an early microlithic assemblage that contained typical blades as well as microliths (Site III).

It might have been expected that, aside from sites at key points on major waterways and even allowing for absences from the uplands, there would have been scatters of find spots from across much of the rest of the inland landscape.

Surprisingly there is only a very thin scatter of occasional finds, usually microliths, even from across Co. Antrim. Interestingly, few small core axes or flake axes are found away from the main river valleys (Woodman *et al.* 2006, fig. 7:9). Few other Earlier Mesolithic assemblages are known, perhaps the most notable being the selection of microliths found during an excavation at Tullywiggan on the edge of the Sperrins (Woodman 1978a, 256–7) where 15 microliths and two retouched bladelets were recovered. Elsewhere, as discussed in Chapter 8, the finds usually consist of strays such as individual microliths, an occasional small conical core that looks as if it would fit into the Earlier Mesolithic, and small scatters of blades that may be of the same age. It is apparent from the discussions in Chapter 4 that there have been very few significant discoveries through development-led excavations. Thus the Earlier Mesolithic is extremely poorly represented!

There is one area which suggests that the absence of sites away from lakes and major rivers may be, in part, due to the absence of the field walkers. In the north Strangford Lough area, many of the Earlier Mesolithic sites are on islands near the northern end of the lough. Often they occur in mixed assemblages and, while the occasional axe has been found, most often it is a distinctive group of small blades and cores that identify this presence. In contrast, Peter Carr (1985; 1987) has discovered two significant inland sites some kilometres from the present Lough (Mount Alexander and Ballymaglaff tds) on ridges overlooking the floodplain of the small Enler River that runs from Dundonald down to Strangford Lough. Neither of the locations is at the sea or overlooking a major river or lake. Unlike many of the Antrim finds, which occur in similar locations and are little more than chance stray finds, these sites seem to have represented substantial occupation. These two sites would normally have evidence of blade production, distinctive cores, microliths and micro-awls, as well as a range of other tools including different types of axes. They show that there is an inland Earlier Mesolithic that waits to be discovered by local field walkers.

There remains the question of the extent to which the inland lake areas would have been used. It is of interest that, in the investigation of various midland bogs such as at Lisheen Mines (Gowen *et al.* 2005), Co. Tipperary, deposits of Early Holocene date were rarely reached, i.e. deposits contemporaneous with the earliest phases of the Irish Mesolithic.

So how much is buried below deposits of later Holocene date? The classic Earlier Mesolithic site of Lough Boora (Ryan 1980), which is of exceptional importance, points to the possibility of the existence of numerous buried sites. This was buried below extensive bogs on the shore of an early lake. In this instance, erosion to a significant depth by a later lake and peat milling lead to its discovery and we can suggest that numerous lakeside sites may lie buried below the midland peat bogs.

What about the sea?

The other obvious question must be whether there was a significant presence along the coasts of Ireland during the Earlier Mesolithic. Coastal sites from the earliest stages of the Mesolithic would often be buried, but do those that survive show a presence which suggests that the sea, as well as inland waterways, were an important resource? The newly discovered Earlier Mesolithic site on Inishtrahull, a small island that lies more than 10 km out from Malin Head, shows the capacity of these early settlers to use the sea and navigate in potentially hostile waters (Fig. 9.4).

There appears, at first sight, to be evidence of a substantial coastal presence during the Earlier Mesolithic. Flake and cores axes were recovered from beach deposits near Holywood *DN 1* on the southern shores of Belfast Lough. One core axe also washed up on the beach at Portstewart. However, the apparent coastal presence is slightly spurious. This is equally true of the island sites at the northern end of Strangford Lough. That these sites currently lie in a coastal context does not necessarily mean that they were placed adjacent to the then contemporaneous coast when occupied. Several of these sites lay in areas where the sea had yet to penetrate.

The most notable example can be seen at the northern end of Strangford Lough. Movius (1940b) recovered some Earlier Mesolithic material in raised beach deposits on Rough Island (Woodman 1978a, 291–3; Pl. XXVIIa). Rough Island, and the nearby Island Hill surface-collected site which also contained Earlier Mesolithic material, would have been small hills or

Fig. 9.4. View from Inishtrahull to the Irish mainland at Malin Head, Co. Donegal (photograph by Kieran Westley).

drumlins that overlooked the estuary of the Comber as it flowed into a coastal plain. O'Sullivan *et al*. (2002, 128) have shown that extensive areas of forest still existed at 9000 cal BP in parts of Strangford Lough and it is highly probable that the sea had not penetrated to the north-western corner of the lough.

One of the largest concentrations of Earlier Mesolithic material has been recovered from the shoreline and below sea level at Eleven Ballyboes *DL3* (Costa *et al*. 2001) in Donegal (Pl. XX). As in the case of Strangford Lough, this site on Inishowen probably overlooked the estuary of an extended River Foyle or lay within the floodplain of that river, rather than being on the shores of Lough Foyle (Pl. XXVIIb).

Although the assemblage from Glynn has all the appearance of being washed up from a nearby settlement site it is highly likely that this site was placed on the banks of a small river running down into a valley floor that pre-dated the incursion of the sea into Larne Lough (see Fig. 8.9). Based on dates obtained further north in Glengarriff (Roe and Swindles 2008, 108–11), during the first part of the Irish Mesolithic sea levels would have still been a few metres below present day and so it is possible that Larne Lough was still a low-lying river valley.

There are, however, other sites which may post-date the microlithic phase. As these do not currently contain clearly diagnostic retouched tools, they are mostly known to be early from their stratigraphic contexts. The most significant is the CF1 chipping floor which was buried under several metres of beach shingle at the Port of Larne and, as discussed in Chapter 8, seems to pre-date 9000 cal BP. Today Larne lies at the entrance between the open sea and a sea lough; in this case the site was placed on an island (Praeger's Island) that lay at the entrance to Larne Lough and may at least have overlooked an outer estuary of a river that ran close by, into the sea. Interestingly, on this island there is no substantial presence of the classic Earlier Mesolithic, with microliths and carefully prepared, soft hammer stone blade production.

The coastal sites therefore present a challenge. One has to admit that it is currently impossible to establish whether coastal areas were used as extensively as they were during the Later Mesolithic: is it just changing sea level has rendered it difficult to find evidence, or is there a lack of coastal exploitation at this period?

It is difficult to quantify the nature of the typical Earlier Mesolithic site, as quite often its presence is predicated on a limited number of blades or even an individual core. There are therefore very few Irish Earlier Mesolithic that fit within the "Comfort Zone" of expected European norms.

Settlement patterns in the Later Mesolithic

Perhaps the biggest difference between the Earlier and Later Mesolithic is that identified by Woodman and Anderson (1990); namely that it is difficult to identify Later Mesolithic settlement sites, particularly base camps, that might be expected to lie outside the low-lying river valley floors and lake edges.

The local distribution of sites in the Later Mesolithic differs in certain respects from the earlier period (Fig. 9.5). Rising sea levels and the accumulation of riverine and lacustrine deposits near, at, or above present day water levels, means that the discovery of Later Mesolithic sites, especially those of the final millennium of the Irish Mesolithic, becomes much easier (see Chapters 4 and 8). While nearly two millennia of intermittent settlement have been identified in Newferry (Woodman 1977a; and see above, Chapter 8), it is difficult to replicate a similar sequence elsewhere, though excavations on or near lake shores such as at Derragh Island *LD1* (Fredengren 2009) do show a similar intermittent presence from around, or just after, 7500 cal BP. Similarly, a series of sites belonging to the Later Mesolithic have been found right round the Irish coast. Those on the northern shores are obviously much more common, especially in the sea loughs from Lough Swilly through to Strangford Lough. However, sites of a similar age from Rockmarshall *LH1* (Mitchell 1947; 1949a) to Ferriter's Cove *KY2* (Woodman *et al.* 1999) in the south-west, to Belderrig *MO1* in Mayo (Warren 2009) show that, in spite of coastal erosion and late/"post-Mesolithic" rises in sea level, there is still some evidence of a coastal presence. The ongoing work by the Lynchs at Fanore More in Co. Clare is also showing that Later Mesolithic sites can survive in coastal locations even when they lie in the most unlikely, at risk, environments.

The nature of the archaeological record of the Irish Later Mesolithic has already been discussed in detail in Chapters 4 and 5, but it is worth emphasising certain aspects before looking at the settlement evidence.

There is a remarkable scatter of sites belonging to the Later Mesolithic where 1–5 objects have been recovered. In fact, throughout much of Ireland, the Later Mesolithic is signalled by individual finds. There are many locations where later artefacts were recovered but these are often single finds that could be axes, picks, Moynagh Points, or just chipping floors, but the most common diagnostic tools are the Later Mesolithic forms. It is noticeable that the finds occurring on the NRA excavations often consist of little more than individual items.

In total, throughout Ireland, there are nearly 250 sites where excavation has produced some evidence of a Later Mesolithic (see Chapter 4). Many lack diagnostic tools in the range of Later Mesolithic forms, and consist of small numbers of blades or cores or even individual Moynagh Points, while, in other cases, the site is marked by a number of ground stone axes. Others are from beach deposits and in some instances they are small chipping floors. Only 49 have produced Later Mesolithic forms. There are some sites with large numbers of artefacts which could be described as persistent places. These

have been referred to quite frequently, most notably Newferry 3 (Woodman 1977a), or some of the Midland sites. There are also a number of sites such as Bay Farm where blade production seems to be the dominant element (Woodman and Johnston 1996). Besides the excavations there are, at least five locations along the Lower Bann where retouched tools and blanks can be numbered in the thousands.

This, however, is only one side of the equation. The manner in which these most obvious tools are distributed across the countryside is illustrated in Table 9.1. This pattern is replicated by surface and chance finds.

We can also add the fact that some of the key sites mentioned come from mixed multi-period assemblages in both excavation and surface collections from both fields and lake shores. For this reason some very simplistic, but hopefully robust, choices of potentially diagnostic artefacts had to be made.

Irrespective of find circumstances, and even making allowances for a less than 100% awareness of the potential presence of these artefacts, there is a pattern here. Many excavated sites are not associated with evidence of on-site manufacture of stone tools. At the very least, one can suggest that these artefacts were not created and used in an expedient manner and then discarded. Rather, when created, they were used, retained and often used again repeatedly. The term curated has often been associated with this type of use (Binford 1977).

Back to the north-east

This curation of artefacts is most apparent in and around the Bann Valley, the area to its east and the east Antrim coast, where Woodman and Anderson (1990) noted the absence of recognisable and substantial Later Mesolithic settlement sites in the Bann Valley. It would seem apparent from both the excavations at Newferry Sites 1 (Movius 1936) and Site 3 (Woodman 1977a) that many of these and other sites are not so much locations for significant periods of habitation but rather places which were returned to intermittently and over long periods of time which may be termed "persistent places". There is a sense that the large number of artefacts represents an accumulation with a few pieces being left on each visit. It can be suggested that this pattern could be extended to other localities in this region. While no excavations have taken place in the Culbane area *DY6*, the impression perhaps tens

Table 9.1. Excavations and the other find spots producing Later Mesolithic forms.

Later Mesolithic forms (numbers found per site)	25+	6–25	2–5	1
Number of excavations	6	9	10	24
Surface/stray, etc. (number of sites)	3	12	42	178
Total	9	21	52	202

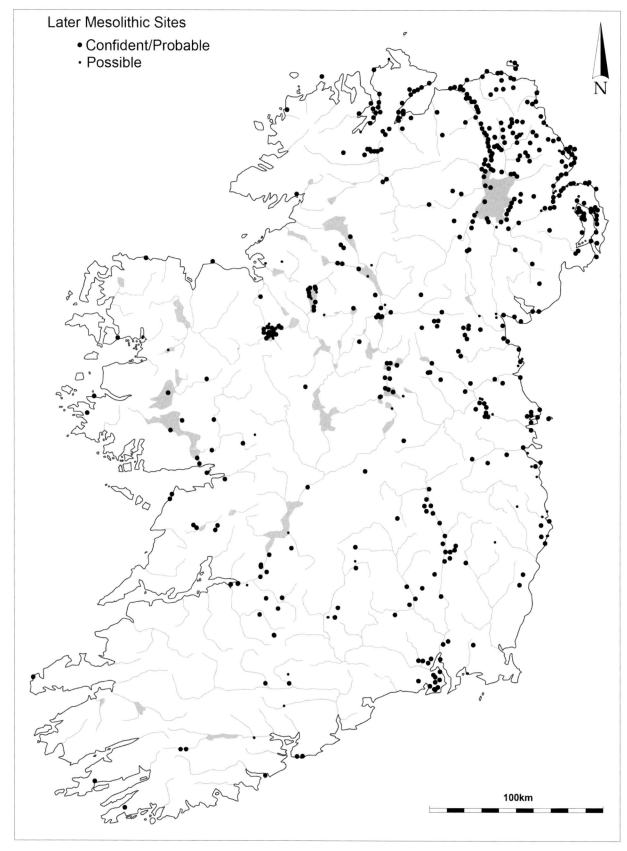

Fig. 9.5. Later Mesolithic sites in Ireland (prepared by Hugh Kavanagh).

of thousands of Later Mesolithic artefacts in the collections (Woodman *et al*. 2006, 281–6, 299–301, 327–8), that the same process had taken place. Here artefacts included large numbers of Butt Trimmed and related forms, large blanks, axes, picks and borers, grind stones as well as range of other stone tools described in Chapter 5.

What is also often not recognised is that these large quantities of artefacts, perhaps as many as 10,000 items, are found only at a limited number of very specific find spots and that very few artefacts were recovered from within much of the very extensive diatomite and other quaternary deposits.

The largest concentrations of artefacts are found at either narrow crossing points or at the locations of fish weirs. See Figure 5.44 for the position of these locations referred to below. These include accumulations at Toome Bar at the exit of the Lower Bann into lough Neagh. It is possible that as many artefacts were also recovered during various dredging operations at Portglenone where much of the material would have been dredged up early in the 19th century, before there was such an extensive tradition of collection. The vicinity of Portglenone Bridge would have been a focus of activity. As noted (Woodman 1978a, 236–9), the same pattern exists in the Kilrea area, where, thanks in particular to the Gracey collection, it is apparent that large quantities of material were found at locations north and south of Kilrea, i.e. at Portna and Movanagher, with much lesser quantities being found in between.

Newferry is slightly enigmatic as it has produced large numbers of artefacts (though not quite in the same numbers as the three locations mentioned above) but the material seems to have lain on ridges in the middle of the floodplain.

Two other observations seem to support this idea that the valley floor sites were "persistent places" rather than habitation sites. First, there is little evidence throughout most of the Newferry 3 sequence, especially above Zone 7 (just after 8000 cal BP), that production of stone artefacts was taking place at that location. This is also evident at the Movius excavation at Newferry Site 1. At these sites, as well as other locations mentioned above, cores and other knapping by-products typical of the Later Mesolithic are virtually absent. There is thus a lack of evidence that extensive flint knapping took place in the Bann Valley during the Later Mesolithic. Secondly, as has been discussed in Chapter 5, there is also a significant concentration of caches of Later Mesolithic artefacts in the same region and it may be that many of the artefacts found in the valley may have been cached, but later disturbed by the winter floods.

A final dimension to the settlement patterns of the Mesolithic of the "North East" is, as noted on numerous occasions (Woodman and Anderson 1990), the apparent production of "blanks" at a series of coastal locations, for example, Bay Farm *(AM 14)* (Woodman and Johnston 1996) or at the Curran Point at Larne. At these locations there is no evidence of the production of axes or other core implements though there are relatively large numbers known (see Chapter 5). This is

a point that will be returned to in the context of the regional distribution of Later Mesolithic find spots in the north-east.

These blanks seem to have been transported for use to other locations across the north-east of Ireland, the most notable being those in the Bann Valley (Woodman and Anderson 1990). Therefore, in many instances settlement sites would be difficult to identify.

The differing ratio between retouched tools, blanks and various forms of industrial by-products is best illustrated in a comparison between Newferry and Bay Farm (Fig. 9.6a) (Woodman and Anderson 1990, fig. 6, 383). Griffiths and Woodman (1987) have also suggested that the Electron Spin Resonance (ESR) analysis of flint artefacts from the Bann Valley, which produced a broad range of signatures, indicated that the raw material was derived from a range of different layers containing flint. This suggested that these blanks were brought into the valley from the east Antrim coast where the beaches contain flint nodules (Pl. XXVIIIa) that derive from an extensive series of flint layers in the adjacent cliff face. In contrast, flint from the west of the Lower Bann tends to come from a narrow series of layers containing flints (see Chapter 2).

Many other activities besides those associated with catching fish may have taken place but, given their location, often in the centre of the valley, it is unlikely that a broad year-round set of activities would have occurred. Though there seems to have been a broad range of implements in use or kept at these sites (see Chapter 5). This does not make them into the archetypal base camp but they do seem important as key locations where many of the lithic artefacts were perhaps left virtually ready for use.

The Toome Bypass site *AM10* (see Chapter 4), where much of the prehistoric activity took place on one large drumlin which was adjacent to and overlooked the rising waters of Lough Neagh, might have been expected to be a major focus of settlement. However, the density of Later Mesolithic artefacts, when spread over an area of 17,000 sq. m., would not, of itself, have indicated such large scale and perhaps intensive settlement. Here, with one exception, there are small scatters of Later Mesolithic forms close to scatters of stake-holes and post-holes There is one large concentration at Feature 5 which, as discussed earlier (see Chapter 4), is both a very enigmatic and substantial structure. There is little clear evidence of tool manufacturing or other forms of maintenance activities that would be expected to be found on many Later Mesolithic campsites. Again, the range of tool types is the same as at the Valley floor locations. If this is a major area of settlement, where perhaps a seasonal series of tasks was carried out, then perhaps we can suggest that settlement sites of the Later Mesolithic will not always be shown in the presence of quantities of artefacts which would have included the manufacture of a range of stone tools.

Therefore, in parts of the north-east of Ireland, much of the archaeological record left behind seems to have consisted of caching; the deposition or loss of a range of usable stone tools. This took place during visits to what could be described as "persistent places".

What is also noticeable is that while large blades/blanks and various types of Butt Trimmed Forms are thinly scattered across the certain landscapes such as mid-Antrim, picks, core-borers and even Bar Forms and notched pieces are only found in the valley floors and in lake and sea-side locations. One has to return to the inconclusive discussion on the purpose of the Later Mesolithic forms and "blanks". It would help if there was a sense of how and why they were used but one does not get the feeling that there was intensive use of the environment away from the valley floors. This is an issue that will be returned to later in this Chapter.

The Later Mesolithic in this part of the north-east seems to be based on a separation between artefact production in some places, and a more intensive use of the valley floors, to where imported blanks and other implements such as axes were brought on numerous repeated and persistent visits (see below). In between is a scatter of stray finds rather than sites. However this may not be valid even for the whole of the north-east.

In trying to establish how different parts of the landscape were used, it might be thought that the simplest way is to look at the different types of tools found at different locations and use them to establish the different activities that took place. There are problems with this approach, however, because tools found in curated assemblages are not made, used and conveniently abandoned all at the same location. In other words we should recognise that artefacts made from scarce raw materials or those that require skill and or a lengthy time to make are likely to have been brought to a particular location, used and unless they have a very specialised function are then taken away when the group or band move on.

The effect of strategies associated with curation are perhaps masked by the very large quantities of later Mesolithic artefacts recovered from particular locations in the Lower Bann. However, in the Maine Valley which lies to the east, the impact at sites like Drumakeely is more obvious. Here, while the site was probably visited on a number of occasions and evidence of at least one structure was uncovered (see Chapter 4) fewer than 15 later Mesolithic forms and large blades or blanks were recovered (Woodman, unpublished report submitted to NAC). Where there is a strategy of curation, i.e. when so much is not only brought to the site but is also taken away, it is very difficult to assess what artefacts might have been present or what activities may have taken place during visits to this location.

There are, of course, some obvious differences between certain sites. For example, through the activities of Willie Stuart of Carnlough, I was attracted to work at nearby Bay Farm where, besides the probable presence of chipping floors, we felt we should attempt to find traces of dwelling sites. At Bay Farm these would probably be set behind both the then shoreline and the chipping floors. Our work produced evidence of actual settlement at other later periods but, in spite of explorations behind and up slope, no clear evidence of Mesolithic dwelling activity was ever found. Were the visits to this particular part of the Antrim coast simply as part of an embedded procurement strategy but one where procurement of raw materials was important? There are other known traces of chipping floors along this coast. This pattern was also evident at NAC's excavations nearby in Carnlough Village Plate.

However, to the north of Bay Farm, near Cushendun, which lies 10 km north of the limit of the Ulster White Limestone (UWL) cliffs that contain flint, a very substantial assemblage was recovered by Declan Hurl during excavations at the medieval tower house of Castlecarra *AM5* (Pl. XXVIIId). Although this is based only on an initial examination of possibly more than 1000 pieces it is remarkably different from the Bay Farm assemblage. Given the fact that it lay under the castle and may have been subject to intermittent exposure and disturbance, it is by and large in a relatively fresh condition and has produced up to 200 blades, many of which are complete. Yet, although there were a large number of small flakes (less than 20 mm across) there were only three cores with a small number of primary cortical flakes. In contrast 12 later Mesolithic forms were identified as well as a small number of other retouched tools. It does not look like material from a knapping floor.

It need not necessarily be that these were all left behind at one time. In effect, for each core there were four Later Mesolithic forms (see below). One of the two most striking aspects of the assemblage is that the blades recovered gave the impression of being those that were to be used rather than the less regular ones from the chipping floor at Bay Farm. However, to the naked eye, quite a number seem to show signs of runs of edge damage and small notches which are so regular that they suggest these implements have been used. The pattern based on the ratios of cores and by-products to blades and retouched tools is more like the Lower Bann but the amount of edge damage is more reminiscent of the Lough Beg cache from near Creagh td and on the shores of Lough Beg *DY8*. In other words these blades were probably used for a different purpose from those recovered from Newferry or Culbane.

To the south of Bay Farm, at the entrance to Larne Lough, it is apparent that the strategy of production at one location and use elsewhere was not quite the same. Chipping floors, which seem again to have been focussed on large blade production, are known from the Curran Point Raised Beach shingles *AM1*. In spite of the attention given to the Curran Point there are relatively few flint core axes from that specific location as well as an absence of axe manufacturing flakes. Most of the nearly 100 core tools come from Larne Lough in general and the majority of them, where there is any documentation, refer to Island Magee. These seem to have been made somewhere else in the vicinity.

Only 1 km away, on the southern side of Larne Lough, there is a different solution. At Ballydown *AM2* (Moore 1999) which lies on Island Magee (see Chapter 4) and under the Neolithic settlement, the excavator uncovered a range of Mesolithic activity areas. It provides a further interesting contrast with Bay Farm which seems to have had such a narrow purpose (Fig. 9.6b). Taking a simple comparison of cores against diagnostic

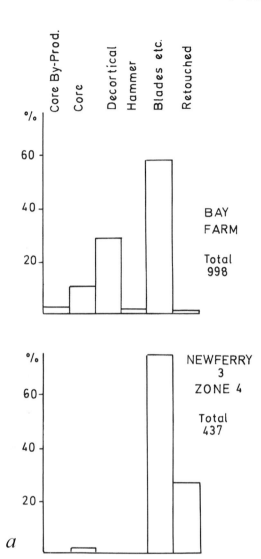

artefact types there is a significant difference between these two sites. At Bay Farm (Fig 9.6a), the site was clearly made up of discarded by-products and blanks with limited numbers of retouched tools or traces of settlement. In the case of Ballydown, although it was not always possible to disaggregate the numbers of artefacts associated with different phases, it could be suggested that approximately 200 cores were associated with the Mesolithic levels. There are some indications that, at Ballydown, the diagnostic retouched tools were somewhat more common and, though not listed here, there was a greater range of other artefact types, including ground stone axes, polissoirs and elongated bevel ended pebbles (see above Chapter 4).

In spite of the profusion of cores and the manufacturing by-products, there seems to have been a higher ratio of retouched tools at Ballydown (Fig. 9.6b). This, and the greater structural evidence, suggests that, even in a relatively small area, sites in coastal regions were being used in different ways. One area on the open coast may have been used on short visits whose primary, though not sole, purpose was to exploit coastal flint resources that lay in the storm beach shingles, while in other coastal areas, such as the sea loughs (in this case in Larne Lough where Knowles collected upwards of 100 large core axes, picks and core borers), slightly different strategies may have been adopted. Even today significant quantities of this latter type of material can be collected from the shores of Island Magee at locations such as Mill Bay.

Therefore, although the east Antrim coast from Larne to Cushendun is often regarded as the springboard for the study of the Irish Mesolithic, on the basis of the previous discussion it could be argued that the north-eastern pattern, i.e. east Coast to Lower Bann, though well-documented, maybe be slightly atypical.

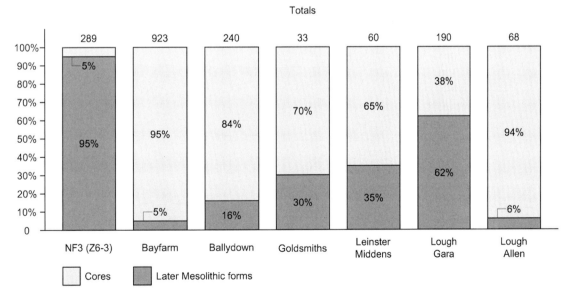

Fig. 9.6. a) Occurrence of different implement types at Bay Farm and Newferry Site 3, Zone 4, b) ratio of cores to retouched stone tools from selected sites (prepared by Hugh Kavanagh).

Perhaps coastal settlement in the very open east coast was partly in areas where marine resources were limited, only seasonally present or needed a particular technology. Perhaps long stay visits were not appropriate? Today, on the land side, the east Antrim coast has a very narrow coastal zone where steep cliffs often reach the sea and where the Antrim Plateau rises quickly to nearly 300 m AMSL (Fig. 9.7). The Antrim glens, with the exception of Glenarriff, by and large create relatively narrow bays. In many areas, the actual intertidal shoreline is usually quite narrow. It is also possible that small rivers such as the Glencloy at Bay Farm had, during earlier times with more forested environments, a smaller water discharge and may therefore not have retained the same fish

populations as that which attracts game fisher men today. It is also remarkable that the Antrim coast has not produced a single shell midden of Mesolithic date, indeed there are no records of shell middens of any date between Larne and Cushendun. One has the sense that, on the land side, "the only way out was up"! But for groups who wished to make extensive use of the Lower Bann, this coastal area provided an unlimited supply of good flint (Pl. XXVIII).

Similarly, sites located in and at the entrance to Larne Lough may have been in an area which offered a broader range of resources and therefore longer periods of settlement may have taken place along the shore. Indeed it may be that the chipping floors found in the raised storm beach shingles of the

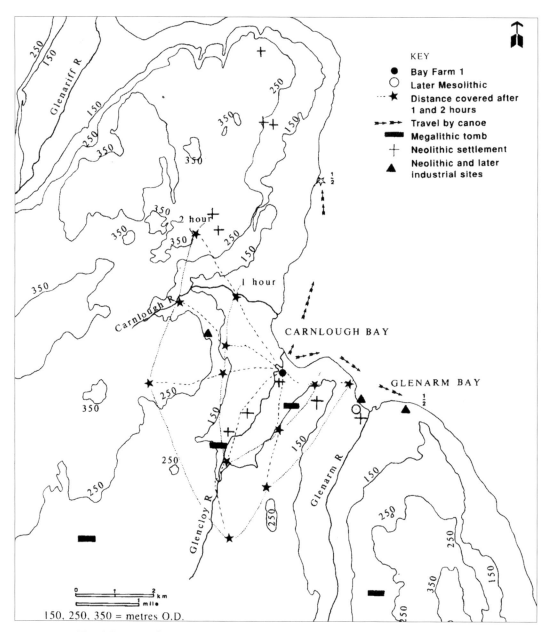

Fig. 9.7. Map of Bay Farm, Glencloy area (after Woodman and Johnston 1996).

Curran Point were the debris left behind by groups from within Larne Lough that were seeking the better quality flint that had selectively survived in the extensive storm beach shingles of what we know today as the Curran Point.

One can also return to Castlecarra. At this stage it is difficult to see how this site fits into a regional picture. Was it part of a coastal movement along the north coast that would have included visits to places such as Bushfoot or Portrush? Certainly even from what has survived of the assemblage recovered at the Bushfoot (Chapter 4) it seems more like Castlecarra than either the Bann Valley assemblages or the so-called industrial sites on the Curran Point or at Bay Farm. It appears that even this small north-eastern area may have seen different strategies in different localities and it was not all simply a question of coast to Lower Bann movements and vice versa.

In one sense the pattern in the Inishowen/Lough Swilly area and, in particular, on Inch Island, is quite similar to that in mid-Antrim. The Dunaff assemblage *DL2*, which appears to be a series of later Mesolithic chipping floors (Addyman and Vernon 1966) lies on the northern edge of the peninsula. This was the first Mesolithic site of significance to be discovered in this part of Donegal. Since then numerous other groups of Later Mesolithic artefacts have been recorded from round the coast of the Inishowen Peninsula. Along the western shores of Lough Foyle, although there is some coastal erosion, numerous groups of Later Mesolithic artefacts have been recorded, especially by local collectors such as McNaught and Gallagher. The largest concentration was recovered at Red Castle *DL7* and, although quantities were found across a large field, much of the material came from a corner of the field adjacent to the coast and a small river. This location produced large numbers of cores, rejuvenation and cortical flakes. However, due to the development of the Magillan sand dunes which cover several square kilometres along the eastern shore of Lough Foyle, little has been found on the eastern side of the Lough. Lough Swilly and the area round Inch Island have produced a number of sites of Later Mesolithic date (see Chapter 4). These, however, are mostly shell middens, but at Baylet on Inch Island *DL5*, in particular, especially during surface collections, large numbers of Later Mesolithic blades, were picked up while there was little evidence of on-site manufacturing. Again this is the difference between locations where flint was available and, perhaps, areas where other resources could be obtained. In general in this area, in spite of extensive field walking by Mc Naught and Kelleher, no artefacts of Mesolithic date have been found away from the coast.

It could be argued that a similar pattern of small scatters of individual artefacts exists at the southern end of the peninsula. Smaller assemblages were found further south, such as at Ballintaggart and Culmore *DY10*, where Lough Foyle narrows into a river estuary. Interestingly, even further south, near Raphoe *DL11* where a very large Neolithic assemblage was recovered from several townlands (Flanagan 1968), Lowry recovered, in total, four Butt Trimmed Forms but no other

evidence of a Later Mesolithic presence. In this case one has to ask whether these artefacts were made from flint procured on the north coast or from flint bands in the UWL that lie on the western slopes on the Sperrins Mountains.

In contrast further south in Strangford Lough, a pattern with some differences seems to emerge. Very significant numbers of Later Mesolithic artefacts has been recovered from this area. Admittedly, this is based primarily on Kirk's surface-collected material and, to a lesser extent, on the Reagan collection. Numerous shell middens have been recorded from this area though many of them may post-date the Mesolithic (Chapter 4). However, if the area was expanded to include a hinterland that contained the Castlereagh Hills to the north and the edge of the drumlin belt to the east, Carr's discovery of Earlier Mesolithic material to the north of Strangford highlights the fact that no scatters of Later Mesolithic artefacts have ever been recovered from higher ground. Thus while, in the Earlier Mesolithic, significant and substantial concentrations of artefacts can be found away from the floodplains on slightly higher ground, there are virtually no traces of concentrations of stone tools of Later Mesolithic date in similar localities.

Again the absence of Later Mesolithic finds from the drumlin belt immediately to the west emphasis the fact that once one moves away from substantial areas of water, whether the sea shore, larger lakes or rivers there are few finds of Later Mesolithic date anywhere in the drumlin belt.

In this area there are numerous locations around the northern end of the Lough where Kirk recovered large quantities of Mesolithic and later material. These include concentrations *DN 4–7* within the vicinity of Island Hill and out onto Rough Island, as well as the Ringneill area and the adjacent Island Reagh, while on the eastern shores a concentration of sites in Ballyuranallen td was named after the home of a local Clergyman (i.e. Goldsmiths: Fig. 9.6b).

The *chaine operatoire* for the manufacture of stone tools tells a story that has more in common with Ballydown rather than sites such as Bay Farm or Red Castle. The Goldsmiths site has been chosen from the Strangford assemblages of Kirk because, in the context of surface collection, there is less evidence of an extensive later presence at that particular place. Further examples from across Ireland are included. These include the Leinster middens i.e. the Rockmarshall middens *LH1*, (Mitchell 1947; 1949a), Sutton midden (Mitchell 1956a; 1972a) and Dalkey Island (Liversage 1968) as well as the assemblages from Loughs Gara and Allen.

The lithics from these sites seem to have a similar character to that noted at Ballydown and can be also be compared to several other coast localities. These suggest that procurement, production and use of stone tools all happened at the same location. It would seem likely that, in the Strangford Lough area, rather than moving across the landscape and acquiring essential raw materials from some considerable distance, many annual activities were carried out in the Strangford/ Ards Peninsula area.

Admittedly these locations in Strangford Lough are only surface collections, but surely the absence of the larger core tools such as picks and the core axes that are typical of the Later Mesolithic must be of some significance. Also, within the Kirk Collection in the National Museums of Northern Ireland (NMNI), which must contain approaching 10,000 artefacts only one ground stone axe is known. Even taking the Ulster Museum's portion of the Kirk collection, it is possible to document nearly 50 Later Mesolithic forms. Indeed, if the very extensive Kirk collection in the National Museum of Ireland (NMI) is taken into consideration, then there are *c.* 250 polished or ground stone axes in the collection. While these include 110 from the adjacent parts of north Down round Kirk's home town of Newtownards at the northern end of Strangford Lough, only four (three from Castle Espie and one from Mahee) came from the shoreline areas where he personally collected extremely large numbers of Later Mesolithic artefacts. Therefore, as there are 100+ Later Mesolithic forms in Kirk's MNI collection, there seems to be very little evidence that ground stone axes played an important role in the Later Mesolithic of the Strangford Lough area. Indeed it is also possible that some of this very small number of axes could belong to the Neolithic period as there is some evidence of a presence of later prehistoric activity in the area. This is a remarkably different ratio from all other regional collections or excavations (Fig. 9.8).

In other words, the strategy apparent between sites such as Bay Farm and those in the Bann Valley floor is only one which may have been used in the Irish Later Mesolithic and indeed, as noted in Chapter 8, that strategy may have only developed in the latter part of the Later Mesolithic.

What was happening in North Leinster?

In general, coastal erosion has probably destroyed large numbers of Mesolithic sites that had existed along the east coast of Ireland. This phenomenon extends from the entrance to Belfast Lough in Co. Down to the most southerly tip of Co. Wexford Coast (see Chapter 4). Later Mesolithic sites exist and are best known from the three excavated sites of Rockmarshall, *LH1* (Mitchell 1948, 49) Sutton *D4* (Mitchell 1956; 1972) and Dalkey Island *D2* (Liversage 1968). Stacpoole found some scatters of artefacts along the north Dublin coast and, as is clear from one very large assemblage recovered in field walking in the Skerries area north of Dublin, it is probable that other major concentrations exist in other bays in the general area. However, the evidence is still relatively sparse in spite of the valiant effort of various collectors such as Hodgers, with some finds from the Dundalk Bay and, to a lesser extent, Stacpoole in north Dublin or some finds made by Frank Mitchell on the south Leinster coast (see Fig. 9.5).

Inland, outside the north-east, it might have been expected that there would have been a similar pattern of extensive discoveries along the rivers. As will be seen, throughout much of the rest of Ireland there is, in many areas, surprisingly little evidence of a riverine Later Mesolithic. It could be argued that the absence of commercial exploitation of quaternary deposits in the floors of many valleys, as happened in the River Bann, has reduced the chance of discovering a significant Later Mesolithic presence at key points along many rivers that may well have had extensive migratory fish populations. There are also several major rivers where dredging and drainage has not taken place.

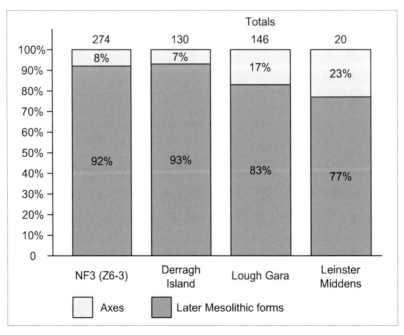

Fig. 9.8. Percentage ratio of Butt Trimmed and related forms to ground stone axes from Newferry Site 3 Zones 6–3, Derragh Island, Leinster Middens and Lough Gara (prepared by Hugh Kavanagh).

Even where drainage has taken place, in general, few distinctive Mesolithic artefacts have been recovered. The most surprising example is the absence of Mesolithic settlement sites or concentrations of artefacts along the River Shannon. Since the 1840s artefacts have been dredged up from the Shannon and the presence of stone axes at key points along the river has been documented as far back as the Wilde's Catalogue of the Museum of the Royal Irish Academy (1857). One must presume, therefore, that the absences of Mesolithic and other materials from other rivers is more a product of the lack of awareness or priority in the recovery of stone age artefacts. Yet,there is a known prehistoric presence in some rivers: i.e. the "polished stone axes". In the context of the large numbers of polished stone axes that occur on known Mesolithic sites, for example 40 from Newferry (Woodman 1977a) and 15 from Ferriter's Cove (Woodman *et al.* 1999) we ignore at our peril the large numbers of axes dredged from many locations within the Shannon catchment, from Cavan to Killaloe *CE2*, as well as possibly smaller groups from places such as Lough Allua *CK6* in west Cork (Mahr 1937). Why should axes from an area such as the Lower Bann include many of presumed Mesolithic date while the same probability is not considered for locations elsewhere?

In recent years the Armagh/Tyrone Blackwater, where axes and related implements had turned up, has produced some Mesolithic material as a result of careful monitoring (Bourke, L. 2001).

In spite of these curious "riverine" absences there is a significant Later Mesolithic presence across the north Midlands. While these tend to concentrate at points where someone took an interest, the evidence for a Later Mesolithic presence has been supplemented closer to the east coast by finds along various motorways.

Good examples were discovered at Clonava, *WH1* and there are also extensive traces of industrial activity at the exit to Lough Derravaragh. These were first found by Frank Mitchell and have recently been discussed by Little (2014, 36–40). Are these typical locations or are the remainder of the sites buried in other types of locations below extensive bogs? Although the quantities are smaller there is also the interesting group of material recovered from dredging along the Inny River, between Loughs Sheelin and Kinale (Little 2010). In this case, as so often, it was through the work of an interested amateur that this material was brought to light.

A contrast in settlement location is provided by the evidence of the long-term investment in sites in a form that suggests lengthy periods of use rather than the remarkable presence of individual Later Mesolithic artefacts scattered across the landscape. The former are the creation of artificial platforms, described in Chapter 5, at both Derragh Island, Lough Kinale *LD1* (Fredengren 2009) and at Moynagh Lough *MH5* (Bradley 1999), with the possibility, as suggested by Fredengren, that numerous small crannógs in Lough Gara may also have their origins in the Later Mesolithic (see Chapter 4). As Fredengren

(2009, 885) noted, they remain a mystery as few traces of fishing activities have been found during excavations at either of the two sites (see below Chapter 10).

Between the inland lakes and what remains of the coastal region that would have existed in the Later Mesolithic, the product of the excavations along the M2 and M3, which run across the north Leinster plain, is beginning to show a linear pattern (see Chapter 4, Figures 4:8 and 9). Besides the scatter of stray finds recovered by chance across this area (Woodman 1978a, 306–26), numerous examples of what appear to be smaller groups of artefacts have been found during excavations. There are also occasional larger sites. These excavations include those such as Clowanstown *MH2*. However here, even allowing for two phases of use (i.e. the platform (context 204) and the earlier fish baskets and associated posts) many of these sites would be regarded as tiny assemblages in comparison with those found elsewhere.

It appears, therefore that there was both a significant presence in this instance on the lakes in particular and occasionally on some of the tributaries of Shannon. This would have been matched by a, now mostly missing, coastal presence (Fig. 9.5).

It has already been pointed out, in the context of the Lower Bann Mesolithic, that activity known from the archaeological record tends to be confined to very specific locations. Therefore, just because there is a substantial river does not mean that its banks will be littered with the traces of Mesolithic habitation. The NRA excavations along the N25 where it crossed the Kilkenny Blackwater River provide an example. At Newrath 34 *KK1* extensive deep excavations produced a small but interesting selection of Later Mesolithic artefacts (Woodman 2011, 201–3). Right out in the floodplain, unless there are fish weirs, the Mesolithic presence will be limited. Yet in this case the most interesting absence is that of a significant Mesolithic presence on either the east or west bank of the river in an area where excavations have shown a significant presence in the Neolithic and Early Bronze Age.

Finally, a curious contrast of two areas

The curious way in which apparent settlement patterns are created is perhaps best illustrated by comparing the north-west loughs i.e. Loughs Gara *SO1/RO1* and Allen, with Limerick/ north Cork (Figs 9.9 and 9.10). They are not, however, "Curiosities" as they provide, in their own way, insights into how the patterns of Mesolithic material in Ireland are often a product of geography and/or the activities of collectors, both amateur and professional.

The former area is one of large loughs set in areas where there are extensive bogs which grew and extended in the periods after the Later Mesolithic, and where permanent grassland is the norm where farming occurs. Here the sites have, once again, been discovered in abundance during times when the lough levels have been lowered, either by nature or by people. After the three north-eastern counties of Derry, Antrim and Down,

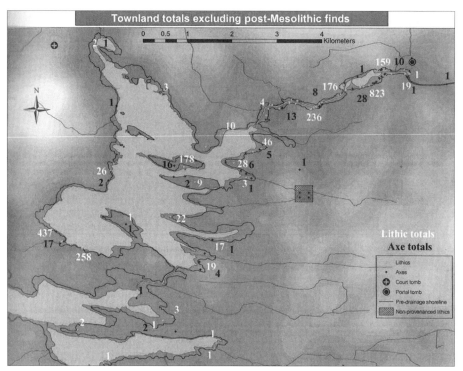

Fig. 9.9. Location of sites identified on the Boyle River/Lough Gara (after Driscoll 2006).

where more than 300 groups of material are known, the three counties of Roscommon, Sligo and Leitrim have produced close to two hundred groups of material (although the lakes have also produced material from later periods and it depends on how one classifies a site when dealing with scatters on a lough shore). This is the second largest concentration of Mesolithic material in Ireland and is the product of only four collectors. In the case of Lough Allen, Driscoll (2006; 2009; Driscoll *et al.* 2014) collected the material while, at Lough Gara, material had been recovered by a number of individuals, including Cross, Raftery, and Mitchell.

Although one often refers to Lough Gara as one complex of sites, there is in this one area along the Boyle River, where it exits from Lough Gara, the largest concentration of Later Mesolithic artefacts to be found in Ireland, aside from the assemblages on the Lower Bann. Indeed more than 1500 artefacts have been recovered along a 4 km length of the shores of the River Boyle just above the point where it flowed into Lough Gara itself (Fig. 9.9).

There are some differences between the concentrations of material on the Lower Bann and the Boyle rivers. As was noted earlier, on the Lower Bann much of the Later Mesolithic material was concentrated at eight particular points along a 50 km stretch. While platforms of Mesolithic date have occasionally been identified in north Leinster, it is highly probable that some of the Crannogs listed along the Boyle River could be similar phenomena and find their origins in the Later Mesolithic. Nothing as substantial as a platform or small crannog has been noted on the Lower Bann.

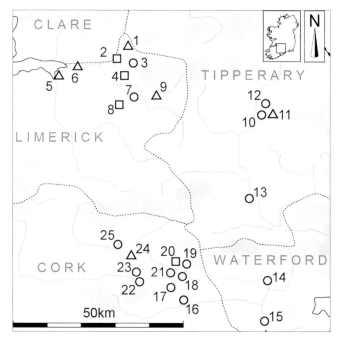

Fig. 9.10. Mesolithic sites in the Limerick and north Cork area. Circles represent Earlier Mesolithic presence, triangles = Later Mesolithic presences, squares = the presence of Earlier and Later Mesolithic material: 1) Annaholty, 2) Hermitage, 3) Annagh Cave, 4) Killuragh Cave, 5) Carrigdirty, 6) Meelick Rock, 7) Rathjordan, 8) Lough Gur, 9) Coologue, 10) Windmill Hill, 11) Owens and Biggs, 12) Monadreela, 13) Ballybrado, 14) Lefanta, 15 Newport, 16)Ballyarra, 17) Ballyoran, 18) Rathhealy, 19) Ballyderown, 20) Gortore, 21) Castlehyde, 22) Castleblagh, 23) Kilcummer, 24) Foley Cave, 25) Ballynamona.

In the context of the Lough Gara area, Cross (1953) makes one interesting observation which seems to imply the possibility that caching of blades and Butt Trimmed Forms was also taking place along the Boyle. He noted (*ibid.*, 93) that: "'Bann Flakes' found in the vicinity were often located as small heaps of varying sizes of flakes". On-site knapping and blade production does not seem to have been particularly common at Lough Gara (see below) and these heaps seem unlikely to be heaps of discarded knapping debris. Could at least some of these heaps be caches of blades and other Later Mesolithic artefacts?

In terms of their lithic assemblages Loughs Gara and Allen are also, in some ways, surprisingly different. In both instances chert seems to be the dominant raw material but with other raw materials ranging from flint, siltstone, and mudstone to Rhyolite and tuff (Driscoll 2006, 224–5).

Leaving aside sporadic and expediently chipped pieces and the fact that Driscoll felt that cores may not have always been recognised by collectors (*ibid.*, 222–3), it is still possible to create, a rough ratio between Later Mesolithic forms and cores and compare the two lakes (see Fig. 9.6b). At Lough Allen the ratio of cores to Later Mesolithic forms is 62:4, while at Lough Gara, Bridgeman (1998, 61) estimated that, in a sample of 1118 pieces of chert and presumably chert-like materials, there were 121 Butt Trimmed Forms as against 69 chert chunks and cores! Thus, there is a variation between Lough Gara, where there seems to have been a high percentage of Later Mesolithic Forms and blanks which were brought to the lake shores, and Lough Allen, where there are indications that artefacts were produced in a different manner. There is no doubt that the Lough Gara area and, in particular, the Boyle River has many similarities with the Lower Bann.

In contrast, the distribution of known sites in Munster is very different. This would already be apparent from the overall distribution maps for the Irish Mesolithic (Plate XII) as there are a relatively limited number of sites and find locations in the Province of Munster, from what would have been expected to be a relatively rich area to the south of the River Shannon. In fact, at a Provincial level, while Ulster has produced nearly 50% of the sites, Leinster and Connaught have each, in very different ways, produced just over 20% of the known find spots. Munster has produced fewer than ten. A closer examination of one portion of the Province shows that this is not simply a question of paucity of finds. The distribution of Mesolithic sites in one area of Counties Limerick/north Cork is apparent. This area is bounded by two of the major rivers in the country (the Shannon and the Cork Blackwater) but lacks any really large loughs. While there are significant areas of pasture there is also, in places, an important role for arable farming. Again, as in the rest of Ireland, there is a virtual absence of upland locations for the Mesolithic of this area. Sites tend to be found close to rivers but mostly on ridges adjacent to the river flood plains. Chance finds are rare, as most of the discoveries come from excavations or field walking. However, as will be apparent from

Figure 9.10, the ratio between numbers of earlier Mesolithic and Later Mesolithic sites and find spots is very different from elsewhere. There is a small but quite significant concentration of Earlier Mesolithic from this area including Killuragh Cave (see Chapters 4 and 8), Hermitage (Collins and Coyne 2006) and along the parts of the Blackwater River, explored by the author in the 1980s. This includes the excavation of the Early Mesolithic site at Kilcummer (Anderson 1993). In contrast there is a surprisingly smaller Later Mesolithic presence in the area and often only individual stray finds are known from excavations, e.g. at Hermitage and Killuragh Cave where one Butt Trimmed Form was recovered from each site. Across most of Ireland the ratio of Earlier to Later Mesolithic is usually about 1:10 while in this area it is almost 2:1. This is likely to be as a result of a very different topography. Earlier Mesolithic sites, as in this area, are often found in fields overlooking rivers. Is the relative absence of Later Mesolithic assemblages due to the lack of large lakes where seasonal fluctuations expose expanses of shorelines where artefacts can be gathered or because the rivers have not been dredged? Unlike the Lower Bann, in this area the valley floor deposits are not exploited for perceived commercial purposes.

One might suggest that the chances of recovery of Mesolithic artefacts are determined by the same factors that were discussed for the Palaeolithic in Chapter 5, i.e. are there landscapes that provide a potential and opportunity for discoveries and is there the presence of persons who are interested? These two local smaller regions which have been discussed here illustrate how patterns of Mesolithic settlement across the "Landscape" are created i.e. by the presence or absence of interested amateurs as well as by the nature of the landscape.

Identifying the local

In trying to gain an appreciation of the manner in which the landscape was used during the latter half of the Irish Mesolithic there is, at least for the author, a slightly un-nerving sense that one is dealing with a phenomenon which seems to have more in common with the British Middle Palaeolithic! Hopefully this is not due to wish fulfilment on the part of the author attempting to either create an Irish Palaeolithic or to more insidiously treat the Irish Later Mesolithic as if it was another variant on a Middle Palaeolithic theme. Objectively however one realizes that there are some similarities. Much of the Later Mesolithic material derives from geological contexts, the artefact types are macrolithic and there was an extensive reliance on hand-held or individually hafted tools. These were produced from blades and flakes that seem to have aspects in common with the Mousterian. There is, as well, a plethora of single finds – whether Bout Coupé handaxes or Butt Trimmed Forms!

If one accepts, for the moment, that it is difficult to find an idealised campsite or base camp then perhaps we can draw on some of the ideas presented by Pettitt and White (2012). In particular, (*ibid.*, 353–62) they have suggested that the distribution of certain Mousterian tools in areas such as Creswell represent activities taking place in "Local Activity Areas" (LOAs).

In the latter part of the Irish Later Mesolithic one might see that there is a case for identifying similar LOA areas. A key part of the activities in these areas would be visits to crucial locations for fishing, trapping, obtaining other plants and vegetable material, as well as places where raw materials such as flint or other stone sources were available. These locations would be the persistent places made up as palimpsests of the accumulation of traces of various activities. Although they would be mostly recognised by these large accumulations of artefacts they could include activities that created substantial hollows, like those found at Newferry (1), stone pavements, like that at the base of Newferry (3) Zone 7, or platforms, like those at Derragh Island or Moynagh Lough.

Many of the known sites which we could regard as persistent places, irrespective of the particular type of landscape in which they are located, seem often to be associated with the same very broad range of artefacts ranging from Later Mesolithic forms through a series of heavier tools including picks and axes, as well as ground stone implements, along with tools made from other coarse stones (see Chapter 5).

On the other hand, one cannot easily delimit individual LOAs even in the Lower Bann though even in the 1970s one could suggest that, away from the Valley floor, the lack of a range of the heavier equipment such as axes, picks, etc. and even bar forms and large notched pieces, could suggest foraging for other resources which would include a range of plants and animals.

Thus, with most of the activities centred in the valley floor, people might also have foraged east over the Long Mountain and into the adjacent Maine River Basin. On the west, or Derry, side the evidence is mostly lacking. "Field walkers" such as McAllister and McErlean have documented numerous valley floor sites but, unfortunately, the massive collection built by Dr Stewart of Portglenone, who travelled extensively in his medical practice round many adjacent parts of east Derry, is mostly been undocumented except for the fact that a significant portion came from what was called his "Upperland" area. Interestingly, even at this level, few diagnostic later Mesolithic implements were included in the material from Upperland.

The shape and make up of these LOAs could vary. Thus in the Strangford area, and perhaps even Larne Lough, one might argue that Later Mesolithic groups simply moved round the sea lough in a planned or even unplanned manner exploiting varying seasonal availabilities.

In some cases, notably Derragh Island, Belderrig and Ferriter's Cove, we are still at the stage of the "Super Site" which provides much new information but occurs in a broader landscape, about which relatively little is known. At this stage, there seems to be an advantage in adopting the term Local Activity Area rather than trying to impose the concept of annual territories which may take very different forms in each

region. Perhaps, in the future, the term LOA might prove to be misleading but, at this stage, it can be seen as a useful concept which can be tested as more sites are investigated (see below).

A question remaining

Did the "base camps" so beloved by many of us exist and, if so, where? Are the ephemeral traces recovered from many sites (Chapter 4) witnesses to the more foraging aspect of Mesolithic lifeways or are they the only surviving remnants of habitation sites such as the scatters of post holes and pits at Toome Bypass? Due to the nature of the way in which the material we find was used, are we missing the obvious fact that these are the last remnants of the localities where human groups normally chose to live? One cannot but have a sense that we are using a grammar from one language to interpret a text encoded in another!

At this stage we should perhaps conclude that, while there is little evidence of a trend towards large sedentary groups as was once thought, we should not presume that there was a regression in life style and economic strategies leading to tiny groupings living in marginal conditions and constantly on the move. If nothing else, the degree of organisation round the persistent places would suggest otherwise. Yet while researching the prehistory of an island, we have to remember that the concept of "Island Pauperisation" is always lurking dangerously in our collective subconscious!

Raw materials and territoriality

There are, as well, some indications of mobility that can be observed from the use of differing raw materials. Torrence (1989) has considered the contrasting role of stone tools amongst the !Kung and the Inuit and suggests that the key factors are not simply centred on the geological aspects of raw material availability. In particular, risk avoidance, may have played an important role and (*ibid.*, 64) Torrence notes that:

> raw materials and manufacturing strategies are the result of careful choices made within the wider context of tool using behaviour … I do not feel that lithic technology is a direct result of the geological setting.

In other words, the strategies adopted by Stone Age hunter-gatherers suggest that safer strategies, that were frequently less than optimum, may have been adopted.

The locations of the flint sources and the distances travelled have not really been addressed so far. The manner in which flint in particular was acquired in the Earlier Mesolithic has already been touched on in Chapter 5, as have the reasons why the initial colonists preferred flint (Chapters 7 and 8). There are changes in the way flint and perhaps other raw materials were used even within the Later Mesolithic.

During the Mount Sandel Facies of the Earlier Mesolithic at least, many procurement and reduction strategies would not

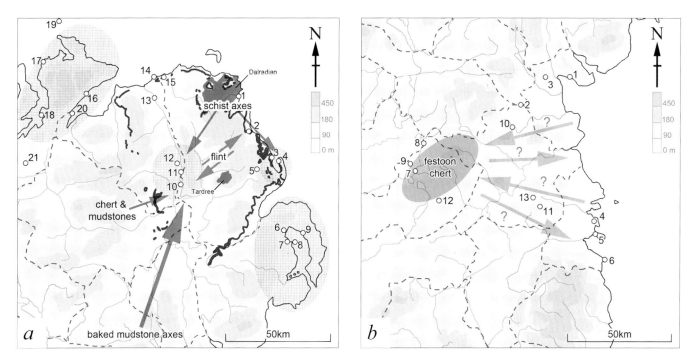

Fig. 9.11. a) sites and possible LOAs or territories in the north-east of Ireland: 1) Castlecarra, 2) Bayfarm, 3) Curran Point, Larne, 4) Ballydown and Mill Bay area, 5) Linford, 6) Island Hill/Roughisland area, 7) Ringneil area, 8) Island Reagh area, 9) Goldsmiths area, 10) Toome Bridge area, 11) Newferry area, 12) Culbane\Portglenone area, 13) Cutts/Sandelford area, 14) Portrush area, 15) Bushfoot area, 16) Redcastle, 17) Dunaff, 18) Baylet, 19) Inishtrahull, 20) Culmore/Ballintaggart, 21) Raphoe, (Lowry Collection) (prepared by Hugh Kavanagh).

b) Sites and territories in north Leinster: 1) Rockmarshall middens, 2) Ballyhoe Lough, 3) Newtown Balreagan, 4) Skerries, 5) Sutton, 6) Dalkey Island, 7) Clonava, 8) Derragh Island/Kinale, 9) Corlanna, 10) Moynagh Lough, 11) Blundelstown, 12) Clowanstown, 13) Leasheamstown (prepared by Hugh Kavanagh).

have differed significantly from those found in much of Western Europe. As discussed in Chapter 5, at Mount Sandel it is clear that flint, either as nodules or core preforms or large flakes, was brought from the coast, which would have been within a day's travel. If boats were used, flint could have been brought to the settlement on an incoming tide in less than 2 hours.

At the other end of the Lower Bann, at the Toome Bypass site, there was also a small scatter of Earlier Mesolithic material. While some of this was probably obtained from the shores of Lough Neagh, some flint with fresh cortex and a distinctive type of banded flint probably came from or near outcrops of flint-bearing UWLF, mostly likely in the Slieve Gallion area, 20 km to the west (Fig. 9.11a).

Flint was not the only raw material used and we should also remember that although the role of ground stone axes in the Later Mesolithic is often emphasised, they also occur earlier. Axes from Mount Sandel, for example, may have come from carboniferous deposits near Ballycastle about 30 km to the east (Woodman and Johnson 1992).

Elsewhere flint was not so easily available, for example in Munster. In this case, aside from very residual pieces – normally of remaniée character – flint had to be obtained from coastal sources. The Blackwater site of Kilcummer (Woodman 1989;

Anderson 1993) relied almost exclusively on flint that must have been transported from the southern coast. The nearest point where this material can be obtained is about 40 km away. In the case of the three Co. Limerick sites, Rathjordan LK3 (Ó Ríordáin 1948), Hermitage LK2 (Collins 2009; Collins and Coyne 2006) and Killuragh Cave LK1 (Woodman 1997), the nearest coastal sources of flint lay 60–80 km away (see Fig. 1.2).

At Lough Boora OY1, flint, although not the dominant material, is present in significant quantities. Although it may have been available some distance inland it is again possible that the main source was from coastal areas that lay more than 100 km to the east. Boats, rather than walks directly over ridges of hill and valleys, may have been the preferred method of travel. The visits to sources, even those within a day's travel, may have been part of a series of embedded procurement strategies where a range of other activities, some of which may have been social, were also being carried out.

Perhaps one can see the significance of these raw materials at two levels. First there is the local, perhaps frequent movement, in the north and east to sources that could be accessed within a day. Were longer trips related to movements taking place within a large annual territory? That seems unlikely. Although there is not enough evidence to test it one might also wonder if the population densities of the Earlier Mesolithic were too low for flint as a raw material to be moved through a complex network of gift exchange. Perhaps, in the Earlier Mesolithic, it is more likely that trips were made by special task groups as part of an embedded procurement strategy.

There is a danger of claiming distant origins for raw materials and even today there can be claims for "northern flint" found on sites that lie exceptionally far from the flint in UWLF of the north! Very often, as has been noted in Chapter 2, the sources can be much more local.

While there is evidence that flint, chert and other raw materials were transported for some distance it is also clear that other sources became more common in the Later Mesolithic. At Ferriter's Cove, besides flint which could be obtained from the local beaches, Rhyolite and siltstone were used alongside a rather intractable local volcanic tuff. Surprisingly, very little imported chert is present. At the same time, the locally available quartzes, which occur in profusion on the local beaches, were almost totally ignored. Aside from the backed blade referred to earlier in Chapter 5 the only artefacts that appear to have been imported were the ground stone axes.

Again, as Martin (2011) has shown in Lough MacNean *FH1*, (see Chapter 2) the local siltstones were preferred to chert which would have to be obtained from some distance away. Although it has yet to be tested, many of the banded cherts and siltstone flakes found in some numbers between Toome and Portglenone may have been obtained from local sources to the west in the Sperrins Mountains. In contrast, the oft-quoted Tardree Rhyolite, which lies within the area delineated in Figure 9.11a, does not seem to have been used, as noted in Chapter 2.

As will have been apparent from discussion earlier in this chapter, in the north-east (especially in relation to the Lower Bann Valley) there seems to have been a heavy reliance on different types of stone being brought to the area (Fig 9.11a). The importation of flint artefacts and blanks has already been discussed in great detail but the significance of some other raw materials is less well known. In general there is almost an acceptance that most of the axes from the Later Mesolithic are made from mudstones or similar types of sedimentary and metamorphosed rocks. Woodman and Johnston (1989) have suggested that the baked mudstone axes derive from sources in the Long/Down Palaeozoic Peneplain (see Fig. 2.10). This is an area that lies south of Lough Neagh and stretches from the shores of Strangford Lough to Granard, close to the Shannon. Unfortunately, alteration within these rocks means that the microfossils that might have led to identification of specific sources have not survived.

At Newferry there appears to have been, in the bottom of the sequence (i.e. before 7000 cal BP), a preference for schist axes (see Chapter 5). These may come from the "Dalradian" geological deposits in the north-east corner of Co. Antrim about 50 km from the southern end of the Lower Bann (Fig. 9.11a). These axes, which were found in some numbers, are particularly susceptible to deterioration and are not likely to have been made on erratic pebbles. There is, therefore, almost certainly an under-representation of axes of this material, however, a few examples and what may have been the poor remnants of axes, of similar material have been found along the east coast of Co. Antrim. The most notable are those found in context 5012 at the Port of Larne. These may date to significantly earlier than 8000 cal BP. This site lies some tens of kilometres from a likely source area. Some possible, much eroded fragments, were also recovered from the Bay Farm excavations (Woodman and Johnston 1996) in Glencloy. I have to admit that, in the context of Bay Farm, this is a thought that occurred to me in retrospect, especially after the discovery at the Port of Larne (Woodman unpublished report). The potential significance to this region is best seen in the fact that 122 out of 198 schist axes (61.6%) (Cooney and Grogan 1994) with some form of known provenience from throughout Ireland are from Co. Antrim.

As discussed in Chapter 2, there is also a tendency to associate cherts with Carboniferous Limestones. There are few chert-bearing carboniferous formations in Northern Ireland though there are several other more local sources. Mudstone flakes and banded cherts appear in the Newferry sequence, 20 in number (see Nawaz 1977) could have come from other sources lying much closer in south Derry or adjacent parts of Tyrone. In fact, there are also probably more than 50, flakes and blades made from a range of different cherts and mudstones from the Toome area, within various collections of lithic artefacts. Occasionally elsewhere, as at Bay Farm, other examples of chert or mudstone flakes have turned up. However these look as if they represent a relatively local usage. Knowles (1912) recorded relatively few examples of these distinctly black rock types from the Bann. In the case of Culbane, which lies only a few kilometres further north, there is a surprising scarcity of black mudstones, silt stone etc. in both the Knowles collections (Woodman *et al.* 2006) and in Vincent McAllister's ongoing project (pers. comm.) in that middle area of the Bann, also centred on Culbane.

In effect the north-east provides evidence of a patchwork of exploitation of a range of resources which may have been brought from some distance and, while their presence is best seen in the Lower Bann Valley, some individual items have been transported across more substantial distances. This suggests a rich knowledge of the region within which Mesolithic groups were living.

The North Strangford area appears, as suggested earlier, quite different with local flint providing most of the raw materials and one should wonder whether some of the few ground stone axes recovered from the area, come from the adjacent Palaeozoic Peneplain.

In the case of the North Leinster area (Figure 9.11b) there are interesting contrasts between the coastal zone, where flint dominates and inland, where many assemblages are dominated by chert. At Rockmarshall and Sutton, where flint in the dominant raw material, there are other occasional flakes and blades of perhaps more local sandstones and volcanics as well as occasional chert flakes and blades. At Dalkey Island (Liversage 1968), where the NMI registration team have documented 32,500 lithic artefacts from all areas of excavation but only 103 are chert. However, much of the lithic material probably dates to the Neolithic and Bronze Age. The team made an interesting observation that chert examples represent 25% of the total of diagnostic Later Mesolithic forms at Dalkey. Thus, although they do not necessarily dominate assemblages in coastal areas, their consistent presence in small numbers must suggest something other than convenience in procurement.

In the central midlands, many sites are close to outcrops containing chert, and assemblages such as those at Clonava *WH 1*, Corlanna *WH 2*, and Derragh Island *LD 1* are dominated by "chert". In fact, at the first two sites, flint or raw materials other than chert are virtually unknown.

At Derragh Island only 6% of the material is flint or other raw material. While there is a Neolithic element present on the site (Fredengren 2009; Sternke and Woodman unpublished) the overwhelming majority of artefacts belong to the Later Mesolithic. Some reduction of cores was taking place at Derragh Lough; the balance between cores (77: including five flint and six quartz), and Later Mesolithic forms (121), is higher than the sites referred to earlier. Even allowing for chert cores shattering down into unrecognisable pieces, it would seem as if a significant portion of the artefacts and blanks were brought to the site. The excavations at Moynagh Lough (Bradley 1991; 1999), which lies roughly midway between the central Midlands and the coast, provided a slightly different balance. Here chert sources lay within 10 km of the site while the coast was only 20 km away. Roughly 2000 lithic items were recovered with, as at Derragh Island, only a very small proportion of the artefacts being made out of flint.

To the south of Moynagh Lough, *MH 10*, at Leashemstown, *MH 13* the Mesolithic levels of a site discovered during water pipeline laying, contained only chert artefacts, again primarily as retouched tools and blanks, while upper levels of Neolithic date contained flint artefacts (G. Warren, pers. comm). At Clowanstown, which is best known for its Mesolithic fish baskets, a number of artefacts were discovered in Mesolithic contexts and others where it was impossible to establish whether they were of Mesolithic or Neolithic date. Here were nine Butt Trimmed Forms, five of which were chert while the remainder were flint. If the total number of flint and chert artefacts from all levels are considered then 13 were found to be of each material (Warren *et al. 2009)*. Elsewhere, smaller numbers of Later Mesolithic artefacts were found. At Blundelstown 3, which was also found during the M3 project, in a sample of nearly 2000 artefacts, just three Later Mesolithic chert pieces were recovered, two of which were distally trimmed and the other a large blade (Farina Sternke pers. comm.). The remainder, which were Neolithic or later in date, were overwhelming made from flint.

At some of these key sites in this region, it is difficult to quantify precisely the numbers of retouched tools or cores, etc. However, as can be seen in the tentative estimates illustrated in Figure 9.11b there seems to be a reverse process from that witnessed in north Antrim. Sites like Clonava exist at, or close to, the chert outcrops such as Knockeyon and seem to be primarily concerned with raw material extraction and artefact production. Further east, sites such as Derragh Island, and perhaps Moynagh Lough, has a mixture of habitation evidence and perhaps was used for other purposes. There was at these locations, though to a lesser extent, some tool production which could have included the early stages in the reduction of blocks of chert. Locations such as Clowanstown and Leashemstown may have been be places visited regularly for particular purposes and to which tools were brought. On the coast, production and use of flint tools was taking place but there were also a limited number of chert artefacts.

In looking at parts of Leinster, the pattern noted in general is that, aside from the not unexpected single stray finds, most assemblages of later Mesolithic artefacts from excavations and field walking alike are quite small. Even Clowanstown could not be regarded as being large. Away from the coast or other large expanses of water, the pattern is not dissimilar to equivalent inland areas in the north-east (see Fig. 9.5).

At this point it is worth noting that similar small assemblages have turned up further south. At Morristownbiller *KE2* a scatter of Later Mesolithic blades has been recovered, again of flint and chert (D. Brennan, pers. comm.). Along the Barrow and adjacent areas, especially around Carlow itself, in the County and adjacent parts of Laois and Kildare, there are also small scatters of artefacts. This pattern is again built up from excavations, including those from work along the M9 and from the Barrow River field walking project (Zvelebil *et al.* 1996) (CW1), in other words, it is probable that flint was being brought from the Leinster coast though either directly or along rivers such as the Liffey.

One of the biggest problems in north Leinster has been the identification of the specific sources of chert used for the manufacture of various artefacts (see Chapter 2). At the moment, one can only assume that most of these derive from sources well to the west of the Leinster coast and that their presence to the east is an, as yet crude, indicator of movements between the coast and interior.

There is also the interesting presence of schist axes in this particular region, notably at Dalkey Island (Liversage 1968) and Sutton (Mitchell 1956; see Chapter 5). However, as yet, no attempt has been made to identify the parent rock from which the axes were made. Similarly, Bradley (1991; 1999) noted that one of the three ground stone axes from Moynagh Lough was green in colour and partially decayed. This description is reminiscent of the condition of the schist axes from Newferry. It seems likely that these axes, because of the manner in which they can deteriorate, are only recovered from excavations, therefore many other examples from fields, bogs etc. would not be noticed. Obviously the biggest problem is trying to establish if all the schist axes come from the one source or whether they were obtained from parent rock in different parts of Ireland. While, at this stage, one could suggest that those from the sites in the northern area derive from the Dalradian rocks, which outcrop in the extreme north-east of Ireland, we need to establish whether the same source was used at sites in north Leinster. If so, then one might be encouraged to look for other indicators that there were other contacts perhaps north and south along the east coast.

Keeping in mind Torrence's 1989 suggestion that geology was only one of the factors that would have to be taken into consideration by Stone Age hunter-gatherers, certain aspects of these raw materials raise issues that have rarely been addressed. In the absence of any statement to the contrary, it would be very easy to slip into a conventional view that raw materials other than flint are substitutes. However, many would regard this as an over-simplification, though one has to wonder why relatively fragile items, such as decarbonated chert, were transported and what the particular value of siltstone flakes might have been. Was there some value in their rarity? If so, they might have been expected to be found across larger areas; or did they have some functional purpose?

The axes certainly suggest that a range of resources was drawn in from quite a large area. At some level, either a complex exchange system developed during the latter half of the Irish Later Mesolithic or small groups travelled across (by Irish standards) quite large distances. The existing information appears to suggest that, in north Leinster, there was some movement of significant groups between the coast and the interior. This could have been almost at the level of the migration of complete bands though it does not preclude movements of smaller groups who were intent on carrying out particular tasks or, similarly, that certain artefacts that survive in the archaeological record were obtained by gift exchange.

There may have been other reasons for visiting these localities as part of an embedded procurement strategy and one must remember that journeys to obtain raw materials for stone tool manufacture were undertaken in order to enable other crucial activities, such as hunting, trapping, collection of vegetable foods, fishing and shellfish collection to take place.

What does all this tell us?

Was raw material procurement part of large-scale movements of whole groups, as would have been implied in the lowlands/uplands movements of northern England (Jacobi 1978), or would it have been one of the tasks of smaller groups who were foraging across a larger landscape? In Ireland the frequent absence of extensive reworking of the flake tools, especially flint examples, and their profusion in certain areas, suggests that the distances needing to be traversed were not perceived as major barriers. Therefore, journeys over land, either from the Antrim coast to the Bann or from the Leinster coast to

the "Lakeland" interior, were trips that could be taken with a degree of convenience and perhaps by a significant portion of any group.

On the other hand, it is possible that other material and artefacts, notably ground stone axes or the Moynagh Points, could have come from sources over 100 km away, and may have been obtained by smaller groups or through an exchange system.

As yet, based on the artefactual evidence, little can be said about the annual territories used in any part of the Mesolithic. While there is significant evidence that shows that there was some degree of movement, the means by which the objects themselves were transported lacks clarity. Perhaps this is in part because of the limited number of excavated sites that provide other indicators of seasonal or longer-term settlement. There is, therefore, little possibility of establishing the balance between movements of "bands" of people, the travels of specialised task groups and the role of gift exchange. In other words, while we know that these were not static communities confined to small areas, there is no clear evidence of, for example, distinctive stylistic differences in tools types (see Chapter 12).

One possibility is that there was a complex relationship between the various needs of these groups, perhaps most notably their quest for food, the procurement methods best suited to obtaining sufficient food and, lastly, the logistical structures needed to obtain the best equipment to carry out these tasks. In this spirit we can look at the way in which we think that the Irish landscape was used. The availability of various raw materials remained the same and it is probable the sources of food did not alter that radically (see below Chapter 10).

The challenge of living in Ireland as Stone Age hunter-gatherers was food availability and finding ways to procure it. The challenge for archaeology is to interpret whether the differences in tool types, reduction strategies and raw materials from area to area are simply the result of different local strategies adapted to the needs of the locality of groups that used the resources of different areas in different ways, or whether the LOAs delineate the core of separate annual territories.

In the Earlier Mesolithic, small nodules and core preforms would have provided the basis for the production of microliths and related items, as well as small axes. The hunting of a range of large mammals was apparently not an option in Ireland and so, to ensure consistent and reliable access to sources such as fish in estuarine, riverine and perhaps lacustrine environments, there may have been the need to build fixed facilities such as weirs and traps. This tactic could also extend to hunting boars and bears (see Chapter 10).

These needs would have required access to quality flint nodules, relatively large chert blocks of greater reliability, or other useful raw materials. These may have only occurred in a limited number of areas. As discussed in Chapter 5, transportation of the necessary large blocks or nodules would have been a difficult task. In the case of certain Native

Australian tribes, the production of numerous elongated, slightly leaf-shaped blades took place at quarries and these were then transported in relatively large numbers. This would be infinitely preferable to carrying large, unworked blocks. The main attribute of these blanks is that they were flexible (Costa *et al.* 2005) and could be used in a number of different ways (see Chapter 5).

The result for parts of the north-east was a complex equation. It was more than a question of obtaining the blanks by visiting the right locality, producing them on the spot, abandoning nodules that suffered from weaknesses such as impurities or internal fractures and then finally selecting those that were most likely to be useful. However, within the Later Mesolithic and with the very simple reduction strategies used on the Antrim coast, it would be unusual, after the removal of cortex, to produce more than 10 reasonable blades from one core and in many cases the figure could be less (see Chapter 5). Therefore, only a small portion of the original weight of the nodule would be removed to the Lower Bann Valley. While one senses that these blanks formed an important part of the assemblage in which all elements could be highly curated, more was required. Other raw materials, or rather finished implements, such as the axes were brought often from considerable distances. The effort in bringing these materials to the Lower Bann suggests that, at certain times of the year, this must have been an area with abundant resources where investment in fixed facilities at certain key points made sense.

In contrast, around Strangford Lough the building of large fixed facilities may not have been required. Here lesser quality flint was somewhat available and if some nodules were poor, others would be found sooner or later. As noted in Chapter 5, small blade-like flakes, which were often quite stubby, could be used alongside the Later Mesolithic forms. Although core tools and ground stone axes exist in this area, they are relatively rare.

North-east Leinster, on the other hand, provides an example of a complex inter-relationship where two types of sources were available, i.e. flint on the east coast and outcrops containing chert at various points inland. It could be argued that this is also an inter-relationship between expedient and curated strategies and may be reflecting the existence of groups moving on a seasonal basis between the coastal area and its resources and an interior of lakes and rivers. In both cases terrestrial and water based resources may have been used.

Along the western side of Ireland it is more difficult to identify patterns of acquisition, reduction and use. At least four major locations can be identified, two of which are sites, namely Ferriter's Cove and Belderrig, while the other two are major lough shore collections, namely Lough Gara and Lough Allen. In these regions, there is the lack of other sites in the vicinity of each locality. It is therefore difficult to track how lithic material was acquired and moved to other locations. In each case one can only see part of the pattern though evidence from Ferriter's Cove suggests a community living entirely in coastal areas on the Dingle peninsula (see Chapter 10).

In Ireland, perhaps due to nature of the landscape in which we grew up, we are inclined to think that 50 km is a great distance and, with certain notable exceptions such as the Neolithic porcelanite axes, we expected artefacts to be moved over relatively short distances. Therefore, movement of certain key resources during the Mesolithic over what seems like long distances may seem unlikely. It is worth remembering that, within European prehistory, there are numerous examples of artefacts or raw materials being transported over much longer distances. For instance, during the Middle and Later Mesolithic in western Norway, axes from the quarries at Bømlo and Flora (Alsaker and Bruen Olsen 1984) were transported in different directions for 200 km along the Norwegian coast while Lihult axes were transported significant distances through the lakes and rivers of Middle Sweden (Bengtsson 2003). Similarly, high quality slate and flint appears to have been exchanged across Lake Onega for distances in excess of 100 km (O'Shea and Zvelibil 1984). The use of water transport could be common to all these examples.

It is probable that during the Later Mesolithic the Lough Neagh/Bann catchment system, whose upper reaches touch on the Erne system and are adjacent to the Shannon system, could have been used to transport axes by boat. The Shannon, the Boyne and the Barrow River systems among others (see Chapter 2) would have been the major arteries across Ireland. There may also have been movements along the coast and possibly across several watersheds and river catchments.

We should also consider whether and how such extensive movement away from the river valleys might have impacted on vegetation and it is worth turning to the evidence gained from palynology in order to assist in understanding how the landscape was used during the Mesolithic.

Vegetation changes and manipulating the environment

The extent of the presence or absence of Mesolithic occupation across a landscape, and how that landscape was used, has often focussed attention on the search for evidence of a human impact which might have survived within the vegetational record. As discussed above, based on a scatter of artefacts there are some indications of a Mesolithic presence away from the coast, rivers and lake shores and one must ask if there is reason to believe that the forested slopes and valleys were used to some extent throughout the Irish Mesolithic?

Given Ireland's limited range of large mammals one might ask, to what purpose would there have been an extensive presence in these areas and why the manipulation of the environment? On a personal basis one can only observe that there have been many claimants that evidence of deliberate manipulation of the environment, such as forest clearances, would be found in Ireland, yet little, actual, substantial evidence has been offered.

Warren *et al.* (2013) have suggested the application of a model based on Smith (1981), who advocated the potential of a diverse range of "environmental engineering" of wild resources used in pre-industrial societies in the Americas. A critique of the suggestion of the importation of bears has already been offered in Chapter 2 but other issues, such as limited cultivation – almost garden horticulture – and woodland management were considered. Much of the suggested evidence for forest clearances or disturbances of the vegetation comes from palynological investigations.

It seems to me that, in examining Smith's (1981) ideas and how they might be applied to Ireland, Warren *et al.* (2013) have taken an overly critical attitude towards the Irish palynological record. There is an implicit assumption that pollen diagrams lack or contain only a few radiocarbon dates and that palynologists could do more (*here lies a certain irony as, on a personal basis, I can remember being informed by environmental scientists that people like me should only excavate at locations where there was a good chance of uncovering deposits where there was good organic preservation!*). This critique makes no allowance for the 75 years+ development of the discipline. www.Ipol.ie lists over 450 pollen diagrams but many of those, especially resulting from analysis carried out by Jessen (1949) or Mitchell (1956) effectively pre-date radiocarbon dating. Most projects were undertaken to help understand vegetational histories or changes to other phenomena such as lake environments. Few were chosen to identify human environmental impact prior to the onset of the Neolithic.

In order to examine this whole question, it would be necessary to choose the appropriate locations and not be overly critical of locations which were not examined: the large concentration of artefacts that drew attention to Ballyhoe Lough, for instance, really only became well known at the end of the 1990s when a substantial number of artefacts were rediscovered by the author in Manchester Museum. So it is not surprising that it was not a candidate for palynological investigation. Similarly, the large concentrations of material round Lough Allen only became known in the mid-2000s, thanks to Killian Driscoll (2009). Coring a lough as large as Lough Allen, in order to detect evidence of human interference with the environment, would be unlikely to produce evidence of a very local event.

The time and costs involved in undertaking an extensive coring survey and all the analyses and radiocarbon dating involved would be very high – perhaps between 50 and 100,000 Euros at current prices! Would we, as archaeologists, be prepared to spend that sum on an exploratory excavation near a lake that seemed to/might contain a record of early vegetational disturbance by humans?

One also has to be realistic in appreciating that the search for pre-Neolithic human disturbances has not necessarily always been fashionable or regarded as a priority. In many cases, as at Lough na Shade near Emain Macha/Navan Fort (Weir 1997, 111–17), the emphasis was, quite naturally, on other events – in that case, on the human impact of later Bronze Age and Iron Age societies – and the possibility of Mesolithic clearance in

an interesting area at the edge of a Drumlin belt was simply not pursued. The instances of research into the nature of the Elm Decline and/or the impact of the first farmers are too numerous to list here. At the other extreme, perhaps one of the most intriguing examples was at Mount Gabriel (Mighall *et al.* 2008), where there were indications of forest clearance during the Mesolithic. In this case the problem was reversed as, while it is just possible that there is a Mesolithic presence in the area, there is no physical evidence for Mesolithic activity.

In examining the track record for the potential to identify traces of early forest disturbance, the Top 25 sites listed in Chapter 4 provide an interesting check list. These demonstrate how difficult it is to find and carry out the types of investigations discussed above. Many of the key sites are in locations where it may not be possible to find deposits suitable for environmental sampling and analysis.

The sites are grouped below dependant on whether or not there were opportunities for palynological investigations in the vicinity and, in some cases, whether there were any significant results. "Deposits" here indicates either bogs or lakes where suitable deposits might be available.

Deposits not available: Ballydown, Baylet, Belderrig, Dalkey Island, Fanore, Hermitage, Kilcummer, Killuragh, Port of Larne.

Deposits searched for and/or not suitable: Bayfarm, Cushendun, The Warren, Mount Sandel (adjacent kettle hole lacked deposits of appropriate period), Spenser Dock, Toome (Creagh).

Sampling not close enough: Derragh Island (Sampling in Lough Kinale).

Sampling undertaken but no clear evidence: Lough Boora, Toome Bypass.

Sampled with possible evidence: Newferry Sites 3 and 4, Clowanstown, Moynagh Lough.

One can begin with the observation that there is little evidence of any extensive vegetation disturbance being created by humans during the Earlier Mesolithic. In part this is because there are so few sites that are older than 8500 years ago. At Mount Sandel, no deposits contemporaneous with the occupation were recorded from the adjacent kettle hole, perhaps due to a prevailing drier, more continental climate (Hamilton *et al.* 1985). Analyses (Hamilton and Brannon 1985) were undertaken on material sub-sampled from bulk samples which were primarily intended for sieving and charcoal extraction. The proximity to the modern surface must make them slightly questionable. In the case of Lough Boora, O'Connell (1980) was able to sample lake deposits within an earlier Holocene lough on whose shores Mesolithic settlement had been located. Here there was no convincing evidence that there had been any significant human alteration to the vegetation round the lake shores.

The very fact that much of the known Later Mesolithic evidence derives from shoreline locations suggests that there should be some evidence that people cleared and altered the vegetation in the immediate vicinity of where they were living.

One might have thought that, if fish weirs were being constructed on a regular basis (see Chapter 4), then some form of woodland management might have existed. As Warren *et al.* (2013) have noted, the evidence for careful woodland management in the form of coppicing of hazel for hurdling, based in particular on the Spenser Docks fish traps, falls into the category of "adventitious coppicing", rather than structured management and harvesting of hazel rods. At Clowanstown, where fish traps or baskets were also found, O'Donnell (2009) suggests that there was no real evidence for coppicing and that the main types of wood used were alder from the lake shore and hazel, which would have been found in the immediate vicinity. Similarly, Lyons' report on the associated plant remains notes the presence of alder, birch and rosewood, further suggesting an opportunistic approach to the manufacture of the fish traps (Lyons 2009).

Evidence for burning of plants, such as reeds and shrubs, on lakeshores can occasionally be found, for instance at Clowanstown (Mossop and Mossop 2009, Appendices 17–19).

There are some locations where a case can be made for some form of human intervention. Palynological investigations were undertaken at Newferry Site 3 and the adjacent Site 4 (Smith and Collins 1971; Smith 1981). Smith was very cautious in identifying unequivocal evidence of clearances in the upper part of the sequence, especially as the local environment was changing with rising water levels and the creation of diatomite flats, but the case for clearances at the base of the sequence was much stronger. In this instance there appears to have been an attempt to lay something such as a stone pavement on shoreline reed swamp peat deposits. This suggests more than a casual short term stay in the area (Woodman 1977a). Based on the increases in light demanding trees such as ash (*Fraxinus*) and willow (*Salix*), along with suggestions that pines were burnt while ferns, which were very common, were noted to exist (and flourish today in stream side forest clearances) Smith (*ibid.*) suggested that

> In view of all these signs of anthropogenic effects, we may perhaps conclude that at this site man also played some role in the establishment of alder. Whether such an effect could have been more widespread however is a question that must be discussed elsewhere.

Therefore, where are significant investments in locations, such as immediately adjacent to the Derragh Island excavations (Fredengren 2009) or on the Boyle River, as well as places where eel weirs were constructed, one might still expect some alteration to the vegetation, even if this did not take the form of a structured and managed use of pollarding.

Locations can be identified which would be worth investigation, such as on small lakes or beside now in-filled lakes in the north Midlands. These include sites in the Top 20 listed above that were adjacent to small lakes (Moynagh Lough

and Clowanstown). In an assessment of the potential of a large area round the Clowanstown site Brooks and Farrell (2009) have identified a number of lakes which have been examined and which would be worth exploring further. These include Moynagh Lough and nearby Ballyhoe Lough. Detailed multi-disciplinary investigations in that particular area would bring a refreshing new perspective to a topic in the types of area that differ from locations by the sea, or beside large expanses of fresh water loughs or major rivers.

In searching for early clearances in Ireland there has been one major change in how we look at the contemporaneous environment. While it had become clearer that there were few large mammals present in Ireland during the Mesolithic (Woodman 1974a) the absence or extreme scarcity of red deer was not fully accepted until the late 1990s (Woodman *et al.* 1997). The assumption of their presence in earlier decades and, in particular, the discussion of Mesolithic clearances and the role of red deer in the Pennines in England (Mellars 1976), could have influenced our view of the Irish Uplands.

Away from shorelines, it is, however, difficult to find any evidence of extensive forest clearance in other parts of landscapes where scatters of Mesolithic artefacts have been noted. There are probably many mountain areas that would not have been suitable for extensive settlement even if there had been a range of large herbivores. However, areas such as that around the Antrim Plateau the Sperrins, parts of the Comeraghs/Knockmealdowns in the south-east or the Cork Kerry Bounds in the south-west have a lot in common with the Pennines (Jacobi *et al.* 1976; Mellars 1985), where the use of fire ecology has been suggested. Yet there is as yet no known Mesolithic presence. In returning (once again!) to Antrim, analysis of the vegetational history obtained at Lough na Trosk, on the margins of the coastal lowlands at 300 m AMSL, by Francis (1987) was undertaken with the intention of establishing not only how the vegetation changed through time but also in the hope of identifying points in time when people using this area interfered with or manipulated the environment in which they lived. No trace of a human interference during the Mesolithic was noted in the record obtained from the Lough. In fact, during fieldwork in this area, in which it was just possible that there would have been a Mesolithic presence and where significant evidence of Neolithic activities became apparent, only one possible Mesolithic artefact was recovered. Similarly, on the occasions where deposits that pre-dated the initial expansion of blanket peat in the Antrim Uplands were examined (Goddard 1971), no indications of forest clearance during the Mesolithic were noted. Further west, on the Sperrins at Beaghmore in Co. Tyrone, which lies at around 200 m AMSL, no traces of interference with the vegetation were noted until around the beginnings of the Neolithic (Pilcher 1969). A similar pattern was noted in the bog adjacent to Ballynagilly, Co. Tyrone (Pilcher and Smith 1979), which again lies at about 200 m AMSL and where extensive traces of Early Neolithic and Beaker settlement were uncovered (Apsimon 1976).

Thus, during the Irish Mesolithic, it is obvious that, while communities did not always tread very lightly, they left a little impact in the vegetational record; there is, as yet, no substantial evidence that they brought about major changes to the forest environment in which they lived.

Conclusion

It is tempting to see the distribution patterns of artefacts as reflecting a very effective series of strategies in procurement of raw materials and their role in the Later Mesolithic economy. Yet, although there has been progress in evaluating how the distribution of Later Mesolithic material reflects the use of the landscape, it seems that we are only beginning to appreciate the complexity of the manner in which the landscape was used. As suggested by Woodman and Anderson (1990) we may still only have a "very partial picture".

Earlier in this chapter certain areas were tentatively defined and the term LOA was suggested. However, one must return to what this means. Can we say that, in certain cases and specific areas, such as some of the sea loughs, the LOA was the territory where most resources, such as food and or raw material, were obtained throughout the year? The significant relative absence of axes within relatively large concentrations of artefacts in the Strangford Lough area raises a question as to whether this absence reflects a lack of need for these tools during seasonal visits to an area where nets and stone built tidal weirs would suffice? As noted above, there are numerous axes in other coastal areas such, as at Ferriter's Cove or perhaps even at Dalkey Island. Why is there this difference?

In contrast the Lower Bann, which could be seen as an LOA, may have been only one part of a much larger region within which specialist task groups may have been dispatched to obtain key resources. While one can sense the presence of LOAs around Midland lakes, could it be that the North Leinster region was exploited through more complex nomadic movements between the coast and interior which took communities through the numerous different environments of rivers and small lakes?

Although the author has often been cautious about assumptions that what is seen in the north-east could be presumed to be equally applicable elsewhere, there are some interesting parallels. The types of material found in such profusion along the Boyle River seem to be remarkably similar to those along parts of the Lower Bann. The scatters of Later Mesolithic forms across parts of north-east Ireland can be paralleled with similar, relatively low density distributions, of artefacts across North Leinster. Similarly, the possibility of regional grouping in areas such as Strangford Lough and the Dingle Peninsula show interesting similarities and differences but they could suggest that there were also some semi-permanent coastal grouping (see Chapter 10).

We can return to Torrence's observations (1989) that stone tools can only appreciated if they are examined in the context of their use, i.e. for manufacturing a range of other artefacts, food procurement or consumption. In the case of the Irish Later Mesolithic there seem to be several least risk solutions. In the north-east, for at least part of the year, the major rivers were a very reliable source of food but without, at least to us, a good range of convenient raw materials. As their locations were probably familiar to communities in the region, then it was less risky to move essential material for stone artefacts to areas where a reliable range of food sources could be obtained. In Strangford, where food could be obtained on a year round basis, the least risk choice was to adapt to using less suitable local erratic flint nodules. The Ferriter's Cove site may be part of a somewhat similar situation on the Dingle Peninsula. Again, as noted above, the information from north Leinster suggests some evidence of movement that could be best described as "interesting and probably very complex"! As usual in archaeology these are working hypotheses that need to be tested.

If the procurement of food and sustenance are, not surprisingly, crucial to the Mesolithic lifeway, then the next question must be, given the distinctive ecological make-up of Early Holocene Ireland, what did communities actually live on and does this contribute our understanding of how Mesolithic peoples lived?

Chapter 10

Food, sustenance and procurement

In addition to matters such as the availability of raw materials, food procurement and various sociological requirements must, in some way, have been taken into consideration and have affected settlement patterns. Usually we focus on the bones of animals, mainly mammals, fish and birds, but often forget about the presence of plant foods – with the exception of hazel nuts. However, Ireland is one of those regions where many of the soils are acidic. A pH of 7 is usually regarded as neutral, but in parts of the north of Ireland, as at Mount Sandel, the pH is regularly recorded as 5 or even lower. Even in the centre of Ireland, where many rocks from the carboniferous area occur, they are often shales and mudstones that combined with acid bogs to create environments where bone does not survive. This is not a problem particular to the Mesolithic. Although there are frequent references to the paucity of Irish Mesolithic faunal remains, Neolithic and Early Bronze Age sites, which are usually dry land sites, rarely include waterlogged areas or shell middens which contain quantities of animal bones in particular. Many settlement sites of a later date also often lack any surviving faunal remains.

Even at sites such as Ferriter's Cove, where the acidity was not so high, the faunal assemblage was in a weathered condition and it is probable that the bones of young animals and many fish bones did not survived intact. In fact, most of the fish bones that survived at Ferriter's Cove had been burnt. For Irish prehistory in general, areas like the Limestone region around Lough Gur, where large quantities of animal bones were recovered, are the exception rather than the norm. In many instances only burnt bone fragments survive and then only where concentrated, as in a hearth or small pit. At Mount Sandel for example (Pl. XXIX), it was apparent that, in very acidic environments, the burnt bones only survived when a significant quantity had accumulated in a feature. Thus, it is probable that the burnt bone from the hearths and pits represent not only a tiny fraction of the total fauna, which has been processed, consumed and discarded, but also a tiny fraction of the burnt material.

In the context of food we often focus on issues that bias the record such as what bone material survives. We should remember that food has a social role, bringing family, band or even larger groups together and that there can be preferences based on taste and texture as well as what is taboo or preferred for religious reasons or constitutes the "hero's portion" – perhaps the reward for bravery in the hunt or the capture of a bird of special significance. Also, organs such as the liver and heart which we consider to be offal may have been highly prized. Today, offering tripe or the Cork version of black pudding ("*Drisheen*") at a meal would cause consternation in most polite circles! In reality we should remember the old saying that the only part of the pig that was not used was the "squeal".

While not all food used in prehistory was cooked, it is surprising how little attention we give to the actual process of preparing, heating, roasting or boiling what was to be eaten though we assume that much of what was consumed was cooked. How often have "hearths" been excavated but been regarded as little more than sources of materials for radiocarbon dating? Hearths will not preserve a record of their use over a long time period but may, at best, contain the remnants of their final use. Perhaps one of the few other signs of use was found at Mount Sandel where small stake-holes occurred round the central hearths. Of course, the discovery of burnt bones and plant remains in a hole does not necessarily mean that it was a cooking hollow.

With these caveats in mind we have to realise that a single chapter on food and the archaeological record from the Mesolithic will have its limitations. This chapter will proceed in a traditional manner i.e. looking at the surviving record to establish what we can say was hunted, fished or collected. It will examine the potential food remains under the headings of a) faunal remains, which will include mammals, birds and fish, b) shellfish and c) plant foods. This is essentially exploring what has survived on various sites. The stable isotope evidence obtained from a very limited number of human remains of Mesolithic date and its implication will also be considered.

The faunal assemblages

It is tempting to see the faunal assemblages, especially the larger ones, as representing an overall picture of the life of Mesolithic communities. However, they are little more than partial snapshots. Because of the impoverished nature of our record we are inclined to focus on identifiable bones but we should remember that there are occasions, perhaps for convenience or purposes of hygiene, when animals are butchered away from dwelling areas. On habitation sites where large numbers of bones are brought back with the flesh still on them then these bone are often broken to obtain marrow or to be used as raw material for certain artefacts such as the bone points.

Some assemblages are more obvious in representing a seasonal, rather than an annual, picture but the evidence from each site also probably only represents a portion of the activities carried out at that particular location. The greatest unknown must be how much was processed off-site. This must have been exceptionally important in the case of fish, such as the salmon and eels, which may have been caught in large numbers at fish weirs and traps. Similarly, trips to seal rookeries probably resulted in animals being killed, butchered and transported back to areas where habitation took place.

As we have seen, Ireland had an extremely limited and unbalanced fauna and while this is often identified in its mammalian fauna it is equally true of fish and, to some extent, the avifauna. There are also a limited number of sites that have produced significant numbers of animal bones. In reality, the total size of the Irish faunal assemblage for the Mesolithic is less than what would be found on many individual sites in mainland Europe.

The available database is also hampered by the fact that sieving was only introduced on Irish sites in the 1970s, therefore the older Leinster midden sites have a bias in what has been recovered and unfortunately it is not possible to return to some of the older sites. The Sutton midden (Mitchell 1956), in particular, has been destroyed while there is probably little left of the of Rockmarshall middens (Mitchell 1947; 1949). The consequences of not sieving were perhaps best illustrated by

Mellars (1978) in his Oronsay project. The Oronsay middens had been investigated in the late 19th century and produced a significant range of sea fish. The 1970s investigations (*ibid.*) included a rigorous programme of sieving, which revealed that the dominant species caught had been Saithe *(Pollachius virens)*. As the bones of Saithe are quite small they had not been noted in the earlier investigations. One might infer from this that, on many sites, bones of smaller mammals and birds, as well as fish, might be under-represented in the record.

The paucity of evidence is further complicated by the fact that many of the excavations were quite limited in extent. Only five sites have produced more than 50 identifiable mammal bones. In Table 10.1 domesticates, which tend (with the exception of Ferriter's Cove) to be intrusive, have been excluded. In some instances, such as Sutton and Rockmarshall, the numbers of mammal bones were very small.

Fish bones, when they occur, are usually found in large numbers but may represent no more than one or two fish. Their full significance will be discussed later but the relative absence of large mammals, other than pigs, is obvious and that fish bones are easily the most common identifiable fragments (Table 10.1).

The faunal remains from the two largest assemblages (Mount Sandel and Lough Boora) are heavily burnt. McCarthy (*et al.* 1999) noted that burnt bones at Ferriter's Cove were an unrepresentative portion of the total faunal remains collected; most of the fish bones were calcined while, in general, the mammal bones, although often in a poor condition, were unburnt. At Polderweg, van Wijngaarden-Bakker *et al.* (2001) have shown that the burnt portion of the assemblage is well below 10% and may be below 1%, and that there can be a variation between species in the ratio of burnt to unburnt bones There is, therefore, no guarantee that there will be an exact correlation between the species caught and those that end up in the fire.

Table 10:1. Faunal remains recovered from major Irish Mesolithic sites.

	Terrestrial and fresh water		Marine		
	Land mammals	*Fish*	*Mammals*	*Fish*	*Birds*
Earlier Mesolithic					
Mount Sandel Upper	329	1800			79
Lough Boora	706	2080			243
Later Mesolithic					
Baylet	7			1220	??
Ferriter's Cove	86			3153	59?
Moynagh	60				
Dalkey II and V	46		22	52	12

It is normal to find that large concentrations of faunal remains come from one of two types of environments. The first are waterlogged deposits that contain large quantities of material dumped out from adjacent settlements, such as at Star Carr (Clark 1954; 1972) or Ringkloster (Andersen 1974; 1994). Many lake-side sites in Zealand, such as at Svaerdborg I (Henriksen 1976), illustrate what happens in these locations, namely that the shoreline is a treasure house of organic material but as one moves onto the slightly higher, drier, habitable ground, much less organic material is found (Fig. 10.1). Moynagh Lough (Bradley 1999) and Derragh Island (Fredengren 2009) provide good Irish examples of waterlogged sites. The second type of environment where preservation can be quite good is within middens. In certain regions caves have provided environments that have preserved a rich and varied range of organic materials but, in Ireland, evidence of Mesolithic use of caves for dwelling is, as noted in Chapter 4, extremely limited.

Mammals

The evidence from the Earlier Mesolithic is confined to Mount Sandel and Lough Boora. In contrast, so far approximately 250 identifiable bones are known from Later Mesolithic contexts. Of the ten known locations, only four sites have produced ten or more identifiable bones (Table 10.2).

As over 90% of the bones from all species are wild boar, it therefore appears that very little can be said about the exploitation of the species, such as hare, otter, bear and dog/wolf, as numbers of bones for each species from each site are in single figures.

Wild boar

The substantial presence of wild boar remains comes from four assemblages. The two largest appear impressive but they consist mostly of fragmentary bones so that even minimum numbers of individuals (MNI) are difficult to estimate. Van Wijngaarden-Bakker (1985) notes that the number of individuals at Mount Sandel could be anywhere between three and 30. Perhaps, from the excavator's perspective, it could be noted that specific pig bones occurred consistently in a large number of pits and hearths, representing numerous different events, and suggest that wild boar was an important sources of food. In spite of the calcined nature of the bones, van Wijngaarden-Bakker found it possible to establish on the basis of the fusion rates of the phalanges that many of the animals at these sites were young adults and that, in the case of Lough Boora, they were about 18 months old and killed in the summer. At Mount Sandel they were slightly older and killed during the winter. Van Wijngaarden-Bakker (*ibid.*) also noted the presence at Mount Sandel of some foetal pig bones which, again, suggests a presence near the end of the winter.

Is this fully representative of the age range of wild boar that were hunted in the Irish Mesolithic? It is possible that

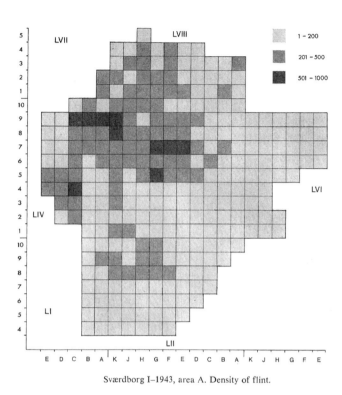

Sværdborg I–1943, area A. Density of flint.

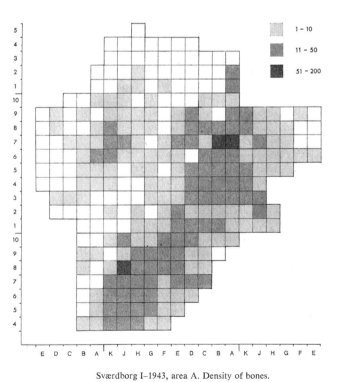

Sværdborg I–1943, area A. Density of bones.

Fig. 10.1. Plan of complementary distributions of faunal remains and lithic from the excavation at Svaerdborg I (Henriksen 1976) by permission of Nationalmuseet/National Museum of Denmark.

Table 10.2. Mammalian remains recovered from Major Irish Mesolithic sites.

Site	Pig	Hare	Canid	Bear	Other
Earlier Mesolithic					
Mount Sandel	322	6 + (3?)	1	–	–
Lough Boora	705	–	(4?)	–	1
Later Mesolithic					
Ferriter's Cove	86	4	1	–	–
Dalkey Island	23	–	18	4	
Baylet	4	–	–	1 + (2?)	3
Moynagh L.	51	–	–	1	3
Sutton	6	–	–	(1?)	–
Others	6	–	1	–	1

different sizes or ages within the same species will be treated in a different manner. Magnell (2003) noted that large, mature wild boar will be butchered and filleted for their meat, perhaps for smoking and storage. The remains, including the bones, will be discarded away from the dwelling. In contrast, piglets will be roasted on the fire and, presumably, their bones would end up in the fire, as seems to have happened at Mount Sandel. Undoubtedly the high number of phalanges at Mount Sandel was a product of burning that left small bones more intact and likely to be identified. Their presence along with recognisable portions of bones from the rest of the body suggests that these younger animals were butchered on-site.

Of the other bone assemblages which date to the Later Mesolithic and are unburnt, at Ferriter's Cove, McCarthy (*et al.* 1999) felt that little could be stated about the minimum numbers of individuals or their age, though it is noticeable that there is no evidence for the presence of very young pigs or old males.

Faunal remains from Derragh Island Site A (Fredengren 2009; in prep.) represent a different type of problem. This site is an artificial platform created by several phases of occupation (see Chapter 4) which "stretch back to 7500–6000 cal BP" (Fredengren 2009, 884). These phases ended in the creation of a stone platform that contained some Neolithic artefacts. The faunal remains which occur primarily in the uppermost layers were in the waterlogged deposits on the edge of the platform and belong to the final stages of the Later Mesolithic, and seem to have been dominated by pig bones, most of which would be wild boar. The uppermost layer contained a Neolithic presence in the form of cattle bones, one of which is dated to the Early Neolithic. It should also be remembered that this material came from a portion of an excavated area of less than 60 sq. m. and must represent only a small portion of the total faunal remains discarded at the site.

At Moynagh Lough, where a large area was excavated, McCormick (2004) has identified a minimum number of four individuals, two of whom were very young, at the most between a few weeks and 2 months old. The other two seem to have been mature individuals that were at least 2 years old. Cut marks indicated that the animals were de-fleshed at the site and the meat was then cooked and consumed. The bones themselves were fractured so that marrow could be obtained. The breaking of bones for marrow would certainly explain the very high numbers of unidentifiable fragments of bone that have been found at a number of sites.

Unfortunately the number of bones from the coastal shell middens is quite small. The largest numbers are from the two middens on Dalkey Island, where the Northern midden produced 10 pieces and the Southern midden produced seven fragments. While Hatting (1968b, 172) felt that it was impossible to ascertain whether any of these were from wild boar, a radiocarbon date from each midden showed that some at least were of Mesolithic age (Woodman *et al.* 1997). In the case of Sutton, the relatively small area of excavations produced two large incisors, which suggest mature males of uncertain age, while an unworn milk molar would have come from a very young pig.

Elsewhere in Europe there is a range of different age distributions for wild boar. At Polderweg, van Wijngaarden-Bakker *et al.* (2001) noted that more than 60% of the boar remains recovered belonged to animals that were 2 years old or more. Similarly, in Denmark at the inland Ertebølle site of Ringkloster in Jutland (Andersen 1974), the carcasses of quite mature wild boar dominated the faunal remains. It does not follow that only mature boar were hunted, indeed two summer short-time Maglemose sites in Zealand show an interesting contrast. It appears that the remains of juvenile boar were found at Svaerdborg I (Aaris-Sørensen 1976, 139) while, at the similar lakeshore site of Ulkestrup, the remains were of animals that were less than 2 years old; in fact some were only a few months old (Richter 1982).

In general the following observations can be made. In spite of the difference in condition between the calcined Earlier Mesolithic material from Mount Sandel and Lough Boora and the unburnt remains from other sites that are of the Later Mesolithic, there is no particular evidence which shows that there was a change in the manner in which wild boar were procured. There is, however, some evidence of procurement in different parts of the year. A case can be made, based on the presence of foetal and very young pigs, for the wild boar from Mount Sandel being hunted in the winter and perhaps the early spring, while the other sites appear to belong to the spring through the summer. From the little evidence available it also seems that young and younger mature pigs were hunted and that there is less evidence for older males and females being hunted. Indeed, a case can be made that the females may have been deliberately excluded and not killed.

On the basis of this relatively slight evidence and as the deliberate human introduction of pigs is not impossible, can we say that pigs were part of a managed economy or that there was a close symbiotic relationship?

Other species

Perhaps the most interesting scarcity from all the faunal assemblages is that of the hare. Even in the late glacial of England (Price 2003, 34), hare would have been trapped quite regularly and was undoubtedly skinned for clothing and taken for food. Although it has not been documented in detail, hare occurs with some frequency in some of the Irish caves.

Similarly, otter bones, which occur at two sites, may represent the bones of animals that were caught for their pelt rather than their food value. The occasional wolf/dog bone, such as those from Mount Sandel and Rockmarshall, again may have been procured for their skins. The stoat, present perhaps from the late glacial, could also have been trapped for its skin. There is no evidence that pine martens, which were caught and skinned on a large scale at Ringkloster in Denmark (Andersen 1974), were available in Ireland during the first half of the Holocene. Finally, there is little clear evidence that red squirrel, pine marten, fox and badgers were present in the Early Holocene and the case for the presence of wolf is still quite equivocal (see Chapter 2).

The interesting case of the bear in Ireland

Perhaps the metaphorical "Elephant in the Room" for the Irish Mesolithic is the bear, which had once been presumed to be extremely rare on archaeological sites but has a consistent presence through the late glacial Interstadial, as well as the Younger Dryas and through the Early Holocene until at least

well into the Bronze Age (see Chapter 2). Not surprisingly, a number of bear bones have turned up that can be dated to the Mesolithic. They occur on at least four archaeological sites, as detailed in Table 10.3.

These may seem to be little more than a sparse or minimal record that could suggest bears were of marginal significance, but Helskog (2012, 217) has recently pointed out that, while bears seem to have played an important role in many hunter-gatherers societies, their skeletal remains tend to be remarkably limited. Nelson (1973), in his study of the Alaskan Kutchin, who primarily hunted the smaller black bears, noted that bears "provide little food but occupy a major role in the minds of the people" (*ibid.*, 115).

There are other examples, such as at least the putatively worked bear bone from Derragh Island (Christina Fredengren, pers. comm.). However identification of human working of bones can be tricky and it is likely that the Derragh bone is a typical example which has been altered through deterioration and canine gnawing at a particularly thin point on the metapodial. (Eva David, pers. comm.). Other examples could include a very fine complete bear incisor from disturbed deposits found during the Liversage (1968) excavations at Dalkey Island, which could also belong to the Mesolithic phase of activity. Some of the others, such as two undated skulls noted by Ball (1849, 416–20) as recovered from "some 8 ft down in a cut away bog" from the borders of Westmeath and Longford could be Early Holocene in date.

It is likely that many other fragmentary bear bones from archaeological excavations could be lying unrecognised and simply dismissed as fragment of large mammal bone. It is therefore significant that it has been suggested that some of the bone points from the Cutts area on the Bann (described in Chapter 5) were made from bear bones (David *et al.* forthcoming.). A major question must be: were these bears deliberately killed and how were these creatures hunted?

The brown bear (*Ursus arctos*) is the mostly widely distributed bear and it varies tremendously in size from Kodiak bears (*Ursus arctos middendorffi*), that can weigh over 600 kg to small Italian examples that weigh less than 100 kg. Perhaps the Irish bears could be compared to the Pyrenean brown bears, where the males can exceed 180 kg and the females can weigh as much as 130 kg.

Table 10.3. Bear bones from Mesolithic contexts.

Site	Bear bones recovered
Baylet	Metapodial, phalanx, 2 limb fragments?
Dalkey Middens	3 phalanges
Moynagh Lough	Metapodial
Sutton	Limb fragment?

Could bears have been caught – though this still leaves the risky business of killing them? Could they have been caught using booby traps, such as deadfalls, as noted by Oswalt (1975, 139–40), or by snares, as suggested by Nelson (1973, 116)? One favoured tactic was to identify where they had been hibernating in their den and then kill them as they exited. In recent times they would often have been shot with a rifle but there are also records of them being killed with knives and spears before the rifle became commonplace.

Many of the Moynagh Points are too thin and fragile for such a task but, based on the idea discussed by Oswalt (1975, 85) that Butt Trimmed Forms were used like some of the large bear hunting spears might seem attractive, except that their profusion on shoreline sites and the thick butt that makes hafting difficult, suggests that their use for that purpose seems unlikely. Doug Bamforth (pers. comm.) has commented on the virtual absence of any wear that would suggest hafting on a wooden shaft (see Chapter 5). This, along with an apparent absence of the types of impact fractures that might be found if these artefacts had been the tips of spears or other projectiles, must regrettably mean that Butt Trimmed tipped bear hunting spears must be put to one side.

Ikeya (2006) has analysed the bear hunting patterns of the Matagai and Ainu of north-eastern Japan and suggested that, at least in that region, trapping bears and documenting the caves where bears could be caught, led to the development of a sense of territoriality where each family had particular hunting sites and where, on the basis of observed patterns of bear movements, traps could be set up. The deadfall traps constructed could contain up to 400 kg of stones. In this region the traps are prepared from late September to mid-November and in general one bear per year is caught. In other parts of the world hunting bears is also seasonal (Helskog 2012, 214), especially in late winter/early spring, perhaps when the animals are beginning to emerge from hibernation.

We are also inclined to assume that methods of capture have to leave some physical presence in the archaeological record; therefore we rarely explore other strategies, such as the use of poisons. Karsten and Knarrström (2003, 188–9) have discussed the possibility that the juice of mistletoe was used, though in their case they were considering that the poison was applied to wooden arrow tips.

Could these animals have been hunted for their meat and skins or are the occasional bones as a result of chance discoveries of dead animals that were kept as trophies or mementoes? There is quite a high incidence of foot bones, which could suggest either trophies or perhaps the retrieval of skins where the foot bones were retained during transport.

As discussed above, large animals may have been butchered away from settlement sites or the residue could be dumped in lakes or bone yards away from the dwellings, therefore their absence from Mount Sandel, where so much of the faunal remains comes from the hearths, is not surprising. In contrast, the bones from the Later Mesolithic middens (i.e. dumps) at

Baylet, Dalkey and Sutton (?), as well as lakeshore sites such as Moynagh, represent a different pattern of disposal. It is interesting that in three instances the bones occur on islands, for example Sutton, on the then island of Howth and Baylet on Inch Island in Lough Swilly, that may perhaps have had a small, temporary population of bears; it seems unlikely that bears would have existed on Dalkey Island. If, in the absence of other large animals, bear bones were used as raw materials, or the bones were smashed for marrow, then it is possible that some of the large unidentified fragments of mammal bones may be have been bear.

Although bear bones occur on some mainland European sites their presence is not as regular as might be imagined. For example, they were not recorded as occurring in either the Star Carr assemblage (Fraser and King 1954) or in that from Polderweg III in the Netherlands (van Wijngaarden-Bakker *et al.* 2001). Both of these are quite large assemblages. Even in a situation where several thousand mammal bones have been recovered the bear bones rarely reached double figures. At Sværdborg 1, Sørensen (1976) documented only eight bear bones out of nearly 3000 fragments identified to mammal species. In Norway, at Kotedalen, the three earliest phases produced a total of 511 identifiable mammal bones, of which six were bear. At Agerod in Sweden (Lepiskaar 1978, table lxxxvi, 242), as on the Irish sites, they were primarily teeth and foot bones.

In summarising the role of the bear in particular there is no doubt that any review has to begin by recognising several important factors. First, for reasons explained earlier, while bears were available throughout the Mesolithic, they have only been found on archaeological sites of the Later Mesolithic. So far approximately 250 identifiable bones are known from Later Mesolithic contexts and of these ten known locations, only four sites have produced ten or more identifiable bones of any specific mammal species. Yet the overall pattern based on the accumulated total from these sites is striking. Bear bones may appear to be scarce but they are, after pig bones and along with the hares, the most frequently recovered species recovered during the Later Mesolithic. This is apart from canid bones, which are mostly dog, and mostly from the Dalkey Island middens.

Brunner (2007), in reviewing the history of bears and especially in their relationship with humans, frequently noted that, besides mystical and shamanistic roles, amongst many societies they were valued as a source of food; as meat and fat as well as raw materials and clothing. Brunner (*ibid.*, 107) has also noted that the Ainu of Hokkaido frequently captured young bear cubs and raised them, a practice which could have existed in Ireland (Figure 10.2).

Sea mammals

Perhaps the greatest surprise must be the absence of sea mammal bones from Ferriter's Cove. The Dalkey Island basal middens, in contrast, have produced between them 19 bones or

Fig. 10.2. a) Saami of bear hunting: drawing of the hunt (by permission of Knut Helskog).

identifiable fragments all of which, with one exception, belong to *Halichoeros gryphus*, the grey seal. The one exception is a vertebra from a dolphin which came from the northern midden. Other individual seal bones were found at Baylet and Rockmarshall. At the moment one must wonder whether extensive killing and butchery of seals would have taken place on an island such as Inishtrahull where, today, there is a particularly large seal colony.

The one whale bone found in the Larne Gravels cannot be assumed to have been in contact with humans of Mesolithic age, but it does remind us that, as with the Yamana of Tierra del Fuego (Piana pers. comm.), the beaching of a whale was something that would attract several groups to the location as the fresh carcass would have been a very important source of food as well as raw materials.

The consequences of the absences

At first sight one is inclined to look simply at how the reduced number of mammal species effects food procurement, but there are further dimensions that also need to be considered. The question of skins and clothing will be discussed later but the examination of the assemblages from waterlogged sites such as Star Carr and the Danish Maglemose sites from Zealand, shows that certain species and particular elements were very important sources of raw material, such as limb bones and the antlers of the Auroch and cervids as well as elk. Obviously one is aware of the range of projectiles, such as barbed and simple points as well as harpoons, but these sites also produced axes, adzes and mattocks made from bone and antler as well as a range of skin-working tools and even antler tips for flint-working (Fig. 10.3; Andersen 1981). Zamostje (Lozovski 1996, 88–91) has,

Fig. 10.2. b) Rock art of bear hunting: plan of rock art (by permission of Knut Helskog).

for example, produced large numbers of beaver jaws whose front teeth were used for wood-working. In this latter instance, the absence of other cutting materials, i.e. lithics such as flint or chert, meant that the beaver jaws were ideal alternatives.

A possibility for Ireland that is now being actively explored is the idea that bear bones, which are particularly robust, were used as the raw material for the manufacture of some of the bone points discussed in Chapter 5. Indeed, as some of the points are in excess of 200 mm in length, it is difficult, in an Irish context, to come up with a suitable alternative. If portions of the bear skeleton were used, then perhaps various elements were broken up to provide raw materials for various

purposes, thus the remnants of the bear skeleton could be lost in unidentifiable mammal bone fragments.

Birds

Perhaps the most significant aspects of the avifauna from Mesolithic sites are 1) they are surprisingly absent from some sites, notably Moynagh Lough, and 2) the larger water fowl that might have been expected at Mount Sandel and Lough Boora are poorly represented.

In the case of most of the coastal sites, only a few bird bones have been recovered. As many of these sites, such as

Dalkey, Sutton and Ferriter's Cove were close to areas where sea birds would have nested, it might have been expected that a significant number of sea bird bones would be recovered. Some excavations were relatively limited and, as a result, small numbers of bones were to be expected but even at Ferriter's Cove only 56 bird bones were recovered and most were burnt beyond identification. It was only possible to identify the presence of guillemot (*Uria aalge*), sea gull, possibly herring gull (*Larus Argentatus*) and gannet (*Sulla bassana*) (McCarthy *et al.* 1999). From the Leinster middens, one puffin (*Fratercula artica*) bone and one from a razorbill or guillemot were the only sea birds identified. It could be argued that the presence of these bones is suggestive of a summer occupation on the coast and that their relative scarcity could also suggest that the coastal presence took place after the breeding season was finished. The occasional blackbird (*Turdus merula*) bone from the Dalkey middens should not be overlooked, as after all blackbirds were regularly consumed in the medieval period. Mount Sandel and Lough Boora have produced some numbers of bones from a diverse range of species. In each case the largest group of bones is represented by the wood pigeon (*Columba palumbus*) but, at Mount Sandel, ducks and divers represent nearly one-third of the bird bones present. The occurrence of grouse (*Lagopus lagopus*) and capercaillie (*tetrao urogallus*), even though rare, suggest that these larger birds could be sought as a major source of food. Perhaps the diversity of species from Mount Sandel could be an indication that the site was used for a considerable period of the year.

It seems, from the very limited evidence, that birds such as the often plump and ungainly wood pigeon and woodcock, along with the grouse and water fowls, could be caught with nets and traps and may have formed an important addition to Mesolithic diets. Wood pigeon today seem almost tame and are often ground-feeders that flock in quite large groups during the breeding season.

One aspect of the Irish avifauna very probably does not relate to food. Mount Sandel has produced six goshawk (*Accipiter gentilis*) and two eagle bones though these are of uncertain species. Lough Boora has added two bones of peregrines. Within the very meagre coastal assemblage of the Dalkey northern midden were three bones of white tailed sea eagle (*Haliaeetus albicilla*), and a further bone of a goshawk. These raptors might have been accidentally caught in traps or nets but it does seem probable that they may have been caught for their plumage, which could be used for display as trophies or even totemic symbols.

In comparison to many European assemblages the avifauna from the Irish Mesolithic seems quite sparse. It is interesting that its relative importance in Ireland seems much greater than elsewhere. In the case of the basal middens from Dalkey, for every bird bone there were approximately, irrespective of whether they were recent domesticates or not, eight mammal bones (Hatting 1968a, 171–3). In the two Earlier Mesolithic assemblages the ratio of bird bones was even higher, thus at

BONE/ANTLER EQUIPMENT OF DOMESTIC USE

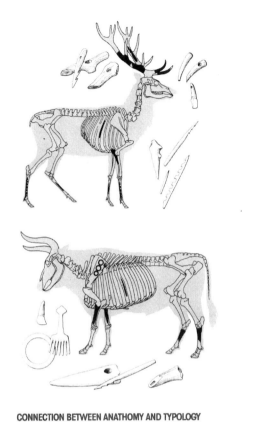

CONNECTION BETWEEN ANATHOMY AND TYPOLOGY

(acc. S.Andersen)

Fig. 10.3. Use of aurochs and deer bones as raw materials for tools (after Anderson 1981).

Lough Boora it was one bird bone for every three mammal bones (1:3) and at Mount Sandel it was four mammal bones for every bird bone (1:4). In comparison to sites in other parts of Europe these ratios are relatively high. In Denmark, the Younger Maglemose site at Ulkestrup in Aamosen (Richter 1982) has a ratio of approximately 1:7, while at Smakerup in Saltbaekvig the ratio was 1:150 (Larsen 2005). Therefore, while we are all aware that one plump wood pigeon does not have the same nutritional value as one pig, and while the Irish sites are both rare and contain few bones, these surviving remains provide a possible indication that birds played a more important role here than elsewhere.

Fish

Fish bones are the most common bones from Irish Mesolithic sites. Again, many are unidentifiable and often the presence of large numbers of vertebrae gives a spurious impression that fish were extremely well represented on Irish sites. The Leinster shell midden sites have produced some fish bones but they are relatively rare and, in the absence of sieving, likely to be unrepresentative. It should be remembered that while individual bones are numerous the minimum number of individuals (MNI) represented can be quite low. At Smakkerup Huse in Denmark, for example, Larsen (2005) estimated that an assemblage containing 9332 identifiable fish bones may represent no more than 22 individuals – and it takes a lot of fish to provide the same amount of food as one boar!

There are, of course, possible pitfalls in assessing the significance of sea fish. First, many species may only be present on a seasonal basis; however, a number of species can be present all year round, both in the lakes and in the sea but can be difficult to catch at certain seasons of the year. These include a number of the key species, such as whiting, i.e. pollack and saithe, which will tend to keep to deeper waters in the winter and not be so easy to catch. This could be equally true of eels which tend to spend much of the winter in the muddy bottoms of loughs and lakes.

While the importance of sieving has been mentioned earlier, routine sieving may not be adequate to recover the bones of certain fish species. The three-spined sticklebacks (*Gasterosteus aculeatus*) are a good example. It is possible that, although they are very small, if caught in reasonable sized shoals, sticklebacks could have been processed to provide an adequate meal. Through a careful sieving programme that was carried out at Ertebølle, where a range of both freshwater and sea fish had been caught, significant evidence in the form of dumps of bones of sticklebacks was recovered (Enghoff 1986). In this instance, samples from a column (N) were taken back for careful analysis

and processed through a series of sieves with mesh down to 0.5 mm in size. The result was that 50% of the bones recovered were of three-spined sticklebacks. Stickleback bones from the main trench excavation constituted only 0.5% of the fish bones recovered! This shows very clearly that, even with routine field sieving where 2.0 mm mesh sieves are used, the bones of certain species will still be missed. Sieving at Clowanstown. albeit in a Neolithic context, produced a number of stickleback bones. Herring is another good example of species whose tiny bones mean that they are often under-represented.

So far five sites have produced significant numbers of fish bones and the Dalkey Island middens can be added to this group. Three of these sites, Ferriter's Cove, Baylet and Port of Larne, are in coastal locations, while one, Mount Sandel, could be described as inner estuary. Only Lough Boora, which is situated in the interior of Ireland has produced any number of fish bones (Table 10.4).

Limited numbers of bones of other species of fish were also recorded from the four sites listed in Table 10.4. In these cases they were either recovered from only one site and/or were in general recorded in very small numbers, i.e. single figures.

Ferriter's Cove: haddock (*Melanogrammus aeglefinus*) 14, ray (Thornback?: *Raja clavata*) 13, shark-type (Elasmobranches) 26, scad (*Trachurus trachurus*) 12, mullet(Mugilidae) 5, salmon 1.

Baylet 1: sea bass 3, halibut (*Hippoglossus hippoglossus*) 15, plaice (*Pleuronectes platessa*) 14, Percidae 3, ray 1.

Port of Larne: sea bass (*Dicentrarchus labrax*) 1.

Dalkey middens: mullet 1.

Table 10.4. Fish remains from coastal sites.

SPECIES	Ferriter's Cove	Baylet	Port of Larne	Dalkey Middens
Wrasse (*Labrus berggyylta*)	1405	–	YES	1
Whiting (*Merlangius merlangus*)	1123	25	YES	–
Cod (*Gadus morrhua*)	57	5	–	1?
Gadidae	221	254	YES	–
Saithe (*Pollachius virens*)	8	30	–	–
Cod/Saithe/Pollack	–	52	–	–
Tope (Galeorhinus galeus)	159	–	Yes	37
Ling (*Molva molva*)	25	–	–	–
Herring (*Clupaea harrangus*)	17	100	–	–
Gurnard (Triglidae)	46	–	–	–
Common eel (*Anguilla anguilla*)	3	18	Yes	–
Conger eel (*Conger conger*)	28	1	Yes	12

Fish bones were also recovered from Rockmarshall: mullet 5+?, sole? (*Solea vulgaris*) 1, tope 5+, while Warren (2008, 21) has noted that wrasse and conger eel, as well as possibly mackerel, have been recovered from his excavations at Belderrig, Co. Mayo.

McErlean (2003b) has provided an historical account of the fish and fishing tradition in Strangford Lough and adjacent parts of the Co. Down coast, albeit in much later periods. His account provides an interesting glimpse of what might have existed at an earlier time round many of the Irish Sea loughs and, while accepting the decline in fish stocks by the beginning of the 19th century, he notes the diversity of fish that would have been available at an earlier date on this stretch of the coast. Even in the early 1800s, the combined Strangford fleet consisted of 180 boats of different types. At an earlier date, large numbers of grey mullet and herring could be caught within the lough, along with plaice and sand eels. Mullet, in particular, would have been present in Strangford Lough for up to 10 months of the year. Eels and flounders, which migrate, can be caught in the autumn and winter. Several other species are found in the lough, although, as demersal species living towards the bottom, they may be difficult to catch at certain times of the year. These include conger eel, plaice and saithe. Further south, in Dundrum Bay, excavations at Anglo-Norman Clough Castle produced large numbers of fish bones – predominantly cod. In this latter instance the whole process of fishing may have been closer to that practised in the 18th century rather than the Mesolithic.

It can, therefore, be presumed that many of the sea loughs round the Irish coast could have, relatively easily, provided large and reliable catches of fish for a significant portion of the year. Perhaps the richness of the sea and the manner in which large numbers of fish could be caught with the simplest technologies is reflected most eloquently in Dobb's 17th century account of fishing at Waterfoot on the Co. Antrim coast (1683: Hill 1978, appx 2):

> This Bay yields a great plenty of fish, as salmon, turbot, plaice, turbot, cod, whiting, mackerel, ling, hallybut, a fish something like turbot, and herring; I have seen people stand upon the shore, some wading little way out, and draw in small nets upon the shore in a dark night, and the lookers on with small bags in their hands, some would throw sand in the faces and eyes of the fishers, others with their bare feet or toes make holes in the nets for the herrings to slip out and so whip them into their bags and away with them.

The three main coastal sites have all produced relatively large numbers of fish bones but, while there was an extensive process of sieving of samples from Ferriter's Cove, the material from the Port of Larne and Baylet came from limited contexts. At Baylet, which had been heavily disturbed (Chapter 4), only a small basal portion of the excavated area of the midden belonged to the Mesolithic and the fish bones came from an area of less than 10 sq. m. in that basal area. Harte (1866) suggested that the original midden stretched for 80 yards (73

m) before the sea level rose with material lying against the slope and that there was a basal Mesolithic layer that ran the full extent of the midden. If so, then the midden may have contained 50–100,000 fish bones. Similarly, at Port of Larne, nearly 2000 fish bones were recovered from one complex of contexts. As at Ferriter's Cove these were primarily calcined fish bones. They were recovered from a number of soil samples that had been sieved. It is possible that many tens of thousands of fish bones still remain in unsieved samples from the Port of Larne!

Unfortunately, Dalkey produced a very small series of fish bones and, based on the experience of the Oronsay middens (Mellars 1978), it is probable that a much broader range of species would have been recovered had sieving taken place.

The range of very common species of fish usually includes wrasse, whiting and gadidae, with smaller numbers of tope. Naturally, given the different types of location, there is some variation between the sites. Both Ferriter's Cove and Port of Larne face out onto the open sea, while Baylet lies some distance up Lough Swilly, nearly 30 km from the open sea. At the latter site, besides the gadidae and saithe/pollack, there was an interesting concentration of herring, with wrasse being virtually unrepresented. Many of the differences could be explained by fishing taking place at different seasons of the year and by slightly different environments pertaining at the various sites.

As can be seen from Table 10.4, the three species which appear to dominate the record are, therefore, wrasse, whiting and pollack/saithe. Wrasse could be caught from the shore in and around some of the rocky bays that lay close to the sites. Whiting and saithe or pollack can be found offshore, though shoals of small young fish could be found closer in. Many of the other fish can also be recovered from similar environments, for example, conger eels, which could be obtained from rock pools, while the tope again seem to be quite young and could have been caught close to the shore. While some interesting individual fish specimens were noted, such as the large conger eel from the Port of Larne (Hamilton Dyer unpublished) and the large portion of tope from Ferriter's Cove, perhaps the most interesting group is the 67 ootoliths of young whiting found in one concentration near hearth F5 at Ferriter's Cove (McCarthy *et al.* 1999, 87). The whiting could have been caught as one event from a shoal that was close in shore. This raises the question as to how the fish were caught: either from the shore with line and hook, or perhaps, by long line fishing from an inshore boat, or with nets. Both McCarthy (*ibid.*) and Parks (in prep.) have noted within the Ferriter's Cove and Baylet assemblages respectively that, where it is possible to estimate the size of fish caught, in general they tend to be of small or medium size and there is little clear evidence that they were caught in large numbers or well off shore.

The two best known so-called inland sites of Mount Sandel and Lough Boora are placed in very different locations. Mount Sandel would have been positioned above the river estuary of the Lower Bann, while Lough Boora would have lain on a lake that is as far inland as it would have been possible, even at 9000 cal BP. A comparison of the fish bone assemblages is given in Table 10.5.

At the time of the main phase of settlement at Mount Sandel, it was probably located just upstream from the inner estuary of the Bann (Batterbee *et al.* 1985, 111–20). It would also have been placed relatively close to the open sea. The site was therefore positioned so as to take advantage of fresh water and brackish environments. Most importantly it was also placed near the Cutts and a ford where salmon migrating upstream could be caught, and the late autumn and early winter downstream migration of eels intercepted (see Chapter 11). Perhaps the most striking aspect of the Mount Sandel fish assemblage is its diversity. Both major migratory species were present. Trout, which may have migrated over short distances or which were almost residential in the area, were also caught. While sea fish are somewhat rarer it is of interest that bones of flounder, a species that could penetrate and live in the estuary, especially in the summer, were also found. Sea bass, probably caught further out near the open sea, were the only other sea fish that were recovered.

From many coastal and island sites round the edge of Europe, there is a significant lack of salmon bones in archaeological contexts of Mesolithic date (see Chapter 7). As McErlean (2003b, 139–40) has observed: "The most effective method of capture was to trap or net them in tidal estuaries where they gathered in huge numbers at predictable times of the year en route to their freshwater spawning grounds."

Went (1963) also noted that, in the north-east of Ireland, it was not until the early 1800s that fixed engines that could be used in the open sea adjacent to the shoreline were introduced from Scotland to exploit the movement of salmon along the coast. The relative absence of salmon from many coastal sites may, in part, be due to the fact that it was, in those areas, more difficult to catch in number while it was simpler to concentrate on the river estuaries. On the other hand, very few Early Mesolithic European sites have been excavated that would have existed, during the Early Holocene, in an estuarine environment.

Table 10.5. Identified fish remains from Mount Sandel and Lough Boora.

SPECIES	Mount Sandel	Lough Boora
Salmon	894	–
Trout	568	709
Salmonidae	43	–
Common eels	122	1371
Flatfish	13	–
Sea bass	144	–

In the Bann Estuary, salmon would have had to congregate and wait for sufficient water discharge to allow them passage through the Cutts. This would have been an ideal location to catch them in large numbers (Pl. XXIXa). The richness of this part of the Lower Bann is best illustrated by Castleroe, which was built in Late Medieval times to protect the fishing rights (Woodman and Mitchel 1993). In 1542 a garrison was placed further downstream at Coleraine to guard the fisheries. As late as the 1850s, when drift netting along the coast would have begun to affect the size of the population, Thompson was able to record (1856), 120 tonnes of salmon being caught every year just downstream from Coleraine at the Cranach (see Kennedy and Vickers 1993, 383; Fig. 5.44). Kennedy and Vickers (*ibid.*, 383) also note that draft nets were used upstream at locations such as Loughan Island and Portglenone. It is tempting to see the use of drift nets for salmon or even eels (see below), but this often required several large boats and/or long nets and we cannot even be sure that the raw materials were available for the manufacture of nets that would be 30 m or more in length.

While evidence of fish traps and weirs has been recovered, for example at Toome or the Spencer Dock site, there would not necessarily have been a need for large fish traps and weirs at Mount Sandel, as simple hand-held baskets and nets thrown into the water at narrow points would have sufficed to catch the salmon or eels. Nets placed in the river or used from boats may also have existed in the Mesolithic. Mitchel (1965) has documented the different ways in which eels can be caught. This includes traps and nets from boats. It would also seem probable that many of the bone points recovered from the Cutts were parts of either Leisters or eel rakes (see Chapter 5).

At the moment it is difficult to judge from modern practices whether, in the past, salmon could have been an important source in Lough Neagh. This is mostly because of disruption to spawning grounds and the role of coastal drift netting. In recent times fishing in Lough Neagh has been overwhelmingly dominated by the pursuit of eels (Woodman and Mitchel 1993).

As noted in Chapter 9, many modern fish traps are in the same locations as large concentrations of Mesolithic artefacts, such as those put in place around Kilrea or at Toome. These were placed to catch eels during their migration to the sea. Although relatively few eel bones were recovered at Mount Sandel, eels were probably an extremely important source of food throughout the Irish Mesolithic. It may be that salmon, which are so well documented in Irish literature, attract greater attention in their mystical role and as "*an Bradan feasa*" or the salmon that gives wisdom. There are, however, good reasons to believe that eels may have played a more important role.

Two other riverine sites have produced quite limited evidence of fishing. One tiny portion of what may have been a similar site was found just upstream from the Cutts, Castleroe (Woodman 1985a, 199); it also produced a small sample of burnt faunal remains. The fish remains were kindly identified by Alwynne Wheeler as salmonids and eels. At Newferry Site 3, one hearth from Zone 4 contained some fish bones (see Chapter

4). In this instance they were kindly identified by Brinkhuizen (see Woodman 1977a, 197), again as salmonids and eels.

The one inland lakeside site which has produced significant numbers of fish bones is Lough Boora. Like Mount Sandel this is a type of site that is rare in the British Isles (Ryan 1980). Again the only bones that survived were heavily burnt. In this instance no traces of salmon were found but bones of trout were recovered. The dominant species present was eel (van Wijngaarden-Bakker 1989).

The fact that trout were found well inland in the Shannon River catchment at Lough Boora, at 9500 cal BP, is of crucial importance. Its presence so far inland, as well as that of late glacial relic species of trout in Lough Melvin and of the Dollaghan and Gillaroo species in Lough Neagh (see Chapter 2) suggests that trout were probably well established by the time humans arrived. The crucial point in the Lough Boora assemblages is the large numbers of eel bones and the absence of salmon. If one returns to recent evidence and takes the Lower Bann and Lough Neagh as the starting point, there seems to have been a much greater emphasis on eel fishing (Mitchel 1965; Woodman and Mitchel 1993). Fishing from boats like the ocean-going "*curragh*" was, at one stage, the occupation of up to 500 fishermen on Lough Neagh. Perhaps the wooden fragment of a canoe found near Lough Neagh at Wood End Lough and dated to the Mesolithic (Fry 2002) is a mute testament to eel fishing of that time. It is significant that all the weirs on the Lower Bann, with the exception of that at the Cutts, were for eel fishing and only the Cutts was used primarily for salmon. The presence of eels in sufficient quantities in many rivers, such as the Mulchair in Limerick (*ibid*.), is shown by the numerous eel forks that have been recovered.

Elsewhere in Ireland, in spite of sieving programmes, fish bones were surprisingly virtually absent from the lakeshore platforms of Moynagh Lough and Derragh Site A. Given the presence of fish remains from Mesolithic sites in the river and lake systems it is hardly likely that there were still no substantial fish populations present within these two lakes as late as the latter half of the Irish Mesolithic (8000–6000 cal BP). Alternatively, is it possible that the lakeside sites were not occupied at the appropriate season for catching fish? The presence of fish baskets at Clowanstown (Chapter 4), on the edge of what had been a small lough, indicates that fishing was taking place on inland loughs and, given the absence of fishbone from Mesolithic levels, it could suggest that they were caught and processed away from habitation sites (a sieving programme produced fish bones from later deposits, in this case levels associated with the Neolithic). As at Lough Boora, the Salmonidae were likely to be trout and the presence of fish of the Coregonus family was also noted. Both of these could have been caught during the Mesolithic. Eel was the dominant species but we can come back to the question of whether the occasional stickleback bone indicates that this species played a significant role in the economy of the Mesolithic. Its presence in substantial numbers at Ertebølle has already been noted and one might wonder whether the small fish traps from Clowanstown might have been used to catch swarms of sticklebacks. Inland evidence for fishing is still quite sparse but one must wonder if *in situ* sites that lie along the course of the Boyle River from Lough Gara would, if excavated, produce clearer evidence for fishing (see Chapter 9).

Other species also survive today in Ireland, notably the river lampreys (*Lampetra fluviatilis*), of which there are three species. Through pollution, however, their numbers have been severely reduced. The lamprey's skeletal structure is based on a softer cartilaginous framework of bones and the chance of the recovery of any remains in an archaeological context is highly unlikely and so the possibility of their presence or use in the Mesolithic is rarely discussed.

Perhaps the absences are the most striking aspects of the fish remains from these early inland sites. Several inland Early Maglemose Danish sites and other sites as far away as eastern Poland (e.g. the pre-Boreal site of Dudka; Guminiski 2003), have produced a range of fish species. The most significant species present was pike. Aside from Wels (*Solaris glanis*), which can exceed 200 kg in weight and is usually found further to the east, pike is the largest freshwater fish in north-west Europe and it must have played a significant role in the economy of many parts of mainland Europe. Clark (1975, 142–4) noted that at Hohlen Viecheln, based on MNI, 32 quite large pike were recovered. Sørensen (1976, 146) noted that, at Svaerdborg I, of the 1013 identifiable fish bones, 1006 are pike. At Ulkestrup, Richter (1982, 167) noted that large pike dominated the 586 fish bones recovered, though he felt that the lack of sieving may have biased retrieval here against smaller bones of fish.

At sites like Polderweg 4, a riverside site in the Netherlands where an intensive sieving programme was undertaken, a very diverse range of fish species was recovered (Beerenhout 2001, table 9:3). From an Irish perspective, it is noticeable that salmon are virtually absent while eels are completely absent at that site. Pike was still the most dominant species, representing 40% of the identifiable remains, while bream and carp were the other major species present. Even from the portion of the site excavated, the minimum numbers index suggests that the remains of at least 400 pike were recovered. Most of the fish seem to have been 0.5–1 m in length, while some were significantly larger. Louwe Kooijmans (2004) noted that, if the site had been fully excavated, possibly up to 10,000,000 fish bones might have been recovered. Thus, the significance of pike in that area can be appreciated. Its absence from Irish waters must therefore have required a very different series of fishing strategies during the Irish Mesolithic.

Besides the absence of many species of freshwater fish, there is a notable lack of a range of fishing equipment (Woodman 2005b). Brinkhuizen (1983) has outlined the range of equipment known from modern folklore and from the archaeological record. The lack of barbed bone points might have been expected given the absence of pike. There is a possibility that much simpler bone points were used during the Mesolithic in Ireland (see Chapter 5), either as fish spears, in the case of the larger blunt pointed examples (perhaps serving the same function as the recent metal examples: see Fig. 5.47) or as rakes, in the case of the narrower ones. These are most likely to have been used to catch eels and perhaps lampreys, probably in the same manner as one might gather up spaghetti today!

The absence of nets and recognisable net floats and sinkers is understandable. In the case of sinkers, some have been dredged up from the River Bann, for example, the triangular shaped and perforated example from Mount Sandel (Woodman 1985a, fig. 35.3), but there is no clear evidence that they are of Mesolithic date. Examples found in the Foyle Estuary are similar to that found at Mount Sandel, however the numerous examples found by May (1939) during the "Bann Dredging", although of a similar shape, had much larger holes drilled through their apex and are almost certainly modern.

Based on personal experience, as a result of observing traditional salmon catching on the Neidin River in Finmark, one should consider simpler explanations. In this instance a net was thrown into a narrow channel within the rapids and numerous large salmon were pulled out (Pl. XXIXb and c). Weights were attached to the net, not simply as sinkers but rather to provide an extra impetus for the throw. Simple river cobbles had been tied round the stones and then attached to the net. The attachments were strips of birch bark and these were simply wound round the cobbles which required no alteration to the surface to help secure the birch bark strips. These cobbles were usually still in place when the nets were pulled back in. Perhaps a small heap of cobbles found just inside the hut area at Mount Sandel had been selected for this purpose. One must ask if the rather curious small arc of stones found in the basal sands of Newferry Site 3 (Zone 9) had a similar purpose (Woodman 1977a; 2009) noted that potential alterations to some cobbles found in the lower Mesolithic deposits could suggest their use as net sinkers and/or that these could have been used to hold down the fish baskets. Movius (1936) also noted a similar presence of large cobbles at Newferry site 1 and some consideration was given to the fact that they were more likely to have been brought there by people rather than by the river. Perhaps on all these sites, on the basis of the Neidin examples, these could have been very simple net sinkers.

The presence of fixed facilities, such as the Dublin Docklands fish weirs, has been discussed (Chapter 4), therefore the only question must be that associated with their purpose. Were they intended to catch sea fish, salmon coming into the estuary, or eels coming downstream? As the fences seem to have been placed parallel to the flow of the estuary the latter seems to be the preferred explanation.

One must assume that the large number of axes found at key locations along the Lower Bann, where in some instances

fish weirs and traps still exist, are a strong indication that there would have been fish weirs created during the Mesolithic, as well as at later dates.

What is of interest is that there are no known fish hooks from Stone Age Ireland. While many fish hooks of Mesolithic date have been discovered in south Scandinavia it may be significant that none has been recovered from the Scottish Late Mesolithic Obanian sites either. Fish hooks could have been made from other materials, such as wood, or fish gorges, including perhaps some of the smallest bone points, could also have been used instead.

Shellfish and shell middens

The convenient image and consistent association of the words 'Mesolithic' and 'middens' has often led to the impression that shellfish formed the dominant element in coastal Mesolithic diets. There are, as noted in Chapter 4, very few clearly documented Mesolithic shell middens. In an Irish context this has been compounded by a common belief that shellfish were a food of last resort during the Great Irish Famine.

The Donegal Ordnance Survey Memoir of the late 1830s paints a different picture when it refers to the fact that significant numbers of shellfish were dredged from the Farland channel in the area of Burt and Inch in Lough Swilly (Day and McWilliams 1997, 147). In folklore, shellfish can also be seen as a common food in coastal communities, thus Sayers (1974, 190–2), in describing life on the Blasket Islands, refers to the roasting of the *báirneach* (limpets) and to stories of disasters and drowning, while Kirby (1990, 10–14) reminisces about how, especially around the time of the low water of spring tide, he was taken to look for shellfish, including "queen scallops" and "black winkles". The collection of shellfish can be an event. Harte (1866) refers to how the "Mountaineers" of Barnesmore came down with their families to Donegal Bay at Easter each year where: "They turned their horses loose, collected mussels, and drank whiskey".

It has long been known that the shells of shellfish bulk large in the archaeological record. Bailey (1978, 39) showed very clearly that large numbers of oysters (52,000) or limpets (31,000) had to be consumed to have eaten the equivalent of a red deer. He also suggests that, if no other food was available, 700 oysters would need to be consumed by one adult each and every day. Milner and Woodman (2001) have also pointed out that ethnographic observations suggest that the consummation of oysters for one meal would create a pile of shells almost one cubic metre in size. Mellars (1978) also showed, during the Oronsay excavations, that without a rigorous programme of sieving the significance of fish will be seriously underestimated and the role of shellfish exaggerated.

Even simple counts of the numbers of each species, no matter how carefully shellfish were recovered during excavation, can be misleading, as observed by McCarthy *et al.* (1999). In particular they noted that limpets and mussels are less robust and fragment very easily. Therefore, their percentage as a total of the shellfish recovered will often appear lower than reality. This can be combined with the fact that the food value of limpets and mussels, as well as cockles, will be higher than periwinkles and whelks per individual.

Numerous authors have highlighted the fact that others factors come into consideration. Meighan (1982) provided a seminal study as to how shellfish were viewed by Native Australian shore dwellers. In particular, she has noted that taste can be important and that, during visits to the beach to collect shellfish, certain species would be ignored in the hope that, with some perseverance, specimens of those which were prized would be found. Moss (2013) has considered the complex social implications and attitudes of the Kwkwaka'wakw and the Tlingit on the Pacific north-west coast of America. This takes many forms, for example, who eats clams relates to some extent on the social standing of the individual families within the village. Within the hierarchy of animals in their origins mythology, the clam, as a legless animal, had no status. It also appears that, while there could be fears over consumption of bad or rotten specimens, they were still an important source of food that clam gardens were created for their cultivation.

In summary, there is much more to shell middens than simply and casually collecting shellfish.

While, in Ireland, many middens that date to the Mesolithic may have been destroyed, the general impression is that none of them could be described as massive (Chapter 4). Not surprisingly, the make-up of the middens reflects the type of shoreline that would have existed in their vicinity. Irrespective of the species of shellfish, it is difficult to envisage any site that would even approach 1000 m³ of shells, yet it is estimated that the Ertebølle midden may have contained more than 3000 m³ of shell and Børnsholm (Andersen 1993) 8000 m³. By the standards of some of the Danish middens, many Irish examples are relatively small. One exception that did survive until recently the midden explored by Mitchell (1956; 1972) at Sutton, which had a length of 100 m running parallel to the beach (Chapter 4, Fig. 4.24b). In spite of the extent of destruction, some of the Lough Swilly middens may have, even in the Mesolithic, been quite extensive. These larger middens tend to be comprised of oyster, as are many of the middens in Strangford Lough.

However, on closer examination, it is apparent that it would be a mistake to over-generalise. Murray (2011, 13–14) has noted that, although they appear to be overwhelming oyster middens, both the Kilnatierney and Rough Island middens contained a mixture of shells. In both, periwinkle was the dominant species and, within the area excavated at the former site, they formed more than 60% of the total. At Rough Island periwinkles constituted 40% of the total and were the most common shell recovered. At Rockmarshall III (Mitchell 1949a) there was no specific count but it appears that the midden contained, besides oyster shell, considerable numbers of other species.

There have been, on occasions, very specific collections of a particular species, especially periwinkles. One midden exposed along a 100 m sea cliff face at Ballymoney td on Lough Swilly contained discrete concentrations of oysters and periwinkles. At Baylet, discrete mounds of periwinkles were found within the oyster midden while separate patches of mussel shells were also recovered. Jim Mallory (pers. comm.) also noted similar concentrations of periwinkles during his excavations at the oyster midden on Rough Island.

Although it cannot be regarded as a shell midden, Ferriter's Cove provided an interesting insight into either the more opportunistic use of shellfish or else a much more targeted use, where different species were sought on different occasions. It has been suggested that the dominant species was whelk (Gibbons and Gibbons 2004). This is based on the fact that whelks constitute the largest numbers of shells recovered during the whole excavation, primarily from two shell mounds (Features 1 and 3). There are, however, ten shell mounds where more than 100 shells were identified. These are much smaller than the two referred to earlier and each could be regarded as representing a separate activity where opportunistic decisions were taken. In this group of ten shell mounds, four species dominate (Table 10.6). In Feature 3, a very large number of fish bones were also recovered which, along with a range of other faunal remains found in and around other shell mounds, emphasises that shellfish were only one of the many resources that were obtained during visits to Ferriter's Cove.

There has been a suggestion that the whelks were collected for the purpose of the production of dye, as happened in historic times (Gibbons and Gibbons 2004). The general consensus is that the meat within each whelk is so tiny and, as documented by Cole (1685), the process of extraction so time consuming that it was rarely pursued outside the Mediterranean. Indeed, it was the difficulties of the process and the rarity of the purple dye that gave whelk its particular value in hierarchical societies. The process also normally required smashing the shells and the examples from Ferriter's Cove were often complete. The whelks at Ferriter's Cove were usually collected and disposed of along with other species and, in many instances, were mixed in with other food debris. There is no evidence that whelks were collected for other purposes than consumption.

Even in the case of the larger middens, it is probable that shellfish were not a source of food that was used all year round or that the middens developed over a long period of time. When the size of these middens is taken into consideration, i.e., examples that exceed 50 m in length, it is probable than shells and other refuse would have been dumped each year on only a small portion of the midden. As Milner (2002) has observed, oysters are usually obtained at or below low water mark, therefore they were more likely to have been collected in the spring when they would be at their best. It may also have been preferable to collect them at the low of spring tides.

If the figures quoted above are taken into consideration it will be apparent that even the larger Mesolithic shell mounds in

Ireland could have been created by a band of 10–15 members, who visited the location on a seasonal basis for a short period of time. There is no reason to think that even a midden such as Sutton could not have been created within the lifetime of a member of this notional band.

Perhaps the one form which has not been given sufficient attention is the smaller shell mounds that may have often been destroyed without being recognised as of particular importance. In the case of Glendhu (Woodman 1985b), an oyster and cockle midden seems to have been the product of a single or, at the most, a double event. Ferriter's Cove is a perfect example of this type of site and presents a cautionary tale (Woodman *et al.* 1999). In this instance the shellfish have been taken from a rocky shore environment and many of these small mounds may represent casual collections of what was available at the time of a short visit. The largest mound, Feature 3, had a maximum dimension of less than 3 m and roughly 20,000 shells of periwinkle, whelk and, to a lesser extent, limpets. Some of the mounds also contained mussels, with an occasional cockle shell being present. In many of these, which were often only about 0.30 m across and usually contained 100–500 shells, there was normally a dominant species. This varied from mound to mound between periwinkles, whelks and limpets. In each heap, however, there were enough other types of shells to suggest that there was a certain amount of casual collection on each occasion (Table 10.6).

Figure 4.18 may be taken to indicate that, instead of each individual heap representing separate visits, different areas of the excavation may have showed a slightly greater concentration of different species. The most notable mounds are the two largest concentrations, Contexts 1 and 3, which contain very large numbers of whelks and, to lesser extent, periwinkles. They are also in the central portion of the site where there are fewer signs of other activities. In contrast very different patterns were noted around several of the fire spots and hearths that were uncovered during the excavation. These concentrations are much smaller and often contain a much more diverse range of species, though limpets are often the most common. There seems to have been a difference between the larger dumps, which accumulated where whelks and periwinkles were being processed in large numbers, and the discarded shellfish from what would seem to have been fireside snacks.

Most of the shellfish consumed at Ferriter's Cove would have been as a dietary supplement but there were several interesting aspects to the shell assemblage. McCarthy (1988) noted that the limpets were often relatively small. While this could be put down to over-exploitation, the relatively small numbers suggest another explanation. It is possible that, for taste reasons or ease of consumption, the smaller limpets, which grew closer to low tide mark, may have been selected because of the fact that they needed a much less developed muscle foot to attach them to the rocks on the shore; therefore they were easier to collect and consume.

There is a temptation to see phenomena such as shell middens as single-purpose or single-season fits all. Most of the faunal indicators from the shell middens suggest that these sites were used during "the summer half of the year" (McCarthy *et al.* 1999, 92). In particular, the fish caught at Ferriter's Cove were likely to have been present during the summer. However, Kimball *et al.* (2009) have suggested, from δ^{18}O analyses of periwinkles from a number of locations at Ferriter's Cove, that they were collected during a cold time of the year. It is of interest that Mannino and Thomas (2007) also indicated, on the basis of δ^{18}O investigations of *M. lineata* shells from several of the layers in the Culverwell midden, that they were collected

Table 10.6. Ferriter's Cove: total numbers of shellfish from main species in larger shell heaps (bold signifies species with largest numbers in each context).

Context	Total	Limpet	Periwinkle	Whelk	Mussel
K-4/-6138	138	60	**12**	**66**	
488	955	75	**678**	169	33
491	290	**125**	84	81	–
1	5385	139	697	**4535**	14
3	19,055	274	8788	**9993**	–
4	515	39	40	**436**	–
6	131	26	54	**163**	–
203	154	11	46	34	**63**
183	1550	**926**	123	494	7
303	138	**97**	9	32	–
372	210	8	**191**	11	–

in the autumn and, in some cases, through to the winter. The emphasis was again on the colder part of the year. This pattern is also evident elsewhere as Colonese *et al*. (2011) have noted that the δ¹⁸O analysis of *Nacella Magellanica* shells at several Yamana sites on the Beagle Channel also indicate that the shells were collected in different seasons of the year. Is it possible that some locations were visited on several occasions during the year and that this could have included visits in summer, autumn and winter?

To summarise, it appears that shellfish played a significant, though not a predominant, role and may have been a key supplement at certain seasons of the year.

Plant foods

Perhaps one of the most obvious statements that can be made about the Irish Mesolithic is that the study of plant remains is still "the poor relation". While some have been identified, until recently no structured, pre-planned sampling strategies for the recovery of plant remains were put in place. At best, extensive *post-hoc* examination and sorting of samples took place. For example, at Mount Sandel, soil samples were taken primarily for the retrieval of fish bones and microliths. Mesolithic sites excavated before Mount Sandel rarely collected or retained soil samples.

One area of research has already been pursued i.e. palynological investigations that might (or might not!) show evidence for forest clearance during the Mesolithic. In the case of Ireland, unlike other parts of Europe, it is difficult to establish why, in the absence of large numbers of browsers, there should be forest clearance. Similarly, Zvelibil (1994, 41–54) has argued for some land clearance for the purpose of primitive horticulture. He has suggested that antler mattocks could be used as hoes. They are mostly found in the river floodplains, however, rather than environments where they might be expected to be used for primitive agricultural purposes. These artefacts do not, in any event, exist in Ireland.

The challenges of plant remains are many. Not only are there issues of recovery but there are also the questions surrounding the survival of plant remains in the archaeological record. If there are questions about the restricted ranges of mammals, freshwater fish and perhaps even birds, then one cannot assume that all plant species present today, would have occurred in Ireland in the first half of the Holocene.

Mears and Hillman (2007), in a television series and book, have shown the rich range of food, especially plant foods, that would have been available during the Mesolithic, but it is evident from the survey carried out by Mason *et al*. (2002), that even at a European level many sites produce quite a small number of identifiable plant remains. Therefore it is not surprising that, in Ireland, aside from hazel nuts, a relatively small number of plant remains have been identified from each site. Warren (*et al*. 2013, table 1) have listed a number of sites where plant remains occur and where some could result from consumption.

One has little choice but to start with the ubiquitous charred hazel nut shells. Hazel shrubs were probably fully established and occurred extensively across Ireland well before 10,000 cal BP. It is of interest that, while charred shells are a frequent occurrence, some sites such as Lough Boora, Derragh Island (Fredengren, pers. comm.), Cushendun (Jessen 1940) and Mitchell's Toome (Creagh) have also produced significant numbers of unburnt complete hazel nuts. So, even in the case of hazel nuts there is a need to distinguish between the *presence* of a species and its consumption.

There are numerous sites which have occasional occurrences of burnt hazel nuts, for example, the Toome Bypass site or Newferry. While Ireland has produced nothing like the very large numbers of burnt hazel nut shell fragments from a single hollow at Staosnaig on the Hebridean island of Colonsay (see below; Mithen 2000, chapter 5:2) occasional small concentrations have been recorded. At Ferriter's Cove (Woodman *et al.* 1999), alongside the small heaps of shells from shellfish there were two small mounds of burnt hazel nut shells.

Larger concentrations were recovered from many of the hearths at Mount Sandel, as well as from some of the smaller pits. The recovery of hazel nut shells from smaller pits and hearths containing some foetal pig bones, as well as young pigs approaching a year old, suggests the use of hazel nuts after a period of storage i.e. until the second half of the winter. When exactly the nuts were harvested must be a matter of some conjecture. Normally they would need to be collected as early as possible due to the likelihood that red squirrels would have moved in and collected them for *their* winter stores. But, as was discussed in Chapter 2, were red squirrels present in Ireland during the Mesolithic?

As McComb (2009, 228) has commented, hazel nuts fulfil the four conditions that made them particularly suitable for storage. These are *abundance* as well as *seasonal availability*, which can be both easily *harvested* and *stored*. McComb (*ibid.*, 229) carried out experiments to ascertain how well they would survive while stored. Where they were stored in pits, especially in baskets placed within soil in the pits, she demonstrated that the hazel nuts could survive reasonably well for 3–4 months providing issues such as damp could be obviated. However, by the following April, i.e. after more than 5 months, they would have deteriorated and mostly become inedible.

In this context, the larger Mount Sandel pits must remain of interest. Pit F.56/1, which cut through the main hut area, is the best known. While Bayliss and Woodman (2009) have shown that the large pits may not always have been contemporaneous with the huts excavated at the site, they were certainly in use in the Earlier Mesolithic (see Chapter 4; Fig. 4.16). At least one, F.74, was deliberately refilled but the other interesting group is that to the west of the huts, i.e. 209/211, where a series of intercutting pits was found. Several of these, like 56/1, were 1 m across and 0.6 m deep (Chapter 4). This may be about the average size and, allowing for the fact that soil, basketry, etc., could take up part of the space, the pits may have contained 100–200,000 nuts or perhaps 50–100 kg of nut meat.

There is also the question as to what circumstances led to the creation and survival of burnt hazel nut shells. McComb (2009, 227) has noted that, if thrown onto an open fire, in general they simply burnt up and disappeared. In contrast, when buried in wood ash and excluded from the air, carbonized fragments, like those from Mount Sandel, were produced. Therefore the remains of hazel nut shell fragments and calcined bones may have been the residue of the last banked fires before the camp was abandoned. During the Mount Sandel re-dating programme, in many instances, even in the 'occupation soil' in the main hollow, it was quite difficult to find even one burnt shell fragment. This suggests that concentrations of burnt hazel nut shells lying within an archaeological site are not likely to have been casual accumulations or the product of inadvertent burning. This raises a slight worry as to how we interpret the occasional burnt hazel nut shell that is seized upon with glee as the potential source of a radiocarbon date? The presence of occasional, in particular, individual, burnt hazel nut shells may not, of themselves, be an indication of a presence just at the time of their autumn harvesting. Given their hardiness they may not even be directly associated with the main phase of use of a particular site.

An artificially created hollow at Staoisnaig on Colonsay produced 30–60,000 burnt fragments of hazel nut shells. Mithen *et al.* (2000, chapter 5:2) suggested that this could represent up to 300,000 hazel nut shells. In this case it should also be remembered that there is no direct evidence that the hollow was actually part of the processing of hazel nuts, rather than being simply a location where the shell fragments were dumped. A hollow of roughly similar size was excavated at Cass ny Hawin (1), on the Isle of Man (Woodman 1987) preserved traces of activities on its floor but most of the artefacts, many of which were in a slightly weathered condition, had been added by nature or humans at a later date. One small patch of burnt hazel nut shells was found on the floor of the hollow.

Mithen *et al.* (2001, 227–9) re-examined the issue and noted, on the basis of experiments, that 12–25% of the hazel nuts shell would become charred during the roasting process and that the kernel within would be inedible. Thus, the charred shells would represent only a small portion of the hazel nuts processed and consumed. Perhaps more interestingly, it appears that charred hazel nut shells are, in fact, discarded waste from nuts that could not be used. Presumably they were discarded in pits, hearths etc.

At Mount Sandel we can note that, while no specific quantification was provided for hearth and pit samples, the totals quantities in each context were relatively small perhaps; at the most 1–200 nuts (Woodman 1985). These seem more likely to be burnt shells created after roasting and perhaps before a meal, as may also have happened at Ferriter's Cove (Woodman *et al.* 1999).

Amongst other plant remains, water lily and apple seeds from Mount Sandel are good examples of plants that were used. The water lily seeds would have to be brought up to the site from the floodplain that lay nearly 30 m below the site and would have constituted a seasonal food. Mears and Hillman (2007) demonstrated that water lily seeds could be ground up to prepare a meal, but if harvested too early in the summer, would produce a particularly unpalatable dish. Their presence on a dry land site 30 m above the river suggests that these were not simply naturally occurring species of plants at a location where people had chosen to live.

Waterlogged sites present a problem as many of the plant remains, most notably phragmites and the rhizomes of other plants, could have been used or may have just been present along the lake shores. On some occasions, however, even the presence in a natural context is an indication of the availability of edible plants. Thus wild raspberry was found at Derragh Island, Cushendun (Jessen 1940) and at Newferry Site 1. *Ranunculus* (lesser celladine) was identified at Derragh Island (McClatchie, in prep.). At the moment these are, at least, indicators of the potential of plant foods. Little (2014, 45–6), has commented Mitchell's list of macro-botanical plant remains from his work at Clonava 1 included not only those listed but several others, such as water sedge (*Carex cf. aquatilis*), Marsh wound-wort (*Stachis palustris*) and guilder rose (*Viburnum opulus*). These, along with the others mentioned earlier, would have been a common choice found on many north-west European Mesolithic sites.

The significance of tubers is even more difficult as they were, in the past, often not recognised, The hollow found at Staosnaig (see above) produced 28 carbonised tuber fragments (against the 30–60,000 carbonised hazel nut shell fragments, but Mason *et al.* (2002) suggested that the processing of tubers may have been of equal importance to the hazel nut harvesting.

Mears and Hillman (2007) provided details of the plant foods that might have been available in Britain during the Mesolithic. There is an assumption that most of these were present during the Mesolithic. Some may only have flourished after farming had been introduced and some may not have arrived in Ireland until a much later date, while others would only survive in waterlogged conditions as they would not have been carbonised. One can only speculate. Is it possible that berries, like the wild red currant, black currant or gooseberry, were already available in Ireland and could have been eaten? Plants such as sea kale or the berries of sea buckthorn, which could have been found on the coast, may also have been consumed. Again, one returns to the question of the consequences of Ireland being isolated as an island for perhaps 15,000 years while mainland Britain would have been a peninsula of the European Continent until well after the beginning of the Holocene.

What is noticeable is that potential food, such as acorns, seem to have no presence in Ireland or Britain. Oak would not have been present in any quantity in the very earliest phases of the Irish Mesolithic (Chapter 2) but, if acorns had been exploited at a later date then, as they require extensive processing including both grinding and washing to leach out acids, it would be expected that some presence of processing sites would have been found by now. This absence of evidence for the extensive processing of acorns is fairly typical of the European Mesolithic and an important reminder that the availability of a certain food source does not necessarily mean that it was gathered and consumed. This would be equally true of many other potential food sources at this date, for example, reed rhizomes.

It is important to realise that many other wild plant foods or raw materials for the manufacture of fibres, etc., cannot simply be collected and consumed or used immediately. They may require extensive preparation before being eaten. Similarly, the production of many other utensils and containers from reeds or plant stalks requires a process that entails several stages. In this case, micro-wear analysis may show what types of tools have been used.

The identification of plant processing equipment, such as grindstones, is another problem that needs to be tackled. The small grindstones from the Bann and elsewhere were probably used for re-sharpening axes Flanagan (1960 and see above Chapter 5) and, in any case, grindstones for use in plant processing might be expected to comprise two stones, an upper and lower, as in the case of Swifterbant culture sites (Devriendt 2013). A better case could be made for some of the other large, flat, often irregular slabs that have turned up at Newferry, Derragh Island or Rockmarshall. Little (2014), however, has made an interesting suggestion that while there is little evidence that Fulachta Fiadh existed in the Irish Mesolithic (see Chapter 4 and Hawkes 2014), based on the identification of heat treated rock fragments recovered from Clonava it is possible that some of them could have been immersed in small pits containing boiling water as part of a process of plant food preparation.

Taking an overview

At this stage it is difficult to see if there has been a major shift through time within the types of resources procured during the Irish Mesolithic. Undoubtedly there were changes in the way a range of resources were procured but, at the same time, certain aspects of Ireland's geographical location, its size and its ecology played a more significant role than any event(s) that took place throughout the 4000 years of the Mesolithic.

Does the surviving archaeological record provide a reasonable indication of the nature of the economy(ies) of the Irish Mesolithic?

As will be apparent from the foregoing discussion, the surviving record only provides a partial picture. This is a combination of what can survive; the methods of disposal of refuse as well as the methods of recovery through excavation. Perhaps the most enigmatic areas are those associated with the fact that resources may often have been processed off-site.

Staple isotope analysis on a few human remains and one dog may provide occasional glimpses that indicate some other possible interpretations should be taken into consideration. In the south-west of Ireland, it was already possible in 1999 to see that there was no one single economy. The $\delta^{13}C$ results from the human remains at Ferriter's Cove ($-14.1‰$) strongly suggested an economy that relied on marine resources while, 80 km inland, the remains of Earlier and Later Mesolithic date from Killuragh Cave had produced $-21‰$, suggesting a more land based diet. In this context it was decided to check the levels of $\delta^{13}C$ from these samples and to include $\delta^{15}N$ as well. In addition to the Ferriter's Cove and Killurgh samples, further samples from Killuragh and the human ulna from the Rockmarshall III midden were all assessed, together with a dog mandible from Dalkey, taken to provide a potential proxy for the human diet. To these we have been able to add a modified human bone dredged from on the Lower Bann at Loughan Island near the Cutts (see Chapter 5). Figure 10.4 and Table 10.7 show that there is no simple pattern.

Besides confirming the marine nature of the diet at Ferriter's Cove, the Dalkey dog bone also reflected a similar consumption of food of marine origin. What was of particular interest was that the results for two other specimens seemed to suggest a more balanced diet in which marine resources played some role but were not dominant. As Rockmarshall is on the outer

Table 10.7. Radiocarbon dates and stable isotope results on humans and dog remains.

Site	$\delta^{13}C$	$\delta^{15}N$	Date cal BP
Killuragh	-21.13‰	11.12‰	9000–8940
Killuragh	-21.50‰	9.52‰	6630–6400
Ferriter's Cove	-13.92‰	16.83‰	6500–4350
Dalkey Island (dog)	-13.71‰	15.23‰	7940–7720
Rockmarshall	-20.12‰	10.70‰	6730–6490
Loughan Island	-19.43‰	10.26‰	7923–7683

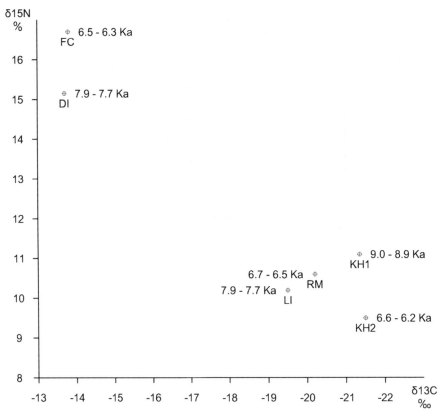

Fig. 10.4. Stable isotopes δ13C and δ15N of human and dog remains: DI = Dalkey Island (dog); FC = Ferriter's Cove; KH = Killuragh Cave samples 1 and 2; RM = Rockmarshall; LI = Loughan Island; dates expressed in terms of 1000 years (ka) (prepared by Hugh Kavanagh).

limits of a small bay looking out over the Irish Sea, a more marine signature might have been expected. However the type of mobility between the coast and inland that was envisaged for the North Leinster area in Chapter 9 would tally with the result for the Rockmarshall ulna. A bone artefact made from human bone from Loughan Island on the Lower Bann, might also have been expected to have shown a more marine signature given its location adjacent to the sea estuary.

It can be no coincidence that many of the major concentrations of Mesolithic artefacts are at locations where eel weirs exist. Eels run downstream to the sea during the later stages of the year. At a time when other sources begin to become scarce eels would still be available and could be caught in large numbers, processed and stored. The role of eels could be crucial in understanding the signatures obtained from the Killuragh samples. In this case the stable isotopes show neither a plant based diet or a marine signature such as that which might have occurred if salmon were relied upon extensively.

Lanting and van der Plicht (1996) noted that freshwater fish, including eels, have an even more negative δ13C signature than plant remains and land based animals. Fischer *et al.* (2007, tables 1 and 3) sampled not only archaeological remains but both the flesh and the bones of present day fish populations. While many

of these species, such as pike or roach, would not be relevant to Ireland, they recorded δ13C results of the flesh of eels of -26‰ to -28‰. This is against -21‰ to -23‰ obtained from humans with a land based diet. Therefore, in some cases, a diet could contain marine species, which would include salmon or perhaps whiting or cod and certainly eels, in addition to food from land based mammals. Eels would have a freshwater signature that would cancel-out or mask the marine signatures and leave an impression of a land based diet. There is, therefore, a strong probability that eels may have played a significant role during the Mesolithic. The very distinctive shape of quite a number of bone points from the River Bann and elsewhere has already been noted. It has been suggested that some examples might be best interpreted as the teeth in rakes while some larger, more bulbous-end forms, are rather like bone versions of some metal spears (Chapter 5). As observed earlier, modern rakes and spears found along the Bann are associated with eel fishing. Another possibility, in the case of Killuragh, is that lampreys, which are still present today in substantial numbers in the nearby Mulchair River, could have formed a substantial part of the diet. In these instances it is possible that communities may not be as entirely bound to the interior of Ireland as was first thought but may have moved between the coast and the interior.

The δ¹⁵N results suggested that, in general, plant foods did not dominate the diet. At the same time, the results from the Dalkey dog and the Ferriter's Cove human seemed to suggest a diet at the upper end of the food chain. Combining the carbon and nitrogen results suggests that sea fish and/or sea mammals formed the main part of the diet. However, before one begins to invent a highly specialised seal hunting economy, it is important to understand that one species consuming another does not necessarily transfer the precise stable isotope signature from what was consumed to the predator.

Fischer *et al.* (2007, 2127) carried out extensive examination of a range of Danish material of both human remains and their food sources. This included modern and archaeological samples from the coast and interior. This included a seal bone which produced δ¹⁵N result of 15.5‰. The authors point out that the values of both δ¹³C and δ¹⁵N in the bone collagen of consumers are different to those of the prey: by 1‰ for the former and 3.5 ‰ for the latter. It would be possible, in the case of a community where seals were the overwhelming source of food, that the δ¹⁵N value could approach 20‰ and perhaps exceed it. This effect has been recorded in Mesolithic humans in southern Norway (Brigitte Skar pers. comm.). Since many sea fish, such as cod, whiting or dab, often produce δ¹⁵N values of 12–13‰, it is highly likely that the people living at Ferriter's Cove would have relied heavily on fish rather than seals. As similar results were recorded for the Dalkey Island dog it is probable those using the island would have relied heavily on sea fish. This is in spite of the comparatively large number of seal bones and the relatively low incidence of fish bones that were recovered from the shell middens there.

The Ferriter's Cove and Dalkey samples can be contrasted with the human remains from Rockmarshall and Loughan Island which would also have been expected to have had a larger marine signature. These results suggest that a smaller portion of the diet of these communities was derived from the sea though, again, one has to wonder about the potential impact of eels on the δ¹³C signature.

It appears that, even though the samples are limited in number, the results of the stable isotope analysis provide a very important counterbalance to the very partial pictures created from other sources of archaeological information. There is, however, little reason to believe, even if there were groups who lived usually on or close to the coast and took most of their sustenance from the sea, that any of these communities specialised in deep sea sources or had a highly developed marine technology. They had a life style that was more sophisticated than the perceived strandlooper economies that were suggested for the Irish Mesolithic in the earlier part of the 20th century. Bjerck (2009, 18) has suggested that coastal communities can be divided into Littoral and Marine economies. Marine economies in Ireland seem to fall at the bottom end of the category, though trips to islands, such has Inistrahull, suggest the capacity to use the open sea. However, where fish and other remains have been found they are dominated by species that

would have been obtainable close to, or even from, the shore. Similarly, while visits to islands such as the Blaskets which lie off West Kerry beyond the end of the Dingle Peninsula or Dalkey may have taken place, they could have been mainly used as a base for fishing or provided an opportunity to exploit seal colonies at their rookeries.

Even though they were not reliant on deep sea fishing it is probable that coastal communities would have used boats for sea-going transport. Although working from a modern environment, a simple catchment analysis for the Glencloy area on the Antrim coast (see Chapter 9) the late John Philips showed that a Canadian style canoe could, in the right conditions, travel from Glencloy North to Glenarriff up to four times more quickly than was possible over land (see Fig. 9.7) (Woodman 1983; Woodman and Johnson 1996).

At the other extreme, shellfish obviously played a part in the diet. However, given the high visibility against the relatively low return of shellfish, the comparatively small size of the surviving middens suggests that they were not necessarily the most important source of food, even for coastal communities. Thus, there is little to suggest that the coastal economy of the Irish Later Mesolithic fell into Bjerck's (2009) "Elaborate Marine" category.

Evidence at Ferriter's Cove has made the case for the existence of communities living in some coastal areas who were highly reliant on marine resources but, beyond that, there is little to suggest other that communities relied heavily on one source of food. Fischer (2003) and more recently Fischer *et al.* (2007) have shown that the analysis of human and dog bones from Ertebølle sites in Denmark, in an area roughly the same size as south-west Ireland, indicates a presence on the coast of people who lived on a highly marine diet but also of others who had drawn most of their food from terrestrial sources. Similarly they have also demonstrated that human and dog remains from inland sites of Middle Mesolithic/Kongemose and Late Mesolithic Ertebølle date have produced marine signatures (*ibid.*, 2144–6).

The limited information from Ireland based on stable isotopes suggest that the use of the sea was not confined to fully sedentary coastal communities, and, mirroring the evidence for the movement of raw materials, indicates some movement between the coast and interior in some areas (Fig. 10.4).

As we have seen, there are numerous indicators that the various forms of salmonids played an important role but perhaps too much emphasis has been given to the Atlantic salmon. In contrast, the role of eels has probably been under-rated and it is possible that, in addition to catching them during their migration to the sea, they were also caught on many inland waterways.

When considering the role of mammals and birds one has the impression that, during the Irish Mesolithic, convenience and opportunism may have played as important a role rather than specialised procurement strategies and diets. The few indications from Ireland suggest that, in the case of the wild boar, younger animals up to 2 years old were much more likely to be caught, though there are cases where older animals were present. While this might be regarded as evidence of a symbiotic or semi-domesticated management of boar, it is more likely that they were easier prey than females with young or fully mature older males.

The presence of many pigeon bones at both Lough Boora and Mount Sandel suggests the easy capture of birds that were likely to have taken up residency near campsites and were consequently easier targets.

MacLean (1993), echoing Clarke (1976), argued that plant foods would have played a very important role but, as Bonsall (1981, 461–5) noted, many plant foods need to be both gathered in large quantities and sometimes require extensive processing. While these plants may have provided important supplements to the daily diet, many would have to be collected in very large numbers to provide a significant staple part of the diet. Zvelebil (1994, 58–9) maintains that a meat based diet could only, in certain circumstances, supply about 50% of the dietary requirements for humans and that plant foods could have contributed 30% or more of their required nutrition. The protein and fat requirements, along with key trace elements, for populations who did not live on the coast would be best supplied by plant foods. Which useful sources of plant based nutrition would have been available in Ireland? It is apparent from Zvelibil (*ibid.*, table I) that water chestnut, which was a very significant food source in many areas, was not present in Britain and Ireland. Acorns may not have been available in significant quantities early in the Irish Mesolithic but hazel nuts were collected and would have had the benefits including availability, ease of processing and storage. Other plant remains have also been recovered, for example apples, but it is unlikely that they would have formed a significant staple part of the diet.

Finally, it is important to remember that diet and health are not simply based upon bulk supply from a few sources. While it is less popular today to rely on protein or carbohydrates, a balanced diet is best obtained from accessing a range of different foods. Carbohydrates and proteins are as essential as simple calorific values, while trace elements and vitamins are also important.

Reflecting on the story so far

This final part of Section 4 will summarise the apparent implications of the last two chapters.

Changes through time

In examining the faunal remains it could not be argued that there was a radical shift in choice within the range of mammals, birds and fish through time. Given the narrow range of species in Ireland, there is always the chance that an incoming human community could, in an island context, cause the extinction of a preferred source of food and thus set in motion a series of

changes in food sources, methods of procurement and, perhaps, changes in how the landscape was utilised. However, Ireland is a particularly large island and, in this case, the extinction scenario seems unlikely (see Woodman 2008, 14–15 for discussion of this topic). Similarly, while some coastal areas changed from valleys to sea loughs, Ireland has remained roughly the same size over the last 10,000 years. Here the change from Boreal to Atlantic forest would not have impacted on the fauna in the same way as it did elsewhere. While numerous small lakes had begun the process of changing to raised bogs and had silted up or begun to be covered with fen peat, numerous, extensive areas of open water remain to this day.

In summary, it appears that the resources available to these earliest inhabitants of Ireland would, for the most part, have remained the same. This would have included the different food sources as well as the raw materials needed to make much of the equipment they required. Changes in the way in which they used the landscape, the manner in which food sources were procured or other raw materials were obtained, would have been through a series of gradual shifts and adaptations, some of which may have been particular to individual regions within the island.

Finding the "Base Camp" or still hunting for the little house on the prairie?

In the context of the transition to farming there has often been a desire to search for evidence of more sedentary settlement. Much of this perspective is based on Rowley-Conway (1983), where it is suggested that large-scale sedentary settlements would be associated with complexity and create situations where adoption of farming would, in the right circumstances, be more likely to take place. It was felt that a case could be made for the Ertebølle culture being regarded as one of these sedentary societies. However, while there has been awareness that many Mesolithic societies were often more complex and richer than had been appreciated in the past (Price and Brown 1985), there has been little unequivocal evidence of large-scale settlements.

In Ireland this issue is compounded by a lack of understanding as to what a base camp should look like in the archaeological record. In spite of the suggestion by Cooney and Grogan (1994, 34) that there should be a growing shift towards larger and more sedentary sites throughout the Mesolithic, there is little clear evidence that such a process took place. This does not mean that the Irish Mesolithic, in particular the Later Mesolithic, population should be seen as a minimal, poorly adapted group of hunter-gatherers. The evidence comes mainly from a series of specialised extraction and production sites but the apparent investment in certain localities and their abilities to extract and move raw materials across significant distances, as well as adapting to local circumstances, surely indicates that Mesolithic communities had successfully overcome the challenges of living on the island of Ireland.

Regional and diverse strategies

Most evidence available for annual territories and mobility comes from the Later Mesolithic. If the evidence from site distribution, the manner in which raw materials were used, organic/food remains recovered from excavations and the limited evidence from stable isotope analyses of human remains are put together they seem to provide a consistent, if not entirely coherent, picture. Taking Torrence's (1989) observation about reliance on least risk strategies into consideration, perhaps the most significant conclusion that one can draw from the data is that there was not one single set of economic and related strategies that was used across the whole island:

1) In the northern area it is apparent that there are both coastal and inland components. The stable isotope results from the Loughan Island human bone again suggest coastal and inland components. If the diet had relied entirely on eels and other freshwater fish, with a lesser marine component, the signature would have been more a quasi-terrestrial one. There is also the strong suggestion that lithic raw materials used in the Lower Bann would have been drawn from both coastal and inland areas, and perhaps even areas in the midlands south of Lough Neagh. In this instance, the least risk solution would have been a reliance on the range of resources based within the Lough Neagh/River Bann catchment system and, in particular, probably on the Lower Bann. With a limited range of lithic resources in the vicinity, it would have been preferable to obtain these by various means from known locations some distance away.

2) It has been argued (Chapter 9) that, in the Strangford Lough area, there may have been one group of communities who were able to fulfil most of their needs within the environs of the sea lough itself. In this area the probable abundance of resources in and around the sea lough could result in a long period of settlement in that area and, as a result, the least risk solution was to use the poorer, but generally

adequate, erratic flint found along the lough's shore. In both areas there is little evidence that raw material, i.e. stone, was imported and it seems that the balance and minimum risk strategies suggested by Torrence (1989) resulted in local communities "shopping local".

3) In contrast, the North Leinster area evidence seems to suggest communities that moved over a significant distance between the coast and the interior. This is reflected in the manner in which artefacts made from materials available in one area consistently appear in some numbers in the other. The stable isotope result from Rockmarshall suggests a mixed coastal and inland based diet. The crucial need in this region must be the identification of chert sources. The δ^{13}C staple isotope results from the Dalkey dog and the Ferriter's Cove human remains, which suggest a heavy reliance on marine resources, are pointers to the possibility that other communities may have lived almost entirely within the vicinity of the sea. Conversely there could be communities living elsewhere that used different environments ,perhaps in very different ways.

4) Evidence from the Limerick/north Cork area has to rely heavily on the Killuragh Cave isotopes. As discussed earlier it is probable that extensive reliance on eels may have masked a coastal component. Although the material comes from the Earlier Mesolithic, the probability that flint was brought from coastal areas suggests either visits to the coast and or some reliance on marine resources.

One could proceed indefinitely with other regional scenarios but I hope that the examples listed here indicate at least one important point – that there is not one Irish Mesolithic economy.

There are other issues that have not really been explored so far. There are questions such as could we improve the way we research the Irish Mesolithic which will be discussed in Chapter 11, while other issues discussed in Chapter 12 are perhaps more speculative!

Part V

Where to Now?

This final part is not an attempt to set the agenda for the future but is, rather, a perspective that provides some personal sense of where priorities could be. Many of the issues discussed below have already been addressed in Conneller and Warren's (2006) Mesolithic Britain and Ireland: New Approaches. In the preface, those editors correctly noted the sad fact that the Mesolithic is often seen as the poor relation to the Upper Palaeolithic and the Neolithic. There is also a tendency to compare regions; thus one aspires to the quality seen in Scandinavia (ibid., 7). However, one has to be aware that the quality of the stratigraphic record (and preservation) found in Denmark represents only one small part of the region. Many parts of northern Scandinavia, for example, offer poor organic preservation but, at the same time, one can walk into Stone Age huts in the "Far North". The changing relative location of the sea and the created raised strandlines, combined with poor soil development, provides opportunities to walk into these Stone Age dwelling structures or up to flint chipping floors lying on the surface; each region has something to offer and it is often the differences between regions that create the greatest contributions. Leaving aside invidious comparisons and, at the risk of being classed as an old fashioned Empiricist, one might quibble with what seems to be (ibid., 10) a slight complacency about the quality of the evidence available and a belief that what we really need better theories.

The view expressed above is not that of all contributors. Milner (2006, 68–9) suggests that many questions have, over the last 50 years, also remained the same and if anything there has been an even greater concentration on the major species of mammals as well as the "boys and arrows" approach (ibid., 82). Jordan (2006, 98–100) has also noted that ethnographic analogies have tended to rely on a very limited number of examples which tend to get repeated ad nauseam!

Perhaps we need to begin by realising that, like most experimental disciplines, archaeology and the related environmental and laboratory disciplines are "a combination of theory and practice". Keeping this in mind, the issues covered in Part V can be considered under two major headings:

1. *Are we carrying out fieldwork and, in particular, excavations in a manner than can address some of the questions that arose earlier in the book. Similarly, are there areas where there could be greater collaboration?*

2. *Are there areas of research and issues that, at the moment, lie outside the priorities and approaches usually considered within Irish Mesolithic studies?*

Before proceeding to the two last chapters it is important to note that many of the concerns raised below are not necessarily specific to Ireland and many of the concerns raised, as well as suggestions, would be similar to those expressed elsewhere in Europe. Thus if the reader peruses the Mesolithic Research and Conservation Framework (Blinkhorn and Milner 2013) it wil be seen that many of the bullet points and issues identified can be reflected throughout "Ireland's First Settlers".

Chapter 11

A critical analysis of fieldwork and methodologies

Can we consider how we get beyond fieldwork that is doomed to simply repeat what we have done before? If not, and in a world where salvage excavation is the main means by which fieldwork obtains new information, then the chances are that any new perspective or insights will have limited opportunity for success. Salvage archaeology, especially when associated with the infrastructural developments that took place during the economic boom of the Celtic Tiger years i.e. during the mid-2000s, has the benefit, as far as research is concerned, of being a tyrannical task master. Field research projects can often be dominated by the desire to do the same, i.e. excavate another better example of what we have worked on before or "find another Star Carr". Excavations determined by the location of industrial estates or the routes of new roads require us to explore the unknown and there is no doubt that, in many instances, whole new vistas can be opened up. In Ireland a particular case in point is the settlement archaeology of the earlier Bronze Age. We still need to ask, in the context of the Irish Mesolithic, have we benefited fully from the 'Celtic Tiger' and are there lessons to be learnt?

There is a lot of value in a very appropriate phrase which has been in existence for 2000 or more years: "New wine in old bottles", i.e. the new wine could lead to the rupturing of the containers. In our case, new ideas which pay no attention to how we work in the field or respect the value of artefacts may not be the best way to proceed. In other words, we are not just dealing with a "text" but rather are both creating and commenting on it. Thus, we need to evaluate how we carry out fieldwork now and consider how it should be carried out in the future. In some ways, the most fundamental problem is the manner in which much field archaeology is undertaken.

Besides middens and, perhaps, caves, Irish Mesolithic sites have a very poor visual presence in the landscape. Ironically, these two more visible types of sites are not the most productive sources of information. Most of the major excavations of Mesolithic sites in Ireland have been undertaken as a result of chance finds or discovery. Many sites have been carefully excavated but one must wonder at times whether they could have been excavated or explored in a different manner.

Issues

1) Is there an awareness of a Mesolithic presence? Are there certain landscapes in which Mesolithic sites are likely to be found?
2) How much is being lost because of a lack of concern about what survives in the topsoil?
3) Do we treat sites seriously or think about the extent of excavation that should be required?
4) Are the recovery techniques normally used adequate for the type of site that is being excavated?

Finding sites

Much of what is included here will be based on the experience and personal observations of the author. Many of these issues are not, however, confined to Ireland and several of the problems of identifying and investigating Mesolithic, or indeed open air Palaeolithic sites, have been considered in a volume edited by Rensink and Peeters (2006).

We all want to find and excavate that perfect site but the reality is that the record of the Mesolithic is mostly made up of small groups of material which are frequently out of context. The challenge is, aside from waiting for an interested amateur, how do we identify locations where Mesolithic material occurs? Is it likely to be a priority? Also, for archaeology in general, is it a priority?

Historically there has always been a strong interest in the final Palaeolithic and Mesolithic in Scandinavia, where it represents the initial known human presence and even the origins of the history of those countries. Elsewhere, in many parts of Europe, the attitude to Mesolithic and other similar types of sites can often be described as "Institutional Inertia" (Fojut 2006, 68–70). The very fact that, in many countries, the protection of the archaeological record is vested in agencies that have the word *Monument* in their title creates its own hierarchy of interests. In other words, sites with no obvious presence, or where a few chance finds have been made in disturbed ground, are often not even documented or are given a low priority.

How often is a serious consideration given to the possibility that there is a chance of Mesolithic settlement existing in a particular locality? Occasionally, as in the case of the Southern Hebrides Mesolithic Project (Mithen 2000), there have been serious attempts to identify localities where Mesolithic settlement might exist. Projects such as the Saltbaekvig Veg Project, which undertook a long-term and intensive review of a relatively small area in north-west Zealand, are relatively uncommon (Gebauer and Price 1990; Fig. 11.1). In this instance, extensive field walking was followed up with a series of excavations focused on a particular series of research issues. Nearer to home is the Seamer Carr Project, initiated by Tim Schadla-Hall (1987). In this instance the presence of a series of British Early Mesolithic sites on the shores of the Early Holocene Lake Pickering, which were in turn adjacent to Star Carr, led to decades of investigation of the environment (Fig. 11.1b). This consisted of testing many different localities for new sites, coring to establish the form and extent of Lake Pickering, as well as a careful examination of floral changes through time. This project is continuing even today (Milner *et al.* 2012). These are, however, locations where there was a decision by archaeologists to work in these particular localities.

In Ireland one must wonder whether, in light of the needs of development-driven excavations, a range of new and different approaches are needed. Where should one look or to what sorts of landscapes should we pay attention? Sensitivity about the potential of certain landscapes is inclined to bring up the riposte: "how can you manage something as ill-defined as a landscape?" The only reply must be that these sites represent 40% of our known history so it is up to the guardians of our archaeological heritage to find a way.

As Fojut (2006, 69) noted in the context of Scotland, Mesolithic sites are often found by "happy accident" and indeed our experience in Ireland is that many of the sites that went on to be excavated were first identified by interested amateurs. In spite of this, should one identify potential hot spots? A simply answer is yes, but that is only a partial solution. In Ireland, it is very apparent that any location at or near a key crossing point of a river, or adjacent to a particularly good point for fishing with either line or traps, must be regarded as a potential location of Mesolithic settlement (see Part II). Similarly, coastal locations on or behind strandlines and river estuaries, as well as areas at the entrance or exit from lakes, are localities where material might survive. These sites need not necessarily be placed on a river bank, especially in the Earlier Mesolithic and so attention would need to extend some distance from the river's edge. Fojut (*ibid.*) noted that, in parts of Scotland, any exploitation of gravels in areas of more than 100 square metres, and which lay 50–200 m above sea level, had close to a 50% chance of producing Mesolithic material. The work of monitoring the building of motorways across Ireland has not, outside the types of areas referred to earlier, produced a significant concentration of Mesolithic settlement, but that does not mean that it did not exist. The small concentration of sites in the tributary of the Barrow in Co. Carlow, i.e. the Burren River, has shown that small scatters of Later Mesolithic

material can be found even some hundreds of metres away from the valley floor (O'Connell forthcoming).

If part of the Mesolithic presence is located away from the classic hot spots, then, as noted in Part II, there is also the problem in Ireland of permanent grassland and, more recently, forestry. In the case of the latter, it would be interesting to know how many artefacts of any period were recovered during drainage trenching prior to the planting of trees. The idea that removal of topsoil by trenching with machinery will unearth Mesolithic sites is also fraught with pitfalls (excusing the pun!). Not least of these problems is the fact that artefacts are rarely found in soil that has been freshly disturbed by machinery, whether of the type used for construction or even through ploughing. Anyone with experience in field walking will know that a freshly ploughed field will rarely produce a significant number of artefacts. If the same field is returned to after several weeks, when the soils have been broken up by natural environmental factors such as rain and frost, the number of artefacts recovered will increase dramatically. There will therefore be few artefacts recovered directly after using mechanical soil prospection, especially when the soil has been lying for only a number of hours. It takes time, just a few days or, at most, weeks before artefacts will begin to appear.

Topsoil finds are usually regarded as of little significance but when artefacts turn up in the topsoil there are many chances that the site has been already been totally obliterated. In one instance in Ireland, a Bronze Age Cinerary Urn was found during the construction of the M8 motorway near Watergrasshill at Killydonoghue in Co. Cork (Sherlock 2013, 88). Ploughing had been intensive so that a significant portion of the upper levels of the subsoil had been removed with the result that only the rim of the urn remained (Fig. 11.2)!

Topsoil (Context 1) finds from excavations or strays may not be the most exciting items but most sites that lie outside the floodplain and below 200 m are likely to have been cultivated quite intensively. Therefore, for periods like the Mesolithic that lack visible monuments or deep foundations, patterns in Ireland will generally be made up from scraps of evidence. When considered in their totality these contribute hugely to our knowledge of the Mesolithic. In other words, each piece of the jigsaw makes an important contribution.

There is still the problem of the permanent grasslands. In Ireland, if trenching is not the best way of finding sites, there is a difficulty exploring grassland areas that can extend over 1000s of square metres if not tens of hectares. Ironically Ireland is both blessed and cursed by the lack of moles; O'Donohue and Lovis (2006) have shown, in their work in the Yorkshire Dales, that up-cast from mole-holes provided indications of areas where Mesolithic and later settlement could be identified. Prospecting with magnetic susceptibility or phosphates can help pinpoint much more ephemeral traces of settlement than those generally found through the usual geophysical prospecting (Doggart 1985). In Belgium, Crombé (2006) experimented with test pitting and coring using a corer of up to 15 cm in diameter

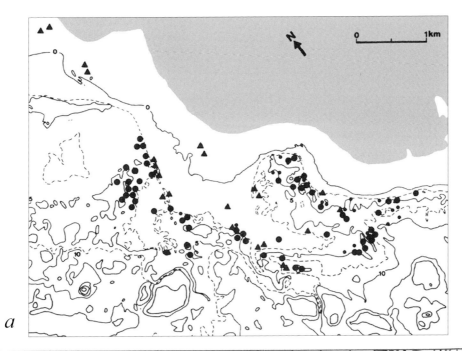

a

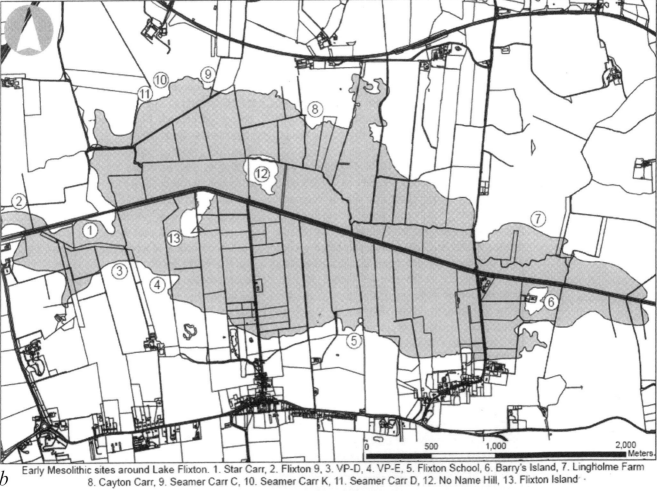

b

Early Mesolithic sites around Lake Flixton. 1. Star Carr, 2. Flixton 9, 3. VP-D, 4. VP-E, 5. Flixton School, 6. Barry's Island, 7. Lingholme Farm 8. Cayton Carr, 9. Seamer Carr C, 10. Seamer Carr K, 11. Seamer Carr D, 12. No Name Hill, 13. Flixton Island

Fig. 11.1. a) The research area at Saltbaek Vig, Zealand, Denmark: triangles = Mesolithic sites, dots = Neolithic sites (after Gebauer and Price 1990), b) The Seamer Carr research area (after Connellar et al. 2009).

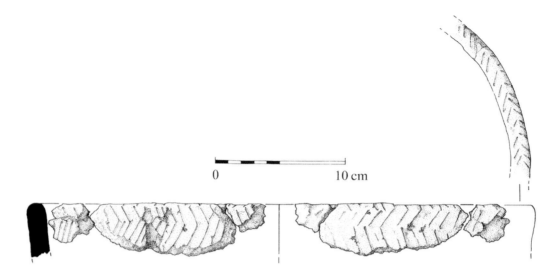

Fig. 11.2. (above and left) Rim of Collared Urn and reconstruction of the original Bronze Age urn burial from Killydonoghue (Sherlock 2013).

across 17 ha and revealed 50 concentrations of artefacts. Of course, one has to have a general sense as to where these techniques could be applied.

There are areas of arable farming which can be prospected through field walking. There can be challenges. As noted in Part I, the tradition of amateur field walking in Ireland has never been particularly strong, therefore, when commercial development is contemplated, archival records, especially in the area of site identification, will probably be of limited help. One of the problems is that outside limited areas, particularly in the north and east, artefact densities can be quite low. As

a result, as was noted during field walking in the Blackwater Valley in Co. Cork where almost all the flint artefacts were imported, most small scatters of lithic artefacts will be difficult to identify (Woodman 1989). Veil's (2006) survey, which analysed the efficacy of relying on surface scatters in Lower Saxony, suggested that only up to 5% of the pieces present in the plough zone could be found through field walking. In fact he noted that often less than 1% is recovered (*ibid.*, 109–12). Veil also noted, however, that in the case of large areas being surveyed and where artefacts are particularly common, specific concentrations can be identified. Also, in a situation where ploughing has effectively destroyed a site, useful information can still be recovered through controlled and proportionate efforts to excavate the topsoil.

A perfect case study of these issues, as noted earlier, was provided by the 350 m long excavation along a drumlin in the floodplain of the Lower Bann adjacent to its exit from Lough Neagh, at Toome Bridge (Chapter 4). This explored an area of approximately 17000 square metres and was an obvious example of a location that would be expected to have attracted settlement through time. In the early stages of the excavation the artefacts from the previously ploughed topsoil were retained by squares defined by a 10 × 10 m grid. This project immediately identified specific areas where it was apparent that a range of activities had taken place in prehistory. This included a perfect example of a problem alluded to by Veil (*ibid.*, 122) in his conclusions; that topsoil material may only contain artefacts from part of the site. In the case of the Toome Bypass site, one particularly rich part of the site lay on a flatter shelf within a slight slope (Dunlop and Woodman 2015). Here it was very apparent that two adjacent squares had experienced very different levels of disturbance. Within this area of the site, as noted in Chapter 4, portions of a large complex structure were uncovered. An area containing significant concentrations of artefacts had survived upslope but the plough had destroyed an originally intact archaeological horizon, therefore there was a high density of finds from the topsoil. Downslope, perhaps where the topsoil was thicker, the archaeological horizon was more intact. Conversely, therefore, artefacts in the topsoil were scarcer but there was proportionately more in the surviving archaeological horizon (Fig. 11.3). In other words, the topsoil material will indicate a presence of settlement but will only give a very partial picture. Ideally we need both the *in situ* archaeology and the topsoil material.

If we remember, however, that our excavations often only explore "the activities of people who dig holes" (Dan Raemarkers pers. comm.) then it is vital that the evidence from the topsoil, with all its flaws, is also taken into consideration.

Therefore, one returns to awareness that in certain areas there could be the remnants of Mesolithic activities still surviving.

It is "utopian" to assume that the full rigour of all these approaches should be used in every instance. Where a case can be made that there is a likelihood that, in a particular type of landscape, a significant prehistoric presence might survive, and then they should be used.

Which areas are worthy of careful exploration and attention?

One approach could be that adopted in the Southern Hebrides Mesolithic Project (SHMP) (Mithen 2000), where P. E. Woodman (2000) assessed the viability of using Predictive Modelling and GIS. The conclusion was that there should be a need for a proper understanding of the concepts and

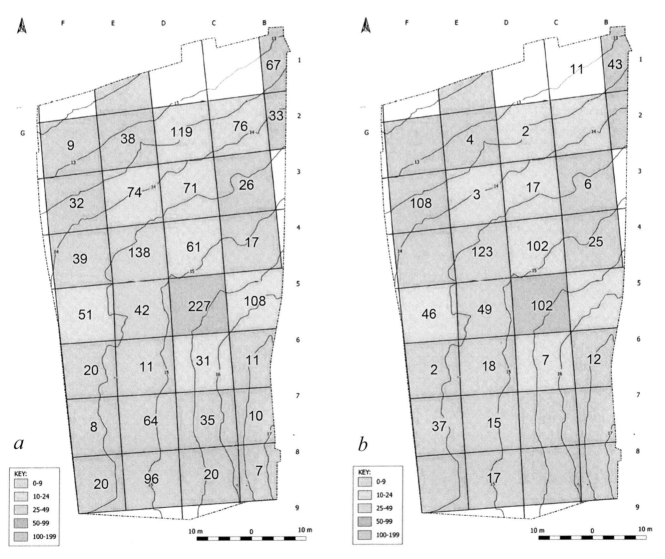

Fig. 11.3. Distribution of artefacts in a) the topsoil and b) in situ *contexts in Area North Toome Bypass (by permission of NAC). (Dunlop and Woodman 2015).*

assumptions of the statistical methods, rather than a simple uncritical acceptance of the results. Even allowing for the limited capacity of these techniques, especially when they are used in regions where the archaeological record is sparse, it was still possible to identify areas where Mesolithic sites were likely to be found. However, as Woodman noted (*ibid.*, 463), even in these particular areas there needs to be a programme of fieldwork, such as test pitting, so that "a comparison can be made between the predicted model and observed Mesolithic site distribution".

Can we identify in Ireland certain types of landscapes where there is potential of the type explored in the SHMP? Can we begin to identify a number of different types of localities where we can both ask relevant questions and expect to find some answers? If so, then perhaps we can begin to work towards establishing some "rules of thumb" that can be used by those who manage our archaeological landscapes. These areas would need to be of a realistic size, perhaps at most 200–300 square kilometres, where sites could or have been found and where there are variations in the landscape.

It goes without saying that all sites that produce some evidence of a Mesolithic presence are important and, similarly, the list does not necessarily consist of areas where the archaeological record is, in each and every case, at risk. They are areas where some sites may have already been found and where, given the nature of farming or other activities, there is a reasonable chance that other sites could be discovered. Thus areas where an important site exists in a vacuum and in an area of extensive peat deposits, either raised bog or blanket peat, or permanent grasslands, would not be considered. There are also some sites that have made an important contribution to the Mesolithic, such as Ferriter's Cove (Woodman *et al.* 1999), Lough Boora (Ryan 1980) or even Belderrig (Warren 2009) but the environment in the general area may not, for various reasons, be conducive to the easy discovery of a range of other sites.

How large or small these areas should be is open to debate. The areas chosen, therefore, are based on localities where there is a reasonable prospect that there would be a useful return for a manageable realistic project.

A Baker's Dozen

We can begin with a more detailed examination of one area which illustrates the potential of looking at the "fine grain".

The Cutts: a local study and a cautionary tale

It is very tempting to expect that any local landscape will, throughout its full extent of time, always be used in a similar manner. The identification of the concentration of Mesolithic artefacts at specific fording/potentially fish trap locations along the Lower Bann are good examples. The area adjacent to Mount Sandel and the Cutts provides a particularly good example of the different ways in which a much smaller area can be used (Fig. 11.4a).

Several specific locations occur within a 2 km stretch of the Bann where the river straddles the Cutts. The most well-known location is that at Mount Sandel, where large concentrations of artefacts belonging to the Earlier Mesolithic (Woodman 1985a) were found and where significant concentration of salmon as well as other fish species which are known to inhabit fish estuaries (Fig. 11.4b).

Two different concentrations of material have been noted from the Bann Estuary. The Knowles Collection contains relatively few Mesolithic artefacts from the area downstream of the Cutts, for example, there are only 11 Butt Trimmed Forms from this whole area. However, immediately below Mount Sandel Fort, on Sandel Ford, a ridge that runs across the Bann, several hundred pieces typical of the Mount Sandel phase have been collected. Contrary to the opinion originally expressed by the author (Woodman 1978a, 227) that this material was washing in from either side of the river, it now seems more likely that these are from settlement sites on a dry ridge extending out into the floor of today's Bann Estuary. Clearly, this was a location on the Bann which could have attracted a presence very early in the Mesolithic, perhaps before and around 9000 cal BP. At this early date the ford may have been a small ridge close to the river itself. At a later date both this location and the site of the huts that overlooked the ford were either less attractive or would have been used in a different manner.

After 8000 cal BP, as sea level rose, the use of the area would have changed. Not only are there few Later Mesolithic artefacts downstream but, as noted in Chapter 5, Whelan (1952) observed, there were no Later Mesolithic artefacts in the immediate vicinity of the rock outcrop of the Cutts, in spite of the profusion of bone points. It appears that these were mostly found further upstream, for example at Loughan Island. As at other locations on the Bann and elsewhere, Later Mesolithic artefacts of Butt Trimmed Forms, axes, etc., seem to have been found at very specific, often narrow, locations.

As May observed (1939), the location where the bone points were recovered appeared anomalous. The logical place where salmon would be sought would be downstream. This is where the fish would wait for the right conditions to navigate "the Cutts" before moving upstream and on to spawning grounds. However, one must wonder if, for a certain time in the middle of the Mesolithic as sea levels rose, eels would have gathered upstream from the Cutts while they were on their downstream voyage to the Sargasso Sea. This pool may have been an ideal location for using forks and rakes to harvest large numbers of eels (Chapter 5). This could explain the rather lower than expected $\delta^{13}C$ of the worked human bone referred to earlier (see also Chapter 10).

What can be learnt from this area is that often only very specific locations may be suitable at any one time; that we should, therefore, be seeking particular spots to look for evidence of a Mesolithic presence; and that through time these types of sought-after locations may have moved. There are also many others areas which are marked on Figure 11.4.

Leaving aside the Cutts/Mount Sandel area, there are additional areas in which there are on-going or potential projects.

1. *North Donegal*, centred on the Inishowen Peninsula. The activities of McNaught and others, as well as both the Lough Foyle Archaeological Project and the Inch Island Prehistoric Landscapes Project have resulted in the identification of numerous sites and the extensive collection of artefacts.

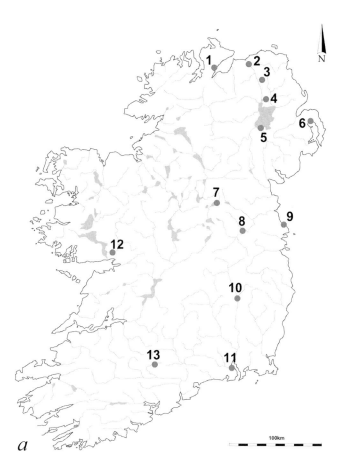

2. *The Kilrea area*, especially the strip of the lower Bann Valley floor between and close to two eel weirs. Here, in addition to the material acquired by the earlier generation of collectors, Walter Gracey built up a very significant collection. Unfortunately, while the provenience of many pieces did not survive, there is still a proportion which was documented to the individual farm and other locations, such as particular bogs.

3. *The Culbane/Portglenone area*, which was the "happy hunting ground" for many collectors (Woodman *et al*. 2006). A number of local amateurs are building up new collections and tying lithic concentrations to areas within specific fields (e.g. McAllister 2008). The inter-relationship is between a partly well-preserved landscape that, historically, is known contain extensive Diatomite deposits which, in turn, contain traces of prehistoric settlement at specific localities. These areas abut onto areas of higher ground as well as parts of the valley where bog filled basins occur. Away from the valley floor are more extensive areas of low rolling arable land. It is known that Dr Stuart of Portglenone (Chapter 9) found significant quantities of stone tools from his "upland" area but, unfortunately, no real data on specific locations have survived.

4. *Lough Neagh, southern shores*, where two majors rivers, the upper Bann and Blackwater exit into Lough Neagh and where artefacts turn up with some regularity. Although there are relatively few known sites in this area, the availability of raw material, the estuaries and extensive series of quaternary deposits that built up as Lough Neagh rose in level, make this an attractive area (Woodman forthcoming Lynn Festschrift).

5. *Strangford Lough, north end*, where, based on the work of Carr of Dundonald, Kirk of Newtownards and Reagan of Greyabbey, there are already large collections of artefacts from many locations. This is an area where there are submerged peat deposits, drumlin environments and extensive areas of farmland running up onto the

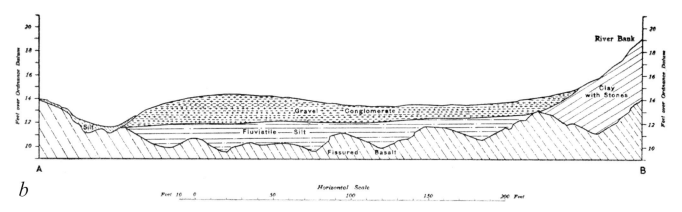

Fig. 11.4. a) "Baker's Dozen" localities (prepared by Hugh Kavanagh), b) Whelan's suggested section through the 1930s' dredged area at the Cutts (after Whelan 1952).

Castlereagh and Holywood Hills at the northern end of Strangford Lough. Research carried out by the Centre for Maritime Archaeology (Coleraine) has shown the interesting possibilities of this region (McErlean *et al.* 2003b).

6. *The Liffey mouth to Rush*, which is an area with important sites, good farmland and estuaries and which calls out for careful inspection even from a passing train. Besides the work of Miss Stacpoole (Woodman 1978a, 309–11), the Sutton excavations (Mitchell 1956a; 1972a) and the Dock Lands fish weirs (McQuade and O'Donnell 2009) perhaps the major concentration of material is that collected by Walsh in the Malahide Skerries area, on the coast just north of Dublin (Fig. 1.2). Although surprisingly little has so far been fully documented from the excavations associated with the NRA M1 construction in this area, there appears again to have been several large lithic assemblages recovered which may contain a significant quantity of Mesolithic artefacts. With the availability of raw materials, an interesting coastal area indented with bays and significant areas of agricultural land, this area should have huge potential.

7. *North-east Meath* is an area where a number of well-known groups of material have been discovered and where developer-led archaeology has doubled the number of locations producing Mesolithic artefacts. It is also an area of extensive arable farming, where access to various raw materials means that visibility of lithic scatters is fairly high. Palynological investigations in the general area have shown the possibility of further environmental investigations.

8. *The Inny at Finnea and adjacent lakes* is an area of extensive waterlogged deposits (Little 2009; 2010). It has been explored since the 1960s both by local amateurs and professional archaeologists (Fredengren 2009). It is possible that the remains of other sites might still survive.

9. *The River Barrow and Co. Carlow*, especially where the Burren River meets the Barrow. The Barrow Valley Project (Zvelibil *et al.* 1996), as well as the building of the N9, has produced an interesting selection of sites. It is a landscape which ranges from the floor of a major river valley through rolling good agricultural land (O'Connell forthcoming).

10. *The confluence of the Suir and Barrow*, which would include the local tributaries such as the Kilkenny Blackwater. This is an area on the northern side of the Ballylough Project (Green and Zvelebil 1990) and where the Waterford City Bypass (N25) exposed numerous sites (Woodman 2011).

11. *North-east Limerick*, including Killuragh Cave, where in spite of the extensive permanent grasslands there appears to be a number of important Earlier Mesolithic sites.

12. *Lough Corrib, southern shores and exit*, is a tantalising area within which artefacts have been recovered over the last 150 years (Driscoll 2006). It is also an area where extensive Quaternary deposits occur and which hold out the possibility that much more is to be recovered from this location.

13. A*n after-thought (between the Funshion and the Awbeg)*, might be a good area to return to. The Cork Blackwater (Woodman 1989, 118–9) is an area of caves, rich rivers and good farmland. Sites are not always easy to find but the potential is shown by work in the 1980s and more recently by excavations at Gortore (O'Donoghue 2011).

Many of these areas include locations where stratified deposits might exist and where there may, in some cases, be a reasonable chance of the preservation of organic materials. This does not represent the total picture of what we want from Mesolithic sites. If organic preservation was the dominant requirement then sites like Mount Sandel would never have been investigated!

What should be expected

As observed earlier, it is unlikely that any individual site will provide a complete picture of life in the Mesolithic. There is, however, still the dream of finding the perfect site which, in Britain, has been categorised as finding "another Star Carr". The actual "near perfect site" will ideally contain a range of areas, including traces of shelters, outdoor activity areas and dumps, preferably in a location where the chuck zone is into waterlogged deposits. These sites are rare, partially because the parts of sites where people habitually lived, i.e. on a dry surface, are often those where the original ground surface has been heavily damaged or entirely destroyed. Sites such as Tågerup in Scania (Karsten and Knarrström 2003; Fig. 11.5), where marine deposits slowly inundated a land surface, buried it, and therefore preserved it intact, are extremely rare but exceptionally important. This site has provided a remarkable combination of the traces of a hut and burials, both of which are dug into the ground and, at the same time on the old land surface, a series of dumps along with a pathway that ran through them. The small island of Vaenget Nord in Zealand, which lay within the silted up Vedbaek Fjord, would be one of the few sites with both the land surface and shoreline deposits preserved intact (Brinch-Petersen 1989). At Gonghusvej 7 in Vedbaek, Zealand, Brinch-Petersen and Meiklejohn (2004) uncovered traces of an oval structure that was 6 × 4 m across and defined by a hearth and a number of stake-holes. This structure dated to about 7000 cal BP. It survived because it was buried beneath 2 m of later deposits.

Few Irish sites fall into the same category as those listed above. Leaving aside that desire for the site with perfect organic preservation, there are a number of sites preserved below a layer of later deposits. They include Lough Boora (Ryan 1980) where the site was recovered from the base of a Bord Na Mona peat milling project, while at Ferriter's Cove (Woodman *et al.* 1999) a range of small shell dumps, slight stake-holes and other features were recovered preserved under several metres of sand. At Bay Farm *in situ* chipping floors and stake-holes were buried below hill wash (Woodman and Johnson 1996). Bog growth had covered chipping floors and a platform at Belderrig. Even in more exposed contexts damage is not necessarily complete. Partial preservation occurred at

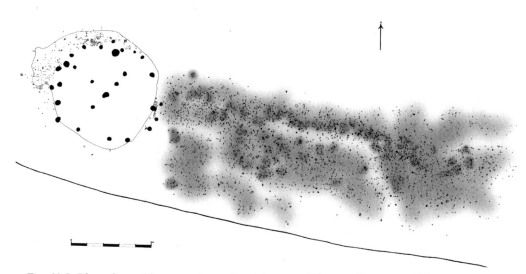

Fig. 11.5. Plan of round house and associated dumps at Tågerup (Karsten and Knarrström 2003).

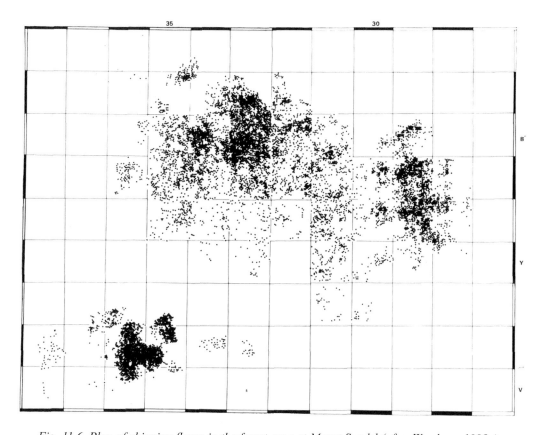

Fig. 11.6. Plan of chipping floors in the forest area at Mount Sandel (after Woodman 1985a).

Toome Bypass, probably because the drumlin had not been intensively ploughed in recent decades. Not all material has been found in ploughed field situations. Even Mount Sandel (Woodman 1985a) provides an interesting case study. A few pit and hearth bottoms survived in the east of the field. Where most of the excavations had taken place the huts had been protected by being in a shallow hollow but much more extensive traces of settlement had been obliterated. In contrast to the west, in the forest area more ephemeral stake-holes and chipping floors had survived, in part, under the field bank and forest soils (Fig. 11.6). These aspects of the site would have been destroyed if those areas had lain within the ploughed field.

It is not only a question of finding the right site but of how the site is excavated. Each generation brings its own expertise and the following observations are based more on personal experience rather than being a set of prescriptive directions.

What is important on the excavation

It may sound pompous, but how should we best approach the task of recovering evidence from the ground?

Sieving

One of the most frequently cited uncertainties surrounds the relative importance of fish and small mammals on many sites. Are absences really genuine or is it simply a lack of the proper recovery techniques? Today, unlike two decades ago, there is usually a healthy programme of flotation and wet sieving of rich organic layers of many types. Besides fish bones or microliths, fine debitage can be as important an indicator of the types of lithic reduction strategies as the finished artefacts. Similarly, as discussed in Chapters 5 and 8, the issue of sieving or lack thereof relates to the important issue of how long Microliths continued to be used. Do they genuinely become rare after a very short period of time or is their scarcity exaggerated by the absence of sieving programmes? Sieving, or more accurately, an organised programme of sieving, is essential.

There is, however, no point in just sieving rich deposits as the relative density of the scatter of any material can only be assured if the same approach is used consistently across the site. In the case of Ferriter's Cove, extensive sieving was carried out on a small midden (Context 3) and numerous small fish bones were recovered but, in order to establish that they were concentrated in that specific area, samples of soil from across the site were also sieved (McCarthy *et al.* 1999, 86). At Mount Sandel, while very careful laboratory based sieving took place of all the organically rich material, everything from occupations layers on the site was at least run through a process of wet sieving using 3mm mesh sieves. Without that programme, distributions of the smaller artefacts across the hut area would have been more a reflexion of the eyesight of the excavators rather than a record of activities carried out by those who had lived there nearly 10,000 years ago

Sieving is, of course, just one technique that should be used, but given that sites will not be defined by obvious structures, where the opportunities arise, other approaches, such as refitting should also be used, as at Ferriter's Cove (see below).

Refitting

In terms of complexity we can return to the observation of "New Wine in old Bottles". It is not just about new perspectives as we often require methodologies which will at least give us a chance of testing our interpretations. As

suggested earlier, this can be as simple as using refitting. This type of analysis has been used on many Stone Age sites. Good examples can be seen in the Pincevent area of France (Leroi-Gourhan and Brezillon 1966; 1972). Here, at Site 1, it could be shown that three hearths might have been used at roughly the same time, while elsewhere, in Unit 34, a case could be made for the remains including hearths and huts being created as a result of separate visits to that particular locality. Even on older excavations, such as at Rormyr II in south-east Norway, it was possible to test the hypothesis that the assemblage, one of the earliest in Norway, was an accumulation of a number of visits. Refitting showed that the assemblage was more likely to have been created in one event (Skar and Coulson 1986).

At Ferriter's Cove (Figs 11.7 and 11.8a) where scatters of animal remains, shells, lithic scatters, etc., were spread along an area of 40 m, it was possible to show that there were likely to have been a number of separate visits to the site. At Bay Farm (Woodman and Johnson 1996; Fig.e 11.8b) refitting suggested that the chipping floors were created during numerous visits to the bay rather than a by-product of massive industrial scale production.

Refitting is, however, about more than determining the number of separate occasions a particular area under excavation has been used. Using simple traditional explanations for artefacts to read in social or ritualistic meanings has its dangers. Finlay (2006) has rightly commented, in the case of the Mount Sandel Microliths, that there is a danger of giving fixed meaning to particular artefact types, such as Microliths, which are likely to have had "multiple biographies".

One example may have implications for sites such as Mount Sandel. Binford's (1983) work at the Palangana site showed that there might be a series of patterns in the debris left behind in the interior of a hut. These would have been created by different actions, such as discussions and particular activities undertaken round the hearth, keeping the sleeping area clean and messy tasks near the entrance.

Certain similar patterns can be seen within the hut at Mount Sandel (Fig. 11.9) which, at the very least, left me feeling that what we were uncovering was not a palimpsest of a large number of visits from before, during and after the use of the main hut area. Murphy (1996) suggested that the same type of male/female division of space referred to earlier may have taken place at Mount Sandel (Fig. 11.10). Welinder (1971, 180) suggested that such a pattern could be seen at the Barre Mose site in Skåne in southern Sweden. Based on the complementary distribution of microburins (associated with Microliths/projectile heads) and scrapers (skin cleaning) there was a male/female division within the hut. It is tempting to read ritualistic divisions of space into this interpretation and there is no doubt that there can be rituals associated with a building and use of dwelling space. However, Skar (1987), through a process of refitting, was able to show that use of certain artefacts may have changed during their life and that

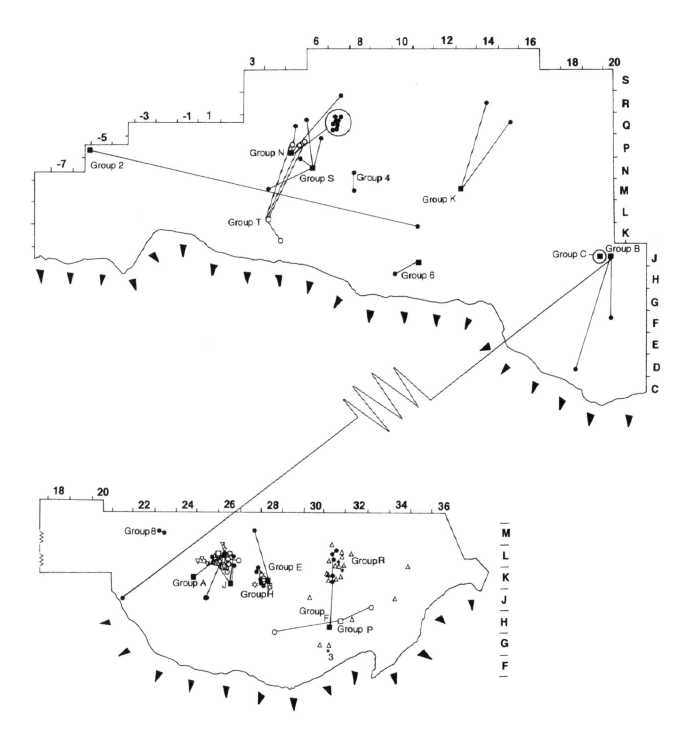

Fig. 11.7. a) Refitting at Ferriter's Cove (Woodman et al. 1999).

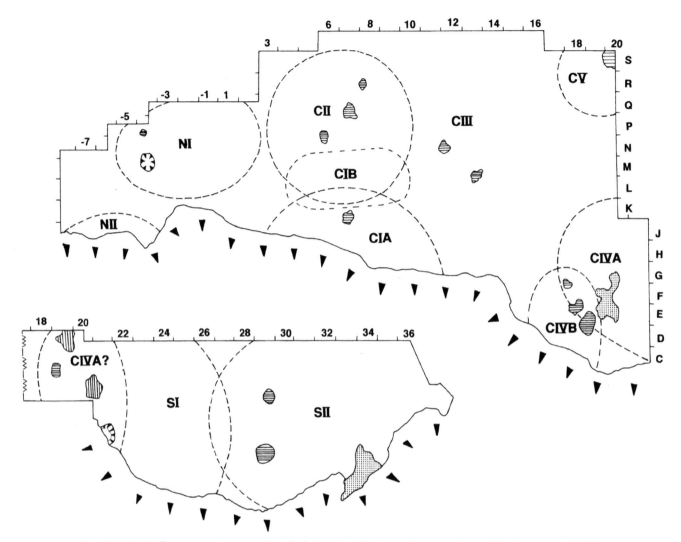

Fig. 11.7. b) Different activity areas identified through refitting at Ferriter's Cove (Woodman et al. 1999).

implements were moved around in a way that suggested a much more flexible use of space than might have been expected. On the basis of the lessons from Barre Mose, any suggestions of behavioural activity such as those proposed for the Mount Sandel hut should be tested through refitting.

The down-side of the simple and effective approach of using refitting has to be tempered with a realisation that it works best with assemblages made up of artefacts, preferably made from distinctively different looking blocks of raw material, where the total is a few hundred or, at worst, a very few thousand!

As often noted, there is a limited return if the realisation of a Mesolithic presence comes late in the excavation or during post-excavation analysis when the specialist reports begin to arrive. The approaches needed must take into consideration, at an early stage, that there may not only be a Mesolithic presence at the location of a particular excavation but that particular questions need to be addressed. In other words,

on-site documentation has to be undertaken with a realisation that our interrogation is only as good as our records.

How extensive an area should be excavated

In recent years, the size of the excavated area tends to be determined by the requirements of the road builder or property developer. Perhaps we could, therefore, ask what we can expect from different types of excavations.

Because of the need for slow, careful recovery strategies, the few sites with waterlogged and less acidic deposits, such as Moynagh Lough (Bradley 1999) and Derragh Lough (Fredengren 2009), suffer from another consequential problem, namely that the area excavated is often quite small. Indeed, given the exceptional quality of information recovered from the latter types of sites, there is a "Catch 22": the care needed to excavate these sites often results in such painstaking excavation

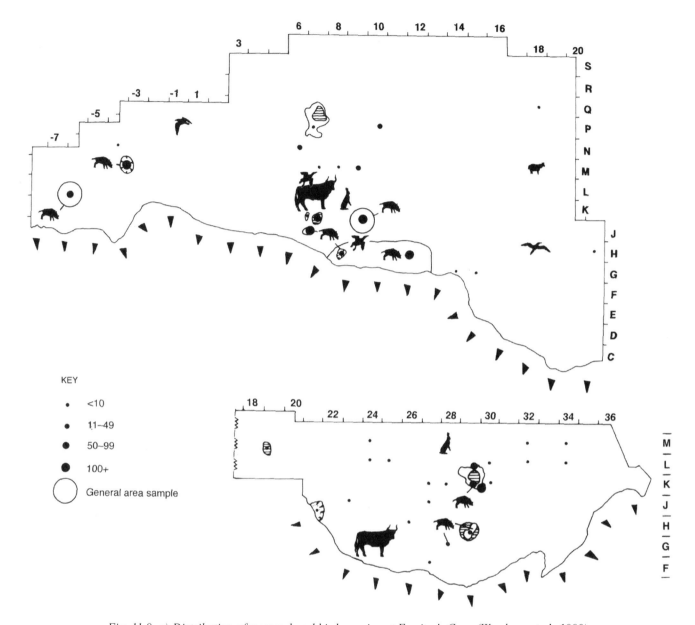

Fig. 11.8. a) Distribution of mammal and bird remains at Ferriter's Cave (Woodman et al. 1999).

that the area shrinks. This raises the question as to whether we are often looking not so much through a keyhole but rather down a drain pipe!

As a result, even where there are challenges in waterlogged and other environments, i.e. where organic preservation is good, it is also necessary to open large areas. At the inland Scanian site of Bökeberg III (Knarrström 2004, 136–7) an area up to 45 m across was opened up while, even in 1943 at the height of World War II, Becker (Henricksen 1976) opened an area at Sværdborg 1(A) that was 25 m across. In summary, anything less than 400 square metres that has not been at least adequately tested, if not fully examined, is not really exploring the whole

potential of the site. It is often impossible to excavate the whole area but sampling of key areas at, for instance, Smakkerup (Price and Gebauer 2005) and Bay Farm (Woodman and Johnston 1996), both tested significant areas and showed that they could still produce crucial stratigraphic information as well as (in the former case) a wealth of ecofacts and artefacts.

The challenge is, therefore, how, using all these painstaking approaches, one can excavate a large enough area in order to explore a representative portion of the site. This presents an awful vista: that the perfect site, which may only represent one season of the yearly round of activities of a Mesolithic group, is so big that it can usually only be excavated as part of a major

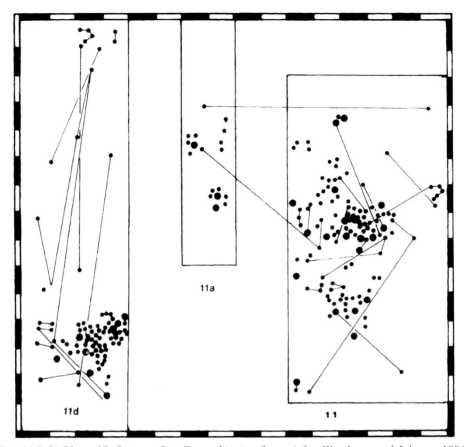

Fig. 11.8. b) Plan of Refitting at Bay Farm chipping floors (after Woodman and Johnson 1996).

infrastructural project such as a motorway, pipeline or railway. At Tågerup (Karsten and Knarrström 2003), for example, 20,000 square metres were explored, while at Polderweg (Louwe Kooijmans 2004) the quantity of material was so large that only a representative sample of material could be sieved. The recent and continuing investigation at Star Carr provides a perfect example of the need to explore large areas. Here, over more than 500 sq. m. have been excavated to date, but the authors have suggested that the area of settlement may have covered nearly 20,000 sq. m. (Conneller *et al.* 2012, fig. 2).

In the case of Ireland, only a few excavations have explored such large areas. Much of the information from these has been explored earlier in this book but it is worth noting that less well-preserved sites, like those on the route of the Toome Bypass excavations, which explored an area in excess of 17,000 sq. m. (Dunlop and Woodman 2015), can also provide differing opportunities to explore the potential of a site. If the bog had not covered the settlement horizon at Lough Boora, where Ryan (1980) explored over 1000 sq. m., one wonders whether it would have been possible to define any areas of activity.

It is tempting to see the discovery of a hut or dwelling activity as the ideal purpose of the excavation yet, as discussed above, many hunter-gatherer camps cover a large area. In the case of

a camp occupied by the Selknam in South America (Coloneze *et al.* 2011), one large hut can be set apart from the dwellings that each family used. Mount Sandel (Woodman 1985a), where at least 700 sq. m. were excavated, provided some opportunity for the identification of differing activitities. For this reason the area around the Mount Sandel excavation site was field walked and phosphate analysis undertaken (Hammond 1985). No other concentrations of Mesolithic artefacts or high levels of phosphates were found in adjacent areas.

The shell midden sites fall into a somewhat similar category where we often hope for simple explanations. These are often seen as dumps that can be mainly explored with careful excavation to produce a very significant range of environmental material. Again, however, the area excavated on many of the midden sites tends to be relatively small and there is an assumption that one or two trenches placed through what is expected to be a horizontally uniform accumulation through time will produce a reasonable picture of the history of the site.

There are many other aspects of shell middens that need to be examined. The most obvious is whether settlement was *on* these sites or nearby, or whether the locations were visited for specific purposes. The monumental task of finding traces of settlement was brought home to a group of us while visiting a

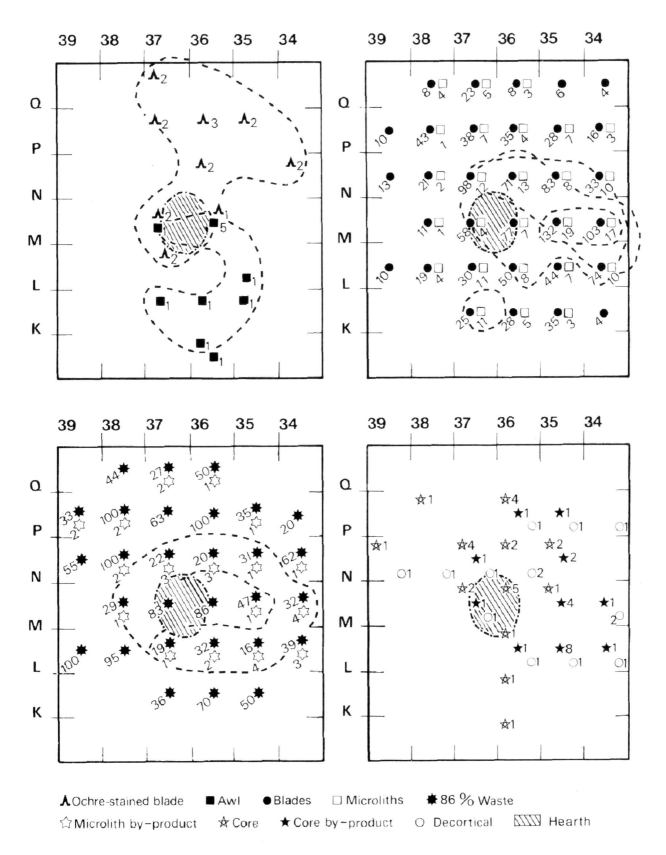

Fig. 11.9. Distribution of different artefacts from the hut area at Mount Sandel (Woodman 1985a).

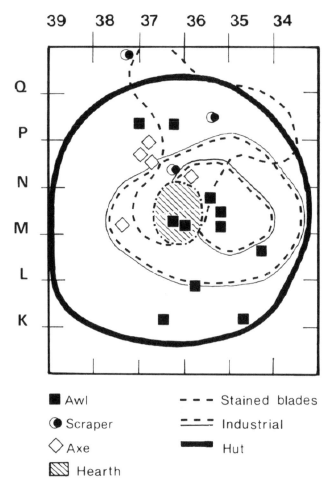

Awl

Scraper

Axe

Hearth

- - - Stained blades

Industrial

Hut

Fig. 11.10. Suggested different activity areas in the hut at Mount Sandel (Woodman 1985a).

number of families collecting oysters in the Mangrove swamps of Senegal (Pl. XXX). The structures on the midden were extremely flimsy and likely to be moved quite frequently. To help clear areas for processing oysters, large heaps of shells were frequently pushed around and mixed up with settlement debris. Therefore, the chances of being able to record traces of dwellings at a later date would be slight. Instead, what would mainly be found would be the remains of fires for boiling shellfish, etc. It also means that, in some cases, the original stratigraphic layering within the midden would be totally disturbed. It is fairly evident that the Irish Mesolithic middens were not the large-scale processing seen in Senegal but many other issues need to be explored (Rowley-Conwy 2013).

Cannon (2013) has attempted some fresh approaches in the exploration of the diverse range of shell middens on the American north-west coast. The nature of the shell middens in that area, whether they were temporary campsites, simple processing sites or significant habitation sites, was explored by coring the middens. This allowed researchers to establish the degree of differences in abundance of parasite eggs present. If

there were large numbers from across the midden a case could be made for short term occupation, whereas, if they were found in large numbers at one specific point then it could be argued that the midden was associated with a long term settlement and that activities such as defecation may have taken place at certain points. Similarly, variation in the presence of intensive activities through differences in rates of fracturing of shells could indicate how much a particular portion of the midden was lived on rather than it just being a dump.

Mesolithic houses: a hard look at the evidence

The reality is that, quite frequently, there are few surviving traces of structures on hunter-gatherer settlements. As discussed in Chapter 4, there is a perfectly natural tendency to see any group of post- or stake-holes as a hut.

An interesting experiment in reconstructing the huts at Mount Sandel has provided certain insights into the problems of reconstructing early dwellings. Children from three primary schools in the Coleraine area carried out this project and the question asked was as follows:

If the skins of large animals were not available in Ireland at that date, notably deer of any type, how were the Mount Sandel huts covered? Given the example of the Saami *Gamma* or winter house where a few very substantial posts were used to support a roof that was primarily constructed of sods, was it possible that some type of turfs or sods were used at Mount Sandel?

The project was a remarkable success, especially given the limited information provided. One instance, where they were not aware of a key fact, was to prove fortunate. A structure of saplings, roughly 4 m across, where branches had been woven to create an inverted basket-shape, was successfully erected and proved capable of supporting a sod wall and roof. The size limitation was based on the fact that the volunteers had found it impossible to bend larger saplings in order to erect a larger structure of this type. However, in the case of the larger Mount Sandel structures, the greater diameter was achieved by placing a number of large saplings into the subsoil at an angle of about 70° and up to 300 mm below the surface. As a result they did not have to be bent over in a tight curve. Indeed, as in the Alacaluf reconstruction published by Bird (1946, 64–6, fig.10), it is possible that a very small number of posts, creating a keel or spine, were put in place first and then slightly smaller stakes were added while lighter branches were finally woven in. Bird observed that these huts were usually 3–4.4 metres in diameter.

Interestingly, parts of this pattern was observed at Mount Sandel where, besides the larger and deeper stake-holes, occasional runs of closely placed smaller ones in between the larger posts were also recorded. The difference seems to be that a larger structure requires some stakes to be set into the ground while a smaller one, such as the experimental hut, can sit very close to the surface and be held down by the weight of the sod walls and roof. The Coleraine volunteers had dug a shallow trench in the soil but no stake-holes were driven into the subsoil to support the structure. The experimental hut not only supported the weight of the sods but a rather large volunteer assistant was able to stand on top of it! (Pl. XXXI). It appears that small versions, such as the Alacaleuf hut, would probably also have left no subsurface traces. Unfortunately this Coleraine experiment did not have time to investigate another solution which was used by the Alacaleuf, namely the use of bark. Here long strips of bark up to 500 mm wide and 2 metres in length were used. Such strips of birch bark have frequently been found below sod roof layers during excavations of Younger Stone Age huts in Arctic Scandinavia.

Unfortunately, as will have been evident in Chapter 4, there are really no other sites in Ireland that provide sufficiently well-preserved traces of structures to offer useful comparisons. The only other known site in Ireland that might have had similar size huts as Mount Sandel was that slightly upstream across the Bann, at Castleroe.

Given the fact that, even when incomplete, the Mount Sandel huts had substantial hearths and stakes that penetrated quite deep into the subsoil, the comparative rarity of similar huts is quite surprising. Kilcorby and Drumakeely, described in Chapter 4, have a preserved record of what would seem to be circular structures but, ultimately, one has to wonder about those occasional pits or hearths like the examples at Cakestown Glebe (see Fig. 4.25b). Could they have been the last remnants of a hearth where traces of a surrounding structure, similar to Kilcorby and Drumakeely, have long since vanished?

Some alternative explanation needs to be found. Evidence from near contemporary hunter-gatherers suggests that the structures on habitation sites were often very flimsy. In Tierra del Fuego, the Yamana and the Selknam often made do with wind breaks while even the Alacaleuf, in adjacent areas of southern Chile, using the building techniques referred to above, did not usually build substantial structures of the size of the huts at Mount Sandel, Howick, East Barnes, etc. (Fig. 11.11). In the Great Lakes area, tribes such as the Sauk and the Ojibwa

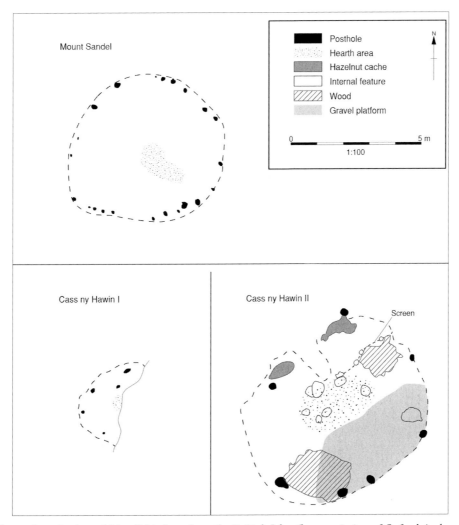

Fig. 11.11. Plans of a selection of Mesolithic huts from the British Isles (by permission of Oxford Archaeology North).

again mostly built structures that were quite light. In Denmark, summer lake shore sites found in locations such as Ulkestrup (Andersen *et al.* 1982) were little more than birch bark floors with a few very light stakes to support a superstructure. The reconstruction of a similar hut found at Lavinge (Jensen 2001, 101) relied on the use of reeds for walls and roofs.

Many of these sites were located on matted reed swamp and give the impression of being very temporary. Yet experimental work in Tierra del Fuego, as well as observations on the excavations of shell midden sites, suggests that the huts could last for a significant length of time. Many of the midden site, which lie along the shores of the Beagle Channel, consist of rings of shell debris that had built up around huts of 3–4 m diameter, a clear indication that that particular spot had been used for perhaps several seasons (Piana and Orquero 2010). Besides observing and excavating these midden sites the excavators examined ethnographic evidence and, over a number of years, carried out a series of experiments (*ibid.*, 266–8). In particular they observed that both poles and branches could be used to form the framework for huts which could then be covered with branches and leaves. Factors such as weather conditions and wind

exposure influenced how they were built. The use or availability of different types of timber, which ranged from thin renewal growth in forests to old, bigger branches in open conditions, would determine whether vaulted or conical structures were built. Above 4 m and especially at 5 m+ diameter, conical huts became impractical and vaulted structures were used.

Piana and Orquero also noted that huts could be left standing and would survive for a number of years (Fig. 11.12) and that they could be re-used with very little repair. Indeed, in the case of the conical huts, these structures could survive for decades. The authors (*ibid.*, 30; 2, e) noted that a photograph taken in the 1970s was of a structure that was erected in 1903/4 (Fig. 11.12b)! In this case, where the stability mostly came from the poles placed in a symmetrical, circular shape rather than being driven or worked into the ground, one wonders whether even in the best conditions any subsurface traces of the site, other than a hearth, would exist.

We should therefore consider whether the Mount Sandel hut, which may have been 5 m or slightly more across, was used for a larger group than one family or had another purpose. Was it a structure that was intended for ritual purposes? While

Fig. 11.12. a) Alacaleuf basket hut under construction, b) real Yamana wigwam type structure built in 1904 and still standing in the 1970s when photographed, c) Yamana ceremonial hut, d) experimental Yamana huts (photographs courtesy of E Piana Conicet).

one should not rely too much on direct comparisons with the ethnographic record, many of the Alacaleuf and Yamana ritual huts, though built in a somewhat similar fashion, tend to be much longer, 12 m or more in length and up to 4 m across. On the other hand it may be that this was more like a Saami "Gama" which was intended to be a more substantial structure, perhaps for use in the less temperate part of the year.

There is also growing evidence that there are a significant number of sunken dwellings in Mesolithic Scandinavia. In some cases, such as the Voullerin houses (Loeffler 2003), which are rectangular and lie on the Arctic Circle in Sweden, they varied between 12 m and 19 m in length, 5–7 m in width and with a depth of up to 0.3 m. Many others are more circular and these are 3–8 m across. It is important to realise, however, that these are not always from the latest stages of the Mesolithic. Thus, while the Tågerup round-house (Fig. 11.5), which is very substantial at up to 8 m across and dated to the Ertebølle, utilised substantial posts rather than stakes and was built within a slight hollow, there are also smaller examples. One of the most notable was that of the Ertebølle example at Nivå on the west coast of Zealand, which was only 3.2 m in diameter (Jensen 2009). One feature that many of these sunken dwellings have in common is that they are usually dug into the subsoil for a depth of up to *c.* 0.3 m, though some, such as

the Mount Sandel hut and the hollow at Star Carr (Conneller *et al.* 2013) are much shallower. Zilhao (2009) noted, very insightfully, that where substantial structures existed they were not found below latitude 50° north and he wondered about the implication of this fact. It seems probable, as Hernek (2003) suggested for the Timmerås site, that these huts with hollows within them could be long-term and/or winter settlement sites.

In general, however, apart from these more impressive substantial huts, the archaeological record and the ethnographic evidence suggest that the evidence for structures will often be very ephemeral. Fortunately we can turn to regions such as northern Scandinavia where the survival of original Stone Age land surfaces is quite common.

In the Norwegian "Older Stone Age" small circular huts 3–4 m across were recovered at numerous sites, such as on the Island of Vega off the north-west coast (Bjerck 1990) or at Mortensnes in Varanger Fjord Finmark (Schancke 1988). In the latter case there were six of these small huts found in close proximity along the arc of a beach ridge (Fig. 11.13). It is possible that these were all in use at the same time. Also in the case of the Mortensnes huts, it was not the locality or the limitations of raw material that restricted the sizes of these structures as, some 2–3000 years later at the beginning of the Younger Stone Age, larger more rectangular huts 6 × 4 m in

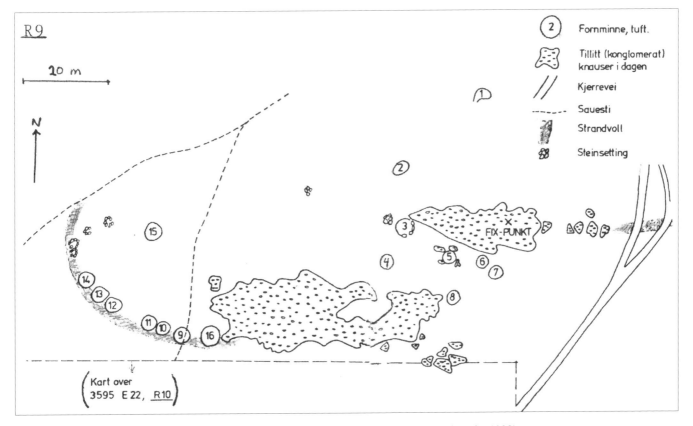

Fig. 11.13. Stone hut circles from Mortensnes (after Schanche 1988).

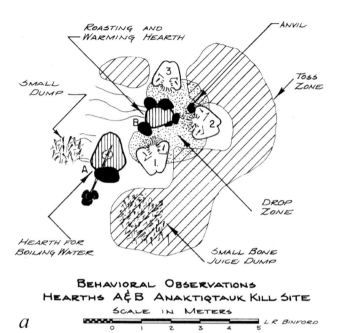

ROASTING AND
WARMING HEARTH

ANVIL

SMALL
DUMP

TOSS
ZONE

3

B

A

2

1

DROP
ZONE

HEARTH FOR
BOILING WATER

SMALL BONE
JUICE DUMP

**BEHAVIORAL OBSERVATIONS
HEARTHS A & B ANAKTIQTAUK KILL SITE**
SCALE IN METERS
0   1   2   3   4   5   L R BINFORD

a

size were built. Several important points can be drawn from these and many other Scandinavian sites of the same age.

1) They were defined by stone rings and, in some cases, by soil or sods. No extensive use was made of stake-holes sunk deep into the ground;
2) They were found in areas of thin, undisturbed soil so that one could presume that nothing of these structures would survive in areas of tillage; and
3) They may have been a product of societies that carried out many of their activities outside the huts.

Taking the implications of point 3) and as was shown earlier from the ethnographic record, many activities may have taken place outside. Scatters of stone tools and their debris may, along with ephemeral traces of fires and small shelters, represent a living area whose articulation would not necessarily indicate the location of the huts. As already noted, this is quite clear at Mount Sandel, where the debris from the chipping floors was being found some metres west of the huts. There are also a number of small groups of stake-holes (1000 and 1006) that are

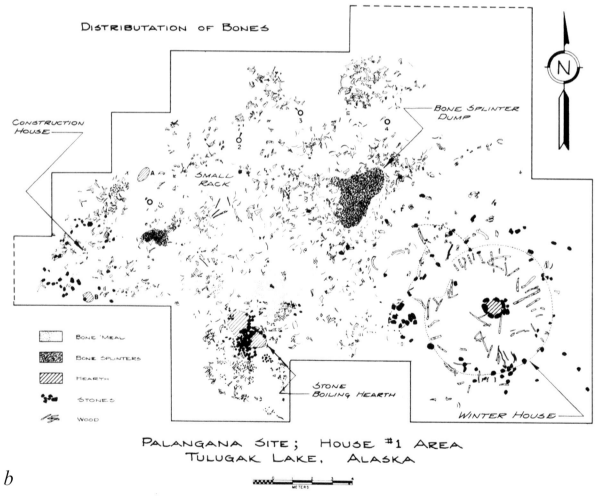

DISTRIBUTATION OF BONES

N

CONSTRUCTION
HOUSE

BONE SPLINTER
DUMP

SMALL
RACK

STONE
BOILING HEARTH

WINTER HOUSE

BONE 'MEAL
BONE SPLINTERS
HEARTH
STONES
WOOD

**PALANGANA SITE; HOUSE #1 AREA
TULUGAK LAKE, ALASKA**

METERS

b

Fig. 11.14. Plan of the Anaktiqtauk and Palangana sites after Binford 1983 (© Thames & Hudson).

placed together and set into the ground at an angle (Woodman 1985a). Perhaps the clearest example of areas of dump or other activities can be seen at Tågerup, in the excavations close to the Ertebølle "round-house" (Karsten and Knarrström 2003), where the excavators estimated that almost 60 instances of dumps of fire-cracked rock, flint waste and discarded tools lay to the west of the round hut (Fig. 11.5). Many of these were probably associated with the hut. In summary, it is very clear that huts only represent one part of the settlement.

In fact there are suggestions that the Fuegians of Tierra del Fuego, whose lifestyle so appalled Darwin, lived by lowering their body temperatures or used sea lion fat to protect them from the cold, so that living in the open air or spending long periods in their boats, as in the case of the Yamana People, was possible. Therefore, for some groups of hunter-gatherer's living in cool temperate regions, substantial dwellings may not have been necessary. In fact one could argue that structures like that at Mount Sandel may have had a special purpose. It is of interest that Coloneso (2011) noted that, at the inland Selknam settlement referred to earlier, there had been a number of small structures but one larger one was placed some distance apart.

It is again quite thought provoking to have a look at some other ethnographic evidence as to how the archaeological record could be created. Binford (1977), in his research on Nunamiut lifestyles, recorded and planned many aspects of their settlement sites. The plan of the Palangana site (Fig. 11.14) shows that a campsite is made up of many activity areas and that major concentrations of refuse are often quite substantial and placed some distance from the hut, which in turn and in spite of its size, would only leave the slightest traces after the location was abandoned. Indeed other traces of outside activities might be a lot more obvious though, as Binford noted, there would be a very different pattern for outside sites, such as at the Anaktiqtauk site where hearths could be surrounded by an inner drop zone and an outer chuck zone. Indeed, the area round Feature 5 at Ferriter's Cove (see chapter 4:19) provides a good example of outside activities. In that case the fact that charcoal was blown off by the south-westerly winds is a clear indication that these activities took place outside.

As noted in Chapter 4, while a few stake-holes do not make a dwelling, it is likely that little groups of post-holes, such as those in the western forest part of Mount Sandel or even some of the alignments, are likely to have been racks for nets, fish drying, etc.

From what we can tell from recent settlement sites of hunter-gatherers, we should expect the Stone Age archaeological record to be much more complex than we had imagined and, on occasions in terms of the area excavated, much larger than the area we are able to excavate. The archaeological record of these hunter-gatherer settlement sites can look very different from those of some later prehistoric societies.

There is one very clear lesson that can be drawn from this survey of the known "habitation structures" of Mesolithic date as well as the cursory survey of some more contemporary hunter-gatherers settlement sites. This lesson is that, while there are certain constraints brought about by human behaviour, *there is no such thing as a specific type of "Mesolithic Hut".* They can vary for all sorts of reasons related to climate, accessibility to raw materials or the way in which life is practised.

Taking the range of archaeological and ethnographic evidence together, we can see that shelters and the evidence they left behind varies (Fig. 11.15):

1) *Simple wigwams* created by poles may leave no traces other than a ring of stones and, as noted by Piana and Orquero (2010), their potential diameter will be limited by the very tall nature of the structure (Fig. 11.13b). This is a particularly large example that had stood for many decades after it was erected in 1903/4.

2) *Basket-shaped structures*, such as that used by the Alacaleuf, may range between 4 m and 6(?) m in diameter. The smaller examples may leave little trace in the ground. Examples like the Mount Sandel huts, because of their angled stake-holes that were placed 200 mm or more into the subsoil, did leave a trace. The depth of the stake-holes and their angled nature would reduce the stress that was created when bending over saplings in order to build a larger structure. Given that these are like inverted woven baskets, the main structural members of the basket may not, as at Mount Sandel, be placed evenly round the potential location for the hut.

3) *Post-built huts* can be larger huts, on occasions exceeding 7 m in diameter. East Barnes and Cass ny Hawin 2 would be good examples of this type of structure. These seem to rely on a number of larger posts placed more evenly round the circumference. The more substantial posts, depending on the angle of the roof, may have been needed to bear the weight of a large heavy roof. In this case, as noted earlier, one has to wonder sometimes, on sites where an irregular pattern of a few post-holes has been recovered, what type of structure was envisaged, or whether they had been used for other purposes.

4) *Sunken dwellings*, where obviously the prime example of this class would be Howick. The slight depressions associated with Mount Sandel and East Barnes may have as much to do with levelling the floor as with creating a hollow. There is a question as to whether smaller hollows, like Cass ny Hawin 1 and Staosnaig, are dwellings though Bjerck (1990), in his investigations on Vega, has noted circular stone structures as small as 3 m across. However as Lothrop (1928, 128) has noted, many of the Yamana huts had a large sunken depression at their centre which could have been up to 500 mm deep and it was in this depression that the fires were placed. The main structural members for building the shelter were placed outside the hollow. In returning to the question of the loss of information from the topsoil and even loss of the upper portion of the original subsoil, one must wonder if the evidence of the outer structural members has been lost through agricultural and other activities.

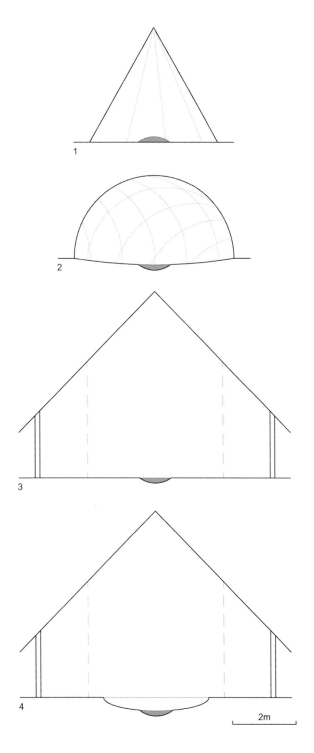

Fig. 11.15. Schematic diagrams of the structures of various potential hut types (prepared by Hugh Kavanagh).

5) *Rectangular structures* are quite common in certain parts of northern Scandinavia but there is less clear evidence for them in these islands. The Toome Bypass Feature 5 is very distinctive and should not be dismissed just because it is made up of deep trenches and a prepared floor. The potential of building a large elongated structure, perhaps for ceremonial purposes, can be seen in the Yamana structure in Figure 11.12.

Figure 11.15 provides a schematic summary of the different hut types with one speculative addition.

Not all known Mesolithic structures can be easily placed within the schema outlined above. The recent and significant discovery of a structure at Star Carr falls into this category (Conneller *et al.* 2012, figs 6 and 7). There is a shallow hollow reminiscent of some of the examples discussed here, e.g. East Barnes or Cass ny Hawin 2, though it is slightly more irregular and has a smaller diameter. However, it is difficult to establish a clear pattern or suggest how it was built. The quite coherent scatter of artefacts associated with the hut clearly shows that this is more than the ploughed out remains of the location of a shelter, as has been found elsewhere.

Well what are we looking for?

Hopefully the previous section illustrates than the fact that habitation sites consist of much more than a hut. It is easy to go with the "Little House on the Prairie" concept. On a more positive note, taking into consideration all the caveats, we need much more than one "Mega/Super site". It should be evident that, no matter what each site can be, it only contains one small part or partial part of story. Thus while some very important sites are waterlogged and contain amazing amounts of information they have to be complimented by others. The differences can be as simple as locations used at different seasons or, in the case of Mount Sandel for example, where there is only one portion of the story of the Earlier Mesolithic. Lots of activities, such as butchering of animals or the gutting of large numbers of some fish, will not always be represented while the sites with fish weirs and baskets, such as Clowanstown (Mossop 2009) or Spenser Dock (McQuade and O'Donnell 2009) provide a different part of the story.

As noted at the beginning of this Chapter many of our "dry land" sites are in locations where the original surface has been partially removed through agricultural activity but as Mick Monk pointed out (Problems in Prehistory Conference 1999, Cork) there are many areas in Ireland, with its heavier soils, where the loss of the original surface has not been as great as in other regions in Europe. These are regions of sandy soils or where deflation of Loess surfaces has had a much greater impact. Thus he observed, even in 1999, that this might partly explain the comparatively numerous instances of Neolithic rectangular houses being discovered in Ireland. So, although we can regret the limited and partial survival of pits, post-holes and hearths described in Chapter 4, in some other parts of Europe not even these scant traces might have survived.

So what would be at the top of my list? Perhaps, first, the one lesson that we should bear in mind is that some of the most important sites that have survived relatively intact have lain beneath a layer of later deposits: whether hill wash, as at Bay Farm, peat deposits like Lough Boora or Belderrig, sand dunes like Ferriter's Cove or even a thick layer of forest soils as in one part of Mount Sandel. A location in one of these environments, especially where the soils are less acidic, such as at Ferriter's Cove, could pay immense dividends. Is it possible that we could combine the Micro-regional areas defined earlier in the Baker's Dozen with the search for locations with neutral subsoil which are buried safely by later deposits? Ultimately, the awareness of both the possibility of discovery of traces of Mesolithic sites and their potential significance cannot be over-emphasised.

Chapter 12

Life and death

Life, death, the universe and everything (as well as little furry creatures from Alpha Centauri)

This is one of those topics where it is easy to be intimidated by what is found elsewhere. Once again one can be envious of sites that vary from cemeteries in the Baltic and Russia to those found along the Atlantic coast in Brittany and Portugal. There are also regions where there are numerous examples of ornaments and mobilary art. There is the existence of rock art and even paintings from the European arctic, as at Alta in Norway (Helskog 1988; Pl. XXXIIa) where extensive naturalistic representations of animals as well as hunting and fishing scenes occur. There must be a question as to why this type of art is not found throughout most of Europe. Indeed absences of Mesolithic rock art are not peculiar to Ireland. Outside Scandinavia and adjacent parts of the Russian federation it is also virtually absent.

Death and its rituals

If one wants to look at issues such as health, life expectations and ritual, it is very useful to start with human remains and the burial or other rituals that are associated with them. Unfortunately, human remains from the Irish Mesolithic are quite rare, indeed there is not one complete non-cremated skeleton that can be convincingly ascribed to the Irish Mesolithic (Meiklejohn and Woodman 2012) and, as noted by Delaney and Woodman (2004), even some of the "possible" Mesolithic skulls preserved in various collections have been shown to be much later in date.

It cannot over-emphasised that funerary ritual can be quite complex without necessarily leaving substantial traces in the form of burials (*ibid.*). In certain areas of the Murray River Valley in Australia, for example, native Australians place the remains of the elderly on rocks or in trees, while the remains of the very young are carried by their mother until they disintegrate (Pretty 1977). Similarly, the Navaho of America dispose of their dead by placing them in niches in cliffs away from the dwellings. In Tierra del Fuego, Ernesto Piana (pers. comm.) estimates that there are few instances of human remains of

the indigenous Yamana population being recovered. Yet their presumed ancestors have lived there for at least 8000 years.

There are some actual cemeteries of Mesolithic date, such as Téviec (Péquart *et al*. 1937), of the coast of Brittany, which would have been placed on a small hilltop set back from the sea, or the island cemetery of Oleni Ostrov in Lake Onega, Russia (Gurina 1956; Fig. 12.1).

It is important to recognise, however, that cemeteries are a relatively rare phenomenon of the Mesolithic and may have been a product of local, very special circumstances. This can be seen even in Denmark where the burials recovered from Vedbaek may have been originally placed in an area of settlement (Albrethsen and Brinch Petersen 1976). There are now a number of other instances in western Zealand of burials being found in areas of settlement. Even in the Vedbaek area, at nearby Gøngehusvej (Brinch Petersen and Meiklejohn 2004), a number of cremation deposits and a child's burial were recovered close to a hut (Fig. 12.2). Similarly, at the settlement sites of Tågerup in Sweden (Karsten and Knarrström 2004) and Polderweg in the Netherlands (Louwe Kooijmans 2001) a number of individual burials were recovered, though in the former case, it could be argued that a separate "cemetery" near to the settlement had come into use towards the end of the Mesolithic.

Irrespective of what happened in the rest of Europe it would appear that the British Isles are somewhat different. As elsewhere, and as Schulting has recently shown (2013) with the Tilbury man dating programme, there may be other unrecognised occasional burials of Mesolithic date to be identified.

In general, in England and Wales a not insignificant number of human remains of Mesolithic date have been recovered, notably those from the south-west (Conneller 2006; Schulting 2013) and these are usually from caves. While Aveline's Hole (Schulting 2005) is obviously the most spectacular, a scatter of remains from other caves, such as those in south Wales, have also turned up human bones of Mesolithic age (Schulting 2009).

In the case of Ireland, the most interesting aspect of the search for Mesolithic human remains must be the absences. If it was to be expected that occasional inhumation burials

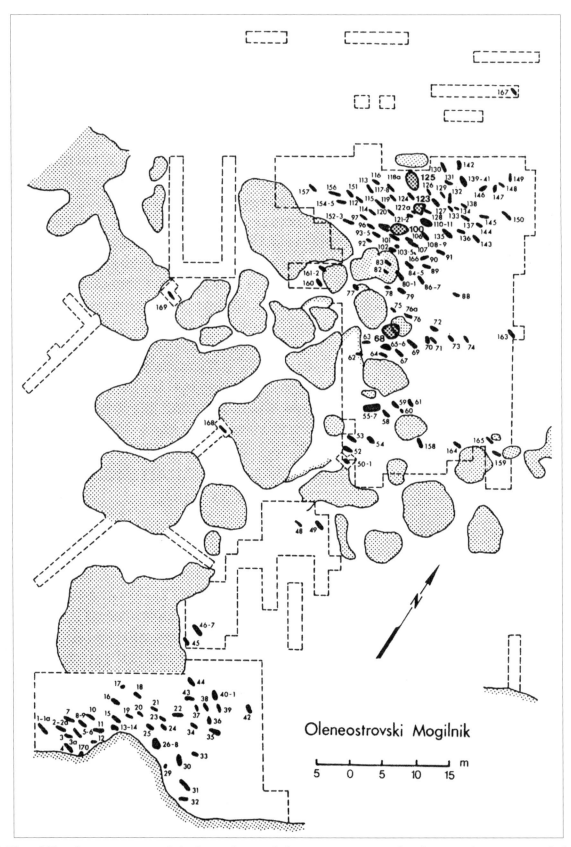

Fig. 12.1. Plan of Oleni Ostrov cemetery on Lake Onega; fine stippled areas represent ground surface irregularities, primarily depressions; graves are marked with bold numerals and stipple indicates the location of upright interments (after Gurina 1956).

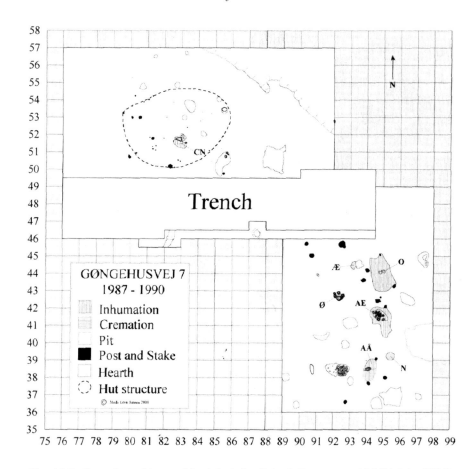

Fig. 12.2. Gøngehusvej hut and burials (after Brinch Petersen and Meiklejohn 2004).

of Mesolithic date existed in Ireland then one or two clear examples might have been found. There are now a sufficient number of excavations of dry land areas where habitation took place, such as Mount Sandel or Toome Bypass, where no graves have been recovered or where, on salvage excavations, there were remnants of pits that one might consider to be graves. Burials that remind us of the humanity of our ancestors, as reflected in the reconstruction drawing from Vedbaek (Knudsen 1980; Fig. 12.3b) are unknown.

More generally it appears that interment in graves was quite a rare phenomenon. In fact the total Irish evidence from excavations of human remains that are clearly of Mesolithic date is exceptionally small. The record consists so far of fewer than ten instances where human remains have been recovered in Ireland. The remains from actual burials comprise those from Hermitage in Co. Limerick. These include the cremation burial in pit A that contained a stone axe and post and is so far unique (Fig. 12.3a; Collins and Coyne 2003; 2006). There are a few other human remains such as an ulna from Rockmarshall, Co. Louth (Woodman *et al.* 1997) and a scatter of teeth and limb fragments from Ferriter's Cove, Co. Kerry (Power 1999) while a reworked human bone was dredged from the Lower Bann at the Cutts.

An interesting comparison can be made in one case, based on Dowd's (2008) survey of Irish caves. This survey and radiocarbon dating programmes of human remains from Irish caves have shown a major concentration of primarily disarticulated individual human bones from the Neolithic and even the Bronze Age. Only Killuragh Cave seems to be the exception. Here human remains of Earlier and Later Mesolithic date (Fibiger in Woodman and Dowd in prep.) were mixed with Neolithic and Bronze Age bones, but it could also be argued that the Mesolithic material present in the cave found its way into it at a much later date. As discussed in Chapter 4, there are, so far, few traces of a Mesolithic presence in the Irish caves

The Islands of the Dead Project (Christina Fredengren pers. comm.) dated 50+ skulls and skeletons from many wetland contexts but has not produced evidence of Mesolithic remains from any context.

Elsewhere, while much attention has focused on burials and cemeteries, there are also numerous instances of the recovery of individual bones but, until recently, there has been "a curious reluctance to acknowledge the ubiquity of disarticulated human bone in the European Mesolithic" (Conneller 2006, 157). This point has recently been emphasised by an exhaustive study carried out by Amy Gray Jones (2011), which illustrated the

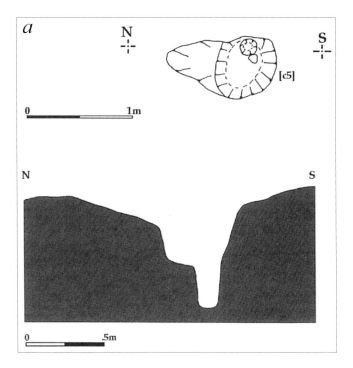

Fig. 12.3. Burials: a) section through cremation burial at Hermitage, Co. Limerick (after Collins and Coyne DATE), b) child burial at Vedbaek (Knudsen 1980).

very extensive distribution of loose human bones throughout the European Mesolithic.

Discoveries in the shell midden at Cnoc Coig on Oronsay suggest that, on occasion, portions of human limbs have been placed in middens. The most famous instance is the series of hand bones placed on a cluster of seal flipper bones (Nolan 1986, 255). Even at the Vedbaek cemetery, individual bones were found sometimes mixed in with midden material. Brinch Petersen (1981, 26) has suggested that eight of these bones, which were broken and had cut marks, had been associated with cannibalism. He suggested that this may have been a ritual process where the power of the deceased as important members of the band was passed on through consuming portions of their body! In other words, these scatters of bones are not just the few bits which we have found while missing burials, but they may represent an important role in Mesolithic societies.

In returning to the bones from Ferriter's Cove, it is tempting to see the human limb bone fragments as a meal eaten while sitting beside the Hearth (Feature 5). However, before someone suggests fireside cannibalism, both in terms of stratigraphy and radiocarbon dating, it must be pointed out that the bones are later than the hearth! Human bones are also not necessarily coming from shell middens, thus, in spite of O'Sullivan's (2002) suggestion that middens were a repository for human remains, this type of site in Ireland, has produced nothing of Mesolithic date (with the exception of one bone from Rockmarshall; Meiklejohn and Woodman 2012). It is also important to remember that the bones from Ferriter's Cove came from a site where shellfish occurred rather than a shell midden. In fact, Irish shell middens of Mesolithic date (Chapter 4) are often quite thin or thrown up against a bank rather than appearing as monuments in the landscape.

The recent publication of numerous burials that have been investigated by the National Museum of Ireland over the last 80 years contains an exhaustive and detailed list of many different types of burials (Cahill and Saekora 2012). For obvious reasons of feasibility this project did not extend to examining the large number of small concentrations of cremated bones, some of which just might pre-date the Neolithic. An initial scan of the reports of the excavations of the last 20 years, in the hope for possible Mesolithic burials that had not been accompanied by diagnostic artefacts, has also produced no potentially interesting burials (see Meiklejohn and Woodman 2012) for a fuller survey of human remains of Mesolithic date as well as examples that have proved not to be of that age). In spite of the lack of any other evidence uncovered so far, of the difficulty in identifying cremation deposits as being potentially of early date and, in particular, of the manner in which the Hermitage cremation burials were first discovered, it would seem possible that there may be other cremation burials of Mesolithic date already recorded or remaining to be discovered in Ireland. There are two sets of human bones from Sramore Cave and Stoney Island that lie on the cusp between the Mesolithic and Neolithic (see below).

Human burials are relatively rare, then, even in mainland Europe and even rarer in Britain and Ireland, but one must wonder whether, given that we have not expected to find them, they occasionally do occur but lie below our perceptual radar. Several factors, such as poor conditions for survival or lack of excavations in locations where relatively substantial settlement had taken place, could contribute to their rarity. This is more than just finding a "trophy" burial as human remains can provide so much information about the life, wellbeing and even death of the people we choose to study. A few skeletons from the Irish Mesolithic would be wonderful but even ten human bones, each from a different site, would be of huge benefit (see Chapter 10).

There are other ways of seeking an understanding of death and the mysteries of the Universe. Some may be quite different from what we expect. The presence of a large number of sculpted amber figures of animals or pendants from Denmark and other parts of the Baltic (Jensen 2001, 128–32; 213–21) are an example. The numerous examples of decorated bone and antler implements from the Baltic must also emphasise the role of decoration and symbolism in Stone Age societies. The cemetery at Oleni Ostrov has produced a series of items, such as the small figures of elk heads as well as snakes, with each specific type being concentrated in one particular part of the cemetery (Gurina 1956; O'Shea and Zvelibil 1984). These must have had, at the very least, totemic significance. Similarly, teeth were sown onto the clothing at Oleni Ostrov (Gurina 1956). The burials at Vedbaek included instances of a necklace or talisman pouch containing mostly teeth of different species including one of an elk, which did not exist at that time in Zealand, as well as bands of various items fastened onto clothing (Fig. 12.4). Often there are much simpler amulets of stone or amber, such as those found in the Netherlands or Britain. While many of the Dutch examples are from graves they are also found elsewhere on the settlement sites.

Newell *et al.* (1990), in their review of potential territories, bands and linguistic groups, relied heavily on personal ornaments and their differences. One of the most striking aspects of that project is that it shows that the great majority of ornaments of all types come from graves, especially those associated with middens in coastal areas (*ibid.*, table 31). The vast majority are made from shells, with much smaller quantities made from teeth and bone.

Instead of looking for similar items in the British Isles, however, one can identify other physical evidence which probably had ritual significance. The 24 antler frontlets found at Star Carr (Clarke 1954), along with several others in Germany, hint at aspects of ritual that no-one could possibly have predicted. Besides these items there are the curious stone figures from Wales, of which some are almost figurine-like. Six unusual and often decorated pebbles were recovered from various locations during the excavations at Rhuddlan in north Wales. Many came from disturbed and later contexts but one, SF2 from pit M90, is a decorated example which might be regarded as having a female figurine-like shape or, if inverted, a phallic shape. The five other fragmentary examples, especially SF1, retained similar decoration (Berridge and Roberts 1994,

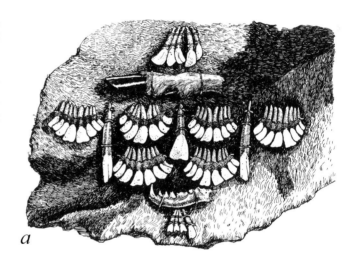

a

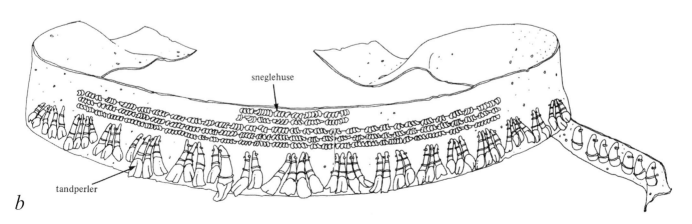

b

Fig. 12.4. Personal decoration from excavations at Vedbaek cemetery, Denmark: a) necklace (after Knudsen 1980), b) decorated band on a dress (Brinch Petersen 1980).

115–54). As Berridge noted, a similar figurine-like example was recovered from Nab Head in Pembrokeshire. David and Walker have also noted that similarly engraved pebbles have been found within a surface collection of British Early Mesolithic artefacts at Triose Head in Cornwall (David and Walker 2004, 314).

a

b

Fig. 12.5. *a) Body painting and Selknam ritual dance (courtesy of E. Piana Conicet), b) Oleni Ostrov figure (after Gurina 1956).*

Nothing similar has been recovered from Ireland though one must wonder about the significance of the small piles of limpets, stacked one on top of the other, which May recovered from the top of the raised beach deposits at Portbraddan Cave in north Antrim (1943, 40). Was this ritual, a child's game, or perhaps a game for adults? Again, pecten shells buried in a small pit under the midden at Baylet (Milner and Woodman in prep.) would seem more likely to be some form of offering rather than rubbish disposal.

In the case of Ireland, the dating of a bone point which was dredged from the Lower Bann at the Cutts presents an interesting example of how little we know. This particular example has been made from a human ulna (see Chapters 5 and 10) and it is always possible that several others from the same location may also be fashioned from human bones. Is this ritual? Insults to an enemy? Or the expedient use of any bones in an island where suitable bones from large mammals were not that conveniently available?

It is well known that so-called "Celtic" societies of Iron Age date invested their beliefs and worship in nature rather than in physical edifices. Similarly, the Saami, as in Varanger Fjord, worshipped the bear stone and held certain mountains, such as Skarv Berget, to be sacred. I have often wondered how Stone Age societies would have reacted to the Vanishing Lake (known either as Lough Aveema or Lough Areema; Fig. 12.6) that lies on the edge of the Antrim Plateau; due to the porosity of the underlying limestone its waters vanish with great regularity. Would they have been mystified by the Shannon Pot? This is the presumed headwater of the Shannon River, a place where water always existed but where there was no surface indication as to where it came from. Natural features in the landscape must have created stories – even the mushroom stones referred to in Chapter 2 (Pl. III). The Giants Causeway (Pl. XXXIIb) would have been the source of speculation and stories while one must wonder at how the groups visiting the beach at Ferriter's Cove would have explained the shape of one of the nearby Blasket Islands i.e. Inish Tuaisceart or "*An Fear Marbh*" (the dead man; Pl. XXXIIc).

The presence of bear bones on Irish sites has also been alluded to earlier. While there may be a simple explanation in terms of butchering practice and the possibility that the skins were returned to settlement sites retaining foot bones, it is also possible that these skins could have been kept for ceremonial purposes. As noted in Chapter 10, to us in the domesticated and civilised regions of the western fringes of Atlantic Europe, an animal such as the bear receives little consideration. It is, however, important to emphasise that the veneration of an animal such as a bear and the use of portions of the body for meat, skins and other raw materials, are not incompatible. Many Native American tribes worshipped the bear; in some instances seeing it as their near cousin, but they also used its body for day-to-day needs, such as food and clothing.

Brunner (2007, 117–24) documents the important role that bears, which had been captured and held in captivity, played

Fig. 12.6. The Vanishing Lake (Photographs © National Museums of Northern Ireland, Collections of the Ulster Museum and Folk & Transport Museum).

in rituals that took place over several days on the banks of the Amur River in Siberia and on its frozen surface. Jordan (2006, 97) also recounts the elaborate rituals of the Siberian Khanty associated with all aspects of their relationships with bears. The significance of the bear amongst the Saami and the manner in which it was reflected in Stone Age rock art in northern Scandinavia has already been discussed in Chapter 10. Its significance in more recent times is illustrated by Figure 10.2, pictures of the ritualistic progress from the bear hunt to the feast and finally the burial.

Obviously, water can be an important element in the rituals of the living. In Ireland so many Mesolithic sites occur near water. Chatterton (2006) has discussed the range of evidence potentially associated with ritual. In the case of water (*ibid.*, 103–12) there are obviously many potential "chicken and egg" situations. For example, are organic remains from waterlogged deposits always ritual deposits or is the nature of the environment in which they were found likely to be the reason for their preservation? How does one decide if the Late Glacial Poulton le Fylde Elk (*ibid.*, 104) is a ritual deposit? If one wants that interpretation should the same explanation be extended to the Prejlup and Vig aurochsen from Denmark, both of which had been pursued and shot at, as there were microliths associated with the skeletons (Jensen 2001, 114–20)? Obviously, as Chatterton (*ibid.*, 108) has rightly noted, there are some finds, such as the tantalising instance of the Hylton log boat, found in northern England in the 19th century and recorded as containing axes and skeletal remains, that require serious consideration.

In Ireland we do not fully understand the reasons for caching a range of Mesolithic and Neolithic artefacts, but one has to wonder about claims that there is a ritual association with water (*ibid.*, 111). It is not usually realised that many of the deposits from the Bann Valley, such as Newferry, Culbane and Portglenone, which are areas from which numerous axes were recovered, were not simple areas of open water. In some cases one can presume that over 1000 axes were originally recovered. The deposits from which they were recovered were created as a relatively shallow spread of winter flood where diatoms within their silica shells were left stranded. As was evident at Newferry 3, however, there are traces of soil horizons present suggesting that the axes were actually left on dry land. These locations are also places where, over thousands of years, eel weirs were erected (see Chapters 9 and 10). It is also possible that the caching of objects was, in part, marking a claim to a particular location and the right to return.

It is also probable that, as in many societies even today, ritual and religion were mixed into day-to-day life. Huts may have been laid out in a prescribed manner, which could have included a specific orientation or a required numbers of posts. Votive offerings, for example at the beginning of a seasonal fish run, would almost certainly have taken place. Some traditions, such as the dance by a group of Selknam illustrated in Figure 12.6, may be something we just have to keep in mind.

In summary, one can, perhaps, get fixated by the quality of evidence in terms of art of various forms, personal ornaments and burials that can be found in certain regions of Europe. There is a danger that, metaphorically, we can become like a group of impoverished Victorian ragamuffins with our noses pressed against the sweet shop window, hoping that we can find a way to share in the feast. There are many other regions where the items described above do not exist. Ireland happens to be one of those regions. So why include this type of evidence? Very simply, it reminds us that we do not have to perceive of our first inhabitants as impoverished creatures living a nasty short and brutish existence.

Living

Naked or clothed?

As mentioned earlier, personal ornaments which might be associated with clothing are not known from the Irish Mesolithic though they do, along with decorative items, exist later in the Irish Stone Age. One interesting group, which is less well known than the more exotic items such as bone and antler pins found in passage Tombs (Bergh and Hensey 2013), comprises small steatite beads that have been found on numerous Irish Early Neolithic sites. No equivalents are known from the Irish Mesolithic. The best we can manage is one pierced cowrie shell from the Baylet shell midden (Nicky Milner pers. comm.). Personal adornment may have also have taken the form of paint or, as suggested by Cahill (2001), albeit in the context of the Bronze Age, tattooing could have taken place as far back as the Mesolithic.

There is also the more mundane matter of clothing. Perhaps it would be salutary to begin by reflecting on *our* expectations. There is no doubt that Darwin and others exploring the Beagle Channel saw indigenous peoples not as viable communities but rather as groups that lacked the normal accoutrements of civilised societies, most notably substantial dwellings and perhaps, in particular as far as European eyes were concerned and given the local climate, the absence of clothing. We can, and will, speculate on clothing but it would appear that groups such as the Yamana had no difficulty living with only simple skins as cloaks for protection or, perhaps, even very little clothing. As mentioned already, it is even suggested that they managed by using sea lion fat and perhaps by being able to adjust their metabolic system to minimise the impact of poor weather conditions. Theirs was a lifestyle and way of dealing with a cold temperate environment which did not, like Ireland, have the benefit of the warming effect of the Gulf Stream. Yet it was apparently adequate for several thousand people and may have endured as a way of life for several thousand years.

It is possible, on the basis of the evidence from elsewhere in Europe that clothing existed in the Irish Mesolithic. Convex scrapers, which were so prolific and used for hide working (among other things) in the Neolithic (Bamforth and Woodman

2004) were rare in the Irish Mesolithic. This did not necessarily mean that people were unable to work skins. There were times in the Danish Maglemose when scrapers were also quite rare and there is no suggestion that they could not work animal hides to prepare them for clothing. In the case of Ireland, clothing could have included seal skins, which would be available in coastal areas. Although they were much smaller, the pelts of wolves (if present), otters and hares could be processed. The remains of large numbers of the last two were recovered at sites such as Polderweg (van Wijngaarden-Bakker *et al.* 2001). There is extensive evidence that pine martens were butchered at sites like Ringkloster (Andersen 1974; 1994; Rowley-Conwy 1994) though as yet there is no clear evidence that pine marten were present in Ireland before the Bronze Age.

The issue of whether our initial inhabitants dressed like the Oleni Ostrov hunter or the Yamana boat people is an interesting question for the future.

The absence of clothing, however, does not mean the absence of richness in ritual and other beliefs, as has already been noted in the Selknam dance performance (Fig. 12.5). Therefore, it is not a question of searching in Ireland for something similar to what has been found elsewhere (though it would be very special if we turned up cemeteries or ornaments); it is the need to keep in mind the possibility of what might be discovered.

Health, life expectancy and well-being

When considering the evidence for illness and cause of death there is, quite naturally, a tendency to concentrate on the more obvious evidence of physical trauma. Evidence includes such well known examples as the triple burial at Vedbaek, where the tip of a bone point was embedded between two of the thoracic vertebrae of one of the mature individuals. At Téviec, a projectile tip was found in a vertebra of one burial. Several authors, such as Lillie (2004, 95), have suggested that the introduction of the bow and arrow may have led to a greater level of violence. In the case of the cemeteries along the Dnieper River Rapids region in Ukraine, where a number of burials in each of three cemeteries of Mesolithic date have microliths embedded in the skeletons, Lillie would argue that there was little evidence for resource stress but suggests that the rapids and pools on rivers such as the Dnieper or Volga could have been locations where conflict over control of resources took place and barriers to passage could be effected. While projectile heads of various sorts have occasionally turned up in skeletal remains elsewhere in Europe they are by no means as prevalent as in the area of the Dnieper River Rapids in Ukraine.

Roksandic (2004, 6), in the introduction to her edited volume, concludes that while evidence for warfare during the Mesolithic appears weak "there is no evidence that the Mesolithic was more or less violent than any other period in (Pre) history". It would seem, in general, that while violence took place there is little evidence of extensive warfare. There is a danger of taking evidence from one group of sites and simply assuming that the same socio-economic structures existed elsewhere.

In spite of the paucity of human remains from Ireland we can still speculate. There is substantial evidence from the ethnographic record that locations on rivers which were prime locations for fishing were constant sources of conflict, therefore one could consider that certain key areas on the Lower Bann, along the Boyle River or on the Shannon at Killaloe could at times be the subject of dispute and conflict. While it might appear to be speculation in the extreme, one might wonder whether the altered human bone found along with other bone implements at the Cutts (see Chapters 5 and 10), could be that of someone who was on the losing side of a dispute here. What better way of making a statement about one's superiority over rival groups than by turning the bones of any enemy into a weapon? Of course, one has to admit that the alternative to this "flight of fancy" could be that it was the ultimate honour to a respected and referred member of one's own band.

What is also apparent is that traumatic injuries did not necessarily lead to death. In the case of the skeletal remains from the Portuguese Sado and Muge middens there is not only evidence of traumatic injury in the form of fractures but, in a significant number of cases, these fractures had healed (Cunha *et al.* 2004). Similarly, Jackes (2004, 23–7) has suggested that, in the case of skeletal remains from several Portuguese middens, there were a significant number of instances of injuries caused by what may have been childhood accidents.

Some of the potential biases have already been referred to earlier but if infant mortality was high then there is no doubt that the surviving evidence, which in the case of young children seems to be very limited, is not entirely representative of a whole population. Aveline's Hole provides a good example of a potential absence. Here Schulting and Wysocki (2005, 192–5) noted lower numbers of young children than might have been expected, though it was unclear whether this was due to survival of immature bones, recovery techniques, or a lack of burial. Even allowing for this type of potential bias, however, some general observations can be made.

In the absence of a significant amount useful of evidence in Ireland, one has to make some inferences from elsewhere, notably from south Scandinavia. In the case of the skeletons from Vedbaek-Bogebakken, the average height of the males was 170 cm, while that of the females was 153 cm (Albrethsen and Brinch Petersen 1976, 20). However it is very easy to generalise from specifics, for example, Schulting and Wysocki (2005, 197) have noted more generalised figures that suggest males in western Europe averaged 163 ± 5.8 cm while females averaged 151 ± 4.6 cm. Were they smaller than Palaeolithic or Neolithic peoples? A comparative sample of Neolithic skeletons from Denmark had average heights of 164 cm and 151 cm respectively (Albrethsen and Brinch Petersen 1976, 20). Meiklejohn and Babb (2011) have suggested, on the basis of a programme of rigorous analysis of a series of long bones dating from the Palaeolithic, Mesolithic and Neolithic of eastern Europe, that there is no convincing evidence of a significant decline in stature through the Stone Age. In later prehistoric periods, up to and including the medieval period, it seems likely that people were generally of a smaller stature than in the Mesolithic and it would have only been in recent centuries that populations would begin, on average, to be taller.

One of the most difficult issues must be establishing the age at death. Today, based on evidence from sites such as Vedbaek, Boldbanner and Skateholm, it is possible to see that for some of the population there was a chance that both males and females could live into their 60s (Albrethsen and Brinch Petersen 1976; Nielsen and Brinch Petersen 1993). While these may be rare instances of long-lived individuals, honoured for their knowledge and experience, their presence shows that there could be an expectation of a long life.

DISEASE AND CURES

Obviously one of the major questions to be answered must be the degree that disease impacted on the lifestyle of Mesolithic peoples. One has to assume that generations of experience and wisdom passed on would have led to a reasonably balanced diet. Many of our diseases may well have evolved into their present form in only the last few millennia. They may have been seemingly harmless viruses that would have mutated and changed. Thus diseases from measles to small pox may not have existed.

Other conditions would also have had to be treated. In some instances these could be a result of pain from accidental fractures or cuts, never mind the possibility of wounds from personal conflict and perhaps also hunting or fishing accidents. These would have included some conditions that resulted from a lifetime engaged in certain tasks, or suffering as a result of inherited conditions, including arthritic conditions or even certain cancers. Similarly, no society is perfect and there can be problems from ingesting the wrong or, perhaps, ill-prepared foods. Lozovski (1996, 38–9) has noted, for example that, in the case of fishing, the lack of proper curing for storage of fish and their consumption can lead to individuals ingesting parasites, such as helminths and other forms of nematodes. Some of these can lead to very acute health problems or ongoing chronic conditions. These conditions could well have played an important part in the health or lack of it of peoples who lived during the Mesolithic period in Ireland.

It is apparent that, in many of the aspects of human health discussed above, there are dangers in making too broad a series of inferences. In reviewing the actual evidence for health and other aspects of well-being, Meiklejohn and Zvelebil (1991, 135–6) have noted the differences between sites in the east i.e. on the Danube, and west, i.e. Portuguese sites such as Moita de Sebastiao. In the former area, the incidence of calculus on the teeth suggests a high protein diet with low carbohydrates which could be associated with the consummation of fish. This was not as evident in the west, where carbohydrates appear to

have played a more imported role. The authors suggest that, in the east, parasitic infestations and rickets would have been prevalent, as would periods of malnutrition. Malnutrition seems to be less prevalent elsewhere, indeed Nielsen and Brinch Petersen (1993, 81) point out that evidence of malnutrition was not prevalent in Danish skeletal remains.

It would be risky to generalise even on a regional basis. The surviving material from Aveline's Hole (Schulting 2005) again provides alternative insights. Often Mesolithic skeletal remains suggest relatively robust persons but the Aveline's Hole material seems to come from a more gracile population. The relatively slight incidence of wear on the teeth, in comparison with teeth from the Neolithic site of Belas Knap and the Mesolithic site of Téviec (McLaughlin 2005), suggests a different, relatively soft diet, though not necessarily one based on fish or other forms of animal protein as there is a low incidence of calculus. Other research on the teeth (Schulting and Wysocki 2005, 199–204) shows evidence of interrupted growth that suggests malnutrition, particularly during childhood years.

One might ask, what has this brief survey of health and well-being in the European Mesolithic got to do with Ireland? First it emphasises how much regional variation there is within the "life ways" of the European Mesolithic. One again returns to the fact that Ireland, as an island with its own distinctive ecology, may have had a way of life that was very different to other parts of Europe and that, in particular, inferences even drawn from Britain may sometimes be inappropriate. Therefore, there is no substitute for the recovery and careful analysis of Mesolithic human remains, to provide important insights into their lifestyle.

In general we can still make certain assumptions. The few human bones from Ireland can provide some indications about the physique of people who lived there. Amongst the human bones that were radiocarbon dated from Killuragh Cave (Woodman and Dowd in prep.) there is a metatarsal from a robust individual, while the human molars from Ferriter's Cove (Power 1999) were heavily worn, suggesting a rough, coarse diet. We can assume that Mesolithic people would be shorter than modern populations, probably by more than 10 cm, and they would have a life expectancy that was, for many, unlikely to exceed their 50s. As with most early societies, infant mortality would have been high. Violence would have existed and accidents happened. Periods of malnutrition would be expected and infections may have been prevalent. In spite of these probable drawbacks, it should be remembered that Mesolithic populations successfully adapted to living in Ireland.

Besides the obvious presence of ill health and death, accumulated wisdom would also have provided cures. We have to assume that antiseptics for cuts, methods of cauterising wounds and certain palliative remedies for pain would have existed. Similarly, even though they may not have been understood in the same way as modern medicine, there would have been remedies for other conditions, whether for coping with indigestion, breathing problems, etc.

While the chances of identifying the substances used may be extremely difficult, these equally important aspects of life must still be taken into consideration. Today, attention is paid to the value of the treasure house of plants to be found in the tropical rain forests but this is of little direct value in considering the world of early postglacial north-western Europe. There is today, even in Ireland, a store of folklore about traditional cures but, as with certain plant remains that can be used as sources of food, there is always the question as to when these particular plants were introduced into Ireland. Many exist in the margins of farmland and may have been brought in relatively recent times, while many medicinal plants were brought back to Western Europe as a result of the Crusades and the knowledge of their use became part of folklore. Some, however, may have been in use for much longer, such as wild roses providing fruit for a potion to cure diarrhoea and leaves to make an eye wash, while yarrow can be used to treat nose bleeds and cuts, as well as help with problems associated with the digestive, urinary and excretory systems. These at least illustrate the range of possibilities for remedies that could have existed in the Stone Age.

While it may be fanciful to look at traditions such as holy wells, one has to wonder whether the potential curative qualities associated with certain water sources would have been identified during the Mesolithic. A remarkable example within south-west Ireland is the tradition that had developed around the waters of Glenagad in Co. Kerry. It is known that this location has been visited during the last few centuries and that the waters were consumed by those thought to be suffering from some forms of insanity. It was only recently that water samples from this location were found to contain significant amounts of lithium, which is used today to combat problems associated with mental health.

Escaping from the western medical model, it is always possible that the well-being of the body was, as in the case of Chinese medicine, Native American traditions, etc., viewed in a very different way from that which has developed from the Renaissance onwards in Europe. The view of the importance of key organs within the body may have been very different from priorities of modern science and one has to assume that through trial and error early populations would have developed a philosophy as to how the body worked and infirmities treated. Indeed, while we accept the idea that earlier societies practised tattooing is it possible, given the existence of small thin needles on many sites, that some could have been used for a form of acupuncture? Perhaps one of the least considered aspects of health and well-being is the role of particular types of stones that are frequently found on sites and usually ignored as curiosities. Yet within medical traditions of certain parts of the world quartz/rock crystal are seen as crystals which would help with healing and would certainly be seen as an aid in traditions such as Reiki.

Regional differences and/or tribal territories

Having explored questions of site location, mobility and food sources there are still the broader issue of speculation such as the question as to whether some of these areas could represent different tribal territories. Finding regional groupings in Ireland, however, is not easy. One also has to ask if these variations are not simply caused by differing accessibility. What do these variations represent?

In spite of some local differences, such as in the use of raw materials discussed in Chapter 9 and variations in the prevalence of one or two tool types, there is a remarkable similarity between the Mesolithic of different regions in Ireland. There may, however, be local differences within the economy of the Irish Mesolithic (see Chapter 10). On the other hand, where artefactual differences are apparent they appear to be based on how raw materials were procured, transported and used, and these seem to be as a result of adaptation to local circumstances rather than being a product of fissioning into different "tribal" groups. There are obviously some differences that are directly associated with variations in raw material or even the presence or absence of suitable materials. There are a few artefacts, such as the core and flake axes, which have limited distributions and are confined to the north and east coastal areas. In contrast, while Trihedral flint picks are common in the north-east, occasional trihedral picks of chert and Rhyolite have been found elsewhere (Chapter 5). It is also of interest that the Moynagh Points, in particular, are remarkably rare in the north-east.

In Ireland what is intriguing is that, as changes in material equipment happened through time, especially 9000–8000 cal BP, it might have been expected that much greater local variation would have emerged. I have to admit that when I moved to Cork I expected to find that the Later Mesolithic would look very different, especially in west Kerry. However it was the similarities that surprised me!

Elsewhere as in Denmark, Vang Petersen (1984; Fig. 12.7a), in examining differences across Denmark in the Late Mesolithic, showed that most of the differences between Jutland and Zealand could be explained, at least in part, by the differences in resources, such as the lack of elk and aurochs in Zealand. At a more local level, however, in eastern Zealand (*ibid.*, fig. 15), there were significant stylistic differences in the form of the flake axes that existed in the Late Ertebølle (Fig. 12.7b)!

How does one balance different or discrete distributions of artefactual evidence with questions such as whether they reflect differing social groups? Peterson (1976, 51), in dealing with tribes and boundaries in Australia, has used two levels that can be identified, or (in our case) assumed:

Two principal levels of groupings: the local group population or band, the regional or cultural area. Between the two, falls a third level composed of congeries of bands united in part by linguistic ties, in part by topography and in part by historical and political links. (*ibid.*)

It is the groupings in the middle that are the difficult ones to establish in the archaeological record. In other words, were

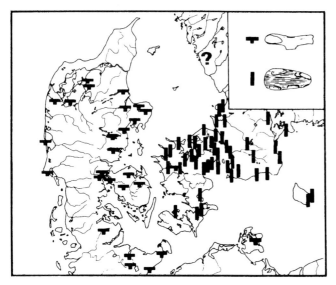

Fig. 11. Distribution of T-shaped red deer antler axes and Limhamn green-stone axes in southern Scandinavia (based partly on Becker 1939 and Jennbert 1984).

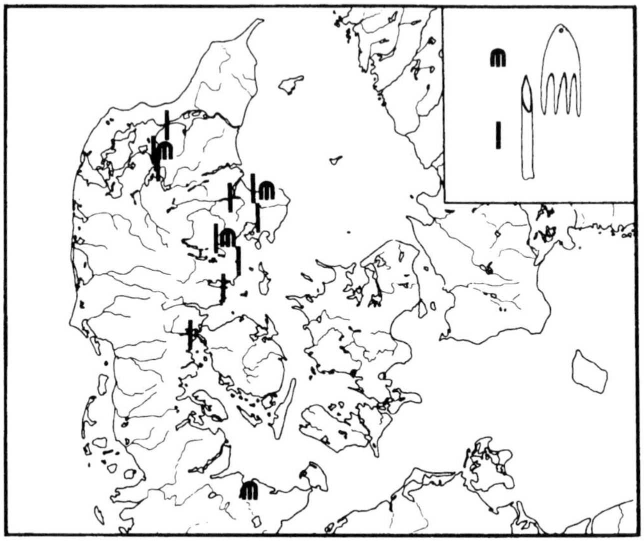

Fig. 12. Distribution of bone combs and bird-bone points dated to the Ertebølle culture in southern Scandinavia.

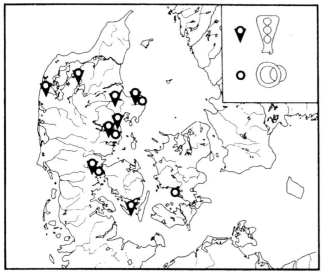

Fig. 13. Distribution of scapulae with circular cuts and bone rings or discs made from scapulae.

Fig. 14. Distribution of straight (type A) and curved (type B) antler harpoons in southern Scandinavia (based partly on Andersen 1971 and 1975).

Fig. 12.7a. Regional distributions of selected objects from the Danish Ertebølle: top left) T-shaped red deer antler and Limhamn greenstone axes in southern Scandinavia, top right) bone combs and bird-bone points, bottom left) scapulae with circular cuts and bone rings or discs made from scapulae, bottom right) straight (type A) and curved (type B) antler harpoons.

there as in Tasmania, tribes and linguistic groups in existence in the Irish Mesolithic (Fig. 12.8; *ibid.*, 62)?

While one can speculate about the total population of Mesolithic Ireland (see below) it is at this stage, virtually impossible to use any information from settlement sites to estimate the size of bands. There are, as discussed earlier, virtually no settlement sites that could be described as intact and, therefore, where it might be possible to provide an

estimate as to how many people would have lived at one location. Mount Sandel might provide an indication that, perhaps for part of the year only, a single hut existed at a time, though one could suggest that these might have been special structures which were set apart from the more numerous and flimsy structures that were normally lived in (see Chapter 11). At other sites where a large area has been opened, such as Lough Boora (Ryan 1980) or Ferriter's Cove (Woodman

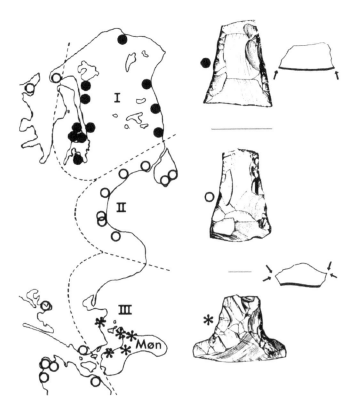

Fig. 12.7b. Local variations in flake axe form during the Ertebolle of East Zealand (both after Vang Petersen 1984).

et al. 1999), traces are much more ephemeral. Are these very temporary stopping spots or are the traces of structures so ephemeral that it was not possible to identify them? This returns us to questions about how we excavate and record information (see Chapter 11).

One could also argue for the "band" as the basic unit of society but that, at key times of the year, for example when certain fish ran, there could have been agglomerations of much larger groups. One could consider that the tens of thousands of Mesolithic artefacts that were used, lost or cached at a number of locations along the Lower Bann or the Boyle River at Lough Gara, indicate that, at important times, larger groups of perhaps several bands would have come together at key points along river valleys. This possibility is not entirely mutually exclusive from the possibility of conflict at the same locations as discussed earlier. Violence at such events, can easily flair.

One can also still speculate on rough estimates of how many people lived in Ireland. Various authors, such as Wobst (1974), have suggested figures which are very rough orders of magnitudes for how hunter-gatherer societies have organised themselves, thus figures such as 25 for a band, 500 for a tribe and perhaps several thousand for a language group, are estimates that are often used. Many authors have noted that tribal areas will vary in size, depending on the topography

and ecology of the region. Figures of one person per 10–20 sq. km are often used but even here there is the assumption that certain areas will attract larger population densities while, in other areas, as in the interior of Tasmania, the population densities will be much lower. In the case of Ireland, where most settlement is concentrated on shores and river banks, the average figure per square kilometre would be misleading. Instead, one could suggest that to retain a long-term, viable population a population of at least 500 would be necessary. Perhaps the suggested figure of 3000–5000 for the human population of Tasmania at the point in time when Europeans arrived (Lourandos 1997, 36) provides a useful rough order of magnitude for Ireland at around 5000 cal BP. This is roughly the figure used in Woodman (1981).

What is difficult to envisage at this stage is how those figures relate to the surviving archaeological record. It is so scant and one has to recognise that much is buried under bogs and in alluvial deposits in river valleys, as well as submerged and eroded away in coastal areas. All these factors limit our possibilities of making estimates. In spite of these problems, a suggested population in the 1000s rather than the 100s seems reasonable.

Can we suggest, therefore, that within Ireland there were groups that conceived of themselves as distinct tribal entities? Ethnographic analogies are always dangerous but they do challenge us to look beyond the artefacts. Three regions that are roughly the same size as Ireland provide interesting parallels.

Tasmania has already been mentioned. At 63,000 sq. km it is marginally smaller than Ireland and, while occupied before 30,000 years ago, it became cut off from mainland Australia at about the beginning of the Holocene (Lourandos 1997, 256). At the time of contact with Europeans it is estimated that up to 5000 native Tasmans were living on the island and these people were in a number of "tribal" territories that seemed to be determined, to some extent, by the geography of a series of river catchments (Peterson 1976, 62–3; Fig. 12.8). In spite of tribal divisions there seems to be little evidence of material culture diversity though, not surprisingly, the archaeological and ethnographic record seems to show that there is different degrees of emphasis on inland and coast resources across the island (Lourandos 1997, chapter 7).

As already noted, in the Magellanic regions round Tierra del Fuego there were, until the 20th century, three or probably four separate though contiguous groups living in an area the size of Ireland (Piana and Orquera 2002). This is a region which is difficult to define. The best known part, Isla Grande, is roughly 45,000 square kilometres but the greater Magellanic area, which extends well into the mainland of South America, could be regarded as being more than 500,000 sq. km. However the relevant area could be considered to be about 100,000 sq. m. Here, each tribe had its own distinct lifestyle and economic basis. The Yamana relied heavily, for most of their 8000 years of existence, on the pursuit of sea lions within the Beagle Channel. To their north-west, the Alacaluf utilised the land and

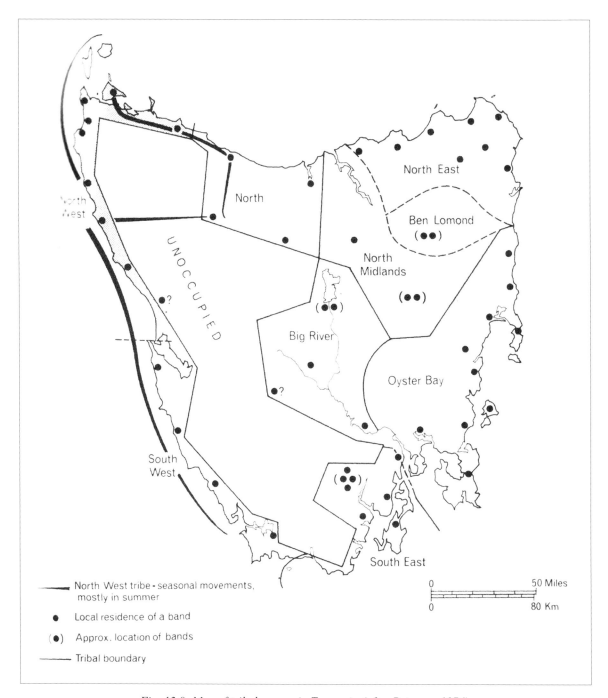

Fig. 12.8. Map of tribal groups in Tasmania (after Peterson 1976).

sea resources within the archipelago on the coast of southern Chile, while the Selknam to their east subsisted mostly by hunting Guanaco (Fig. 12.9). Little is known of the Haush. In each of the three better known groups Martinic (1992) estimates that, at the time of extensive contact with the Europeans in the mid-19th century, there could have been upwards of 3000 persons within each tribe.

In parts of the Fenno-Scandinavia Arctic, three distinct Saami groups lived side by side. These were the Coastal

Saami who lived primarily on marine resources, the Reindeer Saami who, in the modern form, lived primarily by herding reindeer, while the third group, the Skolte Saami, relied more heavily on the resources of the rivers. There are numerous other examples but the manner in which indigenous Saami tribal groups coincided with major river catchments in the Kola Peninsula, which is only marginally smaller than Ireland, again shows the way in which territories and social groups can be influenced by landscape (Fig. 2.10). In this case there is also a major linguistic division between the northern and southern side of the Kola Peninsula.

Authors such as Ames (1985, 159–60) have discussed the question of scalar stress, in particular, the difficulty of communicating and making decisions which increase exponentially as group sizes grow. Therefore, without major societal change it is unlikely that there would have been the social and economic mechanisms to hold together large groups made up of more than about 1000 people. If we propose that several thousand people may have been living in Ireland, then we must assume that there was some form of hierarchy of social organisation in existence and at least some differentiation into bands and probably some form of tribe. It is probable that in Ireland, especially within the latter half of the Irish Mesolithic, there may have been groups who, in different ways, defined themselves as separate from their neighbours. It is unlikely, however, that population levels would have been sufficiently high to allow for the differentiation into language groups.

Perhaps, on the basis of evidence from elsewhere, we could expect some form of regional grouping within Ireland and that the river catchments, lakes and coastline would have determined their form. Yet, beyond that, one must ask whether there is anything in the archaeological record of the Irish Mesolithic that either suggested that there was just one enlarged tribal territory or a series of regional tribes. Already we have seen (Chapters 9 and 10) that the indications from stable isotopes is that a case can be made for a series of local economic strategies, but the artefactual evidence, as already noted, is quite equivocal as it simply shows mobility of some form from one landscape to another. There are two ways of looking at the evidence, though first it should be remembered that tribal boundaries are often porous.

Does the discovery of certain classes of objects over a large region suggest that that region was one tribal/linguistic territory? Mulvaney (1976, maps 4 and 5) has documented the movement of objects, presumably by exchange, of baler and pearl shells across distances of more than 2000 km. While this was mostly through the central Australian desert these objects had been exchanged across many tribal boundaries. Similarly, as shown on his map 6, certain new rites and ceremonies spread quite rapidly over large distances but stopped at certain points.

The possibility that tribal boundaries could be porous at certain times of the year was also documented in south-eastern Australia by Flood (1976). This is a more temperate region with mountains and major river systems, the latter running down to the Pacific Ocean. Here, in an area roughly 500 km long (N/S) and on average of 200 km wide, i.e. roughly the same size as Ireland, there were up to 20 tribal territories. Bogong moth larvae could be obtained at locations in the inland mountain range and, in order to collect and consume these moths, it was usual for members of different tribes to congregate at chosen locations (*ibid.,* 42–4). This entailed those attending the "corroboree" to cross tribal boundaries. The "corroboree" was occasions for feasting, but extensive

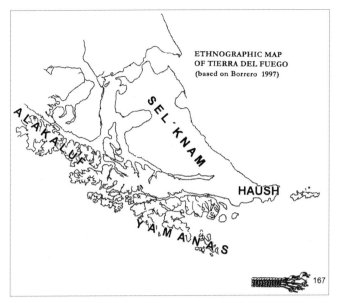

Fig. 12.9. Maps of tribal groups in the Beagle Channel area (after Borrero 1997).

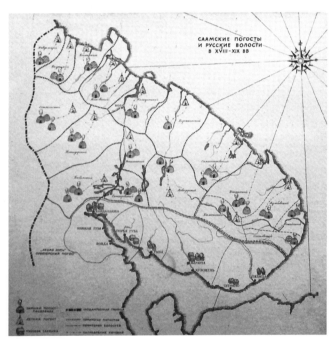

Fig. 12.10. Tribal territories on the Kola peninsula (© Murmansk Museum).

bartering and exchange also took place (*ibid.,* 46). The items exchanged ranged from boomerangs and spears through possum skins to particular stones for axe manufacture, sandstone and perhaps ochre. When this is taken into consideration then one might regard the occasional exotic implement, such as the very distinctive backed knife from Ferriter's Cove (Woodman *et al.* 1999, pl. 4:1) as something that found its way to west Kerry as a product of gift exchange

One cannot presume, therefore, that the distribution of an artefact type or a particular raw material marks a tribal territory. What is of interest is where the distribution of a specific artefact type stops. One interesting example (see Chapter 9) is the complementary distribution of the Bømlo greenstone axes and Flora diabase axes in south-western Norway (Olsen and Alsaker 1984; Fig. 12.11). Ground stone axes obviously also played a very important role in the Irish Later Mesolithic. Perhaps a combination of a careful stylistic examination of their shape and a detailed petrological analysis could identify sources. In this case regional differences might give some indications of tribal boundaries.

However, at the moment, is there, evidence especially within the lithic assemblage, for separate territories in the Irish Mesolithic? Many authors, such as Cooney and Grogan

(1994, 24), have discussed this topic but so far there is little evidence. The implication of the presence of very similar trihedral sectioned picks that have been made from different material and occur throughout Ireland has already been alluded to in Chapter 5.

There is, aside from the work carried out at Aveline's Hole (Price and Schulting 2005, 224–6), little evidence from indicators such as that derived from Strontium Isotopes in the Mesolithic of the western edge of Europe that people moved throughout their lifetime. Again this lack of evidence is partly due to the lack of a suitable range of human remains in places such as Ireland that would make this type of analysis possible.

As discussed elsewhere (Woodman 1981), the more intriguing question is how much Ireland was a separate territorial entity that had limited contacts with other regions, i.e.

a   *b*

Fig. 12.11. a) Locations of axe quarries at Bolo and Flora, b) distribution of stone axes: triangles = Flora, circles = Bomlo (after Olsen and Alsaker 1984).

one of Peterson's (1976) "cultural areas". Many authors have noted that there are, at certain points in time, major distinct boundaries where very different material cultures occur close to a virtual boundary. Britain provides an interesting example. Within virtually all of the main island of Great Britain there seems to be very large areas where much of the same material culture, as reflected in the lithic artefacts, were in use. In the earliest stages of the British Mesolithic, artefacts show a lot of similarity to those in use in adjacent parts of Western Europe, but certainly from, at the latest, 9000 cal BP, Britain retained the use of geometric microliths in composite tools while, in mainland Europe, that technology was being gradually replaced. The retention of composite tools in Britain probably resulted, in part, from the final breaking of the land link with adjacent parts of Europe. However, not only is the use of microliths retained until the end of the Mesolithic but it is difficult to establish clear regional groupings within an island that is more than three times the size of Ireland.

The remarkable differences between the Mesolithic of the islands of Ireland and Britain have often been a source of comment. Contact between areas that were within easy sight of each other would have been possible, even if there was only the limited sea faring capacity. In the case of the Ireland–Scotland connection, the possibility that exchange systems existed in the Mesolithic, as happened at times in the Neolithic and Bronze Age, is very real but there is little actual evidence. On the one hand, in Scotland there was a landscape rich in a range of large mammals that were lacking in Ireland while, on the other hand, there was immediately available a range of lithic resources in Ireland that were relatively scarce in Scotland. Evidence in the form of faunal remains of animals imported into Ireland can be hard to find and there is a remarkable scarcity of Irish artefacts in western and south-western Scotland (Saville 2003) especially when one considers the closeness of Ireland to Scotland.

Were these two social and economic entities sufficiently viable that they did not require exchange at a level that would be observable in the archaeological record?

In contrast, there are much stronger echoes of a connection in the Later Mesolithic of both the Irish and the Manx Mesolithic (McCartan 2003). The basic knapping strategy in the Isle of Man looks similar to that of the "Larnian", but many of the implement types are not quite the same as those found in Ireland. The tanged points that are so common on that island are very different from the Irish examples. The Isle of Man may, like Ireland, be an interesting case study but one with numerous differences between that island and both Britain and Ireland.

One can only observe that there is still much to be done in identifying the different types of lithic materials used, and equally important, in locating their sources. Therefore we still have a long way to go in trying to assess where there are regional territories and discuss their social significance. Perhaps the best area to explore would be the ground stone axes and stone points.

Is this the end of all things?

As noted in the introduction, a lot of time and attention, perhaps too much, has been paid to the question of the "Transition to farming". It is perhaps the most discussed and written about topic in prehistory but on this issue, certainly in the case of Ireland, there is remarkably little clarity.

In one lifetime it has been possible to witness a shift from a presumption that, in Europe at least, farming was spread by migrating farmers (Piggott 1954) to a belief that it was transferred from one group to the next by acculturation, with Mesolithic communities playing the major role. Recently, through the isolation of distinct isotopes and trace elements in human remains, there is recognition that there was movement of people in Postglacial Stone Age Europe. This could reflect intermarriage between different social groups, as suggested by Schulting (2003) for the Breton human remains at Téviec and Hoedic, where it could be argued on the basis of differences in $\delta^{13}C$ that much of the female population came from more inland groups. Similarly, Price *et al.* (2001) have shown that, in a number of locations in Central Europe, there is evidence from analysis of strontium isotopes that some portions of populations, such as within the *Linearbandkeramik*, had moved significant distance during their lifetime. It could be argued that the spread of farming was a complex patchwork of differing processes rather than a simple catch all explanation.

In Ireland, for many years, the general consensus has been that farming was introduced from outside by the arrival of farmers and it is also accepted that the process of 'Neolithisation' was very different to that which took place in Britain. The reasons may be a bit subjective but they are based on a few simple observations. In summary, both the Irish Mesolithic material culture and economy, as well as the ecology of Ireland, are so different from adjacent parts of Europe that it is difficult to understand how a Neolithic culture that is remarkably similar to that of much of southern Britain, could appear in Ireland without some movement of people. In Ireland this includes the appearance of items as mundane as large numbers of convex end scrapers and piercing invasively retouched arrowheads, as well as less emphasis on blade technologies (Woodman 1993b). There is a strong resemblance to the lithic technology of the earliest Neolithic in England and little sign of any continuity from Mesolithic technologies (see Woodman *et al.* 2006, chapter 4, 126–84). These implements, along with carinated bowls that are rather similar to those found in England, and certain common burial and monument traditions, suggest a very strong link with England and Wales (Whittle *et al.* 2011). There also seems to be a shift in the types of raw materials used for stone tools. While mining flint in the Neolithic in Ireland does not seem to have been particularly successful there is no doubt that, in the Neolithic, there was an almost immediate move away from beach flint, with a notable increase in artefacts produced from nodules where the cortex is fresh. Again, very early in the Neolithic, the porcelanite sources of north Antrim were used extensively for the first time for manufacture of certain artefacts, primarily polished stone axes.

A strong case can be made for a fully developed Neolithic existing across Ireland just after 5800 years ago. Cooney *et al.* (2011), in their recent review of the Irish evidence, discussed the significance of the causewayed enclosures that initially may have come into existence after 5800 cal BP and ceased to be used by 5600 cal BP. Unfortunately, this is based on only two sites, one of which has produced some slightly problematic dates (see below). Their review of other forms of evidence, notably 80+ rectangular houses, suggests a well-established Neolithic economy across Ireland by 5700 cal BP. This observation, crucially, represents the final shift away from a belief that the Neolithic presence in any area could be most visibly documented by the occurrence of megalithic tombs and an assumption that these monuments were an integral part of any Neolithic activity. As shown by Schulting et al. (2012) and Bergh and Hensey (2013), court and passage tombs, which are not distributed across the whole island, are in existence certainly by, if not before, *c.* 5600 cal BP.

Therefore, with the notable difference in the use of ritual monuments whose distribution does not coincide with the known geographical distribution of the Early Neolithic, the material culture of this period seems to be remarkably homogeneous and to have been found across much of Ireland within a remarkably short period of time.

Ireland can also be contrasted with Denmark where there is much more evidence of continuity from the Mesolithic to the Neolithic. There is little evidence in Ireland of the type found in the Danish Early Neolithic (Madsen 1986), where there was a series of local or regional variations in the material culture which could suggest adaptations by various indigenous local Mesolithic groups. While domesticated cattle (Woodman and McCarthy 2003) seem to trickle into Ireland, in Denmark, Price and Noe-Nygaard (2009) have documented a distinct horizon for their appearance.

In fact, the shift from Mesolithic to Neolithic in Ireland, while it is not an exact parallel, may have more in common with the Swifterbant culture (Raemarkers 1999; Devriendt 2013), where the shift from hunter-gatherer to farmer may have happened over a period of time with ceramics, domesticated animals and cereals being introduced on a step by step basis. Crucially it is also apparent that while there were LBK influences in the northern region of the Swifterbant, towards the south the Michelsberg culture was of greater influence. Thus even within the Swifterbant culture there may have been different influences from outside in its different regions.

On a more theoretical level, Milner (2010) in her assessment of the changes that took place around and just after "6000 cal BP" suggested that changes took place in a number of different ways and were messy and complex. Similarly, Wickham-Jones (2010, chapter v) has documented the complex series of factors which could have encouraged or inhibited the spread of farming. In the context of these observations associated with

the very beginning of the Neolithic, in Ireland we should also not expect a simple explanation.

At least now one can suggest that there is not a complete information lacuna as suggested by Woodman (2000) though, while a significant number of dates have now been obtained for the 7th millennium cal BP, there is still only few dates from the 200 years on either side of 6000 years ago.

There is some difficulty extending the Mesolithic down as far as 6000 cal BP, while trying to study the origins of the Neolithic from the more mature Neolithic described above is like trying to document the Roman invasion of Britain from Roman amphitheatres or the road network. Transitions are often less distinctive than the fully mature periods on either side of them and can be difficult to identify. In many ways this is one of the lessons that can be learnt from the study of the transition from the Earlier to the Later Mesolithic in Ireland, i.e. transitions are often not obvious and will probably not be clearly signposted.

One of the major outstanding issues must therefore be what was happening in the period between 6200 and 5800 years ago. Was there a significant movement of people into Ireland and should we eventually expect to find a gradual spread of the earliest Neolithic across the island? Alternatively, was there just a small-scale movement which caused a series of changes throughout the island? Or finally, was there a specific period during which the Irish Neolithic emerged? (See Sheridan 2010 for a suggested multi-stage development of an Irish Neolithic).

The following observations can be made. These are based on the fact that there are some forms of evidence that lie within this "transitional" period, but which lie outside the typical sites of both the Neolithic and Later Mesolithic.

1) Evidence for Mesolithic or probable Mesolithic artefacts from after 6200 cal BP are rare. One possible group is a series of blades from a pit at Tinryland, Co. Carlow (O'Connell forthcoming; Sternke and Woodman forthcoming). Similarly, evidence from shell middens at Fanore I is producing dates of a comparable range (Lynch in prep.; Fig. 12.12).

2) The earliest evidence for aspects of what we consider to be Neolithic, in this case bones of domesticated animals, come from sites that either have a major Mesolithic component or could not be regarded as typical of the Neolithic. At Ferriter's Cove cattle bones are well known (Woodman *et al.* 1999). There is some degree of confusion over both the bones and the dates. Two different bones were dated. These were a) a cattle tibia fragment (OxA 3869, 5510±70 BP, 6445–6115 cal BP, southern area; and b) a cattle metatarsal (OxA 8775, 5825±50 BP, 6742–6498 cal BP, central area). The confusion arose because the result from the second sample was obtained at page proof stage during publication of the excavation and so was simply inserted as a footnote in Woodman *et al.* (1999, 14). In retrospect, as the second date was exceptionally early we inquired about re-dating

Fig. 12.12. a) Excavations at Fanore, Co. Clare (photograph by Michael and Clodagh Lynch), b) excavations at Belderrig, Co. Mayo (photograph by Graeme Warren).

the sample. It emerged that the bone, which was a very distinct epiphysis of the metatarsal, had been partially burnt. Therefore, not only was the bone completely used up in the process but, on re-examining the chemical data associated with the dating process, the organic content was very limited and, therefore, the date was not totally reliable. However, the bone itself was associated with an occupation layer adjacent to a fire place (F/5). The hearth and other features including dates from pits and hazel nut shell piles showed that settlement in the area of sample OxA-8775 was associated with intermittent settlement between 6600 and 6100 cal BP. Therefore, there is no doubt that OxA-8775 was a cattle metatarsal fragment and that it would have dated to sometime before 6000 years ago, i.e. before there was an initial Neolithic presence in the area.

3) The presence of cattle bones have also been recovered from the latest phase of the artificial platform at Derragh Island and dated (Fredengren 2009, 884). This platform seems to have been created during the Mesolithic. At Kilgreany Cave (Woodman *et al.* 1997) a cattle bone pre-dates a more substantial Neolithic presence in the cave by several hundred years (OxA- 4269, 5190±80 BP, 6217–5660 cal BP). It is also of interest that the cattle bones from the two latter sites referred to above are much larger than those which are found on Neolithic sites. Perhaps one might even include the sheep bone from Dalkey Island Site II, which produced a date of 5942–5603 cal BP (OxA-4566, 5050±90 BP; Woodman *et al.* 1997).

4) There are sites where evidence for continuity or for a chronological overlap is open to debate. One area, where there have been two good examples, could be described as the *Sligo Phenomenon* where "things seemed to be very early". Burenhult suggested (1984; 2005) that there was evidence that the Carrowmore passage tomb complex had begun well before the appearance of established farming communities, i.e. before 6000 years ago, and while various authors had expressed scepticism, until recently few specific reasons were given for these expressions of doubt. However, Bergh and Hensey (2013), in a recent re-analysis of the dates obtained by Burenhult, concluded that there was little to back claims for such an early date, i.e. based on the unreliability of charcoal dates which were not directly associated with the building of the tombs. The authors noted, on the other hand, that the dating of the bone pins found in significant numbers in several tombs suggested an early use of the monuments well after 6000 years ago. They therefore suggested that the floruit for the Carrowmore tombs lay between 5600 and 5200 cal BP. This still leaves the enigma of the earlier dates from the nearby Magheraboy. (Danaher 2007). The implication of these early dates was discussed at length by Cooney *et al.* (2011, 665–8)

5) It could also be argued that there is evidence of continuity at Clowanstown (Mossop and Mossop 2009). Here, alongside a Neolithic assemblage associated with pottery, diagnostic Neolithic artefacts including leaf lozenge arrowheads and hollow scrapers as well as domesticated animal bones, there was a series of large chert blades and some Butt Trimmed Forms which would seem to have been more at home in the underlying Later Mesolithic levels. Are these evidence of continuity with Neolithic elements grafted on or has there been some mixing of deposits which is not uncommon in shoreline situations?

6) Two groups of human remains that fall into this period cannot be attributed with any certainty to the Mesolithic or Neolithic. These are the bones recovered from Sramore Cave, Co. Leitrim (UB 6407, 5202±39 BP, 6100–5900 cal BP; Dowd 2008) and the burial from Stoney Island, Co. Galway (OxA-2941, 5270±80 BP, 6295–5845 cal BP; generally thought to be the most reliable of a series of dates obtained; Ó Floinn 1995; Brindley and Lanting 1995). One could argue that these could belong to either hunter-gatherers or farmers.

In summary there is no lacuna of information on the transition between the Mesolithic and the Neolithic. There is a lot of evidence but our problem is that we are not sure how to interpret it!

One of the most useful ways of identifying stages at the Mesolithic–Neolithic transition is that of Zvelebil and Rowley-Conwy (1984) who proposed, primarily in the context of the transition to farming in the Baltic region, that we could identify three stages. There were:

1. *Contact stage*: when there is an awareness of the presence of a new economy/material culture etc.
2. *Substitution stage*: when elements of the new life style are imported.
3. *Consolidation stage*: when there is a fully established new economy with, in its broadest sense, a distinctive and perhaps new material culture which can include monuments.

In the case of Ireland, did this change happen over several centuries in the manner outlined above? Was the Irish experience different with minimal stages 1 and a major change with the arrival of new people and an initial different type of Stage 2 i.e. a substituation or an *Adaptation stage* which led to the emergence of the Irish Early Neolithic by 5700 cal BP?

What happened to the natives?

What happened to the indigenous Mesolithic population? There is no firm evidence of Mesolithic settlement associated with a specific distinctive range of Later Mesolithic artefacts which clearly post-dates 6000 cal BP, indeed, as noted above, there is very little evidence of a Mesolithic presence after 6200 cal BP. In general there is a remarkable lack of clearly distinctive Later Mesolithic artefacts on what would be classified as Early Neolithic sites. It is likely that the Irish Mesolithic hunter-gatherers did not all become the farmers. While the change from a hunter-gatherer to a farming economy would result in changes to the material culture, it might have been expected that many of the tool types from the Later Mesolithic would have still proved useful in the Neolithic.

It has often been suggested that diseases introduced by Neolithic people may have led to the demise of the native population. This was very evident in the pandemics that spread through much of the New World with the arrival of Europeans. As Mann (2005, 112–18) has noted, however, part of the problem in the New World might have been what he described as the "Genetics of vulnerability". The Native Americans and other New World populations suffered from two problems. First, due to the lack of exposure to certain pathogens, they had not acquired immunity to a range of diseases. Secondly, it would appear that, with the small initial population of the Americas, their genetic make-up may have provided a limited capacity to respond to new infections. In particular, it would appear that Native Americans have a more limited range of HLA (human leukocytes antigens) which help fight infections. This may have meant that, in the Americas, there was low resistance to newly imported diseases. In the case of the spread of farming to Ireland, unlike the 10,000+ years of separation of the Native Americans, populations in Mesolithic Eurasia may not have diverged to anything like the same degree. Therefore, the immune systems of hunter-gatherers may not have been that different and one must assume that in any area, even Ireland, there is no reason to believe that indigenous populations would have been totally isolated and then, with the arrival of farming, be suddenly subjected to an onslaught of new diseases.

One possibility might be the development of diseases through the process of zoonosis. In this instance, diseases that developed in an environment where people and animals lived in close proximity could provide the opportunity to incubate new forms that were not only virulent but to which the indigenous communities would have had little resistance. Such diseases are at their most prevalent where animals and people share the same living conditions and, as yet, we are nowhere near understanding the nature of Neolithic settlement sites. There is, however, always a possibility that domesticates introduced to Ireland, i.e. cattle, sheep and domesticated pigs, could have brought diseases with them. How were the native population to be exposed to these animals?

In returning to the initial suggestions about population levels in the Irish Mesolithic, there is no doubt that those of us working in the Mesolithic would like to see a substantial population of 5–10,000 persons, but if the numbers were much lower, for example, 1–2000, which would still allow the existence of a sociologically and biologically self-sustaining society, maybe they were simply marginalised by a rapidly burgeoning Neolithic population. Obviously we need to consider the issue of what happened to what Raftery (1951, 70) described as the "Dispossessed Mesolithic".

The range of scenarios could vary from becoming farmers through the development of symbiotic relationship between farmers and foragers to one where "recalcitrant natives" might have been considered as "mere animals" that were to be disposed of in whatever manner was suitable.

Is there a case for a Mesolithic survival?

Is there a reason why two distinctly different lifestyles could not have continued side by side? The two lifestyles were based on economies that were, complementary and usually exploited different parts of the landscape. Of course the Neolithic communities could also have exploited the sea and rivers, but as will be shown below the evidence available from the shell middens suggests that it was done in a more casual manner with a heavier reliance on shellfish and less on fishing.

In areas like the Bann Valley, besides the extremely large numbers of Mesolithic artefacts there are also a smaller but still significant number of Neolithic artefacts. Could "things" have come down to the control of key points for fishing, although one must wonder whether a barter system between hunter-fishers and farmers would have been more effective. Pressure for control of resources may have led to violence. Perhaps, as with the Selknam in Tierra del Fuego 100 years ago, the killing or stealing of animals such as sheep by the hunter-gatherers may have created a situation where, as for the European Argentineans, there were no qualms about killing the "Natives" In Greenland, in the case of the Inuit and Vikings, there was no tolerance of the other community.

With the abandonment of the concept of a "Secondary Neolithic" (Chapter 3), the idea of a "Mesolithic survival" is rarely addressed. When post-5800(?) cal BP sites are found in coastal or valley bottom locations how are they to be explained? Is it instances of Mesolithic survival or Neolithic communities exploiting a range of wild as well as domesticated resources? Indeed was it a more complex series of dynamics?

The sites which are discussed below illustrate some of the complexities association with this transitional period.

Excavations on the Atlantic coast of Co. Clare at Fanore, referred to above (Michael Lynch pers. comm.) have produced axes and fragments along with possible Mesolithic artefacts, such as Moynagh Points. Dates that seem to centre on occupation just after 6000 cal BP.

Settlement on other shell middens also shows a remarkably consistent presence after 6000 cal BP. At Ferriter's Cove, Southern Test Pit (Woodman *et al.* 1999, 170–2) a small scatter of shells, 60 m south of the main excavation, produced a shell date (UB 3761, 5420±24 BP, 6293–6175 cal BP) and a charcoal date (UB 3760, 4820±67 BP, 5747–5316 cal BP). Again, as at the main excavation, no ceramic or diagnostic Neolithic artefacts were recovered, while one used elongated pebble, a hammer stone and some greenstone flakes were found. The fauna, which included fish bones dominated by Ballan wrasse, along with a fused pig bone and a possible hare bone, appears similar to that from the main site. With the absence of ceramics and diagnostic Neolithic stone artefacts are these sites producing evidence for "Mesolithic Survival"?

At Baylet, Co. Donegal, above the Mesolithic levels (Milner and Woodman 2007), above the Later Mesolithic deposits there was a further build-up of midden material (Chapter 4). Some of this accumulation may have begun to take place quite early in the Neolithic. Something similar was noted at Rough Island, Co. Down (James Mallory pers. comm.) where there also was, at least, an Early Neolithic presence in the shell midden. Are these locations where Mesolithic survivors are continuing their existence or were they descendants of Neolithic farmers who simply exploiting the sea shores?

In fact, where it is possible to assess its extent, as at the very large Culeenamore midden in Co. Sligo (Burenhult 1984), deposits of shells over 1 m in thickness accumulated throughout the Neolithic. In the same general area of Ballysadare Bay there are numerous other "post-Mesolithic" shell middens and it is probable that several others date at least in part to the Neolithic (e.g., Tanrego West (Woodman and Milner 2013). Therefore, even allowing for the loss of Mesolithic shell middens during a slightly earlier time of rising sea levels, it appears that shell middens accumulated to a much greater extent in the Neolithic than in the Mesolithic! The major difference is that many of these later midden sites seem to have been created without extensive recourse to other sources such as fish, sea mammals or even sea birds. Therefore, the balance within the economies of the creators of these later middens seems to have been different to the earlier ones.

There are other sites where Neolithic material has been found in contexts which one might normally associate with so-called "Mesolithic" activity. One of the most interesting is the assemblage recovered by O'Sullivan (2001 73–86) at Carrigdirty Rock 5, Co. Limerick, in the Shannon estuary. Here two human bones (a cranium fragment and clavicle) and some cattle bones were recovered among fragments of burnt bone and hazel nut shells in one small area on the intertidal shore. Some of the material was clearly associated with an organic mud. There was also a small scatter of stone tools as well as worked wood and basketry. One date was obtained from the human cranium fragment as well as two from the basketry. These are Early–Middle Neolithic, i.e. somewhere between 3700 and 3300 cal BC (*ibid.*, 76, 78). It would appear that the material belonged to a short period of activity on a former marshy area of reed beds close to the shore of the estuary. O'Sullivan described these people as "Forager Farmers". As part of a project in the area funded by the Heritage Council, three more dates were obtained on a cattle bone, the human

clavicle and cranium, as well as obtaining $\delta^{13}C$ and $\delta^{15}N$ estimates. These new results are sown in Table 12.1.

The dates strongly suggest that much of the material came from that one particular episode or visit, early in the Neolithic. However, there are no strong indications of extensive use of estuarine resources such as sea fish or migrating salmon. As discussed in Chapter 10, extensive reliance on eels would possible produce $\delta^{13}C$ signals in the -20s but so would a land based diet. In this case there are no independent indicators which suggest that these were late surviving Mesolithic "Hunter/Fishers". Perhaps they could best be seen as farmers who foraged?

At other sites, such as Dalkey Island (Woodman *et al.* 1997, 137), although there is little clear evidence that shellfish were still collected after the Mesolithic, there is, as noted earlier, a clear presence of early domesticates within the middens. The excavator (Liversage 1968) also recovered scatters of Earlier Neolithic material, such as pottery and artefacts, on the same locations. Dalkey Island is a small offshore island where coastal foraging would have been taking place. It does not seem to have been a location where visits would have been entirely casual.

Again, at the very top of the sequence at Newferry Site 3 (Woodman 1977a) there is a Neolithic presence. This also occurs at locations such as Culbane, where a significant number of Neolithic artefacts were recovered by Knowles (Woodman *et al.* 2006, chapter 7). Finally, at Belderrig, Co. Mayo, how does one explain the stone pavement that overlies extensive traces of Mesolithic activities dated to 6500–6000 cal BP and, at the same time, is post-dated by a Neolithic presence dating to approximately 5500 cal BP (Warren 2009; Fig. 12.12b)?

At the very least, in locations that had also been used during the Later Mesolithic it would appear that there was a presence during much of the Neolithic. It would, however, also appear that during the Neolithic and later periods, activities in coastal areas were based more on the collection of shellfish and less on an exploitation of the full range of marine resources (Woodman 2005b).

The size of the Neolithic and later middens in areas such as Co. Sligo suggests that in some areas at least the visits were more than short term very occasional casual visits. Sall (2013), although discussing sites of a much later date in Senegal, has shown that in areas where different tribal groups with very different economies lived side by side, shell middens were created in numerous ways. In some cases, certain villages specialised in providing shellfish to their more agrarian

Table 12.1. Radiocarbon dates and stable isotopes from Carrigdirty.

Sample	Lab. ref.	Determination BP	Calibrated date BP or BC?	$\delta^{13}C$	$\delta^{15}N$
Human clavicle	OxA-27217	4750±40	5590–5328	-21.92‰	10.47‰
Human cranium	OxA-27232	4770±40	5594–5333	-22.18‰	10.35‰
Cattle metatarsal	OxA-27216	4775±40	5596–5331	-23.12‰	3.83‰

neighbours while, in other instances, at certain seasons the women moved to locations where shellfish could be collected. It seems likely that shellfish collection became a more specialised activity and it is probable that something similar may have taken place in Ireland. Were these groups who created the large Neolithic middens in Ireland descendants of Mesolithic hunter-gatherers or members of Neolithic communities who were descendants of new arrivals?

Just to confuse matters, one also has to wonder whether there was, even within the Early Neolithic, such a thing as a unitary Neolithic economy. There are some indications from stable isotopes, notably $\delta^{15}N$, that, in some parts of Ireland, cereals and other plant foods were less important than in adjacent parts of Britain (Richards 2000). The evidence from Ceide Fields, Co. Mayo, also suggests that cattle were more important than cereals. Evidence from the large assemblage of human bones from Poulnabrone portal tomb suggests that, in that region on the Burren in Co. Clare, the diet was more omnivorous (Ditchfield 2014, 90). Were there, therefore, regional economic differences in Ireland during the Neolithic and would, as a consequence, the interaction between Mesolithic and Neolithic ways of life have varied from region to region?

The dangers of having simple cultural or economic categories is perhaps also flagged by a reminder that, even in recent times, many of the coastal communities in the west of Ireland had very mixed economies. This is particularly clear in Tómas Ó Crohan's (1951, 97–101) account of his life in the Blasket Islands where there was no division between the (Neolithic) subsistence farming and sheep grazing and the (Mesolithic) activities of fishing and shellfish collecting, as well as the occasional seal hunt. Indeed, until recently, local fishermen/farmers of the Dingle Peninsula caught and sold crayfish to middlemen for sale across the European market. Incidentally, these were so valuable that they were rarely consumed by the families of the fishermen.

How then is this evidence to be interpreted?

Could the Mesolithic have continued after 6000 cal BP and the Neolithic begin at a later date? In this scenario one is left trying to explain the sudden appearance of rectangular houses, such as Cloghers (Kiely 2003), megalithic tombs such as court tombs (Schulting *et al.* 2012) and forest clearances in the context of a fully developed Neolithic material culture.

Could there be an "Experimental"/"Interaction" Stage 2 between an initial Neolithic presence and a surviving final Mesolithic, the presence of the early cattle bones marking the beginning of the phase? This could include some of the elements suggested by Sheridan (2010). Is there an initial, growing, contact along the western seaboard of Ireland first signalled by a) the very early presence of domesticates, then b) by some simple tombs and only then c) by a phase where the full package of carinated bowls, a new lithics assemblage, rectangular structures and certain new tomb types represent

a consolidation phase? From then on there may be different responses to how the hunter-gatherer and farming economies merged.

It is probable that we have over-simplified the issue of invasion versus acculturation. It is likely that human relations on the island of Ireland between approximately 6000 and 55000 cal BP were going through a much complex series of changes and developments than those that we normally discuss. Hopefully access to ancient DNA and perhaps more stable isotopes analysis samples from human remains of both periods will begin to provide some clarity.

Final thoughts

In writing this book the one thread that appears to run through it is that of *attitude*. This is something that may be endemic in Irish archaeology or at least in prehistory. From the middle of the 19th century there was, for a long time, an attitude that there was always a possibility that anything found in Ireland could be as a result of delayed arrivals or be a residual trace of something much older. This is a product of Ireland being a location on the edge of the core research region whose centre stretches from France through to Denmark. Because those regions first developed chronologies and schema of sequences of material culture, we have always been inclined to use them as benchmarks. The same issues could also be found in Scotland and northern Norway, where again, at times, there was a reluctance to accept evidence that initial settlement could begin at an early date. This produces the opposite reaction, i.e. that the most important aspect of the study of early settlement is to show that we have something earlier than conventional wisdom would suggest (see Woodman 1996 for a discussion of the "Shangri la Syndrome" and other problems of working on the edge of Europe). In Ireland this was compounded by a double reluctance, as it was often presumed that the southern half of the country was virtually unoccupied until the Neolithic or even later.

Sometimes there is too much emphasis on questions such as, is there any trace of a Palaeolithic? Or even, is there a possibility of an earlier Mesolithic? This attitude of limited expectations seriously impedes the possibility of the discovery of sites or artefacts from even known phases of the Mesolithic. If there is a limited expectation and if the normal archaeological record is supposed to make itself obvious through the presence of monuments, either extant or disturbed, then chance finds of early artefacts will more likely be treated as curiosities rather than potential indicators of early settlement.

Although it may appear over-critical and contradictory, especially when taking into consideration some comments made above, Irish prehistory has always had the tendency to seek validity by discovering something similar to what has been found in adjacent regions. Phrases such as hoping to find "another Star Carr" or something like the "Tybrind Vig paddle" are quite common, and while the discovery of some exotic artefact(s) would be welcome, it tends to direct us away from the most interesting aspect of the Irish Mesolithic, namely that it is different. It took half my career to realise that this difference was the essential attribute of the Irish Mesolithic. This difference is undoubtedly, in part, due to the fact that the island of Ireland has had a distinctly different ecological dynamic and this is what makes the Irish Mesolithic so interesting and important.

In one way, it is too easy to cringe or apologise for the very large quantities of material that has been picked up on lake shores, dredged out of rivers or been recovered from raised beaches and the inter-tidal shore. Although this material is often in very poor contexts, it also must reflect the nature of settlement and the important exploitation of Irish waterways. It clearly demonstrates how different Ireland was and still is from many other parts of Europe.

Certain regions have ease of access to many Mesolithic sites. These vary from the open exposed surfaces of the arctic and mountainous regions of Scandinavia, through the sandy regions of the northern European plain to the farmlands and uplands of many parts of England. Ireland suffers from extensive cover of bogs and grasslands and in many areas the soils are quite acidic. Yet in Ireland, especially in northern areas, enormous quantities of material have been recovered from within river valley bottoms and some estuaries, as well as certain sea loughs. There are now a small but still significant series of sites that shows the range of fish and other species that were exploited around the coast and in the lakes. There is also growing evidence that there was substantial investment in certain locations, both through the quantities of material found at key points on rivers and as the building of substantial structures along the shores of many lakes. One must also wonder what still lies buried under the still extensive bogs of the Irish midlands.

The range of bone and antler artefacts, some of which are decorated, must be one of the abiding images of the European Mesolithic. Even the Scottish Obanian sites have produced a wealth of such material, such as harpoons and other artefacts. Yet what Ireland has produced is equally interesting, in that alternative ranges of ground stone tools were created. These range from the Moynagh Points through ground stone axes to large possible fish clubs.

One can even point to the fact that Ireland is fortunate in that most artefacts are housed in the two major museums on the island; the National Museum of Ireland in Dublin and what is now the National Museums of Northern Ireland.

As was stated in Chapter 1, it is not the purpose of this book to determine the research strategy of another generation, only to say that there are many questions that still need to be explored and there are many regions where little is known about Mesolithic settlement. Perhaps, if this volume helps change the attitude towards the first 40% of Ireland's known and continuous history, it will have achieved its purpose.

The challenge appears to be the balance between theory and practice. In Ireland we can benefit from seeing the diverse range of evidence that is available from elsewhere. At the same time the benefits of new theoretical perspectives or discoveries from elsewhere can be appreciated but, ultimately, the lesson is that in the island of Ireland, as in so many other regions within Europe, the local environment and research history are of equal importance. Indeed if there is one lesson from the whole history of Ireland it is that its story has been one of adapting new ideas to local circumstances.

In returning to how we want to view our earliest ancestors, the alternatives are best illustrated by images from Tierra del Fuego. Do we favour Hawkesworth's 18th century image of the noble savage (Fig. 12.13a) or the image of the impoverished and to be pitied "Natives" reconstructed at the end of the 19th century in the Jardin Botanique in Paris (Fig. 12.13b). Have things really changed? As discussed in Chapter 3, do we lean towards the Cave Myth or the fall from a Golden Arcadian age?

Fig. 12.13. a) Hawkesworth's 1773 illustration of a Haush encampment, b) reconstruction of a Yamana family and hut at the Jardin Botanique Paris 1900.

BIBLIOGRAPHY

Aaris-Sørensen, K. 1976. A zoological investigation of the bone material from Svaerdborg I. In B. Bille Henricksen, *Svaerdborg I, Excavations 1943–44: A settlement of the Maglemose Period*, 149–160. Arkæoloiske Studier III, Akademisk Forlag Københvn.

Ackerlund, A., Gustaffsson, P., Hammer, D., Lindgren, C., Olsson, E. and Wikell, R. 2003. Peopling a forgotten landscape. In Larsson *et al.* (eds) 2003, xxxiii–xliv.

Adams, A. L. 1876. Report on the exploration of Shandon Cave. *Transactions of the Royal Irish Academy* 26, 187–230.

Adams, A. L., Kinahan, G. H. and Ussher, R. J. 1881. Explorations in the Bone Cave of Ballynamintra, near Cappagh, Co Waterford. *Scientific Transactions of the Royal Dublin Society* 1, 177–226.

Adamson, I. 1991, *The Cruithin,* Pretani Press, Bangor

Addyman, P. V. 1965. Coney Island, Lough Neagh. Prehistoric settlement, Anglo-Norman castle and Elizabethan native fortress. *Ulster Journal of Archaeology* 28, 78–101.

Addyman, P. V. and Vernon, P. D. 1966. A beach pebble industry from Dunaff Bay, Inishowen, Co. Donegal. *Ulster Journal of Archaeology* 29, 6–15.

Agassiz, L. 1840. *Etudes sur les Glaciers.* Jent et Glassman, Neuchatel.

Albrethsen, S. E. and Brinch-Petersen, E. 1976. Excavations of a Mesolithic cemetery at Vedbaek, Denmark. *Acta Archaeologica* 47, 1–28.

Aldhouse-Green, S. H. R. 1993. Lithic finds. In S. Goboland R. C. Turner (eds), *Second Severn Crossings. Archaeological Response: Phase 1 – the Intertidal Zone in Wales*, 45–47. Cadw, Cardiff.

Aldhouse-Green, S., Peterson, R. and Walker, E. A. 2012. *Neanderthals in Wales: Pontnewydd and the Elwy Valley Caves*. Oxbow Books, Oxford.

Alsaker, S. and Bruen Olsen, A. 1984. Greenstone and Diabase utilisation in the Stone Age of western Norway: technological and socio-cultural aspects of axe and adze production and distribution. *Norwegian Archaeological Review* 17(2), 71–103.

Ames, K. 1985. Hierarchies, Stress and logistical strategies among hunter gatherers in the northwestern North America. In T. D. Price and J. A. Brown (eds), *Prehistoric Hunter-Gatherers: The Emergence of Cultural Complexity*, 155–80. Academic Press, New York.

Ames, K. M. 2002. Going by boat: The forager collector continuum at sea. In B. Fitzhugh and J. Habu (eds), *Beyond Foraging and Collecting: Evolutionary Change in Hunter-Gather Settlement Systems*, 19–51. Kluwer Academic/Plenum Publishers, New York.

Andersen, K., Jørgensen, S. and Richter, J. 1982. *Maglemose Hytterne ved Ulkestrup Lyng*. Nordiske Fortidsminder B, Bind 7. Copenhagen.

Andersen, S. H. 1974. Ringkloster: en jysk inlandsboplads med Ertebøllekultur. *Kuml* (1973–4), 10–108.

Andersen, S. H. 1981. *Stenalderen. Jaegerstenalderen*. Sesam, København.

Andersen, S. H. 1987. Tybrind Vig: A submerged Ertebølle settlement in Denmark. In J. M. Coles and A. J. Lawson (eds), *Wetlands in European Prehistory*, 253–280. Clarendon Press, Oxford.

Andersen, S. H. 1993. A stratified Køkkenmødding on the Central Limfjord, North Jutland. *Journal of Danish Archaeology* 10, 59–96.

Andersen, S. H. 1994. Ringkloster, Ertebølle trappers and wild boar hunters in eastern Jutland, A survey. *Journal of Danish Archaeology* 12, 13–59.

Andersen, S. H. and Johansen, E. 1986. Ertebølle revisited. *Journal of Danish Archaeology* 5, 31–61.

Anderson, A. 2003. Entering uncharted waters. In M. Rockman and J. Steele (eds), *Colonization of Unfamiliar Landscapes: the archaeology of adaptations*, 169–189. Routledge, London.

Anderson, C. P. 2000. Mesolithic bevelled pebble tools: a re-evaluation based on assemblages from Dalkey Island, County Dublin, Sutton, County Dublin and Rockmarshall, County Louth. Unpublished MA thesis, University College Cork.

Anderson, E. 1993. The Mesolithic: fishing for answers. In E. Shee-Twohig and M. Ronayne (eds), *Past Perceptions: The Prehistoric Archaeology of South-west Ireland*, 16–24. Cork University Press, Cork.

Anderson, E. 1994. Flint technology in the Irish Later Mesolithic. Unpublished MA thesis, University College Cork.

Anderson, E. 1996. Appendix 1: use wear analysis. In P. C. Woodman and G. J. Johnson, Excavations at Bay Farm 1, Carnlough, Co. Antrim, and the study of the "Larnian" technology, 232–235. *Proceedings of the Royal Irish Academy* 96C, 137–235.

Anderson, T. B. 2004. Southern Uplands-Down-Longford terrain. In W. I. Mitchell (ed.), *The Geology of Northern Ireland: our Natural Foundation* (2nd edn), 9–24. Geological Survey of Northern Ireland, Belfast.

Andreasen, N. H. 2009. Early farmers on the coast: lithic procurement strategies of colonists in the eastern Adriatic in the north west of Europe. In McCartan *et al.* (eds) 2009, 53–60.

Antoine, P., Coutard, J. P., Gibbard, P., Hallegouet, B. Laudtridou, J.-P. and Ozouf, J.-C. 2003. The Pleistocene rivers of the English Channel region. *Journal of Quaternary Science* 18(3–4), 227–43.

Apsimon, A. 1976. Ballynagilly and the beginning and end of the Irish Neolithic. In S. J. de Laet (ed.), *Acculturation and Continuity in Atlantic Europe Mainly During the Neolithic Period and the Bronze Age, Dissertationes Gandensis,* 15–30. Bruges. Ghent

Bailey, G. N. 1978. Shell middens as indicators of postglacial economies: a territorial perspective. In P. Mellars (ed.), *The Early Post-Glacial Settlement of Northern Europe*, 37–64. Duckworth, London.

Ball, R. 1849. Communication by Mr. Ball. *Proceedings of the Royal Irish Academy* 4, 416–20.

Ballin, T. B., Saville, A., Tipping, R. and Ward, T. 2010. An upper Palaeolithic flint and chert assemblage, Howburn Farm, South Lanarkshire: first results. *Oxford Journal of Archaeology* 29(4), 323–60.

Bamforth, D. and Woodman, P. C. 2004. Tool hoards and Neolithic use of the landscape in northeastern Ireland. *Oxford Journal of Archaeology* 23, 21–44.

Barlow, C. and Mithen, S. 2000. The experimental use of elongated pebble tools. In S. Mithen (ed.), *Hunter-Gatherer Landscape Archaeology: The Southern Hebrides Project 1988–98*, 513–22. MacDonald Institute Monograph, Cambridge.

Barnes, B., Edwards, B. J. N., Hallam, J. S. and Stuart, A. J. 1971. Skeleton of a Late Glacial Elk associated with barbed points from Poulton le Fylde, Lancashire. *Nature* 232, 488–89.

Barton, N. 1991. Stone Age Britain. London, English Heritage, Batsford.

Batterbee, R., Scaife, R. G. and Phethean, S. J. 1985. Palaeoecological evidence for sea level change in the Bann estuary in the Early Mesolithic period. In Woodman 1985a, 111–20.

Batty, J. 1938. Some microliths from the Lower Bann Valley. *Ulster Journal of Archaeology* 1, 90–4.

Bayliss, A. and Woodman, P. C. 2009. A new Bayesian chronology for Mesolithic occupation at Mount Sandel, Northern Ireland. *Proceedings of the Prehistoric Society* 75, 101–24.

Beerenhout, B. 2001. Vissen in reptielen. In Louwe Kooijmans (ed.) 2001, 243–76.

Bell, J. 1815. Various relics of antiquities found in Ireland. *Newry Register* 1(4), 293–96.

Bell, J. 1816. Letter from Mr John Bell. *Newry Magazine* 2, 234–40.

Bell, M. 2007. *Prehistoric Coastal Communities: The Mesolithic in Western Britain*. Council for British Archaeology Research Report 149, Council for British Archaeology, York.

Bell, R. and Bennett, S. A. 1923. A recently discovered prehistoric site in Co. Antrim. *Proceedings of the Belfast Naturalists' Field Club*, 1–14.

Bendry, R., Thorpe, N., Outram, A. and van Wijngaarden Bakker, L. H. 2013. The origins of domesticated horses in north-west Europe: new direct dates on the horses of Newgrange Ireland. *Proceedings of the Prehistoric Society* 79, 91–104.

Bengtsson, L. 2003. Knowledge and Interaction in the Stone Age: raw materials for adzes and axes, their sources and distributional patterns. In Larsson *et al.* (eds) 2003, 389–394

Bennett, K. D. 1983. An occurrence of pike (Sorex lucius linné) in the Early Postglacial at Sea Mere, Norfolk and the origins of British Freshwater fish. *Quaternary Newsletter* 41, 7–10.

Bergh, S. 2009. Black is the colour, concave scrapers and passage tombs. In G. Cooney, B. O'Connor and J. Chapman (eds), *Materialitas, Working Stone, Carving Identity*, 105–12. Prehistoric Society Research Papers 3. Prehistoric Society and Oxbow Books, Oxford.

Bergh, S. and Hensey R. 2013. Unpicking the chronology of Carrowmore. *Oxford Journal of Archaeology* 32(4), 343–366.

Berridge, P. 1994. The lithics. In Quinnell *et al.* 1994, 115–31.

Berridge, P. and Roberts, A. 1994. The Mesolithic decorated and other pebble artefacts: synthesis. In Quinnell *et al.* 1994, 95–114.

Bicho, N., Umbelino, C., Detry, C. and Pereira, T. 2010. The emergence of Muge Mesolithic shell middens in central Portugal and the 8000 cal yr BP. *Journal of Island and Coastal Archaeology* 5(1), 86–104.

Binford, L. R. 1977. Forty seven trips. In R. V. S. Wright (ed.), *Stone Tools as Cultural Markers*, 24–36. Australian Institute of Aboriginal Studies, Canberra.

Binford, L. R. 1983. *In Pursuit of the Past*. Thames and Hudson, London.

Bird, J. 1946. The Alaculuf. In J. H. Steward (ed.) *Handbook of South American Indians Vol 1, The Marginal Tribes*, 55–80 Smithsonian Institute, Washington.

Bjerck, H. B. 1986. The Fosna-Nostvet problem: a consideration of archaeological units and chronozones in the south Norwegian Mesolithic period. *Norwegian Archaeological Review* 19, 103–121.

Bjerck, H. B. 1990. Mesolithic site types and settlement patterns at Vega, northern Norway. *Acta Archaeologia* 60, 1–32.

Bjerck, H. B. 1995. The North Sea Continent and the pioneer settlement of Norway. In Fischer (ed.) 1995, 131–44.

Bjerck, H. B. 2009. Colonizing seascapes: comparative perspectives on the development of maritime relations in the Pleistocene/ Holocene transition in the north west of Europe. In McCartan *et al.* (eds) 2009, 16–23.

Blinkhorn, E. and Milner, N. 2013. *Mesolithic Research and Conservation Framework English Heritage*. University of York and Council for British Archaeology, York.

Boate, G. 1725. *The Natural History of Ireland*. Grierson, Dublin.

Bonifay, E. 1998. La Grotte de la Coscia (Macinaggio/Rogliano, Cap Corse) et le probleme du peuplement des îles de Méditerranée Occidentale par l'homme de Néandertal. In G. Camps (ed.), *L'Homme Prehistorique et la Mer*, 133–40. Editions du CTHS, Paris.

Bonsall, C. 1981. The coastal factor in the Mesolithic settlement of north-west England, In B. Gramsch (ed.), *Mesolithikum in Europa*, 451–70. Veröffentlichungen des Museums *für Ur- und Frühgeschichte* Potsdam 14/15, Deutscher Verlag, Berlin.

Borrero, J. M. 1997. The Origins of Ethnographic Subsistence Patterns in Fuego-Patagonia. In C. McEwan, L. A. Borrero and A. Prieto (eds) *Patagonia: Natural History, Prehistory and Ethnography at the Uttermost End of the Earth*, 60–81. Princeton University Press, New Jersey.

Bourillet, J.-F., Reynard, J.-Y., Baltazer, A. and Zaragosi, S. 2003. The "*Fleuve Manche*": the submarine sedimentary features from the outer shelf to the deep sea floor. *Journal of Quaternary Science* 18(3–4), 261–82.

Bourke, L. 2001. *Crossing the Rubicon: Bronze Age Metalwork from Irish Rivers*. Bronze Age Studies 5, Department of Archaeology, National University of Ireland Galway.

Bøe, J. and Nummedal, A. 1936. *Le Finnmarkien: les origins de la civilization dans l'extrêmenord de l'Europe*. Institutet for sammenlignende Kulturforskning, B 32, Oslo.

Bradley, J. 1991. Excavations at Moynagh Lough, County Meath. *Journal of the Royal Society of Antiquaries of Ireland* 121, 5–26.

Bradley, J. 1999. Excavations at Moynagh Lough, Co. Meath, 1997–98. *Ríocht na Mídhe* 10, 1–17.

Bratlund, B. 1996. Archaeozoological comments on final Palaeolithic frontiers in South Scandinavia. In L. Larsson (ed.) *The Earliest*

Settlement of Scandinavia and its Relationship with Neighbouring Areas, 23–33. Acta Archaeologia Lundensia 24. Almquist and Wiksell International, Stockholm.

Bremer, W. 1928. Notes on some objects in the National Collection of Irish Antiquities. *Proceedings of the Royal Irish Academy* 38C, 21–30.

Brennan, E. and Carte, A. 1859. Notice of the discovery of extinct and other animal remains, occurring in a fossil state under limestone at Shandon, near Dungarvan, County of Waterford. *Journal of the Royal Dublin Society* 2, 344–57.

Brett, C. B. 2000. Flint procurement and utilisation in the Burren, Co. Clare. Unpublished MA thesis, University College Cork.

Bridgeland, D. R., Antoine, P., Limondin-Louzet, N., Santisteban, J. I., Westway, R. and White, M. J. 2006. The Palaeolithic occupation of Europe as revealed by evidence from the rivers: data from IGCPP 449. *Journal of Quaternary Science, Special Issue: The Palaeolithic Occupation of Europe: In memory of John J. Wymer* 21(5), 437–56.

Bridgeman, K. A. 1998. Lough Gara: Later Mesolithic Collection. Unpublished MA thesis, University College Cork.

Briggs, C. S. 2007 Prehistory in the 19th century. In S. Pearce (ed.) *Visions of Antiquity: The Society of Antiquaries of London 1707–2007*, 227–66. Society of Antiquaries of London, London.

Brinch Petersen, E. 1973. A Survey of the Late Palaeolithic and Mesolithic of Denmark. In S. Kozłowski (ed.), *The Mesolithic in Europe*, 77–128. Warsaw University Press, Warsaw.

Brinch Petersen, E. 1980. *De døde og deres grave*, Munksgaard, Copenhagen.

Brinch Petersen, E. 1981. *Blev de myrdet alle tre*, Munksgaard, Copenhagen.

Brinch Petersen, E. 1989. Vaenget Nord: excavation, documentation and interpretation of a Mesolithic site at Vedbaek, Denmark. In C. Bonsall (ed.), *The Mesolithic in Europe*, 325–31. John Donald, Edinburgh.

Brinch Petersen, E and Meiklejohn, C. P. 2003. Three cremations and a funeral. In Larsson *et al.* (eds) 2003, 485–94.

Brindley, A. L. and Lanting, J. N. 1995. Irish bog bodies: the radiocarbon dates. In R. C. Turner and R. G. Scaife (eds), *Bog Bodies: New Discoveries and New Perspectives*, 133–136. British Museum Press, London.

Brinkhuizen, D. C. 1983. Some notes on recent pre- and protohistoric fishing gear from northwestern Europe. *Palaeohistoria* 25, 7–54.

Brooks, A. and Farrell, A. Appendix 20: assessment of palaeo-environmental research potential. In Mossop and Mossop 2009.

Brooks, R. J., Bradley, S. J., Edwards, R. J. and Goodwyn, N. 2012. Palaeogeographic maps of Northern Europe during the Post Glacial period. *Journal of Maps* 7, 573–87.

Brunicardi, J. 1914. The shore-dwellers of ancient Ireland. *Journal of the Royal Society of Antiquaries of Ireland* 44, 185–213.

Brunner, B. 2007. *Bears: a Brief History*. Yale University Press, Yale.

Buckland, W. 1823. *Reliquiae diluvianae*. J. Murray, London.

Buick, G. R. 1887. On the development of the knife in flint, as shown by specimens common in Co. Antrim. *Journal of the Royal Society of Antiquaries of Ireland* 18, 241–48.

Buick, G. R. 1891. Fresh facts on prehistoric pottery. *Journal of the Royal Society of Antiquaries of Ireland* 21, 433–42.

Burchell, J. P. T. 1931. Early Neanthropic man and his relation to the Ice Age. *Proceedings of the Prehistoric Society of East Anglia* 6, 253–303.

Burchell, J. P. T. and Reid Moir, J. 1928. *The Early Mousterian Implements of Sligo, Ireland*. W. E. Harrison, Ipswich.

Burchell, J. P. T. and Reid Moir, J. 1932. The evolution and distribution of the hand-axes in north-east Ireland. *Proceedings of the Prehistoric Society of East Anglia* 7, 18–34.

Burenhult, G. 1984. *The Archaeology of Carrowmore: Environmental Archaeology and the Megalithic Tradition at Carrowmore, County Sligo, Ireland*. Thesis and Papers in North European Archaeology 14, Institute of Archaeology, University of Stockholm, Stockholm.

Burenhult, G. 2005. Carrowmore, tombs for hunters. *British Archaeology* 82, 22–7.

Burke, E. 1857. *A Philosophical Enquiry into the Origin of our Ideas of the Sublime and Beautiful*. London.

Burkitt, M. C. 1925. *Prehistory: a Study of Early Cultures in Europe and the Mediterranean Basin*. Cambridge University Press, Cambridge.

Burkitt, M. and Childe, V. G. 1932. A chronological table of prehistory. *Antiquity* 6, 185–205.

Bury, J. B. 1932. *The Idea of Progress: An Inquiry into its Origin and Growth*. Macmillan Company, New York.

Cabot, D. 1997. Essential texts in natural history. In J. W. Foster (ed.), *Nature in Ireland: A Scientific and Cultural History*, 472–97. Lilliput, Dublin.

Cahill, M. 1994. Mr Anthony's bog oak case of Gold Antiquities. *Proceedings of the Royal Irish Academy* 94C, 53–109.

Cahill, M. 2001. Unspooling the mystery. *Archaeology Ireland* 15(3), 8–15.

Cahill, M. and Sikora, M. 2012. *Breaking Ground, Finding Graves – Reports on the Excavations of Burials by the National Museum of Ireland 1927–2006*. National Museum of Ireland, Dublin.

Callaghan, R. and Scarre, C. 2009. Simulating the western Seaways. *Oxford Journal of Archaeology* 28(4), 357–72.

Callow, P. and Cornford, J. M. 1986. *La Cotte de St Brelade 1961–1978. Excavations by C. B. M. McBurney*. Geo Books, Norwich.

Campbell, J. 1977. *The Upper Palaeolithic of Great Britain: A Study of Man and Nature in the Ice Age*. Oxford University Press, Oxford.

Campbell, K. 2003. Arklow Bank Wind Park: Offshore monitoring of Dredging, *www.excavations.ie*

Campbell, K. 2004. Arklow Bank Wind Park, Archaeological monitoring of dredging operations, Turbine Five Access Channel. Unpublished report to G.E. Wind Energy D.J.B.M.A. 01-01-04 (Licence NO. 03E1101).

Carr, P. 1985. An Early Mesolithic site near Dundonald, Co. Down. *Ulster Journal of Archaeology* 48, 122–3.

Carr, P. 1987. An Early Mesolithic site near Comber, Co Down. *Ulster Journal of Archaeology* 50, 157–8.

Cannon, A. 2013. Revealing the hidden dimensions of Pacific Northwest Coast shell middens. In G. N. Bailey, K. Hardy and A. Camara (eds), *Shell Energy*, 21–40, Oxbow Books, Oxford.

Chatterton, R. 2006. Ritual. In Conneller and Warren (eds) 2006, 101–20.

Cheverill, R. C. and Thomas G. S. P. 2010. Extent and timing of the Last Glacial Maximum (LGM) in Britain and Ireland: a review. *Journal of Quaternary Science* 25(4), 535–49.

Chesney, H. 1997. Enlightenment and education. In J. W. Foster (ed.), *Nature in Ireland: A Scientific and Cultural History*, 367–86. Lilliput, Dublin.

Clark, C. D., Hughes, A. L. C., Greenwood, S. L., Jordan, C. and Sejrup, H. P. 2010. Pattern and timing of retreat of the last British-Irish Ice Sheet. *Quaternary Science Reviews* 30, 1–35.

Clark, J. G. D. 1933. The classification of a microlithic culture: the Tardenoisian of Horsham. *Archaeological Journal* 90, 52–77.

Clark, J. G. D. 1936. *The Mesolithic Settlement of Northern Europe.* Cambridge University Press, Cambridge.

Clark, J. G. D. 1954. *Excavations at Star Carr: an Early Mesolithic settlement at Seamer, near Scarborough, Yorkshire.* Cambridge University Press, Cambridge.

Clark, J. G. D. 1972. Star Carr: a case study in bio-archaeology. *Addison Wesley Modules in Anthropology* Module 10, 1–42.

Clark, J. G. D. 1975. *The Earlier Stone Age Settlement of Scandinavia.* Cambridge University Press, Cambridge.

Clarke, A. 2009. Craft specialization in the Mesolithic of northern Britain: the evidence from the coarse stone tools. In Finlay *et al.* (eds) 2009, 12–22.

Clarke, A. and Waddington, C. 2007. Bevelled pebbles, coarse stone tools and ochreous material. In Waddington (ed.) 2007, 110–19.

Clarke, D. L. 1976. Mesolithic Europe: the economic basis. In G. de G. Sieveking, I. H. Longworth and K. E. Wilson (eds), *Problems in Economic and Social Archaeology*, 449–81. Duckworth, London.

Classen, C. 2013. Freshwater shell heaps of the Ohio River Valley, USA. In G. N. Bailey, K. Hardy and A. Camara, (eds), *Shell Energy*, 59–68. Oxbow Books, Oxford.

Cleary, R. M. and Hurley, M. F. 2003. *Cork City Excavations 1984–2000.* Cork City Council, Cork.

Clibborn, E. 1859. On the probable age of flint implements found in gravel beds. *Ulster Journal of Archaeology* 1(7), 324–33.

Coffey, G. and Praeger, R. L. 1904. The Antrim raised beach: A contribution to the Neolithic history of the north of Ireland. *Proceedings of the Royal Irish Academy* 25C, 143–200.

Cole, W. 1685, A letter from Mr William Cole of Bristol, to the Phil. Society of Oxford; containing his observations on the purple fish, *Philosophical Transactions* 15, 1278–86

Coles, B. J. 1998. Doggerland: a speculative survey. *Proceedings of the Prehistoric Society* 64, 45–82.

Coles, J. 1971. The early settlement of Scotland: excavations at Morton, Fife. *Proceedings of the Prehistoric Society* 38, 284–366.

Coles, J. 1983. Excavations at Kilmelfort Cave. *Proceedings of the Society of Antiquaries of Scotland* 113, 11–21.

Collins, A. E. P. 1978. Excavations on Ballygalley Head, County Antrim. *Ulster Journal of Archaeology* 41, 15–32.

Collins, A. E. P. 1983. Excavations at Mount Sandel, lower site, Coleraine, County Londonderry. *Ulster Journal of Archaeology* 46, 1–22.

Collins, T. 2009. Hermitage, Ireland: life and death on the western edge of Europe. In McCartan *et al.* (eds) 2009, 876–9.

Collins, T. and Coyne, F. 2003. Fire and water: Early Mesolithic cremations at Castleconnell, Co. Limerick. *Archaeology Ireland* 17(2), 24–7.

Collins, T. and Coyne, F. 2006. As old as we felt. *Archaeology Ireland* 20(4), 21.

Colonese, A. C., Camarós, E., Verdún, E., Estévez, J, Giralt, S. and Rejas, M. 2011. Integrated archaeozoological research of shell middens: new insights into hunter-gatherer-fisher coastal exploitation in Tierra del Fuego. *Journal of Island and Coastal Archaeology* 6(2), 235–54.

Conneller, C. 2006. Death in Mesolithic Britain and Ireland. In Conneller and Warren (eds) 2006, 139–64.

Conneller, C. 2009a. Transforming bodies: mortuary practice in Mesolithic Britain. In McCartan *et al.* (eds) 2009, 691–97.

Conneller, C. and Warren, G. (eds), 2006. *Mesolithic Britain and Ireland: New Approaches.* Tempus Stroud, Gloucestershire.

Conneller, C. Milner, N., Schadla Hall T., Taylor, B. 2009. Star Carr in the new Millenium. In Finlay *et al.* (eds) 2009, 78–88.

Conneller, C. Milner, N. Taylor, B. and Taylor M. 2012. Substantial settlement in the European Early Mesolithic: new research at Star Carr, *Antiquity*, 86, 100–20

Cook, J. 2003. The discovery of British Antiquity. In K. Sloan (ed.), *Enlightenment: Discovering the World in the Eighteenth Century,* 178–91. British Museum Press, London.

Cook, J. 2012. The elephants in the collection: Sloane and the history of the earth. In A. Walker and M. Hunter (eds), *Books to Bezoars, Sir Hans Sloane, Physician, Naturalist & Collector*, 158–67. British Museum, London.

Cooney, G. 1990. The Mount Oriel Project: an introduction. *County Louth Archaeological and Historical Journal* 22(2), 24–7.

Cooney, G. 2005. Stereo porphyry: quarrying and deposition on Lambay Island, Ireland. In P. Topping and M. Lynott (eds), *The Cultural Landscape of Prehistoric Mines*, 14–29. Oxbow Books, Oxford.

Cooney, G. and Grogan, E. 1994. *Irish Prehistory: a Social Perspective.* Wordwell, Dublin.

Cooney, G., Bayliss, A., Healy, F., Whittle, A., Danaher, E., Cagney, L., Mallory, J., Smyth, J., Kador, T. and O'Sullivan, M. 2011. Ireland. In Whittle *et al.* (eds) 2011, 562–656.

Coope, G. R., Lemdhal, G., Lowe, J. J. and Walker, A. 1998. Temperature gradients in northern Europe during the last glacial–Holocene transition (14–9^{14}C KyrBP) interpreted from coleopteran assemblages. *Journal of Quaternary Sciences* 13, 419–33.

Cooper, L. 2013, Asfordby Leicestershire. In Blinkhorn and Milner 2013, 10–12.

Costa, L. J. 2004. *Corse Préhistorique.* Editions Errante, Paris.

Costa, L. J. 2006. Two long blades from the Bann River Valley. In Woodman *et al.* 206, 238–41.

Costa, L. J., Sternke, F. and Woodman, P. C. 2001. The analysis of a lithic assemblage from Eleven Ballyboes, County Donegal. *Ulster Journal of Archaeology* 60, 1–8.

Costa, L. J., Sternke, F. and Woodman, P. C. 2005. Degeneration or adaptation: The transformation of lithic technology during the Mesolithic in Ireland. *Antiquity* 79(303), 19–33.

Coxon, P. and McGarron, S. G. 2009. Cenezoic: Tertiary and Quaternary (until 11,700 years before 2000). In C. H. Holland and I. A. Sanders (eds), *The Geology of Ireland*, 355–97. Dunedin Press, Edinburgh, 2nd edn.

Cross, R. E. 1953. Lough Gara: a preliminary survey. *Journal of the Royal Society of Antiquaries of Ireland* 83, 93–6.

Crombé, P. 2006. The wetlands of sandy Flanders (northwest Belgium). In Rensink and Peeters (eds) 2006, 41–54.

Crooke, E. 2000. *Politics, Archaeology and the Creation of a National Museum of Ireland: an Expression of National Life.* Irish Academic Press, Dublin.

Cunha, E., Umbelino, C. and Cardoso, F. 2004. About violent interactions in the Mesolithic: the absence of Evidence from the Portuguese shell middens. In M. Roksandic (ed.), *Violent Interactions in the Mesolithic: Evidence and Meaning*, 41–46. British Archaeological Report S237, Archaeopress, Oxford.

Curet, L. A. 2004. Island Archaeology and the study of ancient Caribbean societies. In S. M. Fitzpatrick (ed.), *Voyages of Discovery: the Archaeology of Islands*, 187–201. Praeger Publishers, Westport.

Currant, A. P. and Jacobi, R. M. 1997. Vertebrate faunas from the British Late Pleistocene and the chronology of human settlement, *Quaternary Newsletter* 82, 1–8.

Currant, A. and Jacobi R. M. 2001. A formal mammalian biostratigraphy for the Late Pleistocene of Britain. *Quaternary Science Reviews* 20 1701–1716

Danaher, E. 2007. *Monumental Beginnings: The Archaeology of the Sligo Inner Relief Road.* The National Roads Authority NRA Scheme Monograph 1, Dublin.

Dansgaard., W., Johnsen, S. J., Clausen, H. B., Dahl-Jensen, D., Gundestrup, N. S., Hammer, C. U. *et al.* 1993 Evidence of general instability of past climate from a 250 kyr ice core, *Nature* 364 218–20.

Daniel, G. 1962. *The Idea of Prehistory.* Watts, London.

Dark, P. 1998. Radiocarbon dating of the lake edge deposits. In P. Mellars and P. Dark, *Star Carr in Context*, 119–24. MacDonald Institute Monograph, Cambridge.

Davenport, J. L., Sleeman, D. P. and Woodman, P. C. (eds). 2008. *Mind the Gap: Postglacial Colonization of Ireland*, 45–62. Special Supplement to the *Irish Naturalists' Journal.*

David, A. 1989. Some aspects of the human presence in south-west Wales during the Mesolithic. In C. Bonsall (ed.), *The Mesolithic in Europe*, 241–53. John Donald, Edinburgh.

David, A. 1991. Late Glacial archaeological residues from Wales: a selection, in N. Barton, A. J. Roberts and D. A. Roe (eds), *The Late Glacial in Northwest Europe*, 141–60. Council for British Archaeology Research Report 77 York.

David, A. 1998. Two assemblages of later Mesolithic microliths from Seamer Carr, North Yorkshire: fact and fancy. In N. Ashton, F. Healy and P. Pettitt (eds), *Stone Age Archaeology*, 196–204. Oxbow Monograph 102/Lithic Studies Society Occasional Paper 6, Oxbow Books, Oxford.

David, A. 2007. *Palaeolithic and Mesolithic Settlement in Wales, with Special Reference to Dyfed.* British Archaeological Report 448, Archaeopress, Oxford.

David, A. and Walker E. A. 2004. Wales during the Mesolithic Period. In A. Saville (ed.), *Mesolithic Scotland and its Neighbours: the Early Holocene Prehistory of Scotland, its British and Irish Context, and Some Northern European Perspectives*, 299–338. Society of Antiquaries of Scotland, Edinburgh.

David, E., McCartan S., Mollin, F. and Woodman P. C. forthcoming. The other type of Mesolithic "Pointed bone implements". In Bicho (ed.), *Proceedings of the MUGE 150th Anniversary Conference.* Cambridge Scholars Publishing, Newcastle.

Davis, T. 1846. *Literary and Historical Essays.* Dublin.

Day, R. 1891. Flint axe found near Conna, Co. Cork. *Journal of the Royal Society of Antiquaries of Ireland* 21, 103.

Day, A. and McWilliams, P. (eds) 1997 *Ordnance Survey Memoirs of Ireland Vol. 38: Donegal, 1833–35.* Institute of Irish Studies, Queen's University Belfast.

Delaney, M. and Woodman, P. C. 2004. Searching the Irish Mesolithic for the humans behind the hatchets. In H. Roche, E. Grogan, J. Bradley, J. Coles and B. Rafferty (eds), *From Megaliths to Metals: Essays in Honour of George Eogan*, 6–11. Oxbow Books, Oxford.

Delaney, S. 2000. An investigation into the availability of flint as raw material along the south east coast of Ireland and an examination of a collection of flint implements from the same area. Unpublished MA thesis, University College Cork.

Debenham, N. C., Atkinson, T., Rainer, G., Hebden, N., Higham, T., Housley R., Pettitt, P., Rhodes, E., Rowe, J., Rowe, P. and Zhou, L. P. 2012. Dating. In M. Aldhouse-Green, S. Peterson and E. A. Walker (eds), *Neanderthals in Wales: Pontnewydd and the Elwy Valley Caves*, 283–320. Oxbow Books, Oxford.

Devriendt, I. 2013. Swifterbant stones: The Neolithic stone and flint industry at Swifterbant (the Netherlands). Doctoral Thesis presented at the University of Groningen.

Ditchfield, P. 2014. Stable isotope analysis. In A. Lynch, *Poulnabrone: An Early Neolithic Portal Tomb in Ireland*, 86–92. Archaeological Monograph Series 9, Dublin.

Dobbs, R. 1683. Description of the County of Antrim. Reproduced in G. Hill, 1978 (reprint), *The MacDonnells of Antrim,* appendix 2. Glens of Antrim Historical Society, Ballycastle.

Doggert, R. 1985. A magnetic susceptibility survey. In Woodman 1985a, 99–101.

Doughty, P. 2007. A big mystery: did elephant and hippopotamus roam the Belfast region just before the Ice Age. *Earth Science Ireland* 2, 12–15.

Dowd, M. A. 2002. Kilgreany, Co. Waterford: biography of an Irish cave. *The Journal of Irish Archaeology* 11, 77–98.

Dowd, M. A. 2008. The use of caves for funerary and ritual practices in Neolithic Ireland. *Antiquity* 82, 305–17.

Dowd, M. 2010. Artefacts and bones from Glencurran Cave. *Burren Insight* 2, 10–12.

Dowd, M. 2015. *The Archaeology of Caves in Ireland.* Oxbow Books, Oxford.

Doyle, G. J. and Ó Críodáin, C. 2003. Peatlands – fens and bogs. In M. Otte (ed.), *Wetlands of Ireland: Distribution, Ecology, Uses and Economic Value*, 79–108. UCD Press, Dublin.

Driscoll, K. 2006. The early prehistory of the west of Ireland: investigations into the social archaeology of the Mesolithic west of the Shannon, Ireland. Unpublished M. Litt thesis, National University of Ireland, Galway.

Driscoll, K. 2009. Constructing later Mesolithic landscapes. In Finlay *et al.* (eds) 2009, 101–12.

Driscoll, K. and Warren, G. 2007. Dealing with the quartz problem in Irish lithics research. *Journal of the Lithics Studies Society* 28, 4–14.

Driscoll, K., Menuge, J. and O'Keefe, E. 2014. New materials, traditional practices: a Mesolithic silicified toolkit from Lough Allen, Ireland. *Proceedings of the Royal Irish Academy* 114C, 1–34.

Ducrocq, T. 2010. Elements de chronologie absolue du Mesolithique de la Nord du France. In P. Crombé, M. Van Strydonck, J. Sergant, M. Boudin and M. Bats (eds), *Chronology and Evolution within the Mesolithic of North West Europe, Proceedings of an International Meeting, Brussels, May 30th–1st June 2007*, 345–362. Cambridge Scholars Publishing, Newcastle.

Dugdale, W. 1656. *The Antiquities of Warwickshire.* Thomas Warren, London.

Dumont, J. 1985. A preliminary report on the Mount Sandel micro-wear study. In Woodman 1985a, 61–70.

Dunlop, C. and Woodman, P. 2015. *Excavations of Prehistoric Settlement at Toomebridge, Co. Antrim, Northern Ireland, 2003.* British Archaeological Report 609 Archaeopress, Oxford.

Du Noyer, G. V. 1868. On the worked flint flakes from Carrickfergus and Larne. *Quarterly Journal of the Geological Society* 24, 495.

Du Noyer, G. V. 1869. On the flint flakes of Antrim and Down. *Journal of the Royal Geological Society of Ireland* 2, 169–71.

Edwards, J. and Brooks, A. 2008. The island of Ireland: drowning the myth of an Irish land-bridge? In Davenport *et al.* (eds) 2008, 19–34.

Edwards, C., Suchard, M., Lemey, P., Welch, J., Barnes, I., Fulton, T. l., Barnett, R., O Connell, T., Coxon, P., Monaghan, N., Valdiosera, C., Lorenzen, E., Willersley, E., Baryshnikov, G., Rambaut, A. Thomas, M., Bradley, D. and Shapiro, B. 2011. Ancient hybridization and an Irish origin for the modern polar bear matriline. *Current Biology* 21 1251–8.

Enghoff, I. B. 1986. Freshwater fishing from coastal settlement. *Journal of Danish Archaeology* 5, 62–76.

Eogan, G. 1963. A Neolithic habitation site and megalithic tomb in Townleyhall Townland, Co. Louth. *Journal of the Royal Society of Antiquaries of Ireland* 93, 37–81.

Erdtman, G. 1934. Some indications of the climate and vegetation in northwestern Europe during the Mesolithic age. In *Proceedings of the First International Congress of Prehistoric and Protohistoric Sciences, London August 1932*, 105–107. Oxford University Press, Oxford.

Erlandson, J. M. and Fitzpatrick, S. M. 2006. Oceans, islands and coasts: perspectives on the role of the sea in human prehistory. *Journal of Island and Coastal Archaeology* 1(1), 5–32.

Evans, E. E. 1981. *The Personality of Ireland: Habitat, Heritage and History*. Blackstaff Press, Belfast.

Evans, J. 1867. On some discoveries of stone implements in Lough Neagh, Ireland. *Archaeologia* 41, 397–408.

Fergusson, A. B. 1993. *Utter Antiquity: Perceptions of Prehistory in Renaissance England*. Duke University Press, Durham.

Feynman, R. 1999. Cargo cult science: some remarks on science, pseudo-science and learning how not to fool yourself. In J. Robbins (ed.), *The Pleasure of Finding Things Out: the Best Short Works of Richard P. Feynman*, 205–16. Penguin, London.

Figuier, L. 1863. *La Terre avant la Deluge: Ouvrage contenant 24 vue idéales de paysages de l'ancien mondes dessinées par Riou*. Hachette, Paris.

Finlay, N. 2000a, Microliths in the making in Young R. (ed.), *Mesolithic Lifeways*, 23–31. Leicester University Press Archaeological Monograph 7. Leicester University Press, Leicester.

Finlay, 2000b. Deer prudence. In C. Conneller (ed.), *New Approaches to the Palaeolithic and Mesolithic*, 67–78. Archaeological Review from Cambridge 17(1).

Finlay, N. 2003. Cache and carry: defining moments in the Irish later Mesolithic. In L. Bevan and J. Moore (eds), *Peopling the Mesolithic in a Northern Environment*, 87–94. British Archaeological Report S1157, Archaeopress, Oxford.

Finlay, N. 2006. Gender and personhood. In Conneller and Warren (eds) 2006, 35–60.

Finlay, N., Warren, G. and Wickham-Jones, C. R. 2002. The Mesolithic in Scotland: east meets west. *Scottish Archaeological Journal* 24(2), 101–20.

Finlay, N., McCartan, S., Milner, N. and Wickham-Jones, C. (eds), *From Bann Flakes to Bushmills*. Prehistoric Society Research Papers 1, Oxbow Books,Oxford.

Fischer, A. 1978. På sporet af overgangen mellem palæoliticum og mesoliticum i Sydskandinavien. *Hikuin* 4, 27–50.

Fischer, A. 1989. Hunting with flint tipped arrows: results and experiences from practical experiments. In C. Bonsall (ed.), *The Mesolithic in Europe*, 29–40. John Donald, Edinburgh.

Fischer, A. 1995. *Man and the Sea in the Mesolithic*. Oxbow Books, Oxford.

Fischer, A. 2003. Trapping up the rivers and trading across the sea-steps towards the Neolithisation of Denmark. In Larsson *et al.* (eds) 2003, 405–415.

Fischer, A. 2007. Coastal fishing in Stone Age Denmark – evidence from below and above present day sea level and from human bones. In N. Milner, O. E. Craig and G. N. Bailey (eds), *Shell Middens in Atlantic Europe*, 54–69, Oxbow Books, Oxford.

Fischer, A. Olsen. J. Richards, M. Heinemeier, J. Sveinbjörnsdóttir, A. E. and Bennike, P. 2007 Coast – inland mobility and diet in the Danish Mesolithic and Neolithic: evidence from stable isotope values of humans and dogs. *Journal of Archaeological Science* 34, 2125–50.

Flanagan, L. N. W. 1960. Department of Antiquities, Belfast Museum and Art Gallery. Archaeological acquisitions of Irish origin for the year 1959. *Ulster Journal of Archaeology* 15, 31–59.

Flanagan, L. N. W. 1968. Accumulations of Neolithic flint and stonework from near Raphoe, Co. Donegal. *Ulster Journal of Archaeology* 31, 9–15.

Flood, J. 1976. Man and ecology in the highlands of southwestern Australia. In N. Peterson (ed.), *Tribes and Boundaries in Australia*, 50–72. Australian Institute of Aboriginal Studies, Canberra.

Fojut, N. 2006. Pre-agricultural archaeological sites in Scotland: location, investigation, and preservation. In Rensink and Peeters (eds) 2006, 65–72.

Foster, J. W. 1997. Nature and Nation in the Nineteenth Century. In J. W. Foster (ed.), *Nature in Ireland: A Scientific and Cultural History*, 409–39. Lilliput, Dublin.

Fraser, F. C. and King, J. E. 1954. Faunal remains. In Clark 1954, 70–96.

Francis, E. 1987. The palynology of the Glencloy area. Unpublished PhD thesis, Queen's University Belfast.

Fredengren, C. 2002. *Crannógs*. Wordwell, Bray.

Fredengren, C. 2009. Lake platforms at Lough Kinale – memory reach and place: a discovery programme project in the Irish Midlands. In McCartan *et al.* (eds) 2009, 882–6.

Frere, J. 1800. Account of flint weapons discovered at Hoxne in Suffolk. *Archaeologia* 13, 204–205.

Fry, M. F. 2002. *Coiti. Logboats from Northern Ireland*. Northern Ireland Archaeological Monograph 4, Environment and Heritage Service, Belfast.

Fuglestvedt, I. 2003. Enculturating the landscape beyond Doggerland. In Larsson *et al.* (eds) 2003, 103–7.

Gamble, C. and Kruszynski, R. 2009. John Evans, Joseph Prestwich and the stone that shattered the time barrier. *Antiquity* 83(320), 461–74.

Garrow, D. and Sturt, F. 2011. Grey waters bright with Neolithic Argonauts? Maritime connections and the Mesolithic–Neolithic transition within the western seaway of Britain 5000–3000 BC. *Antiquity* 85(327), 59–72.

Gascoigne, J. 1994. *Joseph Banks and the English Enlightenment*. Cambridge University Press, Cambridge.

Gebauer, A. B. and Price T. D. 1990. The end of the Mesolithic in Eastern Denmark: A preliminary report on the Saltbaek Vig Project. In P. M. Vermeersch and P. Van Peer (eds), *Contributions to the Mesolithic in Europe: Papers Presented at the Fourth International Symposium "The Mesolithic in Europe", Leuven, 1990*, 259–80. Studia Praehistorica Belgica 5. Leuven University Press, Leuven.

Gehlen, B. 2010. A microlithic sequence from Freisack 4, Brandenburg and the Mesolithic in Germany. In P. Crombé, M. Van Strydonck,

J. Sergant, M. Boudinand and M. Bats (eds), *Chronology and Evolution within the Mesolithic of North West Europe Proceedings of an International Meeting, Brussels, May 30th–1st June 2007*, 363–94. Cambridge Scholars Publishing, Newcastle.

Ghilardi, B. and O'Connell, M. 2012. Early Holocene vegetation and climate dynamics with particular reference to the 8.2 event: pollen and macrofossil evidence from a small lake in Western Ireland. *Vegetation History and Archaeobotany* 21, 99–114.

Gibbons, M. and Gibbons, M. 2004. Dyeing in the Mesolithic. *Archaeology Ireland* 17(4), 28–31.

Glavin, T. 2003. *The Last Great Sea: A Voyage Through the Human and Natural History of the North Pacific Ocean*. Greystone Books, Vancouver.

Goddard, A. 1971. Studies of the vegetational changes associated with the initiation of blanket peat accumulation in northeast Ireland. Unpublished PhD thesis, Queen's University, Belfast.

Gooder, J. 2007. Excavation of a Mesolithic house at East Barns, East Lothian, Scotland: an interim report. In C. Waddington and K. Pedersen (eds), *Mesolithic Studies in the North Sea Basin and Beyond*, 49–59. Oxbow Books, Oxford.

Gowen, M. 1988. *Three Irish Gas Pipelines: New Archaeological Evidence in Munster*. Wordwell, Dublin.

Gowen, M., O'Néill, J. and Phillips, M. 2005. *The Lisheen Mines Archaeological Project 1996–1998*. Wordwell, Dublin.

Gould, S. J. 1988. *Time's Arrow, Time's Cycle: Myth and Metaphor in the Discovery of Geological Time*. Penguin, London.

Gould, S. J. 1993a. Fall in the house of Ussher. In S. J. Gould (ed.), *Eight Little Piggies: Reflections in Natural History*, 181–93. W. W. Norton and Company, New York & London.

Gould, S. J. 1993b. On rereading Edmund Halley. In S. J. Gould (ed.), *Eight Little Piggies: Reflections in Natural History*, 168–80. W. W. Norton and Company, New York and London.

Gray, W. 1867. The flint flake foundation of the pre-Adamite theory. *Fourth Annual Report of the Belfast Naturalists' Field Club*, 45–8.

Gray, W. 1879. The character and distribution of the rudely worked flints of the north of Ireland chiefly in Antrim and Down. *Journal of the Royal Historical and Archaeological Association of Ireland* 4(5), 109–43.

Gray, W. 1888. Rough flint celts of the County Antrim. *Journal of the Royal Historical and Archaeological Association of Ireland* 4(8), 505–6.

Gray Jones A. 2011, Dealing with the dead: manipulation of the body in mortuary practices of Mesolithic North West Europe, Phd Thesis presented at the University of Manchester.

Green, H. S. 1984. *Pontnewydd Cave. A Lower Palaeolithic Hominid Site in Wales*. National Museum of Wales, Cardiff.

Green, S. W. and Zvelebil, M. 1990. The Mesolithic colonisation and agricultural transition of south-east Ireland. *Proceedings of the Prehistoric Society* 56, 57–88.

Gregory, N. T. N. 1997. A comparative study of Irish and Scottish log boats. Unpublished PhD Thesis, University of Edinburgh.

Griffiths, D. R. and Woodman, P. C. 1987. Cretaceous chert sourcing in north-east Ireland: preliminary results. In G. de G. Sieveking and M. H. Newcomer (eds), *The Human Uses of Flint and Chert*, 249–52. Cambridge University Press, Cambridge.

Grogan, E. and Eogan, G. 1987. Lough Gur excavations by Seán P. Ó Ríordáin: five enclosed habitation sites of the Neolithic and Beaker period on the Knockadoon peninsula. *Proceedings of the Royal Irish Academy* 87C, 299–506.

Grove White, J. 1915–18, *Historical and Topographical Notes etc on Buttevant, Castletownroche, Doneraile, Mallow and Places in the Vicinity.*

Gurina, N. N. 1956. *Oleneostrovoski Mogilnik.* Materialy I Issledovaniya po Arkheologii SSSR 47, Nauka, Moscow.

Gwynn, A. M., Mitchell, G. F. and Stelfox, A. W. 1942. The explorations of some caves near Castletownroche, Co. Cork. *Proceedings of the Royal Irish Academy* 48B, 371–90.

Hall, M. 1994. *The Cruithin.* Island Pamphlets, Belfast

Hall, V. 2011. *The Making of Ireland's Landscape since the Ice Age.* Collins Press, Cork.

Hamilton, A. and Bannon, D. 1985. Pollen analysis. In Woodman 1985a, 77–9.

Hamilton, A., Dalzell, L. R., Lenehan, B. P. and McDonagh. J. 1985. A palynological investigation of kettle-hole sediments at Mount Sandel. In Woodman 1985a, 185–92.

Hamilton Dyer, S. Unpublished report on faunal remains from Port of Larne excavations, submitted to ADS.

Hammond, F. W. 1985. Chemical analysis of soils. In Woodman 1985a 84–98.

Hanley, K. 2013a. Catalogue of radiocarbon dates. In Hanley and Hurley (eds) 2013, 373–88.

Hanley, K. 2013b. The Mesolithic. In Hanley and Hurley (eds) 2013, 29–41.

Hanley, K. and Hurley, M. F. (eds). 2013. *Generations – The Archaeology from Five National Road Schemes in County Cork.* National Roads Authority, Dublin.

Hansen, K. M. and Pedersen, K. B. 2006. With or without bones – late Palaeolithic hunters in South Zealand. In K. M. Hansen and K. B. Pedersen (eds), *Across the Western Baltic*, 93–110. Sydsjaellands Museum, Vordingborg.

Harkness, R. 1871. The discovery of a kitchen midden at Ballycotton in County Cork. *Proceedings of the British Association for the Advancement of Science* 1870, 151–2.

Harte, W. 1866. On the occurrence of Kjökkenmöddings in the County of Donegal. *Journal of the Royal Geological Society of Ireland* 1, 154–8.

Hassé, L. 1885. A classification of flint flakes, found on the raised beach at Carnlough, Co. Antrim. *Journal of the Royal Society of Antiquaries of Ireland* 17, 153–8.

Hatting, T. 1968a. appendix 1: animal bones from the basal middens. In Liversage 1968, 172–4.

Hatting, T. 1968b. appendix 2: Revised bone lists from Larnian sites at Sutton and Rockmarshall. In Liversage 1968, 174–5.

Haughton, J. P. 1979. *The Atlas of Ireland.* Royal Irish Academy, Dublin.

Hawkes, A. 2014. The beginning and evolution of the *fulacht fia* tradition in Prehistoric Ireland. *Proceedings of the Royal Irish Academy* 114, 89–140

Helskog, K. 1988. *Helleristningene i Alta: Spor etter ritualer og dagligliv i Finnmarks forhistorie.* Alta Museum, Alta.

Helskog, K. 2012. Bears and meaning among Hunter-fisher-gatherers in northern Fennoscandinavia. *Cambridge Archaeological Journal* 22(2), 209–36.

Henriksen, B. B. 1976. *Svaerdborg I Excavations 1943–44: A Settlement of the Maglemose Culture.* Arkæologiske Studier III, Akademisk Forlag, Copenhagen

Herity, M. 1974. *Irish Passage Graves: Neolithic Tomb Builders in Ireland and Britain 2500 B.C.* Irish University Press, Dublin.

Hernek, R. 2003 A Mesolithic winter site with a sunken dwelling from the Swedish coast. In Larsson *et al.* (eds) 2003, 223–9.

Hernek, R. and Nordquist, B. 1995. *Världens Åldasta Tuggummi?* Riksantikvarieämbetet, Stockholm.

Herries Davis, G. L. 1995. *North from the Hook: 150 years of the Geological Survey of Ireland.* Geological Survey of Ireland, Dublin.

Hesjdal, A., Damm, C., Olsen, D. and Storli I. 1996 Arkeologi på Slettnes: Dokumentasjon av 11,000 års bosetning, Tromsø Museums Skrifter 26, Tromso.

Hickey, K. R. 2011. *Wolves in Ireland; a natural and cultural history,* Four Courts Press, Dublin.

Hill, G. 1978. *The MacDonnells of Antrim.* Glens of Antrim Historical Society, Ballycastle.

Hodges, H. W. M. 1953. Some observations on the Mesolithic Period in Ireland. *Ulster Journal of Archaeology* 16, 25–30.

Hodgers, D. 1973. A report on surface finds from Co. Louth. *County Louth Archaeological and Historical Journal* 18, 45–59.

Hodgers, D. 1994. The Salterstown Surface Collection Project. *Journal of the County Louth Archaeological and Historical Society* 23, 240–69.

Hosfield, R. T., Wenban-Smith, F. F. and Pope, M. I. (eds). 2009. *Great Prehistorians: 150 years of Palaeolithic Research, 1859–2009. Lithics* 30

Housley, R. A., Gamble, C. S., Street, M. and Pettitt, P. 1997. Radiocarbon evidence for the Lateglacial human recolonisation of northern Europe. *Proceedings of the Prehistoric Society* 63, 25–54.

Hufthammer, A. K. 1992. De Osteologiske undersøkelensene fra Kotedalen. In H. L. Hjelle, A. K. Hufthammer, P. E. Kaland, A. B. Olsen and E. L. Soltvedt (eds), *Kotedalen – en boplass gjennom 5000 år. Bind 2: Naturvitenskapelige Undersøkelser,* 9–64. Historisk museum, Universitetet i Bergen.

Hurl, D. P. and Murphy, E. M. 1996. Life and death in a County Antrim Tower House. *Archaeology Ireland* 10(2), 20–3.

Ikeya, K. 2006. Mobility and territoriality among hunting-farming trading societies: the case study of bear hunting in mountainous environments of north western Japan. In C. Grier, J. Kim and J. Uchmiya (eds), *Beyond Affluent Foragers: Rethinking Hunter-Gather Complexity,* 34–44. Oxbow Books, Oxford.

Isarin, R. F. B., Renssen, H. and Vandenberghe, J. 1998. The impact of the North Atlantic Ocean on the Younger Dryas climate in Northwestern and Central Europe. *Journal of Quaternary Science* 13(5), 447–53.

Ivens, R. and Simpson, D. D. A. 1988. Excavations at Lislear, Baronscourt, Co. Tyrone. *Ulster Journal of Archaeology* 51, 61–8.

Jackes, M. K. 2004. Osteological evidence for Mesolithic and Neolithic violence: problems of interpretation. In M. Roksandic (ed.), *Violent Interactions in the Mesolithic: evidence and meaning,* 23–40. British Archaeological Report S1237, Archaeopress, Oxford.

Jackson, J. W. 1909. On the diatomaceous deposits of the Lower Bann Valley, Counties Antrim and Derry and the prehistoric implements found therein. *Memoirs and Proceedings of the Manchester Literary and Philosophical Society* 53, 3–18.

Jacobi, R. M. 1976. Britain inside and outside Mesolithic Europe. *Proceedings of the Prehistoric Society* 42, 67–84.

Jacobi, R. M. 1978. Northern England in the eighth millennium BC: an essay. In P. Mellars (ed.), *The Early Post-Glacial Settlement of Northern Europe,* 295–332. Duckworth, London.

Jacobi, R. M. 1980. The Early Holocene settlement of Wales, in J. A. Taylor (ed.), *Culture and Environment in Prehistoric Wales,* 131–206. British Archaeological Report 76, BAR, Oxford.

Jacobi, R. M. 1990. Leafpoints and the British Early Upper Palaeolithic. In J. Kozłowski (ed.), *Les industries foliacées du Paléolithique Superieur Européen,* 271–289. ERAUL, l'Université de Liège.

Jacobi, R. and Higham, T. 2009. The Early Lateglacial re-colonisation of Britain: new radiocarbon evidence from Gough's Cave southwest England. *Quaternary Science Reviews* 28, 1895–1913.

Jacobi, R. M., Higham, T. G. F. and Bronk Ramsey, C. 2006. AMS radiocarbon dating of middle and upper Palaeolithic bone in the British Isles: improved reliability using ultrafiltration. *Journal of Quaternary Science, Special Issue: The Palaeolithic occupation of Europe: In Memory of John J. Wymer* 21(5), 557–74.

Jacobi, R. M, Higham, T. G. F., Haesaerts, P., Jadin, I. and Basell, L. S. 2009. Radiocarbon chronology for the Early Gravettian of Northern Europe: new ams determinations for Maisies-Canal, Belgium. *Antiquity* 84(323), 26–40.

Jacobi, R. M., Tallis, J. H., Mellars, P. A. 1976. The Southern Pennine Mesolithic and the archaeological record. *Journal of Archaeological Science* 3(4), 307–20.

Jenkins, I. 1992. *Archaeologists & Aesthetes.* British Museum, London.

Jensen, J. 2001. *Danmarks Oldtid, Stenalder, 13,000–2000 f. Kr.* Gyldendal, København.

Jensen, J. 2009. A sunken dwelling from the Ertebølle site, Nivå 10, eastern Denmark. In Larsson *et al.* (eds). 2009. *Mesolithic on the Move: Papers Presented at the Sixth International Conference on the Mesolithic in Europe, Stockholm 2000,* 465–72. Oxbow Books, Oxford.

Jessen, K. 1949. Studies in Late Quaternary deposits and flora-history of Ireland. *Proceedings of the Royal Irish Academy* 52B, 85–209.

Johnson, G. 1988. A Later Mesolithic assemblage from Bay Farm, Co. Antrim. Unpublished MA thesis, University College Cork.

Jonsson, L. 1995. Vertebrate fauna during the Mesolithic on the Swedish west coast. In Fischer (ed.) 1995, 147–160.

Jordan, R. 2006. Analogy. In Conneller, C. and Warren (eds) 2006, 83–100.

Juel Jensen, H. 1986. Unretouched blades in the Late Mesolithic of South Scandinavia. *Oxford Journal of Archaeology* 5, 19–33.

Juel Jensen, H. 1994. *Flint Tools and Plant Working: Hidden Traces of Stone Age Technology.* Aarhus University Press, Aarhus.

Kador, T. 2009. Prehistoric chain reactions- stories that help us understand the distant past. In Finlay *et al.* (eds) 2009, 31–41.

Kador, T. 2010. The last of the old: A homogeneous Later Mesolithic Ireland. In B. Finlayson and G. Warren (eds), *Landscapes in Transition,* 147–57. Council for British Research in the Levant, Oxford.

Karsten, P. and Knarrström, B. 2003. *The Tågerup Excavations.* National Heritage Board Sweden, Lund.

Keen, D. H., Hardaker, T. and Lang, O. A. T. 2006. A lower Palaeolithic industry from the cromerian (MIS 13) Baginton formation of Waverly Wood and Wood Farm Pits, Bubbenhall, Warickshire, UK. *Journal of Quaternary Science, Special Issue: The Palaeolithic Occupation of Europe: In Memory of John J. Wymer* 21(5), 457–71.

Kelly, J. G. 2010. Lithology of archaeological artefacts and lithic fragments collected by Gortatole OEC from Lower Lough Macnean, Florenscourt, Co. Fermanagh. Unpublished specialist report for Gabriel Burns, Gortatole OEC, Florenscourt, County Fermanagh.

Kelly, R. 2003. Colonisation of new land by hunter gatherers: expectations and implications based on ethnographic data. In M. Rockman and J. Steele (eds), *Colonization of Unfamiliar Landscapes: the archaeology of adaptations,* 44–58. Routledge, London.

Kelly, T. 2008. The origins of the avifauna of Ireland. In Davenport *et al.* (eds) 2008, 97–107.

Kennedy, K. U. and Vickers, G. J. A. 1993. The fish of Lough Neagh, Part B: Investigations on salmon (*Salmo salar* L.) and eels (*Anguilla anguilla*) in the Lower River Bann. In R. B. Wood and R. V. Smith (eds), *Lough Neagh, the Ecology of a Multipurpose Water Resource*, 397–416. Kluwer Academic, Dortrecht.

Kiely, J. 2003. A Neolithic house at Cloghers, Co. Kerry. In I. Armit, E. Murphy, E. Nelis and D. Simpson (eds), *Neolithic Settlement in Ireland and Western Britain*, 182–7. Oxbow Books, Oxford.

Kimball, M. J. 2000. *Human Ecology and Neolithic Transition in Eastern County Donegal, Ireland*. British Archaeological Report 300, Archaeopress, Oxford.

Kimball, M. J., Showers, M., McCartan, S. and Genna, B. J. 2009. $\delta^{18}O$ analysis of Littorina littorea shells from Ferriter's Cove, Dingle Peninsula: preliminary results and interpretations. In Finlay *et al.* (eds) 2009, 189–97.

Kirby, M. 1990. *Skelligside*. Lilliput, Dublin.

Knarrström, B. 2004. The introduction of culture. In M. Anderson, P. Kartsen, B. Knarrström and M. Svensson (eds), *Stone Age Scania. Significant Places Dug and Read by Contract Archaeology*, 22–70. Riksantikvarieämbetet arkeologiska undersökningar 52, Malmö, Stockholm.

Knight, C. 1845. *Old England: A Pictorial Museum of Regal, Ecclesiastical, Baronial, Municipal and Popular Antiquities*. Charles Knight & Co., Ludgate Street, London.

Knowles, W. J. 1885. Flint implements from the North East of Ireland, *Proceedings of the Royal Irish Academy* 2(2), 436–44.

Knowles, W. J. 1889. Report on the prehistoric remains from the sandhills of the coast of Ireland. *Proceedings of the Royal Irish Academy* 3(1), 173–87.

Knowles, W. J. 1901. The fourth report on the prehistoric remains from the sandhills of the coast of Ireland. *Proceedings of the Royal Irish Academy* 3(6), 331–89.

Knowles, W. J. 1912. Prehistoric stone implements from the River Bann and Lough Neagh. *Proceedings of the Royal Irish Academy* 30C, 195–222.

Knowles, W. J. 1914. The antiquity of man in Ireland, being an account of the older series of Irish flint implements. *Journal of the Royal Anthropological Institute* 44, 83–121.

Knudsen, S. A. 1980, *Livet på Bopladsen*, Munksgaard, København.

Kozłowski, S. K. 2009. Mapping the European Mesolithic. In McCartan *et al.* (eds) 2009, xx–xxvi.

Lagarde, J. L., Amorese, D., Font, M., Lavilla, E. and Dugué, O. 2003. Structural evolution of the English Channel. *Journal of Quaternary Science* 18(3–4), 201–13.

Lanting, J. and van der Plicht, J. 1996. Wathebben Floris V, skelet Swifterbant S2 en visottersengemeen. *Palaeohistoria* 37/38, 491–519.

Larsen, C. S. 2005. The finds: fish bones and shell. In Price and Gebauer 2005, 103–5.

Larsson, L., Kindgren, H., Knutsson, K., Loefler, D. and Akerlund, A. (eds). 2003. *Mesolithic on the Move: Papers Presented at the Sixth International Conference on the Mesolithic in Europe, Stockholm 2000*. Oxbow Books, Oxford.

Lawlor, H. C. 1928. *Ulster: its Archaeology and Antiquities*. R. Carswell and Sons, Belfast.

Legge, A. J. and Rowley-Conwy, P. A. 1988. *Star Carr Revisited: a Re-analysis of the Large Mammals*. Birkbeck College, London.

Leerssen, J. 1996. *Remembrance and Imagination*. Cork University Press, Cork.

Ledwich, E. 1804 . *Antiquities of Ireland*. John Jones, Dublin (2nd edn).

Leonard, H. 1868. Kitchen midden on Omey Island, Co. Galway. *Geological Magazine* 5, 266–8.

Lepiskaar, J. 1978. Bone remains from the Mesolithic settlements Ageröd 1:B and Ageröd 1:D. In L. Larsson, Ageröd 1:B – Ageröd 1:D, A study of Early Atlantic settlement in Scania. *Acta Archaeologica Lundensia* 12, 234–44.

Leroi-Gourhan, A. and Brezillon, M. 1966. L'Habitation magdalénienne No. 1 de Pincevent près Montereau (Seine-et-Marne). *Gallia Préhistoire* 9, 263–385.

Leroi-Gourhan, A. and Brezillon, M. 1972. *Fouilles de Pincevent*. CNRS, Paris.

Lhwyd, E. 1710–12. Several observations relating to the Antiquities and Natural History of Ireland, made by Mr. Edw. Lhwyd, in his travels thro' that Kingdom. In a letter to Dr. Trancred Robinson, Fellow of the College of Physicians and Royal Society. *Philosophical Transactions of the Royal Society* 27, 503–6.

Lillie, M. 2004. Fighting for your life? Violence at the Late glacial to Holocene transition in Ukraine. In M. Roksandic (ed.), *Violent Interactions in the Mesolithic: Evidence and Meaning*, 89–96. British Archaeological Report S1237, Archaeopress, Oxford.

Little, A. 2009. The Island and the Hill: extracting scales of sociability from a Mesolithic chert quarry. In Finlay *et al.* (eds) 2009, 133–42.

Little, A. 2010. Reconstructing memory and meaning: Mesolithic identities and landscapes in the North Midlands. Unpublished PhD thesis, University College Dublin.

Little, A. 2014. Clonava Island revisited: a story of c ooking, plants and re-occupation during the Irish Late Mesolithic, *Proceedings of the Royal Irish Academy* 114, 35–56.

Liversage, G. D. 1957. An object of giant deer antler. *Journal of the Royal Society of Antiquaries of Ireland* 55, 159.

Liversage, G. D. 1968. Excavations at Dalkey Island, Co. Dublin, 1956–1959. *Proceedings of the Royal Irish Academy* 66C, 52–233.

Livingstone, D. N. 1997. Darwin in Belfast: the evolution debate. In J. W. Foster (ed.), *Nature in Ireland: A Scientific and Cultural History*, 387–408. Lilliput, Dublin.

Livingstone, D. N. 2008. *Adams Ancestors: Race Religion and the Politics of Human Origins*. Johns Hopkins University Press, Baltimore.

Loeffler, D. 2003. Some observations concerning the relationship between distribution patterns, floor size and social organisation. In Larsson *et al.* (eds) 2003, 239–48.

Lothrop, S. K. 1928 *The Indians of Tierra del Fuego*, Museum of the American Indian, Heye Foundation, New York.

Lourandos, H. 1997. *Continent of Hunter-Gatherers: New Perspectives in Australian Prehistory*. Cambridge University Press, Cambridge.

Louwe Kooijmans, L. P. (ed.). 2001. *Hardinxveld-Giessendam Polderweg: Een mesolithisch jachtkamp in het rivierengebied (5500–5000 v. Chr.)*. Rapportage Archaelogische Monumentenzorg 83, Utrecht.

Louwe Kooijmans, L. P. 2004. Hardinxveld sites in the Rhine/Meuse Delta, the Netherlands, 5500–4500 cal BC. In McCartan *et al.* (eds) 2004, 608–24.

Lowenthal, D. 1985. *The Past is a Foreign Country*. Cambridge University Press, Cambridge.

Lozoviski, V. M. 1996. *Zamostje 2*. Editions du Cedrac, Treignes.

Lyell, C. 1830–33. *Principles of Geology, Being an Attempt to Explain the Former Changes in the Earth's Surface by Reference to Causes Now in Operation*. John Murray, London.

Lynch, M. 2002. A study of a possible Mesolithic landscape in County Clare. Unpublished MA thesis, University College Cork.

Lyons, S. 2009. Appendix 13: assessment and identification of the plant remains from six woven baskets. In Mossop and Mossop 2009.

Macalister, R. A. S. 1921. *A Text-Book of European Archaeology Vol. 1*. Cambridge University Press, Cambridge.

Macalister, R. A. S. 1928. *The Archaeology of Ireland*. Methuen, London.

Macalister, R. A. S. 1935. *Ancient Ireland: A Study in the Lessons of Archaeology and History*. Methuen, London.

MacGregor, A. 1994. The life, character and career of Sir Hans Sloane. In A. MacGregor (ed.), *Sir Hans Sloane: Collector, Scientist, Antiquary, Founding Father of the British Museum*, 11–44. British Library, London.

MacLean, R. 1993. Eat your greens: an examination of the potential diet available in Ireland during the Mesolithic. *Ulster Journal of Archaeology* 56, 1–8.

McAllister, V. 2008. Lithic material from Ballynease-Macpeake, County Londonderry. *Ulster Journal of Archaeology* 67, 1–13.

McCabe, A. M. 1987. Quaternary deposits and glacial stratigraphy in Ireland. *Quaternary Science Reviews* 6, 259–299.

McCabe, A. M., Coope, G. R., Gennard, D. E. and Doughty, P. 1987. Freshwater organic deposits and stratified sediments between Early and Late Midlandian (Devensian) till sheets at Aghnadarragh, Co. Antrim, Northern Ireland, *Journal of Quaternary Science* 2, 11–33.

McCartan, S. B. 2003. Mesolithic hunter-gatherers in the Isle of Man: adaptations to an island environment. In Larsson *et al.* (eds) 2003, *Mesolithic on the Move. Papers Presented at the Sixth International Conference on the Mesolithic in Europe, Stockholm 2000*, 331–9.

McCartan, S., Schulting, R., Warren, G. and Woodman, P. (eds). 2009. *Mesolithic Horizons: Papers presented at the Seventh international conference on the Mesolithic in Europe, Belfast 2005*. Oxbow Books, Oxford.

McCarthy, A. 1988. An analysis of the marine molluscan remains from Ferriter's Cove, Dingle, Co. Kerry. Unpublished MA thesis, University College Cork.

McCarthy, M. 2008. The faunal remains from Site A. In Doody, M. *The Ballyhoura Hills Project*, 427–42. Discovery Programme Monograph. Wordwell, Dublin.

McCarthy, M., Finlay, N. and McClean, O. 1999. The faunal remains. In Woodman *et al.* 1999, 85–92. Wordwell, Dublin.

McComb, A. M. G. 2009. The ecology of hazel (*Corylus avellana*) nuts in the Irish Mesolithic. In McCartan *et al.* (eds) 2009, 224–31.

McCormick, F. 2004. Hunting Pigs in the Late Mesolithic. In H. Roche, E. Grogan, J. Bradley, J. Coles and B. Raftery (eds), *From Megaliths to Metals, Essays in Honour of George Eogan*, 1–5. Oxbow Books, Oxford.

McDermott, C. nd. Wooden Structure on the Dargle at Killarney Townland, Bray, Co. Dublin. Unpublished Report, Irish Archaeological Wetland Unit.

McDermott, F., Mattey, D. P. and Hawkesworth, C. J. 2005. Corrections to Centennial-scale Holocene climate variability revealed by a high resolution speleotherm $\delta^{18}O$ record from SW Ireland. *Science* 309, 1816.

McDevitt, A. D., Vega, R., Rambau, R. V., Yannic, G., Herman, J. S., Hayden, T. J. and Searle, J. B. 2011. Colonisation of Ireland: revisiting "the pygmy shrew syndrome" using mitochrondrial, Y chromosomal and microsatellite markers. *Heredity* 107, 548–57.

McErlean, T. 2003a. Shellfish and shell middens in Strangford Lough. In T. McErlean, R. McConkey and W. Forsythe (eds), *The Strangford Lough: An Archaeological survey of the maritime cultural Landscape*, 186–199. Northern Ireland Archaeological Monographs 6, The Blackstaff Press, Belfast.

McErlean, T. 2003b. Fish and fishing in Strangford Lough. In McErlean *et al.* (eds) 2003, 132–43.

McErlean, T. and O'Sullivan, A. 2003. Foreshore tidal fish traps. In McErlean *et al.* (eds) 2003, 144–85.

McErlean, T., McConkey, R. and Forsythe, W. (eds). 2003. *The Strangford Lough: An Archaeological Survey of the Maritime Cultural Landscape*. Northern Ireland Archaeological Monograph 6, Blackstaff Press, Belfast.

McGrail, S. 2001. *Boats of the World: From the Stone Age to Medieval Times*, Oxford University Press Oxford.

McGuiness, D. 2010. Druid's Altars, Carrowmore and the birth of Irish Archaeology. *The Journal of Irish Archaeology* 19, 29–31.

McLaughlin, R. 2005. Dental micro wear. In Schulting 2005, 213–23.

McQuade, M. and O'Donnell, L. 2009. The excavation of Late Mesolithic fish trap remains from the Liffey Estuary, Dublin, Ireland. In McCartan *et al.* (eds) 2009, 889–94.

Madsen, T. 1986. Where did all the hunters go? An assessment of an epoch-making episode in Danish prehistory. *Journal of Danish Archaeology* 5, 229–39.

Magnell, O. 2003. Butchering of wild boar (*Sus scrofa*) in the Mesolithic. In Larsson *et al.* (eds) 2003, 670–9.

Mahr, A. 1937. New aspects and problems in Irish prehistory. *Proceedings of the Prehistoric Society* 3, 261–437.

Mallory, J. P. 2013. *The Origins of the Irish*. Thames and Hudson, London.

Mallory, J. P. and Hartwell, B. N. 1997. Down in Prehistory. In L. Proudfoot (ed.), *Down: History and Society*, 1–32. Geography Publications, Dublin.

Mandal, S. 1999a. Polished stone axe catalogue. In Woodman *et al.* 1999, 193–4.

Mandal, S. 1999b. Petrological identification of selected artefacts. In Woodman *et al.* 1999, 201–2.

Mann, C. C. 2005. *1491: New Revelations of the Americas before Columbus*. Vintage, New York.

Mannino, M. A. and Thomas, K. D. 2007. Determining the season of collection of intertidal gastropods from $\delta^{18}O$ analyses of shell carbonates. In N. Milner, O. E. Craig and G. N. Bailey (eds), *Shell Middens in Atlantic Europe*, 110–22. Oxbow Books, Oxford.

Martin, S. W. J. 2011. Final Report on 2009 Archaeological Investigations of Inishee Island, Lough MacNean Lower Co. Fermanagh. Unpublished report submitted to the Northern Ireland Environment Agency, Belfast.

Martinic, M. 1992. *Historia de la Region Magellanica*. Volumen I. Universidad de Magellanes, Punta Arenas.

Mason, S. L. R., Hather, J. G. and Hillman, G. C. 2002. The archaeobotany of European hunter-gatherers: some preliminary investigations. In S. L. R. Mason and J. G. Hather (eds), *Hunter-gatherer Archaeobotany: Perspectives from the Northern Temperate Zone*, 188–96. Institute of Archaeology, University College London.

Mattiangelli, V., McEvoy, B. and Bradley, D. G. 2008. In Davenport *et al.* (eds), 2008, 126–33.

May, A. Mcl. 1939. Some bone points from the River Bann. *Journal of the Royal Society of Antiquaries of Ireland* 69(3), 152–61.

May, A. Mcl. 1943. Portbraddan Cave, County Antrim. *Ulster Journal of Archaeology* 6, 39–60.

Mears, R. and Hillman, G. C. 2007. *Wild Food*. BBC Publications, Hodder & Stoughton, London.

Meighan, B. 1982. *From Shell Bed to Shell Midden*. Institute of Aboriginal Studies, Canberra.

Meiklejohn, C. M. and Babb, J. 2011. Long bone length, stature and time in the European Late Pleistocene and Early Holocene. In R. Pinhasi and J. T. Stock (eds), *Human Bioarchaeology of the Transition to Agriculture*, 153–76. Wiley-Blackwell, Chichester.

Meiklejohn, C. M. and Woodman, P. C. 2012. Radiocarbon dating of Mesolithic human remains in Ireland. *Mesolithic Miscellany* 22(1), 22–41.

Meiklejohn, C. and Zvelebil, M. 1991. Health status of European populations at the transition to agriculture and the implications for the adoption of farming. In H. Bush and M. Zvelebil (eds), *Health in Past Societies. Biocultural Interpretations of Human Skeletal Remains in Archaeological Contexts*, 129–43. British Archaeological Report S567, Archaeopress, Oxford.

Mellars, P. A. 1974. The Palaeolithic and the Mesolithic. In C. Renfrew (ed.), *British Prehistory: a New Outline*, 41–99. Duckworth, London.

Mellars. P. 1976. Fire ecology, animal populations and man: a study of some ecological relationships in prehistory. *Proceedings of the Prehistoric Society*, 42 15–45.

Mellars, P. A. 1978. Excavation and economic analysis of Mesolithic shell middens on the Island of Oronsay (Inner Hebrides). In P. Mellars (ed.), *The Early Post-Glacial Settlement of Northern Europe*, 371–96. Duckworth, London.

Mellars, P. A. 1985. The ecological basis of social complexity in the Upper Palaeolithic of southwestern France. In Price and Brown (eds) 1985, 271–98.

Mendyk, S. A. E. 1989. *Speculum Britanniae: Regional Study, Antiquarianism and Science in Britain until 1700*. University of Toronto Press, Toronto.

Mercer, J. 1971. A regression-time stone workers camp 33 ft O. D. Lussa River, Isle of Jura. *Proceedings of the Society of Antiquaries of Scotland* 103, 1–32.

Mercer, J. 1974. Glenbatrick Waterhole, a microlithic site on the Isle of Jura. *Proceedings of the Society of Antiquaries of Scotland* 105, 9–32.

Mercer, J. 1980. Lussa Wood I: the late glacial and early post-glacial occupation of Jura. *Proceedings of the Society of Antiquaries of Scotland* 110, 1–31.

Mighall, T. M., Timpanny, S., Blackford, J. J., Innes, J. B., O'Brien, C. E., O'Brien, W. and Harrison, S. 2008. Vegetation change during the Mesolithic and Neolithic on the Mizzen Peninsula, Co. Cork, South West Ireland. *Vegetation History and Archaeobotany* 17, 617–28.

Milner, N. J. 2002. Oysters, cockles and kitchen middens: Changing practices at the Mesolithic/Neolithic transition. In P. Miracle and N. J. Milner (eds), *Consuming Passions*, 89–96. MacDonald Institute Monograph, Cambridge.

Milner, N. 2006. Subsistence. In Conneller and Warren (eds) 2006, 61–82.

Milner, N. 2010. Subsistence at 4000–3700 cal BC. In B. Finlayson and G. Warren (eds), *Landscapes in Transition*, 46–54. Council for British Research in the Levant, Oxford.

Milner, N. J. and Woodman, P. C. 2001. Mesolithic middens. *Archaeology Ireland* 15(3), 32–5.

Milner, N. J. and Woodman, P. C. 2005. Looking into the Canon's Mouth. In N. J. Milner and P. C. Woodman (eds), *Mesolithic Studies at the beginning of the 21st Century*, 1–13. Oxbow Books, Oxford.

Milner, N. J. and Woodman, P. C. 2007. Deconstructing the myths of Irish shell middens. In N. Milner, O. E. Craig and G. N. Bailey (eds), *Shell Middens in Atlantic Europe*, 101–10. Oxbow Books, Oxford.

Milner, N., Lane, P. J., Taylor B., Conneller, C. and Schadla-Hall, T. 2012. Star Carr in a Post Glacial Lakescape: 60 years of Research, *Journal of Wetland Archaeology* 11, 1–19

Mitchel, N. C. 1965. The Lower Bann fisheries. *Ulster Folk Life* 11, 1–32.

Mitchell, F. J. G. 2009. The Holocene. In C. H. Holland and I. S. Sanders (eds), *The Geology of Ireland*, 397–404. Dunedin Press, Edinburgh (2nd edn).

Mitchell, G. F. 1941. The reindeer in Ireland. *Proceedings of the Royal Irish Academy* 46B, 183–8.

Mitchell, G. F. 1947. An early kitchen midden in Co. Louth. *County Louth Archaeological Journal* 11, 169–74.

Mitchell, G. F. 1949a. Further early kitchen middens in Co. Louth. *Journal of the County Louth Archaeological and Historical Society* 12, 14–20.

Mitchell, G. F. 1949b. The Larnian Culture: a review. *Journal of the Royal Society of Antiquaries of Ireland* 79, 170–82.

Mitchell, G. F. 1955. The Mesolithic site a Toome Bay, Co. Derry. *Ulster Journal of Archaeology* 18, 1–16.

Mitchell, G. F. 1956a. Post-Boreal pollen diagrams from Irish raised bogs. *Proceedings of the Royal Irish Academy* 57B, 185–251.

Mitchell, G. F. 1956b. An early kitchen midden at Sutton, Co. Dublin. *Journal of the Royal Society of Antiquaries of Ireland* 86, 1–26.

Mitchell, G. F. 1971. The Larnian Culture: a minimal view. *Proceedings of the Prehistoric Society* 37(2), 274–83.

Mitchell, G. F. 1972a. Further excavations of the early kitchen-midden at Sutton, Co. Dublin. *Journal of the Royal Society of Antiquaries of Ireland* 102, 151–73.

Mitchell, G. F. 1972b. Some ultimate Larnian sites in Lake Derravarragh, Co. Westmeath. *Journal of the Royal Society of Antiquaries* 102, 160–73.

Mitchell, G. F. 1986. *Reading the Irish Landscape*. Country House Ireland, Dublin.

Mitchell, G. F. 1989. *Man and Environment in Valentia Island*. Royal Irish Academy, Dublin.

Mitchell, G. F. and Ryan, M. 1997. *Reading the Irish Landscape*, Town House, Dublin.

Mitchell, G. F. and Sieveking, G. de G. 1972. A flint flake, probably of Palaeolithic age from Mell Townland, near Drogheda, Co Louth. *Journal of the Royal Society of Antiquaries of Ireland* 102(2), 174–7.

Mithen, S. 2000. *Hunter-Gatherer Landscape Archaeology: The Southern Hebrides Project 1988–98*. MacDonald Institute Monograph, Cambridge.

Mithen, S., Finlay, N., Carruthers, W., Carter, S. and Ashmore P. 2001. Plant use in the Mesolithic: evidence from Staosnaig, Isle of Colonsay, Scotland, *Journal of Archaeological Science* 28, 223–34.

Molyneux, T. 1697. A discourse concerning the large horns frequently found underground in Ireland, concluding from them that the Great American Deer, call'd the Moose, formerly found in Ireland. *Philosophical Transactions of the Royal Society of London* 19, 489–512.

Molyneux, T. 1701. An essay concerning giants. *Philosophical Transactions of the Royal Society* 22, 487–508.

Molyneux, T. 1714. Remarks upon the aforesaid letter and teeth. *Philosophical Transactions of the Royal Society* 29, 370–84.

Molyneux, T. 1725. A discourse concerning the Danish mounts, forts and towers of Ireland; never before published. In Boate (ed.) 1725, 189–213.

Moore, D. G. 1999. Analysis of the Lithic assemblages from early prehistoric sites along the south Antrim Coast. Unpublished M.Phil thesis, Queen's University Belfast.

Moore, J. 1867. On the antiquity of Man. *Proceedings of the Royal Geological Society of Ireland* 1, 16–29.

Morant, G. 1867. Account of the "finds" at Ballyhoe Lough. *Journal of the Kilkenny Archaeological Society* 6, 8–10.

Moriarty, C. 1997. The early naturalists. In J. W. Foster (ed.), *Nature in Ireland: A Scientific and Cultural History*, 71–90. Lilliput, Dublin.

Mortillet, G. 1867. Promenades Prehistoriques a l'exposition universelle. *Matériaux pour l'histoire positive et philosophique de l'Homme* 5–6, 181–368.

Moss, M. L. 2013. Beyond subsistence: The social and symbolic meanings of shellfish in North Western Coastal Societies. In G. N. Bailey, K. Hardy and A. Camara (eds), *Shell Energy*, 7–20. Oxbow Books, Oxford.

Moss, M. and Erlandson, J. 2009. Life on the edge: Early maritime cultures of the Pacific coast of North America. *Quaternary Science Reviews* 28(23–24), 2539–41.

Mossop, M. 2009. Lake developments in County Meath, Ireland: a Late Mesolithic fishing platform and possible moorings at Clowanstown 1. In McCartan *et al.* (eds) 2009, 889–94.

Mossop, M. and Mossop, E. 2009. *M3 Clonee–North of Kells, Contract 2 Dunshaulin–Navan. Report on the Archaeological Excavation at Clowanstown 1, Co, Meath.* www.M3mortorway.iw/archaeology/section2/clowanstown1/file,16720,en.pdf

Movius, H. L. 1935. Kilgreaney Cave, Co, Waterford. *Journal of the Royal Society of Antiquaries of Ireland* 65, 254–96.

Movius, H. L. 1936. A Neolithic site on the River Bann. *Proceedings of the Royal Irish Academy* 43C, 17–40.

Movius, H. L. 1940a. An early post-glacial archaeological site at Cushendun, Co. Antrim. *Proceedings of the Royal Irish Academy* 46C, 1–48.

Movius, H. L. 1940b. Report on a Stone Age excavation at Rough Island, Strangford Lough, Co. Down. *Journal of the Royal Society of Antiquaries of Ireland* 70, 111–42.

Movius, H. L. 1942. *The Irish Stone Age: Its Chronology, Development and Relationships.* Cambridge University Press, Cambridge.

Movius, H. L. 1953a. Curran Point, Larne, Co. Antrim, the type site of the Irish Mesolithic. *Proceedings of the Royal Irish Academy* 56C, 1–95.

Movius, H. L. 1953b. An historical account of the investigations at Larne. *Ulster Journal of Archaeology* 16, 7–23.

Mulvaney, D. J. 1976. The chain of connection; the Material evidence. In N. Peterson (ed.), *Tribes and Boundaries in Australia*, 72–94. Australian Institute of Aboriginal Studies, Canberra.

Mulvaney, W. T. 1852. Collection of antiquities presented to the Royal Irish Academy on behalf of the Commissioners of Public Works Ireland. *Proceedings of the Royal Irish Academy* 5, xxxi–lxv.

Murphy, E. M. 1996. Possible gender labour divisions at the Mesolithic site of Mount Sandel, County Londonderry, Northern Ireland. *Kvinner I Arkeologi in Norway* 21, 103–24.

Murray, E. 2011. A late Mesolithic shell midden at Kiltierney near Greyabbey, County Down. *Journal of Irish Archaeology* 20, 1–18.

Nawaz, R. 1977. Identification of rock types at Newferry 3 appendix 2. In Woodman 1977a, 197–8. *Proceedings of the Prehistoric Society* 43, 155–99.

Naylor, D. and Shannon, P. M. 2009. Geology of offshore Ireland, In C. H. Holland and I. A. Sanders (eds), *The Geology of Ireland*, 405–60. Dunedin Press, Edinburgh

Nelson, R. K. 1973. *Hunters of the Northern Forest.* University of Chicago Press, Chicago.

Nevile, F. 1714. A letter of Mr Francis Nevile to the Right Reverend St George Lord Bishop of Clogher R. S. S., Ireland, Giving an account of some large teeth lately dugg up in the North of Ireland and by his lordship communicated to the Royal Society. *Philosophical Transaction of the Royal Society of London* 29, 367–70.

Nevill, W. E. 1958. The Carboniferous knoll reefs of East Central Ireland. *Proceeding of the Royal Irish Academy* 59 (B) 285–302.

Newell, R. R., Kielman, D., Constandse-Westermann, T., van Gijn, A. and van der Sanden, W. A. B. 1990. *An Enquiry into the Ethnic Resolutions of Mesolithic Regional Groups: the Study of their Decorative Ornaments in Time and Space.* Brill, Leiden.

Newman, J. H. 1873. *The Idea of a University: Defined and Illustrated.* University of Notre Dame Press (republished 1982).

Nielsen, E. K. and Brinch-Petersen, E. 1993. Burials, people and dogs. In S. Hvass and B. Storgaard (eds), *Digging into the Past: 25 Years of Archaeology in Denmark*, 76–80. Royal Society of Northern Antiquities & Jutland Archaeological Society, Aarhus.

Nolan, R. W. 1986. Cnoc Coig: The spatial analysis of a Late Mesolithic shell midden in Western Scotland. Unpublished PhD thesis , University of Sheffield.

O'Brien, W. 2012. *Iverni: A Prehistory of Cork.* Collins Press, Cork.

Ó Cofaigh, C., Telfer, M. W., Bailey, R. M. and Evans, D. J. A. 2010. Late Pleistocene chronostratigraphy and ice sheet limits, southern Ireland, *Quaternary Science Reviews* 30, 1–20.

O'Connell, A. 2009. Directors first findings from Lismullin 1. In M. B. Deevy and D. Murphy (eds), *Places along the Way: First Findings along the M3*, 21–43. NRA Scheme Monograph 5, National Roads Authority, Dublin.

O'Connell M. 1980. Pollen analysis of a fen peat from a mesolithic site at Lough Boora, *Royal Dublin Society. Journal of Life Sciences* 2, 45–9.

O'Connell, T. 2015. NRA Carlow Bypass. In Teresa Bolger, Colm Moloney and Damian Shiels, *A Journey Along the Carlow Corridor. The archaeology of the M9 Carlow Bypass.* NRA Scheme Monograph 16. National Roads Authority, Dublin.

O'Connor, A. 2007. *Finding Time for the Old Stone Age: A History of Palaeolithic Archaeology and Quaternary Geology in Britain, 1860–1960.* Oxford University Press, Oxford.

Ó Crohan, T. 1951. *The Islandman.* Clarendon Press, Oxford.

O'Donnell, L. 2009. Appendix: wood report. In Mossop and Mossop 2009.

O'Donoghue, J. 2011. Archaeological Excavations Report E2410 – Gortore 1b, Co. Cork Mesolithic, Neolithic and Early Bronze Age activity on the banks of the River Funshion. *Issue 10: Eachtra Journal* (http://eachtra.ie/index.php/journal/issues/10/).

O'Donohoe, R. E. and Lovis, W. A. 2006. Regional sampling and site evaluation strategies for predicting Mesolithic settlement in the Yorkshire Dales. In Rensink and Peeters (eds) 2006, 13–25.

Ó Drisceoil, C. and Jennings, J. 2006. The Dungarvan Cave Project: First Interim Report. *Journal of the Waterford Archaeological and Historical Society* 62, 1–19.

O'Flaherty, R. 1684. *A Cartographic Description of West or H – Ar Connaught.* (ed. J. Hardiman 1846). Irish Archaeological Society, Dublin.

Ó Floinn, R. 1995. Recent research into Irish bog bodies. In R. C. Turner and R. G. Scaife (eds), *Bog Bodies: New Discoveries and New Perspectives*, 137–45. British Museum Press, London.

Ó Floinn R. 2012. Annagh Cave. In Cahill and Sikora (eds) 2012, 17–47.

O'Halloran, C. 2004. *Golden Ages and Barbarous Nations: Antiquarian Debate and Cultural Politics in Ireland, 1750–1800.* Cork University Press, Cork.

O'Kelly, M. J. 1952. Three promontory forts in Co. Cork. *Proceedings of the Royal Irish Academy* 55C, 25–59.

O'Kelly, M. J. 1982. Two ringforts at Garryduff. *Proceedings of the Royal Irish Academy* 63C, 17–125.

O'Laverty, J. 1857. Relative antiquity of stone and bronze weapons. *Ulster Journal of Archaeology* 1(5), 122–7.

O'Laverty, J. 1878. *A History of the Diocese of Down and Connor Vol. I.* James Duffy and Sons, Dublin.

O'Laverty, J. 1884. *A History of the Diocese of Down and Connor Vol. III.* James Duffy and Sons, Dublin.

Olsen, A. B. and Alsaker, S. 1984. Greenstone and diabase utilization in the Stone Age of western Norway: technological and sociocultural aspects of axe and adze production and distribution. *Norwegian Archaeological Review* 17(2), 71–103.

Olsen, B. 1994. *Bosetning og samfunn i Finnmarks forhistorie.* Universitetforlaget, Oslo.

O'Neill, T. 2013. Rath-healy 3: Temporary settlement. In Hanley and Hurley (eds) 2013, 39–40.

Oppenheimer, S. 2006. *The Origins of the British: The New Prehistory of Britain and Ireland from Ice Age Hunter Gatherers to Vikings as Revealed by DNA Analysis.* Robinson, London.

Ó Ríordáin, S. P. 1948. Earthen barrows at Rathjordan, Co. Limerick. *Journal of the Cork Historical and Archaeological Society* 53, 19–32.

Ó Ríordáin, S. P. 1954. Lough Gur excavations: Neolithic and Bronze Age houses on Knockadoon. *Proceedings of the Royal Irish Academy* 53C, 297–459.

Ó Ríordáin, S. P. 1979. *Antiquities of the Irish Countryside.* Methuen, London (5th edn revised by R. De Valera).

O'Shea, J. and Zvelebil, M. 1984. Oleneostrovski mogilnik: reconstructing the social and economic organisation of Prehistoric Foragers in Northern Russia. *Journal of Anthropological Archaeology* 3, 1–40.

O'Sullivan, A. 2001. *Foragers, Farmers and Fishers in a Coastal Landscape: an Intertidal Archaeological Survey of the Shannon Estuary.* Discovery Programme Monograph 5, Dublin.

O'Sullivan, A. 2002. Living with the dead amongst hunter gatherers. *Archaeology Ireland* 16(2), 10–12.

O'Sullivan, A., Forsythe, W. and McErlean, T. 2002. The submerged landscape. In McErlean *et al.* (eds) 2002, 127–31.

O'Sullivan, D. C. 2009. *The Natural History of Ireland by Philip O'Sullivan Beare.* Cork University Press, Cork.

Oswalt, W. H. 1975. *An Anthropological analysis of food gathering technology.* John Wiley and Sons, New York.

Parks, R. nd. Unpubished preliminary report on the faunal remains from the excavations at Baylet Co. Donegal.

Parslow, C. R. 1995. *Rediscovering Antiquity: Karl Weber and the Excavations of Herculaneum, Pompeii and Stabiae.* Cambridge University Press, Cambridge.

Patterson, W. H. 1892. On a newly discovered site for worked flints in the County of Down. *Journal of the Royal Society of Antiquaries of Ireland* 22, 154–5.

Patton, M. 1996. *Islands in Time: Island Sociogeography and Mediterranean Prehistory.* Routledge, London.

Pedersen, L. and Fischer, A. 1997. Stone age fishers on the Halsskov fjord. In L. Pedersen, A. Fischer and B. Aaby (eds), *The Danish Storebælt Since the Ice Age*, 109–208. A/S, Storebælt Fixed Link, Copenhagen.

Pellegatti, P. 2009. Hunter gatherers of the Istrian peninsula: the value of lithic raw material analysis to study small scale colonisation processes. In McCartan *et al.* (eds) 2009, 45–52.

Péquart, M., Péquart, St-J. Boule, M. and Vallois, H. 1937. Téviec: station necropole Mésolithique du Morbihan. *Archives de L'institut de Paléontologie Humaine* 18.

Petersen, V. P. 1984. Chronological and regional variation in the Late Mesolithic of Denmark. *Journal of Danish Archaeology* 3, 7–18.

Peterson, N. 1976. The natural and cultural areas of Aboriginal Australia: a preliminary analysis of population groupings with adaptive significance. In N. Peterson (ed.), *Tribes and Boundaries in Australia*, 50–71. Australian Institute of Aboriginal Studies, Canberra.

Pettitt, P. B. 2007. Cultural context and form of some of the Creswellian images: an interpretative model. In P. B. Pettitt, P. Bahn and S. Ripoll (eds), *Creswell Palaeolithic Cave Art in European Context.* Oxford University Press, Oxford.

Pettitt, P. B. 2008. The British Upper Palaeolithic. In J. Pollard (ed.), *Prehistoric Britain*, 18–57. Blackwell, Oxford.

Pettitt, P. and White, M. 2012. *The British Palaeolithic: Human Societies at the Edge of the Pleistocene World.* Routledge, London.

Piana, E. L. and Orquera L. A. 2002. The canoe people of the South: archaeology of the Magallanes Region of Tierra del Fuego. In C. Odone and P. Mason (eds), *Traditional Cultures: 12 Perspectives on Selknam, Yaghan and Kawesqar*, 165–85. Taller Experimental Cuerpos Pintados, Santiago.

Piana, E. L. and Orquero, L. A. 2010. Shell midden formation at the Beagle Channel (Tierra del Fuego, Argentina). In D. Calado, M. Baldia and M. Boulanger (eds), *Monumental Questions: Prehistoric Megaliths, Mounds and Enclosures*, 263–271. British Archaeological Report S2122, Archaeopress, Oxford.

Piggott, S. 1954. *The Neolithic Cultures of the British Isles.* Cambridge University Press, Cambridge.

Pilcher, J. R. 1969 Archaeology, palaeoecology and 14C dating of the Beaghmore stone circles site. *Ulster Journal of Archaeology* 32, 73–93.

Pilcher, J. R. and Smith, A. G. 1979. Palaeoecological investigations at Ballynagilly, a Neolithic and Bronze Age settlement in County Tyrone, Northern Ireland, *Philosophical Transactions of the Royal Society of London* (B) 286, 345–69.

Pollock, H. N. 2005. *Uncertain Science ... Uncertain World.* Cambridge University Press, Cambridge.

Power, C. 1999. The human remains. In Woodman *et al.* 1999, 102–3.

Praeger, R. L. 1890. Report of a Committee of Investigation on the gravels and the associated beds of the Curran, at Larne, Co. Antrim. *Annual Report and Proceedings of the Belfast Naturalists' Field Club* 2, 198–210.

Praeger, R. L. 1892. Report on the estuarine clays of the north-east of Ireland. *Proceedings of the Royal Irish Academy* 3(2), 212–89.

Praeger, R. L. 1937. *The Way That I Went*. Methuen, London.

Praeger, R. L. 1949. *Some Irish Naturalists*. Dundalgan Press, Dundalk.

Preece, R. C., Coxon, P. and Robinson, J. E. 1986. New biostratigraphic evidence of the postglacial colonisation of Ireland and for Mesolithic forest disturbance. *Journal of Biogeography* 13, 487–509.

Prescott, P. A. 2011. Lithics to landscapes: Hunter-gather tool use, resource exploitation and mobility during the Mesolithic of the Central Pennines. Unpublished PhD thesis, University of Oxford.

Preston, J. 1960. Petrological Indentification of Axe 322:1959a. *Ulster Journal of Archaeology* 23, 55.

Pretty, G. H. 1977. The cultural chronology of the Roonka Flat. In R. V. S. Wright (ed.), *Stone Tools as Cultural Markers: Change, Evolution and Complexity*, 288–331. Australian Institute of Aboriginal Studies, Canberra.

Price, C. R. 2003. *Late Pleistocene and Early Holocene Small Mammals in South West Britain*. British Archaeological Report 347, Archaeopress, Oxford.

Price, T. D. and Brown, J. A. 1985. *Prehistoric Hunter Gatherers: the Emergence of Cultural Complexity*. Academic Press, New York.

Price, T. D. and Gebauer, A. B. 2005. *Smakkerup Huse, A Late Mesolithic Coastal Site in Northwest Zealand, Denmark*. Aarhus University Press, Aarhus.

Price, T. D. and Noe-Nygaard, N. 2009. Early domestic cattle in southern Scandinavia and the spread of the Neolithic in Europe. In Finlay *et al.* (eds) 2009, 198–210.

Price, T. D. and Schulting, R. J. 2005. Strontium isotopes and mobility. In Schulting 2005, 224–6.

Price, T. D., Bentley, R. A., Lunning, J. Gronnenborn, D. and Wahl, J. 2001. Prehistoric human migration in the Linearbandkeramik of central Europe. *Antiquity* 75, 593–603.

Prosch-Danielsen, L. and Høgestøl, M. 1995. A coastal Ahrensburgian site, found at Galta, Rennesøy. In Fischer (ed.) 1995, 123–30.

Prothero, D. R. 1990. *Interpreting the Stratigraphic Record*. Freeman and Company, New York.

Quinn, A. 2013. Rathhealy 3: Temporary Settlement. In Hanley and Hurley (eds) 2013, 36–8.

Quinnell, H. and Blockley, M. R. with Berridge, P. 1994. *Excavations at Rhuddlan, Clwyd 1969–73.* Council for British Archaeology Research Report 95, Council for British Archaeology, York.

Raemaekers, D. C. M. 1999. *The Articulation of a "New Neolithic"*. Leiden University, Leiden.

Raftery, J. 1944. The Bann Flake outside the Bann Valley. *Journal of the Royal Society of Antiquaries of Ireland* 74, 155–9.

Raftery, J. 1951. *Prehistoric Ireland*. Batsford, London.

Raftery, J. 1972. Archaeological acquisitions in the year 1969. *Journal of the Royal Society of Antiquaries* 102, 181–223.

Rankama, T. 2003. The colonisation of northernmost Finnish Lapland and the inland areas of Finmark. In Larsson *et al.* (eds) 2003, 57–64.

Reilly, E. 2008. An ever closing gap? Modern ecological and palaeoecological contributions towards understanding the Irish post-glacial insect fauna. In Davenport *et al.* (eds) 2008, 63–71.

Rensink, E. and Peeters, H. 2006. *Preserving the Early Past: Investigation, Selection and Preservation of Palaeolithic and Mesolithic Sites and Landscapes*. Nederlandse Archeologische Rapporten 31, Rijksdienst voor het Outheidkundig Bodemonderzoek, Amersfoort.

Reeves Smyth, T. 1997. The natural history of Demesnes. In J. W. Foster (ed.), *Nature in Ireland: A Scientific and Cultural History*, 367–86. Lilliput, Dublin.

Reynier, M. 2005. *Early Mesolithic Britain: Origins, Developments and Directions.* British Archaeological Report 393, Archaeopress, Oxford.

Reynolds, J. D. 2008. The colonisation of Ireland by mammals. In Davenport *et al.* (eds) 2008, 109–15.

Richards, M. 2000. Human and faunal stable isotope analyses from Goat's Hole and Foxhole Caves, Gower. In S. Green (ed.), *Paviland Cave and the Red Lady: A Definitive Report*, 71–75. Scarab, Newport.

Richards, M. P. and Mellars, P. A. 1998. Stable isotopes and the seasonality of the Oronsay middens. *Antiquity* 72, 178–84.

Richter, J. 1982. Faunal remains from Ulkestrup lyng øst. In K. Andersen, S. Jorgensen and J. Richter, *Maglemose hytterne ved Ulkestrup Lyng*, 144–77. Nordiske Fortidsminder B, Bind 7, Copenhagen.

Roberts, A. J. 1987. Late Mesolithic occupation of the Cornish Coast at Gwithian: preliminary results. In P. Rowley-Conwy, M. Zvelebil and H. P. Blankholm (eds), *Mesolithic North West Europe: Recent Trends*, 131–137. Department of Archaeology and Prehistory, University of Sheffield.

Rockman, M. 2003. Knowledge and learning in the archaeology of colonisation. In M. Rockman and J. Steele (eds), *Colonization of Unfamiliar Landscapes: the Archaeology of Adaptations*, 3–24. Routledge, London.

Roe, H. M. and Swindles, G. T. 2008. Holocene sea-level history and coastal evolution of Glenarriff, County Antrim. In N. J. Whitehouse, H. M. Roe, S. McCarron and J. Knight (eds), *North of Ireland, Field Guide*, 106–16. Quaternary Research Association, London.

Roebroeks, W. 2006. The human occupation of Europe: where are we? *Journal of Quaternary Science, Special Issue: The Palaeolithic occupation of Europe: In Memory of John J. Wymer* 21(5), 425–36.

Roksandic, M. 2004. Introduction: how violent was the Mesolithic, or is there a common pattern of violent interactions specific to sedentary Hunter-Gatherers? In M. Roksandic (ed.), *Violent Interactions in the Mesolithic: Evidence and Meaning*, 1–8. British Archaeological Report 1237, Archaeopress, Oxford.

Roläo, J. M. and Roksandic, M. 2007. The Muge Mesolithic complex: new results from the excavations. In N. Milner, O. E. Craig and G. N. Bailey (eds), *Shell Middens in Atlantic Europe*, 158–64. Oxbow Books, Oxford.

Rowley-Conwy, P. 1983. Sedentary hunters: the Ertebølle example. In G. Bailey (ed.), *Hunter-gatherer Economy in Prehistory: a European Perspective*, 111–26. Cambridge University Press, Cambridge.

Rowley-Conwy, P. 1994. Meat, furs and skins: Mesolithic animal bones from Ringkloster, a seasonal hunting camp in Jutland. *Journal of Danish Archaeology* 12, 87–98.

Rowley-Conwy, P. 1996. Why didn't Westropp's Mesolithic catch on in 1872? *Antiquity* 70, 940–4.

Rowley-Conway, P. 2013. Homes without houses, some comments on an Ertebølle enigma. In G. N. Bailey, K. Hardy and A. Camara, (eds), *Shell Energy*, 137–55. Oxbow Books, Oxford.

Rudwick, M. J. S. 1995. *Scenes from Deep Time: Early Pictorial Representations of the Prehistoric World*. University of Chicago Press, Chicago.

Ryan, M. 1980. An Early Mesolithic site in the Irish midlands. *Antiquity* 54(210), 46–47.

Sall, M. 2013. Ethnoarchaeology of Senegambian shell middens. In G. N. Bailey, K. Hardy and A. Camara (eds), *Shell Energy*, 183–90. Oxbow Books, Oxford.

Sandmo, A. K. 1986. Råstoff og redskap – mer enn teknisk hjelpemiddel. Om symbolfunksjonen som et aspekt ved materiell kultur. Skisse av etaberlingsforløpet i en nordeuropeisk kystsone 10.000–9.000 BP. Unpublished Magistergrad thesis, University of Tromsø.

Saville, A. 1981. Honey Hill, Elkington: a Northamptonshire Mesolithic site. *Northamptonshire Archaeology* 16, 1–13.

Saville, A. 1999. A cache of flint axeheads and other flint artefacts from Auchenhoan, near Campbeltown, Kintyre, Scotland. *Proceedings of the Prehistoric Society* 65, 83–124.

Saville, A. 2003. A flint core tool from Wig Sands, Kircolm, near Stranraer, and a consideration of the absence of core tools in the Scottish Mesolithic. *Transaction of the Dumfriesshire and Galloway Natural History and Antiquarian Society* 3rd Series 77, 13–22.

Saville, A. 2004. The material culture of Mesolithic Scotland. In A. Saville (ed.), *Mesolithic Scotland and its Neighbours*, 185–220. Society of Antiquaries of Scotland, Edinburgh.

Saville, A. 2008. The beginning of the Later Mesolithic in Scotland. In Z. Sulgostowska and A. J. Tomaszewski (eds), *Man-Millennia-Environment: Studies in Honour of Romauld Schild*, 207–14. Polish Academy of Sciences, Warsaw.

Saville, A. 2009. Speculating on the significance of an axe-head and a bead from Luce Sands, Dumfries and Galloway, South West Scotland. In Finlay *et al.* (eds) 2009, 50–8.

Saville, A. and Ballin, T. B. 2009. Upper Palaeolithic evidence from Kilmelfort Cave Argyll: A revaluation of the evidence. *Proceedings of the Society of Antiquaries of Scotland* 139, 9–45.

Saville, A., Hardy, K., Miket T. B., R. and Ballin, 2012. An Corran, Staffin: a rockshelter with Mesolithic and later occupation. http://www.sair.org.uk./sair51

Sayers, P. 1974. *PEIG: The Autobiography of Peig Sayers of the Great Blasket Island*. Talbot Press, Dublin.

Schadla-Hall, T. 1987. Recent investigations of the Early Mesolithic landscape and settlement in the Vale of Pickering, North Yorkshire. In P. Rowley-Conwy, M. Zvelebil and H. P. Blankholm (eds), *Mesolithic North West Europe: Recent Trends*, 46–55. Department of Archaeology and Prehistory, University of Sheffield.

Schanche, K. 1988. Mortensnes: En Boplass i Varanger. Thesis presented for a Magistergrad avhandling i Arkeologi, University of Tromsø.

Schnapp, A. 1996. *The Discovery of the Past: the Origins of Archaeology*. British Museum, London.

Schulting, R. J. 2003. The marrying kind; evidence for a patrilocal post marital residence pattern in the Mesolithic of southern Brittany. In Larsson *et al.* (eds), 2003, 431–41.

Schulting, R. J. 2005. Pursuing a rabbit in Burrington Cove, North Somerset, stratigraphy and problems. *Proceedings of University of Bristol Speleological Society* 23(3), 171–265.

Schulting, R. J. 2009. Worms Head and Caldey Island (south Wales, UK) and the question of Mesolithic territories. In McCartan *et al.* (eds) 2009, 354–61.

Schulting, R. J. 2013 "Tilbury Man": A Mesolithic skeleton from the Lower Thames. *Proceedings of the Prehistoric Society* 79, 19–38.

Schulting, R. J. and Wysocki, M. 2005. The human bones, etc. In Schulting 2005, 184–213.

Schulting, R. J., Murphy, E., Jones, C. and Warren, G. 2012. New dates from the North and proposed chronology for Irish Court tombs. *Proceedings of the Royal Irish Academy* 112C, 1–54.

Shackleton, N. J. 1987. Oxygen isotopes, ice volume and sea level. *Quaternary Science Reviews* 6, 183–90.

Sherlock, R. 2013. Killydonoghue AR2 Cremation burial pit. In Hanley and Hurley (eds) 2013, 87–9.

Sheridan, A. 2010. The Neolithisation of Britain and Ireland, the Big Picture. In B. Finlayson and G. Warren (eds), *Landscapes in Transition*, 89–105. Council for British Research in the Levant, Oxford.

Simms, M. J. 2009. Permian and Mesozoic. In C. H. Holland and I. A. Sanders (eds), *The Geology of Ireland*, 3111–332. Dunedin Press, Edinburgh.

Simpson, D. D. A. 1993. Stone artefacts from the Lower Bann Valley. *Ulster Journal of Archaeology* 56, 31–43.

Skar, B. 1987. The Scanian Maglemose site Barre Mose – a re-examination by refitting. *Acta Archaeologica* 58, 87–104.

Skar, B. and Coulson, S. 1986. Evidence for behaviour from refitting – a case study. *Norwegian Archaeological Review* 19(2), 90–102.

Sleeman, D. P. 2008. Quantify the prey gap for Ireland. In Davenport *et al.* (eds), 77–82.

Sleeman, D. P., Carlsson, J. and Carlsson, J. E. L. (eds) 2014. *Mind the Gap II, New Insights into the Irish Postglacial*. Irish Naturalist's Journal, Belfast.

Sloane, H. 1727–28 An account of elephants teeth and bones found underground. *Philosophical Transactions of the Royal Society of London* 35, 457–71, 497–514.

Smith, A. G. S. 1981 Palynology of a Mesolithic–Neolithic site in County Antrim, N. Ireland. *IVth International Palynology Conference Lucknow 1976–77* 3, 248–57.

Smith, A. G. S. and Collins, A. E. P. 1971. The stratigraphy, palynology and archaeology of diatomite deposits at Newferry, Co. Antrim, Northern Ireland. *Ulster Journal of Archaeology* 34, 3–25.

Smith, P. 1960. L'Origine de La Terme Mesolithique, *L'Anthropologie* 66, 183–6.

Sørensen, K. A. 1976. A Zoological investigation of the bone material from Sværdborg I-1943. In B. B. Henriksen, *Sværdborg I: excavations 1943–44: A Settlement of the Maglemose Culture*, 137–148. Akademisk Forlag, Copenhagen.

Sørensen, M. and Sternke, F. 2004. Nørregård VI – Lateglacial hunters in transition. In T. Terberger and B. V. Eriksen (eds), *Hunters in a Changing World: Environment and Archaeology of the Pleistocene–Holocene Transition (ca. 11000–9000 B.C.) in Northern Central Europe*, 85–111. Verlag Marie Leidorf GmbH, Rahden/Westf.

Spikens, P. 2008. Mesolithic Europe: glimpses of another world. In G. Bailey and P. Spikens (eds), *Mesolithic Europe*, 1–17. Cambridge University Press, Cambridge.

Stegner, W. 1955. *Wolf Willow*. Penguin, London.

Sternke, F. 2013. The significance of the lithic assemblage. In Hanley and Hurley (eds) 2013, 322–333.

Sternke, F. and Woodman, P. C. 2009. Lithic finds report for 03E0942-Derragh, Co. Longford. Unpublished specialist report for the Discovery Programme, Dublin.

Sternke, F. and Woodman, P. C. 2015. Lithics from NRA Excavations, Carlow. In Teresa Bolger, Colm Moloney and Damian Shiels, *A Journey Along the Carlow Corridor. The archaeology of the M9 Carlow Bypass*. NRA Scheme Monograph 16. National Roads Authority, Dublin.

Stirland, J. 2008. 200,000 year old flint from County Down. *Archaeology Ireland* 22(1), 23.

Stringer, C. 2012. *The Origin of Our Species*. Penguin, London.

Svensson, A., Andersen, K. K., Bigler, M., Clausen, H. B., Dahl-Jensen, D. and Davis, S. M. *et al.* 2008. A 60,000 year Greenland stratigraphic ice core chronology. *Climate of the Past* 4, 57–67.

Takala, H. 2009. The flint collection from the Ristola site in Lahti and the cultural contacts of the earliest Postglacial settlement of southern Finland. In McCartan *et al.* (eds) 2009, 31–7.

Takamiya, H. 2006. An unusual case? Hunter-gatherer adaptations to an Island environment: a case study from Okinawa, Japan. *Journal of Island and Coastal Archaeology* 1(1), 49–66.

Terberger, T. 2006. The Mesolithic Hunter-fisher-gatherers on the North European Plain. In K. M. Hansen and K. B. Pedersen (eds), *Across the Western Baltic*, 111–85. Sydsjaellands Museum, Vordingborg.

Tingle, M. 2013. A new Mesolithic pit site and Beaker feature at Little Dartmouth Farm in Devon. *PAST* 74, 5–6.

Torrence, R. 1989. Re-tooling towards a behavioural theory of stone tools. In R. Torrence (ed.), *Time, Energy and Stone Tools*, 57–66. Cambridge University Press, Cambridge.

Trigger, B. 1989. *A History of Archaeological Thought*. Cambridge University Press, Cambridge.

Troels-Smith, J. 1937. Beile aus dem Mesolithicum Danemarks Einteilungs-versuch. *Acta Archaeologica* 8, 278–95.

van Gijn, A. and Keisers, L. 1999. Microwear analysis. In Woodman *et al.* 1999. *Excavations at Ferriter's Cove 1983–1995: Last foragers, first farmers in the Dingle Peninsula*, 68–70. Wordwell, Dublin.

Van Wijngaarden-Bakker, L. H. 1974, The animal remains from the Beaker settlement at Newgrange, Co. Meath: first report. *Proceedings of the Royal Irish Academy* 74C, 313–83.

Van Wijngaarden-Bakker, L. H. 1985. The faunal remains. In Woodman 1985a, 71–6.

Van Wijngaarden-Bakker, L. H. 1989. Faunal remains and the Irish Mesolithic. In C. Bonsall (ed.), *The Mesolithic in Europe*, 125–33. John Donald, Edinburgh.

Van Wijgaarden-Bakker, L. H., Cavallo, C., van Kolfschoten, Th., Maliepaard, C. H. and Oversteegen, J. F. S. 2001. Zoogdieren, vogels, reptielen. In Louwe Kooijmans (ed.) 2001, 181–242.

Veil, S. 2006. Are Stone Age ploughzone sites third class monuments? Some insights from investigations on Stone Age surface sites in Lower Saxony. In Rensink and Peeters (eds) 2006, 107–26.

Viney, M. 2003. *Michael Viney's Ireland*. Blackstaff Press, Belfast.

Von Rust, A. 1972. *Vor 20,000 Jahren: Rentierjäger der Eiszeit*. Karl Wachholtz Verlag, Neumüster.

Waddell, J. 1991–92. The Irish Sea in prehistory. *The Journal of Irish Archaeology* 6, 29–40.

Waddell, J. 2005. *Foundation Myths: The Beginnings of Irish Archaeology*. Wordwell, Dublin.

Waddington, C. (ed.). 2007. *Mesolithic Settlement in the North Sea Basin: a Case Study from Howick, North-East England*. Oxbow Books, Oxford.

Waddington, C., Bailey, G., Bayliss, A. and Milner, N. 2007. Howick in its North Sea context. In Waddington (ed.) 2007, 201–24.

Walker, E. 2009. Discoveries in Devon: the works of Father John McEnery and William Pengelly. In R. T. Hosfield, F. F. Wenban-Smith and M. I. Pope (eds), *Great Prehistorians: 150 years of Palaeolithic Research, 1859–2009. Lithics* 30, 13–24.

Warren, G. 2003. Living in the trees: Mesolithic people and the woods of Ireland. *Archaeology Ireland* 17(3), 20–3.

Warren, G. 2006. Technology. In Conneller and Warren (eds) 2006, 13–34.

Warren, G. 2008. Fieldwork in Belderrig, Co. Mayo 2004–2008. (http://www.ucd.ie/archaeology/documentstore/ria/belderrig/BDG2008_Retrospective_2004_2008.pdf)

Warren, G. 2009. Belderrig, a new Later Mesolithic and Neolithic landscape in north west Ireland. In Finlay *et al.* (eds) 2009, 143–52.

Warren, G., Little, A. and Stanley, M. 2009. A late Mesolithic scatter from Corlanna, Co. Westmeath, and its place in the Mesolithic landscape of the Irish Midlands. *Proceedings of the Royal Irish Academy* 109C, 1–36.

Warren, G., Daly, D., Laws, S., Menuge, J, O'Keefe, E. and van Gijn, A. 2009. Appendix 6: lithics report. In Mossop and Mossop 2009.

Warren, G., Davis, S., Mcclatchie, M. Sands, R. 2013. The potential role of humans in structuring the wooded landscape of Mesolithic Ireland: a review of data and discussion of approaches. *Vegetational History and Archaeobotany* DOI 10 1007/s00334-013-0417-z.

Watson, J. E., Brooks, S. J., Whitehouse, N., Reimer, P., Birks, H. J. B. and Tuney, C. 2010. Chironomid-inferred late-glacial summer air temperatures from Lough Nadourcan, Co. Donegal, Ireland. *Journal of Quaterny Sciences* 25(8), 1200–10.

Webb, D. A. 1983. The flora of Ireland in its European context. *Journal of Life Sciences* 4, 143–60.

Weir, D. A. 1997. An outline of vegetational history in the Navan area from Late Mesolithic to medieval times. In D. M. Waterman, *Excavations at Navan Fort 1961–71*. HM Stationary Office, Belfast.

Welinder, S. 1971. Tidligpostglacialt Mesolithicum i Skåne. *Acta Archaeologica Lundensia Series in 8° Minore* 1, Studentlitteratur, Lund.

Wenban-Smith, F. F., Bates, M. R. and Schwenninger, J. 2010. Early Devensian (MIS 5d–b) occupation at Dartford, south east England. *Journal of Quaternary Science* 25(8), 1193–9.

Went, A. E. J. 1963. Notes on some fixed engines for the capture of salmon, used in Ireland since 1800. *Journal of the Royal Society of Antiquaries* 93, 151–9.

Went, A. E. J. 1964. The pursuit of salmon in Ireland. *Proceedings of the Royal Irish Academy* 63C, 191–244.

Westley, K. 2013 Taking the plunge. *Archaeology Ireland* 27(4) no. 108, 38–41.

Westley, K. and Woodman, P. C. forthcoming. Irish prehistoric landscapes. In A. Fischer (ed.), *Atlas of European Submerged Prehistoric Sites*. Wiley-Blackwell, London.

Westropp, H. 1866. On the analogous form of implements amongst early and primitive races. *Memoirs of the Anthropological Society of London* 11, 288–93.

Westropp, H. 1872. *Prehistoric Phases; or Introductory Essays on Prehistoric Archaeology*. Bel & Dalby, London.

Wheeler, A. 1978. Why were there no fish remains at Star Carr? *Journal of Archaeological Science* 5, 85–9.

Whelan, C. B. 1930a. The flint industry of the northern Irish (25-foot) raised beach: a preliminary study of its relation to the Asturian Industry of Portugal. *Journal of the Royal Anthropological Institution* 60, 169–84.

Whelan, C. B. 1930b. The tanged flake industry of the River Bann, Co. Antrim. *Antiquaries Journal* 10, 134–8.

Whelan, C. B. 1931. The Asturian Industry of Northern Ireland. *Man* 31, 236.

Whelan, C. B. 1933a. Post-glacial prehistory in Northern Ireland, three recent chronological indications. *Irish Naturalist Journal* 4, 149, 201, 215.

Whelan, C. B. 1933b. The Palaeolithic question in Ireland. In *Report of the XVI International Geological Congress (Washington)*, 1209–18.

Whelan, C. B. 1938. Studies in the significance of the Irish Stone Age: the cultural sequence. *Proceedings of the Royal Irish Academy* 44C, 115–38.

Whelan, C. B. 1952. *A Bone Industry from the Lower Bann*. Northern Ireland Archaeological Monograph 1, HMSO, Belfast.

Whittle, A., Healy, F. and Bayliss, A. (eds). 2011. *Gathering Time: Dating the Early Neolithic Enclosures of Britain and Ireland*. Oxbow Books, Oxford.

Wickham-Jones, C. R. 1990. *Rhum: Mesolithic and Later Sites at Kinloch, Excavations 1984–6*. Society of Antiquaries of Scotland Monograph 7, Edinburgh.

Wickham-Jones, C. R. 2007. Middens in Scottish prehistory; time space and relativity. In N. Milner, O. E. Craig and G. N. Bailey (eds), *Shell Middens in Atlantic Europe*, 86–93. Oxbow Books, Oxford.

Wickham-Jones, C. 2010. *Fear of Farming*. Windgather Press, Oxford.

Wickham-Jones, C. R. and Woodman, P. C. 1998. Studies on the Early settlement of Scotland and Ireland. *Quaternary International* 49–50, 13–20.

Wigfross, J. 1995. West Swedish Mesolithic settlements containing faunal remains – aspects of the topography and economy. In Fischer (ed.) 1995, 197–206.

Wilde, W. 1857. *A Descriptive Catalogue of the Antiquities of Stone, Earthen and Vegetable Materials in the Museum of the Royal Irish Academy*. Royal Irish Academy, Dublin.

Wilde, W. 1860. Upon the unmanufactured animal remains belonging to the Academy. *Proceedings of the Royal Irish Academy* 7, 181–211.

Winchester, S. 2001. *The Map that Changed the World*. Penguin, London.

Windle, B. C. A. 1910. Some prehistoric shore dwellers in Ireland. *Journal of the Ivernian Society* 2, 189–96.

Windle, B. C. A. 1911. A note on some kitchen-middens in the north of Ireland. *Royal Society of Antiquaries of Ireland* 61, 1–4.

Windle, J. F. 1904. A visit to Ballybunion sandhills, Co. Kerry. *Journal of the Limerick Field Club* 2, 243–6.

Wilson, P. 1985. The Postglacial colonisation of Ireland by fish, amphibians and reptiles. In D. P. Sleeman, D. J. Devoy and P. C. Woodman (eds), *Proceedings of the Postglacial Colonisation Conference of Ireland, University College Cork 15–16 October 1983*, 53–8. Occasional Publications of the Irish Biogeographical Society 1, Cork.

Wobst, H. M. 1974. Boundary conditions for Palaeolithic social systems: a simulation approach. *American Antiquity* 39, 147–78.

Woodman, P. C. 1967. A flint hoard from Killybeg. *Ulster Journal of Archaeology* 30, 8–15.

Woodman, P. C. 1974a. The chronological position of the latest phases of the Larnian. *Proceedings of the Royal Irish Academy* 74C, 237–58.

Woodman, P. C. 1974b. Settlement patterns of the Irish Mesolithic. *Ulster Journal of Archaeology* 36–37, 1–16.

Woodman, P. C. 1977a. Recent excavations at Newferry, Co. Antrim. *Proceedings of the Prehistoric Society* 43, 155–99.

Woodman, P. C. 1977b. A narrow blade Mesolithic site at Glynn, County Antrim. *Ulster Journal of Archaeology* 40, 12–21.

Woodman, 1977c. The "Irish Stone Age": a reconsideration, unpublished PhD Thesis, Queen's University Belfast.

Woodman, P. C. 1978a. *The Mesolithic in Ireland*. British Archaeological Report 58, BAR, Oxford.

Woodman, P. C. 1978b. A reappraisal of the Manx Mesolithic. In P. Davey (ed.), *Man and Environment in the Isle of Man*, 333–70. British Archaeological Report 54. BAR, Oxford.

Woodman, P. C., 1980. The other Mesolithic radiocarbon dates. *Journal of the Royal Society of Antiquaries* 110, 160–2.

Woodman, P. C. 1981. The postglacial colonization of Ireland: the human factors. In D. O'Corráin (ed.), *Irish Antiquity: Essays and Studies Presented to Professor M. J. O'Kelly*, 93–110. Tower Books, Cork.

Woodman, P. C. 1983. The Glencloy Project in perspective. In T. Reeves-Smith and F. Hammond (eds), *Landscape Archaeology in Ireland*, 25–34. British Archaeological Report 116, BAR, Oxford.

Woodman, P. C. 1985a. *Excavations at Mount Sandel, 1973–77*. Northern Ireland Archaeological Monograph 2, HMSO, Belfast.

Woodman, P. C. 1985b. Excavations at Glendhu, Co. Down. *Ulster Journal of Archaeology* 48, 31–40.

Woodman, P. C. 1985c. Rescue excavations at Castleroe. In Woodman 1985a, 199–200.

Woodman, P. C. 1986. Problems in the colonisation of Ireland. *Ulster Journal of Archaeology*, 49, 10–17.

Woodman, P. C. 1987. Excavations at Cass Ny Hawin. *Proceedings of the Prehistoric Society* 53, 1–22.

Woodman, P. C. 1988. Prehistoric settlers. In P. Loughrey (ed.), *The People of Ireland*, 11–25. Appletree press/BBC, Belfast

Woodman, P. C. 1989. The Mesolithic of Munster: a preliminary assessment. In C. Bonsall (ed.), *The Mesolithic in Europe: Papers Presented at the 3rd International Symposium*, 116–24. John Donald, Edinburgh.

Woodman, P. C. 1992a. Excavations at Mad Man's Window, Glenarm, Co. Antrim: problems of flint exploitation in east Antrim. *Proceedings of the Prehistoric Society* 58, 77–106.

Woodman, P. C. 1992b. The Komsa Culture, a re-examination of its position in the Stone Age of Finnmark. *Acta Archaeologica* 63, 57–76.

Woodman, P. C. 1993a. The prehistory of south-west Ireland – an archaeological region or a state of mind? In E. Shee-Twohig and M. Ronayne (eds), *Past Perceptions: the Prehistoric Archaeology of South-West Ireland*, 6–15. Cork University Press, Cork.

Woodman, P. C. 1993b. Towards a definition of Irish Early Neolithic assemblages. In N. Ashton and A. David (eds), *Stories in Stone*, 213–18. Lithic Studies Society Occasional Paper 4, Lithic Studies Society, London.

Woodman, P. C. 1996. Archaeology on the edge: learning to fend for ourselves. In T. Pollard and A. Morrison (eds), *The Early Prehistory of Scotland*, 152–61. Edinburgh University Press, Edinburgh.

Woodman, P. C. 1997. Killuragh. In I. Bennett (ed.), *Excavations 1996*, 67–8. Wordwell, Dublin.

Woodman, P. C. 1998a. George Morant and the Mesolithic of Ballyhoe Lough. In M. Ryan (ed.), *Irish Antiquity: Essays in Memory of Joseph Raftery*, 1–16. Wordwell, Dublin.

Woodman, P. C. 1998b. Rosses Point revisited. *Antiquity* 72, 562–70.

Woodman, P. C. 1998c. Pushing the boat out for an Irish Palaeolithic. In N. Ashton, F. Healy and P. Pettitt (eds), *Stone Age Archaeology. Essays in Honour of John Wymer*. Lithic Studies Society Occasional Paper 6/Oxbow Books, Oxford.

Woodman, P. C. 1999. The early Post Glacial settlement of Arctic Europe. In E. Cziela, T. Kersting and S. Pratsch (eds), *Den Bogen Spannen*, 297–312. Beier and Beran, Weisbach.

Woodman, P. C. 2000a. Getting back to basics: transitions to farming in Britain and Ireland. In T. D. Price (ed.), *Europe's First Farmers*, 219–59. Cambridge University Press, Cambridge.

Woodman, P. E. 2000b. A predictive model for Mesolithic site locations on Islay using logistical regression and GIS. In Mithen (ed.) 2000, 445–64.

Woodman, P. C. 2003. Pushing back the boundaries. John Jackson Lecture 2003. *Occasional Papers in Irish Science and Technology* 27, 1–18.

Woodman, P. C. 2004. Retrospect and prospect. In A. Saville (ed.), *Mesolithic Scotland; the Early Holocene Prehistory of Scotland and its European Context*, 285–99. Society of Antiquaries of Scotland, Edinburgh.

Woodman, P. C. 2005a. Too light to be right. In N. Milner and P. C. Woodman (eds), *Mesolithic Studies and the Beginning of the 21st Century*, 126–43. Oxbow Books, Oxford.

Woodman, P. C. 2005b. The exploitation of Ireland's coastal resources: a marginal resource through time? In M. R. Gonzalez-Morales and G. A. Clark (eds), *The Mesolithic of the Atlantic Façade*, 37–56. Anthropological Research Paper 55, Arizona State University, Phoenix.

Woodman, P. C. 2005c. Lithics Report on lithics from excavations at Kilrane, County Kildare, paper submitted to Aegis Archaeology.

Woodman, P. C. 2008. Mind the gap or gaps? In Davenport *et al.* (eds) 2008, 5–18.

Woodman, P. C. 2009. Ireland's place in the European Mesolithic: why its OK to be different. In McCartan, *et al.* (eds) 2009, xxxvi–xlvi.

Woodman, P. C. 2010. Challenging times. In P. Crombé, M. Van Strydonck, J. Sergant, M. Boudin and M. Bats (eds), *Chronology and Evolution within the Mesolithic of North West Europe. Proceedings of an International Meeting, Brussels, May 30th–1st June 2007*, 195–215. Cambridge Scholars Publishing, Newcastle.

Woodman, P. C. 2011. The significance of the lithic assemblages from the archaeological excavations on the N25 Waterford City Bypass. In J. Eogan and E. Shee Twohig (eds), *Cois tSiúire – Nine Thousand Years of Human Activity in the Lower Suir Valley*, 199–206. NRA Scheme Monograph 8, National Roads Authority, Dublin.

Woodman, P. C. 2012. Making yourself at home on an island: the first 1000 Years(+?) of the Irish Mesolithic. *Proceedings of the Prehistoric Society* 78, 1–34.

Woodman, P. C. 2013. The significance of the stone age sites? In Hanley and Hurley (eds) 2013, 51–59.

Woodman, P. C. 2014. Ireland's native mammals: a survey of the archaeological evidence in Sleeman *et al.* (eds) 2014, 28–43.

Woodman, P. C. 2015. The lithic assemblage. In Dunlop and Woodman 2015, 70–125.

Woodman, P. C. Forthcoming a. Lithics from Irish caves. In M. Dowd (ed.), *The Irish Cave Archaeology Project: Studies on Human Remains and Artefacts from Ireland's caves*. Oxbow Books, Oxford.

Woodman, P. C. and Anderson, E. 1990. The Irish Later Mesolithic: a partial picture. In M. P. Vermersch and P. van Peer (eds), *Contributions to the Mesolithic in Europe*, 377–387. Leuven University Press, Leuven.

Woodman, P. C. and Cook J. 2013. Elephant's teeth in the Diocese of Kilmore, *Archaeology Ireland* 27(4) No. 106, 11–14.

Woodman, P. C. and Griffiths, D. R. 1988 The archaeological importance of flint sources in Munster. *Journal of the Cork Historical and Archaeological Society* 252, 66–72.

Woodman, P. C. and Johnson, G. 1996. Excavations at Bay Farm 1, Carnlough, Co. Antrim, and the study of the 'Larnian' technology. *Proceedings of the Royal Irish Academy* 96C, 137–235.

Woodman, P. C. and Johnson, I. 1991–92. A petrological examination of some Mesolithic stone artifacts. *Ulster Journal of Archaeology* 54–5, 134–7.

Woodman, P. C. and McCarthy, M. 2003. Contemplating some awful(ly interesting) vistas: importing cattle and red deer into Prehistoric Ireland. In I. Armit, E. Murphy, E. Nelis and D. Simpson (eds), *Neolithic Settlement in Ireland and Western Britain*, 31–9. Oxbow Books, Oxford.

Woodman, P. C. and Milner, N. 2013. From restaurant to takeaway: placing Sligo shell middens in context. In M. A. Timoney (ed.), *Dedicated to Sligo*, 37–40. Publishing Sligo's Past, Sligo.

Woodman, P. C. and Mitchel, N. C. 1993. Human settlement and economy of the Lough Neagh basin. In R. B. Wood and R. V. Smith (eds), *Lough Neagh, the Ecology of a Multipurpose Water Resource*, 91–111. Kluwer Academic Publishers, Dortrecht.

Woodman, P. C., Anderson, E. and Finlay, N. 1999. *Excavations at Ferriter's Cove 1983–1995: Last Foragers, First Farmers in the Dingle Peninsula*. Wordwell, Dublin.

Woodman, P. C., Doggart, R. and Mallory, J. 1991–92. Excavations at Windy Ridge, Co. Antrim, 1981–82. *Ulster Journal of Archaeology* 54–5, 13–35.

Woodman, P. C., Finlay, N. and Anderson, E. 2006. *The Archaeology of a Collection: The Keiller-Knowles Collection of the National Museum of Ireland*. National Museum of Ireland Monograph 2, Wordwell, Bray.

Woodman, P. C., McCarthy, M. and Monaghan, N. 1997. The Irish Quaternary Faunas Project. *Quaternary Science Reviews* 16, 129–59.

Worsaae, J. J. A. 1845–47. An account of the formation of the Museum of Copenhagen, and general remarks on the classification of the antiquities found in the North and West of Europe. *Proceedings of the Royal Irish Academy* 3, 310–15, 327–44.

WWW.IPOL.IE

Wymer, J. 1962. Excavations at the Maglemosian sites at Thatcham, Berkshire, England. *Proceedings of the Prehistoric Society* 28, 329–61.

Wymer, J. 1968. *Lower Palaeolithic Archaeology in Britain*. John Baker, London.

Wyse Jackson, P. N. 1997. Fluctuations in fortune: three hundred years of Irish geology. In J. W. Foster (ed.), *Nature in Ireland: A Scientific and Cultural History*, 91–114. Lilliput, Dublin.

Yalden, D. 1999, *The History of British Mammals*, Poyser Natural History, London.

Young, R. M. 1892. Antiquarian notes on Bushfoot and Ballymagarry. *Reports and Proceedings of the Belfast Natural History and Philosophical Society*, 37–44.

Zilhao, J. 2009. Dwellings: introduction. In McCartan *et al.* (eds) 2009, 407–8.

Zvelebil, M. 1994. Plant use in the Mesolithic and its role in the transition to farming. *Proceedings of the Prehistoric Society* 60, 35–74.

Zvelebil, M., 2009. The Mesolithic and the 21st century. In McCartan *et al.* (eds) 2009, xlvii–lviii.

Zvelebil, M. and Rowley-Conwy, P. 1984. Transition to farming in northern Europe: a hunter-gatherer perspective. *Norwegian Archaeological Review* 17, 104–28.

Zvelebil, M., Mackiln, M. G., Passmore, D. G. and Ramsden, P. 1996. Alluvial archaeology in the Barrow Valley, south-east Ireland: the Riverford Culture revisited. *Journal of Irish Archaeology* 7, 1–11.

PLATES

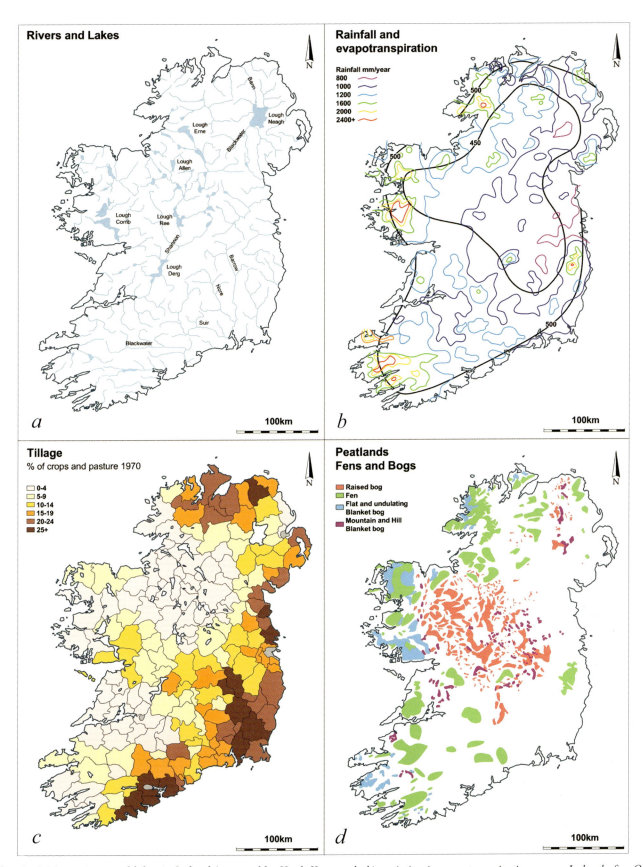

Rivers and Lakes

Lough Erne

Lough Neagh

Blackwater

Lough Allen

Lough Corrib

Lough Ree

Shannon

Lough Derg

Barrow

Nore

Suir

Blackwater

100km

a

Rainfall and evapotranspiration

Rainfall mm/year
800
1000
1200
1600
2000
2400+

500

450

500

500

500

100km

b

Tillage

% of crops and pasture 1970

0-4
5-9
10-14
15-19
20-24
25+

100km

c

Peatlands Fens and Bogs

Raised bog
Fen
Flat and undulating Blanket bog
Mountain and Hill Blanket bog

100km

d

Plate I. a) Major rivers and lakes in Ireland,(prepared by Hugh Kavanagh, b) variation in evapotranspiration across Ireland after Otte 2003, c) Extent of tillage across Ireland in 1970 RIA, d) extent of different forms of peatlands in Ireland (after Doyle and O'Criordain 2003).

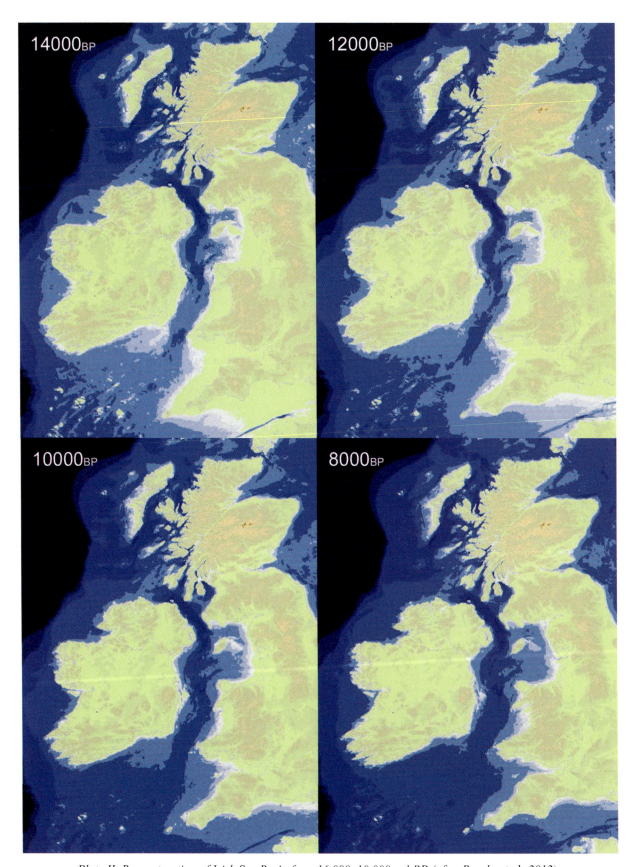

Plate II. Reconstruction of Irish Sea Basin from 16,000–10,000 cal BP (after Brooks et al. *2012).*

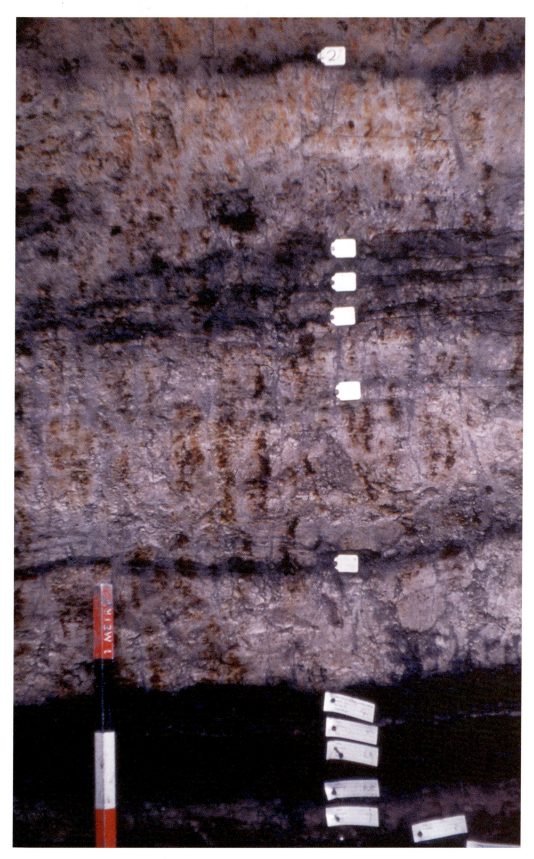

Plate III a) Diatomite and ash layers exposed at Newferry site 3 on the Lower Bann.

Plate III. b) Mushroom stone.

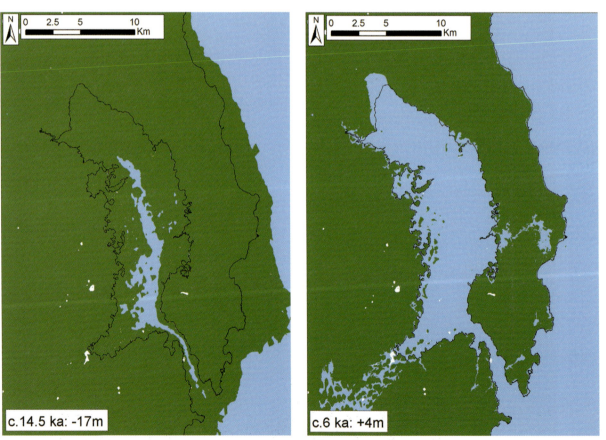

Plate IV. Sea level changes between 14,500 and 6,000 years ago within Strangford Lough, Co. Down Palaeo-sea level position is based on models developed by Brooks et al. (2008), terrestrial topography is from the ASTER global digital elevation model (a product of METI and NASA), offshore bathymetry is based on data from the Joint Irish Bathymetric Survey (a partnership between the Marine and Coastguard Agency and Marine Institute of Ireland), the INFOMAR survey (Marine Institute of Ireland) and the UK Hydrographic Office (photographs supplied by Kieran Westley, Centre for Maritime Archaeology, University of Ulster, Coleraine).

Plate V. a) Sir Thomas Molyneux 1661–1733 (© National Museums of Northern Ireland Collection Armagh County Museum), b) George Du Noyer (by permission of the Royal Society of Antiquaries of Ireland, c) Monsignor Peter O Laverty 1826–1906 (© National Museums of Northern Ireland Collection Ulster Museum), d) stone tools from the shores of Lough Neagh (Evans 1867).

Plate VI. a) William Gray MRIA 1830–1917 (1912), (© National Museums of Northern Ireland Collection Ulster Museum), b) William Knowles, c) Frank Mitchell on Valentia Island (1983).

Plate VII. Excavations at Newferry 1970–71 showing ash spreads which were interleaved within the diatomite deposits.

Plate VIII. Excavations at Mount Sandel, Co. Derry 1973–77: a) general view of the main hut area during excavation 1973, b) excavation through the hedge 1976.

a

b

Plate IX. Excavations at Lough Boora 1976(?): a) general view of the excavation, b) initial discovery of stone axes (courtesy of M. Ryan).

Plate X. a) Location of the Kilcummer Lower Mesolithic site, at the junction of the Blackwater and Awbeg Rivers, Co Cork (courtesy of professor W. O'Brien), b) excavations at Ferriter's Cove, Co. Kerry, in the Central Area 1986.

Plate XI. Changes in Ballyhoe Lough 1830s to 2010 (prepared by Hugh Kavanagh).

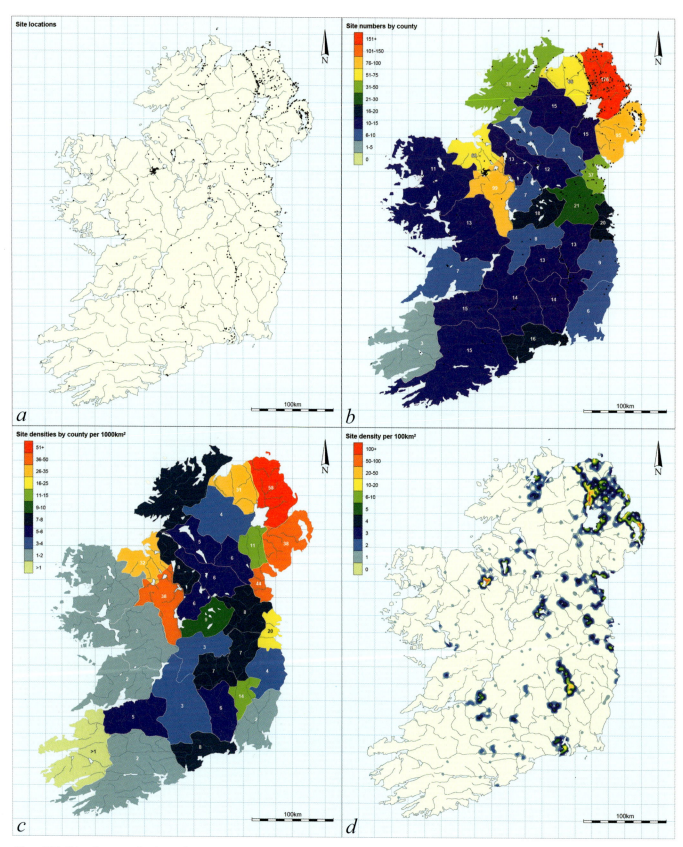

Plate XII. Distribution of: a) site locations, b) number of locations per county, c) number of locations per county per 1000 sq km, d) number of locations per 100 sq. km unit (prepared by Hugh Kavanagh).

Plate XIII. Excavations at Mount Sandel, Co. Derry: a) Central Hearth area and F56/1, b) Fully excavated pit complex F209/211.

Plate XIV. Presumed location of the Young and Swanston excavations at the Bushfoot: a) looking into the quarry area, b) looking out towards the Bush River.

a

b

Plate XV. Excavations along the Toome Bypass, Co. Antrim: a) view of the northern area during excavation, b) excavation, at Drumakeeley, discussions about the Later Mesolithic Settlement site.

Plate XVI a) and b) Excavations at Bay Farm 1981, c) and d) excavations at the Port of Larne 2003 (courtesy of Archaeological Development Services).

Plate XVII a) and b) Portbraddan Cave, Co. Antrim, c) and d) Killuragh Cave, Co. Limerick (photographs by S. Moore).

a

b

Plate XVIII. Lough Swilly, Co. Donegal shell middens: a) Ballymoney, b) Baylet.

Plate XIX. Excavations of platforms at a) Moynagh Lough, Co. Meath, b) Derragh Island, Co. Longford.

Plate XX. Exploration of a submerged landscape at Eleven Ballyboes, Greencastle, Co. Donegal by the Centre for Maritime Archaeology, University of Ulster, Coleraine: a) Bay 1, Eleven Ballyboes, b) CMA team on the beach, May 2012, c) hazel nuts from the surface of the peat deposits in Bay 2, d) selection of Earlier Mesolithic artefacts recovered from Eleven Ballyboes (photographs c) and d) supplied by Kieran Westley Centre for Maritime Archaeology, University of Ulster, Coleraine).

Plate XXI. a) Axe from Gortore, Co. Cork, b) axes and other stone tools from Hermitage, Co. Limerick, the axe from Earlier Mesolithic Burial is in the centre of the photograph (courtesy of Aegis Archaeology).

Plate XXII. a) and b) refitted Early mesolithic c core and flakes found by Vincent McAlister at Culbane, c) assemblage from Ballyderown, Co. Cork (photograph by Hugh Kavanagh).

Plate XXIII. A portion of the cache from Urbal td. Co. Antrim.

10cm

5cm

Plate XXIV. Toome Castle cache (photograph by Hugh Kavanagh).

Plate XXV. Portions of refitted cores from cache (?) recovered on the shores of Lough Beg, Co. Derry.

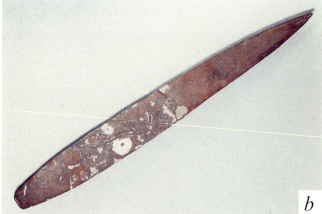

Plate XXVI. a) Point recovered from excavation near Dungannon, Co. Tyrone (courtesy of IAC), b) Moynagh Points dredged from near Minane, Beare Island, Co. Cork (courtesy of National University of Ireland, Galway), c) Moynagh Points from Moynagh Lough (courtesy of John Bradley).

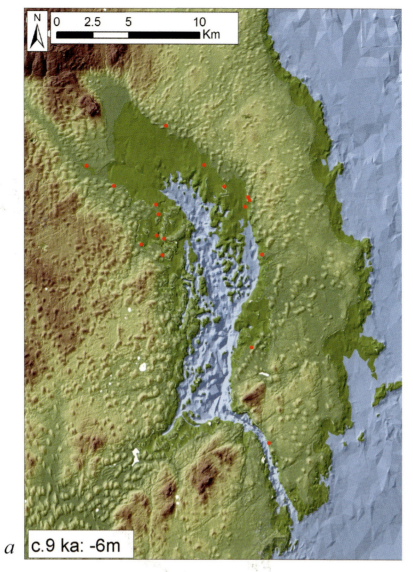

a c.9 ka: -6m

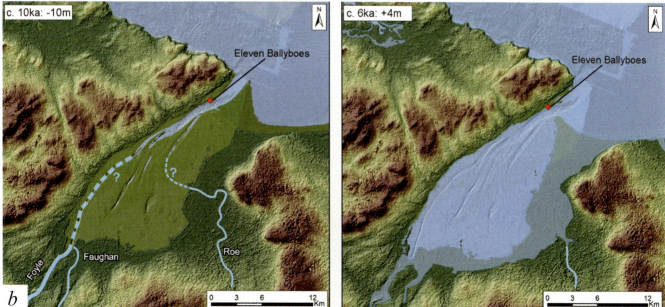

c. 10ka: -10m

Eleven Ballyboes

Foyle Faughan Roe

b

c. 6ka: +4m

Eleven Ballyboes

Plate XXVII. Maps of a) Strangford Lough at 9000 cal BP and b) the Foyle Estuary at (left) 9000 cal BP, (right) 6000 cal BP, showing location of known Earlier Mesolithic sites (prepared by Kieran Westley Centre for Maritime Archaeology, University of Ulster, Coleraine).

Plate XXVIII. a) Flint bands in Ulster White Limestone, Glenarm, Co. Antrim, b) view of Glencloy, Carnlough, Co. Antrim, c) Lough na Trosk, Glencloy, d) Location of Castle Carra near Cushendun.

Plate XXIX. a) Aerial view of Mount Sandel, b) Looking south at the Cutts to the area where the bone points were dredged, c and d) salmon fishing on the Neidin River, Finnmark, Norway.

Plate XXX. Oyster middens, shellfish processing and living on a midden in Senegal.

Plate XXXI. a) Reconstruction of Mount Sandel type hut by pupils from St Malachy's, Sandelford and Irish Society Primary Schools, Coleraine. Built on the grounds of St Malachy's Primary School in collaboration with ecological volunteers and Causeway Heritage Service, b) Rock art at Alta (by permission of Knut Helskog).

Plate XXXII a) Giants Causeway, Co. Antrim 2005, b) An Fear Marbh, Inish Tuaisceart, "The Sleeping Giant" (courtesy of Helene Brennan).

INDEX

Numbers in italics indicate pages with illustrations